Reading

Grade 3, Unit 6

Freedom

D1469228

PEARSON

Scott
Foresman

scottforesman.com

Editorial Offices: Glenview, Illinois • Parsippany, New Jersey • New York, New York
Sales Offices: Boston, Massachusetts • Duluth, Georgia • Glenview, Illinois
Coppell, Texas • Sacramento, California • Mesa, Arizona

We dedicate Reading Street to
Peter Jovanovich.

His wisdom, courage,
and passion for education
are an inspiration to us all.

Accelerated Reader®

Cover Mark Buehner

About the Cover Artist
Mark Buehner's sisters say that he was born with a pencil in his hand. While he was growing up, pulling out pencils, paper, and watercolors was part of his daily routine. He loved poring over the pictures in books and even used to staple his pictures together to make books. He had no idea that what he was doing would eventually become his career. He grew up to become an award-winning illustrator of books for children. He believes he has the best job in the world!

ISBN-13: 978-0-328-24378-5

ISBN-10: 0-328-24378-7

Copyright © 2008 Pearson Education, Inc.

All Rights Reserved. Printed in the United States of America. This publication is protected by Copyright, and permission should be obtained from the publisher prior to any prohibited reproduction, storage in a retrieval system, or transmission in any form by any means, electronic, mechanical, photocopying, recording, or likewise. For information regarding permission(s), write to: Permissions Department, Scott Foresman, 1900 East Lake Avenue, Glenview, Illinois 60025.

Many of the designations used by manufacturers and sellers to distinguish their products are claimed as trademarks. Where those designations appear in this book, and Scott Foresman was aware of a trademark claim, the designations have been printed with initial capitals and in cases of multiple usage have also been marked with either ® or ™ where they first appear.

2 3 4 5 6 7 8 9 10 11 V064 16 15 14 13 12 11 10 09 08 07
CC:N1

Reading

STREET

Where the
Love of
Reading
Begins

Reading Street Program Authors

Peter Afflerbach, Ph.D.
Professor, Department of
Curriculum and Instruction
University of Maryland at
College Park

Camille L.Z. Blachowicz, Ph.D.
Professor of Education
National-Louis University

Candy Dawson Boyd, Ph.D.
Professor, School of Education
Saint Mary's College of California

Wendy Cheyney, Ed.D.
Professor of Special Education
and Literacy, Florida
International University

Connie Juel, Ph.D.
Professor of Education, School of
Education, Stanford University

Edward J. Kame'enui, Ph.D.
Professor and Director, Institute for
the Development of Educational
Achievement, University of Oregon

Donald J. Leu, Ph.D.
John and Maria Neag Endowed
Chair in Literacy and Technology
University of Connecticut

Jeanne R. Paratore, Ed.D.
Associate Professor of Education
Department of Literacy
and Language Development
Boston University

P. David Pearson, Ph.D.
Professor and Dean,
Graduate School of Education
University of California, Berkeley

Sam L. Sebesta, Ed.D.
Professor Emeritus,
College of Education,
University of Washington, Seattle

Deborah Simmons, Ph.D.
Professor, College of Education
and Human Development
Texas A&M University
(Not pictured)

Sharon Vaughn, Ph.D.
H.E. Hartfelder/Southland
Corporation Regents Professor
University of Texas

Susan Watts-Taffe, Ph.D.
Independent Literacy Researcher
Cincinnati, Ohio

Karen Kring Wixson, Ph.D.
Professor of Education
University of Michigan

Components

Student Editions (1–6)

Teacher's Editions (PreK–6)

Assessment
Assessment Handbook (K–6)
Baseline Group Tests (K–6)
DIBELS™ Assessments (K–6)
ExamView® Test Generator CD-ROM (2–6)
Fresh Reads for Differentiated Test Practice (1–6)
Online Success Tracker™ (K–6)*
Selection Tests Teacher's Manual (1–6)
Unit and End-of-Year Benchmark Tests (K–6)

Leveled Readers
Concept Literacy Leveled Readers (K–1)
Independent Leveled Readers (K)
Kindergarten Student Readers (K)
Leveled Reader Teaching Guides (K–6)
Leveled Readers (1–6)
Listen to Me Readers (K)
Online Leveled Reader Database (K–6)*
Take-Home Leveled Readers (K–6)

Trade Books and Big Books
Big Books (PreK–2)
Read Aloud Trade Books (PreK–K)
Sing with Me Big Book (1–2)
Trade Book Library (1–6)

Decodable Readers
Decodable Readers (K–3)
Strategic Intervention Decodable Readers (1–2)
Take-Home Decodable Readers (K–3)

Phonics and Word Study
Alphabet Cards in English and Spanish (PreK–K)
Alphabet Chart in English and Spanish (PreK–K)
Animal ABCs Activity Guide (K)
Finger Tracing Cards (PreK–K)
Patterns Book (PreK–K)
Phonics Activities CD-ROM (PreK–2)*
Phonics Activities Mats (K)
Phonics and Spelling Practice Book (1–3)
Phonics and Word-Building Board and Letters (PreK–3)
Phonics Songs and Rhymes Audio CD (K–2)
Phonics Songs and Rhymes Flip Chart (K–2)
Picture Word Cards (PreK–K)
Plastic Letter Tiles (K)
Sound-Spelling Cards and Wall Charts (1–2)
Strategies for Word Analysis (4–6)
Word Study and Spelling Practice Book (4–6)

Language Arts
Daily Fix-It Transparencies (K–6)
Grammar & Writing Book and Teacher's Annotated Edition, The (1–6)
Grammar and Writing Practice Book and Teacher's Manual (1–6)
Grammar Transparencies (1–6)
Six-Trait Writing Posters (1–6)
Writing Kit (1–6)
Writing Rubrics and Anchor Papers (1–6)
Writing Transparencies (1–6)

Practice and Additional Resources
AlphaBuddy Bear Puppet (K)
Alphasaurus Annie Puppet (PreK)
Amazing Words Posters (K–2)
Centers Survival Kit (PreK–6)
Graphic Organizer Book (2–6)
Graphic Organizer Flip Chart (K–1)
High-Frequency Word Cards (K)
Kindergarten Review (1)
Practice Book and Teacher's Manual (K–6)
Read Aloud Anthology (PreK–2)
Readers' Theater Anthology (K–6)
Research into Practice (K–6)

Retelling Cards (K–6)
Scott Foresman Research Base (K–6)
Skill Transparencies (2–6)
Songs and Rhymes Flip Chart (PreK)
Talk with Me, Sing with Me Chart (PreK–K)
Tested Vocabulary Cards (1–6)
Vocabulary Transparencies (1–2)
Welcome to Reading Street (PreK–1)

ELL
ELL and Transition Handbook (PreK–6)
ELL Comprehensive Kit (1–6)
ELL Posters (K–6)
ELL Readers (1–6)
ELL Teaching Guides (1–6)
Ten Important Sentences (1–6)

Digital Components
AudioText CDs (PreK–6)
Background Building Audio CDs (3–6)
ExamView® Test Generator CD-ROM (2–6)
Online Lesson Planner (K–6)
Online New Literacies Activities (1–6)*
Online Professional Development (1–6)
Online Story Sort (K–6)*
Online Student Editions (1–6)*
Online Success Tracker™ (K–6)*
Online Teacher's Editions (PreK–6)
Phonics Activities CD-ROM (PreK–2)*
Phonics Songs and Rhymes Audio CD (K–2)
Sing with Me/Background Building Audio CDs (PreK–2)
Songs and Rhymes Audio CD (PreK)

My Sidewalks Early Reading Intervention (K)

My Sidewalks Intensive Reading Intervention (Levels A–E)

Reading Street for the Guided Reading Teacher (1–6)

* INTERACTIVE WHITEBOARD READY

Grade 3
Priority Skills

Priority skills are the critical elements of reading—phonemic awareness, phonics, fluency, vocabulary, and text comprehension—as they are developed across and within grades to assure that instructional emphasis is placed on the right skills at the right time and to maintain a systematic sequence of skill instruction.

Key
- ● = Taught/Unit priority
- ◑ = Reviewed and practiced
- ○ = Integrated practice

	UNIT 1 Weeks 1–2	UNIT 1 Weeks 3–5	UNIT 2 Weeks 1–2	UNIT 2 Weeks 3–5
Phonemic Awareness	Phonemic Awareness for Grade 3 appears in *Scott Foresman Intervention*.			
Phonics				
Blend sounds of letters to decode				
Consonants				
Consonant blends and digraphs				●
Short Vowels	●	○	●	○
Long Vowels	◑	○	●	○
r-Controlled Vowels				
Vowel Digraphs		●	○	○
Diphthongs		●	◑	○
Other vowel patterns				
Decode words with common word parts				
Base words and inflected endings	●	●	○	○
Contractions				
Compounds				●
Suffixes and prefixes				
Blend syllables to decode multisyllabic words	●	●	●	●
Fluency				
Read aloud with accuracy, comprehension, and appropriate rate	●	○	●	○
Read aloud with expression/intonation		●	○	●
Attend to punctuation and use appropriate phrasing		●	○	○
Practice fluency in a variety of ways, including choral reading, paired reading, and repeated oral reading	●	●	●	●
Work toward appropriate fluency goals	80–90 WCPM	80–90 WCPM	85–95 WCPM	85–95 WCPM
Vocabulary				
Read high-frequency words and lesson vocabulary automatically	○	○	○	○
Develop vocabulary through direct instruction, concrete experiences, reading, and listening to text read aloud	○	○	○	○
Use word structure to figure out word meaning	●	●	○	○
Use context clues to determine word meaning of unfamiliar words, multiple-meaning words, homonyms, homographs	●	●	●	●
Use grade-appropriate reference sources to learn word meanings	●	○	○	●
Use new words in a variety of contexts	○	○	○	○
Create and use graphic organizers to group, study, and retain vocabulary	○	○	○	○
Classify and categorize words	○	○	○	○
Use descriptive words	●	○	○	○

UNIT 3		UNIT 4		UNIT 5		UNIT 6	
Weeks		**Weeks**		**Weeks**		**Weeks**	
1–2	3–5	1–2	3–5	1–2	3–5	1–2	3–5

(Chart of skill indicator circles — filled, half-filled, and open)

UNIT 3		UNIT 4		UNIT 5		UNIT 6	
90–100 WCPM	90–100 WCPM	95–105 WCPM	95–105 WCPM	102–112 WCPM	102–112 WCPM	110–120 WCPM	110–120 WCPM

Grade 3
Priority Skills

Key
- ● = Taught/Unit priority
- ◐ = Reviewed and practiced
- ○ = Integrated practice

Text Comprehension	UNIT 1 Weeks 1–2	UNIT 1 Weeks 3–5	UNIT 2 Weeks 1–2	UNIT 2 Weeks 3–5
Strategies				
Preview the text	○	○	○	○
Set and monitor purpose for reading	○	○	○	○
Activate and use prior knowledge	●	○	○	○
Make, confirm, and modify predictions				●
Monitor comprehension and use fix-up strategies		●	○	●
Use graphic organizers to focus on text structure, to represent relationships in text, or to summarize text			●	○
Answer questions				
Generate questions				●
Recognize text structure: story and informational		●	○	○
Summarize text by retelling stories or identifying main ideas	●	○	○	○
Visualize; use mental imagery		●	●	○
Make connections: text to self, text to text, text to world	○	○	○	○
Skills				
Author's purpose	◐	○	○	●
Cause and effect				
Compare and contrast				
Draw conclusions		◐	○	●
Fact and opinion				
Follow directions			●	○
Generalize				
Graphic sources (charts, diagrams, graphs, maps, tables)			●	●
Main idea and supporting details		●	●	●
Realism/fantasy	●	●	●	○
Sequence of events	●	●	◐	○
Literary Elements				
Character (Recognize characters' traits, actions, feelings, and motives)	◐	●	●	◐
Plot and plot structure				
Setting	◐	●	○	◐
Theme				

	UNIT 3		UNIT 4		UNIT 5		UNIT 6	
	Weeks		**Weeks**		**Weeks**		**Weeks**	
	1–2	**3–5**	**1–2**	**3–5**	**1–2**	**3–5**	**1–2**	**3–5**
	○	○	○	○	○	○	○	○
	○	○	○	○	○	●	○	○
	○	◐	○	●	○	●	○	○
	○	○	○	○	●	○	○	●
	○	●	○	●	○	●	○	◐
	○	○	○	●	○	○	●	○
		●	●	○	○	○	○	●
	○	●	●	○	○	○	○	○
	●	○	○	○	●	○	●	○
	●	○	○	○	○	●	○	○
	○	○	○	○	○	○	○	●
	○	○	○	○	○	○	○	○
	●	◐	○	○	○	●	○	○
	●	○	●	◐	○	○	●	◐
		●	●	○	●	◐	○	○
	◐	●	○	◐	○	◐	○	○
				●	●	◐	○	●
	●	○	○	○	○	○	◐	○
		●	○	●	◐	○	○	●
	○	◐	●	●	○	○	○	○
	◐	○	○	○	○	○	●	◐
	○	○	○	○	○	○	○	○
	○	○	◐	○	○	●	○	○
	○	○	○	○	○	○	○	○
	◐	○	○	●	◐	○	◐	●
	○	◐	○	◐	○	◐	○	◐
	◐	○	○	●	○	○	◐	●

UNIT 6

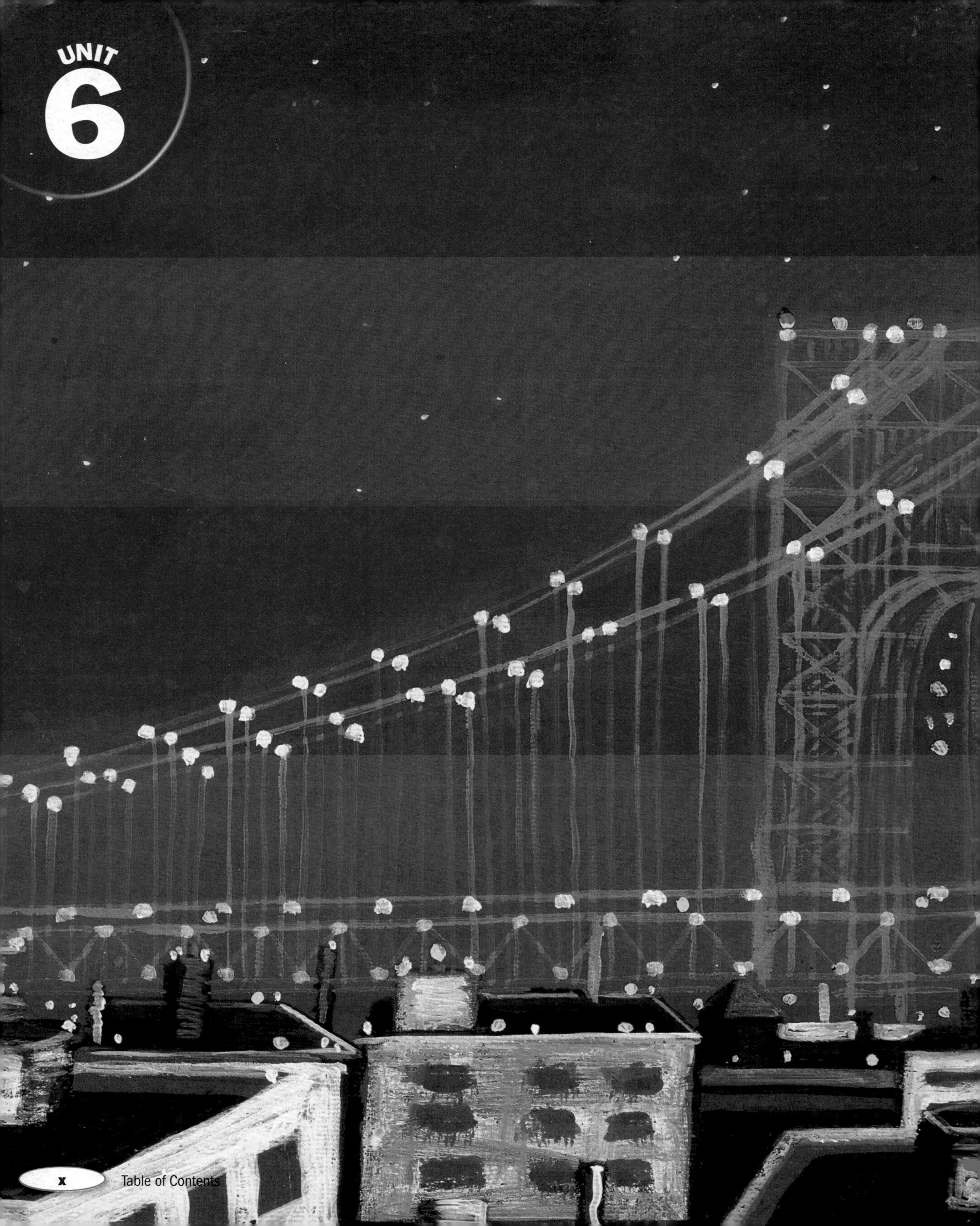

Unit 6
Freedom

Writing and Assessment WA1–WA18

Leveled Resources LR1–LR48

Differentiated Instruction . . . . . . DI•1–DI•60

Teacher Resources TR1–TR40

Unit 1
Dollars and Sense

Writing and Assessment WA1–WA18

Leveled Resources LR1–LR48

Differentiated Instruction . . . . . . DI•1–DI•60

Teacher Resources TR1–TR40

Unit 2
Smart Solutions

Unit 3
People and Nature

freedom

What does it mean to be free?

The Story of the Statue of Liberty

The Statue of Liberty has come to symbolize American freedom.

NARRATIVE NONFICTION

connect to SOCIAL STUDIES

Happy Birthday Mr. Kang

Mr. Kang makes an important decision about his pet bird.

REALISTIC FICTION

connect to SCIENCE

Talking Walls: Art for the People

Artists express freedom through murals.

PHOTO ESSAY

connect to SOCIAL STUDIES

Two Bad Ants

Ants learn the difficulties of a free life.

ANIMAL FANTASY

connect to SCIENCE

Elena's Serenade

Elena learns she has the freedom to follow her dream.

FANTASY

connect to SOCIAL STUDIES

Unit 6
Skills Overview

288–303
The Story of the Statue of Liberty/A Nation of Immigrants

NARRATIVE NONFICTION

What does the Statue of Liberty mean to Americans?

308–331
Happy Birthday Mr. Kang/Back to the Wild

REALISTIC FICTION

When might it be hard to grant freedom?

Reading		WEEK 1	WEEK 2
	Comprehension	**T** ⊙ **Skill** Main Idea and Details **T** ⊙ **Strategy** Text Structure **T** REVIEW **Skill** Cause and Effect	**T** ⊙ **Skill** Cause and Effect ⊙ **Strategy** Graphic Organizers **T** REVIEW **Skill** Plot and Theme
	Vocabulary	**T** ⊙ **Strategy** Word Structure	**T** ⊙ **Strategy** Context Clues
	Fluency	Accuracy, Appropriate Pace/Rate, and Expression	Appropriate Phrasing
Word Work	**Phonics**	Vowels in *tooth, cook*	Schwa
	Spelling and Phonics	Vowel Sounds in *tooth* and *cook*	Schwa
Oral Language	**Speaking/Listening/Viewing**	Use Nonverbal Cues Perception and Understanding of What You Hear	Express an Opinion about Community Issues Help Others Make Their Own Views Clear
Language Arts	**Grammar, Usage and Mechanics**	**T** Capital Letters	**T** Abbreviations
	Weekly Writing	Taking Notes Writing Trait: Focus/Ideas	Outlining Writing Trait: Sentences
	Unit Process Writing	Research Report	Research Report
	Research and Study Skills	Time Line	Maps
Integrate Science and Social Studies Standards		*Time for* SOCIAL STUDIES History Cultures: Symbols Government History	*Time for* SOCIAL STUDIES Cultures Community Responsibility

⊙ Target Skill   **T** Tested Skill

 **Big Idea**

What does freedom mean?

WEEK 3	WEEK 4	WEEK 5
336–353 **Talking Walls/ Nathaniel's Rap** PHOTO ESSAY	358–379 **Two Bad Ants/Hiking Safety Tips** ANIMAL FANTASY	384–407 **Elena's Serenade/ Leading People to Freedom** FANTASY
Why is freedom of expression important?	*When can freedom be a problem?*	*When are you free to follow your dreams?*
T **Skill** Fact and Opinion **T** **Strategy** Answer Questions **T** REVIEW **Skill** Main Idea and Details	**T** **Skill** Plot and Theme **T** **Strategy** Visualize **T** REVIEW **Skill** Cause and Effect	**T** **Skill** Generalize **T** **Strategy** Predict **T** REVIEW **Skill** Main Idea and Details
T **Strategy** Glossary	**T** **Strategy** Word Structure	**T** **Strategy** Context Clues
Read Silently with Fluency and Accuracy	Accuracy, Appropriate Pace/Rate, and Expression	Express Characterization
Syllables *-tion, -sion, -ture*	Multisyllabic Words	Related Words
Words with *-tion, -sion, -ture*	Multisyllabic Words	Related Words
Interview by Presenting a Talk Show View Common Themes of Artwork	Oral Presentation and Evaluation Form Opinion about Messages in Advertisements	Figurative Language Techniques Rhetorical Devices
T Combining Sentences	**T** Commas	**T** Quotations
Informational Paragraph Writing Trait: Organization/Paragraph	Write About a Picture Writing Trait: Word Choice	Write Good Paragraphs Writing Trait: Organization/Paragraphs
Research Report	Research Report	Research Report
Reference Sources	Note-taking	Chart/Table
Time for SOCIAL STUDIES Freedom of Expression Immigration Murals as History	**Time for Science** Life Cycles Environments	**Time for SOCIAL STUDIES** Manufacturing Cultures: Crafts Changes

Unit 6
Monitor Progress

Predictors of Reading Success	WEEK 1	WEEK 2	WEEK 3	WEEK 4
WCPM **Fluency**	Read with Accuracy and Appropriate Pace/ Rate, and Expression 110–120 WCPM	Read with Appropriate Phrasing 110–120 WCPM	Read Silently with Fluency and Accuracy 110–120 WCPM	Read with Accuracy, Appropriate Pace/ Rate, and Expression 110–120 WCPM
Oral Vocabulary **Vocabulary/ Concept Development** (assessed informally)	initials patriotic recruiting	affectionate collar territory	appreciates downhearted pondered	encountered fascinated guilty
Lesson Vocabulary	**Strategy** Word Structure crown liberty models symbol tablet torch unforgettable unveiled	**Strategy** Context Clues bows chilly foolish foreign narrow perches recipe	**Strategy** Glossary encourages expression local native settled social support	**Strategy** Word Structure crystal disappeared discovery goal journey joyful scoop unaware
Retelling **Text Comprehension**	**Skill** Main Idea and Details **Strategy** Text Structure	**Skill** Cause and Effect **Strategy** Graphic Organizers	**Skill** Fact and Opinion **Strategy** Answer Questions	**Skill** Plot and Theme **Strategy** Visualize

282e   Freedom   Target Skill   SuccessTracker/Unit 6 Benchmark Tested Skills

Make Data-Driven Decisions

Data Management
- Assess
- Diagnose
- Prescribe
- Disaggregate

Classroom Management
- Monitor Progress
- Group
- Differentiate Instruction
- Inform Parents

ONLINE CLASSROOM

WEEK 5

Express
Characterization

110–120 WCPM

discouraged
instruments
mellow

🔲 🔘 **Strategy**
   Context Clues

   burro
   bursts
   factory
   glassblower
   puffs
   reply
   tune

🔲 🔘 **Skill** Generalize

🔘 **Strategy**
   Predict

🔲 Manage Data

- Assign the Unit 6 Benchmark Test for students to take online.

- SuccessTracker records results and generates reports by school, grade, classroom, or student.

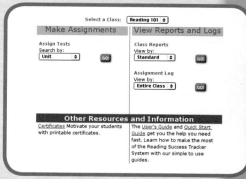

- Use reports to disaggregate and aggregate Unit 6 skills and standards data to monitor progress.

- Based on class lists created to support the categories important for AYP (gender, ethnicity, migrant education, English proficiency, disabilities, economic status), reports let you track adequate yearly progress every six weeks.

🔲 Group

- Use results from Unit 6 Benchmark Tests taken online through SuccessTracker to regroup students.

- Reports in SuccessTracker suggest appropriate groups for students based on test results.

🔲 Individualize Instruction

- Tests are correlated to Unit 6 tested skills and standards so that prescriptions for individual teaching and learning plans can be created.

- Individualized prescriptions target instruction and accelerate student progress toward learning outcome goals.

- Prescriptions include resources to reteach Unit 6 skills and standards.

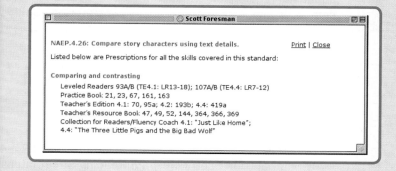

NAEP.4.26: Compare story characters using text details.   Print | Close

Listed below are Prescriptions for all the skills covered in this standard:

Comparing and contrasting

Leveled Readers 93A/B (TE4.1: LR13-18); 107A/B (TE4.4: LR7-12)
Practice Book: 21, 23, 67, 161, 163
Teacher's Edition 4.1: 70, 95a; 4.2: 193b; 4.4: 419a
Teacher's Resource Book: 47, 49, 52, 144, 364, 366, 369
Collection for Readers/Fluency Coach 4.1: "Just Like Home";
4.4: "The Three Little Pigs and the Big Bad Wolf"

Unit 6
Grouping for AYP

Diagnose and Differentiate

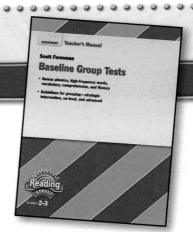

Diagnose
To make initial grouping decisions, use the Baseline Group Test or another initial placement test. Depending on students' ability levels, you may have more than one of each group.

Differentiate

If... student's performance is **Below-Level** **then...** use the regular instruction and the daily Strategic Intervention lessons, pp. DI•2–DI•50.

If... student's performance is **On-Level** **then...** use the regular instruction for On-Level learners throughout each selection.

If... student's performance is **Advanced** **then...** use the regular instruction and the daily instruction for Advanced learners, pp. DI•3–DI•51.

Group Time

On-Level

- Explicit instructional routines teach core skills and strategies.
- Independent activities provide practice for core skills and extension and enrichment options.
- Leveled readers (LR1–48) and decodable readers provide additional reading and practice with core skills and vocabulary.

Strategic Intervention

- Daily Strategic Intervention lessons provide more intensive instruction, more scaffolding, more practice with critical skills, and more opportunities to respond.
- Decodable readers practice word reading skills.
- Reteach lessons (DI•52–DI•56) provide additional instructional opportunities with target skills.
- Leveled readers (LR1–48) build background for the selections and practice target skills and vocabulary.

Advanced

- Daily Advanced lessons provide compacted instruction for accelerated learning, options for investigative work, and challenging reading content.
- Leveled readers (LR1–48) provide additional reading tied to lesson concepts.

Additional opportunities to differentiate instruction:
- Reteach Lessons, pp. DI•52–DI•56
- Leveled Reader Instruction and Leveled Practice, LR1–48
- My Sidewalks on Scott Foresman Reading Street Intensive Reading Intervention Program

4-Step Plan for Assessment

1. Diagnose and Differentiate
2. Monitor Progress
3. Assess and Regroup
4. Summative Assessment

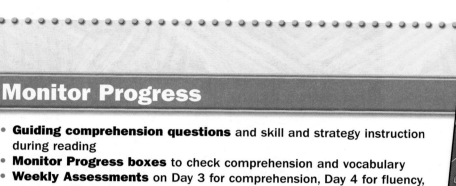

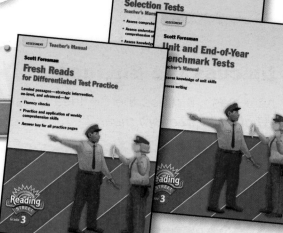

Monitor Progress

STEP 2

- **Guiding comprehension questions** and skill and strategy instruction during reading
- **Monitor Progress boxes** to check comprehension and vocabulary
- **Weekly Assessments** on Day 3 for comprehension, Day 4 for fluency, and Day 5 for vocabulary
- **Practice Book** pages at point of use
- **Weekly Selection Tests** or **Fresh Reads for Differentiated Test Practice**

Assess and Regroup

STEP 3

- **Days 3, 4, and 5 Assessments** Record results of weekly Days 3, 4, and 5 assessments in retelling, fluency, and vocabulary (pp. WA16–17) to track student progress.
- **Unit 6 Benchmark Test** Administer this test to check mastery of unit skills.
- There is no need to regroup at the end of Unit 6. Use weekly assessment information, Unit Benchmark Test performance, and the Unit 6 Assess and Regroup (p. WA18) to assess students' progress. See the time line below.

YOU ARE HERE
Begin Unit 6

SCOTT FORESMAN ASSESSMENT

Group
Baseline Group Test

Regroup
Units 1 and 2

Regroup
Unit 3

Regroup
Unit 4

Regroup
Unit 5

| 1 | 5 | 10 | 15 | 20 | 25 | 30 |

END OF YEAR

OUTSIDE ASSESSMENT

Initial placement — Outside assessment for regrouping — Outside assessment for regrouping

Outside assessments (e.g., **DIBELS**) may recommend regrouping at other times during the year.

Summative Assessment

STEP 4

- **Benchmark Assessment** Use to measure a student's mastery of each unit's skills.
- **End-of-Year Benchmark Assessment** Use to measure a student's mastery of program skills covered in all six units.

Unit 6
Theme Launch

Discuss the Big Idea

As a class, discuss the Big Idea question, *What does freedom mean?*

Explain how freedom is a word and an idea that has different meanings to different people. *(to share one's ideas, from fear, to practice a religion of choice, and so on)*

Ask students why it is important for people to have freedom.

Examples of important freedoms are found in the Bill of Rights. Explain a few of them for students.

Theme and Concept Connections

Weekly lesson concepts help students connect the reading selections and the unit theme. Theme-related activities throughout the week provide opportunities to explore the relationships among the selections, the lesson concepts, and the unit theme.

UNIT 6

Rea
Onl
PearsonSuc

Freedom

What does it mean to be free?

282

CONNECTING CULTURES

Use the following selections to help students learn more about the meaning of the concept of freedom.

The Story of the Statue of Liberty Have students discuss why the statue was created and what it represents to people around the world today.

Talking Walls: Art for the People Have students discuss the different reasons people paint murals. Explain to students that murals use pictures and symbols to tell a story of people, the history of a place, or important celebrations.

The Story of the Statue of Liberty

The Statue of Liberty has come to symbolize American freedom.

NARRATIVE NONFICTION

Paired Selection

A Nation of Immigrants

TEXTBOOK

Happy Birthday Mr. Kang

Mr. Kang makes an important decision about his pet bird.

REALISTIC FICTION

Paired Selection

Back to the Wild: A Talk with a Wildlife Worker

INTERVIEW

Talking Walls: Art for the People

Artists express freedom through murals.

PHOTO ESSAY

Paired Selection

Nathaniel's Rap

POETRY

Two Bad Ants

Ants learn the difficulties of a free life.

ANIMAL FANTASY

Paired Selection

Hiking Safety Tips

EVALUATING SOURCES

Elena's Serenade

Elena learns she has the freedom to follow her dream.

FANTASY

Paired Selection

Leading People to Freedom

EXPOSITORY NONFICTION

283

Unit Inquiry Project

Symbols of Freedom

In the unit inquiry project, students research symbols that represent freedom and then choose one symbol and find out about its history. Students may use print or online resources as available.

The project assessment rubric can be found on p. 408a. Discuss the expectations before students begin the project. [Rubric] [4][3][2][1]

PROJECT TIMETABLE

WEEK	ACTIVITY/SKILL CONNECTION
1	**IDENTIFY QUESTIONS** Students browse a few Web sites or print reference materials to develop an inquiry question about American symbols of freedom.
2	**NAVIGATE/SEARCH** Students conduct effective information searches and look for text and images that can help them answer their questions.
3	**ANALYZE** Students explore Web sites or print materials. They analyze the information they have found to determine whether or not it will be useful to them. Students print or take notes on valid information.
4	**SYNTHESIZE** Students combine relevant information they've collected from different sources to develop an answer to their inquiry questions from Week 1.
	ASSESSMENT OPTIONS
5	**COMMUNICATE** Each student prepares a list of useful resources for other classes who may wish to explore symbols of American freedom. Students may also prepare presentations about their symbols of freedom.

Unit 6
Freedom

What does it mean to be free?

Week 1

Expand the Concept
What does the Statue of Liberty mean to Americans?

Connect the Concept

Develop Language
initials, patriotic, recruiting

Teach Content
History
Cultures: Symbols
Government History

Writing
Taking Notes

Internet Inquiry
Symbols of Freedom

Literature

SOCIAL STUDIES

Week 2

Expand the Concept
When might it be hard to grant freedom?

Connect the Concept

Develop Language
affectionate, collar, territory

Teach Content
Cultures
Community
Responsibility

Writing
Outlining

Internet Inquiry
Granting Freedom to Animals

Literature

Week 3

Expand the Concept
Why is freedom of expression important?

Connect the Concept

Develop Language
appreciates, downhearted, pondered

Teach Content
Freedom of Expression
Immigration
Murals as History

Writing
Informational Paragraph

Internet Inquiry
Freedom of Expression

Literature

SOCIAL STUDIES

Week 4

Expand the Concept
When can freedom be a problem?

Connect the Concept

Develop Language
encountered, fascinated, guilty

Teach Content
Life Cycles
Environments

Writing
Writing About a Picture

Internet Inquiry
Freedom

Literature

Time for Science

Week 5

Expand the Concept
When are you free to follow your dreams?

Connect the Concept

Develop Language
discouraged, instruments, mellow

Teach Content
Manufacturing
Cultures: Crafts
Changes

Writing
Write Good Paragraphs

Internet Inquiry
Following Your Dreams

Literature

SOCIAL STUDIES

Illinois

Planning Guide for Performance Descriptors

The Story of the Statue of Liberty

Reading Street Teacher's Edition pages

Grade 3 English Language Arts Performance Descriptors

Oral Language

Speaking/Listening Build Concept Vocabulary: 284l, 295, 299, 303c
Read Aloud: 284m

1A.Stage C.5. Use a variety of decoding strategies (e.g., phonics, word patterns, structural analysis, context clues) to recognize new words when reading age-appropriate material.
1B.Stage C.13. Read age-appropriate material aloud with fluency and accuracy.

Word Work

Vowel Sounds in *tooth* and *cook:* 303i, 303k–303l

1A.Stage C.8. Use a variety of resources (e.g., dictionaries, thesauruses, indices, glossaries, internet, interviews, available technology) to clarify meanings of unfamiliar words.

Reading

Comprehension Main Idea: 284–285, 288–299, 303b
Text Structure: 288–299

Vocabulary Lesson Vocabulary: 286b, 295, 299, 302
Word Structure: 286–287, 297, 303c

Fluency Model Reading with Accuracy and Appropriate Pace/Rate: 284l–284m, 303a
Choral Reading: 303a

Self-Selected Reading: LR1–9, TR16–17

Literature Genre—Narrative Nonfiction: 288
Reader Response: 300

1A.Stage C.5. Use a variety of decoding strategies (e.g., phonics, word patterns, structural analysis, context clues) to recognize new words when reading age-appropriate material.
1B.Stage C.1. Identify purposes for reading before and during reading.
1B.Stage C.4. Identify explicit main ideas.
1B.Stage C.13. Read age-appropriate material aloud with fluency and accuracy.
1C.Stage C.7. Use text structure (e.g., sequential order, chronological order, problem/solution) to determine most important information.
2A.Stage C.8. Classify major types of nonfiction (e.g., essay, biography, autobiography).
4A.Stage C.6. Respond in an appropriate manner to questions and discussion with relevant and focused comments.

Language Arts

Writing Taking Notes: 303g–303h

Six-Trait Writing Focus/Ideas: 289, 303g–303h

Grammar, Usage, and Mechanics Capital Letters: 303e–303f

Research/Study Time Line: 303n

Technology New Literacies: 303m

3A.Stage C.5. Use appropriate capitalization.
3B.Stage C.1. Use appropriate prewriting strategies (e.g., drawing, webbing, brainstorming, listing, note taking, graphic organizers) to generate and organize ideas with teacher assistance.
5A.Stage C.4. Use text aids (e.g., table of contents, glossary, index, alphabetical order) to locate information in a book.

Unit Skills

Writing Research Report: WA2–9

Poetry: 408–411

Project/Wrap-Up: 412–413

3B.Stage C.1. Use appropriate prewriting strategies (e.g., drawing, webbing, brainstorming, listing, note taking, graphic organizers) to generate and organize ideas with teacher assistance.
3C.Stage C.3. Experiment with different forms of creative writing (e.g., song, poetry, short fiction, play).

This Week's Leveled Readers

Below-Level

1B.Stage C.4. Identify explicit main ideas.
2A.Stage C.2. Identify the setting and tell how it affects the story.

Nonfiction

On-Level

2A.Stage C.8. Classify major types of nonfiction (e.g., essay, biography, autobiography).
4A.Stage C.2. Distinguish among different kinds of information (e.g., fact, opinion, detail, main idea, fantasy, reality).

Nonfiction

Advanced

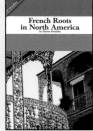

1B.Stage C.4. Identify explicit main ideas.
2A.Stage C.6. Name several characteristics that distinguish fiction from nonfiction.

Nonfiction

Content-Area Illinois Performance Descriptors in This Lesson

Social Studies

14E.Stage C.1. Describe an example where the people of the United States and people from other countries might need to cooperate to solve a common problem.

14E.Stage C.2. Tell about people who have come from other countries to live in the United States.

14F.Stage C.2. Define the concept of "Patriotism."

14F.Stage C.4. Define the concept of "liberty."

14F.Stage C.5. Identify an artistic expression (e.g., song, painting, film) that illustrates the traditions important to our political system and concept of freedom.

18A.Stage C.4. Explain the significance of the cultural diversity of the United States.

18A.Stage C.5. Describe aspects of the community that reflect its cultural heritage.

18C.Stage C.2. Describe the concept of cooperation.

Science

12C.Stage C.2. Apply scientific inquiries or technological designs to analyze simple properties and changes: matching examples of physical and chemical properties to common substances (e.g., mixtures, solutions, solids, liquids, gases).

Math

6C.Stage C.3. Determine whether exact answers or estimates are appropriate for solutions to problems.

7A.Stage C.1. Explain the need for using standard units for measuring.

7A.Stage C.3. Perform simple unit conversions within a system of measurement (e.g., three feet is the same as a yard).

7A.Stage C.4. Describe multiple measurable attributes (e.g., length, mass/weight, time, temperature, area, volume, capacity) of a single object.

Illinois!

A FAMOUS ILLINOISAN
Abraham Lincoln

Abraham Lincoln (1809–1865) was the sixteenth president of the United States. As a child, Lincoln taught himself to read and write. He later moved with his family to Illinois, where he lived for many years. Lincoln was President during the Civil War and wrote the Emancipation Proclamation, a document that helped free enslaved people. He served as President from 1861 until his assassination in 1865. Lincoln is buried in Springfield. The Abraham Lincoln Presidential Library and Museum opened there in 2005.

Students can . . .
Find out more about Abraham Lincoln's early years and put on a play about the life of young Lincoln in Illinois.

A SPECIAL ILLINOIS PLACE
Carl Sandburg Home

Carl Sandburg (1878–1967) was one of the most important American poets. He was born in Galesburg. The home he was born in is now maintained by the Illinois Historic Preservation Agency. Visitors can tour the home and see many of the furnishings that once belonged to the Sandburg family. Sandburg wrote about Illinois in such works as his poem "Chicago" and his autobiography *Always the Young Strangers*.

Students can . . .
Write a poem about the house in which they live.

ILLINOIS FUN FACTS
Did You Know?

- Abraham and Mary Todd Lincoln's house in Springfield was the only house they ever owned. Their son Robert donated it to the state in 1887.

- Central Illinois is known for its rich soil, which is well suited for farming.

- One of the most popular events in Chicago is the annual Air and Water Show along the shores of Lake Michigan.

Students can . . .
Draw a picture of an airplane or boat that they would like to see in the Air and Water Show.

Unit 6
Freedom

EXPAND THE CONCEPT
What does the Statue of Liberty mean to Americans?

CONNECT THE CONCEPT

▶ **Build Background**

initials, patriotic, recruiting

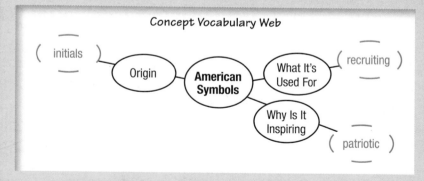

Concept Vocabulary Web

▶ **Social Studies Content**

History; Cultures: Symbols; Government History

▶ **Writing**

Taking Notes

▶ **Internet Inquiry**

Symbols of Freedom

Preview Your Week

What does the Statue of Liberty mean to Americans?

What is interesting or important about the Statue of Liberty?

The Story of the Statue of Liberty

by Betsy & Giulio Maestro

Genre Narrative nonfiction gives information about real people and events in the form of a story. What special event does this selection tell about?

288

289

Student Edition pages 288-299

Audio CD

Genre	Narrative Nonfiction
Vocabulary Strategy	Word Structure
Comprehension Skill	Main Idea
Comprehension Strategy	Text Structure

SOCIAL STUDIES

Paired Selection

Reading Across Texts

Combining Information from Two Sources

Genre

Textbook

Text Features

Photos

Captions

Charts

Social Studies in Reading

A Nation of Immigrants

Textbook

Genre
- A textbook is a source of information.
- Textbooks are used by students from elementary school through college.
- A textbook can be about any subject.

Text Features
- Photos and captions make information clearer.
- Charts often are included to give additional information.

Link to Social Studies
Use the library or the Internet to find out more about why immigrants came to the United States. Copy the chart on page 303, and add a column that tells Why They Came.

For decades, immigrants have come to the United States from almost every other country in the world. Some people wanted freedom or better opportunities. Some came because there was very little food in their home country. Some came to find jobs or to work on farms. Others came because they had no choice.

Many ships that came from Europe arrived first at Ellis Island in New York Harbor. Many immigrants from Asia arrived at Angel Island in San Francisco Bay. Immigrants also entered through other cities, such as Boston, Massachusetts; Galveston, Texas; and New Orleans, Louisiana.

Ellis Island

REVIEW What were some reasons immigrants came to the United States?

302

Times When Many Immigrants Came

Time Period	Where Many Were From
Before 1820	United Kingdom, countries of Western Africa such as those now known as Ghana, Togo, Benin, Nigeria, and Cameroon
1820–1860	Ireland, Germany, United Kingdom, France, Canada
1861–1890	Germany, United Kingdom, Ireland, Canada, Norway/Sweden
1891–1920	Italy, Austria/Hungary, Russia, United Kingdom, Germany
1961–1990	Mexico, Philippines, Canada, Korea, Cuba

Angel Island

Reading Across Texts
Immigrants from which countries would have been the first to see the new Statue of Liberty on Bedloe's Island?

Writing Across Texts Imagine that you are one of those immigrants. Write a journal entry telling your impression of the Statue of Liberty.

Main Idea What is the main idea of this article?

Student Edition pages 302-303

Audio CD

Leveled Readers

Skill Main Idea

Strategy Text Structure

Lesson Vocabulary

Below-Level

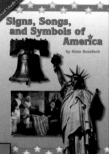

On-Level

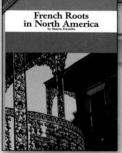

Advanced

ELL Reader

• Concept Vocabulary
• Text Support
• Language Enrichment

Time for **SOCIAL STUDIES**

Integrate Social Studies Standards

• History
• Cultures: Symbols
• Government History

✓ **Read**

The Story of the Statue of Liberty
pp. 288–299

"A Nation of Immigrants"
pp. 302–303

Leveled Readers

Below-Level — **On-Level** — **Advanced**

• Support Concepts — • Develop Concepts — • Extend Concepts

ELL Reader

✓ **Build**
Concept Vocabulary
American Symbols,
pp. 284l–284m

✓ **Teach**
Social Studies Concepts
Location Skills, p. 291
Cultures (Symbols), p. 293

✓ **Explore**
Social Studies Center
Artists/Monuments, p. 284k

Weekly Plan

READING

45–90 minutes

TARGET SKILLS OF THE WEEK

- **Comprehension Skill**
  Main Idea
- **Comprehension Strategy**
  Text Structure
- **Vocabulary Strategy**
  Word Structure

DAY 1
PAGES 284l–286b, 303a, 303e–303h, 303k–303m

Oral Language

QUESTION OF THE WEEK *What does the Statue of Liberty mean to Americans?*

Read Aloud: "Uncle Sam," 284m
Build Concepts, 284l

Comprehension/Vocabulary

Comprehension Skill/Strategy Lesson, 284–285

- Main Idea **T**
- Text Structure

Build Background, 286a

Introduce Lesson Vocabulary, 286b
crown, liberty, models, symbol, tablet, torch, unforgettable, unveiled **T**

Read Leveled Readers

Grouping Options 284f–284g

Fluency

Model Accuracy, Appropriate Pace/Rate, and Expression, 284l–284m, 303a

DAY 2
PAGES 286–295, 303a, 303e–303i, 303k–303m

Oral Language

QUESTION OF THE DAY *What did Bartholdi want the Statue of Liberty to symbolize?*

Word Work

Phonics Lesson, 303i
Vowel Sounds in *tooth* and *cook*

Comprehension/Vocabulary

Vocabulary Strategy Lesson, 286–287

- Word Structure **T**

Read *The Story of the Statue of Liberty,* 288–295

Grouping Options 284f–284g

- Main Idea **T**
- Text Structure **T**
- **REVIEW** Cause/Effect **T**

Develop Vocabulary

Fluency

Choral Reading, 303a

LANGUAGE ARTS

30–60 minutes

Trait of the Week

Focus/Ideas

Grammar, 303e
Introduce Capital Letters **T**

Writing Workshop, 303g
Introduce Taking Notes
Model the Trait of the Week: Focus/Ideas

Spelling, 303k
Pretest for Vowel Sounds in *tooth* and *cook*

Internet Inquiry, 303m
Identify Questions

Grammar, 303e
Develop Capital Letters **T**

Writing Workshop, 303g
Improve Writing: Paraphrasing

Spelling, 303k
Teach the Generalization

Internet Inquiry, 303m
Navigate/Search

DAILY WRITING ACTIVITIES | **Day 1** Write to Read, 284 | **Day 2** Words to Write, 287
Strategy Response Log, 288, 295

DAILY SOCIAL STUDIES CONNECTIONS | **Day 1** American Symbols Concept Web, 284l | **Day 2** Time for Social Studies: Location Skills, 291; Cultures (Symbols), 293
Revisit the American Symbols Concept Web, 295

DAILY SUCCESS PREDICTORS
for Adequate Yearly Progress

Monitor Progress and Corrective Feedback

Vocabulary | Check Vocabulary, *284l*

RESOURCES FOR THE WEEK

- Practice Book 3.2, *pp. 101–110*
- Phonics and Spelling Practice Book, *pp. 101–104*
- Grammar and Writing Practice Book, *pp. 101–104*
- Selection Test, *pp. 101–104*
- Fresh Reads for Differentiated Test Practice, *pp. 151–156*
- The Grammar and Writing Book, *pp. 200–205*

Grouping Options for Differentiated Instruction

Turn the page for the small group lesson plan.

DAY 3
PAGES 296–301, 303a, 303e–303h, 303k–303m

Oral Language

QUESTION OF THE DAY *What does the statue symbolize for many immigrants?*

Comprehension/Vocabulary

Read *The Story of the Statue of Liberty,* 296–300

Grouping Options 284f–284g

- Text Structure
- Word Structure **T**
- Develop Vocabulary

Reader Response

Selection Test

Fluency

Model Accuracy, Appropriate Pace/Rate, and Expression, 303a

Grammar, 303f
Apply Capital Letters in Writing **T**

Writing Workshop, 301, 303h
Write Now
Prewrite and Draft

Spelling, 303l
Connect Spelling to Writing

Internet Inquiry, 303m
Analyze Sources

Day 3 Strategy Response Log, 298
Look Back and Write, 300

Day 3 Social Studies Center: Artists and Monuments, 284k
Revisit the American Symbols Concept Web, 299

DAY 4
PAGES 302–303a, 303e–303h, 303k–303m

Oral Language

QUESTION OF THE DAY *How would you feel coming to the United States to live if you were from another country?*

Word Work

Phonics Lesson, 303j
REVIEW Suffixes *–y, -ish, -hood, -ment* **T**

Comprehension/Vocabulary

Read *"A Nation of Immigrants,"* 302–303

Grouping Options 284f–284g

- Textbook/Text Features
- Reading Across Texts
- Content-Area Vocabulary

Fluency

Paired Reading, 303a

Grammar, 303f
Practice Capital Letters for Standardized Tests **T**

Writing Workshop, 303h
Draft, Revise, and Publish

Spelling, 303l
Provide a Strategy

Internet Inquiry, 303m
Synthesize Information

Day 4 Writing Across Texts, 303

Day 4 Social Studies Center: Artists and Monuments, 284k

DAY 5
PAGES 303a–303h, 303k–303n

Oral Language

QUESTION OF THE WEEK *To wrap up the week, revisit the Day 1 question.*
Build Concept Vocabulary, 303c

Fluency

Read Leveled Readers

Grouping Options 284f–284g

Assess Reading Rate, 303a

Comprehension/Vocabulary

- Reteach Main Idea, 303b **T**
- Steps in a Process, 303b
- Review Word Structure, 303c **T**

Speaking and Listening, 303d
Announcement
Listen to an Announcement

Grammar, 303f
Cumulative Review

Writing Workshop, 303h
Connect to Unit Writing

Spelling, 303l
Posttest for Vowel Sounds in *tooth* and *cook*

Internet Inquiry, 303m
Communicate Results

Research/Study Skills, 303n
Time Line

Day 5 Steps in a Process, 303b

Day 5 Revisit the American Symbols Concept Web, 303c

KEY = Target Skill **T** = Tested Skill

Check Retelling, *301*

Check Fluency WCPM, *303a*

Check Vocabulary, *303c*

SUCCESS PREDICTOR

Small Group Plan *for Differentiated Instruction*

Daily Plan AT A GLANCE

Reading
Whole Group
- Oral Language
- Phonics
- Comprehension/Vocabulary

Group Time
Differentiated Instruction

Meet with small groups to provide:
- Skill Support
- Reading Support
- Fluency Practice

Read

This week's lessons for daily group time can be found behind the Differentiated Instruction (DI) tab on pp. DI·2–DI·11.

Whole Group
- Fluency

Language Arts
- Grammar
- Writing
- Spelling
- Research/Inquiry
- Speaking/Listening/Viewing

Use *My Sidewalks on Reading Street* for Tier III intensive reading intervention.

DAY 1

On-Level	Strategic Intervention	Advanced
Teacher-Led Page DI·3	**Teacher-Led** Page DI·2	**Teacher-Led** Page DI·3
• Develop Concept Vocabulary • **Read** On-Level Reader *Signs, Songs, and Symbols of America*	• Preteach Vowels in *tooth, cook* • **Read** Decodable Reader 26 • **Read** Below-Level Reader *The Statue of Liberty . . .*	• **Read** Advanced Reader *French Roots in North . . .* • Independent Extension Activity

ⓘ Independent Activities
While you meet with small groups, have the rest of the class...

- Visit the Reading/Library Center
- Listen to the Background Building Audio
- Finish Write to Read, p. 284
- Complete Practice Book 3.2 pp. 103–104
- Visit Cross-Curricular Centers

DAY 2

On-Level	Strategic Intervention	Advanced
Teacher-Led Pages 290–295	**Teacher-Led** Page DI·4	**Teacher-Led** Page DI·5
• **Read** *The Story of the Statue of Liberty*	• Practice Lesson Vocabulary • Read Multisyllabic Words • **Read** or Listen to *The Story of the Statue of Liberty*	• Extend Vocabulary • **Read** *The Story of the Statue of Liberty*

ⓘ Independent Activities
While you meet with small groups, have the rest of the class...

- Visit the Reading/Library Center
- Listen to the AudioText for *The Story of the Statue of Liberty*
- Finish Words to Write, p. 287
- Complete Practice Book 3.2 pp. 105–106, 109
- Write in their Strategy Response Logs, pp. 288, 295
- Visit Cross-Curricular Centers
- Work on inquiry projects

DAY 3

On-Level	Strategic Intervention	Advanced
Teacher-Led Pages 296–299	**Teacher-Led** Page DI·6	**Teacher-Led** Page DI·7
• **Read** *The Story of the Statue of Liberty*	• Practice Main Idea and Text Structure • **Read** or Listen to *The Story of the Statue of Liberty*	• Extend Main Idea and Text Structure • **Read** *The The Story of the Statue of Liberty*

ⓘ Independent Activities
While you meet with small groups, have the rest of the class...

- Visit the Reading/Library Center
- Listen to the AudioText for *The Story of the Statue of Liberty*
- Write in their Strategy Response Logs, p. 298
- Finish Look Back and Write, p. 300
- Complete Practice Book 3.2 p. 107
- Visit Cross-Curricular Centers
- Work on inquiry projects

① Begin with whole class skill and strategy instruction.

② Meet with small groups to provide differentiated instruction.

③ Gather the whole class back together for fluency and language arts.

DAY 4

On-Level

Teacher-Led
Pages 302–303

- **Read** "A Nation of Immigrants"

Strategic Intervention

Teacher-Led
Page DI · 8

- Practice Retelling
- **Read** or Listen to "A Nation of Immigrants"

Advanced

Teacher-Led
Page DI · 9

- **Read** "A Nation of Immigrants"
- Genre Study

ⓘ Independent Activities

While you meet with small groups, have the rest of the class...

- Visit the Reading/Library Center
- Listen to the AudioText for "A Nation of Immigrants"
- Visit the Writing and Vocabulary Centers
- Finish Writing Across Texts, p. 303
- Visit Cross-Curricular Centers
- Work on inquiry projects

DAY 5

On-Level

Teacher-Led
Page DI · 11

- **Reread** Leveled Reader *Signs, Songs, and Symbols of America*
- Retell *Signs, Songs, and Symbols of America*

Strategic Intervention

Teacher-Led
Page DI · 10

- **Reread** Leveled Reader *The Statue of Liberty: From Paris to New York City*
- Retell *The Statue of Liberty: From Paris to New York City*

Advanced

Teacher-Led
Page DI · 11

- **Reread** Leveled Reader *French Roots in North America*
- Share Extension Activity

ⓘ Independent Activities

While you meet with small groups, have the rest of the class...

- Visit the Reading/Library Center
- Complete Practice Book 3.2 pp. 108, 110
- Visit Cross-Curricular Centers
- Work on inquiry projects

 E L L

Grouping Place English language learners in the groups that correspond to their reading abilities in English.

Use the appropriate Leveled Reader or other text at students' instructional level.

TIP Send home the appropriate Multilingual Summary of the main selection on Day 1.

ONLINE
PearsonSuccessNet.com

Sharon Vaughn
For ideas on professional development, see the article "The Role of Mentoring . . ." by Scott Foresman author S. Vaughn and M. Coleman.

TEACHER TALK

Modeling is demonstrating a skill for others to imitate. Modeling reading skills often involves thinking aloud as one reads, to make clear the strategies a reader uses to comprehend text.

 Looking Ahead

Be sure to schedule time for students to work on the unit inquiry project "Symbols of Freedom." This week students develop an inquiry question about American symbols of freedom.

Name _____ Date _____

My Work Plan
Put an ☒ next to the activities you complete.

Listening
- ☐ Listen to *The Story of the Statue of Liberty.*
- ☐ Listen to "A Nation of Immigrants."

Writing
- ☐ Design and write a postcard.
- ☐ Design a stamp.

Reading
- ☐ Read a book.
- ☐ Read Ten Important Sentences.
- ☐ Book Club

Social Studies
- ☐ Research a U.S. monument.
- ☐ Make a fact sheet.

Vocabulary
- ☐ Play a word game.

Technology
- ☐ Write about the Statue of Liberty.
- ☐ Save your file.

Independent Practice
- ☐ Practice Book 3.2, pp. 101–110
- ☐ Independent Writing

Inquiry
- ☐ Unit Inquiry
- ☐ Internet Inquiry

Wrap Up Your Week Turn your paper over. Write about what you did at school this week. What did you read? What did you learn about American symbols?

Unit 6 • Week 1 • *The Statue of Liberty* **43**

▲ **Group-Time Survival Guide**
p. 43, Weekly Contract

Customize Your Plan *by Strand*

ORAL LANGUAGE

SOCIAL STUDIES

Concept Development

What does the Statue of Liberty mean to Americans?

CONCEPT VOCABULARY
initials   *patriotic*   *recruiting*

BUILD

❑ **Question of the Week** Introduce and discuss the question of the week. This week students will read a variety of texts and work on projects related to the concept *American symbols*. Post the question for students to refer to throughout the week. **DAY 1** *284d*

❑ **Read Aloud** Read aloud "Uncle Sam." Then begin a web to build concepts and concept vocabulary related to this week's lesson and the unit theme, Freedom. Introduce the concept words *initials*, *patriotic*, and *recruiting* and have students place them on the web. Display the web for use throughout the week. **DAY 1** *284l–284m*

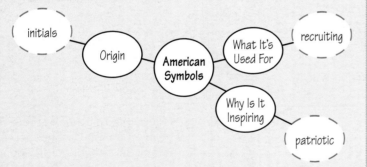

DEVELOP

❑ **Question of the Day** Use the prompts from the Weekly Plan to engage students in conversations related to this week's reading and the unit theme. **EVERY DAY** *284d–284e*

❑ **Concept Vocabulary Web** Revisit the American Symbols Concept Web and encourage students to add concept words from their reading and life experiences. **DAY 2** *295*, **DAY 3** *299*

CONNECT

❑ **Looking Back/Moving Forward** Revisit the American Symbols Concept Web and discuss how it relates to this week's lesson and the unit theme. Then make connections to next week's lesson. **DAY 5** *303c*

CHECK

❑ **Concept Vocabulary Web** Use the American Symbols Concept Web to check students' understanding of the concept vocabulary words *initials*, *patriotic*, and *recruiting*. **DAY 1** *284l*, **DAY 5** *303c*

VOCABULARY

STRATEGY WORD STRUCTURE
A prefix is a group of letters at the beginning of a word that changes the word's meaning. When you come across a word you don't know, look closely to see if the word has a prefix. Use the prefix and base word to help you figure out the word's meaning.

LESSON VOCABULARY

crown	tablet
liberty	torch
models	unforgettable
symbol	unveiled

TEACH

❑ **Words to Know** Give students the opportunity to tell what they already know about this week's lesson vocabulary words. Then discuss word meaning. **DAY 1** *286b*

❑ **Vocabulary Strategy Lesson** Use the vocabulary strategy lesson in the Student Edition to introduce and model this week's strategy, *word structure*. **DAY 2** *286–287*

Vocabulary Strategy Lesson

PRACTICE/APPLY

❑ **Leveled Text** Read the lesson vocabulary in the context of leveled text. **DAY 1** *LR1–LR9*

❑ **Words in Context** Read the lesson vocabulary and apply word structure in the context of *The Story of the Statue of Liberty*. **DAY 2** *288–295*, **DAY 3** *296–300*

❑ **Vocabulary Center** Use a game to practice word meanings. **ANY DAY** *284j*

❑ **Homework** Practice Book 3.2 pp. 104–105. **DAY 1** *286b*, **DAY 2** *287*

Leveled Readers

Main Selection—Nonfiction

❑ **Word Play** Have partners use reference sources to make lists of words that refer to sculpture, with their meanings. Students can draw a picture of a sculpture they found and label it with the appropriate words. **ANY DAY** *303c*

ASSESS

❑ **Selection Test** Use the Selection Test to determine students' understanding of the lesson vocabulary words. **DAY 3**

RETEACH/REVIEW

❑ **Reteach Lesson** If necessary, use this lesson to reteach and review *word structure*. **DAY 5** *303c*

COMPREHENSION

SKILL MAIN IDEA The topic is what a piece of writing is about. The main idea is the most important idea about the topic. Supporting details are small pieces of information that tell about the main idea.

STRATEGY TEXT STRUCTURE Text structure is how a selection is organized and written. To identify the main idea, ask yourself what the paragraph or selection is mostly about. To identify supporting details, look for key words that tell you *who, what, when, where,* and *why* as you read.

TEACH

❑ **Skill/Strategy Lesson** Use the skill/strategy lesson in the Student Edition to introduce and model *main idea* and *text structure.* **DAY 1** *284-285*

❑ **Extend Skills** Teach steps in a process. **ANY DAY** *303b*

Skill/Strategy Lesson

PRACTICE/APPLY

❑ **Leveled Text** Apply *main idea* and *text structure* to read leveled text. **DAY 1** *LR1-LR9*

❑ **Skills and Strategies in Context** Read *The Story of the Statue of Liberty,* using the Guiding Comprehension questions to apply *main idea* and *text structure.* **DAY 2** *288-295,* **DAY 3** *296-300*

Leveled Readers

❑ **Skills and Strategies in Context** Read " A Nation of Immigrants," guiding students as they apply *main idea* and *text structure.* Then have students discuss and write across texts. **DAY 4** *302-303*

Main Selection—Nonfiction

❑ **Homework** Practice Book 3.2 pp. 103, 107, 108. **DAY 1** *285,* **DAY 3** *299,* **DAY 5** *303b*

❑ **Fresh Reads for Differentiated Test Practice** Have students practice *main idea* with a new passage. **DAY 3**

Paired Selection—Nonfiction

ASSESS

❑ **Selection Test** Determine students' understanding of the selection and their use of *main idea.* **DAY 3**

❑ **Retell** Have students retell *The Story of the Statue of Liberty.* **DAY 3** *300-301*

RETEACH/REVIEW

❑ **Reteach Lesson** If necessary, reteach and review *main idea.* **DAY 5** *303b*

FLUENCY

SKILL ACCURACY, APPROPRIATE PACE/RATE AND EXPRESSION Reading accurately means reading the words that are there, not omitting words or substituting words. Reading at an appropriate pace and rate means reading at the right speed—not too fast and not too slow. Reading with expression means reading the words as if you were the character.

TEACH

❑ **Read Aloud** Model fluent reading by rereading " Uncle Sam." Focus on this week's fluency skill, accuracy, appropriate pace/rate and expression. **DAY 1** *284l-284m, 303a*

PRACTICE/APPLY

❑ **Choral Reading** Read aloud selected paragraphs from p. 293 without skipping or changing any words. Then practice as a class by doing three choral readings of the paragraphs. **DAY 2** *303a,* **DAY 3** *303a*

❑ **Paired Reading** Have partners practice reading aloud with accuracy and expression and offering each other feedback. As students reread, monitor their progress toward their individual fluency goals. **DAY 4** *303a*

❑ **Listening Center** Have students follow along with the AudioText for this week's selections. **ANY DAY** *284j*

❑ **Reading/Library Center** Have students reread a selection of their choice. **ANY DAY** *284j*

❑ **Fluency Coach** Have students use Fluency Coach to listen to fluent readings or practice reading on their own. **ANY DAY**

ASSESS

❑ **Check Fluency** WCPM Do a one-minute timed reading, paying special attention to this week's skill—accuracy, appropriate pace/rate and expression. Provide feedback for each student. **DAY 5** *303a*

☑ Customize Your Plan *by Strand*

GRAMMAR

SKILL CAPITAL LETTERS A capital letter is an uppercase letter. Capital letters are used to begin proper nouns, including the days of the week, the months of the year, and people's titles.

TEACH

- ☐ **Grammar Transparency 26** Use Grammar Transparency 26 to teach capital letters. DAY 1 *303e*

Grammar Transparency 26

PRACTICE/APPLY

- ☐ **Develop the Concept** Review the concept of capital letters and provide guided practice. DAY 2 *303e*

- ☐ **Apply to Writing** Have students review something they have written and apply what they have learned about capital letters. DAY 3 *303f*

- ☐ **Test Preparation** Examine common errors in using capital letters to prepare for standardized tests. DAY 4 *303f*

- ☐ **Homework** Grammar and Writing Practice Book pp. 101–103. DAY 2 *303e*, DAY 3 *303f*, DAY 4 *303f*

ASSESS

- ☐ **Cumulative Review** Use Grammar and Writing Practice Book p. 104. DAY 5 *303f*

RETEACH/REVIEW

- ☐ **Daily Fix-It** Have students find and correct errors in grammar, spelling, and punctuation. **EVERY DAY** *303e–303f*

- ☐ **The Grammar and Writing Book** Use pp. 200–203 of The Grammar and Writing Book to extend instruction for using capital letters. **ANY DAY**

The Grammar and Writing Book

WRITING

Trait of the Week

FOCUS/IDEAS To focus means to concentrate on. Good writers focus on a main idea and explain or describe this with strong, supporting details. When you take notes, for example, you write only the most important facts from a piece of writing. You also use your own words to write the facts.

TEACH

- ☐ **Writing Transparency 26A** Use the model to introduce and discuss the Trait of the Week. DAY 1 *303g*

- ☐ **Writing Transparency 26B** Use the transparency to show students how paraphrasing can improve their writing. DAY 2 *303g*

Writing Transparency 26A **Writing Transparency 26B**

PRACTICE/APPLY

- ☐ **Write Now** Examine the model on Student Edition p. 301. Then have students take notes. DAY 3 *301, 303h*, DAY 4 *303h*

  Prompt *The Story of the Statue of Liberty* tells how a sculptor created this famous statue. Think about the most important ideas in the selection. Now write notes about one part of the selection.

Write Now p. 301

- ☐ **Writing Center** Draw and write a picture postcard about the Statue of Liberty to send to a family member. **ANY DAY** *284k*

ASSESS

- ☐ **Writing Trait Rubric** Use the rubric to evaluate students' writing. DAY 4 *303h*

RETEACH/REVIEW

- ☐ **The Grammar and Writing Book** Use pp. 200–205 of The Grammar and Writing Book to extend instruction for capital letters, paraphrasing, and taking notes. **ANY DAY**

The Grammar and Writing Book

SPELLING

GENERALIZATION VOWEL SOUNDS IN *TOOTH* AND *COOK*
The vowel sound in tooth can be spelled *oo*, *ew*, *ue*, and *ui*: *school*, *few*, *glue*, *fruit*. The vowel sound in cook can be spelled *oo* and *u*: *cookie*, *cushion*.

TEACH

☐ **Pretest** Give the pretest for words with vowel sounds in *tooth* and *cook*. Guide students in self-correcting their pretests and correcting any misspellings. DAY 1 303k

☐ **Think and Practice** Connect spelling to the phonics generalization for the vowel sounds in *tooth* and *cook*. DAY 2 303k

PRACTICE/APPLY

☐ **Connect to Writing** Have students use spelling words to write a shopping list. Then review frequently misspelled words: *could, through, took, would.* DAY 3 303l

☐ **Homework** Phonics and Spelling Practice Book pp. 101–104. EVERY DAY

RETEACH/REVIEW

☐ **Review** Review spelling words to prepare for the posttest. Then provide students with a spelling strategy— vowel combinations. DAY 4 303l

ASSESS

☐ **Posttest** Use dictation sentences to give the posttest for words with vowel sounds in *tooth* and *cook*. DAY 5 303l

Spelling Words

1. few*	6. cookie	11. suit
2. school	7. cushion	12. chew
3. true	8. noodle	13. glue
4. goose	9. bookmark	14. Tuesday
5. fruit	10. balloon	15. bushel

Challenge Words

16. bamboo	18. soothe	20. renewal
17. mildew	19. barefoot	

*Word from the selection

PHONICS

SKILL VOWEL SOUNDS IN *TOOTH* AND *COOK* The letters *oo* can stand for the vowel sound in *book*, /u̇/, or in *moon*, /ü/. The letter *u* can stand for short *u* or the vowel sound in *book*, /u̇/. Context provides the clue to pronunciation. The letters *ew*, *ue*, and *ui* can stand for the vowel sound in *moon*, /ü/.

TEACH

☐ **Phonics Lesson** Model how to read words with vowel sounds in *tooth* and *cook*. Then have students practice by decoding longer words and reading words in context. DAY 2 303i

PRACTICE/APPLY

☐ **Homework** Practice Book 3.2, p. 109. DAY 2 303i

RETEACH/REVIEW

☐ **Review Word Parts** Review how to read words with the suffixes *-y*, *-ish*, *-hood*, and *-ment*. Then have students practice by decoding longer words and reading words in context. DAY 4 303j

RESEARCH AND INQUIRY

☐ **Internet Inquiry** Have students conduct an Internet inquiry on symbols of freedom. EVERY DAY 303m

☐ **Time Line** Review ideas related to timelines, such as time order, reading a timeline, and entries. Have students research the construction of a well-known United States monument, and create a timeline that shows important events of the construction. DAY 5 303n

☐ **Unit Inquiry** Allow time for students to develop an inquiry question about American symbols of freedom. ANY DAY 283

SPEAKING AND LISTENING

☐ **Announcement** Have students make a 2-minute announcement about a new sculpture they are unveiling in your city or town. Remind students to be aware of the nonverbal clues they use when speaking, including facial expressions and body language. DAY 5 303d

☐ **Listen to an Announcement** Have students listen to a public service announcement, then answer questions orally or in writing. DAY 5 303d

Resources for
Differentiated Instruction

LEVELED READERS

▶ **Comprehension**
- 🎯 **Skill** Main Idea
- 🎯 **Strategy** Text Structure

▶ **Lesson Vocabulary**
- 🎯 **Word Structure**

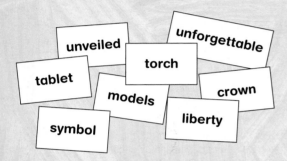

unveiled · unforgettable · torch · tablet · models · crown · symbol · liberty

▶ **Social Studies Standards**
- **History**
- **Cultures: Symbols**
- **Government History**

Leveled Reader Database
ONLINE
PearsonSuccessNet.com

Use the Online Database of over 600 books to

- Download and print additional copies of this week's leveled readers.
- Listen to the readers being read online.
- Search for more titles focused on this week's skills, topic, and content.

On-Level

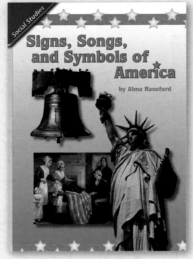

Social Studies

Signs, Songs, and Symbols of America
by Alma Ransford

On-Level Reader

Main Idea
- The **main idea** is the author's most important point about a topic.
- Sometimes the main idea is not stated directly in a selection, but the details of a selection can give you clues.

Directions Read the following passages. Then write down the main idea and list two details from the passage that support your answer.   Possible responses given.

> Our flag has thirteen stripes to remind us of our first colonies. There is a star for each state. The colors all mean something. Red is for hardiness, white is for innocence, blue stands for justice. Betsy Ross sewed the first flag.

1. Main idea: __Everything about our flag is symbolic.__

2. Supporting detail: __Each of the colors stands for something.__

3. Supporting detail: __The thirteen stripes remind us of our colonies.__

> Francis Scott Key watched the British attack during the War of 1812. When he looked out after a terrible battle, he saw that our flag was still waving. This inspired him to write a poem about it, *The Star Spangled Banner*, which was set to music. This song later became our national anthem.

4. Main idea: __Francis Scott Key wrote our national anthem.__

5. Supporting detail: __He was inspired by watching a battle.__

6. Supporting detail: __He wrote a poem that was set to music.__

On-Level Practice TE p. LR5

Vocabulary
Directions Use five of these vocabulary words to write a story about the signs and symbols of America. Then write definitions for the words you don't use in your story.

Check the Words You Know			
__crown	__liberty	__models	__symbol
__tablet	__torch	__unforgettable	__unveiled

1. __Responses will vary.__
_____
_____
_____
_____
_____
_____

2. _____
3. _____
4. _____

On-Level Practice TE p. LR6

Strategic Intervention

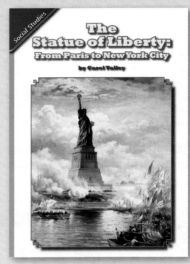

Social Studies

The Statue of Liberty: From Paris to New York City
by Carol Talley

Below-Level Reader

Main Idea
- The main idea is the most important idea about the topic.
- Sometimes the main idea is stated in a sentence, but when it isn't, you have to figure it out and state it in your own words.

Directions Read the following passages from the story *The Statue of Liberty: From Paris to New York City.* Circle the correct main idea in each.

1. What was New York City like in 1886? At night the city was ablaze with light. New York City was the first city in the world lighted by electricity!
   a. New York City was a busy city.
   b. New York in 1886 was full of light.
   c. New York City was the first city to have electricity.

2. The Statue of Liberty was being unveiled. Thousands of New Yorkers watched the unforgettable sight from the shores of Manhattan.
   a. Thousands of New Yorkers came to the shores.
   b. The Statue of Liberty was unveiled.
   c. People like to see new statues.

3. The Paris of today still has much of the charm of the old city. But not everything in Paris is old. There are new parks and gardens. You can ride down wide, tree-lined avenues where you will see new railroad stations, government buildings, and theaters.
   a. Paris has many parks and gardens.
   b. Paris today is a mixture of old and new.
   c. You can have a lot of fun in Paris.

Directions Look at the main ideas written below. Can you think of a supporting detail for each idea? For example, if the main idea is "Bob loves to sing," a supporting detail might be "and he is always giving musical concerts." Try it yourself!
Possible responses given.

4. My dog Skip loves the park. __He loves to play frisbee on the lawn.__
__He loves to roll on the grass. He naps under a tree.__

5. Keeping your teeth clean is important. __You can get cavities if you don't__
__brush. Your teeth won't be healthy. Your teeth won't look good.__

Below-Level Practice TE p. LR2

Vocabulary
Directions Fill in the missing letters for each vocabulary word. Then use the word in a sentence.

Check the Words You Know			
__crown	__liberty	__models	__symbol
__tablet	__torch	__unforgettable	__unveiled

Sentences will vary.

1. __r__wn __crown__

2. __ __b__ __ty __liberty__

3. t__ __ch __torch__

4. __ __for__et__able __unforgettable__

5. m__de__s __models__

6. __ __mbol __symbol__

7. t__ __let __tablet__

8. un__ei__ed __unveiled__

Below-Level Practice TE p. LR3

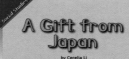
Advanced

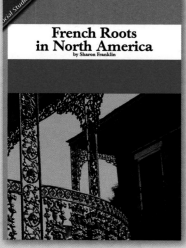

Social Studies

**French Roots
in North America**
by Sharon Franklin

Advanced Reader

Main Idea

- The **main idea** is the most important idea about a reading selection.
- Sometimes it is stated at the beginning, middle, or end of the selection; but sometimes it isn't and you must figure it out yourself.

Directions Below are groups of three sentences. Write *M* next to the sentence that is the main idea and *D* next to the sentences that are the supporting details.

_D_ **1.** No trip to Detroit is complete without a visit to the Henry Ford car museum.

_D_ **2.** Because of the automobile industry, Detroit is called Motor City.

_M_ **3.** Detroit is the home of the automobile industry.

_M_ **4.** In the 1820s, the French fur-trading families began to lose their influence.

_D_ **5.** The first major in the local army was an English-speaking doctor.

_D_ **6.** The population grew to include Germans, Irish, and others.

_M_ **7.** The strongest tradition in St. Lucia is African, but there is a large amount of French culture.

_D_ **8.** French is still spoken in St. Lucia.

_D_ **9.** There is a great deal of French music in St. Lucia.

10. What was the main idea of *French Roots in North America*?

The French have influenced North America.

Advanced Practice TE p. LR8

Vocabulary
Directions Unscramble the vocabulary words. Write the letter of the correct definition on the line.

Check the Words You Know

__assembly line	__bilingual	__descendants	__echo chamber
__fortified	__immigrants	__influences	__strait

_a_ **1.** gualbiiln — bilingual

_d_ **2.** mmgistnari — immigrants

_c_ **3.** stiart — strait

_b_ **4.** fluinensec — influences

_g_ **5.** blyssaem enli — assembly line

_f_ **6.** roftideif — fortified

_e_ **7.** hoec hamcber — echo chamber

_h_ **8.** cendesdants — descendants

a. what you are if you speak two languages

b. things that have effects on someone or something

c. a narrow strip of water that connects two larger bodies of water

d. people who leave one country and settle in another

e. room or space with walls that reflect sound so that an echo is made

f. made stronger against attack

g. in a factory, work passing from one person or machine to the next

h. people who are related to someone who lived in the past

Advanced Practice TE p. LR9

Social Studies

A Gift from Japan
by Cecelia Li

ELL Reader

ELL Poster 26

Teacher's Edition Notes

ELL notes throughout this lesson support instruction and reference additional resources at point of use.

**Teaching Guide
pp. 176–182, 262–263**

- Multilingual summaries of the main selection
- Comprehension lesson
- Vocabulary strategies and word cards
- ELL Reader 3.6.1 lesson

ELL and Transition Handbook

Ten Important Sentences

- Key ideas from every selection in the Student Edition
- Activities to build sentence power

More Reading

Readers' Theater Anthology
- Fluency practice
- Five scripts to build fluency
- Poetry for oral interpretation

Leveled Trade Books

Below-Level

...IF YOUR NAME WAS CHANGED at Ellis Island

Advanced

On-Level

- Extended reading tied to the unit concept
- Lessons in the Trade Book Library Teaching Guide

School + Home

Homework
- Family Times Newsletter
- ELL Multilingual Selection Summaries

Take-Home Books
- Leveled Readers

Family Times

Cross-Curricular Centers

 **Listening**

Listen to the
Selections

MATERIALS `SINGLES`
CD player, headphones,
AudioText CD, Student Edition

Listen to *The Story of the Statue of Liberty* and "A Nation of Immigrants" as you follow or read along in your book. Listen for main ideas about the Statue of Liberty.

If there is anything you don't understand, you can listen again to any section.

 Reading/Library

Read It
Again!

MATERIALS `SINGLES` `PAIRS` `GROUPS`
Collection of books for self-selected reading, reading log

Select a book you have already read. Record the title of the book in your reading log. You may want to read with a partner.

You may choose to read any of the following:

- **Leveled Readers**
- **ELL Readers**
- **Stories written by classmates**
- **Books from the library**
- *The Story of the Statue of Liberty*

TEN IMPORTANT SENTENCES Read the Ten Important Sentences for *The Story of the Statue of Liberty*. Then locate the sentences in the Student Edition.

BOOK CLUB Compose a group letter to the book's authors. Explain why you did or did not like the selection. Include any questions about the Statue of Liberty.

 Vocabulary

Definition
Game

MATERIALS `PAIRS`
Index card with 2 slits, 3" strip of construction paper, dictionary, pencil

Use words from the list below to play a game with a partner.

1. Choose 6 words from the list below. Write the words on the paper strip.
2. Use a dictionary. Write a short definition under each word.
3. Thread the strip through the slits in the index card. Only one word and its definition should show.
4. Without saying the word, give your partner clues to the word's meaning until he or she guesses the word. Take turns.

EARLY FINISHERS Read a word. Have your partner give a sentence using the word correctly.

constructed	monument
engineer	pedestal
fascination	remembrance
harbor	sculptor
immigrants	symbol
independence	unveiled

Scott Foresman Reading Street Centers Survival Kit

Use *The Story of the Statue of Liberty* materials from the
Reading Street Centers Survival Kit to organize
this week's centers.

Writing

Write a Postcard

MATERIALS `SINGLES`
Large index card, writing
and drawing materials

Imagine that you have just visited
the Statue of Liberty and want
to send a postcard to a family
member.

1. Design a postcard. The front of
   the postcard should be a picture.
   You may want to draw the Statue
   of Liberty or the view of New York
   Harbor as you would see it from
   inside the crown.
2. Draw a vertical line down the center
   of the back of the postcard.
3. On the left side of the line, write a
   short message to a family member.
4. Write the person's name and address
   on the right side.
5. Design a stamp for the postcard.

EARLY FINISHERS Make a list of five
to ten interesting facts about the
Statue of Liberty.

> Dear Kayla,
> Today we visited
> the Statue of
> Liberty. We climbed
> 168 steps to go
> inside her.

Social Studies

Artists and Monuments

MATERIALS `SINGLES` `PAIRS`
Books about United States
monuments, Internet access,
paper, pencil

Learn about another United States
monument and share the facts
with classmates.

1. Select a U.S. monument, such as
   Mount Rushmore, the Washington
   Monument, the Lincoln Memorial,
   the Golden Gate Bridge, or the St.
   Louis Gateway Arch.
2. Learn three or four interesting facts
   about the monument's designer.
   Write them on a fact sheet.
3. Display your fact sheet in your
   classroom.

EARLY FINISHERS Trade fact sheets
with a partner. Compare and
contrast the monuments.

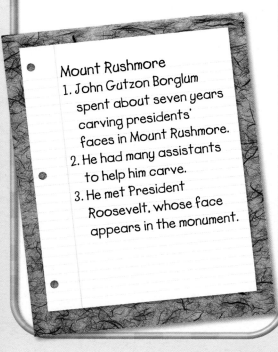

> Mount Rushmore
> 1. John Gutzon Borglum
>   spent about seven years
>   carving presidents'
>   faces in Mount Rushmore.
> 2. He had many assistants
>   to help him carve.
> 3. He met President
>   Roosevelt, whose face
>   appears in the monument.

Technology

Write a Description

MATERIALS `SINGLES`
Computer

Use lesson vocabulary to write
about the Statue of Liberty.

1. Open a word processing program.
2. In your own words, describe the
   Statue of Liberty. Use lesson
   vocabulary from the box below.
3. Save your file.

unveiled	crown
unforgettable	models
torch	liberty
tablet	symbol

EARLY FINISHERS Type new
sentences using vocabulary words.

> The Statue of Liberty is a
> symbol of freedom. She wears
> a crown and carries a torch.
> The torch lights up. The
> statue also holds a tablet.

ALL CENTERS

Concept Vocabulary

initials the first letter of words

patriotic having or showing love and loyal support for your country

recruiting getting people to join

Monitor Progress

Check Vocabulary

If... students are unable to place words on the web,	**then...** review the lesson concept. Place the words on the web and provide additional words for practice, such as *loyal* and *historic*.

SUCCESS PREDICTOR

DAY 1   Grouping Options

Reading

Whole Group

Introduce and discuss the Question of the Week. Then use pp. 284l–286b.

Group Time

Differentiated Instruction

Read this week's Leveled Readers. See pp. 284f–284g for the small group lesson plan.

Whole Group

Use p. 303a.

Language Arts

Use pp. 303e–303h and 303k–303m.

Build Concepts

FLUENCY

MODEL ACCURACY, APPROPRIATE PACE/RATE, AND EXPRESSION As you read "Uncle Sam," read with an appropriate tone. Use your tone of voice to model reading with expression. Use intonation when reading the rhetorical question "Who is he?" Use amusement and excitement as you read the last line.

LISTENING COMPREHENSION

After reading "Uncle Sam," use the following questions to assess listening comprehension.

1. **In a word or two, who is this selection about?** *(Uncle Sam)* **What is the most important idea about this topic?** *(Uncle Sam is a cartoon symbol for the United States of America.)* **Main Idea and Details**

2. **What is one detail that tells more about the main idea?** *(Possible response: He sometimes appears at patriotic gatherings.)* **Main Idea and Details**

BUILD CONCEPT VOCABULARY

Start a web to build concepts and vocabulary related to this week's lesson and the unit theme.

- Draw the American Symbols Concept Web.
- Read the sentence with the word *initials* again. Ask students to pronounce *initials* and discuss its meaning.
- Place *initials* in an oval attached to Origin. Explain that *initials* is related to this concept. Read the sentences in which *patriotic* and *recruiting* appear. Have students pronounce the words, place them on the web, and provide reasons.
- Brainstorm additional words and categories for the web. Keep the web on display and add words throughout the week.

Concept Vocabulary Web

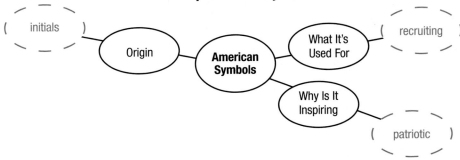

Uncle Sam

by Delno C. West and Jean M. West

Perhaps you've seen him in parades or at a Fourth of July picnic. He sometimes appears at patriotic gatherings clad in a long blue coat, a vest, and red and white striped trousers. He normally wears a beard and a tall striped and starred hat, and he appears to be dressed to look like the American flag. Who is he? He is "Uncle Sam," a cartoon symbol for the United States of America.

There is much debate about who Uncle Sam was and how the symbol came to be. The first mention of him was in a Troy, New York, newspaper article that appeared on September 7, 1813. It seems that a certain meat-processing plant owner named Sam Wilson began stamping the meat sold to the United States Army during the War of 1812 with the letters "U.S." The meatpackers at his plant called Sam Wilson "Uncle Sam," and the story was that the initials "U.S." really stood for "Uncle Sam" Wilson rather than "United States." The nickname stuck, and from then on everything belonging to the United States government began to be called "Uncle Sam's." Soon, cartoonists latched on to this idea, and they began drawing varieties of Uncle Sam in political cartoons. The most famous depictions of Uncle Sam were on World War I and World War II military recruiting posters. Today, no patriotic gathering would be complete without an appearance by someone dressed as Uncle Sam.

Set Purpose

Have students listen for the main idea and details that support the idea that Uncle Sam is a symbol for the United States.

Creative Response

Have students work in small groups to improvise a patriotic event, such as Independence Day. Encourage students to discuss Uncle Sam as a symbol of the country. *Drama*

Build Background Show students the image of Uncle Sam. Explain that he is a symbol of the United States.

Access Content Before reading, share this summary: The Uncle Sam we see today was probably introduced during the War of 1812 when a man named Sam Wilson stamped meat with the initials U.S.

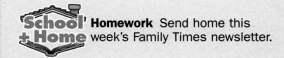

Homework Send home this week's Family Times newsletter.

SKILLS ⟷ STRATEGIES IN CONTEXT

Main Idea
Text Structure

OBJECTIVES

- Determine main idea and identify details.
- Use text structure to identify main idea.

Skills Trace
Main Idea and Details

Introduce/Teach	TE: 3.2 150–151, 198–199, 3.6 284–285
Practice	PB: 3.1 53, 57–58,73, 77–78, 86; 3.2 103, 107–108, 126, 146
Reteach/Review	TE: 3.2 173b, 223b, 233, 241, DI·54; 3.6 303b, 339, 391, 397, DI·52
Test	Selection Test: Unit 6 Benchmark Tests: Units 2, 6

INTRODUCE

Write the topic "Neighbors" and add details: *The Gonzales family moved to the neighborhood from Mexico. The Adams family moved here from Maine. The Buckley family has lived in the neighborhood for 50 years.* Ask what might be the main idea in an article with this topic and details. *(Possible response: People in a neighborhood come from many different places.)*

Have students read the information on p. 284. Explain the following:

- A main idea is what a paragraph or passage is mostly about.
- Supporting details provide more information about a main idea.
- The way in which a passage is organized, or its text structure, can help you identify main ideas.

Use Skill Transparency 26 to teach main idea and text structure.

 The Story of the Statue of Liberty

Comprehension

Skill
Main Idea and Details

Strategy
Text Structure

 Main Idea and Details

Main Idea and Details

- The main idea is the most important idea in a selection or a paragraph.
- The small pieces of information that tell about the main idea are the supporting details.

Main Idea

Supporting Detail **Supporting Detail** **Supporting Detail**

Strategy: Text Structure

Active readers think about how a selection is organized and written. It's a good idea t look for key words in the text, such as *who, what, where, why,* and *when.* These key wo will give you details about the main idea.

Write to Read

1. Read "Coming to America." Then make a graphic organizer like the one above to show the main idea and details.

2. Write a paragraph about where your ancestors came from.

284

Strategic Intervention

Main Idea Help students become familiar with the graphic organizer on p. 284. Begin by presenting a common situation, such as the one in the "Introduce" activity on the page. Model how to fill in the main idea sentence in the graphic organizer. Then invite volunteers to indicate where to write each supporting detail. Explain the graphic organizer's arrow directionality, which helps reinforce the idea that the supporting details give more information about the main idea.

ELL

Access Content

Beginning/Intermediate For a Picture It! lesson on main idea and supporting details, see the ELL Teaching Guide, pp. 176–177.

Advanced Encourage students to share their family's immigration experience. Did their parents and/or grandparents come to America? From where did they come? Why did they come?

Coming to America

The country where you were born is called your *homeland*. People who leave their homeland and come to another country—such as America—are called *immigrants*. America has been called a "Nation of Immigrants." Why?

Everyone who lives in America now (except for Native Americans) once came from somewhere else. This may have happened a very long time ago in your family. Maybe the ones to come to America were your great-great-great-great-great grandparents. Or maybe you and your family arrived here recently.

Immigrants leave their homeland for different reasons. Some came to America looking for religious freedom. Some came to escape war or hunger. Others came for adventure. But mostly, people came looking for a better life for themselves and their children.

The next time you have a coin, turn it over and look for the motto of the United States on the back. The words are in Latin, and they say *E pluribus unum*. They mean "Out of many, one."

People came to America from all over the world, but together, we are one nation!

1 **Strategy** Here is a key word—*why*—that gives you a clue. The next part of this selection will probably answer that question.

2 **Skill** Here is the main idea of this paragraph—people came to America for many reasons. Now read on to find the supporting details.

285

Available as **Skill Transparency** 26

Main Idea and Details · Text Structure

- The **main idea** is the most important idea in a selection or a paragraph.
- The small pieces of information that tell about the main idea are the supporting **details**.
- Look for key words in the text, such as *who, what, where, why,* and *when,* to get **details** about the **main idea.**

Directions Read the following passage and complete the web below.

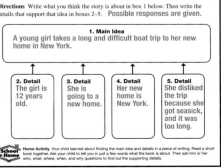

I was getting seasick again. The trip on the boat to America was taking longer than a 12-year-old girl like me ever imagined. I disliked the constant rocking and the smells of all the people crammed together in such a small space. It didn't seem like we'd ever get to the place everyone called *New York*—the place where we'd soon be calling home. Suddenly, people started yelling. I ran outside to see what was going on. There, in front of me, stood a giant statue. They called it the Statue of Liberty. It was beautiful. We were home at last!

Directions Write what you think the story is about in box 1 below. Then write the details that support that idea in boxes 2–5. **Possible responses are given.**

1. Main Idea
A young girl takes a long and difficult boat trip to her new home in New York.

| **2. Detail** The girl is 12 years old. | **3. Detail** She is going to a new home. | **4. Detail** Her new home is New York. | **5. Detail** She disliked the trip because she got seasick, and it was too long. |

School + Home **Home Activity** Your child learned about finding the main idea and details in a piece of writing. Read a short book together. Ask your child to tell you in just a few words what the book is about. Then ask him or her who, what, where, when, and why questions to find out the supporting details.

Practice Book 3.2 p. 103

TEACH

1 **STRATEGY** Discuss how the text structure can help you identify main ideas.

Think Aloud **MODEL** The first paragraph ends with a statement followed by a question. The statement is "America has been called a 'Nation of Immigrants.'" Then the author wrote the question "Why?" This structure gives me a clue. The next sentences will likely give details about the main idea that America is a nation of immigrants.

2 **SKILL** Use paragraph 3 to model how to determine main idea and supporting details.

Think Aloud **MODEL** I ask myself, "What is the paragraph all about?" I decide that the big idea of the paragraph is that people come to America for different reasons. The other sentences in the paragraph give more information about the main idea.

PRACTICE AND ASSESS

STRATEGY Main idea: "America has been called a 'Nation of Immigrants.'" Supporting detail: "Everyone who lives in America now (except for Native Americans) once came from somewhere else."

SKILL Main idea: "People become immigrants for different reasons." Supporting details: Religious freedom, to escape war or hunger, for adventure, to have a better life for themselves and their children.

WRITE Have students complete steps 1 and 2 of the Write to Read activity. You might consider using this as a whole class activity.

Monitor Progress

Main Idea

| **If...** students are unable to complete **Write to Read** on p. 284, | **then...** use Practice Book 3.2 p. 103 to provide additional practice. |

Tech Files ONLINE

For a Web site that explores the history and symbolism of the Statue of Liberty, suggest students use a student-friendly search engine with the keywords *Statue of Liberty history*.

Build Background Use ELL Poster 26 to build background and vocabulary for the lesson concept of the meaning of the Statue of Liberty.

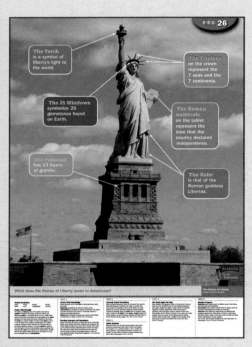

▲ **ELL Poster** 26

Build Background

BEGIN A K-W-L CHART about the Statue of Liberty.

- Give students two to three minutes to write as many things as they can about the Statue of Liberty. Record what students know on the K-W-L chart.

- Give students two minutes to write three questions they would like to answer about the statue. Record questions on the K-W-L chart. Add a question of your own.

- Tell students that, as they read, they should look for the answers to their questions and note any new information to add to the chart.

K	W	L
The Statue of Liberty is big.	When was the Statue of Liberty built?	
The Statue of Liberty is in New York.	What does the Statue of Liberty stand for?	

▲ **Graphic Organizer** 3

BACKGROUND BUILDING AUDIO This week's audio explores Ellis Island and its role in American history. After students listen, discuss what they found out and what surprised them most about Ellis Island.

Background Building Audio

Introduce Vocabulary

DISCUSS THE VOCABULARY

Have students use these steps for reading multisyllabic words. (See the Multisyllabic Word Routine on p. DI·1.)

1 Look for Meaningful Word Parts (base words, endings, prefixes, suffixes, roots) Think about the meaning of each part. Use the parts to read the word. Model: I see *un-* at the beginning of *unforgettable,* and I see *-able* at the end. I know that *un-* means "not" and that *-able* means "able." I know what *forget* means, so *unforgettable* must mean "something you can't forget."

2 Chunk Words with No Recognizable Parts Say each chunk slowly. Then say the chunks fast to make a word. Model: *mod, els—models.*

Share lesson vocabulary with students. Have students locate each word in their glossaries and note each word's pronunciation and meaning. Ask these questions to help clarify word meanings.

Was there anything written on the tablet?

Do you think the bald eagle is a good symbol for the United States?

Who gets to wear the crown?

Were you there when they unveiled the statue?

Was there a torch to light up the cave?

What is the most unforgettable book you ever read?

Were the models made of clay?

Point out that some of this week's words are features of the Statue of Liberty—*tablet, torch, crown.* Ask students what other words they know that might be categorized with the Statue of Liberty. *(Possible response: copper, pedestal, sandals)* **Activate Prior Knowledge**

Continue this activity by having students write their own questions using the vocabulary.

Lesson Vocabulary

WORDS TO KNOW

T **crown** a head covering of precious metal worn by a royal person, such as a queen or king

T **liberty** freedom

T **models** small copies of something

T **symbol** an object, diagram, icon, and so on, that stands for or represents something else

T **tablet** a small, flat surface with something written on it

T **torch** a long stick with material that burns at one end of it

T **unforgettable** so good or so wonderful that you cannot forget it

T **unveiled** removed a veil from; uncovered; revealed

MORE WORDS TO KNOW

pedestal a base on which a column or a statue stands

riveted fastened something with metal bolts

sculptor an artist who make things by cutting or shaping them

T= Tested Word

Vocabulary
Directions Solve each riddle with a word from the box. Write the word on the line.
1. I describe something that you will always remember. What am I? __unforgettable__
2. People who live in a free country have me. What am I? __liberty__
3. Kings and queens wear me on their heads. What am I? __crown__
4. I am another word for uncovered. What am I? __unveiled__
5. I am a light that helps people see in dark caves. What am I? __torch__

Check the Words You Know: liberty, crown, tablet, symbol, unveiled, torch, models, unforgettable

Directions Write the word from the box that best completes each sentence below.
6. The wood carver made two ___ of an airplane. __models__
7. At night we lit a ___ to help us see our campsite. __torch__
8. A flag is a ___ of a country. __symbol__
9. A ___ is a stone that has writing cut into it. __tablet__

Write an Editorial
On a separate sheet of paper, write an editorial about the first time the Statue of Liberty was seen in New York. Write as if you worked for a newspaper. Tell readers how you felt when you first saw the new statue. Use as many vocabulary words as possible. Students' writing should use vocabulary to describe the unveiling of the Statue of Liberty and express their feelings about it.

Home Activity Your child has identified and used vocabulary from The Story of the Statue of Liberty. Read a story together about this or another historical monument. Have a conversation about the monument and its meaning. Encourage your child to use vocabulary words.

▲ **Practice Book 3.2** p. 104

Vocabulary Strategy

OBJECTIVE

 Use word structure to determine the meaning of words with prefixes.

INTRODUCE

Discuss the word structure strategy for prefixes using the steps on p. 286.

TEACH

- Have students read "Emma and Liberty," paying attention to how vocabulary is used.
- Model using word structure to determine the meaning of *unveiled*.

 MODEL I know that *veil* means "to cover with something." I know that the prefix *un-* means "the opposite of" or "not." So the word *unveiled* must mean "to take the cover off something."

Words to Know

liberty

unveiled

crown

torch

tablet

models

symbol

unforgettable

Remember

Try the strategy. Then, if you need more help, use your glossary or a dictionary.

Vocabulary Strategy
for Prefixes

Word Structure When you see a word you don't know, look closely at the word. Does it have *un-* at the beginning? The prefix *un-* makes the word mean "not ____" or "the opposite of ____." For example, *unhappy* means "not happy." You can use the prefix to help you figure out the meaning of the word.

1. Put your finger over *un-*.

2. Look at the base word. Put the base word in the phrase "not ____" or "the opposite of ____."

3. Try that meaning in the sentence. Does it make sense?

Read "Emma and Liberty." Look for words that begin with *un-*. Use the prefix to help you figure out the meanings of the words.

286

DAY 2   Grouping Options

Reading
Whole Group Discuss the Question of the Day. Then use pp. 286–289.

Group Time Differentiated Instruction
Read *The Story of the Statue of Liberty.* See pp. 284f–284g for the small group lesson plan.

Whole Group Use pp. 303a and 303i.

Language Arts
Use pp. 303e–303h and 303k–303m.

Strategic Intervention

Word Structure Encourage students to work in pairs to follow the steps on p. 286 to find the best meaning for each unknown word.

ELL

Access Content Use ELL Poster 26 to preteach vocabulary. Choose from the following to meet language proficiency levels.

Beginning Point out the base word *forget* in *unforgettable*. Tell students that the prefix *un-* means "not." Work with students to define *unforgettable*, as "not able to be forgotten."

Intermediate After reading, students can create a chart with the words and their definitions.

Advanced Teach the lesson on pp. 286–287. Students can report on the names of these different parts of the Statue of Liberty in their home languages.

Resources for home-language words may include parents, bilingual staff members, bilingual dictionaries, or online translation sources.

Emma and Liberty

Emma is visiting New York City. What she wants to see more than anything else is the Statue of Liberty. Emma knows everything about Liberty. She knows why the statue was made, who made it, and when it was unveiled in New York Harbor. She knows how tall it is from its base to its crown, what its torch is made of, and what is written on the tablet. Emma has collected pictures of the statue and made models of it. However, she has never seen the real Liberty.

From Battery Park in lower Manhattan, Emma can see the Statue of Liberty in the distance. She waits in line for the boat that will take her to the island. As the boat gets nearer, Emma imagines what it was like for the immigrants who sailed past Liberty as they arrived in America. At last Emma is standing at Liberty's feet. She tilts her head back to look up at this symbol of freedom. It is an unforgettable moment.

Words to Write

What do you know about the Statue of Liberty or another symbol of America? Write about it. Use as many words from the Words to Know list as you can.

287

PRACTICE AND ASSESS

- Have students determine the meanings of the remaining words and explain how they used base words and prefixes to find the meaning.
- Point out that using base words and prefixes does not work with every word. Students may have to use the glossary or a dictionary to find the exact meaning of some words.
- Have students complete Practice Book 3.2, p. 105.

WRITE Writing should include vocabulary words that describe what the students know about the Statue of Liberty or another symbol of the nation.

Monitor Progress

Word Structure

If... students need more practice with the lesson vocabulary,	**then...** use Tested Vocabulary Cards.

Vocabulary • Word Structure

- A **prefix** is a word part added to the beginning of a word. **Prefixes** can help you figure out the meaning of a word you don't know.
- The **prefix** *un-* means "not" or "opposite of."

Directions Match the word with the prefix *un-* with its meaning.

1. unforgettable — not common
2. unveiled — not divided into pieces
3. unhappy — not something you'll forget
4. unusual — opposite of happy
5. uncut — not covered

Directions Read each pair of sentences. Circle the word that belongs in the blank. Write the word on the line.

6. The laces of her shoes dragged on the ground.
   The laces of her shoes were _untied_   (untied)   uncover

7. Too much sugar is not good for our bodies.
   Eating too many sweets is _unhealthy_   undone   (unhealthy)

8. He just got home from vacation.
   He will _unpack_ his bags.   until   (unpack)

9. The artist takes the beads off the string.
   She will _unstring_ the beads.   (unstring)   upend

10. The main character never tells lies.
    He never says anything that is _untrue_   under   (untrue)

Home Activity Your child has identified and used words with the prefix *un-*. Read a short story or paragraph with your child. Together, look for words with the prefix *un-*. Help your child figure out the meaning of these words.

▲ **Practice Book 3.2** p. 105

Prereading Strategies

OBJECTIVES

- Identify main idea and supporting details to improve comprehension.
- Use text structure to help determine main idea.

GENRE STUDY

Narrative Nonfiction

The Story of the Statue of Liberty is narrative nonfiction. Explain that narrative nonfiction reads like a story but tells about real people and events.

PREVIEW AND PREDICT

Have students preview the selection title and illustrations and discuss the topics or ideas they think this selection will cover. Encourage students to use lesson vocabulary as they talk about what they expect to learn.

Strategy Response Log

Activate Prior Knowledge Ask students if they have ever seen the Statue of Liberty or a picture of it. Invite them to list facts they know about the statue. Students add to their list and monitor their comprehension in the Strategy Response Log activity on p. 295.

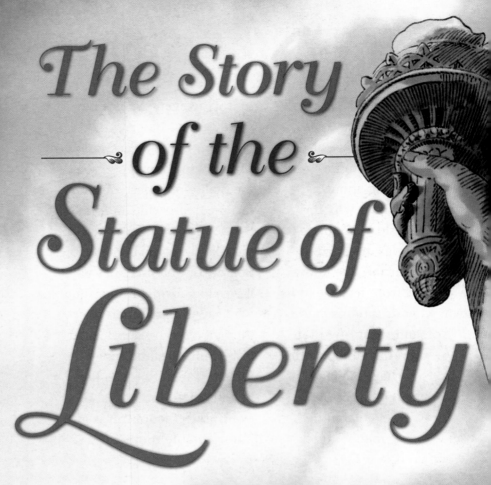

The Story of the Statue of Liberty

by Betsy & Giulio Maestro

Genre

Narrative nonfiction gives information about real people and events in the form of a story. What special event does this selection tell about?

288

ELL

Activate Prior Knowledge Help students understand the concepts of freedom and liberty before they read the selection. Also make sure students understand and can describe a symbol.

Consider having students read the selection summary in English or in students' home languages. See the Multilingual Summaries in the ELL Teaching Guide, pp. 180–182.

What is interesting or important about the Statue of Liberty?

289

SET PURPOSE

Read the first page of the selection aloud to students. Have them consider their preview discussion and tell what they hope to find out as they read.

Remind students to look for main ideas and supporting details as they read.

STRATEGY RECALL

Students have now used these before-reading strategies:

- preview the selection to be aware of its genre, features, and possible content;
- activate prior knowledge about that content and what to expect of that genre;
- make predictions;
- set a purpose for reading.

Remind students to be aware of and flexibly use the during-reading strategies they have learned:

- link prior knowledge to new information;
- summarize text they have read so far;
- ask clarifying questions;
- answer questions they or others pose;
- check their predictions and either refine them or make new predictions;
- recognize the text structure the author is using, and use that knowledge to make predictions and increase comprehension;
- visualize what the author is describing;
- monitor their comprehension and use fix-up strategies.

After reading, students will use these strategies:

- summarize or retell the text;
- answer questions they or others pose;
- reflect to make new information become part of their prior knowledge.

Audio CD AudioText

Guiding Comprehension

1 **Fact and Opinion • Inferential**

Read p. 290. Name one fact and one opinion on the page.

Possible response: Fact: "The Statue of Liberty stands on an island in New York Harbor." Opinion: "She is a beautiful sight to all who pass by her."

2  **Main Idea • Inferential**

Have students determine the main idea and a supporting detail of paragraph 3 on p. 290.

Main Idea: The Statue of Liberty was a special statue to Bartholdi. Detail: The statue was to be a gift to Americans from the French.

Monitor Progress

 **Main Idea**

If... students are unable to determine the main idea and supporting details,	**then...** use the skill and strategy instruction on p. 291.

ONLINE

Students can find out more about the life and work of Frédéric Bartholdi by searching the Internet. Have them use a student-friendly search engine and the keywords *Frédéric Bartholdi.*

The Statue of Liberty stands on an island in New York Harbor. She is a beautiful sight to all who pass by her. Each year, millions of visitors ride the ferry out to the island. They climb to the top of the statue and enjoy the lovely view.

A young French sculptor named Frédéric Auguste Bartholdi visited America in 1871. When he saw Bedloe's Island in New York Harbor, he knew it was just the right place for a statue he wanted to build.

Bartholdi had created many other statues and monuments, but this one was to be very special. It was to be a present from the people of France to the people of America, as a remembrance of the old friendship between the two countries. **1** **2**

290

ELL

Access Content Help students become more familiar with places in the United States and France that are named in the selection. On a map, point out the locations mentioned in the selection, such as New York Harbor and Paris. Help students differentiate between and understand the concepts of an island and a harbor.

When Bartholdi got back to Paris, he made sketches and some small models. The statue would be a woman whom he would call Liberty. She would be a symbol of the freedom in the New World. She would hold a lamp in her raised hand to welcome people who came to America. She would be *Liberty Enlightening the World*.

291

Location Skills

Have students locate New York Harbor and Paris, France, on a world map. Ask them to estimate the distance between the two locations. Explain that New York is a state in the country of The United States of America. The country is on the continent of North America. Paris is in the country of France. The country is on the continent of Europe. Use a ruler and a map scale to figure the approximate distance between the two places. (3,635 miles) Remind students of the distance as they read pp. 290–291.

Time for SOCIAL STUDIES

SKILLS ⟷ STRATEGIES IN CONTEXT

Main Idea

TEACH

- Remind students that a main idea makes an important point about the topic and has at least one supporting detail.
- Supporting details are smaller pieces of information that provide more detail about the main idea.
- Model finding the main idea of p. 290, paragraph 3.

 Think Aloud **MODEL** First I'll see what each sentence in the paragraph is about. Then I'll look for details the sentences have in common. Both sentences are about the Statue of Liberty and why it was special to Bartholdi. If I put the information together, the main idea is that the Statue of Liberty was special to Bartholdi. A detail is that the statue was to be a present from the French to the Americans. This detail explains why the statue was important to him.

PRACTICE AND ASSESS

Have students reread p. 291. Ask which of the following is the main idea for the paragraph. (choice *c*)

a) Bartholdi began work on the Statue of Liberty by making models and sketches.

b) Bartholdi decided the statue would be a woman.

c) Bartholdi decided that the statue would be a symbol of freedom.

Guiding Comprehension

3 **Sequence • Literal**

What was the first step in the construction of the Statue of Liberty?

Building a huge, steel skeleton.

4 REVIEW **Cause and Effect • Inferential**

Why were parts of the Statue of Liberty displayed in the United States before the statue was completed?

Possible response: People paid money to tour the pieces. The money was used to pay for the statue.

Monitor Progress	
REVIEW **Cause and Effect**	
If... students have difficulty identifying the cause and effect relationship,	**then...** use the skill and strategy instruction on p. 293.

The statue would be very large and very strong. Bartholdi wanted people to be able to climb up inside the statue and look out over the harbor from the crown and torch.

Many well-known artists, engineers, and craftsmen gave him ideas about how to build the statue. First, a huge skeleton was constructed from strong steel.

3

Many people worked together in a large workshop. Some worked on Liberty's head and crown. Others worked on her right hand, which would hold the torch.

In her left hand she would hold a tablet with the date July 4, 1776, written on it. This is when the Declaration of Independence was signed.

292

Extend Language Direct students' attention to the words *artists,* *engineers,* and *craftsmen* in the second paragraph on p. 292. Explain the relationship among these three words. Point out how the careers are similar and different.

The arm holding the torch was sent to Philadelphia for America's 100th birthday celebration in 1876. Afterward, it stood in Madison Square in New York City for a number of years.

Liberty's head was shown at the World's Fair in Paris during this time. Visitors were able to climb inside and look around. In this way, money was raised to pay for the statue.

293

Cultures (Symbols)

Time for SOCIAL STUDIES

In a speech, former President Cleveland said, "We will not forget that Liberty has here made her home." The Statue of Liberty is a symbol of freedom, a symbol of the friendship between the U.S. and France, and a symbol of the United States. The statue has additional symbolism. Broken chains at Lady Liberty's feet represent freedom from tyranny or misuse of power. The seven rays in her crown symbolize the seven continents and seas. Can you identify other symbols within the statue?

Cause/Effect REVIEW

TEACH

- Remind students that cause is why something happened. The effect is what happened.

- Explain that clue words, such as *because* and *so,* can help them identify cause and effect, but clue words are not always there. To be a cause and effect relationship, one event must make another happen.

Think Aloud **MODEL** On p. 293, I notice the clue words "in this way." These words may signal a cause and effect relationship. People paid money to climb inside Liberty's head. This is a cause given in the question. The effect is that money was raised.

PRACTICE AND ASSESS

- Have students reread the first two paragraphs on p. 292. Ask them to identify material Bartholdi used to make the Statue of Liberty's skeleton. Invite students to identify the reasons Bartholdi chose steel. *(The statue needed to be very large and very strong. Steel is strong.)*

- To assess, use Practice Book 3.2, p. 106.

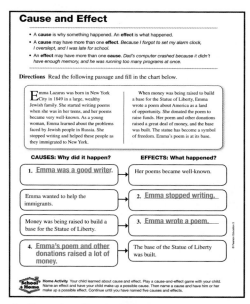

▲ **Practice Book 3.2** p. 106

Guiding Comprehension

5 **Text Structure • Inferential**

How did the authors organize the main ideas in the text for this selection?

Sequential order.

Monitor Progress

Text Structure

If... students have difficulty identifying the main ideas or text structure,	then... use the skill and strategy instruction on p. 295.

---

6 Steps in a Process • Critical

Text to World **Workers created the Statue of Liberty by creating and following a process of steps. Describe a statue, building, or other structure you have seen or read about that was built in a similar way.**

Possible response: The process is like the one workers followed when they built the tall bank building in my community. First, workers built a steel frame. Then they put up a scaffold to work on the outside of the building.

7 Draw Conclusions • Inferential

Why was the completed Statue of Liberty taken apart?

Possible response: It was too large and heavy to ship to the United States. It had to be shipped in smaller pieces.

Then, skin of gleaming copper was put onto the skeleton and held in place with iron straps. As the huge statue grew, all of Paris watched with great fascination.

294

ELL

Activate Prior Knowledge Ask students if they have ever sent or received a fragile package in the mail. Invite them to share how it was packed and why such care was taken. Then relate this information to the dismantling of the Statue of Liberty before shipping.

Finally, in 1884, Liberty was completed. There was a big celebration in Paris. Many famous people came to see her. Only a few had the energy to climb all the way to the crown—168 steps!

Then began the hard work of taking Liberty apart for the long voyage across the Atlantic Ocean. Each piece was marked and packed into a crate. There were 214 crates in all. They were carried by train and then put on a ship to America. **5 6 7**

295

Develop Vocabulary

PRACTICE LESSON VOCABULARY

Have students provide oral responses to each question.

1. **Where is the *tablet* on the Statue of Liberty? What is on the *tablet*?** (In her left hand; the date of America's signing of the Declaration of Independence)
2. **What is a *symbol* for love?** (Possible response: a heart)
3. **Would you wear a *crown* on your head or your feet?** (Your head)

BUILD CONCEPT VOCABULARY

Review previous concept words with students. Ask if students have come across any words today in their reading or elsewhere that they would like to add to the Concept Web.

🔄 SKILLS ◆▶ STRATEGIES IN CONTEXT

Text Structure

TEACH

- Explain to students that authors organize their writing in different ways. Many historical selections and biographies are written in the order the real events occurred.
- Main idea statements can help identify the text structure.
- Words, such as *before, after, first,* and *finally,* sometimes signal a sequential organization.
- Read pp. 294–295. Model how to use the main ideas to determine the text structure.

Think Aloud **MODEL** The selection's main idea is the building and symbolism of the Statue of Liberty. The paragraph on p. 294 uses the words *then* and *as.* These words indicate a sequence of events. The next paragraph uses the word *finally.* The text structure is sequential.

Strategy Response Log

Monitor Comprehension Ask students to revisit their list of facts about the Statue of Liberty. Invite them to add facts they have learned to the list and record any facts or concepts from the selection that they do not understand. Encourage them to reread appropriate pages to clear up their understanding of the text.

EXTEND SKILLS

Word Choice

Tell students that authors often use certain words to set a tone or create an image. The words *skeleton* and *skin* on p. 294 are interesting words to use to describe a statue. Ask students why the authors may have chosen these words. (*Possible response: to remind us that the statue looks like a person*) Explain that the authors use these words to create an image of the statue that we can picture in our heads.

If you want to teach this selection in two sessions, stop here.

Guiding Comprehension

If you are teaching the selection in two days, discuss the main ideas so far and review the vocabulary.

8 Sequence • Inferential
What happened after the statue arrived in New York?

It was reassembled.

9 Vocabulary • Word Structure
What is the meaning of the word *unveiled* on p. 297?

Removed the covering from.

Monitor Progress

Word Structure

If... students are unable to determine the meaning of *unveiled*,	**then...** use the vocabulary strategy instruction on p. 297.

DAY 3 Grouping Options

Reading
Whole Group Discuss the Question of the Day.

Group Time Differentiated Instruction
Read *The Story of the Statue of Liberty.* See pp. 284f–284g for the small group lesson plan.

Whole Group Discuss the Reader Response questions on p. 300. Then use p. 303a.

Language Arts
Use pp. 303e–303h and 303k–303m.

But in America people had lost interest in the Statue of Liberty. Money had run out and work on Bedloe's Island had stopped. The base for the statue was not finished. With the help of a large New York newspaper, the money was raised. People all over the country, including children, sent in whatever they could. By the time the ship reached New York in 1885, it was greeted with new excitement.

8 The work on the island went on, and soon the pedestal was completed. Piece by piece, the skeleton was raised. Then the copper skin was riveted in place. Liberty was put back together like a giant puzzle. The statue had been built not once, but twice!

296

ELL

Access Content Help students understand the use and meaning of the words *skeleton* and *skin* in the last paragraph on p. 296.

At last, in 1886, Liberty was standing where she belonged. A wonderful celebration was held. Boats and ships filled the harbor. Speeches were read, songs were sung. Bartholdi himself unveiled Liberty's face and she stood, gleaming in all her glory, for everyone ⑨ to see. There was a great cheer from the crowd. Then President Grover Cleveland gave a speech.

297

TIME FOR Science

Metals

Ask students why they think copper was used as the skin of the Statue of Liberty. Explain that copper resists the damaging effects of wind, sun, rain, and other elements. Copper is found underground and is mined in the United States, especially in Arizona, Montana, and Utah, and around the world. The largest deposits of copper are found in the Atacama Desert in northern Chile. Much of today's copper is recycled.

VOCABULARY STRATEGY

Word Structure

TEACH

Read p. 297 aloud. Model using word structure to determine the meaning of *unveiled*.

Think Aloud

MODEL I see the word *unveiled* on p. 297. I know that *to veil* something means to cover it. I also know that the prefix *un-* makes a word mean "not ____" or "the opposite of _____." If the opposite of veiling something is unveiling it, then I think *unveiled* means to take the cover off of something.

PRACTICE AND ASSESS

Have students think of a word with a prefix that could be substituted in the third sentence on p. 296. *(unfinished)*

EXTEND SKILLS

Word Choice

Tell students that authors often use special words and phrases to indicate steps in a process. The words *by the time, then,* and *at last* on pp. 296–297 are clue words that indicate a process. Explain that visualizing the steps will help students understand them as they read. Have students identify all of the steps in the process of making the Statue of Liberty.

Guiding Comprehension

10 **Symbolism • Critical**

What does the Statue of Liberty symbolize?

Possible responses: freedom, liberty, friendship.

11 **Text Structure • Critical**

Text to Self **How does the text structure help you summarize what you read? Use a time line, steps in a process chart, or other graphic organizer to write a summary of the selection.**

Possible response: The chronological structure is a way to remember the events in the order in which they happened.

Strategy Response Log

Summarize When students finish reading the selection, provide this prompt: Imagine that a friend has asked what *The Story of the Statue of Liberty* is about. In four or five sentences, explain its important points.

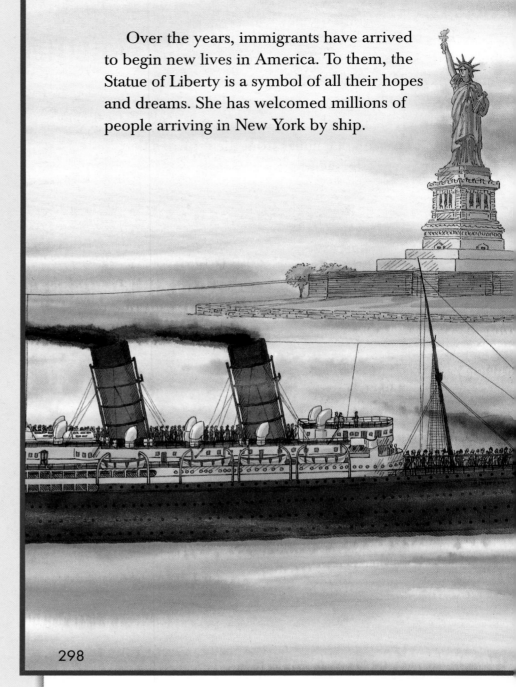

Over the years, immigrants have arrived to begin new lives in America. To them, the Statue of Liberty is a symbol of all their hopes and dreams. She has welcomed millions of people arriving in New York by ship.

298

ELL

Access Content Read the poem on p. 299 with students. Help them understand its meaning and from whose point of view it is written. Ask them to identify why the statue would be a welcome sight to immigrants arriving in the United States.

Every year, on the Fourth of July, the United States of America celebrates its independence. Fireworks light up the sky above New York Harbor. The Statue of Liberty is a truly unforgettable sight—a symbol of all that is America.

"Give me your tired, your poor,
Your huddled masses yearning to breathe free,
The wretched refuse of your teeming shore.
Send these, the homeless, tempest-tost to me,
I lift my lamp beside the golden door!"

–from "The New Colossus" by Emma Lazarus, 1883, placed on a tablet on the pedestal of the Statue of Liberty in 1903

299

Develop Vocabulary

PRACTICE LESSON VOCABULARY

As a class, answer the following sentences orally.

1. **Are people with *liberty* free?** *(Yes)*
2. **Why did Bartholdi make *models* of the statue first?** *(Possible response: He wanted to plan how it would look before he started building it.)*
3. **Name one purpose of a *torch*.** *(Possible response: to give light)*

BUILD CONCEPT VOCABULARY

Review previous concept words with students. Ask if students have come across any words today in their reading or elsewhere that they would like to add to the Concept Web.

STRATEGY SELF-CHECK

Text Structure

Ask students to revisit each page to determine the main ideas and events. Have them use the order of the main ideas to explain the authors' text structure. Students can use the main ideas to complete a graphic organizer (Time Line: Graphic Organizer 22, or Steps in a Process chart: Graphic Organizer 23) and write a summary.

SELF-CHECK

Students can ask these questions to assess their ability to use the skill and strategy.

- Did I accurately identify the main ideas and events from the selection?
- Do the main ideas and events support my classification of the text structure?
- Did I choose a graphic organizer that reflects the text structure?
- To assess, use Practice Book 3.2, p. 107.

Monitor Progress

Main Idea

If... students have difficulty identifying main ideas and text structure,	then... use the Reteach lesson on p. 303b.

Main Idea and Details • Text Structure

- The **main idea** is the most important idea in a selection or a paragraph.
- The small pieces of information that tell about the main idea are the supporting **details**.
- Look for key words in the text, such as *who, what, where, why,* and *when,* to get details about the **main idea**.

Directions Read the following passage. Then answer the questions below.

Where are your ancestors from? Maybe they came from another country. And maybe they came through Ellis Island, which is about a mile outside of New York City. Samuel Ellis owned the island in the 1770s. He sold it to the state of New York, which sold it for use as an immigration station. About 17 million people came through Ellis Island. They were registered and given physicals. A wall was built at Ellis Island that has some of the immigrants' names written on it. Do you want to see if your relatives are there? There are sites online where you can type in your last name. You'll get a list of people who were at Ellis Island who have the same last name.

1. What is this passage about?
   It's about Ellis Island and how many people came to this country through Ellis Island.

2.–4. Name three supporting details about Ellis Island.
   Possible responses:
   2) It was owned by Samuel Ellis.
   3) It was a big immigration station.
   4) There's a wall with immigrants' names on it.

5. Is this passage fiction or nonfiction? How can you tell?
   It's nonfiction. It is written with dates and facts and is about a real place and a real thing that happened.

Home Activity Your child learned about finding the main idea and details in a piece of writing. Watch a TV show with your child. When it's over, have your child tell you what the main idea and some of the supporting details were on the show. Discuss why your child chose the details he or she did.

▲ **Practice Book 3.2** p. 107

Reader Response

Open for Discussion **Personal Response**

MODEL The Statue of Liberty was a gift from France as a symbol of friendship. It is also a symbol of liberty. She is a symbol recognized around the world.

Comprehension Check **Critical Response**

1. Possible response: The authors included details to help the reader visualize the Statue of Liberty and appreciate her size and meaning. **Author's Purpose**

2. Details include: ...well-known artists, engineers, and craftsmen...ideas. Many people worked...the hard work of taking Liberty apart... **Main Idea**

3. Possible responses: First, during this time, then, finally. **Text Structure**

4. Responses will vary but should show an understanding of the words. **Vocabulary**

Look Back and Write For test practice, assign a 10–15 minute time limit. For assessment, see the Scoring Rubric at the right.

Retell

Have students retell *The Story of the Statue of Liberty*.

Monitor Progress
Check Retelling [4][3][2][1] Rubric
If... students have difficulty retelling the selection, **then...** use the Retelling Cards and the Scoring Rubric on p. 301 to assist fluent retelling. SUCCESS PREDICTOR

 ELL

Check Retelling Have students use illustrations and other text features to guide their retellings. Let students listen to other retellings before attempting their own. See the ELL and Transition Handbook.

Reader Response

Open for Discussion Every day in rain, snow, or sunshine the Statue of Liberty stands on her island. Why is she there? Why is she so famous?

1. The authors include details, such as the number of steps to the statue's crown. Why did they do that? Find other details. How do details help you know the Statue of Liberty? **Think Like an Author**

2. Building the Statue of Liberty was a complicated project. Look back at pages 292–295. What details support that fact? **Main Idea and Details**

3. This selection is told in the order in which events happened. What clue words did you notice that helped you recognize the sequential text structure? **Text Structure**

4. Imagine you have a pen pal who has never seen the Statue of Liberty, even in a picture. Write a description for your pen pal. Use words from the Words to Know list. **Vocabulary**

Look Back and Write What does the Statue of Liberty hold in her right hand and in her left hand? Look back at page 292. Why is that important?

Meet authors Betsy and Giulio Maestro on page 420.

300

Scoring Rubric | **Look Back and Write**

Top-Score Response A top-score response will use the information from p. 292 of the selection to tell what the Statue of Liberty holds in her right and left hands and why these things are important.

Example of a Top-Score Response The Statue of Liberty holds a torch in the right hand and a tablet in her left hand. Light from the torch welcomes people to America. The tablet has the date July 4, 1776, on it. This date is important. It is the date the Declaration of Independence was signed.

For additional rubrics, see p. WA10.

Write Now

Take Notes

Prompt

The Story of the Statue of Liberty tells how a sculptor created this famous statue. Think about the most important ideas in the selection.

Now write notes about one part of the selection.

Writing Trait

Good writers **focus** on important **ideas** and support these ideas with strong details.

Notes *focus* only on most important *ideas* in story.

Student Model

> **Notes on *The Story of The Statue of Liberty***
>
> French sculptor Frédéric Auguste Bartholdi
>   visited America in 1871 and saw island in N.Y.
> Decided to make statue as present from France
> S of L shows friendship between US and France
> S of L a symbol of freedom—welcomed people
> She would be "Liberty Enlightening the World"
> S of L large, strong—people could climb inside
> Holds tablet with July 4, 1776
> Arm with torch sent to Philadelphia, 1876
> Liberty's head at Paris World's Fair—visitors paid to
>   climb inside, raised $ for statue

Writer uses own words. Author's words are in quotation marks.

Notes are not always in complete sentences.

Use the model to help you write your own notes.

301

Write Now

Look at the Prompt Explain that each sentence in the prompt has a purpose.

- Sentence 1 presents a topic.
- Sentence 2 suggests students think about the topic.
- Sentence 3 tells what to write—notes.

Strategies to Develop Focus/Ideas

Have students

- mark important ideas in the text with self-stick notes.
- look at the first sentence of each paragraph to find important ideas.
- include only important ideas in notes.

NO: Visitors enjoy lovely view

YES: Statue on island in New York Harbor

For additional suggestions and rubric, see pp. 303g–303h.

Writer's Checklist

- ☑ **Focus** Do notes include only most important ideas?
- ☑ **Organization** Are notes in the same order as ideas in the text?
- ☑ **Support** Are important dates and names included in notes?
- ☑ **Conventions** Are capital letters used where needed? Do punctuation and abbreviations used make sense?

Scoring Rubric | Expository Retelling

Rubric 4 3 2 1	4	3	2	1
Connections	Makes connections and generalizes beyond the text	Makes connections to other events, texts, or experiences	Makes a limited connection to another event, text, or experience	Makes no connection to another event, text, or experience
Author's Purpose	Elaborates on author's purpose	Tells author's purpose with some clarity	Makes some connection to author's purpose	Makes no connection to author's purpose
Topic	Describes the main topic	Identifies the main topic with some details early in retelling	Identifies the main topic	Retelling has no sense of topic
Important Ideas	Gives accurate information about events, steps, and ideas using details and key vocabulary	Gives accurate information about events, steps, and ideas with some detail and key vocabulary	Gives limited or inaccurate information about events, steps, and ideas	Gives no information about events, steps, and ideas
Conclusions	Draws conclusions and makes inferences to generalize beyond text	Draws conclusions about the text	Is able to draw few conclusions about the text	Is unable to draw conclusions or make inferences about the text

Retelling Plan

- ☑ **This week assess Strategic Intervention students.**
- ☐ **Week 2** Assess Advanced students.
- ☐ **Week 3** Assess Strategic Intervention students.
- ☐ **Week 4** Assess On-Level students.
- ☐ **Week 5** Assess any students you have not yet checked during this unit.

Use the Retelling Chart on p. TR17 to record retelling.

Selection Test To assess with *The Story of the Statue of Liberty*, use Selection Tests, pp. 101–104.

Fresh Reads for Differentiated Test Practice For weekly leveled practice, use pp. 151–156.

Retelling

SUCCESS PREDICTOR

Social Studies in Reading

- Examine features of a textbook.
- Practice a test-taking strategy.
- Compare and contrast across texts.

PREVIEW

As students preview "A Nation of Immigrants," have them examine the photos, captions, and chart. After they preview, ask:

- **How can the photos and captions help you understand the text?** *(They make the information clearer.)*
- **What is the purpose of the chart?** *(It gives more information about immigrants.)*

Link to Social Studies

Help students use reference materials such as encyclopedias to find why immigrants came during certain time periods.

DAY 4 Grouping Options

Reading
Whole Group Discuss the Question of the Day.

Group Time Differentiated Instruction
Read "A Nation of Immigrants." See pp. 284f–284g for the small group lesson plan.

Whole Group Use pp. 303a and 303j.

Language Arts
Use pp. 303e–303h and 303k–303m.

Social Studies in Reading

A Nation of Immigrants

Textbook

Genre

- A textbook is a source of information.
- A textbook can be about any subject taught in school.

Text Features

- Photos and captions make information clearer.
- Charts often are included to give additional information.

Ellis Island

Link to Social Studies

Use the library or the Internet to find out more about why immigrants came to the United States. Copy the chart on page 303, and add a column that tells Why They Came.

For decades, immigrants have come to the United States from almost every other country in the world. Some people wanted freedom or better opportunities. Some came because there was very little food in their home country. Some came to find jobs or to work on farms. Others came because they had no choice.

Many ships that came from Europe arrived first at Ellis Island in New York Harbor. Many immigrants from Asia arrived at Angel Island in San Francisco Bay. Immigrants also entered through other cities, such as Boston, Massachusetts; Galveston, Texas; and New Orleans, Louisiana.

★ ———————————————— ★

REVIEW What were some reasons immigrants came to the United States?

302

Content-Area Vocabulary	Social Studies
decades	periods of ten years
immigrants	people who have left their country and come to another country to live
opportunities	chances, especially ones that offer advantages

Times When Many Immigrants Came

Time Period	Where Many Were From
Before 1820	United Kingdom, countries of Western Africa such as those now known as Ghana, Togo, Benin, Nigeria, and Cameroon
1820–1860	Ireland, Germany, United Kingdom, France, Canada
1861–1890	Germany, United Kingdom, Ireland, Canada, Norway/Sweden
1891–1920	Italy, Austria/Hungary, Russia, United Kingdom, Germany
1961–1990	Mexico, Philippines, Canada, Korea, Cuba

Angel Island

Reading Across Texts

Immigrants from which countries would have been the first to see the new Statue of Liberty on Bedloe's Island?

Writing Across Texts Imagine that you are one of those immigrants. Write a journal entry telling your impression of the Statue of Liberty.

Main Idea What is the main idea of this article?

303

TEXTBOOK

Use the sidebar on p. 302 to guide discussion.

- Remind students to carefully examine photos, captions, charts, and graphs as they read textbooks.
- Discuss with students the information they think the textbook will give.

 **AudioText**

CONNECT TEXT TO TEXT

Reading Across Texts

Guide students in a discussion about how to answer the question. Review the appropriate information from both selections before answering the question.

Writing Across Texts Encourage students to use details from the selections and sensory words in their journal entry.

Main Idea

Immigrants from other countries have come to the United States for freedom and better opportunities.

EXTEND SKILLS

Strategies for Nonfiction

Explain that textbooks often have charts with information in an easy-to-read format. Suggest the following test-taking strategy:

1. Read the title and headings in a chart or graph as you preview the selection.
2. When you read a question, check to see whether the text or a chart provides the answer.

Fluency Assessment Plan

☑ **This week assess Advanced students.**

☐ **Week 2** Assess Strategic Intervention students.

☐ **Week 3** Assess On-Level students.

☐ **Week 4** Assess Strategic Intervention students.

☐ **Week 5** Assess any students you have not yet checked during this unit.

Set individual goals for students to enable them to reach the year-end goal.

• Current Goal: 110–120 wcpm

• Year-End Goal: 120 wcpm

Fluency Coach CD To develop fluent readers, use Fluency Coach.

MORE READING FOR

Fluency

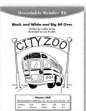

To practice fluency with text comprised of previously taught phonics elements and irregular words, use Decodable Reader 26.

DAY 5   Grouping Options

Reading
Whole Group
Revisit the Question of the Week.

Group Time
Differentiated Instruction
Reread this week's Leveled Readers. See pp. 284f–284g for the small group lesson plan.

Whole Group
Use pp. 303b–303c.

Language Arts
Use pp. 303d–303h and 303k–303n.

ACCURACY, APPROPRIATE PACE/RATE, AND EXPRESSION

Fluency

DAY 1

Model Reread "Uncle Sam" on p. 284m. Explain that you will read at an appropriate rate and use your voice to show expression. Model for students as you read.

DAY 2

Choral Reading Read aloud p. 293. Have students notice how you read without skipping or changing any words. Have students practice as a class, doing three choral readings of p. 293.

DAY 3

Model Read aloud p. 295. Have students notice how you pause at the dash and how your voice changes at the exclamation point. Practice as a class by doing three choral readings of p. 295.

DAY 4

Paired Reading Have partners practice reading aloud p. 297, three times. Students should read with expression and accuracy. Partners should offer each other feedback.

Monitor Progress   Check Fluency wcpm

As students reread, monitor their progress toward their individual fluency goals. Current Goal: 110–120 words correct per minute. End-of-Year Goal: 120 words correct per minute.

If... students cannot read fluently at a rate of 110–120 words correct per minute,
then... make sure students practice with text at their independent level. Provide additional fluency practice, pairing nonfluent readers with fluent readers.

If... students already read at 120 words correct per minute,
then... they need not reread three to four times.

SUCCESS PREDICTOR

DAY 5

Assessment
Individual Reading Rate Use the Fluency Assessment Plan and do a one-minute timed reading of either selection from this week to assess students in Week 1. Pay special attention to this week's skills, accuracy, appropriate pace/rate, and expression. Because this week's selections are nonfiction, students may need to use a slightly slower pace. Provide corrective feedback for each student.

RETEACH

Main Idea

TEACH

Explain to students that the main idea is the "big idea" of a paragraph or selection. Students can complete Practice Book 3.2, p. 108, on their own, or you can complete it as a class. Point out the question in Box 1 and explain that the question is asking for the main idea. The questions in the remaining boxes serve to prompt students to identify details that give more information.

ASSESS

Have partners use p. 297 in their books to determine the paragraph's main idea *(There was a celebration when Liberty was in place in the harbor)* and supporting details *(Bartholdi unveiled Liberty's face, boats filled the harbor, President Cleveland gave a speech)*.

For additional instruction for main idea, see DI·52.

EXTEND SKILLS

Steps in a Process

TEACH

When you tell the steps in a process, you tell the order of steps to finish something or the steps in which something happens.

- Think about what is being made and how it should look after each step.
- Look for clue words, such as *first, next,* and *then.*
- If there are diagrams or illustrations, "match" them to the written steps.

Work with students to identify the steps in the process on p. 292, paragraphs 2 and 3. Have them identify clue words and illustrations that help them visualize and understand the steps in the process.

ASSESS

Have students work individually to reread p. 295. Have them list the steps in the process in paragraph 2 on p. 295. Ask:

1. Did you see a picture in your mind as you read each step?

2. Could you explain the process to someone?

OBJECTIVES

- Determine main idea and supporting details.
- Identify steps in a process.

Skills Trace

Main Idea and Details	
Introduce/Teach	TE: 3.2 150–151, 198–199, 3.6 284–285
Practice	PB: 3.1 53, 57, 58, 73, 77–78, 86; 3.2 103, 107–108, 126, 146
Reteach/Review	**TE: 3.2 173b, 223b, 223, 241, DI•54; 3.6 303b, 339, 391, 397, DI•52**
Test	Selection Test: Unit 6 Benchmark Tests: Units 2, 6

ELL

Access Content Reteach the skill by reviewing the Picture It! lesson on main idea and details in the ELL Teaching Guide, pp. 176–177.

Main Idea and Details

- The **main idea** is the most important idea in a selection or a paragraph.
- The small pieces of information that tell about the main idea are the supporting **details**.
- Look for keywords in the text, such as *who, what, where, why,* and *when,* to get **details** about the **main idea**.

Directions Read the following passage and complete the chart below.

> I stood in line at Ellis Island for a long time. People were speaking different languages all around me. Finally, it was my turn. I told the man my name. Then he asked a question. I didn't know what to answer because I didn't understand English. Another man told me in my own language that he wanted to know if I ever was in prison. I was only 13 years old! He asked me if I was sick, and I said "No." He tried to say my name, but couldn't. He wrote a new name next to mine. The other man told me my new name. "Welcome to America, young lady," he said.

Directions Write the main idea of the passage in box 1. Then write the details that support that idea in boxes 2–5.

1. Main Idea
What is the passage about?
A girl goes through the immigration line at Ellis Island.

2. Detail	3. Detail	4. Detail	5. Detail
Where was the girl? **She was in line at Ellis Island.**	What was one problem the girl had? **She couldn't speak English.**	What was one question the man asked the girl? **The man asked if she had been in prison.**	What happened to the girl's name? **The man changed it because he couldn't say it.**

School + Home Home Activity Your child learned about finding the main idea and details in a piece of writing. Read a newspaper or magazine article with your child. Have him or her tell you what the article was about and give three details that support the main idea.

▲ **Practice Book 3.2** p. 108

Vocabulary and Word Study

VOCABULARY STRATEGY
⊙Word Structure

PREFIXES Remind students that they can use word structure and prefixes to help determine the meaning of unfamiliar words. Have students list any unknown words they encountered as they read *The Story of the Statue of Liberty*. They can create a chart showing the unknown word, its base and prefix, and their definition of the word. Students can confirm word meanings using a dictionary.

Word	Base + Prefix	Meaning
uncover	un + cover	to remove the cover; to reveal
unfinished		
unable		

Sculpture Words

Some words, such as *statue*, have to do with making sculptures, or large free-standing artworks. Have partners use reference sources to make lists of words that refer to sculpture, with their meanings. Students can draw a picture of a sculpture they found and label it with the appropriate words.

Some Sculpture Words

model	statue
mold	figure
skeleton	framework
cast	marble

BUILD CONCEPT VOCABULARY
American Symbols

LOOKING BACK Remind students of the focus question of the week: What does the Statue of Liberty mean to Americans? Discuss how this week's Concept Web of vocabulary words relates to the theme of American symbols. Ask students if they have any words or categories to add. Discuss whether words and categories are appropriately related to the concept.

MOVING FORWARD Preview the title of the next selection, *Happy Birthday Mr. Kang*. Ask students which Concept Web words might apply to the new selection based on the title alone. Put a star next to these words on the web.

Display the Concept Web and revisit the vocabulary words as you read the next selection to check predictions.

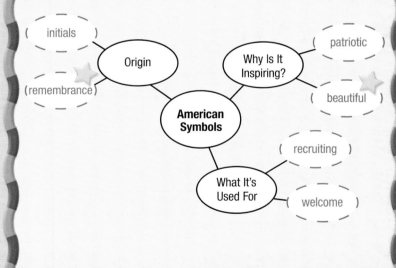

Monitor Progress
Check Vocabulary

If... students suggest words or categories that are not related to the concept,	then... review the words and categories on the Concept Web and discuss how they relate to the lesson concept.

SUCCESS PREDICTOR

Speaking and Listening

SPEAKING

Announcement

SET-UP Have students make a 2-minute announcement about a new sculpture that they are unveiling in your city or town.

PLANNING Have students announce and pretend to unveil a new sculpture. Their announcement will name the sculpture and the artist who created it, and explain why it was created. Encourage students to use descriptive words and offer complimentary opinions about the sculpture. Remind students to be aware of the nonverbal cues they use when they are speaking, including facial expressions and body language. Suggest that students conclude their announcements by asking the audience to applaud the work of the artist.

MULTIMEDIA PRESENTATION Some students may choose to play music in the background during the announcement. Others might decide to show photos or slides of other works of art.

Planning Tips

- Decide what the sculpture looks like.
- Name the artist.
- Think of words that will describe the sculpture.
- Plan kind remarks about the artist and the work of art.

LISTENING

Listen to an Announcement

Have students listen to a public service announcement. Individually, they can answer these questions orally or in writing.

1. **Do you have the same understanding of the situation as the speaker?** *(Possible response: Yes. I know that there are warning signs for cancer.)*

2. **Why do you think this public service announcement was made?** *(Possible response: The announcement was made to help keep people healthy.)*

3. **Do you agree with the ideas presented in the public service announcement? Why or why not?** *(Possible response: Yes. Some people who hear the announcement will go to a doctor to find out more about their health.)*

Support Vocabulary Use the following to review and extend vocabulary and to explore lesson concepts further:
- ELL Poster 26, Days 3–5 instruction
- Vocabulary Activities and Word Cards in ELL Teaching Guide, pp. 178–179

Assessment For information on assessing students' speaking, listening, and viewing, see the ELL and Transition Handbook.

Check Vocabulary

SUCCESS PREDICTOR

Grammar Capital Letters

OBJECTIVES

- Define and identify capital letters.
- Use capital letters in writing.
- Become familiar with capital letter assessment on high-stakes tests.

Monitor Progress

Grammar

| If... students have difficulty with capital letters, | then... see The Grammar and Writing Book pp. 200–203. |

DAILY FIX-IT

This week use Daily Fix-It Transparency 26.

Spiral REVIEW

Grammar Support See the Grammar Transition lessons in the ELL and Transition Handbook.

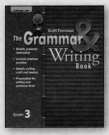

▲ **The Grammar and Writing Book** For more instruction and practice, use pp. 200–205.

DAY 1 Teach and Model

DAILY FIX-IT

1. The classes visits the Washington Monument on tuesday. *(visit; Tuesday)*

2. is the Statue of Liberty or the Washington Monument biggest? *(Is; bigger)*

READING-GRAMMAR CONNECTION

Write this sentence from *The Story of the Statue of Liberty* on the board:

Every year, on the Fourth of July, the United States of America celebrates its independence.

Explain that because *Fourth of July* is the name of a holiday and *United States of America* is the name of a country, the first word and all important words in the names are capitalized.

Display Grammar Transparency 26. Read aloud the definitions and sample sentences. Work through the items.

Capital Letters

Use **capital letters** for proper nouns. Proper nouns include days of the week, months of the year, and holidays. Titles for people and abbreviations of the titles should be capitalized when they are used with a person's name. Do not capitalize titles when they are used by themselves.

Incorrect	The fourth thursday in november is thanksgiving.
Correct	The fourth Thursday in November is Thanksgiving.
Incorrect	My Grandpa visits on hanukkah and independence day.
Correct	My grandpa visits on Hanukkah and Independence Day.

Directions If a sentence has capitalization mistakes, write correctly the words that should have capital letters. If a sentence has no capitalization mistakes, write *C*.

1. Today mr. chang said Americans have many symbols of freedom.
Mr. Chang

2. We eat special cakes at easter.
Easter

3. Americans can display flags on any day from january to december.
January; December

4. One monday in july I spotted a bald eagle.
Monday; July

5. Bald eagles are also a symbol of freedom in the United States.
C

Directions Write the sentences. Use capital letters correctly.

6. Last august my family visited Mount Rushmore.
Last August my family visited Mount Rushmore.

7. In the summer, a ceremony is held there each night from monday through sunday.
In the summer, a ceremony is held there each night from Monday through Sunday.

Unit 6 The Story of the Statue of Liberty   Grammar **26**

▲ **Grammar Transparency** 26

DAY 2 Develop the Concept

DAILY FIX-IT

3. Maria and her daugter came to the United States in november. *(daughter; November)*

4. The Statue of Liberty greated Maria and she. *(greeted; her)*

GUIDED PRACTICE

Review the concept of capital letters.

- Days of the week, months of the year, and holidays begin with a **capital letter.**
- Titles for people and abbreviations of the titles should be capitalized when they are used with a person's name but not when they are used by themselves.

HOMEWORK Grammar and Writing Practice Book p. 101. Work through the first two items with the class.

Capital Letters

Use **capital letters** for proper nouns. Proper nouns include days of the week, months of the year, and holidays. Titles for people should be capitalized when they are used with a person's name. Do not capitalize titles when they are used by themselves.

Incorrect	Last october aunt Rosie and my Uncle gave a party for halloween.
Correct	Last October Aunt Rosie and my uncle gave a party for Halloween.
Incorrect	Does mother's day come earlier than memorial day?
Correct	Does Mother's Day come earlier than Memorial Day?

Directions Write correctly the words that should have capital letters.

1. Last may Mara saw some wonderful sights.
May

2. Mara's mom and aunt lucy took her to the Statue of Liberty.
Aunt Lucy

3. They saw the Liberty Bell in philadelphia on memorial day.
Philadelphia; Memorial Day

Directions Write the sentences. Use capital letters correctly.

4. Bartholdi hoped the statue would be finished by july 4, 1876.
Bartholdi hoped the statue would be finished by July 4, 1876.

5. Only the statue's arm and torch were ready by the fourth of july.
Only the statue's arm and torch were ready by the Fourth of July.

 **Home Activity** Your child learned about capital letters. While looking at a magazine, ask your child to point out three capital letters used for days of the week, months of the year, or holidays.

▲ **Grammar and Writing Practice Book** p. 101

DAY 3   Apply to Writing

DAILY FIX-IT

5. Didnt you climb to the top of the statue on Toosday? *(Didn't; Tuesday)*

6. You cant go to the top anymore but you can go inside the base. *(can't; anymore, but)*

USE CAPITAL LETTERS IN WRITING

Explain that using proper nouns can make writing more specific.

General: We spent the holiday at the statue.

Specific: We spent the Fourth of July at the Statue of Liberty.

• Have students review something they have written to see if they can use proper nouns to make their writing more specific.

HOMEWORK Grammar and Writing Practice Book, p. 102

Capital Letters
Directions Complete each sentence with a proper noun for the word in ( ). Use capital letters correctly. **Possible answers:**
1. One of my favorite holidays is **Labor Day**. (holiday)
2. We celebrate this holiday in **September**. (month)
3. This year my birthday is on **Monday**. (day of the week)
4. The day of the week that I like best is **Friday**. (day of the week)
5. I like the weather in the month of **May**. (month)
6. I do not like the weather in the month of **February**. (month)

Directions Write two sentences about something you do with family members on a particular holiday. Use capital letters correctly.
Possible answer: On Labor Day my family has a picnic with Aunt Linda and Uncle Jim. After lunch, Uncle Jim starts a soccer game.

Home Activity Your child learned how to use capital letters in writing. With your child, recall an event that included many family members. Have your child write a list of the people, using capital letters correctly.

▲ **Grammar and Writing Practice Book** p. 102

DAY 4   Test Preparation

DAILY FIX-IT

7. Fue people had saw the Statue of Liberty until 1886. *(Few; seen)*

8. The statues torch shines over every one. *(statue's; everyone)*

STANDARDIZED TEST PREP

Test Tip

You may be asked to identify which words should be capitalized in a sentence. Remember that days of the week, months of the year, and holidays should be capitalized. Titles for people and abbreviations of the titles should be capitalized when they are used with a person's name. They should not be capitalized when they are used by themselves.

Incorrect: My Aunt came on thursday for thanksgiving with uncle Rob.

Correct: My aunt came on Thursday for Thanksgiving with Uncle Rob.

HOMEWORK Grammar and Writing Practice Book, p. 103

Capital Letters
Directions Mark the letter of the word or words that should be capitalized.
1. The family sailed across the ocean in february.
   A family
   B across
   C ocean
   (D) february
2. On monday the children said good-bye to their grandparents.
   (A) monday
   B good-bye
   C children
   D grandparents
3. On friday the ship arrived in a new country.
   A ship
   (B) friday
   C country
   D new
4. The next day aunt sue took her guests to the city.
   A next day
   (B) aunt sue
   C guests
   D city
5. Their aunt told the family about holidays in america.
   A aunt
   B holidays
   C family
   (D) america
6. She said people enjoy fireworks on independence day.
   A people
   B independence
   (C) independence day
   D fireworks
7. Americans remember explorers on columbus day.
   A explorers
   B voyages
   C remember
   (D) columbus day
8. I hope Grandpa visits us at hanukkah.
   A hope
   B visits
   C us
   (D) hanukkah

Home Activity Your child prepared for taking tests on capital letters. Look at a calendar with your child and have him or her point out capital letters and explain the reasons for their use.

▲ **Grammar and Writing Practice Book** p. 103

DAY 5   Cumulative Review

DAILY FIX-IT

9. When the Statue of Liberty was finaly presented, president Grover Cleveland gave a speech. *(finally; President)*

10. Mr. and mrs. Adams watched fireworks expload in the harbor. *(Mrs.; explode)*

ADDITIONAL PRACTICE

Assign pp. 200–203 in The Grammar and Writing Book.

EXTRA PRACTICE Grammar and Writing Practice Book, p. 147

TEST PREPARATION Grammar and Writing Practice Book, pp. 157–158

ASSESSMENT

CUMULATIVE REVIEW Grammar and Writing Practice Book, p. 104

Capital Letters
Directions If a sentence has capitalization mistakes, write correctly the words that should have capital letters. If a sentence has no capitalization mistakes, write *C*.
1. The Statue of Liberty was repaired in the 1980s. **C**
2. In our town, mr. barnes raised money for the repairs. **Mr. Barnes**
3. Many Americans helped keep the statue on Liberty Island beautiful. **C**
4. People celebrated the restored statue on the fourth of july in 1986. **Fourth of July**
5. They also celebrated in october, 100 years after the original dedication. **October**

Directions Write the sentences. Use capital letters correctly.
6. On monday, the class read poems about freedom.
   On Monday, the class read poems about freedom.
7. A poem by emma lazarus appears on the statue of liberty.
   A poem by Emma Lazarus appears on the Statue of Liberty.
8. Our teacher, ms. adams, says it inspires people from around the world.
   Our teacher, Ms. Adams, says it inspires people from around the world.

Home Activity Your child reviewed capital letters. While outdoors, have your child write the name of a day of the week with correct capitalization using natural objects such as sand, twigs, or pebbles.

▲ **Grammar and Writing Practice Book** p. 104

Writing Workshop Taking Notes

OBJECTIVES

- Identify the characteristics of taking notes.
- Take notes on factual material and paraphrase the facts in the notes.
- Focus on focus/ideas.
- Use a rubric.

Genre Notes
Writer's Craft Paraphrasing
Writing Trait Focus/Ideas

Focus/Ideas Write the following sentences on sheets of paper, one to a sheet. Work with English learners to identify the sentence that doesn't belong: Books can be about anything. Libraries have many books. We will swim after lunch. I read many books this summer.

Writing Trait

FOCUS/IDEAS The notes focus on the most important information in the article.

ORGANIZATION/PARAGRAPHS The notes are organized by topic.

VOICE The writer's voice is clear and knowledgeable.

WORD CHOICE The writer uses precise words that communicate the meaning of the original source.

SENTENCES Brief sentences and sentence fragments are used.

CONVENTIONS Grammar and mechanics are excellent, including use of capital letters.

READING-WRITING CONNECTION

- *The Story of the Statue of Liberty* is narrative nonfiction about the Statue of Liberty.
- Ideas in *The Story of the Statue of Liberty* were paraphrased from the authors' research and from their notes on their research.
- Students will **take notes** on the article by paraphrasing the main ideas of what they read.

MODEL FOCUS/IDEAS Discuss transparency 26A. Then discuss the model and the trait of focus/ideas.

Think Aloud I see that the writer has taken notes on *The Story of the Statue of Liberty*. The writer has paraphrased the most important ideas in one part of the article and has restated them. The notes are in list form and are not always complete sentences. The writer uses abbreviations.

Taking Notes

When you **take notes**, write the most important facts in an article. Try to put ideas into your own words. Put any phrases that you pick up word-for-word in quotation marks.

Notes on *The Story of the Statue of Liberty* (last 4 pages)

Notes are written in list form.

| Americans forgot about the S of L |
| No money to finish the base |

Writer uses abbreviations and does not always use complete sentences.

N.Y. newspaper asked public for money, and statue was finished

Celebration—speeches, songs, speech by Pres. Cleveland—in 1886 when statue was in place. Bartholdi uncovered statue's face

People coming on ships to live in America first see S of L

Writer uses quotation marks to show phrase is a direct quote from the original text.

Fireworks above S of L part of July 4th celebration each year

"a truly unforgettable sight"

Unit 6 The Story of the Statue of Liberty   Writing Model **26A**

▲ **Writing Transparency** 26A

WRITER'S CRAFT
Paraphrasing

Display Writing Transparency 26B. Read the directions and discuss as a group what the word *paraphrase* means and how one paraphrases.

Think Aloud **PARAPHRASING** Tomorrow we will take notes on one part of *The Story of the Statue of Liberty*. I will have to decide which are the most important ideas in the selection and which I should omit. I have to write the notes in my own words, not in the words of the author. I do not have to write in complete sentences, and I can use abbreviations.

GUIDED PRACTICE Some students may need more help paraphrasing. Review a nonfiction article that students have read recently. Help them paraphrase each paragraph.

Paraphrasing

When you take notes on facts in a book or article, you **paraphrase** the article. When you paraphrase, choose the most important facts and restate them in your own words.

- Paraphrase only the main ideas, not unimportant details. Make sure you paraphrase the facts correctly.
- Use your own words, not the words and word order used by the author.
- If a phrase or sentence is especially interesting, write it in quotation marks.

Includes main ideas   Omits important information   Follows original wording too closely

Directions Read the paragraph and each paraphrase. Write the best description from the box for each paraphrase.

The Liberty Bell is a symbol of American freedom. It was made in England and sent to Philadelphia. It cracked on its first ring and was repaired. On July 8, 1776, the bell was rung in honor of adopting the Declaration of Independence. It was rung each July 8 for many years. Today you can see the Liberty Bell at Liberty Bell Pavilion in Philadelphia.

1. The Liberty Bell got cracked on its way from England to America, but Americans fixed it.
Omits important information

2. The Liberty Bell stands for freedom to Americans because it was rung in 1776 when the Declaration of Independence was adopted. The Liberty Bell is still displayed in Philadelphia.
Includes main ideas

Directions Write a paraphrase of the following paragraph.

3. The Washington Monument reminds Americans of our history and our first President, George Washington. The monument is more than 555 feet high and is covered in white marble. It has been one of the most famous sights in Washington, D.C., since it was completed in 1884. Possible answer:
The Washington Monument was finished in 1884 in honor of our first President. It is one of the most famous buildings in our capital.

Unit 6 The Story of the Statue of Liberty   Writer's Craft **26B**

▲ **Writing Transparency** 26B

DAY 3 Prewrite and Draft

READ THE WRITING PROMPT
on page 301 in the Student Edition.

The Story of the Statue of Liberty *tells how a sculptor created this famous statue.*

Think about the most important ideas in the selection.

Now take notes on one part of the selection.

Writing Test Tips
- Decide which facts in the section are most important.
- State the facts in your own words. Do not copy the exact words of the author unless you enclose them in quotation marks.
- Use abbreviations, shortened sentence forms, and sentence fragments.

GETTING STARTED Students can do any of the following:
- With the class, summarize sections orally.
- With a small group, read one paragraph of the article. Discuss which sentences state the main idea and which state supporting details.
- Practice paraphrasing individual sentences in shortened note form.

DAY 4 Draft and Revise

EDITING/REVISING CHECKLIST
on page 301 in the Student Edition.

☑ Do the notes reflect the article's main ideas?

☑ Do the notes paraphrase instead of copy the article's exact words?

☑ Are capital letters used correctly?

☑ Are words with the vowel sounds in *tooth* and *cook* spelled correctly?

See *The Grammar and Writing Book*, pp. 204–209.

Revising Tips

Focus Ideas
- Determine the main idea of each paragraph on which you are taking notes.
- State the main idea in your own words.
- Do not include ideas that are less important supporting details.

PUBLISHING Students can compare their notes in small groups. Some students may wish to revise their work later.

ASSESSMENT Use the scoring rubric to evaluate students' work.

DAY 5 Connect to Unit Writing

Research Report	
Week 1	Taking Notes 303g–303h
Week 2	Outlining 331g–331h
Week 3	Informational Paragraph 353g–353h
Week 4	Write About a Picture 379g–379h
Week 5	Write Good Paragraphs 407g–407h

PREVIEW THE UNIT PROMPT

Write a research report about a monument or statue that symbolizes freedom in the United States. Discuss the monument itself, its history, and why it is important. Find information in sources such as books, magazines, CD-ROMs, and the Internet.

APPLY
- A research report is an informational article based on research.
- The first step in writing a research report is taking notes on information from a variety of sources.

Writing Trait Rubric

	4	3	2	1
Focus/ Ideas	Excellent focus with many vivid supporting details; nothing superfluous	Clear focus with some supporting details; nothing superfluous	Limited focus with a few supporting details; some unrelated details	Unfocused with little support and many unrelated details
	Excellent notes with interesting, well-supported main idea	Notes with adequately supported main idea	Sharper focus on main idea needed in notes	Notes with no clear focus or main idea

AFTER READING

OBJECTIVES

- Associate the vowel sounds in *tooth* and *cook* with the letters that spell them.
- Review words with suffixes *-y*, *-ish*, *-hood*, and *-ment*.
- Blend and read words with the vowel sounds in *tooth* and *cook* and words with suffixes *-y*, *-ish*, *-hood*, and *-ment*.
- Apply decoding strategies: blend longer words.

Generalization

The letters *oo* can stand for the vowel sound in *book*, /u̇/, or in *moon*, /ü/. The letter *u* can stand for short *u* or the vowel sound in *book*, /u̇/. Context provides the clue to pronunciation. The letters *ew*, *ue*, and *ui* can stand for the vowel sound in *moon*, /ü/.

Support Phonics Speakers of Chinese, French, Italian, Korean, Spanish, and Urdu may have difficulty distinguishing the short and long *oo* sounds in *book* (short) and *moon* (long). Help them practice saying and writing word pairs like *cook/cool*, *took/tool*, *shook/shoot*.

See the Phonics Transition Lessons in the ELL and Transition Handbook.

Vowels in *tooth, cook*

Directions Circle each word with the vowel sound in **tooth** or the vowel sound in **cook**. Then write each word in the correct column.

1. Our school took us on a field trip to an art museum.
2. We spent a full day studying famous paintings and statues.
3. We looked at works by some of the art world's true masters.
4. After we returned to class, our teacher asked us to make a few drawings in our notebooks.
5. I sketched a picture of President Lincoln wearing a black wool suit and a very tall hat.

vowel sound in tooth

6. school
7. statues
8. true
9. few
10. suit

vowel sound in cook

11. took
12. full
13. looked
14. notebooks
15. wool

Directions Cross out the one word in each line that does **not** have the vowel sound in **tooth** or the vowel sound in **cook**.

16. ~~build~~   cushion   glue
17. bushel   ~~rocket~~   smooth
18. ~~button~~   bookstore   juice
19. football   stew   ~~story~~
20. balloon   pudding   ~~throat~~

Home Activity Your child identified and wrote words with the vowel sounds in *tooth* (as in *school, few, glue,* and *fruit*) and *cook* (as in *cookie* and *cushion*). Have your child write riddles using words with the vowel sounds in *tooth* and *cook*. Try to guess the answer after your child reads each riddle to you.

▲ **Practice Book 3.2** p. 109

Vowels in *tooth, cook*

TEACH

Remind students that many sounds can be spelled in different ways. Write the words *cook, tooth, put, blew, true,* and *suit.*

- How many vowels do you see in the word *cook?* (2)
- How many vowel sounds do you hear? (1)
- What vowel sound do you hear in *cook?* (/u̇/)
- Which letters stand for that sound? *(oo)*

 MODEL I see that the letters *oo* stand for /u̇/. So the next word must be /tu̇th/. That's not right! The word *tooth* has the vowel sound /ü/, so it looks as if the letters *oo* can stand for /u̇/ or /ü/. The vowel pairs *ew, ue,* and *ui* also stand for /ü/. And *u* is another way to spell /u̇/.

Model blending *put, blew, true,* and *suit.* Then have students blend the words with you.

p u t →   **b l e w** →

t r u e →   **s u i t** →

PRACTICE AND ASSESS

DECODE LONGER WORDS Write these words. Have students read them and then underline the letters that stand for /u̇/ or /ü/.

n<u>ui</u>sance   noteb<u>oo</u>k   amb<u>u</u>sh   shr<u>ew</u>dly

w<u>oo</u>dy   mild<u>ew</u>   untr<u>ue</u>   bamb<u>oo</u>

READ WORDS IN CONTEXT Write these sentences. Have individuals read them and point out words with /u̇/ or /ü/. Words with /u̇/ or /ü/ are underlined.

L<u>oo</u>k at the big kangar<u>oo</u>!

The stories in the n<u>ew</u>spaper were untr<u>ue</u>.

Dr<u>ew</u> p<u>u</u>t blueberries on his cereal.

Fr<u>ui</u>t j<u>ui</u>ce is a g<u>oo</u>d, healthy drink.

To assess, observe whether students pronounce the /u̇/ and /ü/ words correctly.

Review Word Parts

(REVIEW) SUFFIXES -y, -ish, -hood, -ment

CONNECT Write this sentence: *The bright sun gave the fluffy cloud a yellowish glow.*

- We studied the suffixes *-y, -ish, -hood, -ment*.
- Read the sentence to yourself. Raise your hand when you know which words have suffixes. *(fluffy, yellowish)*
- What is the suffix in *fluffy? (-y)* What is the base word? *(fluff)*
- What is the suffix in *yellowish? (-ish)* What is the base word? *(yellow)*

Continue in the same way with the sentence *Teamwork gave everyone a sense of accomplishment and brotherhood.*

PRACTICE AND ASSESS

DECODE LONGER WORDS Have individuals read the following words. Provide help blending the words as needed. Have the suffix and base word identified in each.

sisterhood	guilty	improvement	babyish
government	speedy	chilly	selfish
fiftyish	pavement	motherhood	astonishment

READ WORDS IN CONTEXT Have students read these sentences. Then, to check meaning, have them give their own sentence for the underlined word.

The new mother looks forward to <u>parenthood</u> with <u>excitement</u>.

I thought his <u>statement</u> was very <u>childish</u>.

We watched the <u>tricky</u> magician in <u>amazement</u>.

The children love to play outside on <u>snowy</u>, <u>windy</u> days.

To assess, note how well students read words with the suffixes *-y, -ish, -hood,* and *-ment*.

Vocabulary Tip

You may wish to explain the meanings of these words.

astonishment great surprise
pavement the hard surface of a road

Spelling & Phonics   Vowel Sounds in *tooth* and *cook*

OBJECTIVE

- Spell words with the vowel sounds in *tooth* and *cook*.

Generalization

Connect to Phonics The vowel sound in tooth can be spelled *oo*, *ew*, *ue*, and *ui*: *school, few, glue, fruit*. The vowel sound in cook can be spelled *oo* and *u*: *cookie, cushion*.

Spelling Words

1. few*	9. bookmark
2. school	10. balloon
3. true	11. suit
4. goose	12. chew
5. fruit	13. glue
6. cookie	14. Tuesday
7. cushion	15. bushel
8. noodle	

Challenge Words

16. bamboo	19. barefoot
17. mildew	20. renewal
18. soothe	

*Word from the selection

ELL

Spelling/Phonics Support See the ELL and Transition Handbook for spelling support.

DAY 1   Pretest and Sort

PRETEST

Use the Dictation Sentences from Day 5 to administer the pretest. Read the word, read the sentence, and then read the word again. Guide students in self-correcting their pretests and correcting any misspellings.

Monitor Progress

Spelling

If... students misspell more than 4 pretest words,	then... use words 1–8 for Strategic Intervention.
If... students misspell 1–4 pretest words,	then... use words 1–15 for On-Level practice.
If... students correctly spell all pretest words,	then... use words 1–20 for Advanced Learners.

HOMEWORK Spelling Practice Book, p. 101

Vowel Sounds in *tooth* and *cook*

Generalization The vowel sound in *tooth* can be spelled oo, ew, ue, and ui: school, few, glue, fruit. The vowel sound in cook can be spelled oo and u: cookie, cushion.

Word Sort Sort the list words by the spelling of the vowel sounds in *tooth* and *cook*.

oo (tooth)
1. school
2. goose
3. noodle
4. balloon

ew
5. few
6. chew

ui
7. fruit
8. suit

ue
9. true
10. glue
11. Tuesday

oo (cook)
12. cookie
13. bookmark

u
14. cushion
15. bushel

Challenge Words

oo (tooth)
16. bamboo
17. soothe

ew
18. mildew
19. renewal

oo (look)
20. barefoot

Spelling Words
1. few
2. school
3. true
4. goose
5. fruit
6. cookie
7. cushion
8. noodle
9. bookmark
10. balloon
11. suit
12. chew
13. glue
14. Tuesday
15. bushel

Challenge Words
16. bamboo
17. mildew
18. soothe
19. barefoot
20. renewal

School Home **Home Activity** Your child is learning words with the vowel sound in *tooth* (spelled oo, ew, ue, ui) and the vowel sound in cook (spelled oo, u). To practice at home, have your child say each word and then spell it.

▲ **Spelling Practice Book** p. 101

DAY 2   Think and Practice

TEACH

The vowel sounds in cook and tooth can be spelled several different ways. Write each spelling word on the board. Have students identify each sound and underline the vowel combination that makes that sound.

bal**l<u>oo</u>n**

FIND THE PATTERN Divide the class into small groups and have students write *oo, ew, ue, ui,* and *u* on note cards. Have one student read the list words. Have the others hold up the letters that the words contain.

HOMEWORK Spelling Practice Book, p. 102

Vowel Sounds in *tooth* and *cook*

Spelling Words				
few	school	true	goose	fruit
cookie	cushion	noodle	bookmark	balloon
suit	chew	glue	Tuesday	bushel

Names Write list words to name the pictures.

1. suit
2. fruit
3. bookmark

Categorizing Add a list word to each group.

4. duck, chicken, ___   4. goose
5. cake, pie, ___   5. cookie
6. paste, tape, ___   6. glue
7. Sunday, Thursday, ___   7. Tuesday
8. pillow, pad, ___   8. cushion
9. liter, quart, ___   9. bushel

Rhyming Words Complete each sentence with a list word that rhymes with the underlined word.

10. We grew a few different kinds of vegetables.
11. It's true that blue is my favorite color.
12. I will blow up your balloon soon.
13. The meat in this stew is hard to chew.
14. That doodle you drew looks like a noodle.
15. The school building seems cool today.

School Home **Home Activity** Your child wrote words with the vowel sound in *tooth* (spelled oo, ew, ue, ui) and the vowel sound in cook (spelled oo, u). Have your child pronounce and spell the words with oo.

▲ **Spelling Practice Book** p. 102

DAY 3 Connect to Writing

WRITE A SHOPPING LIST

Ask students to write a list of things to buy, using at least three spelling words. Have students share their lists by reading them aloud to the class or by displaying them on the bulletin board.

Frequently Misspelled Words

through	took
would	could

Although these words seem easy, it is hard for third-graders to spell them correctly because the same sound can be formed by different letter combinations. Alert students to these frequently misspelled words and encourage them to think carefully before they write them.

HOMEWORK Spelling Practice Book, p. 103

Vowel Sounds in _tooth_ and _cook_

		Spelling Words		
few	school	true	goose	fruit
cookie	cushion	noodle	bookmark	balloon
suit	chew	glue	Tuesday	bushel

Proofread a Schedule Kelsey made a schedule. Circle four spelling errors on this week's page. Write the words correctly. Then circle five words that need capital letters.

monday	no school—cuold go to Gym for Kids
tuesday	fruit and cooky sale
wednesday	blow up ballons for party
thursday	Jena's birthday party
friday	Jena's tru birthday

Frequently Misspelled Words
through
took
would
could

1. could   2. cookie
3. balloons   4. true

Proofread Words Fill in a circle to show which word is spelled correctly. Write it.

5. ○ noddle ● noodle ○ noodel   5. noodle
6. ● bookmark ○ bukmark ○ book mark   6. bookmark
7. ○ cushon ● cushion ○ cooshion   7. cushion
8. ○ ballewn ○ ballon ● balloon   8. balloon
9. ○ glew ○ gleu ● glue   9. glue
10. ○ friut ● fruit ○ froot   10. fruit

School + Home Home Activity Your child identified misspelled words with the vowel sound in tooth (spelled oo, ew, ue, u) and the vowel sound in cook (spelled oo, u). Ask your child to write a sentence containing two or more list words.

▲ **Spelling Practice Book** p. 103

DAY 4 Review

REVIEW VOWEL SOUNDS

Have students work individually to create a maze using the spelling words. Each path in the maze can follow words that use the same spelling patterns. Have students exchange their mazes and try to solve each other's puzzles.

Spelling Strategy
Vowel Combinations

Words with these vowel combinations are easier to spell if students picture the words in their minds before spelling them.

HOMEWORK Spelling Practice Book, p. 104

Vowel Sounds in _tooth_ and _cook_

		Spelling Words		
few	school	true	goose	fruit
cookie	cushion	noodle	bookmark	balloon
suit	chew	glue	Tuesday	bushel

Word Puzzle Fill in the missing letters to make list words.

1. c o o k i e
2. n o o d l e
3. s c h o o l
4. g o o s e
5. b o o k m a r k
6. b a l l o o n

Word Search The list words in the box are hidden in the puzzle. Circle and write each word you find.

| few |
| chew |
| true |
| bushel |
| cushion |
| suit |
| glue |
| fruit |

c h e b u s h e l
s t a f r i c h o
u c r s g l u e f
i u e u l i t s r
t s f c e t r t u
g c h e w m s u i
l b u s o u f o t
s u t b g l c e s
c u s h i o n u w

7. bushel
8. suit
9. true
10. glue
11. fruit
12. chew
13. few
14. cushion

School + Home Home Activity Your child has been learning to spell words with the vowel sound in tooth (spelled oo, ew, ue, u) and the vowel sound in cook (spelled oo, u). Ask your child to identify and spell the four list words he or she has the most difficulty spelling.

▲ **Spelling Practice Book** p. 104

DAY 5 Posttest

DICTATION SENTENCES

1. There are a few games left to play.
2. What time does school start?
3. Which answer is true?
4. Jen has a pet goose.
5. Mom always packs fruit in my lunch.
6. May I please have a cookie?
7. There is a cushion on that chair.
8. Do you like noodle soup?
9. You can find your page with a bookmark.
10. I want a red balloon.
11. Dad has a new suit.
12. Please chew your food.
13. I need glue for my project.
14. I was sick on Tuesday.
15. We need a bushel of apples.

CHALLENGE

16. Pandas like to eat bamboo.
17. Wet places can have mildew.
18. Please soothe the baby when she cries.
19. I like to walk barefoot in the grass.
20. I mailed my renewal form yesterday.

OBJECTIVES

- Formulate an inquiry question that is connected to this week's lesson focus.
- Effectively and efficiently find, evaluate, and communicate information related to an inquiry question using electronic sources.

New Literacies

Day 1	Identify Questions
Day 2	Navigate/Search
Day 3	Analyze
Day 4	Synthesize
Day 5	Communicate

NEW LITERACIES

Internet Inquiry Activity

EXPLORE SYMBOLS OF FREEDOM

Use the following 5-day plan to help students conduct this week's Internet inquiry activity on symbols of freedom. Remind students to follow classroom rules when using the Internet.

DAY 1

Identify Questions Discuss the lesson focus question: *What does the Statue of Liberty mean to Americans?* Brainstorm ideas for specific inquiry questions about American symbols of freedom. For example, students might want to learn more about the Statue of Liberty, or how the bald eagle became our national bird. Have students work individually, in pairs, or in small groups to write an inquiry question they want to answer.

DAY 2

Navigate/Search Students begin an Internet search. Have them type keywords related to their inquiry questions. Review how to use an advanced search, which narrows the number of sites. Students can then read the descriptions to select only those sites that contain information relevant to their inquiry questions.

DAY 3

Analyze Have students explore the Web sites they identified on Day 2. Tell them to scan each site for information that helps answer their inquiry questions. Students may need to do additional searching if more information or different information is needed to completely answer inquiry questions. They can print relevant information or take notes.

DAY 4

Synthesize Have students organize the information from Day 3. Remind them that when they organize, they pull information together and arrange it in an orderly, functional way. Organizing information will help students develop answers to their inquiry questions.

DAY 5

Communicate Have students share their inquiry results. They can use a word processing program to create a short informational article about symbols of freedom.

RESEARCH/STUDY SKILLS

Time Line

OBJECTIVES

- Review ideas related to time lines.
- Create a time line.

TEACH

Ask students to name a way that dates of related events can be shown. If necessary, prompt them to mention a time line. Show students a time line, perhaps from a social studies text, as you discuss these ideas.

- Time lines present information in **time order.**
- Read a time line from left to right or from top to bottom.
- Time lines can cover a short period, such as what you did on a particular school day. They can also cover long periods of time—for example, the history of the United States.
- Entries on a time line include a date and a description of what happened on that date. The dates can be specific (January 13, 1956) or general (1887).

Have students research the construction of a well-known United States monument, such as the Lincoln Memorial or Mount Rushmore. If possible, students can do an Internet search to find an appropriate Web site. Otherwise they can browse the library for informative books. Students will create a time line to show important events in the construction of the monument.

Show the time line below on the board and discuss these questions.

1. **What are the beginning and ending dates on this time line?** *(1892 and 1954)*

2. **What does the time line show?** *(Important events in the history of Ellis Island)*

1892 1897 1900   1924   1954

1892	Immigration Center opens on Ellis Island.
1897	Fire destoys original building.
1900	Immigration Center reopens.
1924	National Origins Act is passed. Immigration is reduced.
1954	Immigration Center on Ellis Island closes.

ASSESS

As students collect information for their time lines, check that they use important events. Make sure the time lines follow correct chronological order.

For more practice or to assess students, use Practice Book 3.2, p. 110.

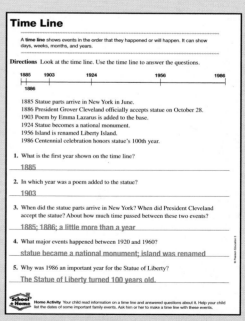

▲ **Practice Book 3.2** p. 110

Assessment Checkpoints *for the Week*

Selection Assessment

Use pp. 101–104 of Selection Tests **to check:**

 Selection Understanding

  Comprehension Skill *Main Idea*

Selection Vocabulary

crown	tablet
liberty	torch
models	unforgettable
symbol	unveiled

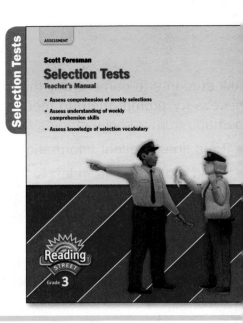

Selection Tests

ASSESSMENT

Scott Foresman
Selection Tests
Teacher's Manual

- Assess comprehension of weekly selections
- Assess understanding of weekly comprehension skills
- Assess knowledge of selection vocabulary

Reading STREET Grade 3

Leveled Assessment

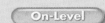
On-Level
Strategic Intervention
Advanced

Use pp. 151–156 of Fresh Reads for Differentiated Test Practice **to check:**

  Comprehension Skill *Main Idea*

 REVIEW **Comprehension Skill** *Character*

Fluency *Words Correct Per Minute*

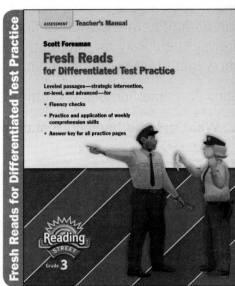

Fresh Reads for Differentiated Test Practice

ASSESSMENT Teacher's Manual

Scott Foresman
Fresh Reads
for Differentiated Test Practice

Leveled passages—strategic intervention, on-level, and advanced—for
- Fluency checks
- Practice and application of weekly comprehension skills
- Answer key for all practice pages

Reading STREET Grade 3

Managing Assessment

Use Assessment Handbook **for:**

 Observation Checklists

 Record-Keeping Forms

 Portfolio Assessment

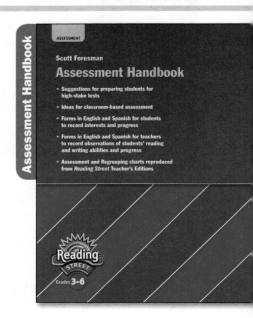

Assessment Handbook

ASSESSMENT

Scott Foresman
Assessment Handbook

- Suggestions for preparing students for high-stake tests
- Ideas for classroom-based assessment
- Forms in English and Spanish for students to record interests and progress
- Forms in English and Spanish for teachers to record observations of students' reading and writing abilities and progress
- Assessment and Regrouping charts reproduced from *Reading Street* Teacher's Editions

Reading STREET Grades 3–6

Illinois

Planning Guide for Performance Descriptors

Happy Birthday Mr. Kang

Reading Street Teacher's Edition pages

Grade 3 English Language Arts Performance Descriptors

Oral Language

Speaking/Listening Build Concept Vocabulary: 304l, 317, 325, 331c
Read Aloud: 304m

1A.Stage C.3. Discuss the meanings of new words encountered in independent and group activities.
1B.Stage C.13. Read age-appropriate material aloud with fluency and accuracy.
2A.Stage C.5. Define unfamiliar vocabulary.

Word Work

Schwa: 331i, 331k–331l

3A.Stage C.8. Use knowledge of letter-sound relationships to spell unfamiliar words.

Reading

Comprehension Cause/Effect: 304–305, 308–325
Graphic Organizer: 304–305, 308–325
Vocabulary Lesson Vocabulary: 306b, 317, 325, 328
Context Clues: 306–307, 319, 331c
Fluency Model Reading with Appropriate Phrasing: 304l–304m, 331a
Choral Reading: 331a
Self-Selected Reading: LR10–18, TR16–17
Literature Genre—Realistic Fiction: 308
Reader Response: 326

1A.Stage C.7. Use content and previous experience to determine the meanings of unfamiliar words in text.
1B.Stage C.1. Identify purposes for reading before and during reading.
1B.Stage C.3. Use a variety of strategies (e.g., K-W-L, anticipation guide, graphic organizer, DR-TA) to connect important ideas in text to prior knowledge and other reading.
1B.Stage C.13. Read age-appropriate material aloud with fluency and accuracy.
2A.Stage C.5. Define unfamiliar vocabulary.
2A.Stage C.7. Classify major types of fiction (e.g., tall tale, fairy tale, fable).
2A.Stage C.9. Classify types of expository text structures (e.g., description, sequence, comparison, cause/effect, problem/solution).

Language Arts

Writing Outlining: 331g–331h
Six-Trait Writing Sentences: 327, 331g–331h
Grammar, Usage, and Mechanics Abbreviation: 331e–331f
Research/Study Maps: 331n
Technology New Literacies: 331m

1C.Stage C.9. Use information from simple tables, maps, and charts to increase comprehension of a variety of age-appropriate materials, both fiction and nonfiction.
3A.Stage C.6. Use appropriate punctuation.
3B.Stage C.1. Use appropriate prewriting strategies (e.g., drawing, webbing, brainstorming, listing, note taking, graphic organizers) to generate and organize ideas with teacher assistance.

Unit Skills

Writing Research Report: WA2–9
Poetry: 408–411
Project/Wrap-Up: 412–413

1B.Stage C.8. Identify genres of poetry.
2A.Stage C.11. Recognize both rhymed and unrhymed poetry.
5A.Stage C.2. Define the focus of the research.
5A.Stage C.3. Collect information relevant to the topic.

This Week's Leveled Readers

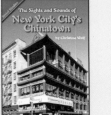

Below-Level

2A.Stage C.9. Classify types of expository text structures (e.g., description, sequence, comparison, cause/effect, problem/solution).
2B.Stage C.1. Apply events and situations in both fiction and nonfiction to personal experiences.

Nonfiction

On-Level

1C.Stage C.8. Explain how authors and illustrators express their ideas.
2A.Stage C.9. Classify types of expository text structures (e.g., description, sequence, comparison, cause/effect, problem/solution).

Nonfiction

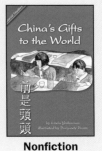

Advanced

1C.Stage C.7. Use text structure (e.g., sequential order, chronological order, problem/solution) to determine most important information.
2A.Stage C.9. Classify types of expository text structures (e.g., description, sequence, comparison, cause/effect, problem/solution).

Nonfiction

Content-Area Illinois Performance Descriptors in This Lesson

Social Studies

14E.Stage C.2. Tell about people who have come from other countries to live in the United States.

16D.Stage C.4. Tell about the origin of a family or community tradition or custom.

16D.Stage C.7. Compare how families and other groups of people lived in a past culture with how families and other groups of people in the community live today.

18A.Stage C.1. Define culture.

18A.Stage C.2. Define ethnicity, and contrast it with culture.

18A.Stage C.3. Identify cultures other than the student's own.

18A.Stage C.4. Explain the significance of the cultural diversity of the United States.

18A.Stage C.5. Describe aspects of the community that reflect its cultural heritage.

Science

12B.Stage C.2. Apply scientific inquiries or technological designs to examine the interdependence of organisms in ecosystems: identifying adaptations that help animals survive in specific or multiple environments; describing the interaction between living and non-living factors in an ecosystem.

Math

7A.Stage C.4. Describe multiple measurable attributes (e.g., length, mass/weight, time, temperature, area, volume, capacity) of a single object.

10C.Stage C.1. Describe events as likely or unlikely and discuss the degree of likelihood using such words as certain, equally likely, and impossible.

Illinois!

A FAMOUS ILLINOISAN
Walter Payton

Walter Payton (1954–1999) is considered one of the greatest running backs in the history of professional football. After attending Jackson State University in Mississippi, Payton signed with the Chicago Bears in 1975. He played thirteen years—his entire career—with the Bears. When he retired in 1987, he held records for the most yards rushed in a career, the most yards gained in one game, and the most rushing touchdowns.

Students can . . .
Create a poster celebrating Walter Payton and the football records he set.

A SPECIAL ILLINOIS PLACE
Abraham Lincoln Presidential Library and Museum

Located in Springfield, the Abraham Lincoln Presidential Library and Museum was officially dedicated in April 2005. This center dedicates more than 200,000 square feet to the history of Illinois and our sixteenth President. At the museum children can try on period clothing, experience some of the chores that children did in Lincoln's time, or compare their height to Lincoln's.

Students can . . .
Find out how tall Abraham Lincoln was and compare their own height to the President's.

ILLINOIS FUN FACTS
Did You Know?

- The University of Illinois has three campuses: one is downstate in Urbana-Champaign, the second is in Chicago, and the third is in Springfield.

- Kaskaskia is located on an island in the Mississippi River. The original settlement is now under water.

- Centralia gets its name from its founder, the Illinois Central Railroad.

Students can . . .
Research Illinois cities that were named for people and make a T-chart with the city name on one side and the person's name on the other.

Unit 6
Freedom

CONCEPT QUESTION
What does it mean to be free?

CONNECT THE CONCEPT

▶ **Build Background**
affectionate, collar, territory

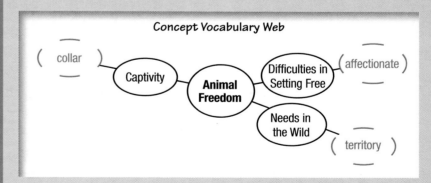

Concept Vocabulary Web

▶ **Social Studies Content**
Cultures, Community, Responsibility

▶ **Writing**
Outlining

▶ **Internet Inquiry**
Granting Freedom to Animals

Preview Your Week

When might it be hard to grant freedom?

HAPPY BIRTHDAY MR. KANG

WRITTEN AND ILLUSTRATED BY SUSAN L. ROTH

Genre **Realistic fiction** has characters and events that are like people and events in real life. Are the characters in this story like anyone you know?

308

WHAT IS SPECIAL ABOUT MR. KANG'S BIRTHDAY?

30

Student Edition pages 308-325

Audio CD

Genre	Realistic Fiction
Vocabulary Strategy	Context Clues
Comprehension Skill	Cause and Effect
Comprehension Strategy	Graphic Organizers

SOCIAL STUDIES

Paired Selection

Reading Across Texts
Compare and Contrast Birds

Genre
Interview

Text Features
Names in Dark Print
Photographs

Science in Reading

Back to the WILD

Interview

Genre
- In an interview, an expert shares his or her knowledge about a subject.
- An interview is written in a question-and-answer format.

Text Features
- The names of the interviewer and the expert answering the questions usually appear in dark print. The names are sometimes abbreviated.
- Photographs often help the reader better understand the subject.

Link to Science
Learn more about animal rescue programs. Use the library or the Internet. Create a brochure that will encourage people to use one program.

A Talk with a Wildlife Worker

by Melissa Blackwell Burke

Animals in the wild are free. They do what comes naturally to them. They don't have people taking care of them. What happens when a wild animal gets sick or hurt? Sometimes people bring such animals to a wildlife clinic. The clinic takes care of the animal until it can care for itself again. The goal is to get the animal back into the wild as soon as possible.

The staff at the Wildlife Medical Clinic at the University of Illinois in Urbana work toward that goal. We spoke to Molly Jean Carpenter, a volunteer at the clinic. She shared her thoughts about working with wildlife and described an

328

Molly Jean Carpenter

MELISSA BLACKWELL BURKE: How do workers decide when an animal needs care in your clinic?
MOLLY JEAN CARPENTER: Concerned citizens rescue animals that have been hurt. Or sometimes they bring in a young animal that isn't being cared for by its kind. We examine the animal from its head to its tail. If the animal can't take care of itself in the wild, we admit it to our clinic. We feed the animals, clean them, and give them any

medicine and care that they need. We do our best to help the animal recover so that it can go back into the wild.

MBB: Why is it so important to return these animals to the wild?
MJC: It's important because that is their home! It is very stressful for a wild animal to lose its freedom. They need to do all the activities that are natural for them, such as running, hunting, or soaring.

Wildlife rescue at work

Cause and Effect What causes animals to be brought to the clinic?

Student Edition pages 328-331

Audio CD

Read It
ONLINE
PearsonSuccessNet.com
- Student Edition
- Leveled Readers

Leveled Readers

◉ **Skill** Cause/Effect
◉ **Strategy** Graphic Organizer
Lesson Vocabulary

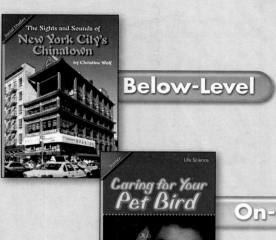

Below-Level

On-Level

Advanced

ELL Reader
- Concept Vocabulary
- Text Support
- Language Enrichment

Raising a
Seeing-Eye Dog
by Anton Economon

Illustrated by Larry Johnson

Integrate Social Studies Standards
- Community
- Responsibility
- Cultures

✓ **Read**

Happy Birthday Mr. Kang
pp. 308—325

"Back to the Wild"
pp. 328–331

Leveled Readers

Below-Level　　**On-Level**　　**Advanced**
- Support Concepts
- Develop Concepts
- Extend Concepts

ELL Reader

Raising a
Seeing-Eye Dog
by Anton Economon

✓ **Build**
Concept Vocabulary
Animal Freedom,
pp. 304I–304m

✓ **Teach**
Social Studies Concepts
Location Skills, p. 311
Hua Mei Bird Garden, p. 315
Immigration, p. 319

✓ **Explore**
Social Studies Center
Exotic Birds, p. 304k

Weekly Plan

READING

45–90 minutes

TARGET SKILLS OF THE WEEK

- **Comprehension Skill**
  Cause/Effect
- **Comprehension Strategy**
  Graphic Organizers
- **Vocabulary Strategy**
  Context Clues

LANGUAGE ARTS

30–60 minutes

Trait of the Week

Sentences

DAY 1
PAGES 304l–306b, 331a, 331e–331h, 331k–331m

Oral Language

QUESTION OF THE WEEK *When might it be hard to grant freedom?*

Read Aloud: "Elsa," 304m
Build Concepts, 304l

Comprehension/Vocabulary

Comprehension Skill/Strategy Lesson, 304–305
- Cause/Effect **T**
- Graphic Organizers

Build Background, 306a

Introduce Lesson Vocabulary, 306b
bows, chilly, foolish, foreign, narrow, perches, recipe **T**

Read Leveled Readers

Grouping Options 304f–304g

Fluency

Model Appropriate Phrasing, 304l–304m, 331a

Grammar, 331e
Introduce Abbreviations **T**

Writing Workshop, 331g
Introduce Outlining
Model the Trait of the Week: Sentences

Spelling, 331k
Pretest for Schwa

Internet Inquiry, 331m
Identify Questions

DAY 2
PAGES 306–317, 331a, 331e–331i, 331k–331m

Oral Language

QUESTION OF THE DAY *Why does Mr. Kang feel a connection with the hua mei?*

Word Work

Phonics Lesson, 331i
Schwa

Comprehension/Vocabulary

Vocabulary Strategy Lesson, 306–307
- Context Clues **T**

Read *Happy Birthday Mr. Kang,* 308–317

Grouping Options
304f–304g

- Cause/Effect **T**
- Graphic Organizers
- Context Clues **T**
- **REVIEW** Plot **T**
  Develop Vocabulary

Fluency

Choral Reading, 331a

Grammar, 331e
Develop Abbreviations **T**

Writing Workshop, 331g
Improve Writing: Including Important Details

Spelling, 331k
Teach the Generalization

Internet Inquiry, 331m
Navigate/Search

DAILY WRITING ACTIVITIES

Day 1 Write to Read, 304

Day 2 Words to Write, 307
Strategy Response Log, 308, 317

DAILY SOCIAL STUDIES CONNECTIONS

Day 1 Animal Freedom Concept Web, 304l

Day 2 Time for Social Studies: Location Skills, 311
Revisit the Animal Freedom Concept Web, 317

DAILY SUCCESS PREDICTORS
for Adequate Yearly Progress

Monitor Progress and Corrective Feedback

Vocabulary — Check Vocabulary, *304l*

RESOURCES FOR THE WEEK

- Practice Book 3.2, *pp. 111–120*
- Word Study and Spelling Practice Book, *pp. 105–108*
- Grammar and Writing Practice Book, *pp. 105–108*

- Selection Test, *pp. 105–108*
- Fresh Reads for Differentiated Test Practice, *pp. 157–162*
- The Grammar and Writing Book, *pp. 206–211*

Grouping Options for Differentiated Instruction

Turn the page for the small group lesson plan.

DAY 3 — PAGES 318–327, 331a, 331e–331h, 331k–331m

Oral Language

QUESTION OF THE DAY *What does Mr. Kang learn from the hua mei?*

Comprehension/Vocabulary

Read *Happy Birthday Mr. Kang, 318–326*

Grouping Options 304f–304g

- Cause/Effect **T**
- Graphic Organizers
- Context Clues **T**
- **REVIEW** Theme **T**
- Develop Vocabulary

Reader Response

Selection Test

Fluency

Model Appropriate Phrasing, 331a

Grammar, 331f
Apply Abbreviations in Writing **T**

Writing Workshop, 327, 331h
Write Now
Prewrite and Draft

Spelling, 331l
Connect Spelling to Writing

Internet Inquiry, 331m
Analyze Sources

Day 3 Strategy Response Log, 324
Look Back and Write, 326

Day 3 Time for Social Studies: Immigration, 319
Revisit the Animal Freedom Concept Web, 325

DAY 4 — PAGES 328–331a, 331e–331h, 331j–331m

Oral Language

QUESTION OF THE DAY *How are animals that live in the wild similar to pets that stay with us in our homes?*

Word Work

Phonics Lesson, 331j
REVIEW Vowel Sounds in *tooth* and *cook* **T**

Comprehension/Vocabulary

Read "Back to the Wild," 328–331

Grouping Options 304f–304g

Interview/Text Features
Reading Across Texts
Content-Area Vocabulary

Fluency

Paired Reading, 331a

Grammar, 331f
Practice Abbreviations for Standardized Tests **T**

Writing Workshop, 331h
Draft, Revise, and Publish

Spelling, 331l
Provide a Strategy

Internet Inquiry, 331m
Synthesize Information

Day 4 Writing Across Texts, 331

Day 4 Social Studies Center: Exotic Birds, 304k

DAY 5 — PAGES 331a–331h, 331k–331n

Oral Language

QUESTION OF THE WEEK *To wrap up the week, revisit the Day 1 question.*
Build Concept Vocabulary, 331c

Fluency

Read Leveled Readers

Grouping Options 304f–304g

Assess Reading Rate, 331a

Comprehension/Vocabulary

- Reteach Cause/Effect, 331b **T**
- Word Choice, 331b
- Review Context Clues, 331c **T**

Speaking and Listening, 331d
Express an Opinion
Listen to Opinions

Grammar, 331f
Cumulative Review

Writing Workshop, 331h
Connect to Unit Writing

Spelling, 331l
Posttest for Schwa

Internet Inquiry, 331m
Communicate Results

Research/Study Skills, 331n
Maps

Day 5 Word Choice, 331b

Day 5 Revisit the Animal Freedom Concept Web, 331c

KEY ☺ = Target Skill **T** = Tested Skill

Comprehension — Check Retelling, *327*

Fluency — Check Fluency WCPM, *331a*

Vocabulary — Check Vocabulary, *331c*

SUCCESS PREDICTOR

Small Group Plan *for Differentiated Instruction*

Daily Plan
AT A GLANCE

Reading
Whole Group
- Oral Language
- Phonics
- Comprehension/Vocabulary

Group Time
Differentiated Instruction

Meet with small groups to provide:
- Skill Support
- Reading Support
- Fluency Practice

Read

This week's lessons for daily group time can be found behind the Differentiated Instruction (DI) tab on pp. DI·12–DI·21.

Whole Group
- Fluency

Language Arts
- Grammar
- Writing
- Spelling
- Research/Inquiry
- Speaking/Listening/Viewing

Use *My Sidewalks on Reading Street* for Tier III intensive reading intervention.

DAY 1

On-Level
Teacher-Led
Page DI·13
- Develop Concept Vocabulary
- **Read** On-Level Reader *Caring for Your Pet Bird*

Strategic Intervention
Teacher-Led
Page DI·12
- Preteach Schwa
- **Read** Decodable Reader 27
- **Read** Below-Level Reader *The Sights and Sounds . . .*

Advanced
Teacher-Led
Page DI·13
- **Read** Advanced Reader *China's Gifts to the World*
- Independent Extension Activity

i **Independent Activities**
While you meet with small groups, have the rest of the class...

- Visit the Reading/Library Center
- Listen to the Background Building Audio
- Finish Write to Read, p. 304
- Complete Practice Book 3.2 pp. 113–114
- Visit Cross-Curricular Centers

DAY 2

On-Level
Teacher-Led
Pages 310–317
- **Read** *Happy Birthday Mr. Kang*

Strategic Intervention
Teacher-Led
Page DI·14
- Practice Lesson Vocabulary
- Read Multisyllabic Words
- **Read** or Listen to *Happy Birthday Mr. Kang*

Advanced
Teacher-Led
Page DI·15
- Extend Vocabulary
- **Read** *Happy Birthday Mr. Kang*

i **Independent Activities**
While you meet with small groups, have the rest of the class...

- Visit the Reading/Library Center
- Listen to the AudioText for *Happy Birthday Mr. Kang*
- Finish Words to Write, p. 307
- Complete Practice Book 3.2 pp. 115–116, 119
- Write in their Strategy Response Logs, pp. 308, 317
- Visit Cross-Curricular Centers
- Work on inquiry projects

DAY 3

On-Level
Teacher-Led
Pages 318–325
- **Read** *Happy Birthday Mr. Kang*

Strategic Intervention
Teacher-Led
Page DI·16
- Practice Cause/Effect and Graphic Organizer
- **Read** or Listen to *Happy Birthday Mr. Kang*

Advanced
Teacher-Led
Page DI·17
- Extend Cause/Effect and Graphic Organizer
- **Read** *Happy Birthday Mr. Kang*

i **Independent Activities**
While you meet with small groups, have the rest of the class...

- Visit the Reading/Library Center
- Listen to the AudioText for *Happy Birthday Mr. Kang*
- Write in their Strategy Response Logs, p. 324
- Finish Look Back and Write, p. 326
- Complete Practice Book 3.2 p. 117
- Visit Cross-Curricular Centers
- Work on inquiry projects

① Begin with whole class skill and strategy instruction.

② Meet with small groups to provide differentiated instruction.

③ Gather the whole class back together for fluency and language arts.

DAY 4

On-Level

Teacher-Led
Pages 328–331

- **Read** "Back to the Wild"

Strategic Intervention

Teacher-Led
Page DI · 18

- Practice Retelling
- **Read** or Listen to "Back to the Wild"

Advanced

Teacher-Led
Page DI · 19

- **Read** "Back to the Wild"
- Genre Study

ⓘ Independent Activities

While you meet with small groups, have the rest of the class...

- Visit the Reading/Library Center
- Listen to the AudioText for "Back to the Wild"
- Visit the Writing and Vocabulary Centers

- Finish Writing Across Texts, p. 331
- Visit Cross-Curricular Centers
- Work on inquiry projects

DAY 5

On-Level

Teacher-Led
Page DI · 21

- **Reread** Leveled Reader *Caring for Your Pet Bird*
- Retell *Caring for Your Pet Bird*

Strategic Intervention

Teacher-Led
Page DI · 20

- **Reread** Leveled Reader *The Sights and Sounds of New York City's Chinatown*
- Retell *The Sights and Sounds of New York City's Chinatown*

Advanced

Teacher-Led
Page DI · 21

- **Reread** Leveled Reader *China's Gifts to the World*
- Share Extension Activity

ⓘ Independent Activities

While you meet with small groups, have the rest of the class...

- Visit the Reading/Library Center
- Complete Practice Book 3.2 pp. 118, 120

- Visit Cross-Curricular Centers
- Work on inquiry projects

Grouping Place English language learners in the groups that correspond to their reading abilities in English.

Use the appropriate Leveled Reader or other text at students' instructional level.

TIP Send home the appropriate Multilingual Summary of the main selection on Day 1.

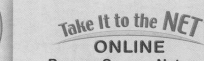

Take It to the NET ONLINE
PearsonSuccessNet.com

P. David Pearson
For ideas and activities to build comprehension, see the article "Comprehension Instruction in the Primary Grades" by Scott Foresman author P. D. Pearson and N. Duke.

TEACHER TALK

Fix-up strategies are strategies readers use when they realize they do not understand something. Adjusting reading rate, rereading, and using a reference source are a few fix-up strategies.

Be sure to schedule time for students to work on the unit inquiry project "Symbols of Freedom." This week students conduct effective information searches that help them answer their questions.

Looking Ahead

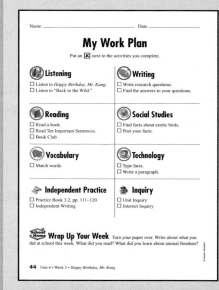

Name _____   Date _____

My Work Plan
Put an ☒ next to the activities you complete.

🎧 Listening
☐ Listen to *Happy Birthday, Mr. Kang.*
☐ Listen to "Back to the Wild."

✏️ Writing
☐ Write research questions.
☐ Find the answers to your questions.

📖 Reading
☐ Read a book.
☐ Read Ten Important Sentences.
☐ Book Club

🌐 Social Studies
☐ Find facts about exotic birds.
☐ Post your facts.

📕 Vocabulary
☐ Match words.

💻 Technology
☐ Type facts.
☐ Write a paragraph.

➤ Independent Practice
☐ Practice Book 3.2, pp. 111–120
☐ Independent Writing

🐦 Inquiry
☐ Unit Inquiry
☐ Internet Inquiry

Wrap Up Your Week Turn your paper over. Write about what you did at school this week. What did you read? What did you learn about animal freedom?

44   Unit 6 • Week 2 • *Happy Birthday, Mr. Kang*

▲ **Group-Time Survival Guide** p. 44, Weekly Contract

Mr. Kang   **304g**

☑ Customize Your Plan *by Strand*

ORAL LANGUAGE

Concept Development

When might it be hard to grant freedom?

CONCEPT VOCABULARY
affectionate   collar   territory

BUILD

❑ **Question of the Week** Introduce and discuss the question of the week. This week students will read a variety of texts and work on projects related to the concept *animal freedom*. Post the question for students to refer to throughout the week. **DAY 1** *304d*

❑ **Read Aloud** Read aloud "Elsa." Then begin a web to build concepts and concept vocabulary related to this week's lesson and the unit theme, Freedom. Introduce the concept words *affectionate, collar,* and *territory* and have students place them on the web. Display the web for use throughout the week. **DAY 1** *304l–304m*

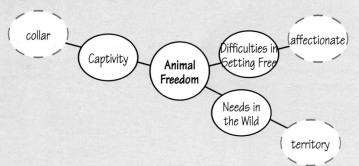

DEVELOP

❑ **Question of the Day** Use the prompts from the Weekly Plan to engage students in conversations related to this week's reading and the unit theme. **EVERY DAY** *304d–304e*

❑ **Concept Vocabulary Web** Revisit the Animal Freedom Concept Web and encourage students to add concept words from their reading and life experiences. **DAY 2** *317,* **DAY 3** *325*

CONNECT

❑ **Looking Back/Moving Forward** Revisit the Animal Freedom Concept Web and discuss how it relates to this week's lesson and the unit theme. Then make connections to next week's lesson. **DAY 5** *331c*

CHECK

❑ **Concept Vocabulary Web** Use the Animal Freedom Concept Web to check students' understanding of the concept vocabulary words *affectionate, collar,* and *territory.* **DAY 1** *304l,* **DAY 5** *331c*

VOCABULARY

STRATEGY CONTEXT CLUES
Context clues are the words and sentences around an unknown word. Sometimes an author uses an antonym as a context clue. An antonym is a word that means the opposite of another word. When you come across a word you don't know, look for an antonym as a context clue. The antonym can help you figure out the meaning of the unfamiliar word.

LESSON VOCABULARY
bows	narrow
chilly	perches
foolish	recipe
foreign	

TEACH

❑ **Words to Know** Give students the opportunity to tell what they already know about this week's lesson vocabulary words. Then discuss word meaning. **DAY 1** *306b*

❑ **Vocabulary Strategy Lesson** Use the vocabulary strategy lesson in the Student Edition to introduce and model this week's strategy, *context clues.* **DAY 2** *306–307*

Vocabulary Strategy Lesson

PRACTICE/APPLY

❑ **Leveled Text** Read the lesson vocabulary in the context of leveled text. **DAY 1** *LR10–LR18*

❑ **Words in Context** Read the lesson vocabulary and apply *context clues* in the context of *Happy Birthday Mr. Kang.* **DAY 2** *308–317,* **DAY 3** *318–326*

Leveled Readers

❑ **Vocabulary Center** Play a game to practice new words. **ANY DAY** *304j*

❑ **Homework** Practice Book 3.2 pp. 114–115. **DAY 1** *306b,* **DAY 2** *307*

Main Selection—Fiction

❑ **Word Play** Have students write and illustrate a short poem using their favorite rhyming words. **ANY DAY** *331c*

ASSESS

❑ **Selection Test** Use the Selection Test to determine students' understanding of the lesson vocabulary words. **DAY 3**

RETEACH/REVIEW

❑ **Reteach Lesson** If necessary, use this lesson to reteach and review *context clues.* **DAY 5** *331c*

① Use assessment data to determine your instructional focus.

② Preview this week's instruction by strand.

③ Choose instructional activities that meet the needs of your classroom.

COMPREHENSION

SKILL CAUSE AND EFFECT A cause is a fact that tells *why* something happened. The word *because* is often a signal of a cause. An effect is a fact that tells *what* happened. The word *so* often signals an effect. Sometimes a cause has more than one effect.

STRATEGY GRAPHIC ORGANIZER A graphic organizer is a chart that readers make to arrange information from a story. Active readers use graphic organizers to help themselves see and understand story information. Use a graphic organizer to fill in the causes and effects as you read the story.

TEACH

❏ **Skill/Strategy Lesson** Use the skill/strategy lesson in the Student Edition to introduce and model *cause and effect* and *graphic organizers.* **DAY 1** *304-305*

Skill/Strategy Lesson

❏ **Extend Skills** Teach word choice. **ANY DAY** *331b*

PRACTICE/APPLY

❏ **Leveled Text** Apply *cause and effect* and *graphic organizers* to read leveled text. **DAY 1** *LR10-LR18*

❏ **Skills and Strategies in Context** Read *Happy Birthday Mr. Kang,* using the Guiding Comprehension questions to apply *cause and effect* and *graphic organizers.* **DAY 2** *308-317,* **DAY 3** *318-326*

Leveled Readers

❏ **Skills and Strategies in Context** Read "Back to the Wild," guiding students as they apply *cause and effect* and *graphic organizers.* Then have students discuss and write across texts. **DAY 4** *328-331*

Main Selection—Fiction

❏ **Homework** Practice Book 3.2 pp. 113, 117, 118. **DAY 1** *305,* **DAY 3** *325,* **DAY 5** *331b*

Paired Selection—Nonfiction

❏ **Fresh Reads for Differentiated Test Practice** Have students practice *cause and effect* with a new passage. **DAY 3**

ASSESS

❏ **Selection Test** Determine students' understanding of the selection and their use of *cause and effect.* **DAY 3**

❏ **Retell** Have students retell *Happy Birthday Mr. Kang.* **DAY 3** *326-327*

RETEACH/REVIEW

❏ **Reteach Lesson** If necessary, reteach and review cause and effect. **DAY 5** *331b*

FLUENCY

SKILL APPROPRIATE PHRASING Appropriate phrasing means reading groups or "chunks" of words that go together, rather than reading word for word.

TEACH

❏ **Read Aloud** Model fluent reading by rereading "Elsa." Focus on this week's fluency skill, appropriate phrasing. **DAY 1** *304l-304m, 331A*

PRACTICE/APPLY

❏ **Choral Reading** Read aloud selected paragraphs from *Happy Birthday Mr. Kang,* reading groups of words rather than word-by-word. Then practice as a class by doing three choral readings of the paragraphs. **DAY 2** *331a,* **DAY 3** *331a*

❏ **Paired Reading** Have partners practice reading aloud groups of words, offering each other feedback. As students reread, monitor their progress toward their individual fluency goals. **DAY 4** *331a*

❏ **Listening Center** Have students follow along with the AudioText for this week's selections. **ANY DAY** *304j*

❏ **Reading/Library Center** Have students reread a selection of their choice. **ANY DAY** *304j*

❏ **Fluency Coach** Have students use Fluency Coach to listen to fluent readings or practice reading on their own. **ANY DAY**

ASSESS

❏ **Check Fluency** WCPM Do a one-minute timed reading, paying special attention to this week's skill—appropriate phrasing. Provide feedback for each student. **DAY 5** *331a*

☑ Customize Your Plan *by Stran*

GRAMMAR

SKILL ABBREVIATIONS An abbreviation is a short form of a word. Many abbreviations begin with a capital letter and end with a period.

TEACH

☐ **Grammar Transparency 27** Use Grammar Transparency 27 to teach abbreviations. **DAY 1** *331e*

Grammar Transparency 27

PRACTICE/APPLY

☐ **Develop the Concept** Review the concept of abbreviations and provide guided practice. **DAY 2** *331e*

☐ **Apply to Writing** Have students review something they have written and apply what they have learned about abbreviations. **DAY 3** *331f*

☐ **Test Preparation** Examine common errors in using abbreviations to prepare for standardized tests. **DAY 4** *331f*

☐ **Homework** Grammar and Writing Practice Book pp. 105–107. **DAY 2** *331e*, **DAY 3** *331f*, **DAY 4** *331f*

ASSESS

☐ **Cumulative Review** Use Grammar and Writing Practice Book p. 108. **DAY 5** *331f*

RETEACH/REVIEW

☐ **Daily Fix-It** Have students find and correct errors in grammar, spelling, and punctuation. **EVERY DAY** *331e–331f*

☐ **The Grammar and Writing Book** Use pp. 206–209 of The Grammar and Writing Book to extend instruction for abbreviations. **ANY DAY**

The Grammar and Writing Book

WRITING

Trait of the Week

SENTENCES Good writing has a natural flow. Different kinds of sentences should make it sound smooth and clear. For example, when you are writing sentences from an outline, keep your topic, audience, and purpose in mind. Include only the important details about your topic.

TEACH

☐ **Writing Transparency 27A** Use the model to introduce and discuss the Trait of the Week. **DAY 1** *331g*

☐ **Writing Transparency 27B** Use the transparency to show students how including important details can improve their writing. **DAY 2** *331g*

Writing Transparency 27A **Writing Transparency 27B**

PRACTICE/APPLY

☐ **Write Now** Examine the model on Student Edition p. 327. Then have students write their own outlines. **DAY 3** *327, 331h*, **DAY 4** *331h*

> **Prompt** *Happy Birthday Mr. Kang* tells about a special bird and a wish. Think about some of the facts in the story. Now use the story and the library or Internet to outline a topic from the story.

Write Now p. 327

☐ **Writing Center** Plan a research report on Chinese American traditions including questions to answer, research, and fact cards. **ANY DAY** *304k*

ASSESS

☐ **Writing Trait Rubric** Use the rubric to evaluate students' writing. **DAY 4** *331h*

RETEACH/REVIEW

☐ **The Grammar and Writing Book** Use pp. 206–211 of The Grammar and Writing Book to extend instruction for abbreviations, including important details, and outlines. **ANY DAY**

The Grammar and Writing Book

SPELLING

GENERALIZATION SCHWA In many words, the schwa in an unaccented syllable gives no clue to its spelling: *above*, *family*, *melon*. The schwa can be spelled in a number of different ways, but it always has the same sound.

TEACH

☐ **Pretest** Give the pretest for words with schwa. Guide students in self-correcting their pretests and correcting any misspellings. **DAY 1** *331k*

☐ **Think and Practice** Connect spelling to the phonics generalization for the schwa sound. **DAY 2** *331k*

PRACTICE/APPLY

☐ **Connect to Writing** Have students use spelling words to write an invitation. Then review frequently misspelled words: *again*, *beautiful*, *upon*. **DAY 3** *331l*

☐ **Homework** Phonics and Spelling Practice Book pp. 105–108. **EVERY DAY**

RETEACH/REVIEW

☐ **Review** Review spelling words to prepare for the posttest. Then provide students with a spelling strategy—vowel combinations. **DAY 4** *331l*

ASSESS

☐ **Posttest** Use dictation sentences to give the posttest for words with schwa. **DAY 5** *331l*

Spelling Words

1. above	6. open	11. sugar
2. another	7. family	12. circus
3. upon	8. travel	13. item
4. animal	9. afraid	14. gallon
5. paper	10. nickel	15. melon

Challenge Words

16. character	18. Oregon	20. dinosaur
17. cardinal	19. particular	

PHONICS

SKILL SCHWA In unaccented (unstressed) syllables, any vowel can stand for the schwa sound, /ə/.

TEACH

☐ **Phonics Lesson** Model how to read words with schwa. Then have students practice by decoding longer words and reading words in context. **DAY 2** *331i*

PRACTICE/APPLY

☐ **Homework** Practice Book 3.2, p. 119. **DAY 2** *331i*

RETEACH/REVIEW

☐ **Review Word Parts** Review how to read words with the vowel sounds in *tooth* and *cook*. Then have students practice by decoding longer words and reading words in context. **DAY 4** *331j*

RESEARCH AND INQUIRY

☐ **Internet Inquiry** Have students conduct an Internet inquiry on granting freedom to animals. **EVERY DAY** *331m*

☐ **Maps** Review terms related to maps, such as *legend* (key), *scale*, *compass rose*, and *landmarks*. Have students work with a partner to locate three or four landmarks on a map of Boston. **DAY 5** *331n*

☐ **Unit Inquiry** Allow time for students to conduct information searches, looking for text and images to help answer their questions. **ANY DAY** *283*

SPEAKING AND LISTENING

☐ **Express an Opinion** Have students deliver a speech that expresses their opinion about a topic that is important in your community. Remind them to give reasons that support their opinion. **DAY 5** *331d*

☐ **Listen to Opinions** Have students listen to opinion speeches, ask questions, and then answer questions. **DAY 5** *331d*

Resources for Differentiated Instruction

LEVELED READERS

► **Comprehension**
- 🎯 **Skill** Cause and Effect
- 🎯 **Strategy** Graphic Organizers

► **Lesson Vocabulary**
- 🎯 **Context Clues**

recipe perches foolish foreign narrow chilly bows

► **Social Studies Standards**
- **Community**
- **Responsibility**
- **Cultures**

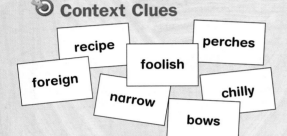

Leveled Reader Database ONLINE

PearsonSuccessNet.com

Use the Online Database of over 600 books to
- Download and print additional copies of this week's leveled readers.
- Listen to the readers being read online.
- Search for more titles focused on this week's skills, topic, and content.

On-Level

Science / Life Science
Caring for Your Pet Bird
by Lana Grace

On-Level Reader

Cause and Effect
- A **cause** is why something happened.
- An **effect** is what happened.

Directions Use *Caring for Your Pet Bird* to fill in each missing cause or effect.

Causes _Possible responses given._	Effects
1. Removing birds from their habitat can make them become extinct. **Why did it happen?**	In the United States it is illegal to import birds from many countries. **What happened?**
2. Zebra finches don't like to be lonely. **Why did it happen?**	Zebra finches are kept in pairs. **What happened?**
3. Most pet birds like the challenge of finding food. **Why did it happen?**	Place interesting treats in different parts of your bird's cage. **What happened?**
4. Birds like to chew on their toys. **Why did it happen?**	Buy bird toys that are nontoxic. **What happened?**
5. Most birds don't like the cold. **Why did it happen?**	Make sure there are no cold drafts near the cage. **What happened?**

🎯 **On-Level Practice** TE p. LR14

Vocabulary

Directions Fill in the blank with the word from the box that matches the definition.

Check the Words You Know
- bows
- foolish
- narrow
- recipe
- chilly
- foreign
- perches

1. **foreign** *adj.* from a country other than your own
2. **perches** *n.* places to view things from high above
3. **bows** *v.* leans forward to show respect
4. **foolish** *adj.* silly; not wise
5. **recipe** *n.* instructions for cooking
6. **narrow** *adj.* having a small width; not very wide
7. **chilly** *adj.* slightly cold

Directions Write a brief paragraph discussing how to care for a pet bird. Use at least three vocabulary words.

Responses will vary.

🎯 **On-Level Practice** TE p. LR15

Strategic Intervention

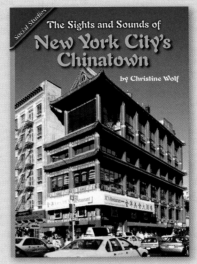
Social Studies / The Sights and Sounds of **New York City's Chinatown**
by Christine Wolf

Below-Level Reader

Cause and Effect
- A **cause** is why something happened.
- An **effect** is what happened.

Directions For each cause, write an effect. Use *The Sights and Sounds of New York City's Chinatown* to help you. The same cause may have different effects.

Causes _Possible responses given._	Effects
1. Many Chinatown residents come from China. **Why did it happen?**	Throughout Chinatown, you can hear people speaking Chinese. **What happened?**
2. Many Chinatown residents come from China. **Why did it happen?**	Many Chinese traditions are maintained in Chinatown. **What happened?**
3. Many young Chinatown residents do not show respect to their elders. **Why did it happen?**	Some older residents of Chinatown are disappointed in the younger generation. **What happened?**
4. Many Chinatown residents want to exercise their minds and bodies. **Why did it happen?**	Some Chinatown residents practice Tai Chi. **What happened?**
5. Some people want to avoid the crowds at the Chinese New Year celebrations. **Why did it happen?**	Some people watch the celebrations from perches high above the city streets. **What happened?**

🎯 **Below-Level Practice** TE p. LR11

Vocabulary

Directions Fill in the blank with the word from the box that matches the definition.

Check the Words You Know
- bows
- foolish
- narrow
- recipe
- chilly
- foreign
- perches

1. **foreign** from a country other than your own
2. **perches** places to view things from high above
3. **bows** leans forward to show respect
4. **foolish** silly; not wise
5. **recipe** instructions for cooking
6. **narrow** having a small width; not very wide
7. **chilly** slightly cold

Directions Write a paragraph about Chinatown as described in *The Sights and Sounds of New York City's Chinatown*. Use at least three vocabulary words.

Responses will vary.

🎯 **Below-Level Practice** TE p. LR12

Advanced

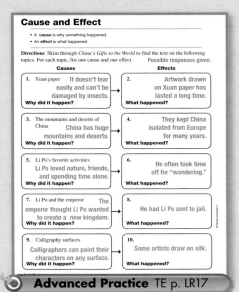

Advanced Reader

China's Gifts to the World
by Linda Yoshizawa

Cause and Effect

- A **cause** is why something happened.
- An **effect** is what happened.

Directions Skim through *China's Gifts to the World* to find the text on the following topics. For each topic, list one cause and one effect.   Possible responses given.

Causes	Effects
1. Xuan paper It doesn't tear easily and can't be damaged by insects. **Why did it happen?**	2. Artwork drawn on Xuan paper has lasted a long time. **What happened?**
3. The mountains and deserts of China China has huge mountains and deserts. **Why did it happen?**	4. They kept China isolated from Europe for many years. **What happened?**
5. Li Po's favorite activities Li Po loved nature, friends, and spending time alone. **Why did it happen?**	6. He often took time off for "wandering." **What happened?**
7. Li Po and the emperor The emperor thought Li Po wanted to create a new kingdom. **Why did it happen?**	8. He had Li Po sent to jail. **What happened?**
9. Calligraphy surfaces Calligraphers can paint their characters on any surface. **Why did it happen?**	10. Some artists draw on silk. **What happened?**

Advanced Practice TE p. LR17

Vocabulary

Directions Fill in the blank with the word from the box that matches the definition.

Check the Words You Know
- bristles   - dialects   - diverse
- expedition   - flourished   - ingredient
- inspiration   - literate   - muffled
- techniques   - translation

1. flourished   *v.* steadily grew, expanded
2. inspiration   *n.* something that stimulates a person to be creative
3. bristles   *n.* the hairs on a brush
4. muffled   *adj.* unable to be heard; wrapped with material to deaden the sound
5. ingredient   *n.* one of several substances mixed together to make a new substance
6. expedition   *n.* a journey with a specific purpose
7. techniques   *n.* methods of doing something

Directions Write a paragraph about China using the words *dialects, diverse, literate,* and *translation.*

Responses will vary.

Advanced Practice TE p. LR18

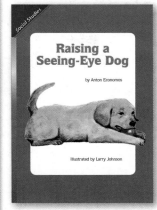

ELL Reader

Raising a Seeing-Eye Dog
by Anton Economos
Illustrated by Larry Johnson

ELL Poster 27

Teacher's Edition Notes

ELL notes throughout this lesson support instruction and reference additional resources at point of use.

Teaching Guide pp. 183–189, 264–265
- Multilingual summaries of the main selection
- Comprehension lesson
- Vocabulary strategies and word cards
- ELL Reader 3.6.2 lesson

ELL and Transition Handbook

Ten Important Sentences
- Key ideas from every selection in the Student Edition
- Activities to build sentence power

More Reading

Readers' Theater Anthology
- Fluency practice
- Five scripts to build fluency
- Poetry for oral interpretation

Leveled Trade Books

Below-Level

Advanced

On-Level

- Extended reading tied to the unit concept
- Lessons in the Trade Book Library Teaching Guide

School + Home

Homework
- Family Times Newsletter
- ELL Multilingual Selection Summaries

Take-Home Books
- Leveled Readers

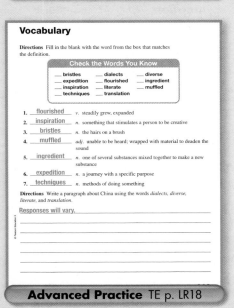

Family Times

Cross-Curricular Centers

Listening

Listen to the *Selection*

MATERIALS · SINGLES
CD player, headphones, AudioText CD, Student Edition

Listen to *Happy Birthday, Mr. Kang* and "Back to the Wild: A Talk with a Wildlife Worker" as you follow or read along in your book. Listen for cause and effect relationships.

If there is anything you don't understand, you can listen again to any section.

Reading/Library

Read It *Again!*

MATERIALS · SINGLES · PAIRS · GROUPS
Collection of books for self-selected reading, reading log

Select a book you have already read. Record the title of the book in your reading log. You may want to read with a partner.

You may choose to read any of the following:

- **Leveled Readers**
- **ELL Readers**
- **Stories written by classmates**
- **Books from the library**
- *Happy Birthday Mr. Kang*

TEN IMPORTANT SENTENCES Read the Ten Important Sentences for *Happy Birthday Mr. Kang*. Then locate the sentences in the Student Book.

BOOK CLUB Write a list of questions about *Happy Birthday Mr. Kang*. Read the questions with a small group and discuss.

Vocabulary

A Nest of *Words*

MATERIALS · SINGLES · PAIRS
Box or other container, 8 plastic eggs, 16 strips of paper, dictionary, pencil

Match a word and its definition to make eggs for the *hua mei*'s nest.

1. **Write each word below on a paper strip.**
2. **Write a definition on separate paper strips. Use your own words for the definitions.**
3. **Put the word and definition strips in the container. Mix them.**
4. **A partner looks through the "nest" and finds a word and its matching definition. He or she puts the two matching strips in an "egg" and places it back in the container.**
5. **Repeat until all "eggs" are complete.**

EARLY FINISHERS "Crack" an "egg." Read the word and definition. Write a sentence with the word.

ceramic	melody
fragrant	restaurant
interrupts	scallions
language	silence

words that people write or speak

language

Scott Foresman Reading Street Centers Survival Kit

Use the *Happy Birthday Mr. Kang* materials from the Reading Street Centers Survival Kit to organize this week's centers.

Writing

Write Fact Cards

MATERIALS SINGLES PAIRS
Paper, research materials, pencil

Plan a research report on Chinese American traditions.

1. On each piece of paper, write a question you want answered in your research report. For example, you might want to find out how Chinese Americans celebrate holidays.
2. Your questions should be about Chinese American traditions, including foods, languages, family, and celebrations.
3. Use research materials to learn the answers to your questions.
4. Write the facts on the fact cards.

EARLY FINISHERS Find China on a world map. Write a paragraph describing the journey an immigrant would take from China to where you live.

How do Chinese Americans celebrate birthdays?

Social Studies

Exotic Birds

MATERIALS SINGLES
Books about birds, Internet access, large sticky notes, globe, pencil

Learn about a bird from a different continent.

1. Learn three or four interesting facts about a bird from the list below. Write them on a sticky note.
2. Attach your facts to the globe on the appropriate continent.

Africa	**Australia**
Emerald cuckoo	Laughing kookaburra
Social weaver	Riflebird
Antarctica	
Rockhopper penguin	**Europe**
Royal albatross	Flycatcher
	Great snipe
Asia	Red kite
Himalayan vulture	**South America**
Okinawa rail	Ibis
	Lear's macaw

EARLY FINISHERS Find the bird's home on a world map. Attach your facts to the correct location on the map.

Laughing Kookaburra
3. can sound like a person laughing

Technology

Write a Report

MATERIALS SINGLES
Computer, printer

Write a report about a bird.

1. Open a word processing program.
2. Type the facts that you learned about your bird.
3. Now write a paragraph using those facts.
4. Print out your report.

EARLY FINISHERS Trade papers with a partner and proofread each other's reports.

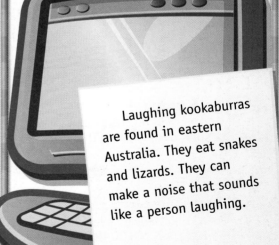

Laughing kookaburras are found in eastern Australia. They eat snakes and lizards. They can make a noise that sounds like a person laughing.

ALL CENTERS

OBJECTIVES

● Build vocabulary by finding words related to the lesson concept.

◐ Listen for cause and effect relationships.

Concept Vocabulary

affectionate loving

collar a leather or plastic band or a metal chain for the neck of a dog or other pet animal

territory an area, such as a nesting ground, in which an animal lives, and which it defends from others of its kind

Monitor Progress

Check Vocabulary

If... students are unable to place words on the web,	then... review the lesson concept. Place the words on the web and provide additional words for practice, such as *game* and *climate*.

SUCCESS PREDICTOR

DAY 1   Grouping Options

Reading
Whole Group
Introduce and discuss the Question of the Week. Then use pp. 304l–306b.

Group Time
Differentiated Instruction
 this week's Leveled Readers. See pp. 304f–304g for the small group lesson plan.

Whole Group
Use p. 331a.

Language Arts
Use pp. 331e–331h and 331k–331m.

Build Concepts

FLUENCY

MODEL APPROPRIATE PHRASING As you read "Elsa," model grouping words together and using commas to read with appropriate phrasing. Select a sentence with a comma, such as "However, we left her where there was plenty of game, hoping that hunger would force her to attack." Read it once, reading each word in a staccato manner. Then reread the sentence using appropriate phrasing, grouping together words. *However / we left her / where there was plenty of game / hoping that hunger / would force her to attack.*

LISTENING COMPREHENSION

After reading "Elsa," use the following questions to assess listening comprehension.

1. **Why does the author go to a place ten miles away from Elsa?** *(Elsa made friends with another lion in the wild.)* **Cause and Effect**

2. **How did the author know Elsa was hunting and eating on her own in the wild?** *(She brought her a buck to eat, but Elsa did not want it.)* **Draw Conclusions**

BUILD CONCEPT VOCABULARY

Start a web to build concepts and vocabulary related to this week's lesson and the unit theme.

• Draw an Animal Freedom Web.

• Read the sentence with the word *affectionate* again. Ask students to pronounce *affectionate* and discuss its meaning.

• Place *affectionate* in an oval attached to Difficulties in Setting Free. Explain that *affectionate* is related to this concept. Read the sentences in which *collar* and *territory* appear. Have students pronounce the words, place them on the web, and provide reasons.

• Brainstorm additional words and categories for the web. Keep the web on display and add words throughout the week.

Concept Vocabulary Web

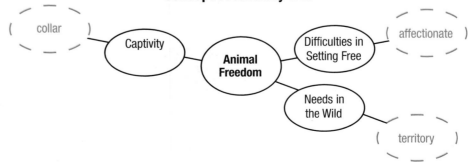

Elsa

by Joy Adamson

The true story of a lioness who was brought up from cubhood by Joy Adamson and her husband, a senior game warden; they taught her to stalk and kill for herself so that she could be set free into the African Jungle. Elsa's sisters were sent to the Rotterdam Zoo, but Elsa and the Adamsons had grown quite fond of each other. Here's how Elsa finally learned how to be free.

Elsa began to show an increasing interest in going off on her own. She was nearly two years old and her voice was getting much deeper. Often she stayed away for two or three days and we knew that she several times joined up with other lions. But she was as affectionate as ever when she saw us again.

We now began to wonder whether we could release Elsa back to the wild instead of sending her to join her sisters, as we had originally intended. It would be an experiment worth trying, and we thought we would take her to a place where there was plenty of game, spend two or three weeks with her, and if all went well leave her.

Elsa traveled in the back of my truck and the morning after our arrival we took off her collar to show her that she was free. She hopped onto the roof of the Land Rover and we set off to explore the territory.

Up to now we had always given her her meat cut up. Although she knew how to retrieve we were not sure whether she knew how to cope with a dead animal, but if she was to be left alone she would have to learn. To our surprise and delight we discovered that even though she had had no mother to teach her she knew exactly what part of an animal was eatable and what should be buried. But she had no idea how to kill. However, we left her where there was plenty of game, hoping that hunger would force her to attack.

But she hated being left on her own and when we went to see her she was terribly hungry and had obviously not eaten since our last visit. After we had given her a meal she fell sound asleep.

We decided to move her to a climate which would suit her better. The new home we chose for her was only some twenty miles from her birthplace. It was a really beautiful place with a river running through it where many wild animals came to drink.

We stayed with her for several months while she learned all the things her own mother would have taught her. One afternoon she refused to go for a walk with us and disappeared until the next morning. We realized she had made friends with a wild lion and that the time had now come.

We therefore drove to another river ten miles away where we planned to spend a week before returning to see how she had managed without us. Although I knew it was for her good, I could not help feeling we were deserting her.

continued on TR1

Set Purpose

Read the introduction aloud. Have students listen for the effect of Elsa's meeting a wild lion.

Creative Response

Encourage students to imagine that they are field reporters observing the release of Elsa. Have them work with a partner. One partner should be a camera person while the other gives a "live" report describing what is taking place. Students should then switch roles. ***Drama***

Build Background Before students listen to the Read Aloud, ask them what they know about lions in Africa.

Access Content Before reading, share this summary: Two people, Joy and George, live in Africa. They have a young lioness named Elsa that they want to set free. This part of the story tells how they know Elsa is ready to be released into the wild.

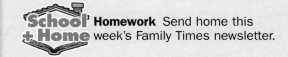 **Homework** Send home this week's Family Times newsletter.

SUCCESS PREDICTOR

SKILLS ↔ STRATEGIES IN CONTEXT

Cause and Effect Graphic Organizers

OBJECTIVES

- Identify cause and effect relationships.
- Use graphic organizers to analyze cause and effect relationships.

Skills Trace	
Cause and Effect	
Introduce/Teach	TE: 3.3 280–281, 3.4 12–13, 3.6 304–305
Practice	PB: 3.1 103, 107, 108, 116; 3.2 3, 7, 8, 16, 26, 106, 113, 117, 118, 136
Reteach/Review	TE: 3.3 303b, 315, DI·55; 3.4 35b, 49, 71, DI·52; 3.6 293, 331b, 373, DI·53
Test	Selection Test: Unit 6; Benchmark Tests: Units 4, 6

INTRODUCE

Write the following on the board: *Because Jennifer left the birdcage open, the bird flew away.* Ask, "What happened?" *(The bird flew away.)* Ask, "Why did it happen?" *(Jennifer left the birdcage open.)*

Have students read the information on p. 304. Explain the following:

- The cause is "why something happened." An effect is "what happened." The cause makes another thing, the effect, happen.
- Using a graphic organizer can help you identify cause and effect relationships.

Use Skill Transparency 27 to teach cause and effect and graphic organizers.

Skill
Cause and Effect

Strategy
Graphic Organizers

 ## Cause and Effect

- An effect is something that happens. A cause is why that thing happens.

- A cause may have more than one effect: *Because I forgot to set my alarm clock, I overslept, and I was late for school.*

- An effect may have more than one cause: *Dad's computer crashed because it didn't have enough memory, and he was running too many programs at once.*

Causes ⟶	Effects

Strategy: Graphic Organizers

A graphic organizer can help you identify and organize information as you read. You can make one like this and fill it in with causes and effects as you read the story.

Write to Read

1. Read "A New Life." Look for causes and effects in the story. Make a graphic organizer like the one above.

2. Fill in your chart as you read the story.

Strategic Intervention

Cause and Effect Provide several examples of simple cause and effect relationships, and have students identify the cause, or "why it happened," and the effect, or "what happened." Then progress to situations in which multiple causes produce one effect and one cause produces multiple effects.

ELL

Access Content

Beginning/Intermediate For a Picture It! lesson on cause and effect, see the ELL Teaching Guide, pp. 183–184.

Advanced Demonstrate how students can check causal relationships by joining the cause and effect and adding *because*. For example, in the last paragraph on p. 305, students may create the following sentence: *Because Rosa was doing well in school and the store was doing well, the Garcías were happy.* Point out that moving *because* to the second part of the sentence makes a false statement; therefore, the cause and effect are correctly identified in the example sentence.

A New Life

"Thank you," said Mr. and Mrs. García, as the customer left the store. "Please come again."

The Garcías repeated these words many times every day, as a steady stream of customers entered and left their small grocery store. Business was good, and the García family was making a good living from the store. Still, at times they were sad because they missed their beautiful little village in northern Mexico. They also missed all of the family members they had left behind when they moved to Chicago.

"¡Hola!" shouted Rosa as she burst through the back door of the store. "I got my report card today. Here it is."

The Garcías looked at the report card and then hugged Rosa. She was doing so well in her new school! And the store was doing well too. They were happy. Yes, they missed their old home in Mexico. But here in Chicago, they had found a better life for themselves and for Rosa.

1 **Skill** The clue word *because* signals a cause. What causes the Garcías to be sad?

2 **Strategy** Here are some more causes and effects. If you made a graphic organizer, you could add this information to it.

305

Available as **Skill Transparency** 27

Cause and Effect • Graphic Organizer

- A **cause** is why something happens. An **effect** is what happens.
- A **cause** may have more than one **effect**. *Because I did not do my homework, I couldn't watch the movie or go outside for recess.*
- An **effect** may have more than one **cause**. *Dad's plants dried up because he left them in the hot sun and did not water them.*
- A **graphic organizer** can help you identify and organize information as you read.

Directions Read the following story. Then fill in the chart below.

Rosa's mother made beautiful tin ornaments. No two were the same. One day, a man asked her to come to the United States to make the ornaments for his business. So Rosa and her mother left Mexico. People loved the ornaments. The man sold everything Rosa's mother made. She was so busy, she had to teach others to make the tin pieces. The man was so happy that he made Rosa's mother a business partner.

CAUSES: Why did it happen?	EFFECTS: What happened?
1. Rosa's mother made beautiful tin ornaments.	A man wanted Rosa's mother to make the ornaments for his business.
The man asked Rosa's mother to come to the United States.	2. Rosa and her mother moved to the United States.
3. People loved the ornaments.	The man sold everything Rosa's mother made.
Rosa's mother was very busy.	4. She had to show others how to make the ornaments.
5. The man was very happy.	The man made Rosa's mother a partner.

Home Activity Your child learned about cause and effect. Read a story together. Ask your child to describe something that happened in the story. Then ask him or her to tell you what caused the effect. Repeat the exercise two or three times.

Practice Book 3.2 p. 113

TEACH

1 SKILL Use paragraph 2 to model how to use clue words to identify a cause and effect relationship.

Think Aloud **MODEL** Sometimes authors use clue words, such as *because, so,* and *since.* However, these words do not always indicate a cause and effect relationship. I must check to see that one event makes another event happen rather than simply coming after an event.

2 STRATEGY Use a graphic organizer to identify and analyze cause and effect relationships.

Think Aloud **MODEL** As I read the last paragraph, I look for events that cause other events to happen. I can record them in a graphic organizer. This helps me decide if the relationships are truly cause and effect. I begin by drawing a cause and effect graphic organizer.

PRACTICE AND ASSESS

SKILL Causes: They miss their home in northern Mexico; they miss their friends who still live in Mexico.

STRATEGY Causes: Rosa is doing well in school; the store is successful. Effect: The Garcías feel happy.

WRITE Have students complete steps 1 and 2 of the Write to Read activity. You might consider using this as a whole class activity.

Monitor Progress

🔁 Main Idea

If... students are unable to complete **Write to Read** on p. 304,	**then...** use Practice Book, 3.2 p. 113 to provide additional practice.

For a Web site that explores types of pet birds, have students use a student-friendly Internet search engine using the keywords *pet birds*.

E L L

Build Background Use ELL Poster 27 to build background and vocabulary for the lesson concept of giving freedom to a pet.

▲ **ELL Poster** 27

Build Background

ACTIVATE PRIOR KNOWLEDGE

BEGIN A STORY PREDICTIONS CHART about *Happy Birthday Mr. Kang*.

• Ask students to read the title of the selection and preview the illustrations.

• Have students think about what they already know about birthdays and pets. Then have them make predictions about the story's events in column 1.

• Students should think about what clues they used to make their predictions and write them in column 2.

• Tell students that after they read the story, they will complete column 3.

Title *Happy Birthday Mr. Kang*		
What might happen?	**What clues do I have?**	**What did happen?**
Mr. Kang will get a bird for his birthday.	The title is *Happy Birthday Mr. Kang*. The illustrations show a man with a bird.	

▲ **Graphic Organizer** 6

BACKGROUND BUILDING AUDIO This week's audio explores why people keep birds as pets. After students listen, discuss what they found out about pet birds and whether they would like to have one.

Background Building Audio

Introduce Vocabulary

WORD RATING CHART

Create word rating charts using the categories *Know, Have Seen,* and *Don't Know.*

Word Rating Chart

Word	Know	Have Seen	Don't Know
bows	✔		
chilly	✔		
foolish		✔	
foreign			
narrow			
perches			
recipe			

▲ **Graphic Organizer** 4

Read each word to students and have them place a check mark in one of the three columns: *Know* (know and can use); *Have Seen* (have seen or heard the word; don't know meaning); *Don't Know* (don't know the word).

Activate Prior Knowledge

Have students share where they may have seen some of these words. Point out that some of this week's words have antonyms, or words that have the opposite meaning *(narrow/wide; chilly/warm).*

Context Clues • Antonyms

Check charts with students at the end of the week and have them make changes to their ratings.

Discuss the meanings of some of the vocabulary words with students. Ask the following questions to clarify word meanings.

- Is the gap in the fence too *narrow* for you to squeeze through?
- Do you have a *recipe* for making these delicious cookies?
- Do I look *foolish* in this costume?

Use the Multisyllabic Word Routine on p. DI·1 to help students read multisyllabic words.

Lesson Vocabulary

WORDS TO KNOW

T **bows** bends the head and body in greeting, respect, worship, or obedience

T **chilly** cold; unpleasantly cool

T **foolish** without any sense; unwise

T **foreign** outside your own country

T **narrow** not wide; having little width

T **perches** comes to rest on something; settles; sits

T **recipe** a set of written directions that shows you how to fix something to eat

MORE WORDS TO KNOW

fragrant having a sweet smell or odor

gingerly with extreme care or caution

sleek soft and shiny; smooth

T= Tested Word

Vocabulary

Directions Match each word with its meaning. Draw a line to connect them.

Check the Words You Know
___narrow   ___foolish
___perches   ___bows
___recipe   ___chilly
___foreign

1. foolish — cool
2. recipe — from a different country
3. narrow — silly
4. chilly — directions for cooking food
5. foreign — skinny

Directions Write the word from the box that best completes each sentence below.

6. Watch the red bird as it _____ on the branch.   perches
7. After he sings, he _____ to the audience.   bows
8. The gap was too _____ for me to squeeze through.   narrow
9. He moved here from a _____ country called Sudan.   foreign
10. My stepmother wrote that _____ for beef stew.   recipe

Write a Recipe
On a separate sheet of paper, write a recipe for something you like to eat or drink. It can be something simple, like chocolate milk or a sandwich. Use as many vocabulary words as possible. Students' writing should use vocabulary in a simple recipe for a food they like.

Home Activity Your child identified and used vocabulary words from *Happy Birthday Mr. Kang.* Have your child plan a menu for dinner or help you prepare food from a written recipe. Encourage your child to use vocabulary words in conversations.

▲ **Practice Book 3.2** p. 114

Vocabulary Strategy

◉ Use context clues and antonyms to determine word meaning.

INTRODUCE

Discuss the strategy of context clues using the steps on p. 306.

TEACH

- Have students read "Mr. Wang's Wonderful Noodles," paying attention to how vocabulary is used.
- Model using context clues to determine the meaning of *narrow*.

MODEL The word *narrow* used on p. 307 is contrasted with the words *wide* and *thick*. So *narrow* must be the opposite of *wide* and *thick*. It means "thin."

Words to Know

narrow

foolish

perches

bows

recipe

chilly

foreign

Remember

Try the strategy. Then, if you need more help, use your glossary or a dictionary.

Vocabulary Strategy
for Antonyms

Context Clues Sometimes when you are reading, you will see a word you don't know. The words around it might help you figure out the meaning. For example, the author may give you an antonym for the word. An antonym is a word that means the opposite of another word. For example, *thin* is the opposite of *thick*. Look for another word that might be an antonym and see if it will help you figure out the meaning of the word you don't know.

1. Look at the words around the unfamiliar word. Perhaps the author used an antonym.

2. Look for words that seem to have opposite meanings. Think about the one word you know.

3. Use that word to help you figure out the meaning of its antonym.

As you read "Mr. Wang's Wonderful Noodles," look for antonyms to help you understand the meanings of the vocabulary words.

306

DAY 2 Grouping Options

Reading
Whole Group Discuss the Question of the Day. Then use pp. 306–309b.

Group Time Differentiated Instruction
Read *Happy Birthday Mr. Kang.* See pp. 304f–304g for the small group lesson plan.

Whole Group Use pp. 331a and 331i.

Language Arts
Use pp. 331e–331h and 331k–331m.

Strategic Intervention

◉ **Context Clues** Have students work in pairs to follow the steps on p. 306. Encourage them to list clues for an unknown word and then decide together the best meaning for it.

 ELL

Access Content Use ELL Poster 27 to preteach vocabulary. Choose from the following to meet language proficiency levels.
Beginning Point out clues on p. 307 that show that *foolish* means "silly."
Intermediate After reading, students can create a two-column chart of words and their antonyms, with meanings for both.
Advanced Teach the lesson on pp. 306–307. Students can report on the names of different types of birds in their home languages.
Resources for home-language words may include parents, bilingual staff members, bilingual dictionaries, or online translation sources.

MR. WANG'S WONDERFUL Noodles

Mr. Wang is the best noodle maker in Shanghai, China. People who like wide, thick noodles may think people who like narrow, thin noodles are foolish. People who like narrow, thin noodles may think people who like wide, thick noodles are not very smart. But everyone agrees on one thing. Mr. Wang's noodles are the best.

When a customer comes to the noodle shop and perches on a stool at the counter, Mr. Wang always bows his head with respect, as if to say "Thank you for coming to my shop."

One day a stranger came into the noodle shop. He said, "Mr. Wang, please bring your noodle recipe to the United States. Make noodles in my restaurant."

The warm shop suddenly felt chilly. People stopped slurping their noodles to listen to Mr. Wang's reply.

Mr. Wang quietly said, "Thank you. But I do not wish to go to a foreign land. I am happy making noodles in China."

Everyone heaved a sigh of relief and went back to slurping Mr. Wang's wonderful noodles.

Words to Write

Write about your favorite food. How does it taste? Why do you like it? Use words from the Words to Know list.

307

PRACTICE AND ASSESS

- Have students determine the meanings of the remaining words and explain the context clues and antonyms they used.
- Point out that context does not work with every word. Students may have to use the glossary or a dictionary to find the exact meaning of some words.
- If you began word rating charts (p. 306b), have students reassess their ratings.
- Have students complete Practice Book 3.2, p. 115.

WRITE Writing should include vocabulary words and describe students' favorite foods.

Monitor Progress

Context Clues

| If... students need more practice with the lesson vocabulary, | then... use Tested Vocabulary Cards. |

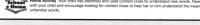

Vocabulary · Context Clues

- Sometimes when you read you see unfamiliar words. The **context**, or words around it, may help you figure out the meaning.
- Look to see if the author used an **antonym**, a word with the opposite meaning, and use that word to help you with the meaning of the unfamiliar word.

Directions Read the paragraph. Then answer the questions below.

My family wanted to eat at a Chinese food restaurant instead of the usual burger place. We had never been to a Chinese restaurant before and were excited to learn about a different culture. We walked in through a narrow hallway that didn't seem wide enough for us to fit. We drank hot tea with dinner, which was perfect because I was chilly. I tried to eat with chopsticks, but felt foolish because I seemed clumsy with them. I thought it was sensible to ask for a fork! After this restaurant becomes an old favorite, maybe my family will again try something new—maybe Brazilian food!

1. What does the word *usual* mean in the passage? What context clue helps?
   normal; different

2. What does the word *narrow* mean in the passage? What context clue helps?
   thin; wide

3. What does the word *chilly* mean in the passage? What context clue helps?
   cold; hot

4. What does the word *foolish* mean in the passage? What context clue helps?
   silly; sensible

5. What does the word *old* mean in the passage? What context clue helps?
   familiar; new

Home Activity Your child has identified and used context clues to understand new words. Read a story with your child and encourage looking for context clues to help her or him understand the meaning of unfamiliar words.

▲ **Practice Book 3.2** p. 115

Prereading Strategies

- Identify cause and effect relationships to improve comprehension.
- Use graphic organizers to analyze cause and effect relationships.

GENRE STUDY

Realistic Fiction

Happy Birthday Mr. Kang is realistic fiction. Explain that realistic fiction is a story that could really happen. The characters encounter real problems that they solve in a realistic manner.

PREVIEW AND PREDICT

Have students preview the selection title and illustrations and discuss the topics or ideas they think this story will cover. Encourage students to use lesson vocabulary as they talk about what they expect to read.

Strategy Response Log

Activate Prior Knowledge Have students write about a time when they wanted to be somewhere else. Perhaps they were sleeping over at a friend's house and missed their own house.

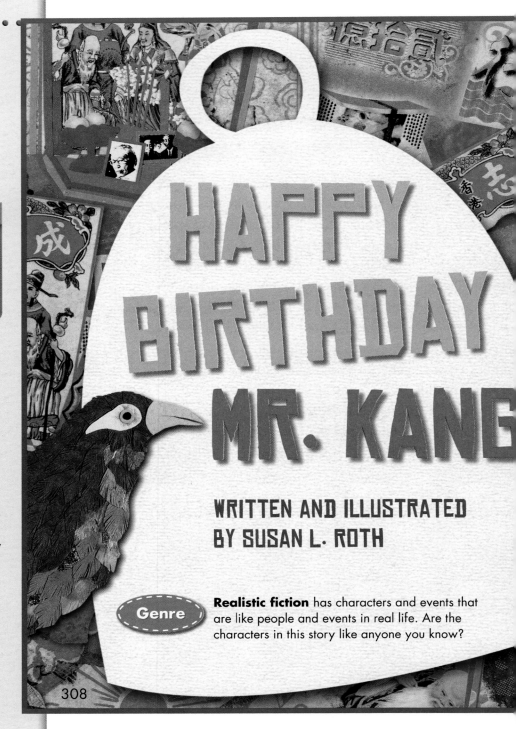

HAPPY BIRTHDAY MR. KANG

WRITTEN AND ILLUSTRATED BY SUSAN L. ROTH

Genre **Realistic fiction** has characters and events that are like people and events in real life. Are the characters in this story like anyone you know?

308

Activate Prior Knowledge Talk with students about how they felt on their first day of school. Explain that Mr. Kang is from another country, and while he enjoys his life in America, he misses his home country.

Consider having students read the selection summary in English or in students' home languages. See the Multilingual Summaries in the ELL Teaching Guide, pp. 187–189.

WHAT IS SPECIAL ABOUT MR. KANG'S BIRTHDAY?

SET PURPOSE

Read the first page of the selection aloud to students. Have them consider their preview discussion and tell what they hope to find out as they read.

Remind students to read for cause and effect relationships.

STRATEGY RECALL

Students have now used these before-reading strategies:

- preview the selection to be aware of its genre, features, and possible content;
- activate prior knowledge about that content and what to expect of that genre;
- make predictions;
- set a purpose for reading.

Remind students that, as they read, they should monitor their own comprehension. If they realize something does not make sense, they can regain their comprehension by using fix-up strategies they have learned, such as:

- use phonics and word structure to decode new words;
- use context clues or a dictionary to figure out meanings of new words;
- adjust their reading rate—slow down for difficult text, speed up for easy or familiar text, or skim and scan just for specific information;
- reread parts of the text;
- read on (continue to read for clarification);
- use text features such as headings, subheadings, charts, illustrations, and so on as visual aids to comprehension;
- make a graphic organizer or a semantic organizer to aid comprehension;
- use reference sources, such as an encyclopedia, dictionary, thesaurus, or synonym finder;
- use another person, such as a teacher, a peer, a librarian, or an outside expert, as a resource.

After reading, students will use these strategies:

- summarize or retell the text;
- answer questions they or others pose;
- reflect to make new information become part of their prior knowledge.

Audio CD **AudioText**

Mr. Kang **309**

Guiding Comprehension

1 **Sequence • Literal**

When did Mr. Kang come to America?

Forty-three years before his grandson was born.

2 **Cause and Effect • Inferential**

Why does Mr. Kang say he is done with cooking?

Possible response: He is older now and wants to retire from his job at the Golden Dragon.

Monitor Progress

Cause and Effect

If... students are unable to determine the cause and effect relationship,	**then...** use the skill and strategy instruction on p. 311.

---

3 **Draw Conclusions • Critical**

Why do you think Mr. Kang wishes to read _The New York Times_ every day?

Possible response: He wants to read to learn about the world. Also, if he spends time reading the paper, it means that he has relaxing free time.

Tech Files
ONLINE

Students can learn more about the Chinese tradition of keeping a caged _hua mei_ by searching the Internet. Have them use a student-friendly search engine and the keywords _hua mei bird_.

310

 ELL

Access Content Tell students that _The New York Times_ is a newspaper. Read the last paragraph on the page with students. Point out that a newspaper delivery person puts the newspaper on Mr. Kang's doorstep each morning.

1 Forty-three years before his grandson, Sam, was born in the New World, Mr. Kang left China and came to America. Every day he chopped scallions, wrapped dumplings, and pulled noodle dough into long and perfect strands for the hungry people who ate at the Golden Dragon Restaurant in New York City.

When Mr. Kang turned seventy, Mrs. Kang had a birthday party for him.

"Make a wish!" said Sam as Mr. Kang shut his eyes, puffed his cheeks, and blew out all the candles on his cake. Everyone clapped and shouted hurray.

"What was your wish?" Sam asked.

"Three wishes," said Mr. Kang. "I want to read *The New York Times* every day. I want to paint poems every day. And I want a bird, a *hua mei,* of my own. I'll feed him every day, and on Sundays I'll take him to Sara Delano Roosevelt Park on Delancey Street. Enough cooking."

2 "Good idea," said Mrs. Kang. "I'll cook for you, and the Golden Dragon Restaurant can get a new cook."

"Grandpa, why do you want a bird in a cage? There are birds all over the place outside," said Sam.

"Sam," said Mr. Kang. "This is not just an American bird in a cage. This is a Chinese bird. My grandfather had a hua mei in a cage. Now I want a hua mei in a cage. And sometimes you and I will take him to Sara Delano Roosevelt Park on Delancey Street together."

And so it is that every morning Mr. Kang finds *The New York Times* on his doorstep. Every morning he reads it while he drinks his tea and eats his sweet and fragrant almond cakes, warm from the oven. **3**

311

Location Skills

Time for SOCIAL STUDIES

Locate China on a world map or globe. On which continent is it located? *(Asia)* Locate New York City on the same map or globe. On which continent is it located? *(North America)* The world is a big place, but throughout history, people have been finding ways to travel between the different continents. In the late 1800s and early 1900s, you could travel from China to New York City by ship across the Pacific Ocean to North America, and then travel on land from the West Coast to the East Coast. Today you can travel much faster from China to New York City by airplane. It takes you across the Pacific Ocean directly to New York City.

SKILLS ◆▶ STRATEGIES IN CONTEXT

Cause and Effect

TEACH

- Remind students that a cause is why something happened. An effect is what happened.

- While sometimes clue words, such as *because, so,* and *since* are used to indicate a cause and effect relationship, these words are not always present. Students should look for one event that makes another event happen.

- Model identifying a cause and effect relationship.

 MODEL I see that Mr. Kang says, "Enough cooking." Why does he want to stop cooking? I skim the text and read that Mr. Kang is celebrating his 70th birthday. His wishes are for things that are relaxing to him. Now that he's older, he probably wants to stop working and have time to do fun things. Mr. Kang's age probably causes his wish to stop cooking.

PRACTICE AND ASSESS

Have students reread p. 311, paragraph 3. Ask them to identify another cause and effect relationship. *(Cause—Mr. Kang blew out all the candles on his cake. Effect—Everyone clapped and shouted hurray.)*

Guiding Comprehension

4 **Setting • Literal**

Where and when does this part of the story take place?

In Mr. Kang's kitchen, in the present.

5 **Vocabulary • Antonyms**

Have students use context clues to determine the meaning of *damp* in p. 312, paragraph 3. Then have them identify an antonym for the word.

Clues: *cleans* the cage with a damp towel, *dries* the cage with a soft cloth. Meaning: slightly wet. Antonym: *dry.*

Monitor Progress	
Antonyms	
If... students have difficulty using context clues to determine the meaning of an antonym for damp,	**then...** use vocabulary strategy instruction on p. 313.

6 **Compare and Contrast • Critical**

What two things does Mr. Kang compare in the second and third sections of the poem on p. 313?

Possible response: Americans born in the United States and immigrants in the United States or in some foreign land.

4 Mr. Kang sits at the kitchen table and thinks about the sun showing through the trees in the park or the moon peeking into his window. He listens to words in his head, then he picks up his brush and paints a poem. Sometimes he paints a poem twice to practice his brushwork. Mrs. Kang hangs the poems on the kitchen cabinets.

And then, after making sure that the door and the windows are shut, Mr. Kang opens his hua mei's cage. Speaking softly, he invites the bird to stand on the table.

Mr. Kang cleans the cage with a damp towel and dries **5** it with a soft cloth. He takes out the hand-painted ceramic water bowl, rinses it, and puts it back in its stand, full of cool, clear water. He washes the hand-painted ceramic food bowl and puts it back, full of his own special recipe of millet coated with egg yolks and mixed with chopped meat. These days this is the only cooking Mr. Kang does.

Last, Mr. Kang takes a small piece of silk cloth, dampens it with water not too hot, not too cold, and gently wipes the sleek gray feathers of his bird. The hua mei walks right back into his cage. He prefers to give himself a bath.

"Never mind, Birdie," says Mr. Kang. "Instead of the bath, I'll read you my poem. I know you can understand. We both left our homeland. We still speak the old language."

Access Content Have students read the first sentence on p. 312. Ask them to describe the image in their mind when they read the words "the sun showing through the trees." Repeat with "the moon peeking into his window." Explain that the moon cannot peek into someone's window. The two phrases have similar meanings. The moonlight shines through Mr. Kang's window the way the sunlight shines through the trees.

Rushing to the Golden Dragon
against a chilly wind,
the icy tears on my cheeks melt
with memories of warm old days.

Those who never left their home
stay safe, wrapped
in the arms of their motherfather land.
When they look out
their narrow windows,
they see their own kitchen gardens.
They know every plum tree, every kumquat,
every blade of grass, each gray pebble.

We, who long ago tossed on cold waters
looking only straight ahead
watch our city mountains
from wide windows, tall rooftops.
Yet our old hearts hold old places.
We save, in old, grown heads,
a full-blown rose in summer,
the sound of bamboo leaves when
the wind is gentle,
the taste of mooncakes. **6**

The hua mei sings his own melody back
Mr. Kang. Mr. Kang closes his eyes to listen.
"Beautiful, Birdie. You are a good poet
d a good friend to me," says Mr. Kang.

313

⟳ **VOCABULARY STRATEGY**

Antonyms

TEACH

Read the third paragraph on p. 312. Model using context clues to determine the meaning of the word *damp* and the identification of an antonym.

Think Aloud — **MODEL** I read the sentence that has the word *damp*. "Mr. Kang cleans the cage with a damp towel and dries it with a soft cloth." The damp towel must be wet for cleaning. That is why the cage needs to be dried with the soft cloth. In the next paragraph, I see the word *dampen*. Mr. Kang dampens a silk cloth "with water not too hot, not too cold." *Damp* must mean "slightly wet." An antonym would be *dry*.

PRACTICE AND ASSESS

Have students read the first stanza of the poem on p. 313. Ask them to find a pair of antonyms and use context clues to identify their meanings. (*Chilly and warm; cold and hot*)

Guiding Comprehension

7 REVIEW **Plot • Inferential**

What conflict do Sam and Mr. Kang have?

Sam thinks Mr. Kang should set the bird free.

Monitor Progress

REVIEW **Plot**

If... students have difficulty identifying the conflict,	**then...** use the skill and strategy instruction on p. 315.

8 **Realism and Fantasy • Inferential**

How do you know the story is a realistic story and not a fantasy? Give an example.

A fantasy is a story about something that could not happen, but this story could really happen. Mr. Kang came from China. He lives in New York City, where his grandson lives. It is a realistic story.

Sam usually comes to visit on Saturdays. If Mr. Kang is cleaning the cage, then the hua mei sings to Sam. Sam holds out his finger, and the hua mei holds on tightly. They stare at each other, each without blinking.

"Did he really fly from China?" Sam asks one time.

"In an airplane," says Mr. Kang. "China is so far, even for a bird."

"You should let him go. Maybe he wants to fly home." **7**

"I don't think he could without an airplane. Anyway, he's like me. Home is here with you. If he went home now, I think he would miss his Sundays on Delancey Street." Mr. Kang puts his arm around Sam's shoulders and hugs him.

"I have a very smart grandson," he sighs. "Maybe one day we can visit China together."

And this is how Mr. Kang spends his days, except for Sundays.

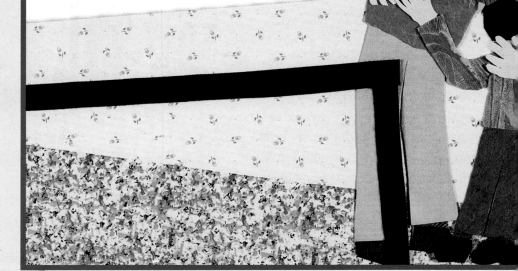

ELL

Access Content Direct students' attention to the next to the last sentence on p. 315. Help them understand the meaning of the phrase "breathes in the morning." Make sure they understand that this is figurative language rather than literal. Mr. Kang does not breathe (exhale and inhale) only in the morning. He breathes the morning air.

On Sundays Mr. Kang gets up when it's dark. He washes his face and puts on his clothes. When he is ready, he picks up the cage by the ring on top. The freshly ironed cover is tied shut, and the bird is still sleeping. As he opens the door to leave the apartment, Mrs. Kang is padding quickly behind him.

"Wait for me!" she calls.

"Shhhh!" says Mr. Kang, but he waits as she closes the door and turns her key.

Mr. Kang and his bird lead the way. He walks gingerly, holding onto the banister to steady himself as he goes down the stairs. Out the door, down the block, across the street he glides, to Sara Delano Roosevelt Park on Delancey Street.

Mrs. Kang follows, three steps behind. She sees her friends and slips away to join them.

Mr. Kang hangs the cage on the fence, stretches his arms, and breathes in the morning.

Mr. Lum arrives with a cage in each hand. "How are you, my friend? How is the bird?" **8**

315

Hua Mei Bird Garden

The *hua mei*, also known as a fighting thrush, is a songbird from the forests of southern China. Today, one place you can come across these birds is at the Sara Delano Roosevelt Park in New York City. Here, a special bird garden has been created. It is a common meeting place for bird owners who can bring their pet songbirds and enjoy the peaceful community garden with its stone paths and greenery. Plants that attract wild birds and posts for the birdcages are located in this garden where the hua mei tradition continues.

SKILLS ⬌ STRATEGIES IN CONTEXT

Plot REVIEW

TEACH

- Remind students that a story's plot describes the major events that happen in the beginning, middle, and end of a story. The events center around a problem or conflict.

- Some plot events are important while some events aren't part of the overall action.

 Think Aloud

MODEL Sam asks about the *hua mei's* home. Sam tells his grandfather that he should let the bird go free. The conflict is that Sam does not want the bird to have to live in a cage.

PRACTICE AND ASSESS

- Have students complete a story map as they read the selection. Make sure they correctly identify the problem presented in the selection.

- To assess, use Practice Book 3.2, p. 116.

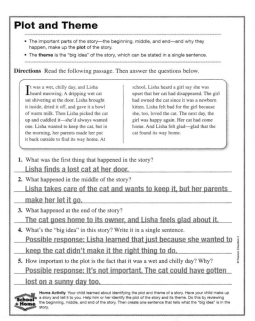

▲ **Practice Book 3.2** p. 116

Guiding Comprehension

9 **Use Graphic Organizers •**
Inferential

Draw a cause and effect graphic organizer on the board. Have students reread Mr. Kang's greeting on p. 316. Ask them what effect seeing Mr. Lum's birdcages has on Mr. Kang and use the information to complete the chart.

Cause: Mr. Kang sees the bird cages in the park. Effect: Mr. Kang remembers his childhood in China.

10 **Character • Critical**

Text to Self **Describe Mr. Kang's character traits. Do you know someone who has similar traits? Explain your answer.**

Possible response: Mr. Kang is thoughtful and poetic. He loves his grandson, Sam. He talks about the past. He enjoys writing and talks a lot about when he was younger.

"We are enjoying the morning," smiles Mr. Kang.

"Mr. Lum!
When I see your cages
resting on the green ivy floor
of Sara Delano Roosevelt Park in New York,

I remember my arm is lifted up to hold
Grandfather's big hand
and that ivy is green
from the Shanghai sun
and that ginkgo tree is blowing
in the soft Shanghai breeze
and that heat in my breast
is from my sweet and fragrant almond cake.
Grandmother slipped it into my pocket,
and it is still there,
warm from her oven." **9**

"Even when you speak a greeting to your friend you are painting a poem," says Mr. Lum. Mr. Kang bows his head.

Today is a special Sunday morning because Sam and Mr. Kang are going to the park together. Sam slept at his grandparents' house last night. It is still dark, and he is rubbing his eyes as he jumps from his bed. Just like Grandpa, he washes his face and puts on his clothes. Together, at dawn's first light, they lift the cage. The cover is still tied, the bird is still sleeping. Sam opens the front door. Grandpa steps out, and Grandma is there right behind him, just as she is every Sunday morning.

"Wait for me!" she says.

316

ELL

Extend Language Have students brainstorm a list of words that can be used to describe character traits. Write their responses on the board. Then have students work together to develop/name categories in which the words belong. They can use the list to help answer question 10.

"Shhhh!" say Mr. Kang and Sam, but they wait as she closes the door. Mrs. Kang takes one extra minute to slip two warm almond cakes into Sam's pocket. Then Sam and Mr. Kang lead the way down the stairs, out the front door, on to the corner, across the street, all the way to Sara Delano Roosevelt Park on Delancey Street. **10**

317

Develop Vocabulary

PRACTICE LESSON VOCABULARY

Students orally respond *yes* or *no* to each question and provide a reason for each answer.

1. **Would you want a coat when it is *chilly?*** (Yes, a coat helps you stay warm.)

2. **Would you need a *recipe* to cook Chinese food?** (Yes, I do not know how to make Chinese food.)

3. **Mr. Kang *bows* to Mr. Lum because Mr. Kang is angry with him. Is this true?** (No, Mr. Kang bows to show appreciation for the compliment.)

BUILD CONCEPT VOCABULARY

Review previous concept words with students. Ask if students have come across any words today in their reading or elsewhere that they would like to add to the Concept Web.

STRATEGY SELF-CHECK

Use Graphic Organizers

Remind students that a cause and effect graphic organizer can help them identify what happened in a selection and why it happened. Modify a problem and solution chart to reflect a cause and effect relationship graphic organizer (Graphic Organizer 20) on the board. Remind students how to read the graphic. Ask them to identify an event from pp. 316–317 and record it in the "What happened?" box. Then have them identify the cause. *(Possible response: "Why did it happen?" Sam is going with his grandparents to the park early on Sunday morning. "What happened?" Sam spent Saturday night at his grandparents' house.)*

SELF-CHECK

Students can ask these questions to assess their ability to use the skill and strategy.

- Did one event cause the other event to happen?

- How does the graphic organizer help me identify the relationship between the cause and the effect?

Monitor Progress

Cause and Effect

If... students have difficulty identifying cause and effect relationships to complete the graphic organizer,	**then...** revisit the skill lesson on pp. 304–305. Reteach as necessary.

Strategy Response Log

Evaluating How do you feel about Mr. Kang keeping the *hua mei* in the cage? Do you think he should keep the bird as a pet or set it free? Explain your thinking.

If you want to teach this story in two sessions, stop here.

Guiding Comprehension

If you teach the story in two days, discuss the main ideas and review vocabulary.

11 🔊 **Vocabulary • Context Clues**

Use context clues to find the meaning of the word *foreign* on page 318.

Clue: "I am happy in this strange land."
Meaning: unfamiliar.

Monitor Progress	
🔊 **Context Clues**	
If... students have difficulty using context to determine the meaning of *foreign*,	**then...** use vocabulary strategy instruction on p. 319.

12 **Author's Purpose • Critical**

Question the Author **Why do you think Susan Roth used the poem on p. 318?**

Possible response: The poem tells the reader that Mr. Kang misses his homeland and loves his grandson.

13 **Compare and Contrast • Inferential**

Reread the second half of p. 319. What comparison does Mr. Kang make?

Mr. Kang compares the bird's life in a cage to his own life working in a restaurant.

DAY 3 Grouping Options

Reading
Whole Group Discuss the Question of the Day.

Group Time Differentiated Instruction
ℝead *Happy Birthday Mr. Kang.* See pp. 304f–304g for the small group lesson plan.

Whole Group Discuss the Reader Response questions on p. 326. Then use p. 331a.

Language Arts
Use pp. 331e–331h and 331k–331m.

As usual, Mrs. Kang follows until she sees her friends. Sam sets the bird cage gently on the ground. Mr. Lum's cages are already hanging.

"Look who's here!" says Mr. Lum. "How are you, Sam? You're getting so big. How old are you?"

"Seven," says Sam.

"Only seven?" says Mr. Lum. "You're handling that cage better than a twelve-year-old would!"

Sam smiles.

11 "An old grandfather does not mind growing old in a foreign land with such a grandson," says Mr. Kang.

"I am happy in this strange land:
I see my grandson planted
in the new, rich earth,
growing straight and smart and tall.
I water him.
The sun shines on his
firm young leaves
as I watch for his flowers
and for his fruit."

12

318

Ⓔ Ⓛ Ⓛ

Activate Prior Knowledge Have students describe how a plant grows. Chorally read the poem on p. 318. Help students understand the poem's meaning. Encourage them to read the poem and explain it in their own words.

"More poems, Mr. Kang," says Mr. Lum. "I think you always speak in poems."

"Your ears are kind to my words, my friend," says Mr. Kang. Two more men with two more cages arrive, then another and yet another. Soon there are twenty-seven cages in the park.

Mr. Kang lets Sam untie the cover. A strand of light passes through the bamboo bars. As the sun climbs, the men and Sam open all the curtains, inch by inch.

A bird calls and is answered by another.

"They sing sad songs," says Sam.

"They sing of their strong young years," says Mr. Lum.

"They sing about their grandfathers," says Mr. Wu.

"Maybe they sing about their grandsons," says Sam.

"They sing about being in their cages," says Mr. Wu. "Probably they want to fly out."

"Like me in my cage," says Mr. Kang. "Like me, making noodles every day for fifty years."

"I would fly out if I were a bird," says Sam.

Mr. Kang stands away from the fence. "Maybe my smart grandson is right. Maybe this bird should be free."

Immigration

Many people from China immigrated to the United States in the mid-1800s. Many came to California in search of gold. Later, they began to look for work in New York and other cities in the East. In New York, they built their own community, which came to be known as Chinatown. The Chinese in Chinatown opened and worked in businesses such as restaurants, laundries, and garment factories. Many American cities today still have sections called Chinatown.

 VOCABULARY STRATEGY

Context Clues

TEACH

Read the paragraph before the poem on p. 318. Then read the poem. Model using context clues to determine the meaning of *foreign*.

Think Aloud

MODEL Mr. Kang says he does not mind growing old in a *foreign* land with Sam. In the first line of the poem, Mr. Kang says he is happy in this *strange* land. I know that Mr. Kang is from China but lives in New York. *Foreign* must mean "strange and unfamiliar."

PRACTICE AND ASSESS

Have students use context clues to determine the meaning of *gently* in the first paragraph on p. 318. *(Clues include: Sam places the cage on the ground; Mr. Lum tells him that he's handling the cage well; gently might mean carefully.)*

EXTEND SKILLS

Metaphor

Explain that a metaphor is a comparison between two unlike things that are alike in at least one way. Writers do not use any words of comparison (such as *like*) when writing metaphors. Have students reread the poem on p. 318. Ask them to find the comparison. *(grandson and a plant)* Encourage students to explain what this comparison tells us about what the grandfather thinks of his grandson.

Guiding Comprehension

14 **Cause and Effect • Inferential**

What caused Mr. Kang to let the *hua mei* go free?

Possible response: Earlier in the story Sam said that the bird should go free. Later, Sam talked about the birds' sad songs. Mr. Kang compares the bird's life to his life. He decides the bird should be free as he is now.

Monitor Progress

Cause and Effect

If... students are unable to identify the cause of Mr. Kang's decision,	**then...** use the skill and strategy instruction on p. 321.

---

15 **Draw Conclusions • Inferential**

Think about what you have read. How has Mr. Kang changed?

Possible response: Mr. Kang wanted a traditional *hua mei* for his birthday. Later, he realizes that, like himself, the bird longs for freedom, so he decides to let the bird go free.

Mr. Kang walks slowly toward his cage.

"Stop!" Mr. Lum puts a hand on his friend's arm. "Mr. Kang, do not be foolish!" The men form a circle around Mr. Kang, and everyone is talking at once. The women rush over.

"Mr. Kang," says Mrs. Kang, "did you forget about your three birthday wishes already? What will you do when you finish painting your poems and there is no bird to sing to you afterwards?"

"Ever since my birthday, I am a free man," says Mr. Kang. "Maybe this hua mei wants to be a free bird. America is the land of the free. Sam says . . ." **14**

"Sam is a seven-year-old American boy," interrupts Mrs. Kang. "He cannot understand old ways."

"But Grandma, it's not fair."

"Sam." Mrs. Kang turns to her grandson. "Sam. This is not something you can understand."

Mr. Kang just shakes his head. He brushes away Mrs. Kang's hands. He brushes away the hands of his friends.

320

E L L

Access Content Read p. 321, paragraph 2, with students. Help them understand the meaning. Make sure they understand that Mr. Kang does not have a problem with his hearing, nor does he have a voice in his heart. He believes setting the bird free is the right thing to do. He will not change his mind by listening to those around him.

Suddenly Sam is frightened. What if Grandma is right? What if Grandpa is sorry after the hua mei flies away? What if the hua mei gets lost? What if he starves? What if he dies?

"Grandpa, wait," says Sam. But Grandpa does not hear. Mr. Kang cannot hear any voice except the voice inside his own head, inside his own heart. He opens the bamboo door.

Mr. Kang's hua mei perches on the threshold of his cage. Perhaps he thinks it's cage-cleaning time. He slowly steps out. He stops to sing a long, sweet note, turns his head to the breeze, and flies into the sky.

Mr. Kang takes off his cap and covers his heart with his hand. For a moment there is silence. Mrs. Kang bends her head and hugs herself. Her mouth is a thin straight line. "Oh, Mr. Kang," she whispers in Chinese. "What can you be thinking?" Sam starts to cry.

"Sam and I are going home to paint poems," says Mr. Kang loudly, in English.

He lifts his empty cage, takes Sam's hand, and together they walk out of the park. Onto the sidewalk, over to the corner, across the street, up the block they walk.

15

SARA D.
ROOSEVELT
PARK

321

Cause/Effect Graphic Organizers

TEACH

Remind students that a cause and effect relationship is not always obvious within a text. In addition, sometimes there are multiple causes that bring about one effect. Model how to determine a cause and effect relationship and use a cause and effect chart (Graphic Organizer 19) to answer question 14.

Think Aloud **MODEL** I will write, "Mr. Kang set the *hua mei* free" in the box that says, "What happened?" I need to find the reason Mr. Kang decided to free the bird. At the beginning, Sam tells Mr. Kang he should let the bird go free. Later, Mr. Kang realizes that keeping the bird in the cage is like his working in the restaurant everyday when he did not want to be there. Mr. Kang says that America is the land of the free and the *hua mei* deserves freedom. These are the causes of, or the reasons for, Mr. Kang's decision to let the bird go free. I can write all of these reasons in the "Why did it happen?" box.

PRACTICE AND ASSESS

Have students reread p. 321 to identify the cause of, or reasons for, Sam's crying. *(The bird flew away.)*

Guiding Comprehension

16 **Draw Conclusions • Inferential**

Why do you think the *hua mei* came back?

Possible response: It was more important for it to be in its home than to fly away. Mr. Kang fed it and treated it well.

17 **REVIEW** **Theme • Inferential**

How does the bird's return relate to the big idea of the story?

Possible response: The big idea of the story is "freedom." The bird was free to fly away, but it came back. It was free to do this.

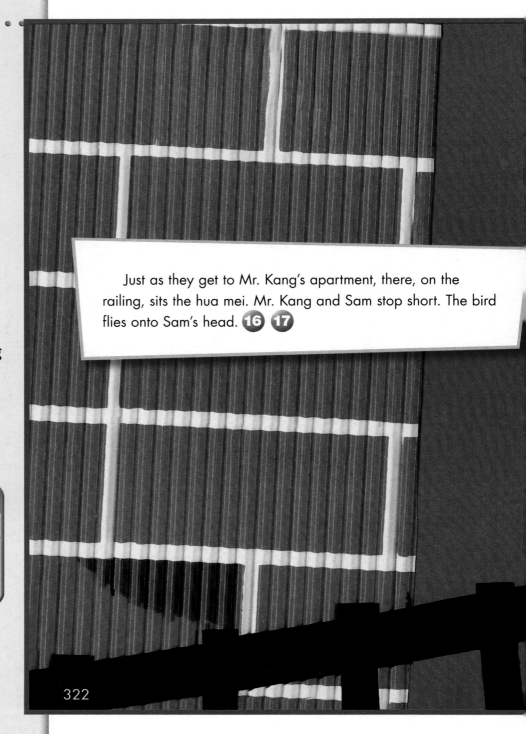

Just as they get to Mr. Kang's apartment, there, on the railing, sits the hua mei. Mr. Kang and Sam stop short. The bird flies onto Sam's head. **16** **17**

322

Monitor Progress	
REVIEW Theme	
If... students have difficulty identify the theme,	**then...** use the skill and strategy instruction on p. 323.

Understanding Idioms As they read the paragraph on p. 322, encourage students to visualize the action. Help them use this technique, along with context clues, to understand the meaning of "stop short."

SKILLS ⟷ STRATEGIES IN CONTEXT

Theme REVIEW

TEACH

Remind students that as they read a story, they should ask themselves, "What does the author want me to learn or know from reading the selection?" The answer to the question describes the big idea of the story.

 MODEL I see that the bird came back to the apartment. Nobody made it come back, so it was free to do it on its own. The big idea of the story is that we all, including Mr. Kang's bird, should have freedom.

PRACTICE AND ASSESS

Ask students to find details in the selection that support the theme, or big idea. Encourage them to identify another selection they have read with the same big idea or something in their own lives that the story reminds them of. *(Responses will vary.)*

323

Guiding Comprehension

18 Theme • Critical

Text to Text **What is the big idea of the poem on p. 324? How does it connect to the big idea of the unit?**

Possible response: The poem says that Mr. Kang was born Chinese but became an American by choice. America is a land of choices and freedoms. The poem relates to the unit theme of freedom.

19 Use Graphic Organizers • Critical

Use a cause and effect chart to describe how receiving a pet bird as a present affected Mr. Kang throughout the story.

Possible responses: Mr. Kang is happy because he has a good pet. On Sundays, he takes the bird to the park to spend time with friends who also have pet birds. Mr. Kang learns a lesson about himself when the bird returns to his apartment.

Strategy Response Log

Summarize When students finish reading the selection, provide this prompt: Imagine that a friend has asked what *Happy Birthday Mr. Kang* is about. In four or five sentences, explain its important points.

Then up the stairs and into the kitchen they run. They sit at the table, coats and caps still on. The hua mei hops onto Sam's paper. Mr. Kang paints his poem as Sam paints his picture. The bird helps.

After forty-three American years
I still speak my native tongue,
but any Chinese ear can hear
that I no longer speak
like a native. Sometimes

even I can hear
the familiar sounds bending
by themselves in my own throat,
coming out strangely,
sounding a little American. Yet

those same words in English suffer more.
I open up
my American mouth and
no one needs to see my face to know
my ship was never Mayflower. But

at home, with even you, my hua mei, peeping
a little like a sparrow,
I sit at my kitchen table, and I paint these words.
They sing out without accent:
We are Americans, by choice. **18**

324

"This is your poem, Birdie," says Mr. Kang, "and Sam, it's your poem too."

Then Mr. Kang looks at Sam's painting. "My grandson is a great artist," he says. He hangs the paintings on the kitchen cabinet and sits back to admire them.

Mrs. Kang walks into the kitchen with her mouth still in that thin straight line, but there is the bird, and suddenly she is smiling.

"Today I'll cook for both of you, and for your hua mei," she says.

And she makes tea, and more sweet and fragrant almond cakes, warm from the oven. **19**

325

Develop Vocabulary

PRACTICE LESSON VOCABULARY

Have students provide oral responses to each question.

1. **Mr. Lum thinks it is *foolish* to let the bird go. What does *foolish* mean?** (*unwise*)
2. **What does a bird do when it *perches*?** (*Rests or sits on something*)
3. **What is an antonym for *narrow*?** (*wide*)

BUILD CONCEPT VOCABULARY

Review previous concept words with students. Ask if students have come across any words today in their reading or elsewhere that they would like to add to the Concept Web.

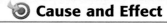 SKILLS STRATEGY SELF-CHECK

Graphic Organizers

- Tell students that graphic organizers such as cause and effect charts can help us organize and understand an author's message.
- Draw a cause and effect chart on the board. Draw multiple boxes for the effects. In the "cause" box, write, "Mr. Kang receives a pet bird for his birthday." Have students think of several effects this event caused.

SELF-CHECK

Students can ask these questions to assess their ability to use the skill and strategy.

- Do I know what happened and why?
- Does my chart include multiple effects?
- To assess, use Practice Book 3.2, p.117.

Monitor Progress

Cause and Effect

If... students have difficulty identifying cause and effect relationships to complete the graphic organizer,	then... use the Reteach lesson on p. 331b.

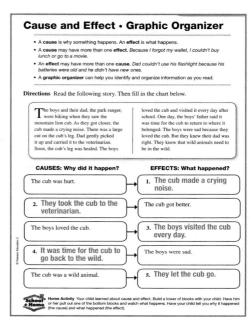

Cause and Effect • Graphic Organizer

- A **cause** is why something happens. An **effect** is what happens.
- A **cause** may have more than one **effect.** *Because I forgot my wallet, I couldn't buy lunch or go to a movie.*
- An **effect** may have more than one **cause.** *Dad couldn't use his flashlight because his batteries were old and he didn't have new ones.*
- A **graphic organizer** can help you identify and organize information as you read.

Directions Read the following story. Then fill in the chart below.

The boys and their dad, the park ranger, were hiking when they saw the mountain lion cub. As they got closer, the cub made a crying noise. There was a large cut on the cub's leg. Dad gently picked it up and carried it to the veterinarian. Soon, the cub's leg was healed. The boys loved the cub and visited it every day after school. One day, the boys' father said it was time for the cub to return to where it belonged. The boys were sad because they loved the cub. But they knew their dad was right. They knew that wild animals need to be in the wild.

CAUSES: Why did it happen? | **EFFECTS: What happened?**

The cub was hurt. → 1. The cub made a crying noise.

2. They took the cub to the veterinarian. → The cub got better.

The boys loved the cub. → 3. The boys visited the cub every day.

4. It was time for the cub to go back to the wild. → The boys were sad.

The cub was a wild animal. → 5. They let the cub go.

Home Activity Your child learned about cause and effect. Build a tower of blocks with your child. Have him or her pull out one of the bottom blocks and watch what happens. Have your child tell you why it happened (the cause) and what happened (the effect).

▲ **Practice Book 3.2** p. 117

Reader Response

Open for Discussion Personal Response

Think Aloud

MODEL I remind myself of the big idea and what Mr. Kang learns during the story. I think the poems are different because Mr. Kang feels one way in the beginning of the story and another way at the end. These poems reflect his feelings.

Comprehension Check Critical Response

1. Responses will vary, but should include valid explanations. ***Author's Purpose***

2. Sam helps Mr. Kang realize that like him, the bird is not free to live its life the way it chooses. ⊙ ***Cause and Effect***

3. Responses will vary, but should include valid explanations. ⊙ ***Use Graphic Organizers***

4. Responses will vary but should show an understanding of the words. ⊙ ***Vocabulary***

Look Back and Write For test practice, assign a 10–15 minute time limit. For assessment, see the Scoring Rubric at the right.

Retell

Have students retell *Happy Birthday Mr. Kang.*

Monitor Progress

Check Retelling [Rubric 4 3 2 1]

| If... students have difficulty retelling the story, | then... use the Retelling Cards and the Scoring Rubric for Retelling on p. 327 to assist fluent retelling. | SUCCESS PREDICTOR |

ELL

Check Retelling Have students use illustrations and other text features to guide their retellings. Let students listen to other retellings before attempting their own. See the ELL and Transition Handbook.

Reader Response

Open for Discussion Read Mr. Kang's first poem out loud. Then read his last poem out loud. Why are the two poems so different from each other?

1. Find the most interesting illustration in the story. Pretend that you are the artist. Explain how and why you made that illustration. **Think Like an Author**

2. What caused Mr. Kang to change his mind about his *hua mei?* **Cause and Effect**

3. Did you create a graphic organizer as you read? If so, tell how it helped you. If not, what kind of graphic organizer could have helped? Tell why. **Graphic Organizer**

4. Write Mr. Kang a note to wish him a happy birthday. Use words from the Words to Know list and from the story. **Vocabulary**

Look Back and Write Sam told his grandfather to make a birthday wish. What did Mr. Kang wish? Look back at page 311. Write about the wish. Use details from the story in your answer.

Meet author **and illustrator Susan L. Roth on page 418.**

326

Scoring Rubric | Look Back and Write

Top-Score Response A top-score response will use details from the selection to tell about Mr. Kang's birthday wish.

Example of a Top-Score Response Mr. Kang has three birthday wishes. Mr. Kang's first wish is to read *The New York Time.* every day. His second wish is to paint poems every day. His thi. wish is to have a *hua mei* bird in a cage. This is a special wish because a *hua mei* is a Chinese bird. It is also special becaus. his grandfather had one. Mr. Kang will feed the bird every day and take it to the park on Sundays.

For additional rubrics, see p. WA10.

Write Now

Outline

Write Now

Prompt

Happy Birthday, Mr. Kang tells about a special bird and a wish.

Think about some of the facts in the story.

Now use the story and the library or Internet to outline a topic from the story.

Writing Trait

Use either phrases or complete **sentences** in your outline, but not both.

Student Model

Important details are shown with Roman numerals.

Information is organized into topics and subtopics.

Hua Mei Bird Garden

I. The garden is located in Sara Delano Roosevelt Park.

II. It has many special features.

  A. There are natural features.

    1. Flowers attract many birds.

    2. There are shrubs from Asia.

  B. There are features made by people.

    1. Stone paths wind through the garden.

    2. People built posts for cages.

Writer used complete <u>sentences</u> instead of phrases in this outline.

Use the model to help you write your own outline.

327

Look at the Prompt Have students identify and discuss key words and phrases in the prompt. *(facts, outline a topic from the story)*

Strategies to Develop Sentences

Have students

- find examples of sentences and phrases and explain how they are different.
- use either phrases or sentences consistently in their outline.

NO: Flowers for many birds

    People send for shrubs from Asia to plant in the garden.

YES: Flowers attract many birds.

    People send for shrubs from Asia to plant in the garden.

For additional suggestions and rubric, see pp. 331g–331h.

Hints for Better Writing

- Carefully read the prompt.
- Choose main ideas for your outline.
- Support your ideas with information and details.
- Use Roman numerals, capital letters, and numbers to organize your outline.
- Proofread and edit your work.

Scoring Rubric — Narrative Retelling

Rubric 4 3 2 1	4	3	2	1
Connections	Makes connections and generalizes beyond the text	Makes connections to other events, stories, or experiences	Makes a limited connection to another event, story, or experience	Makes no connection to another event, story, or experience
Author's Purpose	Elaborates on author's purpose	Tells author's purpose with some clarity	Makes some connection to author's purpose	Makes no connection to author's purpose
Characters	Describes the main character(s) and any character development	Identifies the main character(s) and gives some information about them	Inaccurately identifies some characters or gives little information about them	Inaccurately identifies the characters or gives no information about them
Setting	Describes the time and location	Identifies the time and location	Omits details of time or location	Is unable to identify time or location
Plot	Describes the problem, goal, events, and ending using rich detail	Tells the problem, goal, events, and ending with some errors that do not affect meaning	Tells parts of the problem, goal, events, and ending with gaps that affect meaning	Retelling has no sense of story

Retelling Plan

- ☑ **Week 1** Assess Strategic Intervention students.
- ☑ **This week assess Advanced students.**
- ☐ **Week 3** Assess Advanced students.
- ☐ **Week 4** Assess On-level students.
- ☐ **Week 5** Assess any students you have not yet checked during this unit.

Use the Retelling Chart on p. TR16 to record retelling.

Selection Test To assess with *Happy Birthday Mr. Kang*, use Selection Tests, pp. 105–108.

Fresh Reads for Differentiated Test Practice For weekly leveled practice, use pp. 157–162.

Retelling

SUCCESS PREDICTOR

Science in Reading

OBJECTIVES

- Examine features of an interview.
- Practice a test-taking strategy.
- Compare and contrast across texts.

PREVIEW/USE TEXT FEATURES

As students preview "Back to the Wild," have them identify the names of the interviewer and the expert answering the questions. After they preview, ask:

- **What do the initials MBB and MJC stand for?** (the names of the interviewer, Melissa Blackwell Burke, and the expert, Molly Jean Carpenter)

- **Why are the names, initials, and questions in different colors of type?** (It helps the reader follow the interview and identify who is speaking.)

Link to Science

Help students identify relevant key words to help them locate information about animal rescue programs. If possible, include a local program.

DAY 4 Grouping Options

Reading
Whole Group Discuss the Question of the Day.

Group Time Differentiated Instruction
Read "Back to the Wild." See pp. 304f–304g for the small group lesson plan.

Whole Group Use pp. 331a and 331j.

Language Arts
Use pp. 331e–331h and 331k–331m.

Science in Reading

Back to the WILD

A Talk with a Wildlife Worker

by Melissa Blackwell Burke

Interview

Genre

- In an interview, an expert shares his or her knowledge about a subject.

- An interview is written in a question-and-answer format.

Text Features

- The names of the interviewer and the expert answering the questions usually appear in dark print. The names are sometimes abbreviated.

- Photographs often help the reader better understand the subject.

Link to Science

Learn more about animal rescue programs. Use the library or the Internet. Create a brochure that will encourage people to use one program.

Animals in the wild are free. They do what comes naturally to them. They don't have people taking care of them. What happens when a wild animal gets sick or hurt? Sometimes people bring such animals to a wildlife clinic. The clinic takes care of the animal until it can care for itself again. The goal is to get the animal back into the wild as soon as possible.

The staff at the Wildlife Medical Clinic at the University of Illinois in Urbana work toward that goal. We spoke to Molly Jean Carpenter, a volunteer at the clinic. She shared her thoughts about working with wildlife and described an amazing experience.

328

Content-Area Vocabulary — Science

clinic	a doctor's office or other place that treats sick or injured animals
patient	an animal who is being given medical treatment
wildlife	plants or wild animals living in their natural environment
aggressive	showing readiness to attack

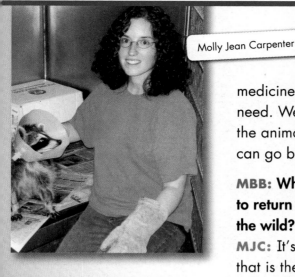

Molly Jean Carpenter

medicine and care that they need. We do our best to help the animal recover so that it can go back into the wild.

MBB: Why is it so important to return these animals to the wild?

MJC: It's important because that is their home! It is very stressful for a wild animal to lose its freedom. They need to do all the activities that are natural for them, such as running, hunting, or soaring.

MELISSA BLACKWELL BURKE:

How do workers decide when an animal needs care in your clinic?

MOLLY JEAN CARPENTER: Concerned citizens rescue animals that have been hurt. Or sometimes they bring in a young animal that isn't being cared for by its kind. We examine the animal from its head to its tail. If the animal can't take care of itself in the wild, we admit it to our clinic. We feed the animals, clean them, and give them any

Wildlife rescue at work

Ⓒ Cause and Effect What causes animals to be brought to the clinic?

329

INTERVIEW

Use the sidebar on p. 328 to guide discussion.

- In an interview, a person asks another person questions. The written interview provides the questions and the expert's responses.

- Ask students to describe how the author chose to use different colored print. Lead them to recognize that the interviewer's and expert's names and initials appear in green and red print. The interviewer's questions appear in bold.

- Discuss with students the best way to read an interview. Consider having two students read p. 329 orally. One person should read the interviewer's questions. The other person should read the expert's responses. Point out that you do not need to read the names of the people each time.

AudioText

Ⓒ Cause and Effect

Citizens rescue animals that are not being cared for by their own kind or that have been hurt.

ELL

Access Content Preview the text with students. Make sure they understand the definition and use of important terms, such as *wild*, *wildlife*, and *clinic*.

Strategies for Nonfiction

USE TEXT FEATURES Explain that students may be asked to read interviews and answer questions about the content on standardized tests. Tell students that they can use the text features, such as the boldface questions, to locate information in the interview. Provide the following strategy.

Use the Strategy

1. Read the test question and make sure you understand what it is asking. Identify a key word or phrase in the question.
2. Scan the interviewer's questions for the key word or phrase.
3. If you do not locate the key word or phrase, skim the expert's response.
4. When you find a match, read the information to find an answer to the test question.

GUIDED PRACTICE Have students discuss how they would use the strategy to answer the following question.

Does Molly Jean Carpenter believe pets should be freed? Why or why not?

INDEPENDENT PRACTICE After students answer the following test question, discuss the process they used to find information.

When does the Wildlife Medical Clinic accept a wild animal for treatment?

Black-footed ferret being released into the wild

Pets depend on people.

330

MBB: If freedom is important for wildlife, should people release their pets into the wild?

MJC: Pets should not be released into the wild because many pets are not suited for a life outdoors. Pets could be hurt by wildlife or weather conditions. They may have a hard time finding food and shelter in the wild. Some pets might even hurt wildlife. It is much safer, for both pets and for wildlife, if pets stay with their owners.

MBB: Tell us about one of your favorite animal success stories at the clinic.

MJC: My favorite patient was a red-tailed hawk named Copernicus. Copernicus was hit by a car. He had a broken wing and a broken leg. He had surgery at the clinic to help his bones heal. We fed and cleaned Copernicus. We gave him treatments every day. He grew stronger and more aggressive. It was his way of

ELL

Test Practice Write the Guided Practice question on the board. Help students identify and underline the key words in the question (pets, freed). You may want to rewrite the question so that the key words match the language in the interviewer's question. (Does Molly Jean Carpenter believe pets should be released into the wild?)

red-tailed hawk in flight

telling us that he wanted to return to the wild. In a couple of months, Copernicus had shown us that he could take care of himself in the wild. We prepared for his release. We found a place with fields and trees where Copernicus could find food and shelter. We took him out of his carrier. He flew straight out into the sky and soared! Then he perched himself at the top of a tall tree. It was an incredible experience that I'll never forget!

REMEMBER: *Wild animals belong in the wild! If you come across a hurt animal, check your phone book for a clinic that helps wild animals and returns them to their homes.*

Reading Across Texts
How was Mr. Kang's *hua mei* different from Copernicus, the red-tailed hawk in this interview?

Writing Across Texts Write a paragraph explaining which bird you think was better off and why.

ⓒ Graphic Organizers Be sure to add information to your graphic organizer.

331

CONNECT TEXT TO TEXT

Reading Across Texts

Discuss similarities and differences between Mr. Kang's *hua mei* and Copernicus, the red-tailed hawk mentioned in the interview. Record students' ideas in a two-column chart on the board.

Writing Across Texts Explain to students that the paragraph is a personal response. There is no right or wrong answer. Students should support their opinion with relevant details.

ⓒ Graphic Organizers

Students can add information about Copernicus to the cause and effect graphic organizer.

ELL

Access Content Discuss with students how the pictures and captions can help them understand the content. Draw attention to the photograph of the red-tailed hawk on p. 331. Have students describe how the image can help them visualize the text on pp. 330–331.

Fluency Assessment Plan

☑ **Week 1** Assess Advanced students.

☑ **This week assess Strategic Intervention students.**

☐ **Week 3** Assess On-Level students.

☐ **Week 4** Assess Strategic Intervention students.

☐ **Week 5** Assess any students you have not yet checked during this unit.

Set individual goals for students to enable them to reach the year-end goal.

• Current Goal: 110–120 WCPM

• Year-End Goal: 120 WCPM

 To develop fluent readers, use Fluency Coach.

MORE READING FOR
Fluency

 To practice fluency with text comprised of previously taught phonics elements and irregular words, use Decodable Reader 27.

DAY 5 Grouping Options

Reading
Whole Group
Revisit the Question of the Week.

Group Time
Differentiated Instruction
Reread this week's Leveled Readers. See pp. 304f–304g for the small group lesson plan.

Whole Group
Use pp. 331b–331c.

Language Arts
Use pp. 331d–331h and 331k–331n.

APPROPRIATE PHRASING
Fluency

DAY 1

Model Reread "Elsa" on p. 304m. Explain that you will group words into appropriate phrases. Model for students as you read.

DAY 2

Choral Reading Read aloud p. 314. Have students notice how you read entire groups of words instead of reading word-by-word. Have students practice as a class, doing three choral readings of p. 314.

DAY 3

Model Read aloud p. 325. Have students notice how you pause at commas and group words appropriately. Practice as a class by doing three choral readings of p. 325.

DAY 4

Paired Reading Have partners practice reading aloud pp. 328–331. Students should read groups of words and offer each other feedback.

Monitor Progress Check Fluency WCPM

As students reread, monitor their progress toward their individual fluency goals. Current Goal: 110–120 words correct per minute. End-of-Year Goal: 120 words correct per minute.

If... students cannot read fluently at a rate of 110–120 words correct per minute,

then... make sure students practice with text at their independent level. Provide additional fluency practice, pairing nonfluent readers with fluent readers.

If... students already read at 120 words correct per minute,

then... they need not reread three to four times.

SUCCESS PREDICTOR

DAY 5

Assessment
Individual Reading Rate Use the Fluency Assessment Plan and do a one-minute timed reading of either selection from this week to assess students in Week 2. Pay special attention to this week's skill, appropriate phrasing. Provide corrective feedback for each student.

RETEACH

⊙ Cause and Effect

TEACH

Review the skill instruction for cause and effect on p. 304. Discuss that the cause is *why* something happens and the effect is *what* happens. Students can complete Practice Book 3.2, p. 118, on their own, or you can complete it as a class. Point out that students will complete exercises in which the answer is either a cause or effect.

ASSESS

Have students reread paragraph 4 on p. 312. Tell them, *After Mr. Kang cleans the cage, the hua mei walks back into it.* Ask students to identify the cause for this effect. *(The hua mei doesn't want Mr. Kang to clean him.)*

For additional instruction for cause and effect, see DI·53.

EXTEND SKILLS

Word Choice

TEACH

Authors select their words carefully. Often authors choose words that help the reader experience the way things look, sound, smell, taste, or feel.

- As you read, consider the author's choice of words.
- Try to see images in your mind as you read.

Read aloud the first paragraph on p. 312. Have volunteers describe why they believe the author chose phrases like "the moon peeking into his window," "listens to words in his head," and "paints a poem."

ASSESS

Have students work with a partner to reread p. 319. Ask:

1. **How do the author's word choices help you understand the story?**

2. **Explain how the author's word choices help you use your senses to better understand the story.**

OBJECTIVES

⊙ Determine cause and effect relationships.

● Describe and explain an author's choice of words.

Skills Trace	
Cause and Effect	
Introduce/Teach	TE: 3.3 280–281, 3.4 12–13, 3.6 304–305
Practice	PB: 3.1 103, 107, 108, 116; 3.2 3, 7, 8, 16, 26, 106, 113, 117, 118, 136
Reteach/Review	**TE: 3.3 303b, 315, DI•52; 3.4 35b, 49, 71, DI•52; 3.6 293, 331b, 373, DI•53**
Test	Selection Test: Unit 6; Benchmark Tests: Units 4, 6

Access Content Reteach the skill by reviewing the Picture It! lesson on cause and effect in the ELL Teaching Guide, pp. 183–184.

Cause and Effect

- A **cause** is why something happens. An **effect** is what happens.
- A **cause** may have more than one **effect**.
- An **effect** may have more than one **cause**.

Directions Read the following passage. Then answer the questions below.

Anthony was just a kid—a kid who had to make a big decision. Anthony's aunt in Italy wanted him to come spend the summer with her family. His parents kept telling him how wonderful it would be for him and how happy it would make his aunt. But Anthony was nervous—he didn't even like sleepovers and could never sleep. How could he go all that way to Italy all by himself? How could he leave his family for two whole months? He really didn't want to go. He barely knew his aunt.

Anthony couldn't sleep. He couldn't eat, and he felt nervous all of the time. Finally, he told his parents that he had decided not to go. Anthony's stomach immediately felt better. He felt calm. He slept well for the first time. He knew he had made the right decision.

1. What effect did worrying about the trip have on Anthony?
   He felt nervous, couldn't eat, and couldn't sleep.

2. How did Anthony feel about going away for the summer?
   He didn't know his aunt well and didn't want to go.

3. What happened to Anthony after he made his decision?
   He felt better.

4. What might be the "big idea" of this story?
   Possible response: In this story, Anthony listens to his feelings and makes the right decision.

Home Activity Your child learned about cause and effect. Do an experiment with your child. If it's hot out, have your child put an ice cube in a bowl outside. Ask him or her what happened to the ice cube after an hour. If it's cold out, put a shallow pan of water outside. Ask him or her what happened to the water after a few hours. Have your child tell the cause and effect of the experiment.

▲ **Practice Book 3.2** p. 118

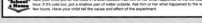

Vocabulary and Word Study

VOCABULARY STRATEGY
Context Clues

ANTONYMS Remind students that they can use antonyms as context clues to determine the meaning of unfamiliar words. Have students list any unknown words they encountered as they read *Happy Birthday Mr. Kang*. They can create a chart showing the unknown word, its antonym, and their definition based on its antonym. Students can confirm word meanings using a dictionary.

Word	Antonym	Meaning
shout	whisper	to say or yell loudly
gently		
silence		

Rhyming Words

Words that have the same ending sounds rhyme. Poems often use rhyming words for example *house* and *mouse*. Have partners use reference sources to make lists of rhyming words. Point out that some words that rhyme have different spellings; others that are spelled the same may not rhyme. Students can write and illustrate a short poem using their favorite rhyming words.

Some Rhyming Words

ants—pants	cage—rage
collar—dollar	glad—sad
sleep—creep	sweet—neat
voice—choice	feather—weather
hug—snug	cake—bake

BUILD CONCEPT VOCABULARY
Animal Freedom

LOOKING BACK Remind students of the focus question of the week: When might it be hard to grant freedom? Discuss how this week's Concept Web of vocabulary words relates to the theme of freedom. Ask students if they have any words or categories to add. Discuss whether words and categories are appropriately related to the concept.

MOVING FORWARD Preview the title of the next selection, *Talking Walls*. Ask students which Concept Web words might apply to the new selection based on the title alone. Put a star next to these words on the web.

Display the Concept Web and revisit the vocabulary words as you read the next selection to check predictions.

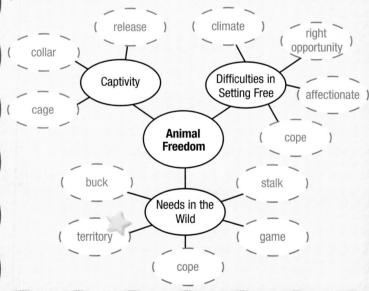

Monitor Progress
Check Vocabulary

If... students suggest words or categories that are not related to the concept,	**then...** review the words and categories on the Concept Web and discuss how they relate to the lesson concept.

SUCCESS PREDICTOR

Speaking and Listening

Express an Opinion

SET-UP Have students deliver a speech that expresses their opinion about a topic that is important in your community.

TOPICS Brainstorm a list of several topics currently being discussed in your community. Topics may include installing a new playground or swimming pool, building a new store, purchasing new park or fire equipment, or planning a skateboard park.

REHEARSE Students should express their opinions clearly. Remind them to give reasons why they feel the way they do. Point out the importance of listening to other viewpoints and asking questions. Encourage students to practice in front of a mirror or a family member to gain confidence. You may wish to videotape their speeches to provide feedback. Give students time to rehearse their opinion speeches.

Delivery Tips
- Make eye contact with the audience.
- Speak clearly.
- Use opinion phrases such as *I believe, I think, my point of view.*
- Support your opinions with facts.

Listen to Opinions

Have students listen to opinion speeches. Encourage students to ask questions. After listening, have students answer these questions.

1. **What is the speaker's opinion?** *(Possible response: The speaker's opinion is that the skateboard park should be built.)*

2. **What questions and answers helped make the speaker's views clear?** *(Possible response: The speaker answered the question about where the park should be located with an opinion of why it should be near the school.)*

3. **Do you agree with the opinion of the speaker? Why or why not?** *(Possible response: No, I don't agree with the speaker. I think the money should be spent on fixing the town's swimming pool.)*

Support Vocabulary Use the following to review and extend vocabulary and to explore lesson concepts further:
- ELL Poster 27, Days 3–5 instruction
- Vocabulary Activities and Word Cards in ELL Teaching Guide, pp. 185–186

Assessment For information on assessing students' speaking, listening, and viewing, see the ELL and Transition Handbook.

Check Vocabulary

SUCCESS PREDICTOR

Grammar **Abbreviations**

OBJECTIVES

- Define and identify abbreviations.
- Use abbreviations in writing.
- Become familiar with abbreviation assessment on high-stakes tests.

Monitor Progress

Grammar

| **If...** students have difficulty with abbreviations, | **then...** see The Grammar and Writing Book, pp. 206–209. |

DAILY FIX-IT

This week use Daily Fix-It Transparency 27.

Spiral REVIEW

Support Grammar See the Grammar Transition lessons in the ELL and Transition Handbook.

▲ **The Grammar and Writing Book** For more instruction and practice, use pp. 206–211.

DAY 1 Teach and Model

DAILY FIX-IT

1. Did Mr Kang's pet fly all the way from China. *(Mr.; China?)*

2. Most birds cant' traval across the ocean. *(can't; travel)*

READING-GRAMMAR CONNECTION

Write this sentence from *Happy Birthday Mr. Kang* on the board:

"Mr. Kang," says Mrs. Kang, "did you forget about your three birthday wishes already?"

Explain that *Mr.* and *Mrs.* are abbreviations. Each begins with a capital letter and ends with a period.

Display Grammar Transparency 27. Read aloud the definitions and examples. Work through the items.

Abbreviations

An **abbreviation** is a shortened form of a word. Many abbreviations begin with a capital letter and end with a period.
- Some titles used for names of people are abbreviations. For example, *Dr.* is the abbreviation for *Doctor*. The title *Miss* is not abbreviated.
  Mr. Mark Elton Lewis   Ms. Susan Wang   Mrs. Carmen Mendoza
- An **initial** is the first letter of a name. It is written with a capital letter and is followed by a period.
  Mr. Mark E. Lewis   S. B. Wang   C. M. Mendoza
- The names of days and months can be abbreviated. *May, June,* and *July* are not abbreviated.

Days of the Week
Sun. Mon. Tues. Wed. Thurs. Fri. Sat.
Months of the Year
Jan. Feb. Mar. Apr. Aug. Sept. Oct. Nov. Dec.

Directions Write each phrase. Be sure to capitalize letters and use periods correctly.
1. ms. Janine Lee   **Ms. Janine Lee**
2. jan 24   **Jan. 24**
3. Dr N D Bond   **Dr. N. D. Bond**
4. thurs, aug 2   **Thurs., Aug. 2**
5. B. c Pepper   **B. C. Pepper**
6. Mon, dec. 13   **Mon., Dec. 13**

Directions Some abbreviations can be used in sentences. Find the words that can be abbreviated in the sentences below. Write the sentences with the abbreviation.
7. Doctor Sanchez showed us his new parrot.
   Dr. Sanchez showed us his new parrot.
8. Mister Davidson can teach parrots to talk.
   Mr. Davidson can teach parrots to talk.

Unit 6 Happy Birthday Mr. Kang   **Grammar 27**

▲ **Grammar Transparency** 27

DAY 2 Develop the Concept

DAILY FIX-IT

3. I allways look at the birds in the cage in dr. Robinson's office. *(always; Dr.)*

4. Ms. Sanchez and him clean the cage dayly. *(he; daily)*

GUIDED PRACTICE

Review the concept of abbreviations.

- **Abbreviations** are often used for words such as days and months and titles used with people's names.

- Abbreviations for days, months, and people's titles are capitalized and end with a period.

HOMEWORK Grammar and Writing Practice Book p. 105. Work through the first two items with the class.

Abbreviations

An **abbreviation** is a shortened form of a word. Many abbreviations begin with a capital letter and end with a period.
- Some titles used for names of people are abbreviations. For example, *Dr.* is the abbreviation for *Doctor*. The title *Miss* is not abbreviated.
  Mr. Don Lee Chang   Ms. Lucy Ruiz   Mrs. Maya Levin
- An **initial** is the first letter of a name. It is written with a capital letter and is followed by a period.
  Mr. Don L. Chang   L. T. Ruiz   M. E. Levin
- The names of days and months can be abbreviated. *May, June,* and *July* are not abbreviated.

Days of the Week
Sun. Mon. Tues. Wed. Thurs. Fri. Sat.
Months of the Year
Jan. Feb. Mar. Apr. Aug. Sept. Oct. Nov. Dec.

Directions Write each abbreviation. Be sure to capitalize letters and use periods correctly.
1. Mrs W. Wenders   **Mrs. W. Wenders**
2. j r Burton   **J. R. Burton**
3. sat, aug 4   **Sat., Aug. 4**
4. ms T j. Matthews   **Ms. T. J. Matthews**

Directions Some abbreviations can be used in sentences. Find the word that can be abbreviated in the sentence below. Write the sentence with the abbreviation.
5. Mister Alexis got a pet bird when he moved to this country.
   Mr. Alexis got a pet bird when he moved to this country.

Home Activity Your child learned about abbreviations. Look through the mail with your child. Have him or her identify abbreviations used for people's names and titles.

▲ **Grammar and Writing Practice Book** p. 105

DAY 3 — Apply to Writing

DAILY FIX-IT

5. This bird has bright feathers and it sings a cheerfull song. *(feathers, and; cheerful)*

6. It's musick makes me feel happy. *(Its; music)*

USE ABBREVIATIONS IN WRITING

Explain that using abbreviations when taking notes or writing outlines saves time and space for writers.

Unabbreviated: Some birds fly south in October or November.

Abbreviated: Some birds fly south in Oct. or Nov.

- Have students review notes or an outline they have written to see if they can use abbreviations that would save time and space.

HOMEWORK Grammar and Writing Practice Book, p. 106

Abbreviations

Directions Write the answer to each question. Use abbreviations correctly. Possible answers:

1. What are your initials?

   S. P. J.

2. What is the abbreviation for the month in which you were born?

   Nov.

3. What are the titles and last names of the adults in your family?

   Dr. Bowen and Mrs. Bowen

4. What is the abbreviation for your busiest day of the week?

   Mon.

5. What is the abbreviation for the month in which your favorite holiday takes place?

   Dec.

6. What is the abbreviation for today's day of the week?

   Wed.

Directions Write two sentences about two adults besides your parents who have taught you important skills or lessons. Use at least two abbreviations.

Possible answer: Mrs. Travers taught me how to set up a tent. Dr. Stanley taught me to be patient with my pets.

Home Activity Your child learned how to use abbreviations in writing. With your child, list some adults who live in your neighborhood. Have your child write their names, using the correct abbreviations for their titles.

▲ **Grammar and Writing Practice Book** p. 106

DAY 4 — Test Preparation

DAILY FIX-IT

7. The women was affraid the bird would fly away. *(were; afraid)*

8. The bird dissappeared on Feb 2. *(disappeared; Feb.)*

STANDARDIZED TEST PREP

Test Tip

You may be asked to identify the correct abbreviation for a word. Remember that abbreviations for words that begin with a capital letter, such as days of the week and months of the year, also begin with a capital letter. All abbreviations end with a period.

Words: Mister Coleman's birthday party—Saturday, January 15.

Abbreviations: Mr. Coleman's birthday party—Sat., Jan. 15.

HOMEWORK Grammar and Writing Practice Book, p. 107

Abbreviations

Directions Mark the letter of the correct abbreviation for each word.

1. Monday
   A mon
   B Mon
   C mon.
   (D) Mon.

2. Mister
   A mr.
   (B) Mr.
   C Mr
   D mr

3. April
   (A) Apr.
   B apr
   C apr.
   D Apr

4. Wednesday
   A wed.
   B wed
   C Wed
   (D) Wed.

5. February
   A feb
   B Feb
   (C) Feb.
   D feb.

6. Doctor
   A dr
   B Dr
   C dr.
   (D) Dr.

7. Richard James
   A RJ.
   B rj.
   (C) R. J.
   D r. j.

8. August
   A aug
   (B) Aug.
   C Aug
   D aug.

9. Saturday
   A sat.
   B sat
   (C) Sat.
   D Sat

10. October
    A oct
    (B) Oct.
    C Oct
    D oct.

Home Activity Your child prepared for taking tests on abbreviations. Have your child write the days of the week, using abbreviations correctly.

▲ **Grammar and Writing Practice Book** p. 107

DAY 5 — Cumulative Review

DAILY FIX-IT

9. The old man feel selfesh because the bird wants its freedom. *(feels; selfish)*

10. Can the bird live out side in the Winter safely? *(outside; winter)*

ADDITIONAL PRACTICE

Assign pp. 206–209 in The Grammar and Writing Book.

EXTRA PRACTICE Grammar and Writing Practice Book, p. 148.

TEST PREPARATION Grammar and Writing Practice Book, pp. 157–158.

ASSESSMENT

CUMULATIVE REVIEW Grammar and Writing Practice Book, p. 108

Abbreviations

Directions Write each sentence correctly. Use correct capitalization and periods for abbreviations.

1. Dr and mrs Hartz have many beautiful pet birds.

   Dr. and Mrs. Hartz have many beautiful pet birds.

2. They will display the birds at the home of mr and Ms Santos.

   They will display the birds at the home of Mr. and Ms. Santos.

3. I am going to see the birds with my friend c. j. Fox.

   I am going to see the birds with my friend C. J. Fox.

4. You can buy tickets at G B Watkins Department Store.

   You can buy tickets at G. B. Watkins Department Store.

Directions The following research notes have initials and abbreviations written incorrectly. Write each note. Correct mistakes in initials and abbreviations.

5. John j Audubon—bird painter

   John J. Audubon—bird painter

6. Born apr 1785

   Born Apr. 1785

7. Wrote book about animals with J Bachman

   Wrote book about animals with J. Bachman

8. Died jan 1851

   Died Jan. 1851

Home Activity Your child reviewed abbreviations. Scan a newspaper with your child and have your child identify abbreviations.

▲ **Grammar and Writing Practice Book** p. 108

Writing Workshop Outlining

OBJECTIVES

- Identify the characteristics of an outline.
- Write an outline on a topic and include important details.
- Focus on sentences.
- Use a rubric.

Genre Outline
Writer's Craft Including Important Details
Writing Trait Sentences

ELL

Sentences Have language learners read their sentences aloud to check rhythm, completeness, and sense. Point out opportunities to change a declarative sentence to another type, or to vary sentence beginnings.

Writing Trait

FOCUS/IDEAS The outline focuses on the topic's most important details.

ORGANIZATION/PARAGRAPHS The outline is organized by main ideas.

VOICE The writer's voice is clear and logical.

WORD CHOICE The writer uses exact words to communicate facts.

SENTENCES Words, phrases, and/or sentences are used.

CONVENTIONS Grammar and mechanics are excellent, including use of abbreviations.

DAY 1 Model the Trait

READING-WRITING CONNECTION

- *Happy Birthday Mr. Kang* is realistic fiction about a man who decides to let his long-caged bird go free.
- Ideas in *Happy Birthday Mr. Kang* are expressed through varied sentences with much sensory detail.
- Students will **outline** facts from the story.

MODEL SENTENCES Discuss Writing Transparency 27A. Then discuss the outline and the writing trait of sentences and phrases.

 Think Aloud The writer has written an outline for a report on pet birds. The outline uses the correct form of using Roman numerals for main topics and capital letters for subtopics. I see that the writer used phrases, words, and sometimes abbreviations in the outline, not complete sentences.

Outline

An **outline** organizes information about a topic. Before writing a research report, use your notes to make an outline.
- For most outlines, use words and phrases, not complete sentences. You may use abbreviations.
- Use Roman numerals for the main topics.
- Use capital letters for subtopics.
- Use numbers for details about the subtopics.

Title tells topic of outline. → **Popular Pet Birds**

I. Parrots
There is no *A* unless there is a *B*, no *1* unless there is a *2*. Details about native homes are included with subtopic.
  A. Native Homes—warm, tropical areas
  B. Appearance
    1. 3 in. to 3 ft. long
    2. Brightly colored
  C. Special Features
Every topic, subtopic, and detail begins with a capital letter.
    1. Noisy, sociable
    2. Can learn to talk

II. Hua Mei
  A. Native Homes—forests of So. China
  B. Appearance
    1. 4–5 in. long
    2. Grayish-yellow with black speckles
  C. Special Features
    1. Can be taught to sing
    2. Name means "painted eyebrows"

Unit 6 Happy Birthday Mr. Kang   Writing Model **27A**

▲ **Writing Transparency** 27A

DAY 2 Improve Writing

WRITER'S CRAFT
Including Important Details

Display Writing Transparency 27B. Work together to decide which are the important details in the outline.

 Think Aloud **INCLUDING IMPORTANT DETAILS** Tomorrow we will write an outline about a topic from the story. I should pick a topic about which I can find many important details. I might use the Sara Delano Roosevelt Park in New York City. I can look for details that tell me where the park is. I can research the size of the park and whether it has playground equipment. These would all be important details.

GUIDED WRITING Some students may need help with important details. Review a nonfiction article that students have read. Help them choose the important details in each paragraph.

Including Important Details

When you write a research report, use the facts in your outline. Keep your topic, audience, and purpose in mind. Then **include the important details** about your topic.

Directions The information below is part of an outline on the hua mei bird. The paragraph that follows it adds unimportant details to the information in the outline. Draw a line through the sentences that have unimportant details.

  I. B. Appearance
    1. 4–5 in. long
    2. Grayish-yellow with black speckles
    3. White marks above eyes
  C. Special Features
    1. Fighting birds
    2. Can be taught to sing
    3. Name means "painted eyebrows"

The hua mei bird is 4 or 5 inches long. ~~Canaries are much more colorful than this bird.~~ It is grayish-yellow with black speckles and unusual white marks above its eyes. These marks led to the bird's name, which is Chinese for "painted eyebrows." The hua mei is a fighting bird. ~~I prefer peaceful birds.~~ People have taught the hua mei bird to sing. ~~Its melody is probably beautiful.~~

Directions Write sentences about the parrot based on the following details.

1. 3 inches to 3 ft. long
2. Brightly colored
3. thick, hooked bill

Possible answer: Parrots can be from three inches to three feet long. They are brightly colored and have thick, hooked bills.

Unit 6 Happy Birthday Mr. Kang   Writer's Craft **27B**

▲ **Writing Transparency** 27B

DAY 3 · Prewrite and Draft

READ THE WRITING PROMPT

on page 327 in the Student Edition.

Happy Birthday Mr. Kang *tells about a special bird and a wish.*

Think about some of the facts in the story.

Now use the story and the library or Internet to outline a topic from the story.

Writing Test Tips

- Take notes on facts in the story and other sources.
- Organize the facts into groups such as *appearance* and *special features.*
- Put the facts into outline form, using words and phrases for headings and subheadings.

GETTING STARTED Students can do any of the following:

- Work in a group and write down all the facts about hua mei birds that are stated or implied in the selection.
- Work with a partner to find articles on the Internet or in the library about hua mei birds or another bird.
- Share information with classmates.

DAY 4 · Draft and Revise

EDITING/REVISING CHECKLIST

☑ Does the outline organize facts into headings and subheadings?

☑ Does the outline include all important details?

☑ Are abbreviations used and punctuated correctly?

☑ Are words with the schwa sound in an unaccented syllable spelled correctly?

See *The Grammar and Writing Book,* pp. 210–213.

Revising Tips

Sentences

- Use abbreviations for some words.
- Use short phrases to support the main subheadings; complete sentences are unnecessary.
- Make sure the ideas are expressed clearly.

PUBLISHING Students can post their outlines on a bulletin board and compare them. Some students may wish to revise their work later.

ASSESSMENT Use the scoring rubric to evaluate students' work.

DAY 5 · Connect to Unit Writing

Research Report	
Week 1	Taking Notes 303g–303h
Week 2	Outlining 331g–331h
Week 3	Informational Paragraph 353g–353h
Week 4	Writing About a Picture 379g–379h
Week 5	Write Good Paragraphs 407g–407h

PREVIEW THE UNIT PROMPT

Write a research report about a monument or statue that symbolizes freedom in the United States. Discuss the monument itself, its history, and why it is important. Find information in sources such as books, magazines, CD-ROMs, and the Internet.

APPLY

- A research report is an informational article based on research.
- The second step in writing a research report is making an outline of the important information in the writer's notes.

Writing Trait Rubric

	4	3	2	1
Sentences	Clear, interesting, unique phrases, used consistently	Clear phrases, used fairly consistently	Limited use of phrases	No use of phrases
	Exceptional variety of content in phrases in outline	Some variety of content in phrases in outline	Needs more variety of content in phrases in outline	Little or no variety of content in phrases in outline

Schwa

TEACH

Remind students that at least one syllable in a multisyllabic word is accented, or stressed. Write the words *about, affect, April, occur,* and *circus.*

- How many syllables do you hear in the word *about?* (2)
- Which syllable is accented, or stressed? (the second)
- What vowel sound do you hear in the accented syllable? (/ou/)
- What vowel do you see in the unaccented syllable? *(a)*
- Do you hear the long *a* sound? (no)
- What sound do you hear? (/ə/)
- /ə/ is the schwa sound.

 MODEL When I read words that have more than one syllable, I see different vowels in the unaccented syllables, but the different vowel letters often stand for the same sound. Vowels in unaccented syllables usually stand for the schwa sound, /ə/. When I'm not sure how to pronounce a multisyllable word, I say the schwa sound for the vowels in the unaccented syllables.

Model blending *affect, April, occur,* and *circus,* stressing the accented syllables. Then have students blend the words with you.

PRACTICE AND ASSESS

DECODE LONGER WORDS Write these words. Have students read them and then underline the letters that stand for the schwa sound.

sist<u>e</u>r   bac<u>o</u>n   <u>a</u>long   <u>u</u>pon

gadg<u>e</u>t   rob<u>i</u>n   met<u>a</u>l   c<u>o</u>mmit

READ WORDS IN CONTEXT Write these sentences. Have individuals read them and point out words with the schwa sound. Words with the schwa sound are underlined.

We stayed in a log <u>cabin</u> at the <u>bottom</u> of a <u>canyon</u>.

I like to put lots of <u>lettuce</u> in my <u>salad</u>.

Would you like to buy a <u>pretzel</u> for a <u>nickel</u>?

The <u>garage</u> was <u>ablaze</u>.

To assess, observe whether students read words with the schwa sound correctly.

Schwa

Directions Choose the word with a vowel that has the same sound as the underlined vowels in **a**bout, tak**e**n, penc**i**l, lem**o**n, and circ**u**s to complete each sentence. Write the word on the line to the left.

afraid — 1. Susan was (afraid/scared) to walk her dog without a leash.

rascal — 2. Every time she opened the front door, the little (puppy/rascal) ran off.

local — 3. One time she took her dog to a (local/nearby) park.

animals — 4. All the (animals/doggies) were fetching or chasing.

around — 5. Susan removed her puppy's leash and let the dog run (around/freely).

paper — 6. When her dog ran off, Susan opened a (paper/plastic) bag and pulled out a treat.

traveled — 7. Susan's dog quickly (traveled/bounded) back.

morsel — 8. Now anytime Susan offers her dog a tasty (biscuit/morsel), it comes racing to her.

Directions Circle the letter in each word that stands for the same sound as the underlined vowels in **a**bout, tak**e**n, penc**i**l, lem**o**n, and circ**u**s.

9. kitch**e**n	12. fam**i**ly	15. gall**o**n	18. **a**go
10. riv**e**r	13. mel**o**n	16. doll**a**r	19. op**e**n
11. s**u**rprise	14. sug**a**r	17. nick**e**l	20. cany**o**n

Home Activity Your child identified and wrote words that contain the vowel sound called schwa, heard in unaccented syllables such as about, taken, pencil, lemon, and circus. Help your child write sentences with words that have this sound. Ask your child to read each sentence and identify the letter that stands for the schwa sound.

▲ **Practice Book 3.2** p. 119

Review Phonics

REVIEW VOWELS in *tooth, cook*

CONNECT Write this sentence: *The food was not good because we put in too little salt.*

- We studied the words with the vowel sounds in *tooth* and *cook*.
- Read the sentence to yourself. Raise your hand when you know which words have the vowel sound in *tooth*. **(food, too)**
- Raise your hand when you know which words have the vowel sound in *cook*. **(good, put)**

Continue in the same way with the sentence *Look at Dad's new blue suit.*

PRACTICE AND ASSESS

DECODE LONGER WORDS Have individuals read the following words. Provide help chunking and blending the words as needed.

pushup	avenue	swimsuit	neighborhood
shampoo	outgrew	overdue	monsoon
cruiser	unscrew	tenderfoot	cushion

READ WORDS IN CONTEXT Have students read these sentences. Then, to check meaning, have them give their own sentence for the underlined word.

Sue's suitcase is full of clothes.

I felt like snoozing, but the bright moonlight kept me awake.

The horses' hoofbeats shook the ground.

The ship's crew knew that a storm was due.

To assess, note how well students read words with the vowel sounds in *tooth* and *cook*.

Generalization

The letters *oo* can stand for the vowel sound in *book*, / u̇ /, or in *moon*, /ü/. The letter *u* can stand for short *u* or the vowel sound in *book*, /u̇ /. Context provides the clue to pronunciation. The letters *ew*, *ue*, and *ui* can stand for the vowel sound in *moon*, /ü/.

Vocabulary Tip

You may wish to explain the meanings of these words.

cruiser	a police car
monsoon	a strong wind and heavy rain
tenderfoot	a person with no experience

Spelling & Phonics *Schwa*

DAY 1 Pretest and Sort

DAY 2 Think and Practice

OBJECTIVE

● Spell words with the schwas.

Generalization

Connect to Phonics In many words, the schwa in an unaccented syllable gives no clue to its spelling: *above, family, melon*. The schwa can be spelled in a number of different ways, but it always has the same sound.

Spelling Words

1. above	9. afraid
2. another	10. nickel
3. upon	11. sugar
4. animal	12. circus
5. paper	13. item
6. open	14. gallon
7. family	15. melon
8. travel	

Challenge Words

16. character	19. particular
17. cardinal	20. dinosaur
18. Oregon	

ELL

Spelling/Phonics Support See the ELL and Transition Handbook for spelling support.

PRETEST

Use the Dictation Sentences from Day 5 to administer the pretest. Read the word, read the sentence, and then read the word again. Guide students in self-correcting their pretests and correcting any misspellings.

Monitor Progress

Spelling

If... students misspell more than 4 pretest words,	then... use words 1–8 for Strategic Intervention.
If... students misspell 1–4 pretest words,	then... use words 1–15 for On-Level practice.
If... students correctly spell all pretest words,	then... use words 1–20 for Advanced Learners.

HOMEWORK Spelling Practice Book, p. 105

Schwa

Generalization In many words, the schwa in an unaccented syllable gives no clue to its spelling: **above, family, melon.**

Word Sort Sort the list words by the letter that stands for the schwa sound. Use a dictionary to help.

a
1. above
2. afraid
3. sugar

e
4. paper
5. open
6. travel
7. nickel
8. item

i
9. family

o
10. gallon
11. melon

u
12. upon
13. circus

a and e
14. another

a and i
15. animal

Spelling Words
1. above
2. another
3. upon
4. animal
5. paper
6. open
7. family
8. travel
9. afraid
10. nickel
11. sugar
12. circus
13. item
14. gallon
15. melon

Challenge Words
16. character
17. cardinal
18. Oregon
19. particular
20. dinosaur

Challenge Words

a and u
16. particular

e and o
17. Oregon

e
19. character

a
18. cardinal

o
20. dinosaur

School + Home Home Activity Your child is learning to spell words with the schwa sound (an unstressed vowel sound such as the a in above). To practice at home, have your child say the word, study it, spell it with eyes closed, and then write it.

▲ **Spelling Practice Book** p. 105

TEACH

The schwa in an unaccented syllable can be spelled in several different ways. Demonstrate this by writing each spelling word on the board. Have students identify the schwa sound and underline the vowel or vowels that make that sound.

nickel

USE THE DICTIONARY Have students copy the list words, look them up in a dictionary, and circle the vowels that are represented by the schwa symbol in the pronunciation key.

HOMEWORK Spelling Practice Book, p. 106

Schwa

Spelling Words

above	another	upon	animal	paper
open	family	travel	afraid	nickel
sugar	circus	item	gallon	melon

Context Clues Write the missing list word.

1. May I have ___ piece of pizza?   1. another
2. I have three dimes and one ___ in my bank.   2. nickel
3. He was eating a slice of ___.   3. melon
4. I wrote a letter on a sheet of green ___.   4. paper
5. My ___ likes to watch football Sunday afternoons.   5. family
6. Please get a ___ of milk.   6. gallon
7. The ___ had clowns and acrobats.   7. circus
8. Is the ___ bowl empty?   8. sugar
9. Each ___ on the list must be done by noon.   9. item
10. Once ___ a time, there was a handsome prince.   10. upon
11. My favorite ___ is the giraffe.   11. animal

Opposites Write the list word that means the opposite.

12. shut   open
13. brave   afraid
14. stay home   travel
15. below   above

| afraid |
| travel |
| above |
| open |

School + Home Home Activity Your child spelled words with the schwa sound (an unstressed vowel sound such as the a in above). Have your child pick a number between 1 and 15. Read the list word with that number and ask your child to spell it.

▲ **Spelling Practice Book** p. 106

DAY 3 Connect to Writing

WRITE AN INVITATION

Ask students to write an invitation to a party, using at least three spelling words. Have students share their invitations by reading them aloud to the class or display them on the bulletin board.

Frequently Misspelled Words

upon   again

beautiful

Although these words seem easy, third-graders are often confused because the same sound is spelled in different ways. Alert students to these frequently misspelled words and encourage them to think carefully before they write them.

HOMEWORK Spelling Practice Book, p. 107

Schwa

Spelling Words				
above	another	upon	animal	paper
open	family	travel	afraid	nickel
sugar	circus	item	gallon	melon

Proofread a Description Jake wrote about an imaginary animal. Circle four words that are spelled incorrectly and two words that should be combined into one compound word. Write the words correctly.

My anamal looks like a lizard with opun wings. It has beutiful colors. It lives above the tree tops. For food it breaks open a mellon. It is not afraid of any thing.

Frequently Misspelled Words
upon
again
beautiful

1. animal   2. open   3. beautiful
4. melon   5. treetops   6. anything

Proofread Words Fill in a circle to show which word is spelled correctly. Write the word.

7. There was an _____ in the paper about our class.   7. item
   ○ itam   ○ itum   ● item
8. Are you _____ you might get lost on the subway?   8. afraid
   ● afraid   ○ ifraid   ○ afraid
9. There are five people in my _____.   9. family
   ● family   ○ famaly   ○ familie
10. The candy cost a _____ each.   10. nickel
   ○ nicle   ○ nickle   ● nickel

School+Home **Home Activity** Your child identified misspelled words with the schwa sound (an unstressed vowel sound such as the a in above). Give clues about a list word. Ask your child to guess and spell the word.

▲ **Spelling Practice Book** p. 107

DAY 4 Review

REVIEW SCHWA

Time students as they write as many list words as they can. Have students exchange papers and check that the words are spelled correctly.

Spelling Strategy
Vowel Combinations

To make words with a schwa easier to spell, encourage students to picture the words in their minds before spelling them.

HOMEWORK Spelling Practice Book, p. 108

Schwa

Spelling Words				
above	another	upon	animal	paper
open	family	travel	afraid	nickel
sugar	circus	item	gallon	melon

Crossword Puzzle
Write list words in the puzzle.

Across
2. something sweet
4. move from place to place
6. a large fruit
8. five cents

Down
1. You write on this.
3. four quarts
5. overhead
7. one more

Word Puzzle The stars in the words below all stand for one vowel. The hearts stand for a different vowel. Can you crack the code? Write the words.

9. ♥ f r ♥ ✻ d   afraid   10. ♥ n ✻ m ♥ l   animal
11. f ♥ m ✻ l y   family   12. ✻ t e m   item

School+Home **Home Activity** Your child has been learning to spell words with the schwa sound. Help your child make up a code and use it to write list words.

▲ **Spelling Practice Book** p. 108

DAY 5 Posttest

DICTATION SENTENCES

1. Hold the ball above your head.
2. May I please have another cookie?
3. The cat sat upon the sofa.
4. A vet is an animal doctor.
5. Please take out a piece of paper.
6. What time does the store open?
7. Sandy has a big family.
8. We travel every year.
9. Ned is afraid of the dark.
10. I have a nickel and a dime.
11. May I have a cup of sugar?
12. I can't wait until the circus comes to town!
13. What is the third item on the list?
14. Mom needs to buy a gallon of milk.
15. The melon was ripe.

CHALLENGE

16. Who is the best character in the story?
17. The cardinal is a red bird.
18. She lives in Oregon.
19. I don't like that particular fruit.
20. The store had a dinosaur display.

OBJECTIVES

- Formulate an inquiry question that is connected to this week's lesson focus.
- Effectively and efficiently find, evaluate, and communicate information related to an inquiry question using electronic sources.

New Literacies

Day 1	Identify Questions
Day 2	Navigate/Search
Day 3	Analyze
Day 4	Synthesize
Day 5	Communicate

NEW LITERACIES

Internet Inquiry Activity

EXPLORE GRANTING FREEDOM TO ANIMALS

Use the following 5-day plan to help students conduct this week's Internet inquiry activity on granting freedom to animals. Remind students to follow classroom rules when using the Internet.

DAY 1

Identify Questions Discuss the lesson focus question: *When might it be hard to grant freedom?* Brainstorm ideas for specific inquiry questions about granting freedom to animals. For example, students might want to find out where baby chicks go after they have been hatched in a classroom, or what happens to the butterflies after a school butterfly release. Have students work individually, in pairs, or in small groups to write an inquiry question they want to answer.

DAY 2

Navigate/Search Teach students how to evaluate Web sites. Explain some factors to consider. Is the information current or out-of-date? Is the site easy to navigate and read? Are there spelling or grammatical errors? Are there distracting pop-up ads? Remind students to consider these factors when selecting sites to analyze.

DAY 3

Analyze Have students explore and analyze information from the Web sites they identified on Day 2. Tell them to scan and analyze information for credibility, reliability, and usefulness. They can print and then highlight relevant information.

DAY 4

Synthesize Have students synthesize information from Day 3. Remind them that when they synthesize, they pull together the relevant ideas from different sources to develop an answer to their inquiry questions.

DAY 5

Communicate Have students share their inquiry results. They can use a word processing program to create a short article for a school newspaper.

RESEARCH/STUDY SKILLS
Maps

OBJECTIVES
- Review terms related to maps.
- Identify locations on a map.

TEACH

Ask students what features they expect to find on the map of a city. Show a city map as you discuss these terms and ideas.

- Some maps show roads. They can show all of the roads for a particular place or just the major roads.

- A map can show important **landmarks** or attractions.

- Maps have a **legend** or **key** that shows what symbols are used.

- A **scale** shows the distance represented by a unit on the map.

Have students work with a partner to study a map of Boston. They should find the terms used above on the map. Ask partners to look for at least three or four landmarks in Boston. Before students work in pairs, use a map of Boston to discuss these questions.

1. **What is the name of a bridge in Boston?** (Possible response: Longfellow Bridge)

2. **What is the name of one of the buildings that lies along the Freedom Trail?** (Possible response: Paul Revere House)

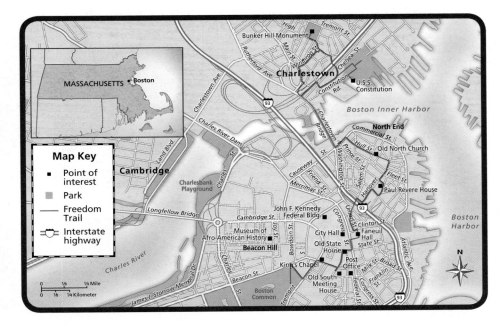

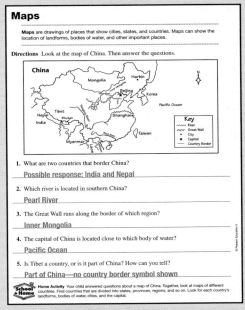

▲ **Practice Book 3.2** p. 120

ASSESS

As students work with the maps, check that they understand the legend and can use it to locate landmarks.

For more practice or to assess students, use Practice Book 3.2, p. 120.

Assessment Checkpoints *for the Week*

Selection Assessment

Use pp. 105–108 of Selection Tests **to check:**

☑ **Selection Understanding**

☑ **Comprehension Skill** *Cause and Effect*

☑ **Selection Vocabulary**

bows	narrow
chilly	perches
foolish	recipe
foreign	

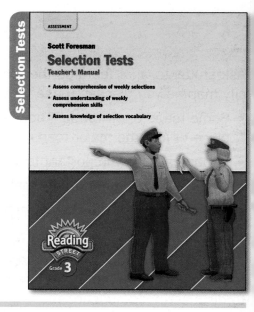

ASSESSMENT
Scott Foresman
Selection Tests
Teacher's Manual
• Assess comprehension of weekly selections
• Assess understanding of weekly comprehension skills
• Assess knowledge of selection vocabulary

Reading STREET Grade 3

Leveled Assessment

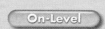 On-Level
Strategic Intervention
Advanced

Use pp. 157–162 of Fresh Reads for Differentiated Test Practice **to check:**

☑ **Comprehension Skill** *Cause and Effect*

☑ **REVIEW Comprehension Skill** *Character*

☑ **Fluency** *Words Correct Per Minute*

ASSESSMENT Teacher's Manual
Scott Foresman
Fresh Reads for Differentiated Test Practice
Leveled passages—strategic intervention, on-level, and advanced—for
• Fluency checks
• Practice and application of weekly comprehension skills
• Answer key for all practice pages

Reading STREET Grade 3

Managing Assessment

Use Assessment Handbook **for:**

☑ **Observation Checklists**

☑ **Record-Keeping Forms**

☑ **Portfolio Assessment**

ASSESSMENT
Scott Foresman
Assessment Handbook
• Suggestions for preparing students for high-stake tests
• Ideas for classroom-based assessment
• Forms in English and Spanish for students to record interests and progress
• Forms in English and Spanish for teachers to record observations of students' reading and writing abilities and progress
• Assessment and Regrouping charts reproduced from *Reading Street* Teacher's Editions

Reading STREET Grades 3–6

Illinois

Planning Guide for Performance Descriptors

Talking Walls: Art for the People

Reading Street Teacher's Edition pages	Grade 3 English Language Arts Performance Descriptors
### Oral Language **Speaking/Listening** Build Concept Vocabulary: 332l, 343, 349, 353c Read Aloud: 323m **Viewing** Analyze Artwork: 353d	**1A.Stage C.7.** Use content and previous experience to determine the meanings of unfamiliar words in text. **1B.Stage C.13.** Read age-appropriate material aloud with fluency and accuracy. **1C.Stage C.8.** Explain how authors and illustrators express their ideas.
### Word Work Words with *-tion, -sion, -ture:* 353i, 353k–353l	**1A.Stage C.5.** Use a variety of decoding strategies (e.g., phonics, word patterns, structural analysis, context clues) to recognize new words when reading age-appropriate material.
### Reading **Comprehension** Fact and Opinion: 332–333, 336–349, 353b Answer Questions: 332–333, 336–349 **Vocabulary** Lesson Vocabulary: 334b, 343, 349 Glossary: 334–335, 345, 353c **Fluency** Model Reading Silently with Fluency and Accuracy; Self-Correct When Reading: 332l–332m, 353a Choral Reading: 353a **Self-Selected Reading:** LR19–27, TR16–17 **Literature** Genre—Photo Essay: 336 Reader Response: 350	**1A.Stage C.5.** Use a variety of decoding strategies (e.g., phonics, word patterns, structural analysis, context clues) to recognize new words when reading age-appropriate material. **1B.Stage C.6.** Differentiate between fact and opinion. **1B.Stage C.9.** Continuously check and clarify for understanding (e.g., reread, read ahead, use visual and context clues) during reading. **1C.Stage C.2.** Use information to generate and respond to questions that reflect higher level thinking skills (e.g., analyzing, synthesizing, inferring, evaluating). **1C.Stage C.8.** Explain how authors and illustrators express their ideas. **2A.Stage C.5.** Define unfamiliar vocabulary. **4A.Stage C.6.** Respond in an appropriate manner to questions and discussion with relevant and focused comments.
### Language Arts **Writing** Informational Paragraph: 353g–353h **Six-Trait Writing** Organization/Paragraphs: 351, 353g–353h **Grammar, Usage, and Mechanics** Combining Sentences: 353e–353f **Research/Study** Reference Sources: 353n **Technology** New Literacies: 353m	**3A.Stage C.1.** Develop a paragraph using proper form (e.g., topic sentence, details, summary/ conclusion sentence). **3A.Stage C.2.** Construct complete sentences. **5B.Stage C.4.** List title, author, and type of resource (e.g., magazine, book, encyclopedia, website, interviewee) used in research. **5C.Stage C.1.** Access and use information from a variety of sources.
### Unit Skills **Writing** Research Report: WA2–9 **Poetry:** 408–411 **Project/Wrap-Up:** 412–413	**2A.Stage C.12.** Discover poetic devices (e.g., rhyme, rhythm, alliteration, onomatopoeia, repetition, simile, metaphor). **3A.Stage C.1.** Develop a paragraph using proper form (e.g., topic sentence, details, summary/ conclusion sentence).

This Week's Leveled Readers

Below-Level

1B.Stage C.6. Differentiate between fact and opinion.
1B.Stage C.9. Continuously check and clarify for understanding (e.g., reread, read ahead, use visual and context clues) during reading.

Fiction

On-Level

1B.Stage C.10. Ask question to clarify understanding.
4A.Stage C.2. Distinguish among different kinds of information (e.g., fact, opinion, detail, main idea, fantasy, reality).

Fiction

Advanced

1B.Stage C.6. Differentiate between fact and opinion.
2A.Stage C.9. Classify types of expository text structures (e.g., description, sequence, comparison, cause/effect, problem/solution).

Nonfiction

Content-Area Illinois Performance Descriptors in This Lesson

Social Studies

14F.Stage C.5. Identify an artistic expression (e.g., song, painting, film) that illustrates the traditions important to our political system and concept of freedom.

16A.Stage C.3. List the important details contained in an image of life in the past.

16A.Stage C.4. Draw a general conclusion about life during a specific period in a specific region or place using a combination of historical sources (e.g., images, artifacts, texts).

16B.Stage C.3. Describe the images/icons on local monuments that commemorate local events or people (e.g., cemetery, slides or pictures of monuments, public buildings).

16D.Stage C.3. Tell about the life of people of various social status in the community/United States in the past.

17C.Stage C.1. Identify how people use tools and machines to obtain resources and change the physical and human environment in their community and in other places.

18A.Stage C.5. Describe aspects of the community that reflect its cultural heritage.

Science

12B.Stage C.2. Apply scientific inquiries or technological designs to examine the interdependence of organisms in ecosystems: describing the interaction between living and non-living factors in an ecosystem.

13B.Stage C.3. Explore the basic occupational categories for direct connections to science and technology: researching past, present and projected future influences of science and technology in job skills, hobbies and home application.

Math

7A.Stage C.4. Describe multiple measurable attributes (e.g., length, mass/weight, time, temperature, area, volume, capacity) of a single object.

7C.Stage C.1. Select and apply appropriate standard units and tools to measure length, area, volume, weight, time, and temperature.

7C.Stage C.2. Determine elapsed time between events.

Illinois!

A FAMOUS ILLINOISAN
Edgar Lee Masters

Edgar Lee Masters (1869–1950) grew up on his grandfather's farm near Lewistown. During the 1890s Masters began writing essays, verses, and plays. He is best known for his book *Spoon River Anthology,* a collection of poems published in 1915. In the book, Masters used the words of individual characters to describe life in a fictitious small town. A play based on the book was presented in 1963 on Broadway.

Students can . . .
Write a story about their community highlighting the words of individual community leaders, similar to what Edgar Lee Masters did in *Spoon River Anthology*.

A SPECIAL ILLINOIS PLACE
Decatur

Decatur is in central Illinois along the Sangamon River. The city was founded in 1829 and named after Stephen Decatur, a U.S. naval hero. Abraham Lincoln gave his first political speech in the city. With the promise of a railroad being built through the town, Decatur grew rapidly between 1836 and 1842. Today Decatur is home to corn and soybean processing plants and several manufacturing industries.

Students can . . .
Research soybeans and write a paragraph on the ways they can be used.

ILLINOIS FUN FACTS
Did You Know?

- Illinois has adopted four different state constitutions; the first in 1818, and others in 1848, 1870, and 1970.

- The Illinois State General Assembly consists of 59 senators and 118 representatives.

- Ninian Edwards was governor of the Illinois Territory. He held the position from 1809 until 1818. He was elected governor of the state of Illinois in 1826.

Students can . . .
Research the Illinois Territory. Have them draw an outline map of the United States and color in the areas that were in the Illinois Territory.

Unit 6
Freedom

CONCEPT QUESTION

What does it mean to be free?

Week 1

What does the Statue of Liberty mean to Americans?

Week 2

When might it be hard to grant freedom?

Week 3

Why is freedom of expression important?

Week 4

When can freedom be a problem?

Week 5

When are you free to follow your dreams?

Week 3

EXPAND THE CONCEPT
Why is freedom of expression important?

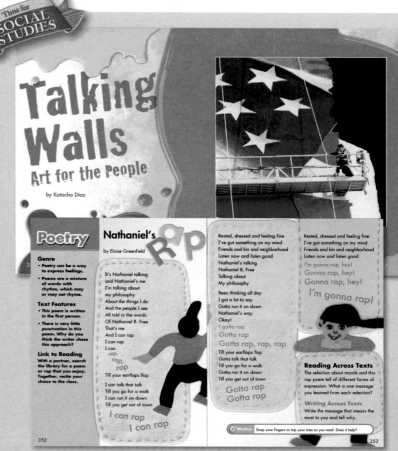

CONNECT THE CONCEPT

▶ **Build Background**
appreciates, downhearted, pondered

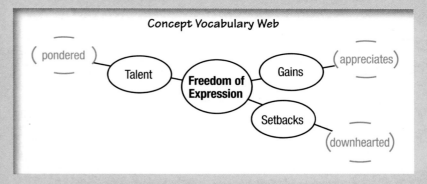

Concept Vocabulary Web

▶ **Social Studies Content**
Freedom of Expression, Immigration, Murals as History

▶ **Writing**
Informational Paragraph

▶ **Internet Inquiry**
Freedom of Expression

Preview Your Week

Why is freedom of expression important?

Talking Walls
Art for the People

by Katacha Diaz

Genre **Photo essays** rely on photographs to help give factual information. What information do you get from the photos in this selection?

336

What do these talking walls have to say?

337

Audio CD

Student Edition pages 336-349

Genre	Photo Essay
Vocabulary Strategy	Glossary
Comprehension Skill	Fact and Opinion
Comprehension Strategy	Answer Questions

SOCIAL STUDIES

Paired Selection

Reading Across Texts
Compare Messages

Genre
Poetry

Text Features
Poetic Elements

Poetry

Genre
• Poetry can be a way to express feelings.
• Poems are a mixture of words with rhythm, which may or may not rhyme.

Text Features
• This poem is written in the first person.
• There is very little punctuation in this poem. Why do you think the writer chose this approach?

Link to Reading
With a partner, search the library for a poem or rap that you enjoy. Together, recite your choice to the class.

Nathaniel's Rap
by Eloise Greenfield

It's Nathaniel talking
and Nathaniel's me
I'm talking about
my philosophy
About the things I do
And the people I see
All told in the words
Of Nathaniel B. Free
That's me
And I can rap
I can
rap,
rap
Till your earflaps flap

I can talk that talk
Till you go for a walk
I can run it on down
Till you get out of town

I can rap
I can rap

Rested, dressed and feeling fine
I've got something on my mind
Friends and kin and neighborhood
Listen now and listen good
Nathaniel's talking
Nathaniel B. Free
Talking about
My philosophy

Been thinking all day
I got a lot to say
Gotta run it on down
Nathaniel's way
Okay!
I gotta rap
Gotta rap
Gotta rap, rap, rap
Till your earflaps flap
Gotta talk that talk
Till you go for a walk
Gotta run it on down
Till you get out of town
Gotta rap
Gotta rap

Rested, dressed and feeling fine
I've got something on my mind
Friends and kin and neighborhood
Listen now and listen good
I'm gonna rap, hey!
Gonna rap, hey!
Gonna rap, hey!
I'm gonna rap!

Reading Across Texts
The selection about murals and this rap poem tell of different forms of expression. What is one message you learned from each selection?

Writing Across Texts
Write the message that means the most to you and tell why.

Rhythm Snap your fingers or tap your toes as you read. Does it help?

352

Student Edition pages 352-353

Audio CD

Read It
ONLINE
PearsonSuccessNet.com

• Student Edition
• Leveled Readers

Leveled Readers

Skill Fact and Opinion

Strategy Answer Questions

Lesson Vocabulary

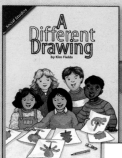

Below-Level

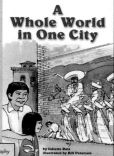

On-Level

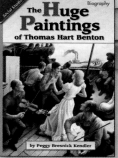

Advanced

ELL Reader

• Concept Vocabulary
• Text Support
• Language Enrichment

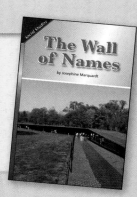

The Wall of Names

Integrate Social Studies Standards

• Freedom of Expression
• Immigration
• Murals as History

✓ Read

Talking Walls: Art for the People
pp. 336–349

"Nathaniel's Rap"
pp. 352–353

Leveled Readers

Below-Level • Support Concepts
On-Level • Develop Concepts
Advanced • Extend Concepts

ELL Reader

✓ Build
Concept Vocabulary
Freedom of Expression,
pp. 332l–332m

✓ Teach
Social Studies Concepts
Artists/Cultures, p. 339
Immigrants, p. 341
Freedom of Speech, p. 345

✓ Explore
Social Studies Center
Plan a Mural, p. 332k

Weekly Plan

My Lesson Planner ONLINE
PearsonSuccessNet.com

READING

45–90 minutes

TARGET SKILLS OF THE WEEK

- **Comprehension Skill**
  Fact and Opinion
- **Comprehension Strategy**
  Answer Questions
- **Vocabulary Strategy**
  Glossary

LANGUAGE ARTS

30–60 minutes

Trait of the Week

Organization/Paragraphs

DAY 1
PAGES 332l–334b, 353a, 353e–353h, 353k–353m

Oral Language

QUESTION OF THE WEEK *Why is freedom of expression important?*

Read Aloud: "Indescribably Arabella," 332m
Build Concepts, 332l

Comprehension/Vocabulary

Comprehension Skill/Strategy Lesson, 332–333
- Fact and Opinion **T**
- Answer Questions

Build Background, 334a

Introduce Lesson Vocabulary, 334b
encourages, expression, local, native, settled, social, support **T**

Read Leveled Readers

Grouping Options 332f–332g

Fluency

Model Reading Silently with Fluency and Accuracy, 332l–332m, 353a

---

Grammar, 353e
Introduce Combining Sentences **T**

Writing Workshop, 353g
Introduce Informational Paragraph
Model the Trait of the Week: Organization/Paragraphs

Spelling, 353k
Pretest for Words with *-tion, -sion, -ture*

Internet Inquiry, 353m
Identify Questions

Day 1 Write to Read, 332

Day 1 Freedom of Expression Concept Web, 332l

DAY 2
PAGES 334–343, 353a, 353e–353i, 353k–353m

Oral Language

QUESTION OF THE DAY *What does it mean to have freedom of artistic expression*

Word Work

Phonics Lesson, 353i
Syllables *-tion, -sion, -ture*

Comprehension/Vocabulary

Vocabulary Strategy Lesson, 334–335
- Glossary **T**

Read *Talking Walls: Art for the People,* 336–343

Grouping Options 332f–332g

- Fact and Opinion **T**
- Answer Questions
- **REVIEW** Main Idea and Details **T**

Develop Vocabulary

Fluency

Silent Reading, 353a

Grammar, 353e
Develop Combining Sentences **T**

Writing Workshop, 353g
Improve Writing: Topic Sentences

Spelling, 353k
Teach the Generalization

Internet Inquiry, 353m
Navigate/Search

Day 2 Words to Write, 335
Strategy Response Log, 336, 343

Day 2 Time for Social Studies: Artists Speak for Their Cultures, 339; Immigrants, 341; Revisit the Freedom of Expression Concept Web, 343

DAILY WRITING ACTIVITIES

DAILY SOCIAL STUDIES CONNECTIONS

DAILY SUCCESS PREDICTORS
for Adequate Yearly Progress

Monitor Progress and Corrective Feedback

Vocabulary Check Vocabulary, *332l*

332d

RESOURCES FOR THE WEEK

- Practice Book 3.2, *pp. 121–130*
- Word Study and Spelling Practice Book, *pp. 109–112*
- Grammar and Writing Practice Book, *pp. 109–112*

- Selection Test, *pp. 109–112*
- Fresh Reads for Differentiated Test Practice, *pp. 163–168*
- The Grammar and Writing Book, *pp. 212–217*

Grouping Options for Differentiated Instruction

Turn the page for the small group lesson plan.

DAY 3   PAGES 344-351, 353a, 353e-353h, 353k-353m

Oral Language

QUESTION OF THE DAY *Why would a community want a mural?*

Comprehension/Vocabulary

Read *Talking Walls: Art for the People,* 344–350

Grouping Options 332f–332g

- Fact and Opinion **T**
- Answer Questions
- Glossary **T**
- Develop Vocabulary

Reader Response

Selection Test

Fluency

Model Reading Silently with Fluency and Accuracy, 353a

Grammar, 353f
Apply Combining Sentences in Writing **T**

Writing Workshop, 351, 353h
Write Now
Prewrite and Draft

Spelling, 353l
Connect Spelling to Writing

Internet Inquiry, 353m
Analyze Sources

Day 3 Strategy Response Log, 348
Look Back and Write, 350

Day 3 Time for Social Studies: Freedom of Speech (Bill of Rights), 345; Revisit the Freedom of Expression Concept Web, 349

DAY 4   PAGES 352-353a, 353e-353h, 353j-353m

Oral Language

QUESTION OF THE DAY *What are some reasons you like to write, scribble, paint, draw, or pretend?*

Word Work

Phonics Lesson, 353j
REVIEW Schwa **T**

Comprehension/Vocabulary

Read "Nathaniel's Rap," 352–353

Grouping Options 332f–332g

Poetry/Text Features

Reading Across Texts

Content-Area Vocabulary

Fluency

Choral Reading, 353a

Grammar, 353f
Practice Combining Sentences for Standardized Tests **T**

Writing Workshop, 353h
Draft, Revise, and Publish

Spelling, 353l
Provide a Strategy

Internet Inquiry, 353m
Synthesize Information

Day 4 Writing Across Texts, 353

Day 4 Social Studies Center: Plan a Mural, 332k

DAY 5   PAGES 353a-353h, 353k-353n

Oral Language

QUESTION OF THE WEEK *To wrap up the week, revisit the Day 1 question.*
Build Concept Vocabulary, 353c

Fluency

Read Leveled Readers

Grouping Options 332f–332g

Assess Reading Rate, 353a

Comprehension/Vocabulary

- Reteach Fact and Opinion, 353b **T**
- Rhythm/Cadence, 353b
- Review Glossary, 353c **T**

Speaking and Viewing, 353d
Interview
Analyze Artwork

Grammar, 353f
Cumulative Review

Writing Workshop, 353h
Connect to Unit Writing

Spelling, 353l
Posttest for Words with *-tion, -sion, -ture*

Internet Inquiry, 353m
Communicate Results

Research/Study Skills, 353n
Reference Sources

Day 5 Rhythm/Cadence, 353b

Day 5 Revisit the Freedom of Expression Concept Web, 353c

KEY ⟳ = Target Skill   **T** = Tested Skill

Comprehension   Check Retelling, *351*

Fluency   Check Fluency WCPM, *353a*

Vocabulary   Check Vocabulary, *353c*

SUCCESS PREDICTOR

Small Group Plan for Differentiated Instruction

Daily Plan AT A GLANCE

Reading
Whole Group
- Oral Language
- Phonics
- Comprehension/Vocabulary

Group Time
Differentiated Instruction

Meet with small groups to provide:
- Skill Support
- Reading Support
- Fluency Practice

Read

This week's lessons for daily group time can be found behind the Differentiated Instruction (DI) tab on pp. DI·22–DI·31.

Whole Group
- Fluency

Language Arts
- Grammar
- Writing
- Spelling
- Research/Inquiry
- Speaking/Listening/Viewing

Use My Sidewalks on Reading Street for Tier III intensive reading intervention.

DAY 1

On-Level
Teacher-Led
Page DI·23
- Develop Concept Vocabulary
- Read On-Level Reader *A Whole World in One City*

Strategic Intervention
Teacher-Led
Page DI·22
- Preteach Syllables -tion, -ture
- Read Decodable Reader 28
- Read Below-Level Reader *A Different Drawing*

Advanced
Teacher-Led
Page DI·23
- Read Advanced Reader *The Huge Paintings of . . .*
- Independent Extension Activity

(i) Independent Activities
While you meet with small groups, have the rest of the class...

- Visit the Reading/Library Center
- Listen to the Background Building Audio
- Finish Write to Read, p. 332
- Complete Practice Book 3.2 pp. 123–124
- Visit Cross-Curricular Centers

DAY 2

On-Level
Teacher-Led
Pages 338–343
- Read *Talking Walls: Art for the People*

Strategic Intervention
Teacher-Led
Page DI·24
- Practice Lesson Vocabulary
- Read Multisyllabic Words
- Read or Listen to *Talking Walls: Art for the People*

Advanced
Teacher-Led
Page DI·25
- Extend Vocabulary
- Read *Talking Walls: Art for the People*

(i) Independent Activities
While you meet with small groups, have the rest of the class...

- Visit the Reading/Library Center
- Listen to the AudioText for *Talking Walls: Art for the People*
- Finish Words to Write, p. 335
- Complete Practice Book 3.2 pp. 125–126, 129
- Write in their Strategy Response Logs, pp. 336, 343
- Visit Cross-Curricular Centers
- Work on inquiry projects

DAY 3

On-Level
Teacher-Led
Pages 344–349
- Read *Talking Walls: Art for the People*

Strategic Intervention
Teacher-Led
Page DI·26
- Practice Fact and Opinion and Answer Questions
- Read or Listen to *Talking Walls: Art for the People*

Advanced
Teacher-Led
Page DI·27
- Extend Fact and Opinion and Answer Questions
- Read *The Talking Walls: Art for the People*

(i) Independent Activities
While you meet with small groups, have the rest of the class...

- Visit the Reading/Library Center
- Listen to the AudioText for *Talking Walls: Art for the People*
- Write in their Strategy Response Logs, p. 348
- Finish Look Back and Write, p. 350
- Complete Practice Book 3.2 p. 127
- Visit Cross-Curricular Centers
- Work on inquiry projects

① Begin with whole class skill and strategy instruction.

② Meet with small groups to provide differentiated instruction.

③ Gather the whole class back together for fluency and language arts.

On-Level
Teacher-Led
Pages 352–353
• **Read** "Nathaniel's Rap"

Strategic Intervention
Teacher-Led
Page DI · 28
• Practice Retelling
• **Read** or Listen to "Nathaniel's Rap"

Advanced
Teacher-Led
Page DI · 29
• **Read** "Nathaniel's Rap"
• Genre Study

 DAY 4

ⓘ Independent Activities

While you meet with small groups, have the rest of the class...

• Visit the Reading/Library Center
• Listen to the AudioText for "Nathaniel's Rap"
• Visit the Writing and Vocabulary Centers
• Finish Writing Across Texts, p. 353
• Visit Cross-Curricular Centers
• Work on inquiry projects

On-Level
Teacher-Led
Page DI · 31
• **Reread** Leveled Reader *A Whole World in One City*
• Retell *A Whole World in One City*

Strategic Intervention
Teacher-Led
Page DI · 30
• **Reread** Leveled Reader *A Different Drawing*
• Retell *A Different Drawing*

Advanced
Teacher-Led
Page DI · 31
• **Reread** Leveled Reader *The Huge Paintings of Thomas Hart Benton*
• Share Extension Activity

 DAY 5

ⓘ Independent Activities

While you meet with small groups, have the rest of the class...

• Visit the Reading/Library Center
• Complete Practice Book 3.2 pp. 128, 130
• Visit Cross-Curricular Centers
• Work on inquiry projects

Grouping Place English language learners in the groups that correspond to their reading abilities in English.

Use the appropriate Leveled Reader or other text at students' instructional level.

TIP Send home the appropriate Multilingual Summary of the main selection on Day 1.

Take It to the NET™ ONLINE
PearsonSuccessNet.com

P. David Pearson
For research on comprehension, see the article "Comprehension Instruction" by Scott Foresman author P. D. Pearson and L. Fielding.

TEACHER TALK

A **rubric** is a guide for assessing a task or writing assignment. It typically describes the qualities of a good, average, and poor product along a scaled continuum.

Looking Ahead

Be sure to schedule time for students to work on the unit inquiry project "Symbols of Freedom." This week students analyze information to determine how useful it is. They take notes on valid information.

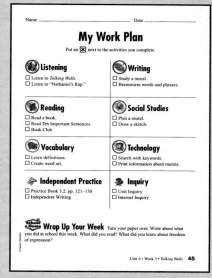

Name _____ Date _____

My Work Plan
Put an ☒ next to the activities you complete.

🎧 Listening
☐ Listen to *Talking Walls*.
☐ Listen to "Nathaniel's Rap."

✏️ Writing
☐ Study a mural.
☐ Brainstorm words and phrases.

📖 Reading
☐ Read a book.
☐ Read Ten Important Sentences.
☐ Book Club

🌎 Social Studies
☐ Plan a mural.
☐ Draw a sketch.

📕 Vocabulary
☐ Learn definitions.
☐ Create word art.

💻 Technology
☐ Search with keywords.
☐ Print information about murals.

✍️ Independent Practice
☐ Practice Book 3.2, pp. 121–130
☐ Independent Writing

🔍 Inquiry
☐ Unit Inquiry
☐ Internet Inquiry

📋 Wrap Up Your Week Turn your paper over. Write about what you did at school this week. What did you read? What did you learn about freedom of expression?

Unit 6 • Week 3 • *Talking Walls* **45**

▲ **Group-Time Survival Guide**
p. 45, Weekly Contract

ORAL LANGUAGE

SOCIAL STUDIES

Concept Development

Why is freedom of expression important?

CONCEPT VOCABULARY

appreciates   downhearted   pondered

BUILD

- ☐ **Question of the Week** Introduce and discuss the question of the week. This week students will read a variety of texts and work on projects related to the concept *freedom of expression*. Post the question for students to refer to throughout the week. **DAY 1** *332d*

- ☐ **Read Aloud** Read aloud "Indescribably Arabella." Then begin a web to build concepts and concept vocabulary related to this week's lesson and the unit theme, Freedom. Introduce the concept words *appreciates, downhearted,* and *pondered* and have students place them on the web. Display the web for use throughout the week. **DAY 1** *332l–332m*

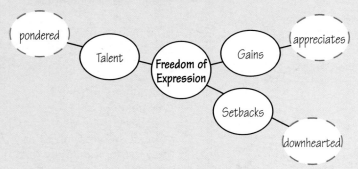

DEVELOP

- ☐ **Question of the Day** Use the prompts from the Weekly Plan to engage students in conversations related to this week's reading and the unit theme. **EVERY DAY** *332d–332e*

- ☐ **Concept Vocabulary Web** Revisit the Freedom of Expression Concept Web and encourage students to add concept words from their reading and life experiences. **DAY 2** *343,* **DAY 3** *349*

CONNECT

- ☐ **Looking Back/Moving Forward** Revisit the Freedom of Expression Concept Web and discuss how it relates to this week's lesson and the unit theme. Then make connections to next week's lesson. **DAY 5** *353c*

CHECK

- ☐ **Concept Vocabulary Web** Use the Freedom of Expression Concept Web to check students' understanding of the concept vocabulary words *appreciates, downhearted,* and *pondered.* **DAY 1** *332l,* **DAY 5** *353c*

VOCABULARY

☐ **STRATEGY GLOSSARY** A glossary is a part of a book, usually at the back, where important words from the book and their meanings are listed. The words are listed in alphabetical order. When you come across an unfamiliar word while you are reading, check in the book's glossary for the word.

LESSON VOCABULARY

encourages   settled
expression   social
local   support
native

TEACH

- ☐ **Words to Know** Give students the opportunity to tell what they already know about this week's lesson vocabulary words. Then discuss word meaning. **DAY 1** *334b*

- ☐ **Vocabulary Strategy Lesson** Use the vocabulary strategy lesson in the Student Edition to introduce and model this week's strategy, using a *glossary.* **DAY 2** *334–335*

Vocabulary Strategy Lesson

PRACTICE/APPLY

- ☐ **Leveled Text** Read the lesson vocabulary in the context of leveled text. **DAY 1** *LR19–LR27*

Leveled Readers

- ☐ **Words in Context** Read the lesson vocabulary and apply using a glossary in the context of *Talking Walls: Art for the People.* **DAY 2** *336–343,* **DAY 3** *344–350*

- ☐ **Vocabulary Center** Show word meaning through pictures. **ANY DAY** *332j*

Main Selection—Nonfiction

- ☐ **Homework** Practice Book 3.2 pp. 124–125. **DAY 1** *334b,* **DAY 2** *335*

- ☐ **Word Play** Have partners use reference sources to make lists of art-related words and their meanings or examples. Students can create art using one of the art forms they researched. **ANY DAY** *353c*

ASSESS

- ☐ **Selection Test** Use the Selection Test to determine students' understanding of the lesson vocabulary words. **DAY 3**

RETEACH/REVIEW

- ☐ **Reteach Lesson** If necessary, use this lesson to reteach and review using a *glossary.* **DAY 5** *353c*

COMPREHENSION

SKILL FACT AND OPINION   A fact is a statement that tells something that can be proved true or false. You can prove a fact by reading or asking an expert. An opinion is a statement that tells someone's ideas or feelings. Words that tell feelings, such as *should* or *best,* are clues to opinions.

STRATEGY ANSWER QUESTIONS   To determine that a statement is a fact, notice that a fact is very often the answer to a question you have asked yourself. To determine that a statement is an opinion, notice if the statement includes words such as *great, best,* and *worst.*

TEACH

❑ **Skill/Strategy Lesson** Use the skill/strategy lesson in the Student Edition to introduce and model *fact and opinion* and *answering questions.* **DAY 1** 332–333

❑ **Extend Skills** Teach rhythm/cadence. **ANY DAY** 353b

Skill/Strategy Lesson

PRACTICE/APPLY

❑ **Leveled Text** Apply *fact and opinion* and *answering questions* to read leveled text. **DAY 1** LR19–LR27

Leveled Readers

❑ **Skills and Strategies in Context** Read *Talking Walls: Art for the People,* using the Guiding Comprehension questions to apply *fact and opinion* and *answering questions.* **DAY 2** 336–343, **DAY 3** 344–350

❑ **Skills and Strategies in Context** Read "Nathaniel's Rap," guiding students as they apply *fact and opinion* and *answering questions.* Then have students discuss and write across texts. **DAY 4** 352–353

Main Selection—Nonfiction

❑ **Homework** Practice Book 3.2 pp. 123, 127, 128. **DAY 1** 333, **DAY 3** 349, **DAY 5** 353b

Paired Selection—Poetry

❑ **Fresh Reads for Differentiated Test Practice** Have students practice *fact and opinion* with a new passage. **DAY 3**

ASSESS

❑ **Selection Test** Determine students' understanding of the selection and their use of fact and opinion. **DAY 3**

❑ **Retell** Have students retell *Talking Walls: Art for the People.* **DAY 3** 350–351

RETEACH/REVIEW

❑ **Reteach Lesson** If necessary, reteach and review fact and opinion. **DAY 5** 353b

FLUENCY

SKILL READING SILENTLY WITH FLUENCY AND ACCURACY   Reading silently means reading only to yourself. When you read silently, you try to read fluently—smoothly, without stopping after every word or phrase—and accurately, reading the words accurately and self-correcting when you misread.

TEACH

❑ **Read Aloud** Model fluent reading by rereading "Indescribably Arabella." Focus on this week's fluency skill, reading silently with fluency and accuracy. **DAY 1** 332l–332m, 353a

PRACTICE/APPLY

❑ **Silent Reading** Read aloud selected paragraphs from *Talking Walls: Art for the People,* self-correcting when you misread a word. Then have students practice carefully reading the page silently two times. **DAY 2** 353a, **DAY 3** 353a

❑ **Choral Reading** Choral read "Nathaniel's Rap" three times, reading with rhythm and expression. As students reread, monitor their progress toward their individual fluency goals. **DAY 4** 353a

❑ **Listening Center** Have students follow along with the AudioText for this week's selections. **ANY DAY** 332j

❑ **Reading/Library Center** Have students reread a selection of their choice. **ANY DAY** 332j

❑ **Fluency Coach** Have students use Fluency Coach to listen to fluent readings or practice reading on their own. **ANY DAY**

ASSESS

❑ **Check Fluency** WCPM Do a one-minute timed reading, paying special attention to this week's skill—reading silently with fluency and accuracy. Provide feedback for each student. **DAY 5** 353a

GRAMMAR

SKILL COMBINING SENTENCES When you combine sentences, you join two short sentences that are about the same topic, and make them into longer sentences.

TEACH

☐ **Grammar Transparency 28** Use Grammar Transparency 28 to teach combining sentences.
DAY 1 *353e*

Grammar Transparency 28

PRACTICE/APPLY

☐ **Develop the Concept** Review the concept of combining sentences and provide guided practice. DAY 2 *353e*

☐ **Apply to Writing** Have students review something they have written and apply what they have learned about combining sentences. DAY 3 *353f*

☐ **Test Preparation** Examine common errors in combining sentences to prepare for standardized tests. DAY 4 *353f*

☐ **Homework** Grammar and Writing Practice Book pp. 109–111. DAY 2 *353e*, DAY 3 *353f*, DAY 4 *353f*

ASSESS

☐ **Cumulative Review** Use Grammar and Writing Practice Book p. 112. DAY 5 *353f*

RETEACH/REVIEW

☐ **Daily Fix-It** Have students find and correct errors in grammar, spelling, and punctuation.
EVERY DAY *353e–353f*

☐ **The Grammar and Writing Book** Use pp. 212–215 of The Grammar and Writing Book to extend instruction for combining sentences. **ANY DAY**

The Grammar and Writing Book

WRITING

Trait of the Week

ORGANIZATION/PARAGRAPHS Organization is the way a writer arranges main ideas and details in a paragraph. A careful writer tells about events and details in order. For example, a well-written paragraph includes a topic sentence that states the main idea, sentences that tell important supporting details, and a concluding sentence.

TEACH

☐ **Writing Transparency 28A** Use the model to introduce and discuss the Trait of the Week. DAY 1 *353g*

☐ **Writing Transparency 28B** Use the transparency to show students how topic sentences can improve their writing.
DAY 2 *353g*

Writing Transparency 28A **Writing Transparency 28B**

PRACTICE/APPLY

☐ **Write Now** Examine the model on Student Edition p. 351. Then have students write their own informational paragraph. DAY 3 *351, 353h*, DAY 4 *353h*

> **Prompt** *Talking Walls* describes special murals. Think about a kind of art that you know well. Now write an informational paragraph about this kind of art.

Write Now p. 351

☐ **Writing Center** Write a description of your favorite mural from the selection and how the mural makes you feel. **ANY DAY** *332k*

ASSESS

☐ **Writing Trait Rubric** Use the rubric to evaluate students' writing. DAY 4 *353h*

RETEACH/REVIEW

☐ **The Grammar and Writing Book** Use pp. 212–217 of The Grammar and Writing Book to extend instruction for combining sentences, topic sentences, and informational paragraphs. **ANY DAY**

The Grammar and Writing Book

SPELLING

GENERALIZATION WORDS WITH -TION, -SION, -TURE Many words end in syllable patterns -tion, -sion, or -ture: ac*tion*, divi*sion*, crea*ture*.

TEACH

☐ **Pretest** Give the pretest for words with -tion, -sion, and -ture. Guide students in self-correcting their pretests and correcting any misspellings. **DAY 1** *353k*

☐ **Think and Practice** Connect spelling to the phonics generalization for words with -tion, -sion, and -ture. **DAY 2** *353k*

PRACTICE/APPLY

☐ **Connect to Writing** Have students use spelling words to write a report. Then review frequently misspelled words: *we're, were.* **DAY 3** *353l*

☐ **Homework** Phonics and Spelling Practice Book pp. 109–112. **EVERY DAY**

RETEACH/REVIEW

☐ **Review** Review spelling words to prepare for the posttest. Then provide students with a spelling strategy—common syllable patterns. **DAY 4** *353l*

ASSESS

☐ **Posttest** Use dictation sentences to give the posttest for words with -tion, -sion, and -ture. **DAY 5** *353l*

Spelling Words

1. question
2. creature
3. furniture
4. division
5. collision
6. action
7. direction
8. culture
9. vacation
10. mansion
11. fiction
12. feature
13. sculpture
14. vision
15. celebration*

Challenge Words

16. fascination
17. legislature
18. manufacture
19. possession
20. declaration

*Word from the selection

PHONICS

SKILL SYLLABLES -TION, -SION, -TURE Recognizing -tion, -sion, and -ture will help you chunk and decode longer words.

TEACH

☐ **Phonics Lesson** Model how to read words with syllables -tion, -sion, and -ture. Then have students practice by decoding longer words and reading words in context. **DAY 2** *353i*

PRACTICE/APPLY

☐ **Homework** Practice Book 3.2, p. 129. **DAY 2** *353i*

RETEACH/REVIEW

☐ **Review Phonics** Review how to read words with schwa. Then have students practice by decoding longer words and reading words in context. **DAY 4** *353j*

RESEARCH AND INQUIRY

☐ **Internet Inquiry** Have students conduct an Internet inquiry on freedom of expression. **EVERY DAY** *353m*

☐ **Reference Sources** Review terms related to a telephone directory, such as *telephone numbers, local area, area code, business listings,* and *yellow pages.* Have students work with a partner to use telephone directories to discuss the book's organization and look up listings. **DAY 5** *353n*

☐ **Unit Inquiry** Allow time for students to analyze information to determine how useful it is, and then take notes on valid information. **ANY DAY** *283*

SPEAKING AND VIEWING

☐ **Interview** Have students work in small groups to act out a talk show, with one student acting as host and the others as guests. Help students recall appropriate behavior as both host and guests. **DAY 5** *353d*

☐ **Analyze Artwork** Have students study the photograph of the U.S. Capitol mural "Declaration of Independence, 1776" on p. 348. With partners, they can answer questions orally or in writing. **DAY 5** *353d*

Resources for Differentiated Instruction

LEVELED READERS

▶ **Comprehension**

🔊 **Skill** Fact and Opinion

🔊 **Strategy** Answer Questions

▶ **Lesson Vocabulary**

🔊 **Glossary**

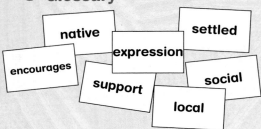

native · settled · expression · encourages · support · social · local

▶ **Social Studies Standards**

• Freedom of Expression
• Immigration
• Murals as History

Leveled Reader Database ONLINE

PearsonSuccessNet.com

Use the Online Database of over 600 books to

• Download and print additional copies of this week's leveled readers.
• Listen to the readers being read online.
• Search for more titles focused on this week's skills, topic, and content.

On-Level

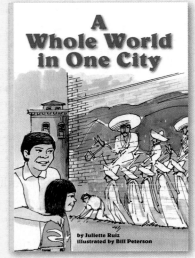

A Whole World in One City
by Juliette Ruiz
Illustrated by Bill Peterson

On-Level Reader

Fact and Opinion

• A statement of **fact** is a statement that can be proved true or false.
• A statement of **opinion** is a statement of someone's judgment, belief, or way of thinking about something. Although statements of opinion cannot be proved true or false, they can be supported or explained.

Directions Write *F* beside statements of fact and *O* beside statements of opinion.

1. _F_ Chicago has many different neighborhoods.
2. _O_ It's much more fun to take the bus or the train.
3. _O_ Mexican ice cream tastes better than regular ice cream.
4. _F_ Pilsen is the largest Mexican neighborhood in any city in the country.
5. _O_ The Polish neighborhood has better food than the Mexican neighborhood.
6. _O_ It is better to feel like you're not stuck in just one place.
7. _F_ The streets were filled with pagodas, fish markets, and restaurants.
8. _O_ The Chicago Food Market has the best fish.

Directions Write your own opinion of what it would be like to live in a city with many different cultures.

Responses will vary.

🔊 **On-Level Practice** TE p. LR23

Vocabulary
Directions Fill in the blank with the word that best completes each sentence.

Check the Words You Know
__encourages __expression __local __native
__settled __social __support

1. She doesn't play much with other kids. She is not very ___social___
2. Lily shopped at the ___local___ fish market in her neighborhood.
3. Lily's family moved to many places, then ___settled___ in Chicago.
4. Lily's grandmother ___encourages___ her to keep a diary.
5. I was born in Chicago, so that makes me a ___native___ of Chicago.
6. At first, Lily did not ___support___ her family's move to Chicago.
7. When Lily saw the colorful neighborhood, she had an excited ___expression___ on her face.

Directions Use the words *encourages, social, local,* and *expression* in a short paragraph about your community.

Responses will vary.

On-Level Practice TE p. LR24

Strategic Intervention

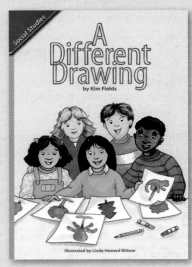

Social Studies

A Different Drawing
by Kim Fields
illustrated by Linda Howard Bittner

Below-Level Reader

Fact and Opinion

• A statement of **fact** is a statement that can be proved true or false.
• A statement of **opinion** is a statement of someone's judgment, belief, or way of thinking about something.

Directions Write *F* beside statements of fact and *O* beside statements of opinion.

1. _F_ Trees have leaves and branches.
2. _O_ There is only one way that you should draw a tree.
3. _O_ Sue's trees were better than the other kids' trees.
4. _F_ Mr. Martinez encouraged his students to do their best.
5. _O_ You should do what other kids tell you to do.
6. _F_ There are all sorts of trees.
7. _O_ All trees should not look like lollipops.
8. _F_ Freedom of expression means that we can express ourselves in many different ways.

Directions Read the statement: Sue's drawings are better than everyone else's drawings. Is this a fact or an opinion? Why?

9–10. Opinion: It is a statement of someone's judgment.

🔊 **Below-Level Practice** TE p. LR20

Vocabulary
Directions Write the word that best completes each sentence.

Check the Words You Know
__encourages __expression __local __native
__settled __social __support

1. A great painting can be an ___expression___ of joy.
2. I was born and raised in this town. I am a ___native___
3. They discussed the problem and ___settled___ it by coming to an agreement.
4. Sue ___encourages___ the other kids to draw the trees any way they like.
5. Nat talked to many kids. He is very ___social___
6. Sue went to the ___local___ art supply store to buy markers.
7. Mr. Martinez will ___support___ you, no matter how you draw a tree.

Directions Use the words *local, support,* and *expression* in a short paragraph.

Paragraphs will vary.

Below-Level Practice TE p. LR21

Advanced

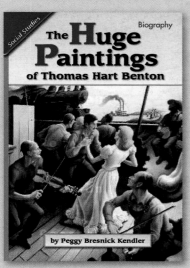

Advanced Reader

The Huge Paintings of Thomas Hart Benton
by Peggy Bresnick Kendler

Fact and Opinion

- A statement of **fact** is a statement that can be proved true or false.
- A statement of **opinion** is a statement of someone's judgment, belief, or way of thinking about something.

Directions Write *F* beside statements of fact and *O* beside statements of opinion. Then explain what makes the statement a fact or an opinion.

____F____ 1. Thomas Hart Benton is a famous muralist.
Many people have written about him; many people know him.

____O____ 2. Thomas Hart Benton is the best of the American muralists.
You cannot prove it, but you can compare him to other artists and like his art more.

____F____ 3. His father wanted his son to go into politics.
His father sent him to military school and expressed a desire for him to go into politics.

____O____ 4. Art institutes are better schools than military institutes.
You cannot prove that this is true.

____O____ 5. New York City is the best place for an artist to live.
You cannot prove this is true.

Advanced Practice TE p. LR26

Vocabulary
Directions Draw a line from the word to its meaning.

Check the Words You Know
- ally
- appreciate
- encouraged
- enlisted
- expression
- legacy
- mural
- native
- social
- support

1. ally — *n.* a local resident
2. appreciate — *n.* example, illustration, or demonstration
3. enlisted — *n.* backing, encouragement, help
4. encouraged — *n.* a friend or helper
5. expression — *v.* gave support to
6. legacy — *n.* a large wall painting
7. mural — *n.* a gift left by someone
8. native — *v.* to be grateful for
9. social — *v.* joined or signed on
10. support — *adj.* relating to human society

Directions Using at least two of the vocabulary words above, write one statement of fact and one statement of opinion.

Responses will vary.

Advanced Practice TE p. LR27

ELL

ELL Reader

The Wall of Names
by Josephine Marquardt

ELL Poster 28

Teacher's Edition Notes
ELL notes throughout this lesson support instruction and reference additional resources at point of use.

Teaching Guide pp. 190–196, 266–267
- Multilingual summaries of the main selection
- Comprehension lesson
- Vocabulary strategies and word cards
- ELL Reader 3.6.3 lesson

ELL and Transition Handbook

Ten Important Sentences
- Key ideas from every selection in the Student Edition
- Activities to build sentence power

More Reading

Readers' Theater Anthology
- Fluency practice
- Five scripts to build fluency
- Poetry for oral interpretation

Leveled Trade Books

Below-Level

On-Level

Advanced

- Extended reading tied to the unit concept
- Lessons in the Trade Book Library Teaching Guide

School + Home

Homework
- Family Times Newsletter
- ELL Multilingual Selection Summaries

Take-Home Books
- Leveled Readers

Family Times

Cross-Curricular Centers

Listening

Listen to the Selections

MATERIALS `SINGLES`
CD player, headphones, AudioText CD, Student Edition

Listen to *Talking Walls: Art for the People* and "Nathaniel's Rap" as you follow or read along in your book. Listen for facts and opinions.

If there is anything you don't understand, you can listen again to any section.

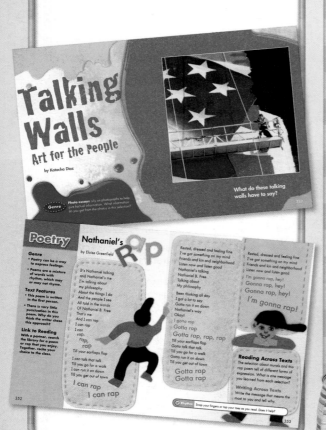

Reading/Library

Read It Again!

MATERIALS `SINGLES` `PAIRS` `GROUPS`
Collection of books for self-selected reading, reading log

Select a book you have already read. Record the title of the book in your reading log. You may want to read with a partner.

You may choose to read any of the following:

- **Leveled Readers**
- **ELL Readers**
- **Stories written by classmates**
- **Books from the library**
- *Talking Walls: Art for the People*

TEN IMPORTANT SENTENCES Read the Ten Important Sentences for *Talking Walls: Art for the People*. Then locate the sentences in the Student Edition.

BOOK CLUB Write a letter to a reading penpal. Describe your favorite mural from the selection. Then explain what the mural "says" to you.

Vocabulary

Word Pictures

MATERIALS `SINGLES`
Paper, art supplies, dictionary

Use a word in a work of art to show the meaning of the word.

1. Choose a word from the list below.
2. Use the dictionary to learn the meaning of the word.
3. Think of something you could draw that would show the meaning of the word. Use the word in the art.
4. Do this for at least two more words.

EARLY FINISHERS Write a paragraph describing your artwork. Be sure to include the word and its definition in your description.

celebration	political
democracy	recycle
education	success
expressions	symbolize
muralist	villages

Scott Foresman Reading Street Centers Survival Kit

Use the *Talking Walls: Art for the People* materials
from the Reading Street Centers Survival Kit
to organize this week's centers.

Writing

Describe A MURAL

MATERIALS
Paper, pencil

`PAIRS`
`GROUPS`

Tell about your favorite mural from the selection.

1. Decide on a mural to describe.
2. Spend two minutes studying the mural.
3. Brainstorm a list of words and phrases about the mural. Your ideas may tell about what is shown in the mural. They may also tell how the mural makes you feel. Record your ideas on paper.

EARLY FINISHERS Write about a mural you would paint in your neighborhood.

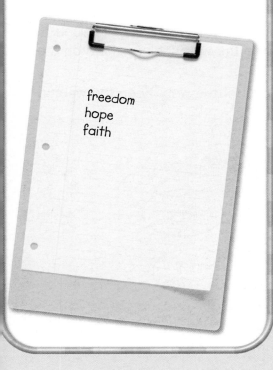

Social Studies

Plan a Mural

MATERIALS
Art materials, paper

`SINGLES`
`PAIRS`
`GROUPS`

Plan a mural for your school or community.

1. Decide where you want your mural to appear. It may be on a wall at school or in your community.
2. Think of important events to feature in the mural. If the mural will be at school, include events that are important to your school's history. Some ideas are the opening of the school, a visit from a special person, and a Veteran's Day celebration.
3. Draw a sketch of the mural on art paper.

EARLY FINISHERS Write a paragraph describing the images in the mural.

Technology

Art Search

MATERIALS
Computer, printer

`SINGLES`
`PAIRS`

Search the Internet for different neighborhood murals.

1. With a partner, discuss keywords you can use to find pictures of different murals.
2. Type your keywords into a search engine to find pictures of neighborhood murals.
3. Print out some of your favorites.

EARLY FINISHERS Write a description of a mural you found. Tell why you liked or disliked it.

ALL CENTERS

Talking Walls **332k**

OBJECTIVES

- Build vocabulary by finding words related to the lesson concept.
- Listen for statements of fact and opinion.

Concept Vocabulary

appreciates admires greatly, values

downhearted low in spirit, depressed

pondered reflected or considered with thought and care

Monitor Progress

Check Vocabulary

| **If...** students are unable to place words on the web, | **then...** review the lesson concept. Place the words on the web and provide additional words for practice, such as *discouraged* and *satisfaction*. |

SUCCESS PREDICTOR

DAY 1 Grouping Options

Reading
Whole Group
Introduce and discuss the Question of the Week. Then use pp. 332l–334b.

Group Time
Differentiated Instruction
Read this week's Leveled Readers. See pp. 332f–332g for the small group lesson plan.

Whole Group
Use p. 353a.

Language Arts
Use pp. 353e–353h and 353k–353m.

Build Concepts

FLUENCY

MODEL READING SILENTLY WITH FLUENCY AND ACCURACY As you read "Indescribably Arabella," model how to read with fluency and how to self-correct when you misread a word. Read the first paragraph, mispronouncing words such as *ordinary* and *indescribably*. Model how to self-correct by using context clues and knowledge of word parts. Explain that though you model by reading aloud, you use the same technique when reading silently.

LISTENING COMPREHENSION

After reading "Indescribably Arabella," use the following questions to assess listening comprehension.

1. **What is one statement of opinion about Arabella?** *(She is not a good painter.)* **What is one statement of fact about Arabella?** *(She threw away her paints, costumes, and dance shoes.)* **Fact and Opinion**

2. **When you heard this story, what did you learn about people?** *(Possible response: Different people appreciate different types of expression.)* **Theme**

BUILD CONCEPT VOCABULARY

Start a web to build concepts and vocabulary related to this week's lesson and the unit theme.

- Draw a Freedom of Expression Concept Web.
- Read the sentence with the word *appreciates* again. Ask students to pronounce *appreciates* and discuss its meaning.
- Place *appreciates* in an oval attached to Gains. Explain that *appreciates* is related to this concept. Read the sentences in which *downhearted* and *pondered* appear. Have students pronounce the words, place them on the web, and provide reasons.
- Brainstorm additional words and categories for the web. Keep the web on display and add words throughout the week.

Concept Vocabulary Web

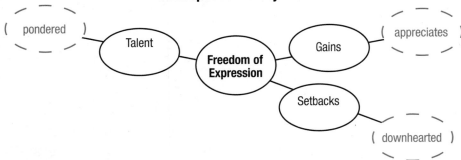

Indescribably Arabella

by Jane Gilbert

Arabella Anastasia was not an ordinary girl. She was, well, indescribably Arabella. One day Arabella decided to be famous. She pondered on how to do it and…all of a sudden she knew!

"I shall become a famous painter." So she painted and painted and painted. And she tried to make her paintings as beautiful as all the other paintings she had seen. But her colors always ran together and the lines were always crooked.

"I am sorry," her art teacher said, "but you will never be a famous painter." So Arabella went home and put her paintings away.

And she pondered and pondered on how to become famous. All of a sudden she knew!

"I shall become a famous actress." Arabella Anastasia was not an ordinary person, you must remember. She was, well, indescribably Arabella. And she did want to become famous so badly! So she acted and acted and acted. And she tried to act like all the other famous actors she had seen. But her entrances were always late and she could never remember her lines.

"I am sorry," her acting teacher said, "but you will never be a famous actress." Arabella tried not to be downhearted. With her last few pennies she bought a ballet dress and dancing slippers.

"I will teach myself to dance," she said. And she practiced…and practiced and practiced and practiced…till she could leap and whirl and kick and stand on her toes like all the other famous dancers she had seen.

But no one would even look at Arabella dance. The people in the Big Offices just laughed at her short legs and her funny little voice because she was, well, indescribably Arabella, and they turned her away from their doors.

"Oh, dear!" cried Arabella. "I shall never become famous!" And she went out to the trash and threw out her paints, and her costumes, and her dancing slippers.

Two people who were very lonely and very sad were passing by, and they said to her, "Why are you doing that, my dear?"

"No one appreciates me," Arabella said, and she sat down and told her whole story. The two people, who were very lonely and very sad, took Arabella Anastasia, her paints, her costumes, and her dancing slippers home with them.

"Now please paint a picture for us, Arabella." So Arabella Anastasia painted her own kind of picture. It was of their cat, and it was the most unusual picture that the two people had ever seen. They hung it right up over their fireplace.

"Now act out a little play for us, Arabella." So Arabella Anastasia acted in her own kind of way, and it was the most unusual performance that the two people had ever seen. They clapped and clapped.

continued on TR1

Set Purpose

Have students listen for statements of fact and opinion about Arabella.

Creative Response

Reread the selection aloud. As you read, have students act out Arabella's feelings as she thinks, comes up with an idea, tries the idea, and is told she is not talented. **Drama**

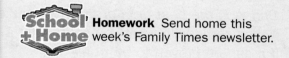

Activate Prior Knowledge Before students listen to the Read Aloud, ask them what they know about being famous.

Access Content Before reading, share this summary: Arabella Anastasia tries different ways to be famous. People tell her she is not talented. Then she meets two people that appreciate her talents.

School + Home **Homework** Send home this week's Family Times newsletter.

SKILLS ⟷ STRATEGIES IN CONTEXT

Fact and Opinion
Answer Questions

OBJECTIVES

 Distinguish between statements of fact and opinion.

 Use facts to answer questions.

Skills Trace	
Fact and Opinion	
Introduce/Teach	TE: 3.4 86–87, 3.5 170–171, 3.6 332–333
Practice	PB: 3.2 33, 37, 38, 63, 67, 68, 86, 96, 123, 127, 128
Reteach/Review	TE: 3.4 111b, DI·55; 3.5 193b, 229, 265, DI·53; 3.6 353b, DI·54
Test	Selection Test, Unit 6

INTRODUCE

Read the following sentence aloud to students: *Spring is the best time of the year.* Ask students if they agree with what you said. Then ask them if it can be proven to be true.

Have students read the information on p. 332. Explain the following:

- A statement of fact can be proven to be true or false.

- A statement of opinion is a statement of someone's judgment, belief, or way of thinking about something.

- Facts and opinions in a passage may be used to answer test questions.

Use Skill Transparency 28 to teach fact and opinion and how to answer questions.

Talking Walls
Art for the People

Comprehension

Skill
Fact and Opinion

Strategy
Answer Questions

 Fact and Opinion

- A statement of fact tells something that can be proved true or false. You can find proof by reading, observing, or asking an expert.

- A statement of opinion tells ideas or feelings about something.

- Words such as *great, best,* and *worst* can be clues to statements of opinion.

Statement	Fact or Opinion?

 Strategy: Answer Questions

Good readers know where to look for answers to questions. Specific facts are particularly easy to locate. Sometimes the answer is right there in the text. Other times, you will have to combine what you already know with what is in the text. A fact in the text could be an answer to a question you are asked.

Write to Read ✏

1. Read "Paint." Look for statements of fact and statements of opinion in the article.

2. Make a chart like the one above. Fill in your chart as you read the article.

332

Strategic Intervention

 Fact and Opinion Have students work in small groups to complete p. 332. Encourage them to discuss whether each statement is a fact or an opinion.

ELL

Access Content

Beginning/Intermediate For a Picture It! lesson on fact and opinion, see the ELL Teaching Guide, pp. 190–191.

Advanced Before students read "Paint," demonstrate, through an experiment or a sequence of pictures, how paint is made. Help students become familiar with the terms *pigment, powder, liquid,* and *resin.*

Paint is one of the greatest things in the world. But what is it?

Paint has two main parts. The first is pigment, which is a powder that gives the paint its color. The other main part is a liquid, such as water. The liquid usually has something called a resin dissolved in it. To make paint, the pigment and the liquid are mixed together. After you paint a surface, the liquid part of the paint dries but the pigment stays on the surface. You should always buy the cheapest paint you can find.

1 **Skill** Here is a statement of fact. How can you tell?

People have been making and using paints for thousands of years. When people lived in caves, some of them used paints to make pictures on the walls. These paintings were a lot better than some of the modern art hanging in museums. Today, people still use paint to make pictures on walls. These pictures are called murals.

2 **Strategy** If you were asked the question "How long have people been making and using paints?" here's where you would find the answer—right there in the text.

333

Available as **Skill Transparency** 28

TEACH

1 **SKILL** Use paragraphs 1 and 2 to model differentiating between fact and opinion.

 MODEL As I read, I look for statements of fact and statements of opinion. I know that some statements of opinion may be written to sound like statements of fact. As a good reader, I have to recognize the difference.

2 **STRATEGY** Use the last paragraph to model answering a question.

 MODEL I read the question, "How long have people been making and using paints?" I believe this is a "Right There" question. I scan the text looking for the key words "people" and "making and using paints."

PRACTICE AND ASSESS

SKILL I know this is a statement of fact because it can be proven true. I can find proof by reading something else about making paint, observing someone making paint, or asking an expert.

STRATEGY People have been making paints for thousands of years.

WRITE Have students complete steps 1 and 2 of the Write to Read activity. You might consider using this as a whole class activity.

Monitor Progress

🔄 Fact and Opinion

If... students are unable to complete **Write to Read** on p. 332,	then... use Practice Book, 3.2 p. 123 to provide additional practice.

Fact and Opinion · Answer Questions

- A **statement of fact** tells something that can be proved true or false. You can prove it true or false by reading, observing, or asking an expert.
- A **statement of opinion** tells your ideas or feelings. It cannot be proved true or false.
- Words such as *great*, *best*, and *worst* can be clues to **statements of opinion**.

Directions Read the following passage and use the information to complete the Fact and Opinion Chart below.

What do *flesh, Prussian blue,* and *Indian red* have in common? They were all crayon colors. Some crayon colors were retired because they were dull. But *flesh, Prussian blue,* and *Indian red* were changed by one crayon maker for other reasons.

Peach replaced *flesh.* Everyone knows that skin comes in many shades, not just in one color. *Prussian blue* was changed to *midnight blue.* Most kids don't know much about Prussia.

Indian red is now *chestnut.* Some people thought the name stood for the skin color of Native Americans. Indian red is actually the name of an oil paint made in India that has a reddish color.

Directions Write the statements of fact from the passage in the left column. Write the statements of opinion in the right column.

Fact and Opinion Chart

Facts	Opinions
1. Flesh, Prussian blue, and Indian red were crayon colors.	4. Everyone knows that skin comes in many shades.
2. Some crayon colors were retired.	5. Most kids don't know much about Prussia.
3. Indian red is the name of a reddish oil paint made in India.	6. Some crayon colors were dull.

Home Activity Your child learned about the difference between statements of fact and statements of opinion. Choose a food your child likes and ask him or her to tell you about the food using three statements of fact and three statements of opinion.

Practice Book 3.2 p. 123

Tech Files
ONLINE

For a Web site that explores the life and work of a muralist featured in the selection, have students use a student-friendly search engine to do an Internet search using the muralist's name. For example, students can use the keywords *Hector Ponce mural.*

ELL

Build Background Use ELL Poster 28 to build background and vocabulary for the lesson concept of freedom of expression in a free society.

▲ **ELL Poster** 28

Build Background

ACTIVATE PRIOR KNOWLEDGE

BEGIN A WEB about freedom of expression.

- Have students write "freedom of expression" in the hub of the web. Ask them to think about what they know about freedom of expression, including why we value it in the United States. They should consider different forms of artistic expression.

- Tell students that, as they read, they should look for details about artistic expression and add information to the web.

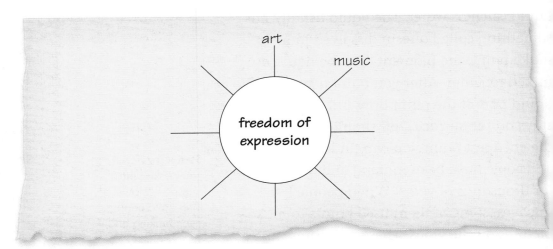

art

music

freedom of expression

▲ **Graphic Organizer** 14

BACKGROUND BUILDING AUDIO This week's audio presents an interview with a muralist. After students listen, discuss what they found out and what surprised them most about the muralist's work.

Background Building Audio

Introduce Vocabulary

WORD RATING CHART

Create word rating charts using the categories *Know*, *Have Seen*, and *Don't Know*.

Word Rating Chart

Word	Know	Have Seen	Don't Know
native		✔	
expression			✔
settled			
encourages			
support			
social			
local			

▲ **Graphic Organizer** 4

Read each word to students and have them place a check in one of the three columns: *Know* (know and can use); *Have Seen* (have heard or seen the word; don't know meaning); *Don't Know* (don't know the word).

Activate Prior Knowledge

Have students share where they may have seen some of these words. Point out that some of this week's words have a long vowel in the first syllable *(native, social, local)* and follow the syllable pattern V/CV.

Syllable Pattern V/CV

Check graphic organizers with students at the end of the week and have them make changes to their ratings.

Use the Multisyllabic Word Routine on p. DI·1 to help students read multisyllabic words.

Lesson Vocabulary

WORDS TO KNOW

T **encourages** gives someone courage or confidence; urges on

T **expression** the act of putting into words or visual medium

T **local** about a certain place, especially nearby; not far away

T **native** belonging to someone because of that person's birth

T **settled** set up the first towns and farms in an area

T **social** concerned with human beings as a group

T **support** to help; aid

MORE WORDS TO KNOW

canvas a type of cloth, often made of cotton

murals large paintings painted directly on a wall

residents people who live in a place

T = Tested Word

Vocabulary

Directions Match each word with its meaning. Draw a line to connect them.

Check the Words You Know
- encourages
- native
- settled
- social
- local
- expression
- support

1. support — provide help
2. native — someone born in a place
3. social — having to do with other people
4. encourages — urges
5. expression — a statement of an idea

Directions Write the word from the box that best completes each sentence below.

6. We moved to the United States and _____ in Houston. **settled**

7. My father always _____ me to study hard. **encourages**

8. My parents are active in _____ neighborhood sports. **local**

9. My cousin was born in Madrid, so she is a _____ of Spain. **native**

10. My parents _____ my team by cheering at all of my games. **support**

Write a Description
On a separate sheet of paper describe a painting that you think would look good on the wall of a building in your neighborhood. Use as many vocabulary words as possible. Students' writing should use vocabulary in a description of wall paintings they would like to see.

Home Activity Your child has identified and used vocabulary words from *Talking Walls: Art for the People*. Take a walking tour of your neighborhood. Encourage your child to use this week's vocabulary words as you talk about what you see.

▲ **Practice Book 3.2** p. 124

Vocabulary Strategy

🔵 Use a glossary to define unfamiliar words.

INTRODUCE

Discuss the glossary strategy for unfamiliar words using the steps on p. 334.

TEACH

- Have students read "Class Art," paying attention to how vocabulary is used.
- Model using a glossary to determine the meaning of *expression*.

Think Aloud **MODEL** The word *expression* begins with *ex*, so I look under these letters in the glossary. The next letter is *p*, then *r*. I find the word, but it has two definitions. I use each definition in the sentence and choose the one that makes sense. Here it is: "the act of putting into words or visual medium."

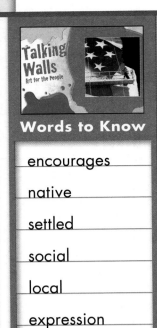

Words to Know

encourages
native
settled
social
local
expression
support

Vocabulary Strategy
for Unfamiliar Words

Glossary Sometimes you can use a glossary to find the meaning of an unknown word. A glossary is a list of important words in a book and their meanings. The words are listed in alphabetical order. The glossary is usually at the back of the book.

1. Turn to the glossary at the back of the book.

2. Use the first letters of the word to help you find it in the glossary.

3. Read the meaning of the word. Then try the meaning in the sentence. Does it make sense?

As you read "Class Art," use the glossary to find out the meanings of the vocabulary words.

334

DAY 2 Grouping Options

Reading

Whole Group Discuss the Question of the Day. Then use pp. 334–337.

Group Time Differentiated Instruction
Read *Talking Walls: Art for the People.* See pp. 332f–332g for the small group lesson plan.

Whole Group Use pp. 353a and 353i.

Language Arts
Use pp. 353e–353h and 353k–353m.

Strategic Intervention

🔵 **Glossary** Have students work in pairs to follow the steps on p. 334. Encourage them to list the words and their meanings, as given in a glossary.

ELL

Access Content Use ELL Poster 28 to preteach vocabulary. Choose from the following to meet language proficiency levels.

Beginning Point out the order of the letters in the word *native*. Have students use the letter order to find the word in a glossary and read its meaning.

Intermediate After reading, students can create their own glossary for the vocabulary words, listing them in alphabetical order and with a definition for each.

Advanced Teach the lesson on pp. 334–335. Students can make a glossary of these words as they are used in their home languages.

Resources for home-language words may include parents, bilingual staff members, bilingual dictionaries, or online translation sources.

Class Art

Ms. Ramsey's students are excited. They are planning to paint a mural on one wall in their classroom. Ms. Ramsey encourages the students to talk about what they will paint on the mural. Everyone has a different idea. Julio's family came to the United States from Mexico. He wants to paint something about his native country and his new country. Mary wants to paint something about the community's history. Her family settled here a long, long time ago. Gerrard thinks the mural should show the social life of the people who live in the community. Diana thinks the mural should be more about global, not local, issues. It should show how the community is part of the world. How can the students get all these ideas on one mural? Ms. Ramsey points out that the mural should be an expression of the group's interests and beliefs. She says that with a little planning, the students can paint a mural that will support everyone's ideas.

Words to Write

Imagine you and your classmates are going to paint a mural. Tell what you think the mural should show. Use words from the Words to Know list.

335

PRACTICE AND ASSESS

- Have students determine the meanings of the Words to Know and explain how they found their meanings in a glossary.
- Have students revise their Word Rating charts, reassessing their ratings.
- Have students complete Practice Book 3.2, p. 125.

WRITE Writing should include vocabulary words that describe the things that the student would put in the mural.

Monitor Progress

Glossary

If... students need more practice with the lesson vocabulary,	**then...** use Tested Vocabulary Cards.

Vocabulary • Reference Sources

- Sometimes you can use a **glossary** to find the meaning of an unknown word.
- A **glossary** is an alphabetical list of important words in a book.

Directions Look carefully at the partial glossary page below. The words are listed in alphabetical order, and guide words are at the top of the page. Use this glossary page to answer the questions.

send • synonym

set•tle (set'l), VERB.
  1. to move to and live in a place.
  2. to sink to the bottom of a liquid.

sketch (skech),
  1. NOUN. a quick drawing.
  2. VERB. to draw something quickly, to describe briefly.

so•cial (sō'shəl), ADJECTIVE.
  1. involving friends.
  2. related to human society.
  NOUN. a kind of party

sup•port (səpôrt'), VERB.
  1. to help or encourage.
  2. to provide with money.

sym•bol (sim'bəl), NOUN.
  1. something that stands for something else. 2. a sign.

1. Which word can be used to describe something an artist may make?
   sketch

2. Find the word *support*. Which meaning of *support* is used in this sentence: *I always support my friends in whatever they do.*
   to help or encourage

3. What are the guide words for this page?
   send and synonym

4. Which of these words would you find on this page? *safety, separate, section, tablet*
   separate

5. Which of these words would you **not** find on this glossary page? *seldom, slipper, speck, shove*
   seldom

Home Activity Your child identified and used new words by using a glossary to find their meanings. Read a nonfiction book that contains a glossary with your child and encourage using the glossary to find the meanings of unfamiliar words.

▲ **Practice Book 3.2** p. 125

Prereading Strategies

- Distinguish between fact and opinion to improve comprehension.
- Answer questions to distinguish between fact and opinion.

GENRE STUDY

Photo Essay

Talking Walls: Art for the People is a photo essay. A photo essay is a collection of photographs about one topic. The photographs and the text give information about the topic.

PREVIEW AND PREDICT

Have students preview the selection title and photographs. Ask students how walls might "talk." Encourage students to use lesson vocabulary as they talk about what they expect to learn.

Strategy Response Log

Generate Questions Write two questions that you want answered as you read the selection. Students will answer their questions in the Strategy Response Log activity on p. 343.

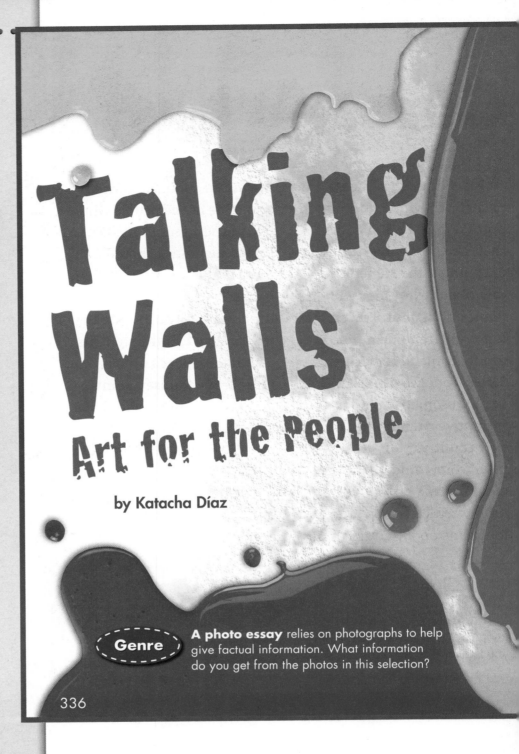

Talking Walls
Art for the People

by Katacha Díaz

Genre

A photo essay relies on photographs to help give factual information. What information do you get from the photos in this selection?

336

ELL

Activate Prior Knowledge Lead a picture walk through the selection. Encourage students to describe what they see in each photograph.

Consider having students read the selection summary in English or in students' home languages. See the Multilingual Summaries in the ELL Teaching Guide, pp. 194–196.

What do these talking walls have to say?

337

SET PURPOSE

Read the first page of the selection aloud to students. Have them consider their preview discussion and tell what they hope to find out as they read.

Remind students to look for facts and opinions as they read.

STRATEGY RECALL

Students have now used these before-reading strategies:

- preview the selection to be aware of its genre, features, and possible content;
- activate prior knowledge about that content and what to expect of that genre;
- make predictions;
- set a purpose for reading.

Remind students to be aware of and flexibly use the during-reading strategies they have learned:

- link prior knowledge to new information;
- summarize text they have read so far;
- ask clarifying questions;
- answer questions they or others pose;
- check their predictions and either refine them or make new predictions;
- recognize the text structure the author is using, and use that knowledge to make predictions and increase comprehension;
- visualize what the author is describing;
- monitor their comprehension and use fix-up strategies.

After reading, students will use these strategies:

- summarize or retell the text;
- answer questions they or others pose;
- reflect to make new information become part of their prior knowledge.

 **AudioText**

Guiding Comprehension

1 (REVIEW) **Main Idea and Details •**
Inferential

Reread p. 338, paragraph 3. What is the main idea and one supporting detail?

Main idea: Muralists paint many different kinds of murals. Supporting detail: "Others show special celebrations and community festivals."

Monitor Progress

(REVIEW) **Main Idea and Details**

If... students are unable to determine the main idea and supporting detail,	**then...** use the skill and strategy instruction on p. 339.

2 **Classify/Categorize • Critical**
Look at the mural shown on p. 339. How would you classify it using the descriptions and categories given on p. 338, paragraph 3?

Possible response: This is an outside mural that shows people celebrating.

Tech Files
ONLINE

Students can find out more about murals by searching the Internet. Have them use a student-friendly search engine and the keyword *mural*.

Immigrants travel to America from all over the world. They leave behind homes and villages in their native countries for the promise of a better life and for the freedom this country has to offer.

The people in America enjoy many different kinds of freedom, including the freedom of artistic expression. Writers, musicians, dancers, and artists are free to speak their minds through their art — in any way they choose. Do you know that some painters use walls as their canvas? These painted walls are called murals and are often painted in public places for all the people of the community to see.

1 Muralists are asked by a town, school, or business to create a work of art on a wall. Muralists paint many different kinds of murals. Some are inside, some are outside. Some tell the history of a town and everyday life of the people who settled there. Others show special celebrations and community festivals. Still others depict symbols of American freedom and democracy at work. All are great examples of artistic expression at its best. **2**

"Community of Music," Long Beach, California ▶

338

ELL

Extend Language Write the words *mural, murals, muralist,* and *muralists* on the board. Help students read each one. Give students the definition of "mural." Then help them understand the definition of the other words and how they are related.

SKILLS ⟷ STRATEGIES IN CONTEXT

Main Idea and Details REVIEW

TEACH

- Remind students that the main idea is what a paragraph or selection is mostly about. Supporting details give more information.

- Identifying the main idea helps us be better readers and understand what we read.

- Model identifying the main idea on p. 338, paragraph 3.

Think Aloud **MODEL** The topic of the paragraph is murals. The second sentence tells the most important idea, or the main idea, of the paragraph. Other sentences give more information about the main idea.

PRACTICE AND ASSESS

- Have students reread p. 338, paragraph 2. Ask which of the following is the main idea. (*Choice b*)

    a) The people in America enjoy many different kinds of freedom.

    b) Painted walls are called murals and are often painted in public places.

- To assess, use Practice Book 3.2, p. 126.

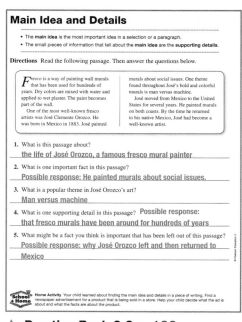

▲ **Practice Book 3.2** p. 126

Artists Speak for Their Cultures

Time for SOCIAL STUDIES

Artists often show images that reflect their cultures. They can depict the world around them or paint scenes from their community's history or mythology. Artists like Edgar Degas included images of Parisian life. Degas's paintings of ballet dancers, theaters, and cafés show us what life was like for some in France in the late 1800s. Muralist Diego Rivera used images of Mexican history and customs in his work. Jacob Lawrence's paintings show us the accomplishments and importance of African American hero Harriet Tubman. Other Lawrence works show us scenes from life in Harlem, his neighborhood in New York City. With their creations, artists leave lasting observations about their cultures.

339

Guiding Comprehension

3 **Text Structure • Inferential**

What did the author use for the heading on the page? Why?

Possible response: The author chose the title of the mural to be the heading for the text on the page. It helps readers understand that the text on the page is about this mural.

4 **Fact and Opinion • Critical**

What is one statement of fact about the photograph on p. 341? What is your opinion of the photograph?

Possible response: Fact: The mural was painted by Hector Ponce. Opinion: The mural represents all Latin American immigrants.

Monitor Progress

Fact and Opinion

If... students have difficulty distinguishing between fact and opinion,	then... use the skill and strategy instruction on p. 341.

EXTEND SKILLS

Text Features of Photo Essay

Remind students that authors organize their texts in different ways. Have students identify the features in the selection, including the headings, text, and photos. Then ask them to analyze the photo essay's text features and describe the selection's organization.

3 **Immigrant**

4 On the walls of a meat market in Los Angeles is a mural about immigrants painted by Hector Ponce. It tells the history of the people who live in the Pico and Hoover neighborhood. This mural, titled "Immigrant," shows the Statue of Liberty just beyond reach and Latin American immigrants working hard to provide for their families. Do you see a woman with young children, a man selling bags of oranges, a seamstress, and a man looking for cans to recycle?

Hector Ponce, the artist, came from El Salvador more than 15 years ago. He says, "My mural shows what's in the hearts of many people who come to this country looking for a better life."

▲ "Immigrant," Los Angeles, California ▶

340

Activate Prior Knowledge Encourage students to share what they learned through reading *The Story of the Statue of Liberty*. Invite them to share ideas about why Hector Ponce chose to include The Statue of Liberty in his mural "Immigrant."

Immigrants

Between 1897 and 1938, many immigrants to the United States entered through New York City's Ellis Island. Immigrants who arrived by steamship from across the Atlantic went through medical tests before being allowed to enter the country. At the peak of immigration, thousands of new arrivals were received each day. In the 1920s, immigration was cut back, and in 1954, Ellis Island was closed and remained unused for over 30 years. In 1990, after an eight-year rebuilding project, Ellis Island reopened as the Ellis Island Immigration Museum. Over 100 million Americans can trace their ancestry to someone who passed through Ellis Island. Now tourists can relive their ancestors' immigration experiences through exhibits and use the museum's database to view the steamship lists on which their family members' names appear.

SKILLS ↔ STRATEGIES IN CONTEXT

Fact and Opinion

TEACH

- Remind students that a statement of fact is a statement that can be proven true or false. A statement of opinion is a statement of someone's judgment, belief, or way of thinking about something. Statements of opinion can be supported or explained.

- Clue words, such as *worst, should,* and *all,* can signal a statement of opinion.

- Model distinguishing between a statement of fact and a statement of opinion relating to the top photograph on p. 341.

MODEL I know that Hector Ponce painted the mural. This is a statement of fact that can be proven true or false. I could check in a book or consult an expert to determine if the statement is true or false. A statement of opinion can be explained, but it cannot be proven true or false. I could say that the mural represents all Latin American immigrants. That is a statement of opinion that can be explained but not proven true or false.

PRACTICE AND ASSESS

Have students identify a statement of fact and a statement of opinion on p. 340. (Statement of fact: "Hector Ponce, the artist, came from El Salvador more than 15 years ago." Statement of opinion: "He says, 'My mural shows what's in the hearts of many people who come to this country looking for a better life.'")

Talking Walls **341**

Guiding Comprehension

5 Draw Conclusions • Critical

Text to World **Why do you think a muralist would want to talk with the people of the community before he paints a mural there?**

Possible response: A muralist sometimes paints murals showing things important to the community. Talking to people who live there helps the muralist understand what is important to them.

6 Answer Questions • Inferential

Reread the last sentence on p. 342. Is this a statement of fact or a statement of opinion? How do you know?

This is a statement of opinion. It is someone's belief and can be supported. It cannot be proven true or false.

7 Theme • Inferential

What is the theme of "Reach High and You Will Go Far"?

Possible answers: Growing; success through education.

Reach High and You Will Go Far

Before artist Joshua Sarantitis creates a mural, he talks with the people of the community. He listens to their stories about the neighborhood. He interprets their stories by making sketches, and then he makes plans for the painting of the mural. **5**

Over the years, Sarantitis has created many public murals across America, including "Reach High and You Will Go Far." This mural honors the hopes and dreams of the many children who live in a downtown neighborhood in Philadelphia. The painting is beautiful. It shows a young girl with her arms held high. Her hands and fingers become a tree rising over the building. The artist fashioned the top of the tree as a billboard extending above the roof to show how **7 6** people can grow and change. The mural encourages children to reach for the future through education.

"Reach High and You Will Go Far,"
Philadelphia, Pennsylvania ▶

342

ELL

Understanding Idioms Help students understand the meaning of the title of the mural. Have them restate the meaning in their own words. For example: "learn a lot in school and you will succeed in what you try."

HIGH AND YOU WILL GO FAR
...hua Sarantitis & EDMAP
...erica Mendosamichi and Joy Epute

343

 STRATEGY SELF-CHECK

Answer Questions

Have students identify a statement of fact and a statement of opinion in the text on p. 342. Remind them to use the Answer Questions strategy when distinguishing between statements of fact and opinion. Students should answer the "On My Own" question of "Can the statement be proven true or false?" *(Possible responses: Statement of opinion: The painting is beautiful. Statement of fact: It shows a young girl with her arms held high.)*

SELF-CHECK

Students can ask themselves these questions to assess their ability to use the skill and strategy.

- Did I distinguish between statements of fact and statements of opinion as I read?
- Did I answer the question "Can the statement be proven true or false?" for each statement?
- Did I answer the question with a complete and correct response?

Monitor Progress	
Fact and Opinion	
If... students have difficulty distinguishing between fact and opinion,	**then...** revisit the skill lesson on pp. 332–333. Reteach as necessary.

 Strategy Response Log

Answer Questions Have students revisit their questions in their Strategy Response Log and answer them if possible.

If you want to teach this selection in two sessions, stop here.

Develop Vocabulary

PRACTICE LESSON VOCABULARY

Have students provide oral responses to each question.

1. **What do we mean when we say people *settled* somewhere?** (*When you* settle *somewhere, you choose to live there.*)
2. **Painting is one form of *expression*. Can you think of another?** (*Dance is another form of* expression.)
3. **Who is someone that *encourages* you?** (*My teacher* encourages *me to do my best.*)

BUILD CONCEPT VOCABULARY

Review previous concept words with students. Ask if students have come across any words today in their reading or elsewhere that they would like to add to the Concept Web.

Guiding Comprehension

If you are teaching the selection in two days, discuss the main ideas so far and review the vocabulary.

8 Compare and Contrast • Critical

How are the murals "A Shared Hope" and "Reach High and You Will Go Far" alike?

Possible response: They both show students the importance of education.

9 Vocabulary • Glossary

How can you use a glossary to learn the meaning of the word "support" on p. 345, paragraph 1?

A glossary is at the back of some books. It lists words in alphabetical order and gives a definition of each word.

Monitor Progress
⟳ **Glossary**

If... students have difficulty using a glossary to learn the meaning of unknown words,	**then...** use the vocabulary strategy instruction on p. 345.

DAY 3 Grouping Options

Reading
Whole Group Discuss the Question of the Day.

Group Time Differentiated Instruction
Read *Talking Walls: Art for the People.* See pp. 332f–332g for the small group lesson plan.

Whole Group Discuss the Reader Response questions on p. 350. Then use p. 353a.

Language Arts
Use pp. 353e–353h and 353k–353m.

A Shared Hope

Paul Botello was 8 years old when he began helping his older brother, David, paint murals. Paul loved painting murals and was inspired to become an artist like his brother. When Paul graduated from high school, he went on to college to study art. Today he creates and paints murals, and he teaches art too!

Paul painted a special mural called "A Shared Hope" for an elementary school in Los Angeles, California. Most of the students at Esperanza School are immigrants from Central America. The mural speaks to the schoolchildren. It tells them that education is the key to success. **8**

344

ELL

Extend Language Help students understand the meaning of unfamiliar phrases such as "The mural speaks to the students" and "the building blocks of life."

At the top of the mural, a teacher helps guide her students over the building blocks of life. Students are standing at the bottom of the painting holding objects that symbolize their future. Their parents stand behind to help guide and support them.

Teachers, students, and parents from the school posed for the artist and his assistants as they created the mural.

"Education, hope, and immigration are my themes," says Paul Botello. "People immigrate to the United States because they hope for a better life. Through education, a better life can be accomplished."

"A Shared Hope," Los Angeles, California

345

Freedom of Speech (Bill of Rights)

The first ten amendments, or changes, to the Constitution of the United States are called The Bill of Rights. They address the rights of individual citizens. Many people think one subject of the first amendment—freedom of speech—is our most important right because what we express defines who we are. The amendment allows you to share your opinions with others. It is still hotly debated in courts and among citizens because we all have different ideas about what "freedom of speech" means. Some people want to limit speech that can hurt or offend people, but others say that not one person can decide if an opinion is offensive to someone else.

VOCABULARY STRATEGY
Glossary

TEACH

- Remind students that a glossary often appears in nonfiction books. It provides an alphabetical list of words from the text and gives their definitions.

- Model using the glossary to learn the meaning of the unknown word *support*.

Think Aloud **MODEL** I read the sentence "Their parents stand behind to help guide and support them." I do not know the meaning of the word *support*. I know that the glossary lists words in alphabetical order, so I will turn toward the end of the glossary to find words that begin with *s*. I locate the word *support* and read the definition. ("to help; aid")

PRACTICE AND ASSESS

Have students use the glossary to locate the meaning of the word *murals*. Point out that though the word *murals* appears in the text, the singular *mural* appears in the glossary.

Guiding Comprehension

10 🎯 **Fact and Opinion • Inferential**

"Dreams of Flight" is David Botello's best work. Is this a statement of fact or opinion? How do you know?

This is a statement of opinion. It cannot be proven true or false. It is someone's belief.

Monitor Progress
🎯 **Fact and Opinion**

If... students are unable to differentiate between statements of fact and opinion,	then... use the skill and strategy instruction on p. 347.

11 **Paraphrase • Inferential**

In your own words, tell the meaning of David Botello's mural "Dreams of Flight."

Possible response: "Dreams of Flight" encourages students to believe in themselves and follow their dreams.

Dreams of Flight

David Botello—the older brother of Paul—loved to paint and dreamed of becoming an artist. When he was in the third grade, he and his art partner, Wayne Healy, painted a mural of a dinosaur in art class. Little did David know that that dinosaur mural was the first of many murals he would paint with Wayne.

Years later, the childhood friends, now both artists, decided to go into business together painting murals. David and Wayne often create and paint murals together, but not always.

David painted a large mural called "Dreams of Flight" at Estrada Courts, a public housing project in Los Angeles. He says, "I've always wanted this mural to speak to the children who see it, and to say, 'Your dreams can come true.'"

346

ELL

Fluency Help students read sentences with appropriate pausing. For example, the first sentence on p. 346 should be read: David Botello / the older brother of Paul / loved to paint / and dreamed of / becoming an artist. Make sure students do not "chunk" "loved to paint and dreamed" because this changes the meaning of the sentence.

It's interesting to note that when the artist repainted the mural seventeen years after it was originally completed, he changed one of the children from a boy to a girl. Much had changed over the years, and the artist wanted all children to know that girls can dream of flying model airplanes too. It is the artist's hope that over time the mural will inspire many of the children who see it to work hard and follow their dreams. **10** **11**

"Dreams of Flight," Los Angeles, California

Fact and Opinion Answer Questions

TEACH

- Remind students that a fact can be proven true or false. When reading, we must decide if a statement is fact or opinion. Then we should decide if facts are true or false.

- State a fact about the weather that is false, such as "It is 120° outside." Ask students to determine whether the statement is a fact or opinion. Lead them to recognize that the statement is a fact, but it is false. You can read a thermometer to check the accuracy of the statement.

- Model distinguishing between statements of fact and statements of opinion.

Think Aloud

MODEL I read a statement and ask myself, "Can it be proven true or false?" It cannot be proven to be true or false if there is no source to prove or disprove it. It is not a statement of fact. Then I ask myself, "Is the statement someone's belief that can be supported, but cannot be proven true or false?" Yes, it is someone's belief. I may agree or disagree with the statement, but it cannot be proven true or false.

PRACTICE AND ASSESS

Have students identify a statement of fact from pp. 346–347. *(Possible response: Statement of fact: David painted a large mural called "Dreams of Flight."*

Guiding Comprehension

12 **Details and Facts • Literal**

Where can you see Allyn Cox's mural "Declaration of Independence, 1776"?

In the U.S. Capitol in Washington, D.C.

13 **Answer Questions • Critical**

Text to Self **Which mural in the selection is your favorite? How does the mural "talk" to you?**

Possible response: My favorite mural is "Reach High and You Will Go Far." It reminds me to set high goals and work to achieve them.

14 **Summarize • Inferential**

Explain how murals are "talking walls."

Possible response: Murals are painted on *walls*. They do not really *talk*, but the art has a message.

Strategy Response Log

Summarize When students finish reading the selection, provide this prompt: Imagine that you want to tell a friend what *Talking Walls: Art for the People* is about. In four or five sentences, explain its important points.

Talking Walls

Cities, large and small, invite artists to paint special murals in public places for everyone to see. Murals are talking walls; they speak to the people.

Community murals tell stories of personal, political, and social beliefs of the local residents. Some murals inspire or amuse us, while others stir our hearts.

"Declaration of Independence, 1776" was painted by Allyn Cox in the U.S. Capitol, Washington, D.C. **12**

348

ELL

Understanding Idioms Read the last sentence on p. 348 with students. Help them understand the meaning of the term "stir our hearts."

From sea to shining sea, the artists who create art for the people are instrumental in reminding Americans everywhere of the freedoms that help our democracy work. **13** **14**

Muralists use scaffolding to reach large murals.

The "American Flag" mural was painted by Meg Saligman in Philadelphia, Pennsylvania. ▼

349

Develop Vocabulary

PRACTICE LESSON VOCABULARY

Have students orally respond to each question and provide a reason for each answer.

1. **What is your *native* country?** (*Responses will vary.*)
2. **You have a friend that lives in another state. Is that *local*?** (*No, another state is usually not in or near our community. It is not local.*)
3. **Is going to a birthday party a *social* activity?** (*Yes, you have a party with other people.*)

BUILD CONCEPT VOCABULARY

Review previous concept words with students. Ask if students have come across any words today in their reading or elsewhere that they would like to add to the Concept Web.

 STRATEGY SELF-CHECK

Answer Questions

Have students identify their favorite mural from the selection. As they formulate their responses and explanations, have them identify their statements as fact or opinion and explain their reasoning.

SELF-CHECK

Students can ask themselves these questions to assess their ability to use the skill and strategy.

- Did I make a statement of opinion about my favorite mural?
- How do I know it is a statement of opinion rather than a statement of fact?
- To assess, use Practice Book 3.2, p. 127.

Monitor Progress
🔁 **Fact and Opinion**

If... students are having difficulty distinguishing between fact and opinion as they answer questions,	then... use the Reteach lesson on p. 353b.

Fact and Opinion • Answer Questions

- A **statement of fact** tells something that can be proved true or false. You can prove it true or false by reading, observing, or asking an expert.
- A **statement of opinion** tells your ideas or feelings. It cannot be proved true or false.

Directions Read the following passage. Then answer the questions below.

Guernica was a small city in Spain. The people who lived there didn't want to be under Spanish rule. At first, they held meetings under an oak tree. The tree became a symbol of freedom. Later, they built a place to meet behind the tree. Soldiers attacked the city during the Spanish Civil War and destroyed it—all except for the tree and the building. It was good that they were not destroyed.

Pablo Picasso, a famous artist, painted a mural about the bombing. He thought that war was a terrible waste and tried to show it in the mural. All the people, animals, and buildings in the mural were painted in black and white. Many people believe that this mural was Picasso's greatest work of art.

1. Write one statement of fact about the oak tree.
   Possible response: It was where the people held meetings.

2. Write one statement of opinion about the oak tree.
   Possible response: It was good that it wasn't destroyed.

3. Write one statement of fact about Picasso's mural.
   Possible response: The mural is painted in black and white.

4. Write one statement of opinion about Picasso's mural.
   Possible response: Some people believe it was his best work.

5. Answer the question: *Why did Picasso paint the mural in only black and white?*
   Possible response: Maybe Picasso thought it would make it very dramatic.

Home Activity Your child learned about the difference between statements of fact and statements of opinion. Read a story with your child. Have him or her write three statements of fact and three statements of opinion about the story. For example, FACT: The story is about three pigs. OPINION: They were too young to go out on their own.

▲ **Practice Book 3.2** p. 127

Reader Response

Open for Discussion Personal Response

Think Aloud **MODEL** I would make a list of people and events that have been important in my life, then paint everyone having fun and celebrating.

Comprehension Check Critical Response

1. Students should read sentences that provide more information about a featured mural. ***Author's Purpose***

2. Possible response: Ask the muralists whether the facts are true or false. Clue word: *best* 🔊 ***Fact and Opinion***

3. The book states that Paul and David Botello live in California. 🔊 ***Answer Questions***

4. Responses will vary but should show an understanding of the words and an explanation of the sentence. 🔊 ***Vocabulary***

 Look Back and Write For test practice, assign a 10–15 minute time limit. For assessment, see the Scoring Rubric at the right.

Retell

Have students retell *Talking Walls: Art for the People*.

Monitor Progress

Check Retelling [Rubric 4 3 2 1]

If... students have difficulty retelling the selection,	then... use the Retelling Cards and the Scoring Rubric on p. 351 to assist fluent retelling.

SUCCESS PREDICTOR

 **ELL**

Check Retelling Have students use photographs and other text features to guide their retellings. Let students listen to other retellings before attempting their own. See the ELL and Transition Handbook.

Reader Response

Open for Discussion Look once more at the murals shown in this article. Now it is your turn. Describe an important mural you would plan and paint.

1. An author can help you look at art. Read sentences by Katacha Díaz that help you understand and enjoy the art in this article. **Think Like an Author**

2. This selection is full of facts. What could you do to prove that these are true facts? Now look on page 338. What clue word signals an opinion on this page? **Fact and Opinion**

3. This selection tells about two brothers who are both muralists. Who are they and where do they live? Is the answer in the book or in your head? **Answer Questions**

4. Explain this statement: Murals are a public form of artistic expression. Use words from the Words to Know list and from the selection. **Vocabulary**

 Look Back and Write Why did David Botello change his mural after 17 years? Look back at page 347. Use information from the selection to support your answer.

Meet author Katacha Diaz on page 416.

Scoring Rubric | **Look Back and Write**

Top-Score Response A top-score response will use information from p. 347 of the selection to explain why David Botello changed his mural after 17 years.

Example of a Top-Score Response David Botello saw that many things had changed. His mural was 17 years old. He changed the mural by making one of the children a girl rather than a boy. He did this to help children see that both boys and girls can dream of flying.

For additional rubrics, see p. WA10.

Write Now

Informational Paragraph

Prompt

Talking Walls describes special murals. Think about a kind of art that you know well. Now write an informational paragraph about this kind of art.

Writing Trait

Organize your writing by arrranging your ideas in a **paragraph.**

Paragraph begins with sentence that grabs readers' attention.

Sequence words help <u>organize</u> steps in process.

Last sentence returns to topic of art mentioned in opening sentence.

Student Model

Clay can't move by itself, but a special kind of art can make clay look like it's moving. Clay animation begins with a story. Then an artist draws pictures like a cartoon and uses the pictures to make characters out of clay. Next, the artist films the characters. After moving the characters a tiny bit each time, the artist takes a picture. Later, when you watch the film, the clay characters look like they're moving. This kind of art takes a long time to make, but it's fun to watch clay come to life!

Use the model to help you write your own informational paragraph.

Write Now

Look at the Prompt Explain that each sentence in the prompt has a purpose.

- Sentence 1 presents a topic.
- Sentence 2 suggests students think about the topic.
- Sentence 3 tells what to write—an informational paragraph.

Strategies to Develop Organization/ Paragraphs

Have students

- use clear supporting details.
- use transitions such as *first, because,* and *when* to relate ideas.
  <u>Because</u> Zoe wants a certain blue, she mixes two colors.
- add a strong conclusion.
  A blank canvas has become a work of art.

For additional suggestions and rubric, see pp. 353g–353h.

Writer's Checklist

☑ **Focus** Does the topic stay the same through the entire paragraph?

☑ **Organization** Does the paragraph have a strong beginning and a clear conclusion?

☑ **Support** Do all details support the topic of the paragraph?

☑ **Conventions** Is the first sentence of the paragraph indented?

351

Scoring Rubric — Expository Retelling

Rubric 4 3 2 1	4	3	2	1
Connections	Makes connections and generalizes beyond the text	Makes connections to other events, texts, or experiences	Makes a limited connection to another event, text, or experience	Makes no connection to another event, text, or experience
Author's Purpose	Elaborates on author's purpose	Tells author's purpose with some clarity	Makes some connection to author's purpose	Makes no connection to author's purpose
Topic	Describes the main topic	Identifies the main topic with some details early in retelling	Identifies the main topic	Retelling has no sense of topic
Important Ideas	Gives accurate information about events, steps, and ideas using details and key vocabulary	Gives accurate information about events, steps, and ideas with some detail and key vocabulary	Gives limited or inaccurate information about events, steps, and ideas	Gives no information about events, steps, and ideas
Conclusions	Draws conclusions and makes inferences to generalize beyond the text	Draws conclusions about the text	Is able to draw few conclusions about the text	Is unable to draw conclusions or make inferences about the text

Retelling Plan

☑ **Week 1** Assess Strategic Intervention students.

☑ **Week 2** Assess Advanced students.

☑ **This week assess Strategic Intervention students.**

☐ **Week 4** Assess On-level students.

☐ **Week 5** Assess any students you have not yet checked during this unit.

Use the Retelling Chart on p. TR17 to record retelling.

Selection Test To assess with *Talking Walls: Art for the People,* use Selection Tests, pp. 109–112.

Fresh Reads for Differentiated Test Practice For weekly leveled practice, use pp. 163–168.

Retelling

SUCCESS PREDICTOR

Poetry

PREVIEW/USE TEXT FEATURES

As students preview "Nathaniel's Rap," have them identify the point of view and the punctuation. Ask:

- **How do you know the poem is written in the first person?** (The use of words such as me, I'm, my, and I.)

- **There are no commas or end marks in the first part of this poem. As a reader, how do you know when to pause?** (You pause before lines that begin with capital letters.)

Link to Reading

Provide children with examples of children's poetry. Encourage them to pay attention to the punctuation when reading a poem aloud.

DAY 4 Grouping Options

Reading
Whole Group Discuss the Question of the Day.

Group Time Differentiated Instruction
Read "Nathaniel's Rap." See pp. 332f–332g for the small group lesson plan.

Whole Group Use pp. 353a and 353j.

Language Arts
Use pp. 353e–353h and 353k–353m.

Poetry

Nathaniel's Rap
by Eloise Greenfield

Genre

- **Poetry can be a way to express feelings.**

- **Poems are a mixture of words with rhythm, which may or may not rhyme.**

Text Features

- **This poem is written in the first person.**

- **There is very little punctuation in this poem. Why do you think the writer chose this approach?**

Link to Reading

With a partner, search the library for a poem or rap that you enjoy. Together, recite your choice to the class.

It's Nathaniel talking
and Nathaniel's me
I'm talking about
my philosophy
About the things I do
And the people I see
All told in the words
Of Nathaniel B. Free
That's me
And I can rap
I can rap
I can
rap,
rap,
rap
Till your earflaps flap

I can talk that talk
Till you go for a walk
I can run it on down
Till you get out of town

I can rap
I can rap

Content-Area Vocabulary	**Social Studies**
philosophy	the way one thinks and lives one's life
rap	a music style in which rhythmic speech is chanted to music
kin	family members

d, dressed and feeling fine
got something on my mind
ds and kin and neighborhood
n now and listen good
aniel's talking
aniel B. Free
ng about
hilosophy

thinking all day
a lot to say
a run it on down
aniel's way
v!
tta rap
tta rap
tta rap, rap, rap
our earflaps flap
a talk that talk
ou go for a walk
a run it on down
ou get out of town

Gotta rap
Gotta rap

Rested, dressed and feeling fine
I've got something on my mind
Friends and kin and neighborhood
Listen now and listen good

I'm gonna rap, hey!

Gonna rap, hey!

Gonna rap, hey!

I'm gonna rap!

Reading Across Texts

The selection about murals and this rap poem tell of different forms of expression. What is one message you learned from each selection?

Writing Across Texts

Write the message that means the most to you and tell why.

 Rhythm | Snap your fingers or tap your toes as you read. Does it help?

353

POEM

Use the sidebar on p. 352 to guide discussion.

- A poem has rhythm and may or may not include rhymes.
- When you read a poem, emphasize the rhythm. The author often uses punctuation to help you know when to pause.
- Discuss with students how a rap sounds.

 **AudioText**

CONNECT TEXT TO TEXT

Reading Across Texts

Encourage discussion about the artistic expression in both selections. Record the "messages" in a list on the board for the Writing Across Texts activity.

Writing Across Texts Explain that there is not a right or wrong answer. We all appreciate art in different ways.

Rhythm

Demonstrate how clapping or toe-tapping helps you read the poem with the correct rhythm.

EXTEND SKILLS

Punctuation in Poetry

Explain that poets often use punctuation to help readers recite and understand a poem. Suggest that students read the first part of a poem and look for punctuation. Each line may not be a sentence. Use punctuation and capitalization to help you read the poem correctly.

Fluency Assessment Plan

- ☑ **Week 1** Assess Advanced students.
- ☑ **Week 2** Assess Strategic Intervention students.
- ☑ **This week assess On-Level students.**
- ☐ **Week 4** Assess Strategic Intervention students.
- ☐ **Week 5** Assess any students you have not yet checked during this unit.

Set individual goals for students to enable them to reach the year-end goal.
- Current Goal: 110–120 WCPM
- Year-End Goal: 120 WCPM

 **Fluency Coach CD** To develop fluent readers, use Fluency Coach.

MORE READING FOR
Fluency

 To practice fluency with text comprised of previously taught phonics elements and irregular words, use Decodable Reader 28.

DAY 5 Grouping Options

Reading
Whole Group
Revisit the Question of the Week.

Group Time
Differentiated Instruction
Reread this week's Leveled Readers. See pp. 332f–332g for the small group lesson plan.

Whole Group
Use pp. 353b–353c.

Language Arts
Use pp. 353d–353h and 353k–353n.

READING SILENTLY WITH FLUENCY AND ACCURACY
Fluency

DAY 1

Model Reread "Indescribably Arabella" on p. 332m. Explain that good silent readers focus on the material they are reading. Good readers read words correctly and self-correct when they misread a word. Model for students as you first read aloud and then read silently.

DAY 2

Silent Reading Read aloud p. 344. Tell students that good silent readers read carefully and correct words that they read incorrectly. Have students notice how you self-correct when you misread a word. Have students read p. 344 silently two times.

DAY 3

Model Silent Reading Read aloud p. 347. Have students notice how you self-correct as you read aloud and then silently. Have students practice reading this page silently three times.

DAY 4

Choral Reading Choral read "Nathaniel's Rap," pp. 352–353, three times. Students should read with rhythm and expression.

Monitor Progress | Check Fluency WCPM

As students reread, monitor their progress toward their individual fluency goals. Current Goal: 110–120 words correct per minute. End-of-Year Goal: 120 words correct per minute.

If... students cannot read fluently at a rate of 110–120 words correct per minute,
then... make sure students practice with text at their independent level. Provide additional fluency practice, pairing nonfluent readers with fluent readers.

If... students already read at 120 words correct per minute,
then... they need not reread three to four times.

SUCCESS PREDICTOR

DAY 5

Assessment
Individual Reading Rate Use the Fluency Assessment Plan and do a one-minute timed reading of either selection from this week to assess students in Week 3. Pay special attention to this week's skill, reading silently with fluency and accuracy. Provide corrective feedback for each student.

RETEACH

Fact and Opinion

TEACH

Review the difference between a statement of fact and a statement of opinion. Tell students that even when they read nonfiction, authors sometimes include opinions. Students should remember that a statement of fact can be proven to be correct or incorrect while an opinion gives thoughts or ideas and are not right or wrong. Students can complete Practice Book 3.2, p. 128, on their own, or you can complete it as a class. Students may need to paraphrase or rewrite statements.

ASSESS

Have partners use p. 338 in their books to determine a statement of fact and a statement of opinion. *(Fact—Some murals are inside and others are outside. Opinion—All are great examples of artistic expression at its best.)*

For additional instruction for fact and opinion, see DI•54.

EXTEND SKILLS

Rhythm/Cadence

TEACH

Rhythm is the pattern of sounds in speech or writing. Many poems have an obvious rhythm. However, all writing has rhythm.

• To understand a selection's rhythm, it is best to read aloud.

• Use punctuation as a guide as to when to stop, pause, and continue.

Work with students to identify the rhythm in the last paragraph on p. 338. Invite them to read the paragraph aloud to hear the flow of the language.

ASSESS

Have students work individually to read aloud the first paragraph on p. 346. Encourage them to identify the flow of language. Ask:

1. **Did you use punctuation clues to help you read with the correct rhythm?**

2. **Did reading aloud help you recognize the rhythm?**

OBJECTIVES

○ Distinguish between statements of fact and opinion.

● Identify rhythm in selections.

Skills Trace	
Fact and Opinion	
Introduce/Teach	TE: 3.4 86-87, 3.5 170-171, 3.6 332-333
Practice	PB: 3.2 33, 37, 38, 63, 67, 68, 86, 96, 123, 127, 128
Reteach/Review	**TE: 3.4 111b, DI•55; 3.5 193b, 229, 265, DI•53; 3.6 353b, DI•54**
Test	Selection Test, Unit 6

Access Content Reteach the skill by reviewing the Picture It! lesson on fact and opinion in the ELL Teaching Guide, pp. 190–191.

Fact and Opinion

• A **statement of fact** tells something that can be proved true or false. You can prove it true or false by reading, observing, or asking an expert.
• A **statement of opinion** tells your ideas or feelings. It cannot be proved true or false.

Directions Read the following passage and use the information to complete the Fact and Opinion Chart below.

Angel Island was the main immigration station in the West. Mostly Chinese immigrants came through Angel Island. Some were there for weeks and some for months. That's a long time to wait. Years later, the buildings were supposed to be torn down. It's a good thing they weren't because Chinese writing was found on the walls. The writing was carved into the walls where the people stayed. The writing turned out to be poems. Who wrote these poems? Why were they written? They were written by the immigrants. They told the stories of their long wait.

Directions Write the statements of fact from the passage in the left column. Write the statements of opinion in the right column.

Facts	Opinions
1. Angel Island was the main immigration station in the West.	4. Waiting for weeks and months is a long time to wait.
2. Some Chinese immigrants stayed there for a long time.	5. It was a good thing that the buildings weren't torn down.
3. Poems written in Chinese were found on the walls.	

6. Who wrote the poems, and what were they about?
<u>People waiting to enter the United States wrote them about their experiences while they waited.</u>

School + Home Home Activity Your child learned about the difference between statements of fact and statements of opinion. Help your child write a poem about a recent experience he or she had. Discuss the poem's statements of fact and statements of opinion.

▲ **Practice Book 3.2** p. 128

Vocabulary and Word Study

UNFAMILIAR WORDS Remind students that they can use the glossary at the back of a book to find the meaning of some unfamiliar words. Have students list any unknown words they encountered as they read *Talking Walls.* They can create a chart showing the unknown word and its glossary definition.

Word	Glossary Definition
immigrants	people who enter a new country to live after having left their native country
festival	
honors	

Art Words

Some words, such as *painter,* refer to visual art. Have partners use reference sources to make lists of art-related words and their meanings or examples. Students can create art using one of the art forms they researched.

Some Art Words

painting: a painted picture	ceramics:
mural:	photography:
sculpture:	enamel:
mobile:	watercolor:
collage:	etching:

BUILD CONCEPT VOCABULARY
Freedom of Expression

LOOKING BACK Remind students of the focus question of the week: Why is freedom of expression important? Discuss how this week's Concept Web of vocabulary words relates to the theme of freedom of expression. Ask students if they have any words or categories to add. Discuss whether words and categories are appropriately related to the concept.

MOVING FORWARD Preview the title of the next selection, *Two Bad Ants.* Ask students which Concept Web words might apply to the new selection based on the title alone. Put a star next to these words on the web.

Display the Concept Web and revisit the vocabulary words as you read the next selection to check predictions.

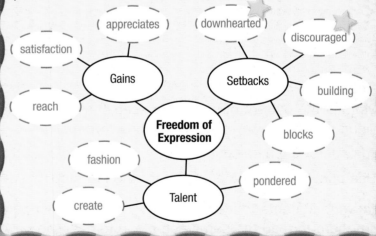

Monitor Progress

Check Vocabulary

If... students suggest words or categories that are not related to the concept,	then... review the words and categories on the Concept Web and discuss how they relate to the lesson concept.

SUCCESS PREDICTOR

Speaking and Viewing

Interview

SET-UP Groups of students act out talk shows having one host and several guests. Students who portray guests decide what they do for a living and why they have been invited. Hosts prepare questions they will ask during the interview.

REHEARSE Remind students to wait for questions to be asked or answered before they ask another question or respond. Remind hosts to listen closely to answers and to look directly at the person to whom they are speaking. Provide time for students to rehearse their talk shows.

SPACE Help students set up a stage area similar to those seen on television talk shows. The host is seated in a chair to one side, often with a desk, and several chairs are placed to one side of the host for the guests. Notice that usually the guests sit to the host's right.

Rehearsal Tips

- Look at the person you are speaking to.
- Ask questions in a logical order.
- Make sure an answer is completed before asking the next question.
- Express interest in guests and vice versa.

Analyze Artwork

Have students study the photograph of the U.S. Capitol mural "Declaration of Independence, 1776" on p. 348. With partners, they can answer these questions orally or in writing.

1. **What are the men doing?** *(The men are shaking hands, sitting around a table, and signing their names on the Declaration of Independence.)*

2. **This mural is in the U.S. Capitol. If this mural could talk, what would it say?** *(Responses will vary.)*

3. **How do you think people feel when they look at this painting? Why?** *(Possible response: People feel proud and happy to be living in America. Seeing the mural reminds them of the history of our country and why we have freedom.)*

Support Vocabulary Use the following to review and extend vocabulary and to explore lesson concepts further:
- ELL Poster 28, Days 3–5 instruction
- Vocabulary Activities and Word Cards in ELL Teaching Guide, pp. 192–193

Assessment For information on assessing students' speaking, listening, and viewing, see the ELL and Transition Handbook.

Grammar Combining Sentences

OBJECTIVES

- Define combining sentences.
- Use sentence combining in writing.
- Become familiar with sentence combining assessment on high-stakes tests.

Monitor Progress

Grammar

If... students have difficulty with combining sentences,	then... see The Grammar and Writing Book pp. 212–215.

DAILY FIX-IT

This week use Daily Fix-It Transparency 28.

Spiral REVIEW

Support Grammar See the Grammar Transition lessons in the ELL and Transition Handbook.

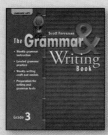

▲ **The Grammar and Writing Book**
For more instruction and practice, use pp. 212–217.

DAY 1 Teach and Model

DAILY FIX-IT

1. Carlos and Maria created a mural about they're cullture. *(their; culture)*

2. The class helped Carlos and she with the desine. *(her; design)*

READING-GRAMMAR CONNECTION

Write these sentences from *Talking Walls* on the board:

The mural speaks to the school children. It tells them that education is the key to success.

Explain that the two sentences could be combined into one sentence: *The mural speaks to the school children and tells them that education is the key to success.*

Display Grammar Transparency 28. Read aloud the definitions and sample sentences. Work through the items.

Combining Sentences

When you **combine sentences,** you join two sentences that are about the same topic. You make them into one sentence.
- You can join two simple sentences and make a compound sentence. Add a comma and a conjunction such as *and, but,* or *or.*
  Our class will paint a mural. We don't know when.
  Our class will paint a mural, but we don't know when.
- You can combine two sentences that have the same subject.
  The mural had bright colors. The mural showed many people.
  The mural had bright colors and showed many people.
- You can combine two sentences that have the same predicate.
  Michael liked the mural. I liked the mural.
  Michael and I liked the mural.

Directions Combine each pair of short sentences into a compound sentence. Use a comma and the conjunction in ( ).

1. People in France explored caves. They found murals. (and)
   <u>People in France explored caves, and they found murals.</u>

2. Were the murals painted by modern people? Were they painted by cave people long ago? (or)
   <u>Were the murals painted by modern people, or were they painted by cave people long ago?</u>

Directions Combine each pair of sentences. Use the underlined words only once in your new sentence.

3. Horses were painted on the cave murals. Other animals were painted on the cave murals.
   <u>Horses and other animals were painted on the cave murals.</u>

4. The cave artists were creative. The cave artists were talented.
   <u>The cave artists were creative and talented.</u>

Unit 6 Talking Walls   Grammar **28**

▲ **Grammar Transparency** 28

DAY 2 Develop the Concept

DAILY FIX-IT

3. The classes paints the mural on a large wall of the shcool. *(paint; school)*

4. We didnt know what great artests we had. *(didn't; artists)*

GUIDED PRACTICE

Review how to combine sentences.

- **Combine sentences** by joining two sentences about the same topic.
- Combine two simple sentences into a compound sentence by adding a comma and a conjunction.
- Combine two sentences that have the same subject by combining the predicates. Combine two sentences that have the same predicate by combining the subjects.

HOMEWORK Grammar and Writing Practice Book p. 109. Work through the first two items with the class.

Combining Sentences

When you **combine sentences,** you join two sentences that are about the same topic. You make them into one sentence.
- You can join two simple sentences and make a compound sentence. Add a comma and a conjunction such as *and, but,* or *or.*
  Jen painted a tree. I painted a flower.
  Jen painted a tree, and I painted a flower.
- You can combine two sentences that have the same subject.
  Jen painted the sky blue. Jen colored the grass green.
  Jen painted the sky blue and colored the grass green.
- You can combine two sentences that have the same predicate.
  Jen worked on the mural. I worked on the mural.
  Jen and I worked on the mural.

Directions Combine each pair of sentences into a compound sentence. Use a comma and the conjunction in ( ).

1. Some murals show famous people. Our mural shows ordinary people. (but)
   <u>Some murals show famous people, but our mural shows ordinary people.</u>

2. I will show you the mural. You can find it yourself. (or)
   <u>I will show you the mural, or you can find it yourself.</u>

Directions Combine the pair of sentences. Use the underlined words only once in the new sentence.

3. Diego Rivera came from Mexico. Diego Rivera painted murals in America.
   <u>Diego Rivera came from Mexico and (*or* but) painted murals in America.</u>

 Home Activity Your child learned about combining sentences. Point out two short related sentences in a book you are reading with your child. Have your child combine the sentences.

▲ **Grammar and Writing Practice Book** p. 109

DAY 3 Apply to Writing

DAILY FIX-IT

5. The class's mural feachures a celebration, and is painted in bright colors. *(features; celebration and)*

6. The mural is the most biggest piece of art in the neighbor hood. *(the biggest; neighborhood)*

USE SENTENCE COMBINING

Explain that combining sentences can help writers avoid wordiness caused by repeating subjects and predicates.

Wordy: The artists painted a bright background. The artists drew people at a celebration.

Less Wordy: The artists painted a bright background and drew people at a celebration.

• Have students review written work to see if they can combine sentences to avoid wordiness.

HOMEWORK Grammar and Writing Practice Book, p. 110

Combining Sentences

Directions Combine each pair of simple sentences into a compound sentence. Add a comma and the conjunction *and, but,* or *or.*

1. People painted murals long ago. They still paint murals today.
People painted murals long ago, and they still paint murals today.

2. Some murals are painted outside. Most murals are painted inside.
Some murals are painted outside, but most murals are painted inside.

3. You can make a mural with paint. You can use bits of glass.
You can make a mural with paint, or you can use bits of glass.

4. One artist can make a mural. Many artists can work together.
One artist can make a mural, or many artists can work together.

Directions Write two simple related sentences about murals. Then combine the sentences to make one compound sentence.
Possible answer: Some immigrants have painted murals. The pictures show their feelings about America. Some immigrants have painted murals, and the pictures show their feelings about America.

Home Activity Your child learned how to combine sentences in writing. Have your child write two short sentences on the same topic on construction paper, cut them out, and combine them on another sheet of paper, adding a comma and a conjunction such as *and*.

 ▲ **Grammar and Writing Practice Book** p. 110

DAY 4 Test Preparation

DAILY FIX-IT

7. Carlos begun a sculpchure to go with the mural. *(began; sculpture)*

8. He is making it out of clay and he will finish it next tuesday. *(clay, and; Tuesday)*

STANDARDIZED TEST PREP

Test Tip

You may be asked to identify the correct way to combine two sentences. Remember that when two simple sentences are made into a compound sentence, a comma must be added before the conjunction. Commas are not added when two subjects or two predicates are combined.

Incorrect: Jay drew and Mary painted. Jay painted the mural, and made a sculpture.

Correct: Jay drew, and Mary painted. Jay painted the mural and made a sculpture.

HOMEWORK Grammar and Writing Practice Book, p. 111

Combining Sentences

Directions Mark the letter of the words that complete each sentence correctly.

1. Julia planned a _____ painted it.
   A mural, And the class
   B mural, or the class
   C mural, and the class
   D mural and the class

2. The mural is about our _____ is so interesting.
   A town, And it
   B town, and it
   C town, or it
   D town and it

3. The mural is not _____ has many scenes.
   A huge, but it
   B huge, But it
   C huge but it
   D huge, or it

4. Tim _____ painted the park.
   A and Lee
   B , and Lee
   C and, Lee
   D and Lee,

5. You can use yellow _____ can use red.
   A paint, Or you
   B paint or you
   C paint, or you
   D paint but you

6. The pictures are _____ bright.
   A big, and
   B big, and
   C , big and
   D big and

7. You can paint a _____ can paint a house.
   A tree but you
   B tree or you
   C tree, Or you
   D tree, or you

8. People look at the _____ love it.
   A mural, or they
   B mural, and they
   C mural, And they
   D mural and they

9. The mural was hard _____ was worth it.
   A work, but it
   B work but it
   C work, But it
   D work or it

10. We will paint a mural next _____ will be even better.
   A year but it
   B year, And it
   C year, and it
   D year and it

Home Activity Your child prepared for taking tests on combining sentences. Have your child show you pairs of short related sentences from a school paper and explain how to combine them.

 ▲ **Grammar and Writing Practice Book** p. 111

DAY 5 Cumulative Review

DAILY FIX-IT

9. The mural was a success and the class will paint unother soon. *(success, and; another)*

10. What subjec will they choose for the next mural. *(subject; mural?)*

ADDITIONAL PRACTICE

Assign pp. 212–215 in The Grammar and Writing Book.

EXTRA PRACTICE Grammar and Writing Practice Book, p. 149.

TEST PREPARATION Grammar and Writing Practice Book, pp. 157–158.

ASSESSMENT

CUMULATIVE REVIEW Grammar and Writing Practice Book, p. 112

Combining Sentences

Directions Combine each pair of sentences into a compound sentence. Use a comma and the conjunction in ( ).

1. Many painters created murals in the 1960s. This art form is still popular today. (and)
Many painters created murals in the 1960s, and this art form is still popular today.

2. Many murals show real people. Some murals show imaginary characters. (but)
Many murals show real people, but some murals show imaginary characters.

3. You can paint a mural on wet plaster. You can use canvas. (or)
You can paint a mural on wet plaster, or you can use canvas.

Directions Combine each pair of sentences. Use the underlined words only once in your new sentence.

4. That mural shows many different people. That mural pictures several events.
That mural shows many different people and pictures several events.

5. A mural can entertain people. A mural can teach people.
A mural can entertain people or (*or* and) teach people.

6. Public buildings are good places for murals. Parks are good places for murals.
Public buildings and parks are good places for murals.

Home Activity Your child reviewed combining sentences. While looking at a magazine or newspaper, ask your child to combine pairs of related sentences in two different ways.

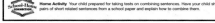 ▲ **Grammar and Writing Practice Book** p. 112

Writing Workshop Informational Paragraph

OBJECTIVES

- Identify the characteristics of an informational paragraph.
- Write an informational paragraph with a topic sentence.
- Focus on organization/paragraphs.
- Use a rubric.

Genre Informational Paragraph
Writer's Craft Topic Sentences
Writing Trait Organization/ Paragraphs

Organization/Paragraphs Make sure English learners can decode words in the prompt. Work with students to complete a cloze sentence that addresses the prompt and could be used to launch writing.

Writing Trait

FOCUS/IDEAS The paragraph focuses on important facts about the main idea.

ORGANIZATION/PARAGRAPHS The paragraph includes a topic sentence that states the main idea, supporting details, and a concluding sentence.

VOICE The writer's voice is unique and knowledgeable.

WORD CHOICE The writer uses exact words to communicate facts.

SENTENCES Sentence lengths and kinds are varied. Evidence of sentence combining is present.

CONVENTIONS Grammar and mechanics are excellent, including use of sentence combining.

DAY 1 Model the Trait

READING-WRITING CONNECTION

- *Talking Walls: Art for the People* is a photo essay about murals that are displayed all across America.
- *Talking Walls: Art for the People* consists of well-developed paragraphs that state a main idea and include supporting details.
- Students will write an **informational paragraph** about an art form.

MODEL ORGANIZATION/PARAGRAPHS
Discuss Writing Transparency 28A. Then discuss the model and the writing trait of organization/paragraphs.

Think Aloud The writer has written an informational paragraph about murals. The topic sentence asks a question to get the reader's attention and tells the paragraph's main idea. Other sentences in the paragraph give supporting details. The concluding paragraph sums up the main idea.

> **Informational Paragraph**
>
> An **informational paragraph** gives facts on a topic. It usually begins with a topic sentence that states the main idea of the paragraph. The other sentences in the paragraphs give details that support the main idea. A concluding sentence sums up the paragraph.
>
> **Large Art**
>
> *Topic sentence gets readers' interest and tells paragraph's main idea.* — What is big and bright and enjoyed by many people? A mural is an art form that has all these traits. A mural is a painting on a large surface such as a wall, either inside or outside. The pictures on a mural tell a story. A mural may show events in history, such as the history of Native Americans. It may show famous people, such as jazz musicians. The bright colors and vivid styles of murals attract everyone's attention. Many famous artists have painted murals. People like you and me can paint murals too. Murals are artworks for everyone.
>
> *Other sentences give facts about main idea.*
>
> *Conclusion sums up paragraph's main idea.*
>
> Unit 6 Talking Walls — Writing Model **28A**

▲ **Writing Transparency** 28A

DAY 2 Improve Writing

WRITER'S CRAFT
Topic Sentences

Display Writing Transparency 28B. Read the directions and work together to decide which topic sentence goes with which details.

Think Aloud **TOPIC SENTENCES**
Tomorrow we will write informational paragraphs about art forms that we like. I want to be sure that I include a strong topic sentence that will get the reader's attention. Maybe I'll ask a question in the topic sentence. This sentence should also tell the main idea of the paragraph. I might even use a strong adjective that tells how I feel when I look at this type of art.

GUIDED WRITING Some students may need more help with topic sentences. Work with them to identify such sentences in the reading selection.

> **Topic Sentences**
>
> A **topic sentence** tells the main idea of a paragraph. The topic sentence is often the first sentence of an informational paragraph.
>
> **Directions** Read the three topic sentences. Write the sentence that would be the best topic sentence for each group of details.
> **Topic Sentences**
> Many artists have painted murals.
> Murals are not hard to make.
> You can see murals in many different places.
>
> 1. Put a big piece of white paper on a bulletin board. Decide on a topic such as school sports. Have each person paint one scene for the mural.
>   <u>Murals are not hard to make.</u>
>
> 2. Some murals are painted on skyscrapers near city highways. Others are painted in neighborhood parks or inside public buildings.
>   <u>You can see murals in many different places.</u>
>
> 3. People who lived in caves long ago painted murals. An Italian artist, Michelangelo, painted a famous mural on a ceiling in the 1500s. Many Americans painted murals in the 1960s.
>   <u>Many artists have painted murals.</u>
>
> **Directions** Write a topic sentence for the following details.
>   Some murals show important people. Others show beautiful places. Still others show events from history.
>   <u>Possible answer: Murals have many different subjects.</u>
>
> Unit 6 Talking Walls — Writer's Craft **28B**

▲ **Writing Transparency** 28B

DAY 3 — Prewrite and Draft

READ THE WRITING PROMPT

on page 351 in the Student Edition.

Talking Walls *describes special murals.*

Think of a kind of art that you know well.

Now write an informational paragraph about this kind of art.

Writing Test Tips

- Use a strong topic sentence that tells exactly what the paragraph will be about.
- Use precise words that help readers understand the facts.
- Organize the details logically, such as in time order or space order.

GETTING STARTED Students can do any of the following:

- Write down all the facts they already know about the art form.
- Work with a partner to make a concept web with the name of the art form in the center.
- Work with a group to discuss various art forms.

DAY 4 — Draft and Revise

EDITING/REVISING CHECKLIST

☑ Does the paragraph begin with a topic sentence that states the main idea?

☑ Do the paragraph's details support the main idea?

☑ Are some sentences combined to avoid wordiness?

☑ Are words with *-tion, -sion,* and *-ture* spelled correctly?

See *The Grammar and Writing Book,* pp. 216–221.

Revising Tips

Organization/ Paragraphs

- Begin with a topic sentence that states the paragraph's main idea.
- Organize the details in a logical order such as time order or space order.
- End with a concluding sentence that sums up the paragraph.

PUBLISHING Students can read their paragraphs aloud in small groups. Some students may wish to revise their work later.

ASSESSMENT Use the scoring rubric to evaluate students' work.

DAY 5 — Connect to Unit Writing

Research Report

Week 1	Taking Notes 303g–303h
Week 2	Outlining 331g–331h
Week 3	Informational Paragraph 353g–353h
Week 4	Writing About a Picture 379g–379h
Week 5	Write Good Paragraphs 407g–407h

PREVIEW THE UNIT PROMPT

Write a research report about a monument or statue that symbolizes freedom in the United States. Discuss the monument itself, its history, and why it is important. Find information in sources such as books, magazines, CD-ROMs, and the Internet.

APPLY

- A research report is an informational article based on research.
- A research report is made up of informational paragraphs.

Writing Trait Rubric

	4	3	2	1
Organization/ Paragraphs	Ideas well developed from beginning to end; strong closure	Ideas that progress from beginning to end; good closure	Some sense of movement from beginning to end; weak closure	No sense of movement from beginning to end or closure
	Paragraph organized with exceptional logic	Paragraph organized adequately	Paragraph not clearly organized	Paragraph not organized

OBJECTIVES

- Associate the common syllables *-tion, -sion,* and *-ture* with the letters that spell them.
- Review words with the schwa sound.
- Blend and read words with the common syllables *-tion, -sion,* and *-ture* and words with the schwa sound.
- Apply decoding strategies: blend longer words.

ELL

Support Phonics The suffix *-tion* has similar forms in other languages, including French *(-tion)*, Spanish *(-ción, -sión)*, Haitian Creole *(-syon)*, and Portuguese *(çäo)*. Children can look for cognates for *–tion* words in other languages. For example, the English word *direction* is *direction* in French, *dirección* in Spanish, *direksyon* in Haitian Creole, and *direção* in Portuguese.

See the Phonics Transition Lessons in the ELL and Transition Handbook.

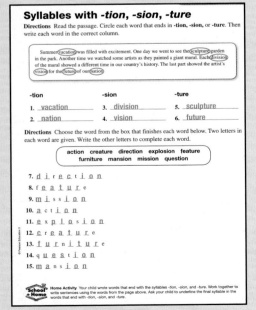

Syllables with *-tion, -sion, -ture*

Directions Read the passage. Circle each word that ends in **-tion, -sion,** or **-ture**. Then write each word in the correct column.

Summer vacation was filled with excitement. One day we went to see the sculpture garden in the park. Another time we watched some artists as they painted a giant mural. Each division of the mural showed a different time in our country's history. The last part showed the artist's vision for the future of our nation.

-tion	-sion	-ture
1. vacation	3. division	5. sculpture
2. nation	4. vision	6. future

Directions Choose the word from the box that finishes each word below. Two letters in each word are given. Write the other letters to complete each word.

action creature direction explosion feature
furniture mansion mission question

7. d i r e c t i o n
8. f e a t u r e
9. m i s s i o n
10. a c t i o n
11. e x p l o s i o n
12. c r e a t u r e
13. f u r n i t u r e
14. q u e s t i o n
15. m a n s i o n

School + Home **Home Activity** Your child wrote words that end with the syllables -tion, -sion, and -ture. Work together to write sentences using the words from the page above. Ask your child to underline the final syllable in the words that end with -tion, -sion, and -ture.

▲ **Practice Book 3.2** p. 129

Syllables *-tion, -sion, -ture*

TEACH

Remind students that they have learned common word parts that appear in many different words. Write the words *question, vision,* and *culture*.

- How many syllables do you hear in *question?* (2)
- What is the first syllable? *(ques)*
- What is the second syllable? *(tion)*
- Which syllable have you seen in many other words? *(tion)*

 Think Aloud

MODEL When I need to sound out a word like *question,* I look for word parts I already know. I've seen *-tion* in lots of words, so I don't have to stop to figure out that syllable. The syllable *-tion* is a helpful syllable to know. So are the common syllables *-sion* and *-ture.*

Model blending *question, vision,* and *culture.* Then have students blend the words with you.

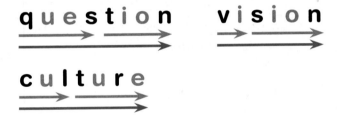

PRACTICE AND ASSESS

DECODE LONGER WORDS Write these words. Have students read them and then underline the syllables *-tion, -sion,* and *-ture.*

expan<u>sion</u>   relation<u>ship</u>   signa<u>ture</u>   comprehen<u>sion</u>

exhaus<u>tion</u>   struc<u>ture</u>   subtrac<u>tion</u>   varia<u>tion</u>

READ WORDS IN CONTEXT Write these sentences. Have individuals read them and point out words with the syllables *-tion, -sion,* and *-ture.* Words with these syllables are underlined. To check meaning, have students give their own sentence for the underlined words.

The class got <u>permission</u> to visit the <u>nature</u> center.

We will show our <u>invention</u> at the science <u>convention.</u>

Each storyteller told a different <u>version</u> of the <u>traditional</u> folk tale.

Did you complete the <u>revision</u> of your <u>picture</u> book yet?

To assess, observe whether students read words with the syllables *-tion, -sion,* and *-ture* correctly.

Review Phonics

REVIEW SCHWA

CONNECT Write this sentence: *A parrot sat on Pirate John's hat.*

- We studied the schwa sound in unaccented syllables.
- Read the sentence to yourself. Raise your hand when you know which words have the schwa sound. *(parrot, Pirate)*
- Which vowel stands for the schwa sound in *parrot*? *(o)*
- Which vowel stands for the schwa sound in *Pirate*? *(a)*
- Does the schwa sound appear in accented or the unaccented syllables? (unaccented)

Continue in the same way with the sentence *Do you happen to have pencils we can use?*

PRACTICE AND ASSESS

DECODE LONGER WORDS Have individuals read the following words. Provide help chunking and blending the words as needed.

fossil	Scotland	gather	pedal
ketchup	instant	lion	shovel
father	budget	forest	lemon

READ WORDS IN CONTEXT Have students read these sentences. Then, to check meaning, have them give their own sentence for the underlined word.

Ben dreamed he saw a <u>dragon</u> in the <u>kitchen</u>.

We <u>often</u> <u>travel</u> to the beach in <u>August</u>.

Mom's <u>muffins</u> won a <u>medal</u> at the fair.

My <u>sister</u> and I ate the whole <u>melon</u>.

To assess, note how well students read words with the schwa sound.

Generalization

In unaccented (unstressed) syllables, any vowel can stand for the schwa sound, /ə/.

Vocabulary TIP

You may wish to explain the meanings of these words.

budget a plan for spending and saving money
fossil the preserved remains of an animal or plant
rapid quick

Spelling & Phonics   Words with *-tion, -sion, -ture*

OBJECTIVE

● Identify and spell words with the syllable patterns *-tion, -sion,* and *-ture.*

Generalization

Connect to Phonics Many words end in syllable patterns *-tion, -sion,* or *-ture*: ac*tion*, divi*sion*, crea*ture*.

Spelling Words

1. question
2. creature
3. furniture
4. division
5. collision
6. action
7. direction
8. culture
9. vacation
10. mansion
11. fiction
12. feature
13. sculpture
14. vision
15. celebration*

Challenge Words

16. fascination
17. legislature
18. manufacture
19. possession
20. declaration

*Word from the selection

ELL

Spelling/Phonics Support See the ELL and Transition Handbook for spelling support.

PRETEST

Use the Dictation Sentences from Day 5 to administer the pretest. Read the word, read the sentence, and then read the word again. Guide students in self-correcting their pretests and correcting any misspellings.

Monitor Progress

Spelling

If... students misspell more than 4 pretest words,	then... use words 1–8 for Strategic Intervention.
If... students misspell 1–4 pretest words,	then... use words 1–15 for On-Level practice.
If... students correctly spell all pretest words,	then... use words 1–20 for Advanced Learners.

HOMEWORK Spelling Practice Book p. 109

Words with *-tion, -sion, -ture*

Generalization Many words end in syllable patterns *-tion, -sion,* or *-ture*: action, division, creature.

Word Sort Sort the list words by their syllable pattern.

-tion
1. question
2. action
3. direction
4. vacation
5. fiction
6. celebration

-sion
7. division
8. collision
9. mansion
10. vision

-ture
11. creature
12. furniture
13. culture
14. feature
15. sculpture

Spelling Words
1. question
2. creature
3. furniture
4. division
5. collision
6. action
7. direction
8. culture
9. vacation
10. mansion
11. fiction
12. feature
13. sculpture
14. vision
15. celebration

Challenge Words
16. fascination
17. legislature
18. manufacture
19. possession
20. declaration

Challenge Words

-tion
16. fascination
17. declaration

-sion
18. possession

-ture
19. legislature
20. manufacture

School Home Home Activity Your child is learning to spell words that end with -tion, -sion, and -ture. To practice at home, have your child look at the spelling of the word, cover and write the word, and then check the spelling.

▲ **Spelling Practice Book** p. 109

TEACH

Many words end in *-tion, -sion,* or *-ture*. Introduce these words to students by writing each list word on the board. Have students identify the different syllable patterns at the end of each word, and underline each one.

que*stion*

USE THE DICTIONARY Have students use a dictionary to find other words with these endings.

HOMEWORK Spelling Practice Book p. 110

Words with *-tion, -sion, -ture*

Spelling Words

question	creature	furniture	division	collision
action	direction	culture	vacation	mansion
fiction	feature	sculpture	vision	celebration

Opposites Write the missing list word. It will be the opposite of the underlined word.

1. The hero in this book lives in a shack.   1. mansion
2. At first, I had trouble with multiplication.   2. division
3. Let me interrupt with a statement about wind power.   3. question
4. Jed left for his usual job.   4. vacation
5. This story is true.   5. fiction

Context Clues Write the last word of the sentence.

6. The situation called for quick action .
7. The school nurse tested everyone's vision .
8. Her cheery smile is her best feature .
9. In art class, Tami made a plaster sculpture .
10. Please come to my birthday celebration .
11. We bought some used furniture .
12. An armadillo is an odd creature .
13. We walked in the wrong direction .
14. The toy robots had a collision .
15. Nature was important in the Aztec culture .

School Home Home Activity Your child wrote words that end with -tion, -sion, and -ture. Have your child underline these endings in the list words.

▲ **Spelling Practice Book** p. 110

DAY 3 — Connect to Writing

WRITE A REPORT

Ask students to write a report about a favorite topic, using at least three spelling words. Have students share their reports by reading them aloud to the class, or displaying them on the bulletin board.

Frequently Misspelled Words

we're   were

Third-graders are often confused by these words because they look alike, but have different pronunciations, spellings, and meanings. Point out that *we're* is a contraction for *we are*. Alert students to these frequently misspelled words and encourage them to think carefully before they write them.

HOMEWORK Spelling Practice Book, p. 111

Words with *-tion, -sion, -ture*

Spelling Words

question	creature	furniture	division	collision
action	direction	culture	vacation	mansion
fiction	feature	sculpture	vision	celebration

Proofread a Description Gina's class is studying local history. Circle four spelling errors. Write the words correctly. Then write the two incomplete sentences as one sentence.

Mr. and Mrs. Hill (we're) very important in the history of our town. They built the Hill (manshun) in 1880. It still has the original (furnichure). Many people tour the house when they are on (vacasion). My favorite feature. Is the dolphin sculpture.

Frequently Misspelled Words
we're
were

1. ___were___   2. ___mansion___
3. ___furniture___   4. ___vacation___
5. ___My favorite feature is the dolphin sculpture.___

Proofread Words Circle the word that is spelled correctly. Write it.
6. I have a (question) quesion.   6. ___question___
7. It's fun to learn about a new calture (culture) 7. ___culture___
8. An eagle has excellent vishun (vision) 8. ___vision___
9. We had a big (celebration) celebrasion. 9. ___celebration___
10. Which (direction) direcsion is the library? 10. ___direction___

Home Activity Your child identified misspelled words that end with *-tion, -sion,* and *-ture.* Give clues about a list word. Ask your child to guess and spell the word.

▲ **Spelling Practice Book** p. 111

DAY 4 — Review

REVIEW WORDS WITH *-tion, -sion, -ture*

Have students work individually or in pairs to create crossword puzzles using the spelling words. Students may exchange their puzzles with other student pairs and try to solve each other's puzzles.

Spelling Strategy
Common Syllable Patterns

Students should memorize these common syllable patterns so they are familiar when the students are spelling words.

HOMEWORK Spelling Practice Book, p. 112

Words with *-tion, -sion, -ture*

Spelling Words

question	creature	furniture	division	collision
action	direction	culture	vacation	mansion
fiction	feature	sculpture	vision	celebration

Complete the Phrase Finish the list of things people do. Use words from the box.

celebration	1. plan a ___celebration___
direction	2. read ___fiction___
fiction	3. call for ___action___
question	4. take a ___vacation___
action	5. ask a ___question___
vacation	6. change ___direction___

Missing Vowels The vowels in these list words are missing. Write the vowels to complete each word. Write each word.

7. d _i_ v _i_ s _i_ o n   7. ___division___
8. sc _u_ lpt _u_ r _e_   8. ___sculpture___
9. cr _e_ _a_ t _u_ r _e_   9. ___creature___
10. c _o_ ll _i_ s _i_ o n   10. ___collision___
11. m _a_ ns _i_ _o_ n   11. ___mansion___
12. f _e_ _a_ t _u_ r _e_   12. ___feature___
13. c _u_ lt _u_ r _e_   13. ___culture___
14. f _u_ r n _i_ t _u_ r _e_ 14. ___furniture___
15. v _i_ s _i_ o n   15. ___vision___

Home Activity Your child has been learning to spell words that end with *-tion, -sion, -ture.* Ask your child to identify and spell the five most difficult list words.

▲ **Spelling Practice Book** p. 112

DAY 5 — Posttest

DICTATION SENTENCES

1. I have a question about the test.
2. The creature in the movie was very scary!
3. Mom and Dad will buy new furniture.
4. Do you know your division facts?
5. The car was in a bad collision.
6. The story had a lot of action.
7. What direction should we walk?
8. I'd like to learn about that culture.
9. What did you do on your vacation?
10. Ed lives in a mansion.
11. I like to read fiction stories.
12. The show will feature songs about stars.
13. Let's look at the sculpture.
14. He has good vision.
15. Her birthday was a big celebration.

CHALLENGE

16. I have a fascination with bugs.
17. The legislature meets on Tuesday.
18. We manufacture boxes.
19. She has the kitten in her possession.
20. She made a declaration to the class.

OBJECTIVES

- Formulate an inquiry question that is connected to this week's lesson focus.
- Effectively and efficiently find, evaluate, and communicate information related to an inquiry question using electronic sources.

New Literacies

Day 1	Identify Questions
Day 2	Navigate/Search
Day 3	Analyze
Day 4	Synthesize
Day 5	Communicate

NEW LITERACIES

Internet Inquiry Activity

EXPLORE FREEDOM OF EXPRESSION

Use the following 5-day plan to help students conduct this week's Internet inquiry activity on freedom of expression. Remind students to follow classroom rules when using the Internet.

DAY 1

Identify Questions Discuss the lesson focus question: *Why is freedom of expression important?* Brainstorm ideas for specific inquiry questions about freedom of expression. For example, students might want to learn more about the First Amendment and find several examples of what free speech means, including verbal, non-verbal, visual, and symbolic expressions. Have students work individually, in pairs, or in small groups to write an inquiry question they want to answer.

DAY 2

Navigate/Search Start a simple Internet search. After students have compiled a list of the sites they would like to analyze, review how to bookmark Web sites, which allows quick access. Students may bookmark the sites today but will not analyze them until Day 3. Remind students that they need a teacher's permission before they bookmark Web sites.

DAY 3

Analyze Students will explore the Web sites they identified on Day 2. Tell them to analyze each site for information that helps answer their inquiry questions. Students can then print and highlight relevant information or take notes.

DAY 4

Synthesize Have students synthesize information from Day 3. Remind them that when they synthesize, they combine relevant ideas and information from different sources to develop answers to their inquiry questions.

DAY 5

Communicate Have students share their inquiry results. They can use a word processing program to create a short review of the First Amendment or a definition of freedom of expression.

RESEARCH/STUDY SKILLS
Reference Sources

TEACH

OBJECTIVES

- Review terms related to a telephone directory.
- Look up listings in a telephone directory.

Ask students to name some reference sources they are familiar with and to tell what kind of information the sources contain. If it is not mentioned, explain that a telephone directory is a reference that we use often. Show a telephone directory and define the following terms and ideas.

- A **telephone directory** is a book of telephone numbers for an area. It is organized alphabetically by last name.
- The listings in a telephone directory are located in a **local** area.
- Some telephone directories have a **business listing.** It is a separate alphabetical list of businesses in the local area.
- Many telephone directories have a section called the **yellow pages.** Businesses can advertise in the yellow pages of a telephone directory.

Have students work with a partner, using telephone directories. Ask partners to go through the book, discuss how it is organized, and list the different kinds of information it contains. Have them look in the yellow pages to find two businesses that sell art supplies. Discuss these questions with the class.

1. **Where are the yellow pages located in the telephone directory?** *(in the back)*

2. **How would you locate a business that sells art supplies?** *(Look up* art *in the yellow pages and see if there are listings for art supply stores.)*

Artists' Materials and Supplies

All About Art
10 Shore Rd Lakeville 555-2790

CASEY'S ART
Everything for the serious artist
1356 Main St.
Milton
555-4890

ASSESS

As students work with the telephone directory, check that they recognize the different sections of the book. Make sure they know how to look up listings alphabetically.

For more practice or to assess students, use Practice Book 3.2, p. 130.

Reference Sources

People use reference sources to find information about a topic. One kind of reference source is a **telephone directory.** It is a book of telephone numbers for an area. Businesses are often listed separately in a business listing. Businesses can advertise in a telephone directory's **yellow pages** section.

Directions Use the yellow page section shown here to answer the questions.

> **Bicycles–Dealers & Repairs**
>
> Artie's Cycles–Sales and Service in Hyde Park
> 1234 E. 12th Street Chicago   773-123-0981
> Bicycles for Everyone–Sales and Repairs
> 2543 W. Pear Street Chicago   773-555-8934
> Eduardo's Bike Shop–Parts and Accessories
> 18 W. Ellison Avenue Chicago   773-233-5988
> Jennings on Wheels–Largest Inventory of Used Bikes in Chicago
> 324 S. 10th Street Chicago   773-595-2342
> Recreational Biking–Used Bikes for Less
> 18 N. Clyburn Chicago   773-232-1800

1. Would a listing for Geraldo Bicycles appear before or after Eduardo's Bike Shop in this telephone directory?
   after

2. What is the telephone number for Bicycles for Everyone?
   773-555-8934

3. Where would you go for a bicycle if you wanted to save money? Explain.
   Possible response: Recreational Biking—It sells used bikes.

4. After which business listing would Montrose Cycles appear?
   after Jennings on Wheels

5. On which street is Artie's Cycles?
   12th Street

School + Home Home Activity Your child learned how and why people use reference sources. He or she also discovered how a telephone directory is organized. Show your child several reference sources and discuss how they are organized and what kind of information they have.

▲ **Practice Book 3.2** p. 130

Assessment Checkpoints *for the Week*

Selection Assessment

Use pp. 109–112 of Selection Tests **to check:**

 Selection Understanding

 Comprehension Skill *Fact and Opinion*

 Selection Vocabulary

encourages	*settled*
expression	*social*
local	*support*
native	

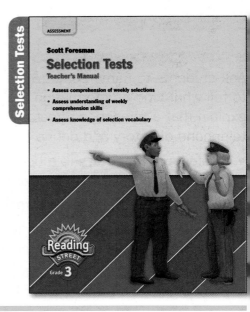

ASSESSMENT

Scott Foresman
Selection Tests
Teacher's Manual

- Assess comprehension of weekly selections
- Assess understanding of weekly comprehension skills
- Assess knowledge of selection vocabulary

Reading STREET Grade 3

Leveled Assessment

On-Level

Strategic Intervention

Advanced

Use pp. 163–168 of Fresh Reads for Differentiated Test Practice **to check:**

 Comprehension Skill *Fact and Opinion*

 REVIEW Comprehension Skill *Character*

 Fluency *Words Correct Per Minute*

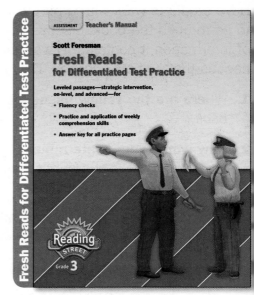

ASSESSMENT   Teacher's Manual

Scott Foresman
Fresh Reads for Differentiated Test Practice

Leveled passages—strategic intervention, on-level, and advanced—for

- Fluency checks
- Practice and application of weekly comprehension skills
- Answer key for all practice pages

Reading STREET Grade 3

Managing Assessment

Use Assessment Handbook **for:**

 Observation Checklists

 Record-Keeping Forms

 Portfolio Assessment

ASSESSMENT

Scott Foresman
Assessment Handbook

- Suggestions for preparing students for high-stake tests
- Ideas for classroom-based assessment
- Forms in English and Spanish for students to record interests and progress
- Forms in English and Spanish for teachers to record observations of students' reading and writing abilities and progress
- Assessment and Regrouping charts reproduced from *Reading Street* Teacher's Editions

Reading STREET Grades 3-6

Illinois

Planning Guide for Performance Descriptors

Two Bad Ants

Reading Street Teacher's Edition pages

Grade 3 English Language Arts Performance Descriptors

Oral Language

Speaking/Listening Build Concept Vocabulary: 354l, 367, 375, 379c
Read Aloud: 354m

Viewing Analyze Classified Ads: 379d

1A.Stage C.8. Use a variety of resources (e.g., dictionaries, thesauruses, indices, glossaries, internet, interviews, available technology) to clarify meanings of unfamiliar words.

1B.Stage C.13. Read age-appropriate material aloud with fluency and accuracy.

Word Work

Multisyllable Words: 379i, 379k–379l

1A.Stage C.2. Use word analysis (root words, inflections, affixes) to identify words.

Reading

Comprehension Plot and Theme: 354–355, 358–375, 379b
Visualize: 354–355, 358–375

Vocabulary Lesson Vocabulary: 356b, 367, 375
Word Structure: 356–357, 365, 379c

Fluency Model Reading with Accuracy and Appropriate Pace/Rate: 354l–354m, 379a
Choral Reading: 379a

Self-Selected Reading: LR28–36, TR16–17

Literature Genre—Animal Fantasy: 358
Reader Response: 376

1A.Stage C.7. Use content and previous experience to determine the meanings of unfamiliar words in text.

1B.Stage C.1. Identify purposes for reading before and during reading.

1B.Stage C.9. Continuously check and clarify for understanding (e.g., reread, read ahead, use visual and context clues) during reading.

1B.Stage C.13. Read age-appropriate material aloud with fluency and accuracy.

1C.Stage C.2. Use information to generate and respond to questions that reflect higher level thinking skills (e.g., analyzing, synthesizing, inferring, evaluating).

2A.Stage C.1. Identify the theme (e.g., friendship, cooperation, sharing, change, exploration) in selected stories and books.

2A.Stage C.5. Define unfamiliar vocabulary.

2A.Stage C.7. Classify major types of fiction (e.g., tall tale, fairy tale, fable).

Language Arts

Writing Write About a Picture: 379g–379h

Six-Trait Writing Word Choice: 377, 379g–379h

Grammar, Usage, and Mechanics Commas: 379e–379f

Research/Study Note-Taking: 379n

Technology New Literacies: 379m

3A.Stage C.6. Use appropriate punctuation.

3B.Stage C.1. Use appropriate prewriting strategies (e.g., drawing, webbing, brainstorming, listing, note taking, graphic organizers) to generate and organize ideas with teacher assistance.

3C.Stage C.1. Use the writing process for a variety of purposes (e.g., narration, exposition, persuasion).

Unit Skills

Writing Research Report: WA2–9

Poetry: 408–411

Project/Wrap-Up: 412–413

3B.Stage C.3. Use stages of the writing process (e.g., prewriting, drafting, revising, editing, publishing) to develop paragraphs with focus, organization, elaboration, and integration.

3C.Stage C.3. Experiment with different forms of creative writing (e.g., song, poetry, short fiction, play).

This Week's Leveled Readers

Below-Level

1C.Stage C.1. Use evidence in text to form questions and verify predictions.

2B.Stage C.4. Discuss works that have a common theme.

Fiction

On-Level

2A.Stage C.1. Identify the theme (e.g., friendship, cooperation, sharing, change, exploration) in selected stories and books.

2B.Stage C.1. Apply events and situations in both fiction and nonfiction to personal experiences.

Fiction

Advanced

1C.Stage C.5. Make comparisons across reading selections (e.g., themes, topics, story elements).

2A.Stage C.3. Identify the elements of plot by retelling the story (i.e., problem, attempts to solve problem, or resolution of problem).

Fiction

Content-Area Illinois Performance Descriptors in This Lesson

Science

12A.Stage C.1. Apply scientific inquiries or technological designs to explore past and present life forms and their adaptations: suggesting why changes over time for individuals and groupings of plants and animals happened.

12B.Stage C.2. Apply scientific inquiries or technological designs to examine the interdependence of organisms in ecosystems: identifying adaptations that help animals survive in specific or multiple environments; describing the interaction between living and non-living factors in an ecosystem; predicting what can happen to organisms if they lose different environmental resources or ecologically related groups of organisms.

12C.Stage C.1. Apply scientific inquiries or technological designs to examine the flow of energy: describing how energy in different forms affects common objects in common events.

Math

6A.Stage C.1. Represent, order, and compare whole numbers to demonstrate an understanding of the base-ten number system.

7C.Stage C.2. Determine elapsed time between events.

10C.Stage C.1. Describe events as likely or unlikely and discuss the degree of likelihood using such words as certain, equally likely, and impossible.

Social Studies

14D.Stage C.2. Describe a situation wherein the common good supercedes the interests of individuals.

17D.Stage C.1. Illustrate how technological developments have been used to alter the physical environment of the local community (e.g., of or about automobiles, electricity, and computers by using pictures and stories).

18C.Stage C.3. Describe how individuals work together to obtain food, clothing, and shelter.

Illinois!

A FAMOUS ILLINOISAN
Allan Pinkerton

Allan Pinkerton (1819–1884) was born in Scotland. He came to Chicago in 1842 and moved to Dundee soon after. Pinkerton became deputy sheriff of Kane County in 1846. He then became deputy sheriff of Cook County and moved back to Chicago. In 1850 Pinkerton started his own detective agency, called the Pinkerton National Detective Agency. The agency was very successful in solving high-profile crimes, including stopping an assassination attempt against Abraham Lincoln in 1861.

Students can . . .
Create an advertising poster for the Pinkerton National Detective Agency.

A SPECIAL ILLINOIS PLACE
Chicago Botanic Garden

The Chicago Botanic Garden is located in Glencoe. It is home to twenty-three types of gardens, including a Japanese garden and an English walled garden. The Chicago Botanic Garden opened to visitors in 1972. Operated by the Chicago Horticultural Society and owned by the Forest Preserve District of Cook County, it includes 385 acres of land and water and has a tram for visitors to ride. More than 900,000 people visit the garden each year to view the gardens or take gardening classes.

Students can . . .
Create a brochure that includes gardening tips from the Chicago Botanic Garden's web site.

ILLINOIS FUN FACTS
Did You Know?

• The first governor of Illinois was Shadrach Bond. He served one term, from 1818 to 1822.

• The earliest people living in Illinois built huge mounds. The remains of several thousand mounds exist today throughout the state.

• Monks Mound in the Cahokia Mounds State Historic Site is the largest mound in the United States.

Students can . . .
Find pictures of mounds in Illinois. Have them use gravel and clay to create a model of a mound and write a sentence to describe its purpose.

Unit 6
Freedom

CONCEPT QUESTION
What does it mean to be free?

Week 1
What does the Statue of Liberty mean to Americans?

Week 2
When might it be hard to grant freedom?

Week 3
Why is freedom of expression important?

Week 4
When can freedom be a problem?

Week 5
When are you free to follow your dreams?

EXPAND THE CONCEPT
When can freedom be a problem?

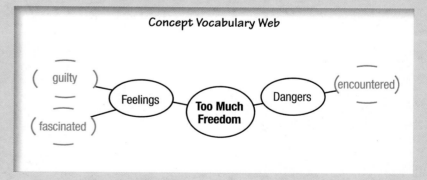

CONNECT THE CONCEPT

▶ **Build Background**
encountered, fascinated, guilty

Concept Vocabulary Web

- guilty
- fascinated
- Feelings
- Too Much Freedom
- Dangers
- (encountered)

▶ **Science Content**
Life Cycles, Environments

▶ **Writing**
Writing About a Picture

▶ **Internet Inquiry**
Freedom

Preview Your Week

When can freedom be a problem?

Two Bad Ants

by Chris Van Allsburg

Genre An **animal fantasy** is a story with animal characters that behave like humans. What is unusual about these ants?

358

Who are these two bad ants, and what do they do?

358

Audio CD

Student Edition pages 358-375

Genre Animal Fantasy
Vocabulary Strategy Word Structure
Comprehension Skill Plot and Theme
Comprehension Strategy Visualize

Paired Selection

Reading Across Texts
Apply Hiking Tips

Genre
Evaluating Sources

Text Features
Links
Last Three Letters of Address

Reading Online
Use URL map: PearsonSuccessNet.com

Evaluating Sources

Genre
• The Internet has a lot of information, but not all sources can be trusted.
• You need to learn how to tell which information is good and which is not.

Text Features
• Information following a link can help you decide whether a Web site might be useful.
• Web addresses ending in .gov or .org are usually good. Ask for help if you are not sure about a site.

Link to Social Studies
Search through newspapers and magazines for travel articles. Share what you learn with the class.

Hiking Safety Tips

You are going on a camping trip. With camping comes freedom, but also dangers. You must prepare a list of hiking safety tips. You decide to use the Internet to help you.

For more practice
Take It to the Net

378

You type the keyword "hiking" into an Internet search engine. The first two sites probably won't help. But the third site looks promising, so you click on Staying Safe on the Trail.

Search Engine   hiking   Search

Hiking Clothes. Outfit your family with these cute hiking shirts.
Footwear. We have 100% leather hiking boots, just what you're looking for
Staying Safe on the Trail. Hiking is fun but beware of plants that . . .

The list goes on. You print it out. Now you can enjoy the freedom of hiking in safety.

STAYING SAFE
A few tips will help you enjoy the freedom of a family hike in safety.

Drinking Water Don't hike anywhere without it, especially on hot days. Even the clearest stream water may not be safe.

Snacks Bring them to eat when you take breaks. Good hiking snacks include granola bars, trail mix, and crackers.

Poison Plants Beware of poison ivy and poison oak. Oil from the leaves can make you break out in a rash and blisters.

poison oak

Reading Across Texts
Which of these hiking tips could have helped the two bad ants?

Writing Across Texts Write a letter to the ants giving them these tips.

Visualize Try to visualize some of these dangers on the trail.

Student Edition pages 378-379

Audio CD

Read It
ONLINE
PearsonSuccessNet.com
• Student Edition
• Leveled Readers

TIME FOR Science

Leveled Readers

🎯 **Skill** Plot and Theme
🎯 **Strategy** Visualize
Lesson Vocabulary

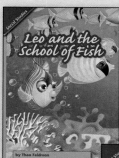

Below-Level

On-Level

Advanced

ELL Reader
· Concept Vocabulary
· Text Support
· Language Enrichment

Lorita's Adventure
by Magali Jaramillo
Illustrated by Freddie Levin

Integrate Science Standards
• Life Cycles
• Environments

✓ **Read**

Two Bad Ants
pp. 358–375

"Hiking Safety Tips"
pp. 378–379

Leveled Readers

Below-Level **On-Level** **Advanced**
• Support Concepts • Develop Concepts • Extend Concepts

ELL Reader

Lorita's Adventure

✓ **Build**
Concept Vocabulary
Too Much Freedom,
pp. 354l–354m

✓ **Teach**
Science Concepts
Species, p. 361
Ant Classes, p. 363
Vortex, p. 369
Life Cycles, p. 373

✓ **Explore**
Science Center
Ant Bodies, p. 354k

Weekly Plan

READING

45–90 minutes

TARGET SKILLS OF THE WEEK

- **Comprehension Skill**
  Plot and Theme
- **Comprehension Strategy**
  Visualize
- **Vocabulary Strategy**
  Word Structure

LANGUAGE ARTS

30–60 minutes

Trait of the Week

Word Choice

DAY 1
PAGES 354l–356b, 379a, 379e–379h, 379k–379m

Oral Language

QUESTION OF THE WEEK *When can freedom be a problem?*

Read Aloud: "The Boy Who Stopped Time," 354m
Build Concepts, 354l

Comprehension/Vocabulary

Comprehension Skill/Strategy Lesson, 354–355
- Plot and Theme **T**
- Visualize

Build Background, 356a

Introduce Lesson Vocabulary, 356b
crystal, disappeared, discovery, goal, journey, joyful, scoop, unaware **T**

Read Leveled Readers

Grouping Options 354f–354g

Fluency

Model Accuracy, Appropriate Pace/Rate, and Expression, 354l–354m, 379a

---

Grammar, 379e
Introduce Commas **T**

Writing Workshop, 379g
Introduce Writing About a Picture
Model the Trait of the Week: Word Choice

Spelling, 379k
Pretest for Multisyllabic Words

Internet Inquiry, 379m
Identify Questions

DAY 2
PAGES 356–367, 379a, 379e–379i, 379k–379m

Oral Language

QUESTION OF THE DAY *Why do the two ants decide not to return home?*

Word Work

Phonics Lesson, 379i
Multisyllabic Words

Comprehension/Vocabulary

Vocabulary Strategy Lesson, 356–357
- Word Structure **T**

Read *Two Bad Ants,* 358–367

Grouping Options
354f–354g

- Plot and Theme **T**
- Visualize
- Word Structure **T**
- **REVIEW** Cause and Effect **T**
  Develop Vocabulary

Fluency

Echo Reading, 379a

Grammar, 379e
Develop Commas **T**

Writing Workshop, 379g
Improve Writing: Elaborating

Spelling, 379k
Teach the Generalization

Internet Inquiry, 379m
Navigate/Search

DAILY WRITING ACTIVITIES	**Day 1** Write to Read, 354	**Day 2** Words to Write, 357 Strategy Response Log, 358, 367
DAILY SCIENCE CONNECTIONS	**Day 1** Too Much Freedom Concept Web, 354l	**Day 2** Time for Science: Species, 361; Ant Classes, 363; Revisit the Too Much Freedom Concept Web, 367

DAILY SUCCESS PREDICTORS
for Adequate Yearly Progress

Monitor Progress and Corrective Feedback

Vocabulary Check Vocabulary, *354l*

Grouping Options for Differentiated Instruction

Turn the page for the small group lesson plan.

DAY 3
PAGES 368–377, 379a, 379e–379h, 379k–379m

Oral Language

QUESTION OF THE DAY *Why do the two ants decide to return to their home?*

Comprehension/Vocabulary

Read *Two Bad Ants, 368–376*

Grouping Options 354f–354g

- Plot and Theme **T**
- Visualize
- Word Structure **T**
- **REVIEW** Cause and Effect **T**
- Develop Vocabulary

Reader Response

Selection Test

Fluency

Model Accuracy, Appropriate Pace/Rate, and Expression, 379a

Grammar, 379f
Apply Commas in Writing **T**

Writing Workshop, 377, 379h
Write Now
Prewrite and Draft

Spelling, 379l
Connect Spelling to Writing

Internet Inquiry, 379m
Analyze Sources

Day 3 Strategy Response Log, 374
Look Back and Write, 376

Day 3 Time for Science: Vortex, 369; Life Cycles, 373; Revisit the Too Much Freedom Concept Web, 375

DAY 4
PAGES 378–379a, 379e–379h, 379j–379m

Oral Language

QUESTION OF THE DAY *What does the expression "with freedom comes responsibility" mean?*

Word Work

Phonics Lesson, 379j
REVIEW Syllables –tion, -sion, -ture **T**

Comprehension/Vocabulary

Read *"Hiking Safety Tips," 378–379*

Grouping Options 354f–354g

Evaluating Sources/Text Features

Reading Across Texts

Fluency

Paired Reading, 379a

Grammar, 379f
Practice Commas for Standardized Tests **T**

Writing Workshop, 379h
Draft, Revise, and Publish

Spelling, 379l
Provide a Strategy

Internet Inquiry, 379m
Synthesize Information

Day 4 Writing Across Texts, 379

Day 4 Time for Science: Safety, 379

DAY 5
PAGES 379a–379h, 379k–379n

Oral Language

QUESTION OF THE WEEK *To wrap up the week, revisit the Day 1 question.*
Build Concept Vocabulary, 379c

Fluency

Read Leveled Readers

Grouping Options 354f–354g

Assess Reading Rate, 379a

Comprehension/Vocabulary

- Reteach Plot and Theme, 379b **T**
- Setting, 379b
- Review Word Structure, 379c **T**

Speaking and Viewing, 379d
Description
Analyze Classified Ads

Grammar, 379f
Cumulative Review

Writing Workshop, 379h
Connect to Unit Writing

Spelling, 379l
Posttest for Multisyllabic Words

Internet Inquiry, 379m
Communicate Results

Research/Study Skills, 379n
Note-taking

Day 5 Setting, 379b

Day 5 Revisit the Too Much Freedom Concept Web, 379c

KEY = Target Skill **T** = Tested Skill

Comprehension **Check Retelling,** *377*

Fluency **Check Fluency** WCPM, *379a*

Vocabulary **Check Vocabulary,** *379c*

SUCCESS PREDICTOR

Small Group Plan for Differentiated Instruction

Daily Plan AT A GLANCE

Reading
Whole Group
- Oral Language
- Phonics
- Comprehension/Vocabulary

Group Time
Differentiated Instruction

Meet with small groups to provide:
- Skill Support
- Reading Support
- Fluency Practice

Read

This week's lessons for daily group time can be found behind the Differentiated Instruction (DI) tab on pp. DI·32–DI·41.

Whole Group
- Fluency

Language Arts
- Grammar
- Writing
- Spelling
- Research/Inquiry
- Speaking/Listening/Viewing

Use My Sidewalks on Reading Street for Tier III intensive reading intervention.

DAY 1

On-Level	Strategic Intervention	Advanced
Teacher-Led *Page DI·33*	Teacher-Led *Page DI·32*	Teacher-Led *Page DI·33*
• Develop Concept Vocabulary	• Preteach Multisyllabic Words	• **Read** Advanced Reader *A Fantastic Field Trip*
• **Read** On-Level Reader *Goldilocks and the Three Bears*	• **Read** Decodable Reader 29	• Independent Extension Activity
	• **Read** Below-Level Reader *Leo and the School of Fish*	

ⓘ Independent Activities
While you meet with small groups, have the rest of the class...

- Visit the Reading/Library Center
- Listen to the Background Building Audio
- Finish Write to Read, p. 354
- Complete Practice Book 3.2 pp. 133–134
- Visit Cross-Curricular Centers

DAY 2

On-Level	Strategic Intervention	Advanced
Teacher-Led *Pages 360–367*	Teacher-Led *Page DI·34*	Teacher-Led *Page DI·35*
• **Read** *Two Bad Ants*	• Practice Lesson Vocabulary	• Extend Vocabulary
	• Read Multisyllabic Words	• **Read** *Two Bad Ants*
	• **Read** or Listen to *Two Bad Ants*	

ⓘ Independent Activities
While you meet with small groups, have the rest of the class...

- Visit the Reading/Library Center
- Listen to the AudioText for *Two Bad Ants*
- Finish Words to Write, p. 357
- Complete Practice Book 3.2 pp. 135–136, 139
- Write in their Strategy Response Logs, pp. 358, 367
- Visit Cross-Curricular Centers
- Work on inquiry projects

DAY 3

On-Level	Strategic Intervention	Advanced
Teacher-Led *Pages 368–375*	Teacher-Led *Page DI·36*	Teacher-Led *Page DI·37*
• **Read** *Two Bad Ants*	• Practice Plot and Theme and Visualize	• Extend Plot and Theme and Visualize
	• **Read** or Listen to *Two Bad Ants*	• **Read** *Two Bad Ants*

ⓘ Independent Activities
While you meet with small groups, have the rest of the class...

- Visit the Reading/Library Center
- Listen to the AudioText for *Two Bad Ants*
- Write in their Strategy Response Logs, p. 374
- Finish Look Back and Write, p. 376
- Complete Practice Book 3.2 p. 137
- Visit Cross-Curricular Centers
- Work on inquiry projects

---

① Begin with whole class skill and strategy instruction.

② Meet with small groups to provide differentiated instruction.

③ Gather the whole class back together for fluency and language arts.

DAY 4

On-Level	Strategic Intervention	Advanced
Teacher-Led *Pages 378–379*	**Teacher-Led** *Page DI · 38*	**Teacher-Led** *Page DI · 39*
• **Read** "Hiking Safety Tips"	• Practice Retelling • **Read** or Listen to "Hiking Safety Tips"	• **Read** "Hiking Safety Tips" • Genre Study

ⓘ Independent Activities

While you meet with small groups, have the rest of the class...

- Visit the Reading/Library Center
- Listen to the AudioText for "Hiking Safety Tips"
- Visit the Writing and Vocabulary Centers
- Finish Writing Across Texts, p. 379
- Visit Cross-Curricular Centers
- Work on inquiry projects

DAY 5

On-Level	Strategic Intervention	Advanced
Teacher-Led *Page DI · 41*	**Teacher-Led** *Page DI · 40*	**Teacher-Led** *Page DI · 41*
Reread Leveled Reader *Goldilocks and the Three Bears* Retell *Goldilocks and the Three Bears*	• **Reread** Leveled Reader *Leo and the School of Fish* • Retell *Leo and the School of Fish*	• **Reread** Leveled Reader *A Fantastic Field Trip* • Share Extension Activity

ⓘ Independent Activities

While you meet with small groups, have the rest of the class...

- Visit the Reading/Library Center
- Complete Practice Book 3.2 pp. 138, 140
- Visit Cross-Curricular Centers
- Work on inquiry projects

 Grouping Place English language learners in the groups that correspond to their reading abilities in English.

Use the appropriate Leveled Reader or other text at students' instructional level.

TIP Send home the appropriate Multilingual Summary of the main selection on Day 1.

Take It to the NET™ ONLINE
PearsonSuccessNet.com

Connie Juel
For research on the importance of phonemic awareness for early reading success, see the article "Learning to Read and Write" by Scott Foresman author Connie Juel.

TEACHER TALK

Paired reading is a method of repeated reading in which two students take turns reading aloud to each other.

Be sure to schedule time for students to work on the unit inquiry project "Symbols of Freedom." This week students will combine information to develop answers to their inquiry questions.

Looking Ahead

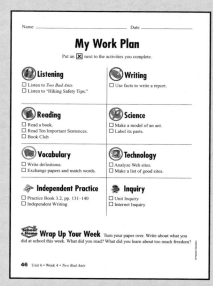

Name	Date
My Work Plan	

Put an ☒ next to the activities you complete.

🎧 Listening
☐ Listen to *Two Bad Ants.*
☐ Listen to "Hiking Safety Tips."

✏️ Writing
☐ Use facts to write a report.

📖 Reading
☐ Read a book.
☐ Read Ten Important Sentences.
☐ Book Club

🔬 Science
☐ Make a model of an ant.
☐ Label its parts.

📚 Vocabulary
☐ Write definitions.
☐ Exchange papers and match words.

💻 Technology
☐ Analyze Web sites.
☐ Make a list of good sites.

✐ Independent Practice
☐ Practice Book 3.2, pp. 131–140
☐ Independent Writing

🔍 Inquiry
☐ Unit Inquiry
☐ Internet Inquiry

Wrap Up Your Week Turn your paper over. Write about what you did at school this week. What did you read? What did you learn about too much freedom?

46 Unit 6 • Week 4 • *Two Bad Ants*

▲ **Group-Time Survival Guide**
p. 46, Weekly Contract

ORAL LANGUAGE

 Science

Concept Development

When can freedom be a problem?

CONCEPT VOCABULARY

encountered   *fascinated*   *guilty*

BUILD

❑ **Question of the Week** Introduce and discuss the question of the week. This week students will read a variety of texts and work on projects related to the concept *too much freedom.* Post the question for students to refer to throughout the week. **DAY 1** *354d*

❑ **Read Aloud** Read aloud "The Boy Who Stopped Time." Then begin a web to build concepts and concept vocabulary related to this week's lesson and the unit theme, Freedom. Introduce the concept words *encountered, fascinated,* and *guilty* and have students place them on the web. Display the web for use throughout the week. **DAY 1** *354l-354m*

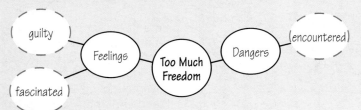

DEVELOP

❑ **Question of the Day** Use the prompts from the Weekly Plan to engage students in conversations related to this week's reading and the unit theme. **EVERY DAY** *354d-354e*

❑ **Concept Vocabulary Web** Revisit the Too Much Freedom Concept Web and encourage students to add concept words from their reading and life experiences. **DAY 2** *367,* **DAY 3** *375*

CONNECT

❑ **Looking Back/Moving Forward** Revisit the Too Much Freedom Concept Web and discuss how it relates to this week's lesson and the unit theme. Then make connections to next week's lesson. **DAY 5** *379c*

CHECK

❑ **Concept Vocabulary Web** Use the Too Much Freedom Concept Web to check students' understanding of the concept vocabulary words *encountered, fascinated,* and *guilty.* **DAY 1** *354l,* **DAY 5** *379c*

VOCABULARY

↻ **STRATEGY WORD STRUCTURE**
Word structure means the way that parts of a word are put together. A prefix is a group of letters at the beginning of a word that changes the word's meaning. A suffix is a group of letters added at the end of a word that changes the word's meaning. When you come across a word you don't know, look closely to see if the word has a prefix or a suffix that can help you figure out the word's meaning.

LESSON VOCABULARY

crystal	journey
disappeared	joyful
discovery	scoop
goal	unaware

TEACH

❑ **Words to Know** Give students the opportunity to tell what they already know about this week's lesson vocabulary words. Then discuss word meaning. **DAY 1** *356b*

❑ **Vocabulary Strategy Lesson** Use the vocabulary strategy lesson in the Student Edition to introduce and model this week's strategy, *word structure.* **DAY 2** *356-357*

Vocabulary Strategy Lesson

PRACTICE/APPLY

❑ **Leveled Text** Read the lesson vocabulary in the context of leveled text. **DAY 1** *LR28-LR36*

❑ **Words in Context** Read the lesson vocabulary and apply *word structure* in the context of *Two Bad Ants.* **DAY 2** *358-367,* **DAY 3** *368-376*

Leveled Readers

❑ **Vocabulary Center** Make word puzzles for classmates. **ANY DAY** *354j*

❑ **Homework** Practice Book 3.2 pp. 134–135. **DAY 1** *356b,* **DAY 2** *357*

Main Selection—Fiction

❑ **Word Play** Have partners use reference sources to make lists of insect words and their meanings. Students can make illustrated bug dictionaries using their words. **ANY DAY** *379c*

ASSESS

❑ **Selection Test** Use the Selection Test to determine students' understanding of the lesson vocabulary words. **DAY 3**

RETEACH/REVIEW

❑ **Reteach Lesson** If necessary, use this lesson to reteach and review *word structure.* **DAY 5** *379c*

COMPREHENSION

SKILL PLOT AND THEME A plot is the important events that happen in a story. The story's plot has a beginning, a middle, and an end. A theme is the point the author is trying to make. The theme can be told in a sentence.

STRATEGY VISUALIZE When you visualize, you make pictures in your mind as you read a story. As you read, picture in your mind what happens at the story's beginning, middle, and end. Visualizing will help you keep track of the story's plot.

TEACH

☐ **Skill/Strategy Lesson** Use the skill/strategy lesson in the Student Edition to introduce and model *plot and theme* and *visualizing*. DAY 1 354–355

☐ **Extend Skills** Teach setting. ANY DAY 379b

Skill/Strategy Lesson

PRACTICE/APPLY

☐ **Leveled Text** Apply *plot and theme* and *visualizing* to read leveled text. DAY 1 LR28–LR36

Leveled Readers

☐ **Skills and Strategies in Context** Read *Two Bad Ants*, using the Guiding Comprehension questions to apply *plot and theme* and *visualizing*. DAY 2 358–367, DAY 3 368–376

Main Selection—Fiction

☐ **Skills and Strategies in Context** Read "Hiking Safety Tips," guiding students as they apply *plot and theme* and *visualizing*. Then have students discuss and write across texts. DAY 4 378–379

Paired Selection—Nonfiction

☐ **Homework** Practice Book 3.2 pp. 133, 137, 138. DAY 1 355, DAY 3 375, DAY 5 379b

☐ **Fresh Reads for Differentiated Test Practice** Have students practice *plot and theme* with a new passage. DAY 3

ASSESS

☐ **Selection Test** Determine students' understanding of the selection and their use of *plot and theme*. DAY 3

☐ **Retell** Have students retell *Two Bad Ants*. DAY 3 376–377

RETEACH/REVIEW

☐ **Reteach Lesson** If necessary, reteach and review *plot and theme*. DAY 5 379b

FLUENCY

SKILL ACCURACY, APPROPRIATE PACE/RATE AND EXPRESSION Accuracy is identifying words correctly as you read, and reading without omitting words or substituting words. Appropriate pace and rate means reading at the right speed—not too fast and not too slow. Reading with expression means reading the words as if you were the character.

TEACH

☐ **Read Aloud** Model fluent reading by rereading "The Boy Who Stopped Time." Focus on this week's fluency skill, accuracy, appropriate pace/rate and expression. DAY 1 354l–354m, 379a

PRACTICE/APPLY

☐ **Echo Reading** Read aloud selected paragraphs from *Two Bad Ants*, emphasizing expression as you read. Then practice as a class, doing three echo readings of the paragraphs. DAY 2 379a

☐ **Choral Reading** After you model reading p. 363, have students choral read three times. DAY 3 379a

☐ **Paired Reading** Partners practice reading aloud with accuracy and offering each other feedback. As students reread, monitor their progress toward their individual fluency goals. DAY 4 379a

☐ **Listening Center** Have students follow along with the AudioText for this week's selections. ANY DAY 354j

☐ **Reading/Library Center** Have students reread a selection of their choice. ANY DAY 354j

☐ **Fluency Coach** Have students use Fluency Coach to listen to fluent readings or practice reading on their own. ANY DAY

ASSESS

☐ **Check Fluency** WCPM Do a one-minute timed reading, paying special attention to this week's skill—accuracy, appropriate pace/rate and expression. Provide feedback for each student. DAY 5 379a

GRAMMAR

SKILL COMMAS A comma is a punctuation mark that is used to separate words in a sentence, or parts of a sentence. A comma also separates part of a letter, the month and day in a date, and the city and state in an address.

TEACH

☐ **Grammar Transparency 29** Use Grammar Transparency 29 to teach commas. **DAY 1** *379e*

Grammar Transparency 29

PRACTICE/APPLY

☐ **Develop the Concept** Review the concept of using commas and provide guided practice. **DAY 2** *379e*

☐ **Apply to Writing** Have students review something they have written and apply what they have learned about commas. **DAY 3** *379f*

☐ **Test Preparation** Examine common errors in the use of commas to prepare for standardized tests. **DAY 4** *379f*

☐ **Homework** Grammar and Writing Practice Book pp. 113–115. **DAY 2** *379e*, **DAY 3** *379f*, **DAY 4** *379f*

ASSESS

☐ **Cumulative Review** Use Grammar and Writing Practice Book p. 116. **DAY 5** *379f*

RETEACH/REVIEW

☐ **Daily Fix-It** Have students find and correct errors in grammar, spelling, and punctuation. **EVERY DAY** *379e-379f*

☐ **The Grammar and Writing Book** Use pp. 218–221 of The Grammar and Writing Book to extend instruction for using commas. **ANY DAY**

The Grammar and Writing Book

WRITING

Trait of the Week

WORD CHOICE Words are a writer's handiest tools. For example, when you describe a picture, use precise nouns and vivid adjectives. Your description will be interesting and lively.

TEACH

☐ **Writing Transparency 29A** Use the model to introduce and discuss the Trait of the Week. **DAY 1** *379g*

☐ **Writing Transparency 29B** Use the transparency to show students how elaborating can improve their writing. **DAY 2** *379g*

Writing Transparency 29A   **Writing Transparency 29B**

PRACTICE/APPLY

☐ **Write Now** Examine the model on Student Edition p. 377. Then have students write their own picture descriptions. **DAY 3** *377, 379h*, **DAY 4** *379h*

> **Prompt** *Two Bad Ants* describes the adventures of two ants. Think about a picture in the story you find interesting. Now write about that picture, using vivid words.

Write Now p. 377

☐ **Writing Center** Using the facts about ants provided, write a paragraph for a research report about ants. **ANY DAY** *354k*

ASSESS

☐ **Writing Trait Rubric** Use the rubric to evaluate students' writing. **DAY 4** *379h*

RETEACH/REVIEW

☐ **The Grammar and Writing Book** Use pp. 218–223 of The Grammar and Writing Book to extend instruction for commas, elaborating, and picture descriptions. **ANY DAY**

The Grammar and Writing Book

① Use assessment data to determine your instructional focus.

② Preview this week's instruction by strand.

③ Choose instructional activities that meet the needs of your classroom.

SPELLING

GENERALIZATION MULTISYLLABIC WORDS When spelling words with many syllables, look carefully at each word part. Multisyllabic words can be divided into smaller parts for spelling and pronunciation.

TEACH

❏ **Pretest** Give the pretest for words with multiple syllables. Guide students in self-correcting their pretests and correcting any misspellings. **DAY 1** *379k*

❏ **Think and Practice** Connect spelling to the phonics generalization for multisyllabic words. **DAY 2** *379k*

PRACTICE/APPLY

❏ **Connect to Writing** Have students use spelling words to write an editorial. Then review frequently misspelled words: *everybody, everything.* **DAY 3** *379l*

❏ **Homework** Phonics and Spelling Practice Book pp. 113–116. **EVERY DAY**

RETEACH/REVIEW

❏ **Review** Review spelling words to prepare for the posttest. Then provide students with a spelling strategy—word combinations. **DAY 4** *379l*

ASSESS

❏ **Posttest** Use dictation sentences to give the posttest for words with multiple syllables. **DAY 5** *379l*

Spelling Words

1. leadership	6. remarkable*	11. impossibly
2. gracefully	7. carefully	12. reappeared
3. refreshment	8. unbearably*	13. unprepared
4. uncomfortable	9. ownership	14. oncoming
5. overdoing	10. unacceptable	15. misbehaving

Challenge Words

16. outrageous	18. undoubtedly	20. disadvantage
17. incomprehensible	19. independence	

*Word from the selection

PHONICS

SKILL MULTISYLLABIC WORDS When reading an unfamililiar multisyllabic word, first look for "chunks" you know. Then use phonics skills to decode any parts that remain.

TEACH

❏ **Phonics Lesson** Model how to read words with multiple syllables. Then have students practice by decoding longer words and reading words in context. **DAY 2** *379i*

PRACTICE/APPLY

❏ **Homework** Practice Book 3.2, p. 139. **DAY 2** *379i*

RETEACH/REVIEW

❏ **Review Word Parts** Review how to read words with the syllables *-tion, -sion,* and *-ture.* Then have students practice by decoding longer words and reading words in context. **DAY 4** *379j*

RESEARCH AND INQUIRY

❏ **Internet Inquiry** Have students conduct an Internet inquiry on freedom. **EVERY DAY** *379m*

❏ **Note-taking** Review terms and ideas related to note-taking, such as keeping notes brief, including the most important information, and using your own words. Have students work in pairs, one partner reading from a science or social studies book while the other takes notes, then switching roles. **DAY 5** *379n*

❏ **Unit Inquiry** Allow time for students to combine information to develop answers to their inquiry questions. **ANY DAY** *283*

SPEAKING AND VIEWING

❏ **Description** Have students write descriptions of their bedrooms as seen by ants. Remind them to use the notes they wrote in Look Back and Write on p. 376 to help them think of other descriptive words and phrases. **DAY 5** *379d*

❏ **Analyze Classified Ads** Have students choose four or five classified ads in newspapers. Then have them answer questions orally or in writing. **DAY 5** *379d*

Resources for
Differentiated Instruction

LEVELED READERS

▶ **Comprehension**
- 🔄 **Skill** Plot and Theme
- 🔄 **Strategy** Visualize

▶ **Lesson Vocabulary**
- 🔄 **Word Structure**

discovery journey crystal goal unaware joyful scoop disappeared

▶ **Science Standards**
- • Life Cycles
- • Environments

Leveled Reader Database
ONLINE
PearsonSuccessNet.com

Use the Online Database of over 600 books to
- • Download and print additional copies of this week's leveled readers.
- • Listen to the readers being read online.
- • Search for more titles focused on this week's skills, topic, and content.

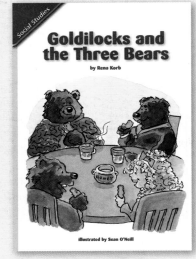

Social Studies
Goldilocks and the Three Bears
by Rena Korb

illustrated by Sean O'Neill

On-Level Reader

Plot and Theme
- • The **plot** is an organized pattern of events.
- • The **theme** is the "big idea" of a story.

Directions Fill in the table below, which will guide you through a summary of the plot and end with your naming the theme of *Goldilocks and the Three Bears.*
Possible responses given.

Title _Goldilocks and the Three Bears_

This story is about _Goldilocks, Dad Bear, Mom Bear, and Billy Bear._
(name the characters)

This story takes place _in the house of the Bear family._
(where and when)

The action begins when _Mom Bear makes oatmeal that is too hot to eat. The family goes for a walk while it cools._

Then, _Goldilocks wanders by their house. She goes inside to taste the oatmeal._

Next, _she tastes the oatmeal, breaks their chairs and a crystal animal, and falls asleep in Billy Bear's bed._

After that, _the Bears return and find the things she's broken. They also find her asleep in Billy Bear's bed. She wakes up, says she's sorry, and runs off._

The story ends when _Billy Bear stops her and says he forgives her._

Theme: _It is best to respect the property of others._

🔄 **On-Level Practice** TE p. LR32

Vocabulary
Directions Fill in the blank with the word from the box that fits best.

Check the Words You Know
__crystal __disappeared __discovery __goal
__journey __joyful __scoop __unaware

1. Mom Bear made breakfast with one large _scoop_ of oatmeal.
2. Goldilocks _disappeared_ from the Bears' house in a rush.
3. Goldilocks did not knock the _crystal_ vase off the shelf.
4. The thought of oatmeal for breakfast made Papa Bear feel _joyful_.
5. The Bears were _unaware_ that Goldilocks was upstairs sleeping.
6. The _goal_ of the Bears' walk was to let the oatmeal cool.
7. The Bears made a big _discovery_ when they returned home.
8. Goldilocks will be more careful on her next _journey_.

Directions Write a brief paragraph discussing Goldilocks's visit to the Bears' house, using as many vocabulary words as possible.
Responses will vary.

🔄 **On-Level Practice** TE p. LR33

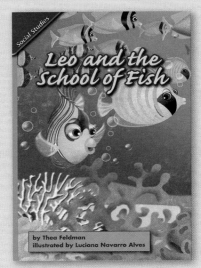

Social Studies
Leo and the School of Fish
by Thea Feldman
illustrated by Luciana Navarro Alves

Below-Level Reader

Plot and Theme
- • The **plot** is an organized pattern of events.
- • The **theme** is the "big idea" of a story.

Directions Fill in the graphic organizer about the story elements in *Leo and the School of Fish.*

Title _Leo and the School of Fish_

This story is about _a fish named Leo_
(name the characters)

This story takes place _under the sea; a time like today_
(where and when)

The action begins when _Leo swims away from the school to look at a ship._

Then, _Leo confronts a lantern fish._

Next, _he confronts a moray eel._

After that, _he gets caught in a net but is able to swim through it._

The story ends when _he rejoins the school._

Theme: _It's best to stick with the group._

🔄 **Below-Level Practice** TE p. LR29

Vocabulary
Directions Fill in the blank with the word from the box that fits best.

Check the Words You Know
__crystal __disappeared __discovery __goal
__journey __joyful __scoop __unaware

1. Leo didn't listen to his friend Gil and set off on his _journey_.
2. The fisherman tried to _scoop_ the fish out of the water with the net.
3. The flashing _crystal_ caught Leo's eye.
4. Leo was hoping to make an exciting _discovery_ on his adventure.
5. The fish in the school were _joyful_ when Leo returned safely.
6. Leo swam so fast it looked as if he _disappeared_.
7. Leo's _goal_ was to explore the ship.
8. Leo was _unaware_ of what would happen on his journey.

Directions Write a brief paragraph discussing Leo's journey, using as many vocabulary words as possible.
Responses will vary.

🔄 **Below-Level Practice** TE p. LR30

Advanced

Life Science

A Fantastic Field Trip

by C. Truman Rogers
illustrated by Dan Bridy

Advanced Reader

Plot and Theme

- The **plot** is an organized pattern of events.
- The **theme** is the "big idea" of a story.

Directions Fill in the table below, which will guide you through a summary of the plot and end with your naming the theme of *A Fantastic Field Trip*. Possible responses given.

1. **Title** _A Fantastic Field Trip_

2. This story is about _the Bug Kids (Emma, Jacob, Kayla, Luke, Carlos, Lily), Mr. Edwards, Mrs. Appleby, and Elvis._
   (name the characters)

3. This story takes place _at the school and at the Entomological Zoo._
   (where and when)

4. The action begins when _the Bug Kids take off in the school van for the zoo. They arrive at their hotel, where they spend one night._

5. Then _at the Entomological Zoo, they visit the butterflies, and some are huge._

6. Next, _they visit wasps and cicadas, which are also huge._

7. After that, _they visit fleas that can jump 150 feet._

8. The story ends when _they return home._

9. Theme: _One should have respect for insects._

Advanced Practice TE p. LR35

Vocabulary

Directions Fill in the blank with the word from the box that fits best.

Check the Words You Know
__announcement __budge __entomological
__exhibition __expenses __nuisances

1. We heard the __announcement__ that blared "Put on your sunglasses!"
2. The __entomological__ zoo was a place that was all about bugs.
3. The Bug Kids raised money to pay for their trip's __expenses__.
4. They tried to open the door but it wouldn't __budge__.
5. The entomological __exhibition__ housed many gigantic insects.
6. Although insects can be fascinating, some of them can be __nuisances__.

Directions Write a brief paragraph discussing the Bug Kids' trip to the Entomological Zoo, using as many vocabulary words as possible.

Responses will vary.

Advanced Practice TE p. LR36

Lorita's Adventure

by Magali Jaramillo
Illustrated by Freddie Levin

ELL Reader

ELL Poster 29

Teacher's Edition Notes

ELL notes throughout this lesson support instruction and reference additional resources at point of use.

**Teaching Guide
pp. 197–203, 268–269**

- Multilingual summaries of the main selection
- Comprehension lesson
- Vocabulary strategies and word cards
- ELL Reader 3.6.4 lesson

ELL and Transition Handbook

Ten Important Sentences

- Key ideas from every selection in the Student Edition
- Activities to build sentence power

More Reading

Readers' Theater Anthology

- Fluency practice
- Five scripts to build fluency
- Poetry for oral interpretation

Leveled Trade Books

Below-Level

On-Level

Advanced

- Extended reading tied to the unit concept
- Lessons in the Trade Book Library Teaching Guide

School + Home

Homework

- Family Times Newsletter
- ELL Multilingual Selection Summaries

Take-Home Books

- Leveled Readers

Family Times

Cross-Curricular Centers

Listen to the Selection

MATERIALS SINGLES
CD player, headphones,
AudioText CD, student book

Listen to *Two Bad Ants* and "Hiking Safety Tips" as you follow or read along in your book. Listen for the main events in the story. Identify the story's theme.

If there is anything you don't understand, you can listen again to any section.

Read It Again!

MATERIALS SINGLES PAIRS GROUPS
Collection of books for self-selected reading, reading log

Select a book you have already read. Record the title of the book in your reading log. You may want to read with a partner.

You may choose to read any of the following:

- **Leveled Readers**
- **ELL Readers**
- **Stories written by classmates**
- **Books from the library**
- *Two Bad Ants*

TEN IMPORTANT SENTENCES Read the Ten Important Sentences for *Two Bad Ants*. Then locate the sentences in the Student Edition.

BOOK CLUB Read "Meet the Author and Illustrator" on p. 377. Read other books by Van Allsburg and share your favorites with a group. Discuss how the texts and illustrations are the same and different across his books.

Word Match

MATERIALS PAIRS
Paper, art supplies, dictionary

Use words and definitions to make a puzzle for a classmate.

1. **Choose five words from the list below. Write them on a piece of paper.**
2. **Use a dictionary to learn their meanings. Write each definition on the paper in an order different from the words.**
3. **Exchange papers with a partner. Match words with definitions.**

EARLY FINISHERS Think of different ways to sort the words you gave clues for. Make lists to show your sorting.

antennae	fountain
chamber	frightening
delicious	sparkling
echo	temperature
entrance	treasure

Writing

 Science

 Technology

Write a Report

MATERIALS   `SINGLES`
Paper, pencil

Write a paragraph for a research report that tells about ants.

1. Read the facts about ants below.
2. Use the facts to write a paragraph that tells about how ants communicate.

Ant Facts
- social insects
- live in colonies
- antennae to smell, touch, taste, and hear
- give off chemicals with smells
- smells carry a message about food or danger

EARLY FINISHERS Write a list of questions about animal communication that you would like to have answered.

Ants trade messages with each other using their antennae to smell, touch, taste, and hear. They also can give off smells that tell about food or danger.

Danger!   *Yikes!*

Ant Bodies

MATERIALS   `SINGLES`
Books on ants, Internet access, art supplies

Learn about an ant's body.

1. Use the resources to learn about an ant's body parts.
2. Make a model of an ant.
3. Label its body parts. Write a short sentence to tell about each body part.

EARLY FINISHERS List five interesting facts you learned about ants while researching their body parts.

Antennae—An ant uses its antennae to smell, touch, hear, and taste.

Analyze Web Sites

MATERIALS   `PAIRS`
Computer, paper, pencil or pen

Find a Web site about ants and decide if it is a reliable source.

1. Use a search engine to find Web sites with facts about ants.
2. With a partner, discuss which sites seemed more reliable and why.
3. Make a list of good Web sites that you found. Describe why you trust them.

EARLY FINISHERS Write a paragraph listing some of the facts that you found on a reliable Web site.

Search Engine

ants

 **ALL CENTERS**

Concept Vocabulary

encountered met someone or something unexpectedly

fascinated held a great interest in

guilty knowing or showing that you have done something wrong

Monitor Progress

Check Vocabulary

If... students are unable to place words on the web,	then... review the lesson concept. Place the words on the web and provide additional words for practice, such as *sadness* and *forbidden*.

SUCCESS PREDICTOR

DAY 1   Grouping Options

Reading
Whole Group
Introduce and discuss the Question of the Week. Then use pp. 354l–356b.

Group Time
Differentiated Instruction
Read this week's Leveled Readers. See pp. 354f–354g for the small group lesson plan.

Whole Group
Use p. 379a.

Language Arts
Use pp. 379e–379h and 379k–379m.

Build Concepts

FLUENCY

MODEL ACCURACY, APPROPRIATE PACE/RATE, AND EXPRESSION As you read "The Boy Who Stopped Time," model reading accurately, at an appropriate pace, and with expression. You can read the mother's voice in paragraph 2 in a stern manner. Model regular speech when reading dialogue. Emphasize pauses indicated by punctuation such as commas and ellipsis.

LISTENING COMPREHENSION

After reading "The Boy Who Stopped Time," use the following questions to assess listening comprehension.

1. **What problem does Julian have at the beginning of the story?** *(He has to go to bed every night at 7:30.)* **Plot and Theme**

2. **What is the big idea of the story?** *(It is better to obey the rules than to be alone.)* **Plot and Theme**

BUILD CONCEPT VOCABULARY

Start a web to build concepts and vocabulary related to this week's lesson and the unit theme.

- Draw a Too Much Freedom Web.
- Read the sentence with the word *encountered* again. Ask students to pronounce *encountered* and discuss its meaning.
- Place *encountered* in an oval attached to Dangers. Explain that *encountered* is related to this concept. Read the sentences in which *fascinated* and *guilty* appear. Have students pronounce the words, place them on the web, and provide reasons.
- Brainstorm additional words and categories for the web. Keep the web on display and add words throughout the week.

Concept Vocabulary Web

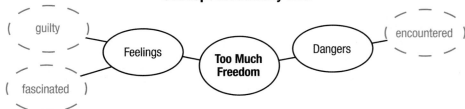

The Boy Who Stopped Time

by Anthony Tabor

No matter how much fun he was having, every night at 7:30, when the clock on the living room wall went *ding-dong*, Julian had to go to bed.

One summer evening, just before bedtime, Julian asked his mom if he could stay up late to watch a special TV show. "No, Julian," she said. "You need your rest more than you need that show. When the big hand gets to the six, it's off to bed with you." She left the living room to tuck in his little sister, AnnaRose.

Julian watched the clock's pendulum swing back and forth until the big hand slid past the five. Then he went to the window. Outside, his father was piling stones in the yard. And from his sister's bedroom he heard his mother begin a lullaby. Julian suddenly had a wonderful idea. He pushed a chair beneath the clock, then climbed up and opened the clock's face. He took a deep breath . . . and stopped the pendulum. A strange hush fell over the house.

He tiptoed down the hall to his sister's room. There in the shadows was his mom, leaning over AnnaRose's crib. Her mouth was open as if she were singing, and AnnaRose was smiling up at her. Everything looked perfectly normal, except his mom and his sister were both as still and quiet as statues. Julian backed out of the room, amazed at what he had done, and ran outside.

He found his dad with arms outstretched by the rock pile, his eyes fixed on a big rock he had just thrown. Julian called to him but got no reply. Looking at his dad made Julian feel guilty. He had not intended to have *everything* stop, only the clock. Maybe he should start the clock again, even though he would have to go to bed.

But on the way back to the house he thought of not having to go to bed. The more he thought about it the better he liked the idea. If he didn't start the clock he never had to go to bed again. So . . . instead of going inside he walked slowly around the house, fascinated by the eerie stillness.

Down by the creek that edged their land, he encountered a magnificent buck deer. It was twice his height, with a huge rack of antlers. Julian had to use a stepladder from the shed to reach its back. Up there he felt like the king of all he saw, and he wished he could make the deer move from the creek and race over the countryside. He looked at his house and his father by the stone pile. He could still go anywhere and do anything he wanted. He decided to take his bike up the driveway to the main road, where he was strictly forbidden to go.

Before leaving, he stopped at the house, gave his mom a secret kiss good-bye, and took some cookies for the trip. He pedaled fearlessly out onto the main road and didn't stop until he was almost a mile away, at the first intersection. He had never been this far on his own before. Julian stopped at the library. It was still

continued on TR1

Set Purpose

Read the title aloud and have students set their own purposes for reading.

Creative Response

Encourage students to work with a partner to write a script for the next night at Julian's house. Have students decide whether or not Julian will stop time again and the adventures he will have if he does. Invite students to present their script to the class. *Drama*

ELL

Build Background Before students listen to the Read Aloud, show them a picture of a clock with a pendulum. Discuss how it works.

Access Content Before reading, share this summary: A young child, Julian, stops time so that he will not have to obey his mother and go to bed at 7:30. Julian learns that even though he's awake, it isn't fun to be alone.

School + Home **Homework** Send home this week's Family Times newsletter.

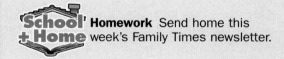

Vocabulary

SUCCESS PREDICTOR

Plot and Theme
Visualize

OBJECTIVES

- Identify a story's plot and theme.
- Visualize plot events to improve comprehension.

Skills Trace
Plot and Theme

Introduce/Teach	TE: 3.4 112–113, 3.6 354–355
Practice	PB: 3.2 43, 47, 48, 116, 133, 137, 138
Reteach/Review	TE: 3.4 137b, DI·56, 3.6 315, 379b, DI·55
Test	Selection Test: Unit 6

INTRODUCE

Read the following short story aloud to students: *There was a thunderstorm last night. Our electricity went out. I thought I saw a monster in the corner. Then the electricity came back on. I saw that what I thought was a monster was only a pile of dirty clothes!* Ask students to identify the "big idea" of the story. *(Possible response: Your eyes can play tricks on you at night.)* Then ask students to describe the beginning, middle, and end of the story.

Have students read the information on p. 354. Explain the following:

- Identifying the plot is like summarizing the story.

- Remember that a story's plot tells the beginning, middle, and end. A theme is the "big idea" of the story. It can be told in only a phrase or sentence.

- When you visualize the important events, or the plot, you can better understand what is happening in the story.

Use Skill Transparency 29 to teach plot and theme and visualize.

Comprehension

Skill
Plot and Theme

Strategy
Visualize

Plot and Theme

- The important events in a story make up the plot.

- The plot has a beginning, a middle, and an end.

- The "big idea" of the story is called the theme.

- The theme can be stated in a single sentence.

(Beginning) → (Middle) → (End)

Strategy: Visualize

Good readers use their imaginations to picture what is happening at the beginning, the middle, and the end of a story. As you read, pretend you are watching a movie of the story inside your head! This will help you keep track of the plot.

Write to Read

1. Read "The Ant and the Beetle." Make a graphic organizer like the one above to show the plot of the story.

2. Write the theme—or moral—of the story, using just one sentence.

354

Strategic Intervention

Plot and Theme Remind students that a story's theme can be told in one sentence. It is the point that the author is trying to make. A story's plot is its most important events. It tells the action at the beginning, middle, and end of the story. Provide students with short stories. Work with them to identify the plot sequence and the theme.

ELL

Access Content

Beginning/Intermediate For a Picture It! lesson on plot and theme, see the ELL Teaching Guide, pp. 197–198.

Advanced Before students read "The Ant and the Beetle," review with them the characteristics of a fable. Remind them that in a fable, the author gives human characteristics to animals in order to teach a moral or lesson. The lesson is sometimes stated at the end of the story.

The Ant and the Beetle

Adapted from Aesop's "The Fox and the Crow"

Annie Ant was famished. She stole a piece of cheese from an abandoned picnic and scrambled up to sit on a rock. She was about to eat the cheese when she noticed a beetle nearby.

The beetle had been spying on her, and having grown tired of his dull menu of leaves, he wanted the cheese for himself. He made a plan.

"My, my, I have never seen such a beautiful ant. From the tip of your antennae to the end of your abdomen, you are simply gorgeous!" flattered the beetle.

Annie thought, "Finally, someone who appreciates my true beauty."

"It is a shame," said the beetle. "Such a beauty must be delicate. Surely, you are not strong enough to help the other ants."

Now Annie Ant was insulted. How dare he suggest she was weak. "Hmph! I can lift this rock that is twice my size," she said.

Annie Ant set down the cheese and lifted the rock over her head. ●

The beetle grabbed the cheese and began to scurry away. "Yes, you are very strong, but you are also very foolish." ●

1 **Strategy** Here is a good place to visualize. What picture do you have in your mind of Annie Ant?

2 **Skill** In a fable, the theme is usually a lesson to be learned. It is called the *moral*. What lesson did the ant learn at the end of this story?

355

Available as **Skill Transparency** 29

TEACH

1 **STRATEGY** Model how to visualize the events of a story.

Think Aloud **MODEL** Annie Ant tells the beetle she "can lift this rock that is twice my size." That helps me see a picture of Annie in my head. She is sitting on a rock. The rock is as big as two ants.

2 **SKILL** Discuss identifying a story's theme.

Think Aloud **MODEL** Visualizing helped me understand the story's beginning, middle, and end. It helped me identify the important events. I ask myself, "What was the author trying to tell me?" I know that the answer is not right there in the text. I will have to put the theme into my own words. I also know the story is a fable. Fables usually teach a lesson. The lesson is the theme.

PRACTICE AND ASSESS

STRATEGY Possible response: I see Annie Ant struggling to lift a rock. She is angry at the beetle for insulting her. She is looking at him as if to say, "I told you so!"

SKILL Do not let your pride make you foolish.

WRITE Have students complete steps 1 and 2 of the Write to Read activity. You might consider using this as a whole class activity.

Monitor Progress

Plot and Theme

| If... students are unable to complete **Write to Read** on p. 354, | then... use Practice Book 3.2 p. 133 to provide additional practice. |

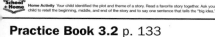

Plot and Theme • Visualize

- The important events in a story make up the **plot** with a beginning, middle, and end.
- The "big idea" of the story is called the **theme**. It can be stated in a single sentence.
- As you read, form a picture in your mind about what is happening in the story.

Directions Read the following story. Then fill in the chart below.

The ants felt sorry for the grasshopper. He'd saved no food and was starving. So they shared what they had. The grasshopper swore he'd remember their kindness and repay them someday. When summer came, the ants were playing outside and accidentally hurt themselves. How would they gather their food? Just then the grasshopper stopped by. When he heard what happened, he told the ants to climb on his back. The ants told the grasshopper where to go and what to gather. Soon the trio had all the food they needed for the winter ahead.

What happened at the beginning of the story?
1. The ants shared their food with the grasshopper.

What happened in the middle of the story?
2. The ants hurt themselves and couldn't gather food.

What happened at the end of the story?
3. The grasshopper helped the ants gather food.

4. What is the "big idea" of this story? Responses may vary.
Help others because one day you might need someone to help you.

5. On a separate sheet of paper, draw what you picture in your mind as you finish reading this story.
Possible drawing: The grasshopper with two ants on its back.

Home Activity Your child identified the plot and theme of a story. Read a favorite story together. Ask your child to retell the beginning, middle, and end of the story and to say one sentence that tells the "big idea."

Practice Book 3.2 p. 133

Tech Files ONLINE

For a Web site that explores life in an ant colony, have students use a student-friendly search engine to do an Internet search using the keywords *ant colony*.

ELL

Build Background Use ELL Poster 29 to build background and vocabulary for the lesson concept of too much freedom.

▲ **ELL Poster** 29

Build Background

ACTIVATE PRIOR KNOWLEDGE

BEGIN A T-CHART about freedom.

- Have students label the left column "Freedom is good when..." Have them label the right column "Too much freedom can be bad when..."
- Explain how to read and complete the columns. Point out that the column heads are sentence starters.
- Allow students time to consider when they have freedom in their lives and when this freedom is good for them. Have them record their ideas in the first column.
- Then have students consider when having too much freedom can be bad. Have them record their ideas in the second column.
- Remind students to add information to their T-chart as they read the selection.

Freedom is good when...	Too much freedom can be bad when...
I can choose what healthy foods to eat for dinner.	I choose to eat only sweets for dinner.

▲ **Graphic Organizer** 25

BACKGROUND BUILDING AUDIO This week's audio presents an interview with entomologist Mark DuBois. After students listen, discuss what they found out and what surprised them most about the work of an entomologist.

Background Building Audio

Introduce Vocabulary

WORD MEANING CHART

Create a word meaning chart for the Words to Know, using the categories *Word, Meaning,* and *Sentence.* Use a three-column chart. Have students write meanings for each word, based on what they think it means. Then have them write a sentence for each word. They should underline the Words to Know in their sentences. Students should share where they may have seen some of these words.

Activate Prior Knowledge

Word Meaning Chart

Word	Meaning	Sentence
1. journey	a trip	She went on a long journey across Africa.
2. goal		
3. crystal		

▲ **Graphic Organizer** 26

Have students look up each word in the glossary to verify that their meanings are correct. If not, they should write a new sentence using the correct meaning.

Ask students what the words *unaware, disappeared,* and *joyful* have in common. (*They all have prefixes or suffixes.*) Then ask them what the base words for these words are (*aware, appear, joy*), and if prefixes or suffixes can be added to any other words from the list. (Possible responses: *crystallize, rediscovery*)

Prefixes and Suffixes

Encourage students to use the words in their writing during the week.

Use the Multisyllabic Word Routine on p. DI·1 to help students read multisyllabic words.

Lesson Vocabulary

WORDS TO KNOW

T crystal a hard, solid piece of some substance that is naturally formed on flat surfaces and angles

T disappeared vanished completely; stopped existing

T discovery something found out

T goal something desired

T journey a long trip from one place to another

T joyful causing or showing joy; glad; happy

T scoop a tool like a small shovel used to dig up things

T unaware not aware; unconscious

MORE WORDS TO KNOW

hovered stayed in one place

twilight the faint light reflected from the sky before sunrise and after sunset

violently acting or doing something with great force

T= Tested Word

Vocabulary

Directions Read each sentence. Write the meaning of the underlined word.

Check the Words You Know	
___goal	___discovery
___scoop	___crystal
___journey	___joyful
___disappeared	___unaware

1. They used a scoop to pour the birdseed into the feeder. tool like a shovel
2. The hikers were on a journey over the mountain. a trip
3. My goal this summer is to learn how to swim. something desired
4. I saw the ant carry a crystal of salt. solid naturally formed substance
5. The chipmunk disappeared among the rocks. vanished from view

Directions Match each word on the left with its meaning. Draw a line from the word to its definition.

6. discovery — not noticing
7. joyful — something new you find
8. unaware — full of happiness
9. disappeared — was no longer seen

Write a Narrative

On a separate sheet of paper, write a narrative about visiting another planet. Write about being very small compared with other things on the planet. Use as many vocabulary words as possible.

Narrative should use vocabulary words to tell about visiting another planet.

Home Activity Your child identified and used vocabulary from *Two Bad Ants.* Read a story about insects to your child. Then discuss the story using this week's vocabulary words.

▲ **Practice Book 3.2** p. 134

Vocabulary Strategy

INTRODUCE

Discuss the word structure strategy for prefixes and suffixes using the steps on p. 356.

TEACH

- Have students read "How Ants Find Food," paying attention to how vocabulary is used.
- Model using word structure to determine the meaning of *disappeared.*

Think Aloud **MODEL** The base word in *disappeared* is *appear*, which means "to be seen or visible." The prefix *dis-* means "not." So *disappeared* probably means "not to be visible, or to vanish from sight."

Words to Know

goal
discovery
scoop
crystal
journey
joyful
disappeared
unaware

Remember

Try the strategy. Then, if you need more help, use your glossary or a dictionary.

Vocabulary Strategy
for Prefixes and Suffixes

Word Structure When you see a word you don't know, look closely at the word. Does it have a prefix or suffix? The prefixes *un-* or *dis-* at the beginning of a word make the word mean "not ___" or "the opposite of ___." For example, *unhappy* means "not happy," and *disagree* means "the opposite of agree." The suffix *-ful* at the end of a word makes a word mean "full of." For example, *joyful* means "full of joy." You can use *un-, dis-,* or *-ful* to help you figure out the meaning of a word you don't know.

1. Put your finger over the prefix or suffix.

2. Look at the base word. Put the base word in the appropriate phrase:
"not___" for *un-*
"the opposite of ___" for *dis-*
"full of ___" for *-ful*

3. Try that meaning in the sentence. Does it make sense?

Read "How Ants Find Food." Look for words that have a prefix or suffix. Use the prefix or suffix to help you figure out the meanings of the words.

356

Strategic Intervention

Word Structure Have students work in pairs to follow the steps on p. 356. Encourage them to list base words and their prefixes or suffixes and then decide together the best meaning for them.

ELL

Access Content Use ELL Poster 29 to preteach vocabulary. Choose from the following to meet language proficiency levels.

Beginning Point out the word structure of *unaware. Aware* means "to be conscious of something." The prefix *un-* means "not." So *unaware* means "not to be conscious of something."

Intermediate After reading, students can create a two-column chart showing base words with their prefixes or suffixes, and the meaning of each.

Advanced Teach the lesson on pp. 356–357. Students can report on the prefixes and suffixes used with words in their home languages.

Resources for home-language words may include parents, bilingual staff members, bilingual dictionaries, or online translation sources.

How Ants Find Food

Ants are social insects. Like wasps and bees, they live in large groups called colonies. The queen ant lays all the eggs, and the worker ants build the nest, look for food, care for the eggs, and defend the nest.

Ants that look for food are called scouts. Their goal is to find food and report the locations to the ants back at the nest. Suppose a scout ant makes this discovery: Someone has left out a scoop of sugar. The scout carries a sugar crystal back to the nest. On its return journey, the scout ant also leaves a scent trail leading from the food to the nest. When the other ants realize that the scout has found food, they become very excited. They seem joyful about the news. Many ants follow the scout's trail back to the food. They swarm over the sugar, picking up all the crystals. In a short time, all of the sugar has disappeared, and so have the ants. It happens so quickly that often people are unaware that ants were ever there at all.

Words to Write

Write about the jobs you think a worker ant does. Use words from the Words to Know list.

357

PRACTICE AND ASSESS

- Have students determine the meanings of the remaining words and explain how they used word structure and prefixes and suffixes to find the meanings.
- Point out that word structure does not work with every word. Students may have to use the glossary or a dictionary to find the exact meaning of some words.
- Have students review their Word Meaning Chart, refining their use of the vocabulary words in their sentences.
- Have students complete Practice Book 3.2, p. 135.

WRITE Writing should include vocabulary words that describe the type of work a worker ant probably does.

Monitor Progress

Word Structure

If... students need more practice with the lesson vocabulary,	then... use Tested Vocabulary Cards.

Vocabulary • Word Structure

- A **prefix** is a word part added to the beginning of a word. A **suffix** is added to the end of a word. **Prefixes** and **suffixes** can help you figure out the meaning of a word you don't know.
- The **prefixes** *un-* and *dis-* mean "not" or "the opposite of." The **suffix** *-ful* means "full of."

Directions Read each pair of sentences. Circle the word that has the same meaning as the underlined words.

1. The girl pushed ahead of me in line. That is <u>not fair</u>.
   (unfair)   unhappy

2. Climbing this mountain is too hard. I am <u>not able</u> to do it.
   disease   (unable)

3. My father did not climb the ladder. He is <u>full of fear</u> high above the ground.
   under   (fearful)

4. He does not keep his word. That's why I <u>do not trust</u> him.
   (distrust)   untrue

5. That dog is mean. I <u>do not like</u> her.
   hateful   (dislike)

Directions Read each sentence. Circle the underlined word that best fits the sentence.

6. My room is in such (disorder)/unclear, I can't find anything.

7. A hammer is a very unused/(useful) tool for nailing things together.

8. My mother (disapproves)/unlike of my staying up late.

9. The strong man had a very unfair/(powerful) handshake.

10. Please (unzip)/disappear your jacket and hang it in the closet.

School + Home Home Activity Your child identified and used prefixes and suffixes to understand new words. Read a story or magazine article together and encourage looking for words with prefixes and suffixes. Help your child use prefixes and suffixes to understand the meaning of unfamiliar words.

▲ **Practice Book 3.2** p. 135

Prereading Strategies

GENRE STUDY

Animal Fantasy

Two Bad Ants is an animal fantasy. In this type of story, animals are personified, or represented as people. In an animal fantasy, the animals can talk, live in houses, have feelings, or lead lives similar to human lives.

PREVIEW AND PREDICT

Have students preview the selection title and illustrations and predict what the story will be about. Encourage students to use lesson vocabulary as they talk about what they expect to read.

Predict Have students predict why the ants in the story are bad. Students will check their predictions in the Strategy Response Log activity on p. 367.

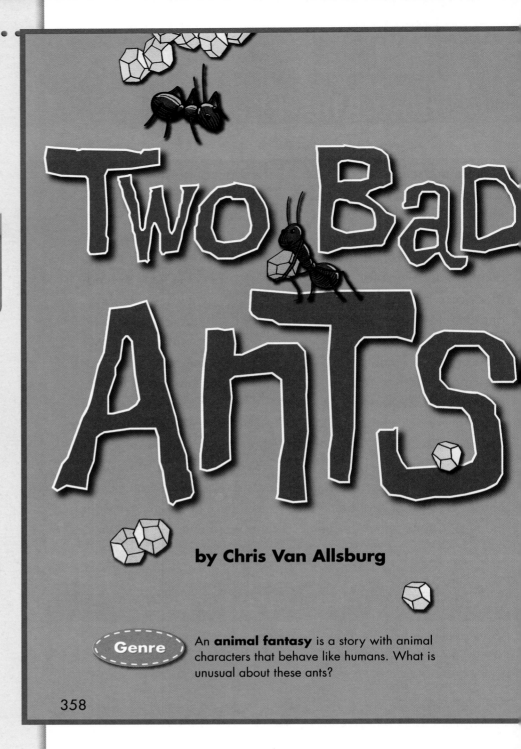

Two Bad Ants

by Chris Van Allsburg

Genre An **animal fantasy** is a story with animal characters that behave like humans. What is unusual about these ants?

358

⊖⊔⊔

Access Content Lead students on a picture walk through the story to reinforce vocabulary, such as *crystal* (p. 360), *goal* (p. 365), *scoop* (p. 367), and introduce the story's setting and plot development.

Consider having students read the selection summary in English or in students' home languages. See the Multilingual Summaries in the ELL Teaching Guide, pp. 208–210.

Who are these two bad ants,
and what do they do?

359

SET PURPOSE

Read the first page of the selection aloud to students. Have them consider their preview discussion and tell what they hope to find out as they read.

Remind students to read for elements of plot and theme of the story.

STRATEGY RECALL

Students have now used these before-reading strategies:

- preview the selection to be aware of its genre, features, and possible content;
- activate prior knowledge about that content and what to expect of that genre;
- make predictions;
- set a purpose for reading.

Remind students that, as they read, they should monitor their own comprehension. If they realize something does not make sense, they can regain their comprehension by using fix-up strategies they have learned, such as:

- use phonics and word structure to decode new words;
- use context clues or a dictionary to figure out meanings of new words;
- adjust their reading rate—slow down for difficult text, speed up for easy or familiar text, or skim and scan just for specific information;
- reread parts of the text;
- read on (continue to read for clarification);
- use text features such as headings, subheadings, charts, illustrations, and so on as visual aids to comprehension;
- make a graphic organizer or a semantic organizer to aid comprehension;
- use reference sources, such as an encyclopedia, dictionary, thesaurus, or synonym finder;
- use another person, such as a teacher, a peer, a librarian, or an outside expert, as a resource.

After reading, students will use these strategies:

- summarize or retell the text;
- answer questions they or others pose;
- reflect to make new information become part of their prior knowledge.

Audio CD AudioText

Guiding Comprehension

1 **Setting • Literal**

Where and when does the beginning of the story take place?

Underground in an ant home, late in the day.

2 **REVIEW Cause and Effect • Inferential**

What was the cause of the ants' decision to make a long and dangerous journey?

The queen wanted more crystals.

Monitor Progress	
REVIEW Cause and Effect	
If... students are unable to determine the cause and effect relationship,	**then...** use the skill and strategy instruction on p. 361.

use the skill and strategy instruction on p. 361.

Tech Files
ONLINE

Students can find out more about ant communication by searching the Internet. Have them use a student-friendly search engine and the keywords *ant communication*.

---

1 The news traveled swiftly through the tunnels of the ant world. A scout had returned with a remarkable discovery—a beautiful sparkling crystal. When the scout presented the crystal to the ant queen, she took a small bite, then quickly ate the entire thing.

She deemed it the most delicious food she had ever tasted. Nothing could make her happier than to have more, much more. The ants understood. They were eager to gather more crystals because the queen was **2** the mother of them all. Her happiness made the whole ant nest a happy place.

ELL

Build Background Help students understand the workings of an ant colony, including their home, way of life, and communication.

It was late in the day when they departed. Long shadows stretched over the entrance to the ant kingdom. One by one the insects climbed out, following the scout, who had made it clear—there were many crystals where the first had been found, but the journey was long and dangerous.

361

Species

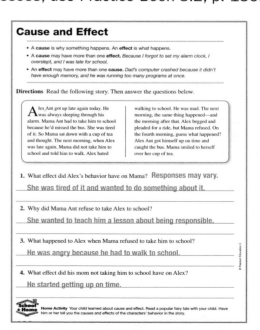

There are about 10,000 different kinds of ants. They can be grouped according to their way of life. Army ants hunt insects and spiders. Slave makers raid other ants' nests. They take young ants that later work in the slave makers' colony. Harvester ants collect and store seeds. Dairy ants and honey ants eat a sugary liquid called honeydew that they gather from insects and plants. What kind of ants might the two bad ants be?

SKILLS ◆ STRATEGIES IN CONTEXT

Cause and Effect REVIEW

TEACH

- Remind students that understanding cause and effect relationships can help them better understand why characters do certain things.
- A cause is something that makes another thing happen. An effect is what happened.
- Model identifying the causal relationship.

Think Aloud **MODEL** I know the effect: The ants go on a long and dangerous journey. I need to find out why. I read that because the queen wanted more crystals, the ants went to get more. This is the cause of their journey.

PRACTICE AND ASSESS

- Have students reread the last two sentences on p. 360 and identify a causal relationship. Remind them to ask themselves "What happened?" and "Why did it happen?" *(Effect— The ants are eager to gather more crystals for the queen. Cause—The queen is the mother of them all.)*
- To assess, use Practice Book 3.2, p. 136.

Cause and Effect

- A **cause** is why something happens. An **effect** is what happens.
- A **cause** may have more than one **effect**. *Because I forgot to set my alarm clock, I overslept, and I was late for school.*
- An **effect** may have more than one **cause**. *Dad's computer crashed because it didn't have enough memory, and he was running too many programs at once.*

Directions Read the following story. Then answer the questions below.

Alex Ant got up late again today. He was always sleeping through his alarm. Mama Ant had to take him to school because he'd missed the bus. She was tired of it. So Mama sat down with a cup of tea and thought. The next morning, when Alex was late again, Mama did not take him to school and told him to walk. Alex hated walking to school. He was mad. The next morning, the same thing happened—and the morning after that. Alex begged and pleaded for a ride, but Mama refused. On the fourth morning, guess what happened? Alex Ant got himself up on time and caught the bus. Mama smiled to herself over her cup of tea.

1. What effect did Alex's behavior have on Mama? Responses may vary.
   She was tired of it and wanted to do something about it.

2. Why did Mama Ant refuse to take Alex to school?
   She wanted to teach him a lesson about being responsible.

3. What happened to Alex when Mama refused to take him to school?
   He was angry because he had to walk to school.

4. What effect did his mom not taking him to school have on Alex?
   He started getting up on time.

School + Home **Home Activity** Your child learned about cause and effect. Read a popular fairy tale with your child. Have him or her tell you the causes and effects of the characters' behavior in the story.

▲ **Practice Book 3.2** p. 136

Guiding Comprehension

 3 🎯 **Plot • Critical**

What happens at the beginning of the story that is important?

The ants leave their colony and journey into the woods in search of more crystals for the queen.

Monitor Progress	
🎯 **Plot**	
If... students have difficulty identifying the beginning of the plot sequence,	**then...** use the skill and strategy instruction on p. 363.

4 **Simile • Literal**

Reread the last sentence in paragraph 1 on p. 363. What does the author say the crickets' chirping sounds like?

Distant thunder.

3 They marched into the woods that surrounded their underground home. Dusk turned to twilight, twilight to night. The path they followed twisted and turned, every bend leading them deeper into the dark forest.

362

ELL

Access Content Help students understand the setting by examining the second sentence on p. 362. Guide students in understanding the meaning of the words *dusk* and *twilight* and how they compare to night.

More than once the line of ants stopped and anxiously listened for the sounds of hungry spiders. But all they heard was the call of crickets echoing through the woods like distant thunder.

Dew formed on the leaves above. Without warning, huge cold drops fell on the marching ants. A firefly passed overhead that, for an instant, lit up the woods with a blinding flash of blue-green light.

363

Ant Classes

Some species of ants, like the two bad ants, live in underground tunnels. There are three classes of ants in a colony. The queen lays eggs. The male ants are generally winged. The workers, all female, build the nest, gather food, take care of the young, and fight enemies.

Plot

TEACH

- Remind students that stories have a beginning, a middle, and an end. Stories also have a problem. The problem often occurs at the beginning of the story.

- Explain to students that as they read, they should decide which events are important to the story and which do not further the action.

- Model identifying the beginning of the story.

Think Aloud **MODEL** I must decide which of the sentences at the beginning of the story are important. The ants leave their home to go on a long and dangerous journey. They are going to find crystals and take them to the queen. This is important to the story line. It presents the problem the ants will face.

PRACTICE AND ASSESS

Have students reread p. 363 and identify any important events. Be sure students understand that while these details make the story more interesting and help the reader better understand the ants' journey, they are not key to the plot sequence.

EXTEND SKILLS

Simile

Tell students that authors sometimes use similes to compare two different things that are alike in some way. A simile uses the words *like* or *as*. Have students use similes to elaborate descriptions and incorporate figurative wording in their own writing.

Guiding Comprehension

5 Setting • Inferential

At the beginning of the story, the ants were at their home. Where does this part of the story take place?

The ants have left the forest and are entering a building.

6 Compare and Contrast • Inferential

How is the building different from the ants' home?

The familiar smells of dirt, grass, and rotting plants are not in the building. There is no wind and there is a ceiling instead of the sky.

7 Vocabulary • Word Structure

Reread the first sentence in paragraph 2 on p. 365. How does the suffix -y change the meaning of the word *shine*?

Shine is a verb that means "to give out light." Dropping the *e* and adding the suffix *-y* changes the word *shine* to *shiny*. The new word describes how the surface looks.

Monitor Progress
Word Structure

If... students have difficulty understanding the meaning of the suffix,	then... use vocabulary strategy instruction on p. 365.

At the edge of the forest stood a mountain. The ants looked up and could not see its peak. It seemed to reach right to the heavens. But they did not stop. Up the side they climbed, higher and higher.

The wind whistled through the cracks of the mountain's face. The ants could feel its force bending their delicate antennae. Their legs grew weak as they struggled upward. At last they reached a ledge and crawled through a narrow tunnel.

5

364

ELL

Activate Prior Knowledge Have students describe what they see in the illustrations on pp. 364–365. Help students use their previous knowledge of buildings and homes to understand the content on the pages. For example, make sure students understand that the "mountain" mentioned in the first sentence on p. 364 is not a real mountain. It is how the ants view the building.

When the ants came out of the tunnel they found themselves in a strange world. Smells they had known all their lives, smells of dirt and grass and rotting plants, had vanished. There was no more wind and, most puzzling of all, it seemed that the sky was gone.

They crossed smooth shiny surfaces, then followed **7** the scout up a glassy, curved wall. They had reached their goal. From the top of the wall they looked below to a sea of crystals. One by one the ants climbed down into the sparkling treasure.

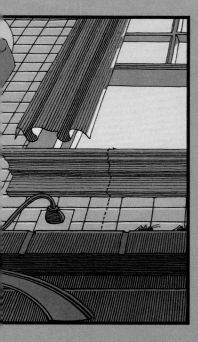

365

VOCABULARY STRATEGY

Word Structure

TEACH

- Explain to students that they can help themselves understand unfamiliar words by using word structure.

- Remind students that a suffix is a word part that is added to the end of a word. A suffix changes the meaning of the word.

- Write the word *fear* on the board and have students identify the meaning of the word. Then add the suffix *-less*. Have students read the word and tell how the meaning of the word changes with the addition of the suffix.

- Model using knowledge of word structure to determine the meaning of *shiny*.

Think Aloud **MODEL** I recognize the word part *shine* in the word *shiny*. I know that it means "to give off light." I see that the suffix *-y* has been added to the word *shine*. Adding the suffix changes the meaning of the word. The new word *shiny* means "bright." *Shiny* must describe the surface the ants are on. It is bright.

PRACTICE AND ASSESS

Have students use word structure to determine the meaning of *glassy* on p. 365. They should recognize the meaning of the base word *glass* and how the suffix *-y* changes the meaning of the word from a noun (naming word) to an adjective (describing word).

Guiding Comprehension

8 **Character • Critical**

What clues in the story help us know what the two ants are like? How would you describe the ants?

Clues: The two ants do not go back home with the other ants. They want to have all the crystals and be able to eat them every day. They are greedy.

9 **Realism and Fantasy • Critical**

Text to Text **What other animal fantasy does *Two Bad Ants* remind you of?**

Responses will vary but should name an animal fantasy with similar characteristics.

10 **Visualize • Inferential**

Which details helped you picture what happened to the ants in the morning?

Possible response: A giant silver scoop plunged into the crystals, shoveled up the ants and crystals, and lifted them high into the air.

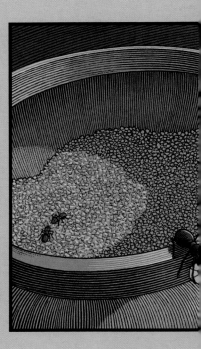

Quickly they each chose a crystal, then turned to start the journey home. There was something about this unnatural place that made the ants nervous. In fact they left in such a hurry that none of them noticed the two small ants who stayed behind.

"Why go back?" one asked the other. "This place **8** may not feel like home, but look at all these crystals."

"You're right," said the other. "We can stay here and eat this tasty treasure every day, forever." So the two ants ate crystal after crystal until they were too full to move, and fell asleep. **9**

366

ELL

Access Content Help students understand the events of the story. Make sure they understand that it is being told from an ant's perspective.

Daylight came. The sleeping ants were unaware of changes taking place in their new-found home. A giant silver scoop hovered above them, then plunged deep into the crystals. It shoveled up both ants and crystals and carried them high into the air. **10**

The ants were wide awake when the scoop turned, dropping them from a frightening height. They tumbled through space in a shower of crystals and fell into a boiling brown lake.

367

Develop Vocabulary

PRACTICE LESSON VOCABULARY

Have students provide oral responses to each question.

1. **Is a *crystal* shiny or dull?** *(A crystal is shiny.)*
2. **What kind of *journey* did the ants make?** *(The ants' journey was long and dangerous.)*
3. **What was the *goal* of the ants' journey?** *(The ants' goal was to bring more crystals to the queen.)*

BUILD CONCEPT VOCABULARY

Review previous concept words with students. Ask if students have come across any words today in their reading or elsewhere that they would like to add to the Concept Web.

 STRATEGY SELF-CHECK

Visualize

Have students identify the important plot events that they have read so far in the story. Remind them to use the visualizing strategy as they read to create a picture in their minds. Point out that they should use all of their senses as they use the strategy. Visualizing helps readers comprehend and enjoy the text.

Read the first paragraph on p. 367 aloud to students. Pause after each statement and have students describe the picture they see in their mind. As appropriate, students should describe what they see, hear, smell, taste, and feel.

SELF-CHECK

Students can ask these questions to assess their ability to use the skill and strategy.

- Did I identify important events from the story?
- Did words and illustrations help me visualize story events?
- How does visualizing help me understand and enjoy a story?

Monitor Progress
🎯 **Plot**

If... students have difficulty recognizing important events in the plot sequence,	**then...** revisit the skill lesson on pp. 354–355. Reteach as necessary.

Strategy Response Log

Check Predictions Provide the following prompt: *Was your prediction accurate? Revise your old prediction or make a new prediction about the rest of the selection.*

If you want to teach this selection in two sessions, stop here.

Guiding Comprehension

If you are teaching the selection in two days, discuss the main ideas so far and review the vocabulary.

11 **Details and Facts • Inferential**
What "lake" are the ants in? What "cave" are they flowing into?

Lake—cup of coffee; cave—someone's mouth.

12 **Vocabulary • Prefixes and Suffixes**
Have students reread the paragraph on p. 369. Ask them to identify a word that has a prefix, then explain the meaning of both the prefix and the word.

Possible response: Disappeared; *dis-: not;* disappeared: not seen anymore.

DAY 3 **Grouping Options**

Reading
Whole Group Discuss the Question of the Day.

Group Time Differentiated Instruction
Read *Two Bad Ants.* See pp. 354f–354g for the small group lesson plan.

Whole Group Discuss the Reader Response questions on p. 376. Then use p. 379a.

Language Arts
Use pp. 379e–379h and 379k–379m.

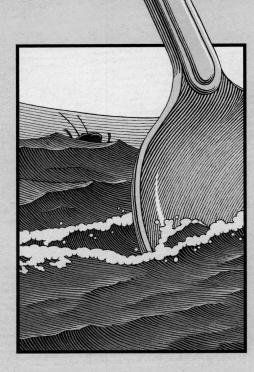
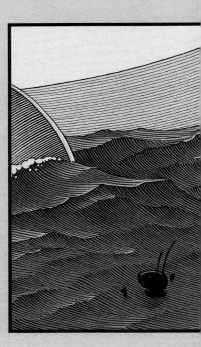

Then the giant scoop stirred violently back and forth. Crushing waves fell over the ants. They paddled hard to keep their tiny heads above water. But the scoop kept spinning the hot brown liquid.

Around and around it went, creating a whirlpool that sucked the ants deeper and deeper. They both held their breath and finally bobbed to the surface, gasping for air and spitting mouthfuls of the terrible, bitter water.

368

Context Clues Help students use context clues and visualizing to learn the meaning of the word *bobbed* in the second paragraph on p. 368. Point out clues, such as "sucked the ants deeper and deeper," "held their breath," "bobbed to the surface," and "gasping for air and spitting out mouthfuls of the terrible, bitter water."

Then the lake tilted and began to empty into a cave. The ants could hear the rushing water and felt themselves pulled toward the pitch-black hole. **11** Suddenly the cave disappeared and the lake became **12** calm. The ants swam to the shore and found that the lake had steep sides.

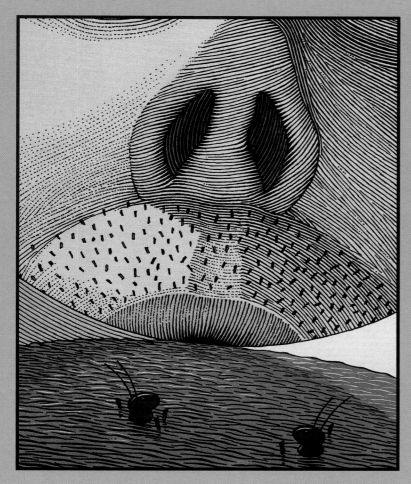

369

Vortex

The ants in the story got caught in a whirlpool, or vortex, in the coffee mug. This was the result of the spoon stirring the coffee in a circular motion. This motion creates a funnel similar to a tornado. You can make your own tornado using two plastic soda bottles and water. Learn how to make a vortex by searching online.

VOCABULARY STRATEGY

Prefixes and Suffixes

TEACH

- Remind students that a prefix, like a suffix, is a word part that changes the meaning of the word. Emphasize that a prefix is added to the beginning of the word and a suffix is added to the end of the word. Explain that students can remember this because the prefix *pre-* means "before." Therefore, a prefix goes *before* a word.

- Remind students that along with context clues, the meaning of common prefixes and suffixes can help them understand unfamiliar words.

- Model identifying the word with a prefix on p. 369.

Think Aloud **MODEL** The word *disappeared* begins with the prefix *dis-*. I know that this prefix means "not." I also see the base word *appear* in the word *disappeared*. I know that *appear* means "to be seen." *Disappeared* must mean "to no longer to be seen."

PRACTICE AND ASSESS

Have children reread the last sentence on p. 368. Ask them to identify a word with a suffix. Then have them identify the meaning of the suffix and the meaning of the word. *(Mouthfuls, -ful: full of; mouthfuls: mouths full of something)*

Two Bad Ants **369**

Guiding Comprehension

13 **Point of View • Critical**

Question the Author **Whom does the author choose to tell the story? Why do you think he chose this method?**

The author chose a narrator who is not a character in the story but maybe another ant because the descriptions are from an ant's point of view. The author probably chose the method to make the story more entertaining.

 Plot • Literal

Describe the major events that occur on pp. 370–371.

The ants climb out of the coffee cup and hide inside a piece of bread inside an electric toaster. The ants cook with the toast and then are thrown out when the toast pops up.

Monitor Progress	
Plot	
If... students are unable to identify the events important to the plot,	then... use the skill and strategy instruction on p. 371.

They hurried down the walls that held back the lake. The frightened insects looked for a place to hide, worried that the giant scoop might shovel them up again. Close by they found a huge round disk with holes that could neatly hide them.

370

ELL

Extend Language Read the last sentence on p. 371 with students. Write the word *rocketed* on the board. Remind students that a rocket is a vehicle that travels into space. In the sentence on p. 371, the word is used as an action verb. Help students understand the meaning of the word *rocketed* as used in the sentence. *(soared quickly)*

But as soon as they had climbed inside, their hiding place was lifted, tilted, and lowered into a dark space. When the ants climbed out of the holes, they were surrounded by a strange red glow. It seemed to them that every second the temperature was rising.

It soon became so unbearably hot that they thought they would soon be cooked. But suddenly the disk they were standing on rocketed upward, and the two hot ants went flying through the air. 13 14

371

SKILLS ↔ STRATEGIES IN CONTEXT

Plot
Visualize

TEACH

- Remind students that using the visualizing strategy can help them identify events that are important to the plot.
- Reread p. 370. Have students use the visualizing strategy to describe the events.
- Model the procedure for the events on p. 371.

Think Aloud **MODEL** As I read, I try to visualize the events. The illustrations help me know that the "huge round disk with holes" is a piece of bread in a toaster. When you press the lever down on a toaster, the bread lowers into the machine. I read "When the ants climbed out of the holes, they were surrounded by a strange red glow." I see a picture in my mind of the ants crawling out of the bread. They are inside a toaster and see a red glow. Then the toast pops up. I can see the ants flying through the air. Now that I have visualized the events, I can retell the important parts.

PRACTICE AND ASSESS

Have students work in pairs to read the text on pp. 370–371 and use the visualizing strategy to help them identify the major plot events. *(The ants were in a piece of bread in the toaster. The toaster popped up the toast and the ants went flying through the air.)*

Guiding Comprehension

15 **Vocabulary • Prefixes and Suffixes**
Reread p. 372. Have students name one word with a prefix and two words with suffixes. Ask them to identify the meaning of each word.

Possible response: Word with prefix: refresh-ing (*make fresh again*); words with suffixes: powerful (*full of power*), slowly (*state of being slow*)

16 (REVIEW) **Cause and Effect • Critical**
What caused the ants to be "caught in a whirling storm of shredded food and stinging rain"?

The ants fell into the drain. Someone turned on the garbage disposal.

Monitor Progress	
(REVIEW) **Cause and Effect**	
If... students are unable to determine the cause and effect relationship,	**then...** use the skill and strategy instruction on p. 373.

17 **Onomatopoeia • Inferential**
Reread the last paragraph on p. 373. Which word sounds like the meaning of the word?

Whirling.

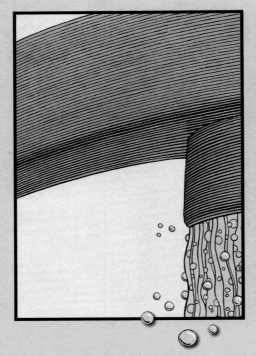

They landed near what seemed to be a fountain—a waterfall pouring from a silver tube. Both ants had a powerful thirst and longed to dip their feverish heads into the refreshing water. They quickly climbed along the tube.

As they got closer to the rushing water the ants felt a cool spray. They tightly gripped the shiny surface of the fountain and slowly leaned their heads into the falling stream. But the force of the water was much too strong. **15**

372

ELL

Extend Language Work with students to identify the words with pre-fixes and/or suffixes. Students should practice analyzing the word parts and determining the meanings of the words.

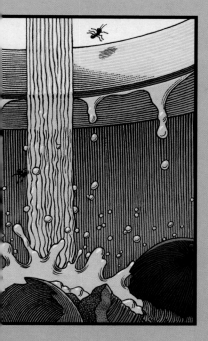

The tiny insects were pulled off the fountain and plunged down into a wet, dark chamber. They landed on half-eaten fruit and other soggy things. Suddenly the air was filled with loud, frightening sounds. The chamber began to spin.

The ants were caught in a whirling storm of shredded **16** **17** food and stinging rain. Then, just as quickly as it had started, the noise and spinning stopped. Bruised and dizzy, the ants climbed out of the chamber.

 TIME FOR Science

Life Cycles

In the story, the two bad ants' lives were in danger. In real life, a queen ant lays eggs. The egg hatches. Out comes a worm-like larva with no eyes. The larva grows and sheds it skin. It spins a cocoon. An adult ant comes out of the cocoon. This process takes about two months. Some queen ants can live for 15 years. Worker ants can live for 7 years.

SKILLS ⟷ STRATEGIES IN CONTEXT

Cause and Effect REVIEW

TEACH

- Remind students that a cause is "why something happened" and an effect is "what happened."
- Draw a cause and effect graphic organizer (Graphic Organizer 19) on the board. Then model identifying the cause and effect relationship.

Think Aloud **MODEL** The question asks me to find a cause. The effect is given. I will write "The ants get caught in a whirling storm of shredded food and stinging rain" in the graphic organizer. I must read and use what I already know to identify the cause. I know that the ants fell into the sink. I know that in some sinks there is a garbage disposal that spins and chops up food. Someone turned on the garbage disposal. I will write that in the "cause" part of the graphic organizer. When the disposal was turned on, the ants went spinning in the sink.

PRACTICE AND ASSESS

Have students identify the effect of the ants leaning into the running water from the faucet. *(The powerful water pulled them in and down the drain.)*

Guiding Comprehension

18 ⊙ **Visualize • Inferential**

What details help you understand how the ants feel at the end of the story?

Possible responses: "Joyful sounds," "the two ants felt happier than they'd ever felt before," "their home," "where they were meant to be."

19 **Character • Critical**

Text to Self **How do the ants feel at the end of the story? When have you felt the same way?**

Although responses may vary, encourage students to draw connections between the ants' appreciation for their home and a similar experience in their own lives.

Strategy Response Log

Summarize When students finish reading the selection, provide this prompt: Imagine that you want to tell a friend what *Two Bad Ants* is about. In four or five sentences, explain its important points.

In daylight once again, they raced through puddles and up a smooth metal wall. In the distance they saw something comforting—two long, narrow holes that reminded them of the warmth and safety of their old underground home. They climbed up into the dark openings.

But there was no safety inside these holes. A strange force passed through the wet ants. They were stunned senseless and blown out of the holes like bullets from a gun. When they landed, the tiny insects were too exhausted to go on. They crawled into a dark corner and fell fast asleep.

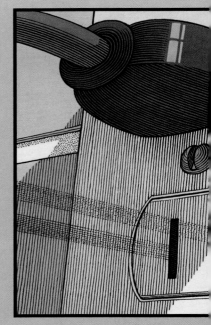

374

ELL

Fluency Read pp. 374–375 chorally with children. Before reading, model how to pause when reading sentences with dashes.

Night had returned when the battered ants awoke to a familiar sound—the footsteps of their fellow insects returning for more crystals. The two ants slipped quietly to the end of the line. They climbed the glassy wall and once again stood amid the treasure. But this time they each chose a single crystal and followed their friends home.

Standing at the edge of their ant hole, the two ants listened to the joyful sounds that came from below. They knew how grateful their mother queen would be when they gave her their crystals. At that moment, the two ants felt happier than they'd ever felt before. This was their home, this was their family. This was where they were meant to be. **18** **19**

375

Develop Vocabulary

PRACTICE LESSON VOCABULARY

Have students provide oral responses to each question.

1. The ants almost *disappeared* when the man drank his coffee. What is the meaning of *disappeared*? (*Not appeared, vanished*)
2. What sounds did the ants hear that they thought were *joyful*? (*Sounds from their ant home*)
3. What *scoop* were the ants afraid of? (*A spoon*)

BUILD CONCEPT VOCABULARY

Review previous concept words with students. Ask if students have come across any words today in their reading or elsewhere that they would like to add to the Concept Web.

 STRATEGY SELF-CHECK

Visualize

Have students identify the main events from pp. 374–375, using the visualizing strategy to help them. Use Practice Book 3.2, p. 137.

SELF-CHECK

Students can ask these questions to assess their ability to use the skill and strategy.

- Did I use my senses to visualize as I read?
- Did I identify the solutions chosen to solve the ants' problems in the story?
- Do I understand the events that happened at the beginning, middle, and end of the story?

Monitor Progress
Plot

If… students are having difficulty visualizing the major plot events,	**then…** use the Reteach lesson on p. 379b.

Plot and Theme · Visualize

- The important events in a story make up the **plot** with a beginning, middle, and end.
- The "big idea" of the story is called the **theme**. It can be stated in a single sentence.
- As you read, form a picture in your mind about what is happening in the story.

Directions Read the following story. Then answer the questions below.

Two ants journeyed out with the goal of finding food. They saw a tiny door to a tunnel and disappeared inside. There they found piles and piles of delicious food. Each ant took as much as he could carry. Then the two turned back toward the doorway. When they got there, however, neither could get out.

Each had so much food, squeezing through the tunnel's door was impossible. Try as they might, they could not squeeze through the tunnel's door holding all the food they'd found. Finally, each ant let go of half of its load. Only then were they able to squeeze through the doorway and go home.

1. What happened at the beginning of the story?
   Two ants went out in search of food.
2. What happened in the middle of the story?
   The ants found food but couldn't get back out of the door because they were carrying too much.
3. What happened at the end of the story?
   The ants had to put down some of the food so they could get through the doorway of the tunnel and go home.
4. What is the "big idea" of the story?
   Possible response: Don't take on more than you can handle.
5. Describe how you picture the two ants trying to get out of the tunnel.
   Possible response: I see two ants with pieces of food stuck on their legs, under their necks, and in their mouths.

School + Home **Home Activity** Your child identified the plot and theme of a story. The next time you watch a movie with your child, have him or her tell you what happened at the beginning, middle, and end of the movie. Then help your child figure out the "big idea" of the movie.

▲ **Practice Book 3.2** p. 137

Two Bad Ants **375**

Reader Response

Open for Discussion **Personal Response**

Think Aloud **MODEL** The ants walk in line through the woods. They climb into a house and jump into a bowl of sugar. Two stay to eat sugar. Someone scoops them into coffee and almost drinks them. The ants climb into a toaster, into a sink, are blown out of an outlet, and go home.

Comprehension Check **Critical Response**

1. Responses should include parts of the story from an ant's point of view. **Author's Purpose**

2. The problem is that the ants are in danger. It is resolved when the other ants return for more sugar and the two bad ants follow them home. The ants learned to appreciate their own home and way of life. **Plot**

3. Responses should include a description of the ants in the disposal. **Visualize**

4. Responses should show an understanding of the words and plot. **Vocabulary**

Look Back and Write For test practice, assign a 10–15 minute time limit. For assessment, see the Scoring Rubric at the right.

Retell

Have students retell *Two Bad Ants.*

Monitor Progress

Check Retelling (Rubric 4 3 2 1)

If... students have difficulty retelling the story,	then... use the Retelling Cards and the Scoring Rubric for Retelling on p. 377 to assist fluent retelling.

SUCCESS PREDICTOR

Check Retelling Have students use illustrations and other text features to guide their retellings. Let students listen to other retellings before attempting their own. See the ELL and Transition Handbook.

Reader Response

Open for Discussion You are a scientist tracking these two bad ants. Tell everything you see them do in this story.

1. How does the author and illustrator make you see the world the way ants see it? Read parts of the story to show what you mean. **Think Like an Author**

2. The decision the ants make leads to a huge problem for them. What is it, and how is it resolved? What do you think the ants learned from their experience? **Plot and Theme**

3. What picture did you have in your mind as you read page 373? How did visualizing help you understand what you were reading? **Visualize**

4. What might the two bad ants have to say about their adventure? Write a journal entry. Use words from the Words to Know list. **Vocabulary**

Look Back and Write Look back at pages 367–369 to find "a boiling brown lake," "a giant scoop," and "a cave." Write a note to tell the ants what these things really are.

Meet author **and illustrator** **Chris Van Allsburg on page 421.**

Scoring Rubric | **Look Back and Write**

Top-Score Response A top-score response uses pp. 367–36[ ] of the selection to identify "a boiling brown lake," "a giant scoop," and "a cave" and to tell the ants what these things really are.

Example of a Top-Score Response The "giant scoop" that sho[ ]eled you up was really a spoon. The person used the spoon to scoop out sugar and dump it into a cup of coffee. That "boiling brown lake" was the hot coffee. The "cave" you were almost pulled into was the person's mouth.

For additional rubrics, see p. WA10.

Write Now
Writing About a Picture

Prompt

Two Bad Ants describes the adventures of two ants.
Think about a picture in the story you find interesting.
Now write about that picture, using vivid words.

Student Model

Picture being described is identified.

Word choice includes exact nouns, strong verbs, and vivid adjectives.

Different kinds and lengths of sentences add variety to description.

> To an ant, a small cup of coffee could seem like an enormous lake. A picture in Two Bad Ants shows ants, a cup of coffee, and the person drinking the coffee. Two ants are floating in a wavy pool of coffee. The cup is tipped toward another giant thing, the person's mouth. Huge lips are slurping coffee. What is that large prickly thing? It must be a mustache! Two long, shadowy holes are the person's nostrils. Notice that an ant's point of view is very different from ours.

Use the model to help you write about a picture.

Write Now

Look at the Prompt Have students identify and discuss key words and phrases in the prompt. *(picture in the story, write about that picture, vivid words)*

Strategies to Develop Word Choice

Have students

- list details about the picture and choose the most interesting ones to use.
- make a concept web for the five senses.
- replace dull words with precise ones.

NO: drinking coffee

YES: slurping coffee

NO: dark places

YES: shadowy holes

For additional suggestions and rubric, see pp. 379g–379h.

Hints for Better Writing

- Carefully read the prompt.
- Use a graphic organizer to plan your writing.
- Support your ideas with information and details.
- Use words that help readers understand.
- Proofread and edit your work.

377

Scoring Rubric | Narrative Retelling

Rubric 4 3 2 1	4	3	2	1
Connections	Makes connections and generalizes beyond the text	Makes connections to other events, stories, or experiences	Makes a limited connection to another event, story, or experience	Makes no connection to another event, story, or experience
Author's Purpose	Elaborates on author's purpose	Tells author's purpose with some clarity	Makes some connection to author's purpose	Makes no connection to author's purpose
Characters	Describes the main character(s) and any character development	Identifies the main character(s) and gives some information about them	Inaccurately identifies some characters or gives little information about them	Inaccurately identifies the characters or gives no information about them
Setting	Describes the time and location	Identifies the time and location	Omits details of time or location	Is unable to identify time or location
Plot	Describes the problem, goal, events, and ending using rich detail	Tells the problem, goal, events, and ending with some errors that do not affect meaning	Tells parts of the problem, goal, events, and ending with gaps that affect meaning	Retelling has no sense of story

Retelling Plan

- ☑ **Week 1** Assess Strategic Intervention students.
- ☑ **Week 2** Assess Advanced students.
- ☑ **Week 3** Assess Strategic Intervention students.
- ☑ **This week assess On-Level students.**
- ☐ **Week 5** Assess any students you have not yet checked during this unit.

Use the Retelling Chart on p. TR16 to record retelling.

Selection Test To assess with *Two Bad Ants*, use Selection Tests, pp. 113–116.

Fresh Reads for Differentiated Test Practice For weekly leveled practice, use pp. 169–174.

SUCCESS PREDICTOR

Reading Online

- Evaluate online sources.
- Compare and contrast across texts.

PREVIEW/USE TEXT FEATURES

As students preview "Hiking Safety Tips," have them describe what they see on p. 379. Ask:

- **What is shown on the first computer screen on p. 379?** *(Results of a search for* hiking.*)*
- **How can you tell if one of the sites has useful information?** *(Read the description.)*

If students have trouble identifying Internet features, use the Technology Tools.

Link to Social Studies

Discuss with students the use of relevant key words. Brainstorm a list of key words to use.

Evaluating Sources

Use the sidebar on p. 378 to guide discussion. Discuss with students the importance of using a reliable source, such as a .gov site, when obtaining information.

 AudioText

DAY 4 Grouping Options

Reading
Whole Group Discuss the Question of the Day.

Group Time Differentiated Instruction
Read "Hiking Safety Tips." See pp. 354f–354g for the small group lesson plan.

Whole Group Use pp. 379a and 379j.

Language Arts
Use pp. 379e–379h and 379k–379m.

Reading Online
New Literacies: **PearsonSuccessNet.com**

Hiking Safety Tips

Evaluating Sources

Genre
- **The Internet has a lot of information, but not all sources can be trusted.**
- **You need to learn how to tell which information is good and which is not.**

Text Features
- **Information following a link can help you decide whether a Web site might be useful.**
- **Web addresses ending in .gov or .org are usually good. Ask for help if you are not sure about a site.**

Link to Social Studies
Search through newspapers and magazines for travel articles. Share what you learn with the class.

You are going on a camping trip. With camping comes freedom, but also dangers. You must prepare a list of hiking safety tips. You decide to use the Internet to help you.

For more practice
Take It to the Net
PearsonSuccessNet.com

378

TECHNOLOGY TOOLS

Evaluating Internet Resources

Domain name: The suffix after a URL. Some common domain names are .com (for a business), .edu (for a school), .gov (for government Web sites), and .org (for organizations).

Keyword: A word or set of words used to find information about a larger subject.

Link A connection from one Web page to another. If you click on a link, the Internet browser will connect to another page.

You type the keyword "hiking" into an Internet search engine. The first two sites probably won't help. But the third site looks promising, so you click on Staying Safe on the Trail.

Search Engine

| hiking | **Search** |

Hiking Clothes. Outfit your family with these cute hiking shirts . . .

Footwear. We have 100% leather hiking boots, just what you're looking for . . .

Staying Safe on the Trail. Hiking is fun but beware of plants that . . .

File   Edit   View   Favorites   Tools   Help

http://

The list goes on. You print it out. Now you can enjoy the freedom of hiking in safety.

STAYING SAFE

A few tips will help you enjoy the freedom of a family hike in safety.

Drinking Water Don't hike anywhere without it, especially on hot days. Even the clearest stream water may not be safe.

Snacks Bring them to eat when you take breaks. Good hiking snacks include granola bars, trail mix, and crackers.

Poison Plants Beware of poison ivy and poison oak. Oil from the leaves can make you break out in a rash and blisters.

poison oak

Reading Across Texts
Which of these hiking tips could have helped the two bad ants?

Writing Across Texts Write a letter to the ants giving them these tips.

Visualize Try to visualize some of these dangers on the trail.

379

Strategies for Navigation

USE HEADINGS Explain to students that they should evaluate the results of their Internet searches. They can skim the headings to find the names of the Web sites they can visit. If they find a promising heading, they can read the description that follows to predict if the Web site will be useful.

Use the Strategy
1. Read the page, skimming headings.
2. Read the descriptions after a few of the headings. Ask yourself, "Does this sound like a useful Web site? Will it contain the answer to my question?"
3. When you find a description that looks helpful, click on the link to visit that Web site.

PRACTICE Think about the ways you evaluate sources at home and at school.

- Think of several companies, organizations, government agencies, or schools that might have informative Web sites.
- The next time you need to conduct research on the Internet, try searching for the Web sites of specific organizations that might be able to help you.

Guided Practice If there is time, have students log on to the Internet. Show them how to evaluate sources. Help students make connections between the steps they are doing and related vocabulary terms.

Visualize

After students read "Staying Safe" ask them to use what they have learned about the visualize strategy to engage senses as they describe the dangers orally.

CONNECT TEXT TO TEXT

Reading Across Texts
Have students explain their answer.

Writing Across Texts Encourage students to include tips from the selection as well as their own tips for hiking.

Safety

TIME FOR Science

One way to stay safe is to read signs and warning labels. Some products have warning labels. Provide examples of warnings for students to read.

Fluency Assessment Plan

- ☑ **Week 1** Assess Advanced students.
- ☑ **Week 2** Assess Strategic Intervention students.
- ☑ **Week 3** Assess On-Level students.
- ☑ **This week assess Strategic Intervention students.**
- ☐ **Week 5** Assess any students you have not yet checked during this unit.

Set individual goals for students to enable them to reach the year-end goal.

- Current Goal: 110–120 wcpm
- Year-End Goal: 120 wcpm

 **Fluency Coach CD** To develop fluent readers, use Fluency Coach.

MORE READING FOR Fluency

 To practice fluency with text comprised of previously taught phonics elements and irregular words, use Decodable Reader 29.

DAY 5 Grouping Options

Reading
Whole Group
Revisit the Question of the Week.

Group Time
Differentiated Instruction
Reread this week's Leveled Readers. See pp. 354f–354g for the small group lesson plan.

Whole Group
Use pp. 379b–379c.

Language Arts
Use pp. 379d–379h and 379k–379n.

ACCURACY, APPROPRIATE PACE/RATE, AND EXPRESSION

Fluency

DAY 1

Model Reread "The Boy Who Stopped Time" on p. 354m. Explain that you will read at an appropriate pace, not too fast and not too slowly. You will read accurately and with expression. Model for students as you read.

DAY 2

Echo Reading Read aloud p. 360. Have students notice expression in your voice. Have students practice as a class, doing three echo readings of p. 360.

DAY 3

Model Read aloud p. 363. Have students notice how you pause at commas and how you read at an appropriate rate. Practice as a class by doing three choral readings of p. 363.

DAY 4

Paired Reading Partners practice reading aloud p. 365, three times. Students should read with accuracy and offer each other feedback.

Monitor Progress | Check Fluency WCPM

As students reread, monitor their progress toward their individual fluency goals. Current Goal: 110–120 words correct per minute. End-of-Year Goal: 120 words correct per minute.

If... students cannot read fluently at a rate of 110–120 words correct per minute,
then... make sure students practice with text at their independent level. Provide additional fluency practice, pairing nonfluent readers with fluent readers.

If... students already read at 120 words correct per minute,
then... they need not reread three to four times.

SUCCESS PREDICTOR

DAY 5

Assessment
Individual Reading Rate Use the Fluency Assessment Plan and do a one-minute timed reading of either selection from this week to assess students in Week 4. Pay special attention to this week's skills, accuracy, appropriate pace/rate, and expression. Provide corrective feedback for each student.

RETEACH

Plot and Theme

TEACH

Review the difference between a story's plot and theme. Remind students that when explaining a story's plot, they should include the most important details about the beginning, middle, and end. Students can complete Practice Book 3.2, p. 138, on their own, or you can complete it as a class. Point out that questions 1–3 ask about the story's plot. Question 4 asks about the story's theme.

ASSESS

Have students review *Two Bad Ants*. Ask them to describe the story's plot *(Beginning—On a trip to find crystals, two ants decide not to return home so they can always enjoy the crystals; Middle—The two ants encounter dangers in their new home; End—The two ants return home, happy to be there)* and theme *(don't take what you have for granted)*.

For additional instruction for plot and theme, see DI·55.

EXTEND SKILLS

Setting

TEACH

The setting is the time and place of a story. The author may state the setting. Often readers have to use details in the story to identify the story's time and place. A story's setting can influence what happens to characters.

- Look for clues in the story that describe the setting.
- As you read, see if the setting affects the characters and plot.

Read aloud the first paragraph on p. 360. Have volunteers identify the setting. Then ask students to describe clues that help them identify the setting.

ASSESS

Have students work with a partner to reread pp. 364–365. Ask:

1. **Did the author state where the ants were, or did you use clues to identify the location? Which clues?**

2. **How would the events change if the story took place in another location, such as a forest?**

OBJECTIVES

- Identify a story's plot and theme.
- Identify a story's setting.

Skills Trace	
Plot and Theme	
Introduce/Teach	TE: 3.4 112, 113; 3.6 354, 355
Practice	PB: 3.2 43, 47, 48, 116, 133, 137, 138
Reteach/Review	**TE: 3.4 137b, DI•56, 3.6 315, 379b, DI•55**
Test	Selection Test: Unit 6

Access Content Reteach the skill by reviewing the Picture It! lesson on plot and theme in the ELL Teaching Guide, pp. 197–198.

Plot and Theme

- The important events in a story make up the **plot** with a beginning, middle, and end.
- The "big idea" of the story is called the **theme**. It can be stated in a single sentence.
- As you read, form a picture in your mind about what is happening in the story.

Directions Read the following story. Then fill in the chart below.

A crow was thirsty, but she couldn't find a drop of water. She spotted a broken pitcher on the side of the road. She looked inside. Some water lay at its bottom. The crow's beak was too short to reach down into the pitcher. She turned her head from side to side. She walked in a circle around the pitcher. Finally, she pushed the pitcher with her beak until it fell over. At last, she could reach the water. With the pitcher on its side, she could drink all the water.

What happened at the beginning of the story?

1. A crow looked for something to drink and found a pitcher with some water in it.

What happened in the middle of the story?

2. The crow's beak was too short to reach the bottom of the pitcher where the water was, so she pushed the pitcher over.

What happened at the end of the story?

3. The crow finally reached the water in the pitcher and drank.

4. What is the "big idea" of this story? Responses may vary.
If you really need or want something, you'll find a way to get it.

Home Activity Your child identified the plot and theme of a story. Write a short story together about a real or imaginary pet. Help identify what happens at the beginning, middle, and end of the story. Ask your child to state the "big idea."

▲ **Practice Book 3.2 p. 138**

SUCCESS PREDICTOR

Vocabulary and Word Study

VOCABULARY STRATEGY
Word Structure

PREFIXES AND SUFFIXES Remind students that they can use word structure to determine the meaning of words with prefixes and suffixes. Have students list any unknown words they encountered as they read *Two Bad Ants*. They can create a chart showing the unknown word, its prefix or suffix, and their definition of the word based on its word structure. Students can confirm word meanings using a dictionary.

Word	Base + prefix or suffix	Meaning
unnatural	un + natural	not natural
mouthful		
disorder		

Bug Words

Some words, such as *ant*, have to do with bugs, or insects. Have partners use reference sources to make lists of insect words and their meanings. Students can make illustrated bug dictionaries using their words.

Some Bug Words

wasp	beetle
butterfly	hornet
nest	mosquito
termite	ladybug

BUILD CONCEPT VOCABULARY
Too Much Freedom

LOOKING BACK Remind students of the question of the week: When can freedom be a problem? Discuss how this week's Concept Web of vocabulary words relates to the theme of too much freedom. Ask students if they have any words or categories to add. Discuss if words and categories are appropriately related to the concept.

MOVING FORWARD Preview the title of the next selection, *Elena's Serenade*. Ask students which Concept Web words might apply to the new selection based on the title alone. Put a star next to these words on the web.

Display the Concept Web and revisit the vocabulary words as you read the next selection to check predictions.

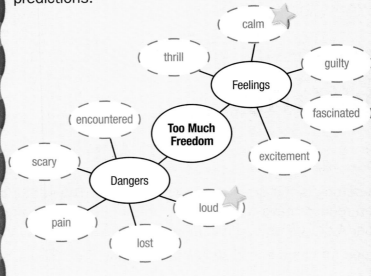

Monitor Progress

Check Vocabulary

If... students suggest words or categories that are not related to the concept,	**then...** review the words and categories on the Concept Web and discuss how they relate to the lesson concept.

SUCCESS PREDICTOR

Speaking and Viewing

SPEAKING

Description

SET-UP Have students use the note they wrote in Look Back and Write on p. 376 to help them think of other descriptive words and phrases when they write descriptions of their bedroom as seen by ants.

ORGANIZATION Have students begin their descriptions with an exciting statement about what their bedroom looks like from an ant's perspective. Students can then imagine the ants crawling to other areas in the room. They may wish to begin at the bedroom door and work their way around the room. Encourage students to include details that support their descriptions. Suggest that students conclude their descriptions with a one-sentence summary of what the room looks like from an ant's perspective.

ASSESSMENT After students deliver their oral descriptions, have them reflect on and assess their performance as speakers. Did they speak loudly and clearly? Did they maintain audience interest? Were there parts of the speech that could have been better? What will they do differently the next time they speak?

VIEWING

Analyze Classified Ads

Have students choose four or five classified ads in newspapers. Then have them answer these questions orally or in writing.

1. **What condition do you expect, based on the words the seller uses to describe the items?** *(Possible response: I think the lawnmower will be in poor condition because the ad says it needs work.)*

2. **How do the writers of the ads use language to create clear visual images?** *(Possible response: The writers use descriptive words to help you visualize the item for sale.)*

3. **Do you trust that the items are exactly as they are described?** *(Possible response: I think the video game will be exactly as it's described because the name of the game is included in the description.)*

ELL

Support Vocabulary Use the following to review and extend vocabulary and to explore lesson concepts further:
• ELL Poster 29, Days 3–5 instruction
• Vocabulary Activities and Word Cards in ELL Teaching Guide, pp. 199–200

Assessment For information on assessing students' speaking, listening, and viewing, see the ELL and Transition Handbook.

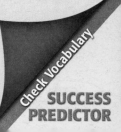

Check Vocabulary

SUCCESS PREDICTOR

Grammar Commas

Monitor Progress

Grammar

If... students have difficulty with commas,	then... see The Grammar and Writing Book, pp. 218–221.

DAILY FIX-IT

This week use Daily Fix-It Transparency 29.

Spiral REVIEW

Support Grammar See the Grammar Transition lessons in the ELL and Transition Handbook.

▲ **The Grammar and Writing Book**
For more instruction and practice, use pp. 218–223.

DAY 1 Teach and Model

DAILY FIX-IT

1. Dr Allen studys insects in his lab. (*Dr.; studies*)

2. He carefuly looks at ants, bees and butterflies. (*carefully; bees,*)

READING-GRAMMAR CONNECTION

Write this sentence on the board:

Suddenly their hiding place was lifted, tilted, and lowered into a dark space.

Explain that the **commas** are used to separate the words in a series, in this case, the verbs *lifted, tilted,* and *lowered.*

Display Grammar Transparency 29. Read aloud the definitions and sample sentences. Work through the items.

Commas

Use a **comma** and a conjunction to join two sentences.
  I went outside, and I saw some ants.
Use **commas** to separate words in a series.
  The ants were small, brown, and active.
Use a **comma** after the greeting and the closing of a friendly letter.
  Dear Ellie,
  Your friend,
Use a **comma** between the name of a city and a state in an address.
  Casper, WY 82602   Cleveland, Ohio
Use a **comma** to separate the month and day from the year.
  April 28, 2007

Directions Write *C* if commas are used correctly in the sentence. Write *NC* if commas are not used correctly.

1. Scientists have found ant fossils and they think they are millions of years old. — **NC**
2. Ants are social insects, and they live in groups called colonies. — **C**
3. Rooms in ant nests include the queen's chamber, nurseries and storage rooms. — **NC**

Directions Write each sentence. Add commas where they are needed.

4. I finished my report on ants on October 3 2006.
I finished my report on ants on October 3, 2006.

5. An ant's sting is painful but it isn't poisonous.
An ant's sting is painful, but it isn't poisonous.

6. That scientist lives in Miami Florida.
That scientist lives in Miami, Florida.

Unit 6 Two Bad Ants   Grammar **29**

▲ **Grammar Transparency** 29

DAY 2 Develop the Concept

DAILY FIX-IT

3. Ants are remarkabel insects but sometimes they are pests. (*remarkable; insects,*)

4. They will go after the littlest crums in you're kitchen. (*crumbs; your*)

GUIDED PRACTICE

Review the concept of using commas.

- Use a **comma** and a conjunction to join two sentences.
- Use commas to separate words in a series.
- Use a comma after the greeting and the closing of a friendly letter.
- Use a comma between a city and a state, between the day and year in a date, and after introductory words in a sentence.

HOMEWORK Grammar and Writing Practice Book, p. 113. Work through the first two items with the class.

Commas

Use a **comma** and a conjunction to join two sentences.
  There was a crumb on the table, and the ant crawled toward it.
Use **commas** to separate words in a series.
  We had sandwiches, cookies, and fruit at the picnic.
Use a **comma** after the greeting and the closing of a friendly letter.
  Dear Jake,
  Your friend,
Use a **comma** between the name of a city and a state in an address.
  Chico, CA 95926   Berea, Kentucky
Use a **comma** to separate the month and day from the year.
  July 21, 2006

Directions Write *C* if commas are used correctly in the sentence. Write *NC* if commas are not used correctly.

1. Some kinds of ants are army ants, honey ants, and dairying ants. — **C**
2. Army ants travel in lines and they hunt other insects. — **NC**
3. Dear Amy — **NC**

Directions Write each sentence. Add commas where they are needed.

4. Some ants eat other insects but many do not.
Some ants eat other insects, but many do not.

5. The newspaper had an article about ants on November 14 2005.
The newspaper had an article about ants on November 14, 2005.

 Home Activity Your child learned about commas. Have your child point out five commas in a book that you are reading together.

▲ **Grammar and Writing Practice Book** p. 113

DAY 3 Apply to Writing

DAILY FIX-IT

5. We learned about ants's strenth, and it is amazing. *(ants'; strength)*

6. Did you know an ant can lift something ten times heavyer than its body. *(heavier; body?)*

USE COMMAS IN WRITING

Explain that using commas correctly makes writing clearer and more easily understood by readers.

Unclear: The ants found sugar cookies and cake in the kitchen.

Clear: The ants found sugar, cookies, and cake in the kitchen.

- Have students review something they have written to see if they can use commas to make their writing clearer.

HOMEWORK Grammar and Writing Practice, Book p. 114

Commas

Directions Answer each question with a complete sentence. Make your writing clear by using commas correctly. **Possible answers:**

1. In what city and state do you live?
   I live in Nashville, Tennessee.

2. What month, day, and year were you born?
   I was born May 14, 1999.

3. What are three of your favorite colors?
   My favorite colors are yellow, green, and orange.

4. What are three of your favorite foods?
   My favorite foods are pizza, spaghetti, and yogurt.

5. What are two activities you do in your free time? Answer with a compound sentence.
   I ride my bike, and I play soccer with my friends.

Directions Write a sentence listing three traits of ants. Use commas correctly.
   Possible answer: Ants are small, hard-working, and strong.

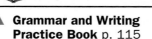 **Home Activity** Your child learned how to use commas in writing. Have your child write a sentence naming three animals that he or she has, using commas correctly.

▲ **Grammar and Writing Practice Book** p. 114

DAY 4 Test Preparation

DAILY FIX-IT

7. The Masons and Marks went to a lake cabin for a vacasion on March 16 2005. *(vacation; 16,)*

8. The families was unprapared for the ants and other insects there. *(were; unprepared)*

STANDARDIZED TEST PREP

Test Tip

You may be asked to identify the correct locations for commas in a sentence. Remember that a comma goes before the conjunction in a compound sentence and between the day of the month and the year in a date. A comma goes after each word in a series, including before the conjunction that joins the words.

Incorrect: Juan ran and, I walked.

We passed a park, a store and a school.

Correct: Juan ran, and I walked.

We passed a park, a store, and a school.

HOMEWORK Grammar and Writing Practice Book, p. 115

Commas

Directions Mark the letter of the words that complete the sentence correctly.

1. The ants march along _____
   (A) grass, bushes, and trees
   B grass bushes and trees
   C grass, bushes and trees
   D grass bushes, and trees

2. The ants carry _____
   A crumbs, salt and sugar
   B crumbs salt and sugar
   (C) crumbs, salt, and sugar
   D crumbs salt, and sugar

3. Some ants _____ lay eggs.
   A work and others
   (B) work, and others
   C work, And others
   D work And others

4. The ants are _____
   A red black and brown
   B red, black and brown
   C red black, and brown
   (D) red, black, and brown

5. I drew these ants on _____
   A March 8 2005
   B March, 8, 2005
   (C) March 8, 2005
   D March 8 2005,

6. I saw many ants in _____
   A Atlanta Georgia
   (B) Atlanta, Georgia
   C Atlanta, Georgia,
   D Atlanta Georgia,

7. We had a picnic with _____
   (A) salad, fruit, and juice
   B salad fruit and juice
   C salad, fruit and juice
   D salad fruit, and juice

8. Some _____ came to the picnic too.
   A ants bees and flies
   B ants bees, and flies
   C ants, bees and flies
   (D) ants, bees, and flies

9. Bees _____ crawled.
   A flew and ants
   (B) flew, and ants
   C flew, And ants
   D flew And ants

10. I like _____ doesn't.
    A insects but Rob
    B insects, But Rob
    C insects But Rob
    (D) insects, but Rob

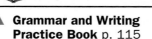 **Home Activity** Your child prepared for taking tests on commas. Have your child show you some sentences from a school paper or ad and explain why they need commas or not.

▲ **Grammar and Writing Practice Book** p. 115

DAY 5 Cumulative Review

DAILY FIX-IT

9. Tommy found a anthill out side his house. *(an; outside)*

10. He staring at the tiny creetures for hours. *(was staring; creatures)*

ADDITIONAL PRACTICE

Assign pp. 218–221 in The Grammar and Writing Book.

EXTRA PRACTICE Grammar and Writing Practice Book p. 150.

TEST PREPARATION Grammar and Writing Practice Book pp. 157–158.

ASSESSMENT

CUMULATIVE REVIEW Grammar and Writing Practice Book, p. 116

Commas

Directions Fix the comma errors in the sentences in the letter. If a phrase or sentence does not have a comma error, write C.

1. Dear Lisa
   Dear Lisa,

2. We looked at ants bees and butterflies in science class.
   We looked at ants, bees, and butterflies in science class.

3. I love butterflies but I am not crazy about ants.
   I love butterflies, but I am not crazy about ants.

4. Tomorrow we will study frogs lizards and snakes.
   Tomorrow we will study frogs, lizards, and snakes.

Directions Write each sentence. Add commas where they are needed.

5. My brother went to camp on July 10 2005.
   My brother went to camp on July 10, 2005.

6. He loves insects and he was happy to live in a tent.
   He loves insects, and he was happy to live in a tent.

7. In his tent he saw spiders ants and flies.
   In his tent he saw spiders, ants, and flies.

 **Home Activity** Your child reviewed commas. Have your child look at letters and envelopes in the mail and point out commas used in dates and addresses.

▲ **Grammar and Writing Practice Book** p. 116

Writing Workshop Writing About a Picture

OBJECTIVES

- Identify the characteristics of writing about a picture.
- Write about a picture by elaborating on its features.
- Focus on word choice.
- Use a rubric.

Genre Writing About a Picture
Writer's Craft Elaborating
Writing Trait Word Choice

Word Choice Pair an English learner with a proficient English speaker to discuss pictures in books or magazines. Have them list colorful words from the discussion to use in their writing.

Writing Trait

IDEAS/FOCUS The paragraph focuses on details in a picture.

ORGANIZATION/PARAGRAPHS The details are arranged in a logical order.

VOICE The writer's voice is observant and original.

WORD CHOICE The writer uses vivid and precise words *(blades of grass, tiny grains)* to describe a picture.

SENTENCES Sentences of different lengths and kinds are used.

CONVENTIONS Grammar and mechanics are excellent, including use of commas.

READING-WRITING CONNECTION

- *Two Bad Ants* is an animal fantasy about two ants that behave like humans.
- Animal fantasies often include interesting illustrations that come to life through the story's telling.
- Students will **write about a picture** in the story by using vivid and precise words to describe it.

MODEL WORD CHOICE Discuss Writing Transparency 29A. Discuss the model in terms of the writing trait of word choice.

 I see that the writer has written a paragraph about an interesting picture in *Two Bad Ants.* The first sentence gets the reader's attention with a general description. The next sentences elaborate with use of vivid descriptive words. The concluding sentence sums up why this picture is especially interesting.

Writing About a Picture

When you **write about a picture,** you describe the picture's details. You may explain why you think the picture is especially interesting, beautiful, or creative.

A Big World

Topic sentence gets readers' interest and describes picture.

Huge creatures with antennae and six legs march through a dark forest covered with rocks and gravel. But wait! The huge

Next sentences use vivid descriptive words to elaborate on picture's traits.

creatures are really tiny ants. The forest is really blades of grass. The rocks and gravel are tiny grains of sand and dirt. This is a picture in *Two Bad Ants,* and it shows how big the world must look to ants. The picture shows a line of black ants marching along a white path. The ants are drawn in correct proportion to the grass. Yet people never see the ground and the grass from the ants'

Conclusion sums up why the picture is interesting.

point of view. This picture gives people a whole new view of the world.

Unit 6 Two Bad Ants   Writing Model **29A**

▲ **Writing Transparency** 29A

WRITER'S CRAFT
Elaborating

Display Writing Transparency 29B. Read the directions and work together to decide how to best elaborate the sentences on the transparency.

 ELABORATING Tomorrow we will write a paragraph about a picture in *Two Bad Ants.* I will elaborate on the main idea by writing specific details. I want to include details and examples to describe what I see in the picture. I can describe colors, sizes, and shapes. I can include sensory details in my paragraph.

GUIDED WRITING Some students may need more help with elaborating. Review some paragraphs from other selections and discuss with students the methods of elaboration used in the paragraphs.

Elaborating

When you **elaborate,** you write details to support your main idea. Use specific words to show what you are describing. Replace words and phrases such as *things* and *a lot of* with specific words.
No   Those ants carried a lot of things.
Yes Those ants carried hundreds of cake crumbs.

Directions Choose words from the box to replace the underlined word or words in each sentence. Write the new sentence.

> like a weight lifter picking up a huge barbell   books and magazine articles
> sugar crystals many times their weight   a huge bread crumb   ten times its size

1. Once I saw an ant carrying something.
Once I saw an ant carrying a huge bread crumb.

2. The bread crumb was very big.
The bread crumb was ten times its size.

3. Ants can lift heavy things.
Ants can lift sugar crystals many times their weight.

4. This is neat.
This is like a weight lifter picking up a huge barbell.

5. I want to read a lot of stuff about ants.
I want to read books and magazine articles about ants.

Directions Elaborate the following topic sentence by writing two details. Use specific words.

Ants come in many different colors and sizes.
Possible answer: Many ants are black or brown, and some ants are rusty red like autumn leaves. Ants may be the size of a pinhead, or they may be more than an inch long.

Unit 6 Two Bad Ants   Writer's Craft **29B**

▲ **Writing Transparency** 29B

DAY 3 — Prewrite and Draft

READ THE WRITING PROMPT

on page 377 in the Student Edition.

Two Bad Ants *describes the adventures of two ants.*

Think about a picture in the story you find interesting.

Now write about that picture, using vivid words.

Writing Test Tips

- Use a strong topic sentence that makes a generalization about the picture's main traits.
- Write details that illustrate these traits.
- Think of one detail that is especially appealing.

GETTING STARTED Students can do any of the following:

- Choose a picture and list details they observe in the picture.
- Read the story with a partner, then close the book and discuss a picture that made a big impression.
- Work with a group to discuss the story's pictures.

DAY 4 — Draft and Revise

EDITING/REVISING CHECKLIST

☑ Does the paragraph focus on a picture?

☑ Are facts, details, and/or examples used to elaborate the picture?

☑ Are commas used correctly for clarity?

☑ Are multisyllabic words spelled correctly?

See *The Grammar and Writing Book,* pp. 222–227.

Revising Tips

Word Choice

- Use precise words to relate facts.
- Use vivid nouns, verbs, and adjectives in descriptive details.
- Use prepositions to make details more specific.

PUBLISHING With a partner, students can show the picture they chose and read their paragraphs aloud. Some students may wish to revise their work later.

ASSESSMENT Use the scoring rubric to evaluate students' work.

DAY 5 — Connect to Unit Writing

Research Report

Week 1	Taking Notes 303g–303h
Week 2	Outlining 331g–331h
Week 3	Informational Paragraph 353g–353h
Week 4	Writing About a Picture 379g–379h
Week 5	Write Good Paragraphs 407g–407h

PREVIEW THE UNIT PROMPT

Write a research report about a monument or statue that symbolizes freedom in the United States. Discuss the monument itself, its history, and why it is important. Find information in sources such as books, magazines, CD-ROMs, and the Internet.

APPLY

- A research report is an informational article based on research.
- Writers use various types of elaboration in a research report.

Writing Trait Rubric

	4	3	2	1
Word Choice	Vivid style created by use of exact nouns, strong verbs, exciting adjectives, and clear figurative language	Some style created by strong and precise words	Little style created by strong, precise words; some lack of clarity	Word choice vague or incorrect
	Uses strong, specific words that make description unusually clear and lively	Uses some specific words that make description clear	Needs more precise word choice to create style and clarity in description	Description made dull or unclear by poor word choice

OBJECTIVES

- Use word parts to decode multi-syllabic words.
- Review words with the common syllables *-tion*, *-sion*, and *-ture*.
- Blend and read multisyllabic words and words with the syllables *-tion*, *-sion*, and *-ture*.
- Apply decoding strategies: blend longer words.

Support Phonics Speakers of mono-syllable languages such as Cantonese, Hmong, Khmer, Korean, and Vietnamese may have difficulty understanding that multisyllabic words are single words. Help children practice saying and writing words with prefixes and suffixes as single words.

See the Phonics Transition Lessons in the ELL and Transition Handbook.

Multisyllabic Words

Directions Each word below has one or more word parts added to the beginning or end of the base word. Underline the base word. Then write a sentence that uses the whole word. Sentences will vary.

1. uncomfortable My shoes are uncomfortable.
2. carefully Please handle the china carefully.
3. disagreement We had a disagreement about what game to play.
4. reappeared My lost glove suddenly reappeared.
5. unprepared I was unprepared for the surprise quiz.
6. endlessly The baby cries endlessly.
7. distasteful That medicine is distasteful.
8. unfriendly She is unfriendly and won't talk to anyone.
9. unplugged A toaster won't work if it is unplugged.

Directions Each base word below has a word part added to the beginning and end. Separate each base word from the other word parts and write each part on a line.

		Base Word		
10. un	+ self	+ ish	= unselfish
11. un	+ law	+ ful	= unlawful
12. dis	+ honest	+ ly	= dishonestly
13. re	+ new	+ able	= renewable
14. re	+ fresh	+ ment	= refreshment
15. dis	+ trust	+ ful	= distrustful

Home Activity Your child identified multisyllabic words, such as uncomfortable, carefully, and disagreement. Challenge your child to add word parts to a base word such as play to see how many new words can be made (for example, replay, playful, playfully, overplay, and player).

▲ **Practice Book 3.2** p. 139

Multisyllabic Words

TEACH

Remind students that prefixes and suffixes can be added to base words. Review meanings of affixes studied. Write the words *rewrite*, *hopeful*, and *unlikely*.

- What is the base word in *rewrite*? *(write)*
- What other word part do you see in *rewrite*? (the prefix *re-*)
- What is the base word in *hopeful*? *(hope)*
- What other word part do you see in *hopeful*? (the suffix *-ful*)

 MODEL When I come to a longer word, I expect it to be hard to read, but when I look more closely, I often notice a prefix, a suffix, or both. When I divide the word and look at each word part, the word becomes much easier. The longer word *unlikely* has three parts that I know: the prefix *un-*, the base word *like*, and the suffix *-ly*.

Model blending *rewrite*, *hopeful*, and *unlikely*. Then have students blend the words with you.

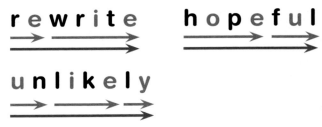

PRACTICE AND ASSESS

DECODE LONGER WORDS Write these words. Have students divide the words into word parts and then read them aloud.

dis/grace/ful   over/act/ing   out/smart/ed   lion/ess

mid/summer   alarm/ing/ly   hope/ful/ly   un/kind/ness

READ WORDS IN CONTEXT Write these sentences. Have individuals read them and point out words with prefixes and suffixes. Words with prefixes and suffixes are underlined. To check meaning, have them give their own sentence with the underlined word.

We thought our team had won, but we were <u>misinformed</u>.

No one <u>distrusted</u> the new <u>governor</u>.

After the table was <u>refinished</u>, it looked as good as new.

The <u>artist</u> <u>carefully</u> set up the easel.

To assess, observe whether students identify and pronounce words with suffixes and prefixes correctly.

Phonics

Review Word Parts

REVIEW SYLLABLES *-tion, -sion, -ture*

Vocabulary TiP

You may wish to explain the meanings of these words.

alteration	change
apprehension	fear, nervousness
stature	size, importance

CONNECT Write this sentence: *Our intention was to capture the stray dog for its owner.*

- We studied the common syllables *-tion, -sion,* and *-ture.*
- Read the sentence to yourself. Raise your hand when you know which words have *-tion, -sion,* or *-ture.* *(intention, capture)*
- What is the common syllable in *intention? (-tion)*
- What is the common syllable in *capture? (-ture)*

Continue in the same way with the sentence *Ron made a good impression because he was very mature.*

PRACTICE AND ASSESS

DECODE LONGER WORDS Have individuals read the following words. Model chunking and blending the words one syllable at a time from left to right as needed.

constellation	miniature	apprehension	session
tension	repetition	stature	alteration
vulture	culture	extension	restriction

READ WORDS IN CONTEXT Have students read these sentences. Then, to check meaning, have them give their own sentence for the underlined word.

Jen won the <u>multiplication</u> <u>competition</u>.

<u>Agriculture</u> is a business that deserves our <u>attention</u>.

In the trial, the prisoner made a <u>sensational</u> <u>admission</u>.

Did the teacher <u>mention</u> that we may use a <u>dictionary</u>?

To assess, note how well students read words with the common word syllables *-tion, -sion,* and *-ture.*

Spelling & Phonics Multisyllabic Words

OBJECTIVE

● Spell multisyllabic words.

Generalization

Connect to Phonics When spelling words with many syllables, look carefully at each word part. Multisyllabic words can be divided into smaller parts for spelling and pronunciation.

Spelling Words

1. leadership	9. ownership
2. gracefully	10. unacceptable
3. refreshment	11. impossibly
4. uncomfortable	12. reappeared
5. overdoing	13. unprepared
6. remarkable*	14. oncoming
7. carefully	15. misbehaving
8. unbearably*	

Challenge Words

16. outrageous	18. undoubtedly
17. incomprehen-sible	19. independence
	20. disadvantage

*Words from the selection

Spelling/Phonics Support See the ELL and Transition Handbook for spelling support.

DAY 1 Pretest and Sort

PRETEST

Use the Dictation Sentences from Day 5 to administer the pretest. Read the word, read the sentence, and then read the word again. Guide students in self-correcting their pretests and correcting any misspellings.

Monitor Progress	
Spelling	
If... students misspell more than 4 pretest words,	**then...** use words 1–8 for Strategic Intervention.
If... students misspell 1–4 pretest words,	**then...** use words 1–15 for On-Level practice.
If... students correctly spell all pretest words,	**then...** use words 1–20 for Advanced Learners.

HOMEWORK Spelling Practice Book, p. 113

Multisyllabic Words

Generalization When spelling words with many syllables, look carefully at each word part.

Word Sort Sort the list words by the number of syllables the word has.

3 syllables
1. leadership
2. gracefully
3. refreshment
4. carefully
5. ownership
6. reappeared
7. unprepared
8. oncoming

4 syllables
9. overdoing
10. remarkable
11. unbearably
12. impossibly
13. misbehaving

5 syllables
14. uncomfortable
15. unacceptable

Challenge Words

3 syllables
16. outrageous

6 syllables
20. incomprehensible

4 syllables
17. undoubtedly
18. independence
19. disadvantage

Spelling Words
1. leadership
2. gracefully
3. refreshment
4. uncomfortable
5. overdoing
6. remarkable
7. carefully
8. unbearably
9. ownership
10. unacceptable
11. impossibly
12. reappeared
13. unprepared
14. oncoming
15. misbehaving

Challenge Words
16. outrageous
17. incomprehensible
18. undoubtedly
19. independence
20. disadvantage

Home Activity Your child is learning to spell words with many syllables. To practice at home, have your child pronounce each word syllable by syllable before spelling it.

▲ **Spelling Practice Book** p. 113

DAY 2 Think and Practice

TEACH

Multisyllabic words can be divided into parts to make spelling easier. Demonstrate this by writing the spelling words on the board and having students sound out the syllables of each word. Guide students in breaking the word into syllables to show the different parts.

grace + ful + ly = gracefully

FIND THE PATTERN Have students look for and identify base words in each spelling word.

HOMEWORK Spelling Practice Book, p. 114

Multisyllabic Words

Spelling Words

leadership	gracefully	refreshment	uncomfortable	overdoing
remarkable	carefully	unbearably	ownership	unacceptable
impossibly	reappeared	unprepared	oncoming	misbehaving

Missing Syllables Add the missing syllables and write the list words.

1. The deer moved grace____. — 1. gracefully
2. He was __bear__ rude. — 2. unbearably
3. Watch out for __com__ cars. — 3. oncoming
4. That is a __mark__ carving! — 4. remarkable
5. Juice is my favorite __fresh__. — 5. refreshment
6. Sam is __fort__ in crowds. — 6. uncomfortable
7. Do the addition care____. — 7. carefully
8. He took a lead____ position. — 8. leadership
9. She gets tired from __do__. — 9. overdoing
10. Sue was __pos__ stubborn. — 10. impossibly

Definitions Write the list word with the same meaning as the underlined words.

11. He was not prepared for the test. — 11. unprepared
12. The sun appeared again from behind the clouds. — 12. reappeared
13. The puppy kept behaving badly. — 13. misbehaving
14. My score on the test was not acceptable. — 14. unacceptable
15. He claimed to be the owner of the stray cat. — 15. ownership

Home Activity Your child spelled words with many syllables. Have your child draw lines to divide the list words into syllables.

▲ **Spelling Practice Book** p. 114

DAY 3 — Connect to Writing

WRITE AN EDITORIAL

Have students write an editorial expressing their opinion about a subject. Their editorials should use as many spelling words as possible. Have students read their editorials aloud, or post them on the bulletin board for everyone to see.

Frequently Misspelled Words

everybody   everything

These words are difficult for third-graders to spell. Alert students to these frequently misspelled words and encourage them to break down each word into its smaller part before spelling.

HOMEWORK Spelling Practice Book, p. 115

Multisyllabic Words

Spelling Words				
leadership	gracefully	refreshment	uncomfortable	overdoing
remarkable	carefully	unbearably	ownership	unacceptable
impossibly	reappeared	unprepared	oncoming	misbehaving

Proofread an Explanation Olivia wrote about how to bowl. Circle four spelling errors. Write the words correctly. Then add the missing comma.

Bowling is a remarkable sport. Almost (every body) likes it.
You should start with good equipment. Don't use a ball that is (unbeareably) heavy and don't settle for (unconfortable) shoes.
When it's your turn, swing the ball back gracefully as you walk toward the pins. Let go when you reach the line. Always aim (carefuly) at the pins.

Frequently Misspelled Words

everybody
everything

1. __everybody__   2. __unbearably__
3. __uncomfortable__   4. __carefully__

Correct the Words Write the correct spelling of each misspelled word.

5. unaceptable   5. __unacceptable__
6. oncomeing   6. __oncoming__
7. missbehaving   7. __misbehaving__
8. inpossibly   8. __impossibly__
9. reapeared   9. __reappeared__
10. leedership   10. __leadership__

School Home **Home Activity** Your child is learning to spell words with many syllables. Have your child write a sentence using two or more of the list words.

▲ **Spelling Practice Book** p. 115

DAY 4 — Review

REVIEW MULTISYLLABIC WORDS

Have students work in pairs to create a word search puzzle featuring the spelling words. Students can exchange their puzzles with other groups to solve each puzzle.

Spelling Strategy
Multisyllabic Words

If students concentrate on spelling each syllable of a long word, it will be easier for them to spell the whole word.

HOMEWORK Spelling Practice Book, p. 116

Multisyllabic Words

Spelling Words				
leadership	gracefully	refreshment	uncomfortable	overdoing
remarkable	carefully	unbearably	ownership	unacceptable
impossibly	reappeared	unprepared	oncoming	misbehaving

Word Maze Draw a path through the maze. Follow the three-syllable words. Write the words.

ownership   reappeared
carefully   misbehaving
impossibly   leadership
refreshment   gracefully
unbearably   overdoing
unprepared   uncomfortable   oncoming
unacceptable   remarkable

1. __unprepared__   2. __gracefully__   3. __leadership__
4. __carefully__   5. __refreshment__   6. __ownership__
7. __reappeared__   8. __oncoming__

Syllable Scramble Rearrange the syllables to make a list word.

9. un a bear bly   9. __unbearably__
10. hav mis ing be   10. __misbehaving__
11. cept un a ble ac   11. __unacceptable__
12. ing o do ver   12. __overdoing__

School Home **Home Activity** Your child has been learning to spell words with many syllables. Help your child scan a page of a magazine or newspaper to find the word(s) with the most syllables.

▲ **Spelling Practice Book** p. 116

DAY 5 — Posttest

DICTATION SENTENCES

1. We need someone with good <u>leadership</u>.
2. Tina walks so <u>gracefully</u>!
3. Where is the <u>refreshment</u> stand?
4. This shirt is very <u>uncomfortable</u>.
5. Be careful about <u>overdoing</u> your workout.
6. That is a <u>remarkable</u> family.
7. Walk <u>carefully</u> near the wet paint.
8. The music is <u>unbearably</u> loud.
9. We have <u>ownership</u> of the car.
10. The torn book was <u>unacceptable</u>.
11. The shelf is <u>impossibly</u> high.
12. The sun <u>reappeared</u> after the storm.
13. I was <u>unprepared</u> for the test.
14. I see an <u>oncoming</u> train.
15. The twins are always <u>misbehaving</u>.

CHALLENGE

16. What an <u>outrageous</u> thing to say!
17. That story was <u>incomprehensible</u>.
18. This is <u>undoubtedly</u> the biggest piece of cake.
19. <u>Independence</u> means freedom.
20. I find it a <u>disadvantage</u> to be so tall.

OBJECTIVES

- Formulate an inquiry question that is connected to this week's lesson focus.
- Effectively and efficiently find, evaluate, and communicate information related to an inquiry question using electronic sources.

New Literacies

Day 1	Identify Questions
Day 2	Navigate/Search
Day 3	Analyze
Day 4	Synthesize
Day 5	Communicate

NEW LITERACIES

Internet Inquiry Activity

EXPLORE FREEDOM

Use the following 5-day plan to help students conduct this week's Internet inquiry activity on freedom. Remind students to follow classroom rules when using the Internet.

DAY 1

Identify Questions Discuss the lesson focus question: *When can freedom be a problem?* Brainstorm ideas for specific inquiry questions about the problems that come with too much freedom. For example, students might want to find out what society would be like if there were no laws, or what might happen if they had no bedtime or television rules. Have students work individually, in pairs, or in small groups to write an inquiry question they want to answer.

DAY 2

Navigate/Search Have students begin a simple Internet search. Review the meanings of endings in URLs, or domain endings. Remind students that looking at these domain endings helps them determine the credibility of the Web site and the reliability of the information.

DAY 3

Analyze Have students explore the Web sites they identified on Day 2. Have them scan the sites for information that will help answer their inquiry questions. Tell students to analyze information and decide if it is relevant to their question. Students can print pages that contain useful information and highlight relevant details.

DAY 4

Synthesize Have students synthesize information from Day 3. Remind them that when they synthesize, they integrate important and relevant ideas from various sources to create answers to their inquiry questions.

DAY 5

Communicate Have students share their inquiry results. They can use a word processing program to write a letter about having too much freedom.

Note-taking

TEACH

Ask students to describe what they do when they read something new that they have to remember. If no one mentions it, present the note-taking strategy. Discuss these ideas about note-taking.

- Taking notes can help you learn and remember new information. You can take notes from reading or from words that people say.

- Notes should be brief. They should include the most important facts and information.

- Do not copy the exact words you read or hear. You will remember the ideas better if you state them in your own words.

- The organization of your notes is important. Arrange notes about the same or similar subject together.

Have students work in pairs using a science or social studies textbook. One student reads two or three paragraphs from the book while the partner takes notes on the information. Partners then switch roles. After both students have had a turn taking notes, they review their work.

To model this activity, read the paragraph below to students, have them take notes, and discuss these questions.

1. What are some keywords in this paragraph? *(mosquito, egg, larva, pupa, adult)*

2. Where do mosquitoes live in the first part of the life cycle? *(in the water)*

Life Cycle of a Mosquito

Mosquitoes lay their eggs in water. The water source can be small, such as in a bird feeder. It might be a large source like a marshland area. The egg forms a larva, which also lives in the water. During this stage, the larva feeds on microorganisms. Next, the larva becomes a pupa. The pupa does not feed, but it is quite active. Finally, the adult comes out of the pupa case and lives its life on land.

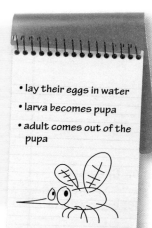

- lay their eggs in water
- larva becomes pupa
- adult comes out of the pupa

ASSESS

As students take notes, check that they have recorded important ideas and that the notes are in their own words.

For more practice or to assess students, use Practice Book 3.2, p. 140.

Note-taking

Note-taking while reading and studying can help you learn and remember new information. The notes should be brief and include the most important facts or information from the text.

Directions Read the paragraph and take notes by writing about the most important ideas.

The Ant Colony

Ants are social insects that live in groups, or colonies. In most ant colonies, there are three castes, or classes, of ants. The castes include the queen, the workers, and the males. The queen's job is to lay eggs. Some colonies have only one queen, while others have several queens. The queen does not rule the colony.

Workers have many jobs. They care for the queen and for the young ants. Workers repair, build, and defend the nest. They also gather food for the colony.

Male ants do not do any work for the colony. They live for only a short time, and their only job is to mate with young queens.

1. ant colony

   ant colony—group of ants living together

2. caste

   caste—classes of ants

3. queen

   queen—lays eggs in the colony

4. workers

   workers—care for nest, queen and young; gather food

5. males

   males—mate with queens; live for only a short time

School + Home Home Activity Your child read a selection and took notes on the most important ideas. Find a paragraph from an encyclopedia or textbook. Ask your child to identify and take notes on the most important information in the paragraph.

▲ **Practice Book 3.2** p. 140

Assessment Checkpoints *for the Week*

Selection Assessment

Use pp. 113–116 of Selection Tests **to check:**

 Selection Understanding

 Comprehension Skill *Plot and Theme*

 Selection Vocabulary

crystal	journey
disappeared	joyful
discovery	scoop
goal	unaware

ASSESSMENT
Selection Tests

Scott Foresman
Selection Tests
Teacher's Manual

• Assess comprehension of weekly selections
• Assess understanding of weekly comprehension skills
• Assess knowledge of selection vocabulary

Reading STREET
Grade 3

Leveled Assessment

- On-Level
- Strategic Intervention
- Advanced

Use pp. 169–174 of Fresh Reads for Differentiated Test Practice **to check:**

 Comprehension Skill *Plot and Theme*

 REVIEW **Comprehension Skill** *Character*

 Fluency *Words Correct Per Minute*

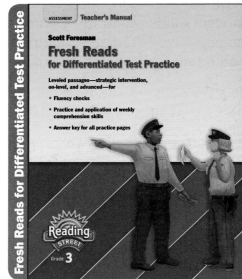

ASSESSMENT Teacher's Manual

Scott Foresman
Fresh Reads
for Differentiated Test Practice

Leveled passages—strategic intervention, on-level, and advanced—for
• Fluency checks
• Practice and application of weekly comprehension skills
• Answer key for all practice pages

Reading STREET
Grade 3

Managing Assessment

Use Assessment Handbook **for:**

 Observation Checklists

 Record-Keeping Forms

 Portfolio Assessment

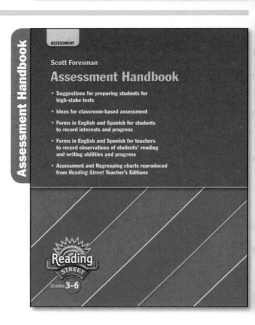

ASSESSMENT

Scott Foresman
Assessment Handbook

• Suggestions for preparing students for high-stake tests
• Ideas for classroom-based assessment
• Forms in English and Spanish for students to record interests and progress
• Forms in English and Spanish for teachers to record observations of students' reading and writing abilities and progress
• Assessment and Regrouping charts reproduced from *Reading Street* Teacher's Editions

Reading STREET
Grades 3–6

Illinois

Planning Guide for Performance Descriptors

Elena's Serenade

Reading Street Teacher's Edition pages	Grade 3 English Language Arts Performance Descriptors
Oral Language **Speaking/Listening** Build Concept Vocabulary: 380l, 393, 400, 407c Read Aloud: 380m	**1A.Stage C.3.** Discuss the meanings of new words encountered in independent and group activities. **1B.Stage C.13.** Read age-appropriate material aloud with fluency and accuracy. **2A.Stage C.5.** Define unfamiliar vocabulary.
Word Work Related Words: 407i, 407k–407l	**1A.Stage C.4.** Use synonyms and antonyms to define words.
Reading **Comprehension** Generalize: 380–381, 384–400, 407b Predict: 380–381, 384–400 **Vocabulary** Lesson Vocabulary: 382b, 393, 400, 404 Context Clues: 382–383, 389, 407c **Fluency** Model Expressing Characterization: 380l–380m, 407a Reader's Theater: 407a **Self-Selected Reading:** LR37–45, TR16–17 **Literature** Genre—Fantasy: 384 Reader Response: 401	**1A.Stage C.5.** Use a variety of decoding strategies (e.g., phonics, word patterns, structural analysis, context clues) to recognize new words when reading age-appropriate material. **1B.Stage C.2.** Make predictions about text events before and during reading and confirm, modify, or reject predictions after reading. **1B.Stage C.13.** Read age-appropriate material aloud with fluency and accuracy. **1C.Stage C.6.** Interpret concepts or make connections through analysis, evaluation, inference, and/or comparison. **2A.Stage C.5.** Define unfamiliar vocabulary. **2A.Stage C.6.** Name several characteristics that distinguish fiction from nonfiction.
Language Arts **Writing** Write Good Paragraphs: 407g–407h **Six-Trait Writing** Organization/Paragraphs: 402–403, 407g–407h **Grammar, Usage, and Mechanics** Quotation: 407e–407f **Research/Study** Chart/Table: 407n **Technology** New Literacies: 407m	**1C.Stage C.9.** Use information from simple tables, maps, and charts to increase comprehension of a variety of age-appropriate materials, both fiction and nonfiction. **3A.Stage C.1.** Develop a paragraph using proper form (e.g., topic sentence, details, summary/conclusion sentence). **3A.Stage C.4.** Use end marks, commas, and quotation marks.
Unit Skills **Writing** Research Report: WA2–9 **Poetry:** 408–411 **Project/Wrap-Up:** 412–413	**2A.Stage C.12.** Discover poetic devices (e.g., rhyme, rhythm, alliteration, onomatopoeia, repetition, simile, metaphor). **3A.Stage C.10.** Proofread and revise one's own work.

This Week's Leveled Readers

Below-Level

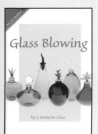

Glass Blowing
by J. Matteson Claus

Nonfiction

1B.Stage C.5. Make connections from text to text, text to self, text to world.

1C.Stage C.6. Interpret concepts or make connections through analysis, evaluation, inference, and/or comparison.

On-Level

Traditional Crafts of MEXICO
by Mary Miller

Nonfiction

1C.Stage C.5. Make comparisons across reading selections (e.g., themes, topics, story elements).

1C.Stage C.6. Interpret concepts or make connections through analysis, evaluation, inference, and/or comparison.

Advanced

Biography

Jackie Robinson
by Morgan Lloyd

Nonfiction

1B.Stage C.3. Use a variety of strategies (e.g., K-W-L, anticipation guide, graphic organizer, DR-TA) to connect important ideas in text to prior knowledge and other reading.

1C.Stage C.6. Interpret concepts or make connections through analysis, evaluation, inference, and/or comparison.

Content-Area Illinois Performance Descriptors in This Lesson

Social Studies

15A.Stage C.3. List jobs people do to earn wages.

15A.Stage C.4. Identify producers of goods and services in the community.

16A.Stage C.6. Tell why the location of where an event occurred helps to explain why and how it happened.

16D.Stage C.4. Tell about the origin of a family or community tradition or custom.

16D.Stage C.7. Compare how families and other groups of people lived in a past culture with how families and other groups of people in the community live today.

17C.Stage C.1. Identify how people use tools and machines to obtain resources and change the physical and human environment in their community and in other places.

18A.Stage C.5. Describe aspects of the community that reflect its cultural heritage.

18C.Stage C.1. Describe the concept of conflict.

18C.Stage C.2. Describe the concept of cooperation.

Science

12B.Stage C.2. Apply scientific inquiries or technological designs to examine the interdependence of organisms in ecosystems: describing the interaction between living and non-living factors in an ecosystem.

12C.Stage C.1. Apply scientific inquiries or technological designs to examine the flow of energy: contrasting the transmission of sound through different materials.

Math

7A.Stage C.4. Describe multiple measurable attributes (e.g., length, mass/weight, time, temperature, area, volume, capacity) of a single object.

7C.Stage C.2. Determine elapsed time between events.

10C.Stage C.1. Describe events as likely or unlikely and discuss the degree of likelihood using such words as certain, equally likely, and impossible.

Illinois!

A FAMOUS ILLINOISAN
Ronald W. Reagan

Ronald W. Reagan (1911–2004) was born in Tampico, and he spent much of his childhood in Dixon. He served two terms as the fortieth President of the United States. Reagan began his adult life as an actor. He appeared in dozens of movies. Reagan served as governor of California from 1967 until 1975. He was elected President in 1980.

Students can . . .
Find out more about Ronald Reagan and create a time line highlighting important events in his life.

A SPECIAL ILLINOIS PLACE
Cairo

Cairo (KAY-roh) was established in 1818. It got its name because some people thought its location looked like the area around Cairo (KY-roh), Egypt. Cairo is a shipping center for the Mississippi and Ohio Rivers. Bridges over both rivers connect Cairo with Kentucky and Missouri. Cairo served as the headquarters for General Ulysses S. Grant during the western campaigns in the Civil War.

Students can . . .
Locate Cairo on an outline map of Illinois. Have students suppose they are an officer in the Civil War and write a short report describing why Cairo would be an important location to control.

ILLINOIS FUN FACTS
Did You Know?

- The Illiniwek Confederation of Native Americans in the 1600s included the Cahokia, Kaskaskia, Michigamea, Peoria, and Tamaroa peoples.

- The first permanent settlement in the region that is now Illinois was the town of Cahokia in 1699.

- The first European settlers in what is now Illinois were French. France owned the land at the time.

Students can . . .
Research what the first French settlers might have seen when they arrived in the area that is now Illinois. Have students report their findings in the form of a journal entry.

Unit 6
Freedom

CONCEPT QUESTION
What does it mean to be free?

Week 1
What does the Statue of Liberty mean to Americans?

Week 2
When might it be hard to grant freedom?

Week 3
Why is freedom of expression important?

Week 4
When can freedom be a problem?

Week 5
When are you free to follow your dreams?

EXPAND THE CONCEPT
When are you free to follow your dreams?

Time for
SOCIAL STUDIES

CONNECT THE CONCEPT

▶ **Build Background**
discouraged, instruments, mellow

Concept Vocabulary Web

discouraged — Feelings — **Freedom to Create** — Description of End Result — instruments
mellow

▶ **Social Studies Content**
Manufacturing; Cultures: Crafts; Changes

▶ **Writing**
Write Good Paragraphs

▶ **Internet Inquiry**
Following Your Dreams

Elena's Serenade **380a**

Preview Your Week

When are you free to follow your dreams?

Genre **Fantasy** is a made-up story that could never happen. What makes this story a fantasy?

384

What happens when Elena plays her serenade?

Student Edition pages 384-400

Genre **Fantasy**

Vocabulary Strategy Context Clues

Comprehension Skill Generalize

Comprehension Strategy Predict

Paired Selection

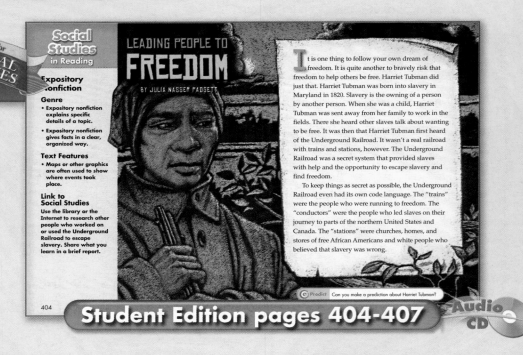

Reading Across Texts
Compare Types of Freedom

Genre
Expository Nonfiction

Text Features
Maps

Student Edition pages 404-407

Read It

ONLINE
PearsonSuccessNet.com

- Student Edition
- Leveled Readers

Leveled Readers

Skill Generalize

Strategy Predict

Lesson Vocabulary

Below-Level

On-Level

Advanced

ELL Reader

- Concept Vocabulary
- Text Support
- Language Enrichment

Time for
SOCIAL STUDIES

Integrate Social Studies Standards

- Manufacturing
- Cultures: Crafts
- Changes

✓ Read

Elena's Serenade
pp. 384–400

"Leading People to Freedom"
pp. 404–407

Leveled Readers

Below-Level **On-Level** **Advanced**

- Support Concepts
- Develop Concepts
- Extend Concepts

ELL Reader

✓ Build
Concept Vocabulary
Freedom to Create,
pp. 380l–380m

✓ Teach
Social Studies Concepts
Location Skills, p. 387
Women in the Workforce,
p. 389
Glassblowing, p. 395
Economic Opportunity, p. 405

✓ Explore
Social Studies Center
Working for Change, p. 380k

Weekly Plan

READING

45–90 minutes

TARGET SKILLS OF THE WEEK

Comprehension Skill
Generalize

Comprehension Strategy
Predict

Vocabulary Strategy
Context Clues

LANGUAGE ARTS

30–60 minutes

Trait of the Week

Organization/Paragraphs

DAY 1
PAGES 380l–382b, 407a, 407e–407h, 407k–407m

Oral Language

QUESTION OF THE WEEK   *When are you free to follow your dreams?*

Read Aloud: "Manuelo the Playing Mantis," 380m
Build Concepts, 380l

Comprehension/Vocabulary

Comprehension Skill/Strategy Lesson, 380–381
  Generalize **T**
  Predict
Build Background, 382a
Introduce Lesson Vocabulary, 382b
burro, bursts, factory, glassblower, puff, reply, tune **T**

Read Leveled Readers

Grouping Options 380f–380g

Fluency

Model Characterization,
380l–380m, 407a

Grammar, 407e
Introduce Quotations **T**

Writing Workshop, 407g
Introduce Write Good Paragraphs
Model the Trait of the Week:
  Organization/Paragraphs

Spelling, 407k
Pretest for Related Words

Internet Inquiry, 407m
Identify Questions

DAY 2
PAGES 382–393, 407a, 407e–407i, 407k–407m

Oral Language

QUESTION OF THE DAY   *What effect does Elena's music have on the animals she meets?*

Word Work

Phonics Lesson, 407i
Related Words

Comprehension/Vocabulary

Vocabulary Strategy Lesson, 382–383
  Context Clues **T**

Read *Elena's Serenade,* 384–393

Grouping Options
380f–380g

  Generalize **T**
  Predict
  Context Clues **T**
  REVIEW Main Idea **T**
  Develop Vocabulary

Fluency

Readers' Theater, 407a

Grammar, 407e
Develop Quotations **T**

Writing Workshop, 407g
Improve Writing with Strong Conclusions

Spelling, 407k
Teach the Generalization

Internet Inquiry, 407m
Navigate/Search

DAILY WRITING ACTIVITIES

Day 1   Write to Read, 380

Day 2   Words to Write, 383
Strategy Response Log, 384, 393

DAILY SOCIAL STUDIES CONNECTIONS

Day 1   Freedom to Create Concept Web, 380l

Day 2   Time for Social Studies: Location Skills, 387; Women in the Workforce, 389; Revisit the Freedom to Create Concept Web, 393

DAILY SUCCESS PREDICTORS
for Adequate Yearly Progress

Monitor Progress and Corrective Feedback

Vocabulary   Check Vocabulary, 380l

RESOURCES FOR THE WEEK

- Practice Book 3.2, *pp. 141–150*
- Phonics and Spelling Practice Book, *pp. 117–120*
- Grammar and Writing Practice Book, *pp. 117–120*

- Selection Test, *pp. 117–120*
- Fresh Reads for Differentiated Test Practice, *pp. 175–180*
- The Grammar and Writing Book, *pp. 224–229*

Grouping Options for Differentiated Instruction
Turn the page for the small group lesson plan.

DAY 3
PAGES 394–403, 407a, 407e–407h, 407k–407m

Oral Language

QUESTION OF THE DAY *How does Elena's music create and guide the swallow that takes her home?*

Comprehension/Vocabulary

Read *Elena's Serenade, 394–401*

Grouping Options
380f–380g

- Generalize **T**
- Predict
- Context Clues **T**
- REVIEW Main Idea **T**
- Develop Vocabulary

Reader Response
Selection Test

Fluency

Model Characterization, 407a

Grammar, 407f
Apply Quotations in Writing **T**

Writing Workshop, 402–403, 407h
Write Now
Prewrite and Draft

Spelling, 407l
Connect Spelling to Writing

Internet Inquiry, 407m
Analyze Sources

Day 3 Strategy Response Log, 398
Look Back and Write, 401

Day 3 Time for Social Studies: Glassblowing, 395
Revisit the Freedom to Create Concept Web, 400

DAY 4
PAGES 404–407a, 407e–407h, 407j–407m

Oral Language

QUESTION OF THE DAY *In what ways do freedoms cost more than what even money can buy?*

Word Work

Phonics Lesson, 407j
REVIEW Prefixes and Suffixes **T**

Comprehension/Vocabulary

Read "Leading People to Freedom," 404–407

Grouping Options
380f–380g

Expository Nonfiction/
Text Features
Reading Across Texts
Content-Area Vocabulary

Fluency

Readers' Theater, 407a

Grammar, 407f
Practice Quotations for Standardized Tests **T**

Writing Workshop, 407h
Draft, Revise, and Publish

Spelling, 407l
Provide a Strategy

Internet Inquiry, 407m
Synthesize Information

Day 4 Writing Across Texts, 407

Day 4 Time for Social Studies: Economic Opportunity, 405

DAY 5
PAGES 407a–407h, 407k–407n

Oral Language

QUESTION OF THE WEEK *To wrap up the week, revisit the Day 1 question.*
Build Concept Vocabulary, 407c

Fluency

Read Leveled Readers

Grouping Options 380f–380g

Assess Reading Rate, 407a

Comprehension/Vocabulary

- Reteach Generalize, 407b **T**
- Details and Facts, 407b
- Review Context Clues, 407c **T**

Speaking and Listening, 407d
Song, Rap, or Poem
Listen to Song or Poem

Grammar, 407f
Cumulative Review

Writing Workshop, 407h
Connect to Unit Writing

Spelling, 407l
Posttest for Related Words

Internet Inquiry, 407m
Communicate Results

Research/Study Skills, 407n
Chart/Table

Day 5 Details and Facts, 407b

Day 5 Revisit the Freedom to Create Concept Web, 407c

KEY = Target Skill **T** = Tested Skill

Comprehension Check Retelling, *403*

Fluency Check Fluency wcpm, *407a*

Vocabulary Check Vocabulary, *407c*

SUCCESS PREDICTOR

Small Group Plan for Differentiated Instruction

Daily Plan AT A GLANCE

Reading
Whole Group
- Oral Language
- Phonics
- Comprehension/Vocabulary

Group Time
Differentiated Instruction

Meet with small groups to provide:
- Skill Support
- Reading Support
- Fluency Practice

Read

This week's lessons for daily group time can be found behind the Differentiated Instruction (DI) tab on pp. DI·42–DI·51.

Whole Group
- Fluency

Language Arts
- Grammar
- Writing
- Spelling
- Research/Inquiry
- Speaking/Listening/Viewing

Use My Sidewalks on Reading Street for Tier III intensive reading intervention.

DAY 1

On-Level
Teacher-Led
Page DI·43
- Develop Concept Vocabulary
- **Read** On-Level Reader *Traditional Crafts of Mexico*

Strategic Intervention
Teacher-Led
Page DI·42
- Preteach Related Words
- **Read** Decodable Reader 30
- **Read** Below-Level Reader *Glass Blowing*

Advanced
Teacher-Led
Page DI·43
- **Read** Advanced Reader *Jackie Robinson*
- Independent Extension Activity

ⓘ Independent Activities
While you meet with small groups, have the rest of the class...

- Visit the Reading/Library Center
- Listen to the Background Building Audio
- Finish Write to Read, p. 38
- Complete Practice Book 3.2 pp. 143–144
- Visit Cross-Curricular Centers

DAY 2

On-Level
Teacher-Led
Pages 386–393
- **Read** *Elena's Serenade*

Strategic Intervention
Teacher-Led
Page DI·44
- Practice Lesson Vocabulary
- Read Multisyllabic Words
- **Read** or Listen to *Elena's Serenade*

Advanced
Teacher-Led
Page DI·45
- Extend Vocabulary
- **Read** *Elena's Serenade*

ⓘ Independent Activities
While you meet with small groups, have the rest of the class...

- Visit the Reading/Library Center
- Listen to the AudioText for *Elena's Serenade*
- Finish Words to Write, p. 383
- Complete Practice Book 3.2 pp. 145–146, 149
- Write in their Strategy Response Logs, pp. 384, 393
- Visit Cross-Curricular Centers
- Work on inquiry projects

DAY 3

On-Level
Teacher-Led
Pages 394–400
- **Read** *Elena's Serenade*

Strategic Intervention
Teacher-Led
Page DI·46
- Practice Generalize and Predict
- **Read** or Listen to *Elena's Serenade*

Advanced
Teacher-Led
Page DI·47
- Extend Generalize and Predict
- **Read** *Elena's Serenade*

ⓘ Independent Activities
While you meet with small groups, have the rest of the class...

- Visit the Reading/Library Center
- Listen to the AudioText for *Elena's Serenade*
- Write in their Strategy Response Logs, p. 398
- Finish Look Back and Write, p. 401
- Complete Practice Book 3.2 p. 147
- Visit Cross-Curricular Centers
- Work on inquiry projects

① Begin with whole class skill and strategy instruction.

② Meet with small groups to provide differentiated instruction.

③ Gather the whole class back together for fluency and language arts.

DAY 4

On-Level
Teacher-Led
Pages 404–407
- **Read** "Leading People to Freedom"

Strategic Intervention
Teacher-Led
Page DI·48
- Practice Retelling
- **Read** or Listen to "Leading People to Freedom"

Advanced
Teacher-Led
Page DI·49
- **Read** "Leading People to Freedom"
- Genre Study

ⓘ Independent Activities

While you meet with small groups, have the rest of the class...

- Visit the Reading/Library Center
- Listen to the AudioText for "Leading People to Freedom"
- Visit the Writing and Vocabulary Centers

- Finish Writing Across Texts, p. 407
- Visit Cross-Curricular Centers
- Work on inquiry projects

DAY 5

On-Level
Teacher-Led
Page DI·51
- **Reread** Leveled Reader *Traditional Crafts of Mexico*
- Retell *Traditional Crafts of Mexico*

Strategic Intervention
Teacher-Led
Page DI·50
- **Reread** Leveled Reader *Glass Blowing*
- Retell *Glass Blowing*

Advanced
Teacher-Led
Page DI·51
- **Reread** Leveled Reader *Jackie Robinson*
- Share Extension Activity

ⓘ Independent Activities

While you meet with small groups, have the rest of the class...

- Visit the Reading/Library Center
- Complete Practice Book 3.2 pp. 148, 150

- Visit Cross-Curricular Centers
- Work on inquiry projects

Grouping Place English language learners in the groups that correspond to their reading abilities in English.

Use the appropriate Leveled Reader or other text at students' instructional level.

TIP Send home the appropriate Multilingual Summary of the main selection on Day 1.

Take It to the NET ONLINE
PearsonSuccessNet.com

Sharon Vaughn
For research on intervention, see the article "Group Size and Time Allotted to Intervention" by Scott Foresman author S. Vaughn and S. Linan-Thompson.

TEACHER TALK

In **Readers' theater,** students read text aloud dramatically to an audience, with minimal or no props.

Be sure to schedule time for students to work on the unit inquiry project "Symbols of Freedom." This week students prepare lists of resources for other classes who may wish to explore symbols of American freedom.

Looking Ahead

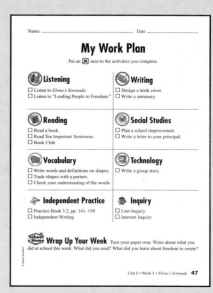

▲ **Group-Time Survival Guide**
p. 47, Weekly Contract

☑ Customize Your Plan *by Strand*

<table>
<tr><td>ORAL LANGUAGE</td><td>VOCABULARY</td></tr>
</table>

ORAL LANGUAGE

SOCIAL STUDIES

Concept Development

When are you free to follow your dreams?

CONCEPT VOCABULARY
discouraged   instruments   mellow

BUILD

☐ **Question of the Week** Introduce and discuss the question of the week. This week students will read a variety of texts and work on projects related to the concept *freedom to create*. Post the question for students to refer to throughout the week. DAY 1 *380d*

☐ **Read Aloud** Read aloud "Manuelo the Playing Mantis." Then begin a web to build concepts and concept vocabulary related to this week's lesson and the unit theme, Freedom. Introduce the concept words *discouraged, instruments,* and *mellow* and have students place them on the web. Display the web for use throughout the week. DAY 1 *380l–380m*

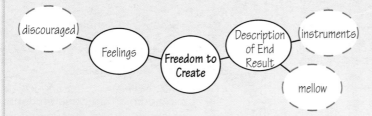

DEVELOP

☐ **Question of the Day** Use the prompts from the Weekly Plan to engage students in conversations related to this week's reading and the unit theme. **EVERY DAY** *380d–380e*

☐ **Concept Vocabulary Web** Revisit the Freedom to Create Concept Web and encourage students to add concept words from their reading and life experiences. DAY 2 *393*, DAY 3 *400*

CONNECT

☐ **Looking Back/Moving Forward** Revisit the Freedom to Create Concept Web and discuss how it relates to this week's lesson and the unit theme. Then make connections to next week's lesson. DAY 5 *407c*

CHECK

☐ **Concept Vocabulary Web** Use the Freedom to Create Concept Web to check students' understanding of the concept vocabulary words *discouraged, instruments,* and *mellow*. DAY 1 *380l*, DAY 5 *407c*

VOCABULARY

🔊 **STRATEGY CONTEXT CLUES** Context clues are the words and sentences around an unknown word. Sometimes an author uses a synonym as a context clue to explain an unfamiliar word. A synonym is a familiar word that has the same or almost the same meaning as another word. When you come across a word you don't know, look for a synonym as a context clue. The synonym can help you figure out the meaning of the unfamiliar word.

LESSON VOCABULARY
burro   puff
bursts   reply
factory   tune
glassblower

TEACH

☐ **Words to Know** Give students the opportunity to tell what they already know about this week's lesson vocabulary words. Then discuss word meaning. DAY 1 *382b*

Vocabulary Strategy Lesson

☐ **Vocabulary Strategy Lesson** Use the vocabulary strategy lesson in the Student Edition to introduce and model this week's strategy, *context clues*. DAY 2 *382–383*

PRACTICE/APPLY

☐ **Leveled Text** Read the lesson vocabulary in the context of leveled text. DAY 1 *LR37–LR45*

Leveled Readers

☐ **Words in Context** Read the lesson vocabulary and apply *context clues* in the context of *Elena's Serenade*. DAY 2 *384–393*, DAY 3 *394–401*

Main Selection—Fiction

☐ **Vocabulary Center** Use a dictionary to complete an art project involving new words. **ANY DAY** *380k*

☐ **Homework** Practice Book 3.2 pp. 144–145. DAY 1 *382b*, DAY 2 *383*

☐ **Word Play** Have partners use reference sources to make lists of words of things that are made of glass and their definitions. Students can illustrate their favorite glass-related words. **ANY DAY** *407c*

ASSESS

☐ **Selection Test** Use the Selection Test to determine students' understanding of the lesson vocabulary words. DAY 3

RETEACH/REVIEW

☐ **Reteach Lesson** If necessary, use this lesson to reteach and review *context clues*. DAY 5 *407c*

① Use assessment data to determine your instructional focus.

② Preview this week's instruction by strand.

③ Choose instructional activities that meet the needs of your classroom.

COMPREHENSION

⊙ SKILL GENERALIZE   When you generalize, you tell how several things are alike. For example, a generalization might tell how all the characters in a story are alike. Often, clue words such as *most, many, all,* or *few* signal that a statement is a generalization.

⊙ STRATEGY PREDICT   To predict means to make a guess based on information in a piece of writing. Make generalizations as you read, then use the generalization to help you predict what might happen next in the story.

TEACH

☐ **Skill/Strategy Lesson** Use the skill/strategy lesson in the Student Edition to introduce and model *generalizing* and *predicting.*   **DAY 1** 380-381

☐ **Extend Skills** Teach details and facts. **ANY DAY** 407b

Skill/Strategy Lesson

PRACTICE/APPLY

☐ **Leveled Text** Apply *generalizing* and *predicting* to read leveled text. **DAY 1** LR37-LR45

☐ **Skills and Strategies in Context** Read *Elena's Serenade,* using the Guiding Comprehension questions to apply *generalizing* and *predicting.*   **DAY 2** 384-393, **DAY 3** 394-401

Leveled Readers

☐ **Skills and Strategies in Context** Read "Leading People to Freedom," guiding students as they apply *generalizing* and *predicting.* Then have students discuss and write across texts.   **DAY 4** 404-407

Main Selection—Fiction

☐ **Homework** Practice Book 3.2 pp. 143, 147, 148.   **DAY 1** 381,   **DAY 3** 400,   **DAY 5** 407b

☐ **Fresh Reads for Differentiated Test Practice** Have students practice *generalizing* with a new passage. **DAY 3**

Paired Selection—Nonfiction

ASSESS

☐ **Selection Test** Determine students' understanding of the selection and their use of *generalizing.*   **DAY 3**

☐ **Retell** Have students retell *Elena's Serenade.*   **DAY 3** 401-403

RETEACH/REVIEW

☐ **Reteach Lesson** If necessary, reteach and review *generalizing.* **DAY 5** 407b

FLUENCY

SKILL CHARACTERIZATION   Characterization is the way an author describes and portrays a character. You show characterization by reading as if you are the character, making changes in your voice to bring the character to life.

TEACH

☐ **Read Aloud** Model fluent reading by rereading " Manuelo the Playing Mantis." Focus on this week's fluency skill, characterization. **DAY 1** 380l-380m, 407a

PRACTICE/APPLY

☐ **Readers' Theater** Read aloud selected paragraphs from *Elena's Serenade,* reading with characterization. Have students practice doing readers' theater readings of p. 387 in groups of three: a narrator, Pedro, and Elena. **DAY 2** 407a

☐ **Paired Reading** Have partners take turns being Elena and the burro as they read p. 389. **DAY 3** 407a

☐ **Readers' Theater** Groups of three practice reading aloud p. 399 with characterization, readers' theater style. As students reread, monitor their progress toward their individual fluency goals. **DAY 4** 407a

☐ **Listening Center** Have students follow along with the AudioText for this week's selections. **ANY DAY** 380j

☐ **Reading/Library Center** Have students reread a selection of their choice. **ANY DAY** 380j

☐ **Fluency Coach** Have students use Fluency Coach to listen to fluent readings or practice reading on their own. **ANY DAY**

ASSESS

☐ **Check Fluency** wcpm Do a one-minute timed reading, paying special attention to this week's skill—characterization. Provide feedback for each student. **DAY 5** 407a

GRAMMAR

SKILL QUOTATIONS   A quotation is a sentence that tells the exact words that a speaker has said. Quotation marks are used at the beginning and end of a quotation. A comma separates the quotation from the rest of the sentence.

TEACH

❑ **Grammar Transparency 30** Use Grammar Transparency 30 to teach quotations. DAY 1 *407e*

Grammar Transparency 30

PRACTICE/APPLY

❑ **Develop the Concept** Review the concept of quotations and provide guided practice. DAY 2 *407e*

❑ **Apply to Writing** Have students review something they have written and apply what they have learned about using quotations. DAY 3 *407f*

❑ **Test Preparation** Examine common errors in using quotations to prepare for standardized tests. DAY 4 *407f*

❑ **Homework** Grammar and Writing Practice Book pp. 117–119.
DAY 2 *407e*,   DAY 3 *407f*,   DAY 4 *407f*

ASSESS

❑ **Cumulative Review** Use Grammar and Writing Practice Book p. 120. DAY 5 *407f*

RETEACH/REVIEW

❑ **Daily Fix-It** Have students find and correct errors in grammar, spelling, and punctuation. **EVERY DAY** *407e-407f*

❑ **The Grammar and Writing Book** Use pp. 224–227 of The Grammar and Writing Book to extend instruction for using quotations. **ANY DAY**

The Grammar and Writing Book

WRITING

Trait of the Week

ORGANIZATION/PARAGRAPHS   Organization is the structure, or arrangement, of your information and ideas. A careful writer gives the main idea in a topic sentence. He or she organizes the details in a clear, logical order, then ends with a strong conclusion.

TEACH

❑ **Writing Transparency 30A** Use the model to introduce and discuss the Trait of the Week. DAY 1 *407g*

❑ **Writing Transparency 30B** Use the transparency to show students how strong conclusions can improve their writing. DAY 2 *407g*

Writing Transparency 30A   **Writing Transparency 30B**

PRACTICE/APPLY

❑ **Write Now** Examine the model on Student Edition pp. 402–403. Then have students write their own paragraphs. DAY 3 *402–403, 407h*, DAY 4 *407h*

> **Prompt** *Elena's Serenade* describes a girl who makes special music. Think about a character or person you know well. Now write a paragraph about that person, using logical organization.

Write Now pp. 402–403

❑ **Writing Center** Design a book cover for *Elena's Serenade* including the title, author, illustrator, a picture, and a short summary of the story. **ANY DAY** *380k*

ASSESS

❑ **Writing Trait Rubric** Use the rubric to evaluate students' writing. DAY 4 *407h*

RETEACH/REVIEW

❑ **The Grammar and Writing Book** Use pp. 224–229 of The Grammar and Writing Book to extend instruction for quotations, strong conclusions, and paragraphs. **ANY DAY**

The Grammar and Writing Book

SPELLING

GENERALIZATION RELATED WORDS   Related words often have parts that are spelled the same but pronounced differently: *cloth, clothes.*

TEACH

☐ **Pretest** Give the pretest for related words. Guide students in self-correcting their pretests and correcting any misspellings. **DAY 1** *407k*

☐ **Think and Practice** Connect spelling to the phonics generalization for related words. **DAY 2** *407k*

PRACTICE/APPLY

☐ **Connect to Writing** Have students use spelling words to write a story. Then review frequently misspelled words: *want, whole.* **DAY 3** *407l*

☐ **Homework** Phonics and Spelling Practice Book pp. 117–120. **EVERY DAY**

RETEACH/REVIEW

☐ **Review** Review spelling words to prepare for the posttest. Then provide students with a spelling strategy—related words. **DAY 4** *407l*

ASSESS

☐ **Posttest** Use dictation sentences to give the posttest for related words. **DAY 5** *407l*

Spelling Words

1. cloth	6. ability	11. please
2. clothes	7. mean	12. pleasant
3. nature	8. meant	13. sign
4. natural	9. deal	14. signal
5. able	10. dealt	15. signature

Challenge Words

16. equal	18. equator	20. majority
17. equation	19. major	

*Word from the selection

PHONICS

SKILL RELATED WORDS   Some words are related and are spelled the same but pronounced differently.

TEACH

☐ **Phonics Lesson** Model how to read related words. Then have students practice by decoding longer words and reading words in context. **DAY 2** *407i*

PRACTICE/APPLY

☐ **Homework** Practice Book 3.2, p. 149. **DAY 2** *407i*

RETEACH/REVIEW

☐ **Review Word Parts** Review how to read words with prefixes and suffixes. Then have students practice by decoding longer words and reading words in context. **DAY 4** *407j*

RESEARCH AND INQUIRY

☐ **Internet Inquiry** Have students conduct an Internet inquiry on following your dreams. **EVERY DAY** *407m*

☐ **Chart/Table** Review terms and ideas related to charts and tables, such as the synonymous terms (chart, table), the chart's title, horizontal rows and vertical columns, and row and column labels. Have students create a table to organize data after a discussion about dream jobs. **DAY 5** *407n*

☐ **Unit Inquiry** Allow time for students to prepare lists of resources for other classes who may wish to explore symbols of American freedom. **ANY DAY**

SPEAKING AND LISTENING

☐ **Song, Rap, or Poem** Have students recite a poem from memory or perform a song or rap for the class. **DAY 5** *407d*

☐ **Listen to Song or Poem** Have students listen to their classmates recite a poem, song, or rap, then answer questions orally. **DAY 5** *407d*

Resources for
Differentiated Instruction

LEVELED READERS

▶ **Comprehension**
- 🎯 **Skill** Generalize
- 🎯 **Strategy** Predict

▶ **Lesson Vocabulary**
- 🎯 **Context Clues**

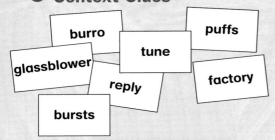

burro puffs tune glassblower reply factory bursts

▶ **Social Studies Standards**
- • Manufacturing
- • Cultures: Crafts
- • Changes

Leveled Reader Database ONLINE

PearsonSuccessNet.com

Use the Online Database of over 600 books to
- Download and print additional copies of this week's leveled readers.
- Listen to the readers being read online.
- Search for more titles focused on this week's skills, topic, and content.

Social Studies

Traditional Crafts of MEXICO

by Mary Miller

On-Level Reader

Generalize
- To **generalize** is to make a broad statement or rule that applies to many examples.
- When you make a generalization, you look for similarities or differences among facts and examples in the text.

Directions Complete the graphic organizer below. Find facts and examples from the text that support the generalization.

Generalization Many Mexican crafts, first made by ancient Indian groups, are still made the same way.

Supporting Examples

1. The Maya made pottery.
2. The Aztecs made pottery, cloth, baskets, and metal work.
3. Today, there are Mexican folk artists.
4. Today, pottery is made without a wheel.
5. Today, people carve wood by hand.
6. People still embroider.

Directions Write a generalization about Mexican crafts. Then write three facts that support the generalization. **Possible responses given.**

Generalization:
7. Most modern Mexican crafts are colorful.

Supporting examples:
8. Some pottery is green, blue, yellow, and mauve.
9. Weavers use natural dyes to make colorful baskets.
10. Some masks are decorated with colorful feathers.

🎯 **On-Level Practice** TE p. LR41

Vocabulary
Directions Choose a word from the box that best completes each sentence.

Check the Words You Know
- burros
- factory
- puff
- tune
- burst
- glassblower
- reply

1. I can play a beautiful ___tune___ on my flute.
2. *Arboles de la vida,* "trees of life," are known for their ___burst(s)___ of leaves and clay figures.
3. When decorating masks, people use a ___puff___ of yarn to represent hair.
4. Many poor people moved closer to a ___factory___ in hopes of getting a job.
5. Some Mexicans travel using ___burros___.
6. If you asked me if I would like to go to Mexico, I would ___reply___ "Yes!"
7. The ___glassblower___ sells his colorful vases at the market.

Directions Using as many vocabulary words as possible, write two generalizations about traditional Mexican crafts.

Responses will vary.

🎯 **On-Level Practice** TE p. LR42

Social Studies

Glass Blowing

by J. Matteson Claus

Below-Level Reader

Generalize
- To **generalize** is to make a broad statement or rule that applies to many examples.
- When you make a generalization, you look for similarities or differences among facts and examples in the text.

Directions Complete the graphic organizer below. Find facts from the text that support the generalization.

Generalization Blowing glass is usually difficult to do by hand.

Possible responses given.

Supporting Examples

1. Need very hot furnace—2500°F.
2. Need safety goggles and gloves
3. Cannot blow too gently
4. Cannot blow too hard
5. Glass breaks easily
6. Must be cooled slowly

Directions Write a generalization about glass factories. Then write three facts that support the generalization. **Possible responses given.**

7. Generalization:
Factories can easily make many identical glass objects.

8–10. Supporting examples:
Factories use machines; machines are controlled by computers; factories use molds.

🎯 **Below-Level Practice** TE p. LR38

Vocabulary
Directions First unscramble each word. Then use the word in a sentence.

Check the Words You Know
- burros
- factory
- puff
- tune
- bursts
- glassblower
- reply

Possible responses given.

1. etnu ___tune___
The musician played a beautiful tune on her guitar.

2. tbsru ___bursts___
When you blow too hard through the rod, the glass bubble bursts.

3. fufp ___puff___
You need to puff through a rod to make a bubble.

4. yrfaotc ___factory___
Glass bottles are made in a factory.

5. orbusr ___burros___
Burros were used to pull wagons.

6. ypelr ___reply___
I will reply to your question when I finish this work.

7. bssalgrewol ___glassblower___
A glassblower wears safety goggles and gloves.

🎯 **Below-Level Practice** TE p. LR39

Advanced

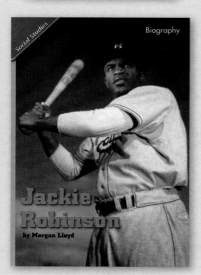

Advanced Reader

Generalize

- To **generalize** is to make a broad statement or rule that applies to many examples. When you make a generalization, you look for similarities or differences among facts and examples in the text.

Directions Read the following passage. Then answer the questions below.

> After he retired from baseball, Jackie and his wife Rachel participated in voter registration drives to register African American voters. They raised money to support Martin Luther King, Jr.'s organization, the Southern Christian Leadership Conference (SCLC). Jackie spoke out against segregation and tried to get other athletes involved in the Civil Rights Movement. He once said, "A life is not important except for the impact it has on other lives." Jackie's life was dedicated to service.

What generalization did the author make about Jackie's life?

1. Jackie's life was dedicated to service.

What four facts and examples from the passage support the generalization?

2. participated in voter registration drives
3. raised money to support the SCLC
4. spoke out against segregation
5. tried to get other athletes involved in the Civil Rights Movement

Directions Write your own generalization about Jackie Robinson. Then write four examples that support the generalization. Possible responses given.

Generalization:

6. Jackie Robinson was a role model.

Supporting examples:

7. Jackie was a talented athlete.
8. Jackie did not react to insults.
9. Jackie was involved in the Civil Rights Movement.
10. He worked to help others.

Advanced Practice TE p. LR43

Vocabulary

Directions Synonyms are words that have similar meanings. Draw a line to match the synonyms.

Check the Words You Know

___ adversity	___ descending	___ discrimination
___ guise	___ legacy	___ scholarships
___ segregated	___ sharecropper	___ strike

1. discrimination — a. protest—an act that shows disapproval
2. guise — b. heritage—lasting customs of a group of people
3. strike — c. awards—prizes given for achievement
4. scholarships — d. bias—unfair dislike
5. legacy — e. charade—a false act

Directions Antonyms are words that have the opposite meaning. Draw a line to match the antonyms.

6. adversity — f. planter—a plantation owner
7. descending — g. integrated—to become joined or combined
8. discrimination — h. ascending—moving upward
9. segregated — i. privilege—a special advantage or right
10. sharecropper — j. easiness—without challenge

Advanced Practice TE p. LR44

ELL

ELL Reader

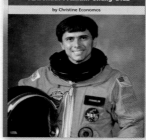

ELL Poster 30

Teacher's Edition Notes

ELL notes throughout this lesson support instruction and reference additional resources at point of use.

Teaching Guide pp. 204–210, 270–271
- Multilingual summaries of the main selection
- Comprehension lesson
- Vocabulary strategies and word cards
- ELL Reader 3.6.5 lesson

ELL and Transition Handbook

Ten Important Sentences
- Key ideas from every selection in the Student Edition
- Activities to build sentence power

More Reading

Readers' Theater Anthology
- Fluency practice
- Five scripts to build fluency
- Poetry for oral interpretation

Leveled Trade Books

- Extended reading tied to the unit concept
- Lessons in the Trade Book Library Teaching Guide

School + Home

Homework
- Family Times Newsletter
- ELL Multilingual Selection Summaries

Take-Home Books
- Leveled Readers

Cross-Curricular Centers

Listening

Listen to the Selection

MATERIALS `SINGLES`

CD player, headphones, AudioText CD, Student Edition

Listen to *Elena's Serenade* and "Leading People to Freedom" as you follow or read along in your book. When you are finished, make generalizations about Elena and the animals she meets.

If there is anything you don't understand, you can listen again to any section.

Reading/Library

Read It Again!

MATERIALS `SINGLES` `PAIRS` `GROUPS`

Collection of books for self-selected reading, reading log

Select a book you have already read. Record the title of the book in your reading log. You may want to read with a partner.

You may choose to read any of the following:

- **Leveled Readers**
- **ELL Readers**
- **Stories written by classmates**
- **Books from the library**
- *Elena's Serenade*

TEN IMPORTANT SENTENCES Read the Ten Important Sentences for *Elena's Serenade*. Then locate the sentences in the Student Edition.

BOOK CLUB Write a review of the story. Include what you liked and what you did not like. Give examples to support your opinions.

Classroom Library

Vocabulary

Words in Glass Shapes

MATERIALS `SINGLES` `PAIRS`

Paper, pencil, scissors, dictionary

Write words and definitions on different shapes.

1. Elena blew glass in different shapes. Draw and cut out two stars, two birds, and two butterflies.
2. Pick six words from the list below. Write each word on a different shape.
3. Use the dictionary to learn the meaning of each word you chose. On the back of each shape, write a definition of the word.
4. Trade shapes with a partner. Read the word on the front and give a definition. Then turn the shape over and check your answer.

EARLY FINISHERS Create a short fantasy using words you chose.

borrow	overtake
burro	serenade
coyote	soldier
declares	tourist
furnace	trousers

"burro"

burro

a small donkey

Scott Foresman Reading Street Centers Survival Kit

Use the *Elena's Serenade* materials from the Reading Street Centers Survival Kit to organize this week's centers.

Writing

Social Studies

Technology

Write a Book COVER

MATERIALS SINGLES
Paper, pencil

Design a book cover for *Elena's Serenade*.

1. Fold a piece of paper in half.
2. Write the title on the front cover. Also write the author's and illustrator's names. Include a picture that goes with the story.
3. On the back cover, write a summary of the story.

EARLY FINISHERS On the inside front cover, write facts about the author. Also make up quotations and reviews from fictional people who have read the book.

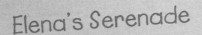

Author: Campbell Geeslin
Illustrator: Ana Juan

Working for Change

MATERIALS SINGLES PAIRS GROUPS
Paper, pencil

Plan an improvement to your school.

1. Elena changed her father's mind about her glassblowing abilities. Changes were made at her house. What could be done to improve something at your school?
2. Decide what change you would like to see in your school.
3. Write a letter to the principal. Explain the change you would like to see. Tell why it is important. Give at least three convincing reasons why the change should be made.

EARLY FINISHERS What would your school be like if the principal agreed to make the change you suggest? Draw a picture to show what would happen after the improvement. Write a short paragraph to support your picture.

> Dear Mrs. Rodriguez,
> We are concerned about the amount of trash students throw away at school. People throw away things like paper, which we can recycle. We think we should all do things to help the world. If we have recycling containers, it will be easy for people to throw away less.
> Sincerely,
> Amanda Martin

Group Story

MATERIALS GROUPS
Computer

Write a group story on the computer.

1. One person writes a sentence about another adventure Elena could have.
2. Each group member adds another sentence to the story.

EARLY FINISHERS Print out and illustrate the story.

Elena wondered what happened to her animal friends. She set out one day for a walk. She thought she could find the coyote.

OBJECTIVES

- Build vocabulary by finding words related to the lesson concept.
- Listen for ideas that can help you generalize.

Concept Vocabulary

discouraged feeling less hopeful about something

instruments devices for producing musical sounds

mellow soft and rich; not harsh

Monitor Progress

Check Vocabulary

If... students are unable to place words on the web,	then... review the lesson concept. Place the words on the web and provide additional words for practice, such as *down-hearted* and *musician*.

SUCCESS PREDICTOR

DAY 1 — Grouping Options

Reading

Whole Group
Introduce and discuss the Question of the Week. Then use pp. 380l–382b.

Group Time

Differentiated Instruction
Read this week's Leveled Readers. See pp. 380f–380g for the small group lesson plan.

Whole Group
Use p. 407a.

Language Arts
Use pp. 407e–407h and 407k–407m.

Build Concepts

FLUENCY

MODEL CHARACTERIZATION As you read "Manuelo the Playing Mantis," use different voices for each character. Point out to students that the size of the animal character influences the voice you choose. In addition, their words and actions, which indicate their personality, can influence the tone of voice you choose to use. You may use an authoritative yet choppy, high-pitched voice for the cricket.

LISTENING COMPREHENSION

After reading "Manuelo the Playing Mantis," use the following questions to assess listening comprehension.

1. **What generalization can you make about Debby?** *(Possible response: She is thoughtful and caring.)* **Generalize**

2. **What generalization can you make about Manuelo?** *(Possible response: He does not give up easily.)* **Generalize**

BUILD CONCEPT VOCABULARY

Start a web to build concepts and vocabulary related to this week's lesson and the unit theme.

- Draw a Freedom to Create Concept Web.
- Read the sentence with the word *discouraged* again. Ask students to pronounce *discouraged* and discuss its meaning.
- Place *discouraged* in an oval attached to Feelings. Explain that *discouraged* is related to this concept. Read the sentences in which *instruments* and *mellow* appear. Have students pronounce the words, place them on the web, and provide reasons.
- Brainstorm additional words and categories for the web. Keep the web on display and add words throughout the week.

Concept Vocabulary Web

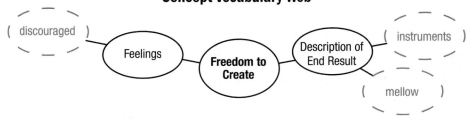

Manuelo the Playing Mantis

by Don Freeman

One warm summer evening in Cloverdale Meadow, a lonely praying mantis named Manuelo stood still as a stick listening to beautiful music coming over the hill. Manuelo had attended these outdoor concerts many times before, and he knew the shapes and sounds of all the different instruments. His favorite sounds were those of the flute, the trumpet, the harp, and the cello.

Manuelo wished that he, too, could be a musician.

When the concert was over, he climbed down from his perch in the thicket and went home to the pond. Hopefully, Manuelo started rubbing his legs against his wings, the way crickets and grasshoppers and katydids do whenever they sing. But as hard as he rubbed, he heard only silence—and the clicking of a cricket coming nearer and nearer.

"Clickety click!" it chirped. "A mantis can't make music the way I can!" And then, just as quickly as it had appeared, it disappeared behind the tall grass.

"There must be something I can do!" Manuelo sighed to himself.

Close by, he spied a trumpet vine clinging to a wall. "Just the thing!" he cried. "I'll play a horn!"

After snipping off a trumpet flower he held it up the way any fine trumpet player does, and began to blow. He blew and blew and blew until he grew blue in the face. Once again, not a single sound could he make!

Poor Manuelo sat there feeling very sad. He loved music so much, and yet he could not make any.

Manuelo was discouraged and almost ready to give up trying when he heard something whirring high above his head. "Take heart, my good fellow," said a thin, wispy voice. "I know how you feel. I can't make music either."

Turning his head completely around, Manuelo looked up and saw a spindly spider suspended by a thread from a branch above. "My name is Debby Webster, and I've been watching you all evening," she said as she slid down lower and lower until she hung directly in front of Manuelo's face. "If you will do as I tell you, maybe together we can make a cello. First you must fetch me an empty walnut shell and a stick with a curlicue on the end."

Without asking any questions, Manuelo went about searching everywhere. In hardly any time at all, he found half a walnut shell and a stick with a curlicue on one end. Tucking them both under his arms, he rushed back to his spindly spider friend.

"Now, my good mantis," said Debby, "if you will fix the stick tightly to the shell I will spin some strong strings for you."

continued on TR1

Set Purpose

Have students listen for ideas that can help them make generalizations about Manuelo and Debby.

Creative Response

Have small groups of students write a script for a continuation of the story. They may include a scene in which Manuelo meets the cricket or Debby again. Invite groups to dramatize their script. *Drama*

Build Background Before students listen to the Read Aloud, ask them what they know about insects and musical instruments.

Access Content Before reading, share this summary: Manuelo the praying mantis wants to make music. He tries different ways and cannot make a sound. With help from a spider, Manuelo makes an instrument and plays it well.

School + Home **Homework** Send home this week's Family Times newsletter.

SKILLS ⟷ STRATEGIES IN CONTEXT

Generalize
Predict

OBJECTIVES

- Make generalizations.
- Use generalizations to make predictions.

Skills Trace
Generalize

Introduce/Teach	TE: 3.3 354–355, 3.4 60–61, 3.6 380–381
Practice	PB: 3.1 133, 137, 138; 3.2 23, 27, 28, 36, 46, 56, 143, 147, 148
Reteach/Review	TE: 3.3 379b, DI·55; 3.4 85b, 101, 127, DI·54; 3.5 161; 3.6 407b, DI·56
Test	Selection Tests: Unit 6 Benchmark Test: Unit 4

INTRODUCE

Write the following details on the board: *Northern Mexico receives little rainfall. The days are hot, and nights are cool. Southern Mexico has different regions. The "hot land" has hot summers and mild winters. The "cold land" has cold temperatures.* Ask students to come up with a true statement about Mexico's climate in general. *(Possible response: Mexico's climate is different in different regions.)*

Have students read the information on p. 380. Explain the following:

- When you generalize, you form a conclusion. You make a broad statement or rule that applies to many examples.
- As you read, make generalizations. You can use them to help you make predictions about what will come next.

Use Skill Transparency 30 to teach generalize and predict.

Comprehension

Skill
Generalize

Strategy
Predict

 ## Generalize

- When you read, you may be given ideas about things or people. Sometimes, you can make a general statement about all of them together.
- This statement might tell how the things or people are all alike in some way.

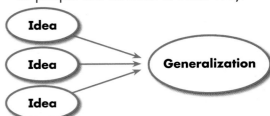

 ## Strategy: Predict

Good readers think about what will come next as they read. Ask yourself: What has the author said about the topic so far? What else might I find out about? Try to take the ideas you've already read and make a generalization about or predict what will come next.

Write to Read

1. Read "Glassblowing." Look for ideas that tell how several things or people are all alike in some way.

2. Make a graphic organizer like the one above. Fill in your graphic organizer as you read the article.

380

Strategic Intervention

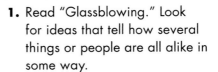

Generalize Explain that when making a generalization, students should list ideas that are related in some way or that have a common topic. The generalization should be a statement about what the ideas generally have in common. Discuss the similarities and differences between making a generalization, drawing a conclusion, and summarizing.

ELL

Access Content

Beginning/Intermediate For a Picture It! lesson on generalizing, see the ELL Teaching Guide, pp. 204–205.

Advanced Have students examine the title of the selection on p. 381. Have them use their knowledge of compound words to predict the meaning of the term *glassblowing.* Correct any misunderstandings students may have.

Glassblowing

Syrian glassworkers invented the art of glassblowing more than 2,000 years ago. This method of shaping glass has changed very little since that time. The glassblower uses a hollow metal pipe that is about five feet long. On one end of the pipe is a mouthpiece. On the other end is a gob of hot melted glass. The worker blows air into the pipe, which causes the glass to expand into a hollow bubble. The worker then shapes the glass bubble into a container of some kind.

Sometimes the glassblower shapes the glass using a mold, as the ancient Syrians often did. But the basic process is the same. After blowing the glass into a bubble, the worker guides the bubble into a mold. Then, the worker blows through the pipe again until the glass bubble takes on the shape of the mold.

Today, glassblowing is often done by machines instead of people. But the basic process has stayed the same. All glassblowing requires melted glass and blowing air.

1 Strategy Here is a good place to predict. What do you think you will find out about next?

2 Skill The word *all* is a clue to a generalization. What generalization can you make about glassblowing?

381

Available as **Skill Transparency** 30

TEACH

1 STRATEGY Use the first paragraph to model how to make a prediction.

Think Aloud **MODEL** I have just read a generalization. I read that generally the method of shaping glass has remained the same for more than 2,000 years. I can use the generalization to make a prediction about what I will read next.

2 SKILL Discuss how to use ideas to generalize.

Think Aloud **MODEL** I know that words such as *all*, *none*, *usually*, and *some* can signal a generalization. I see the word *all* in the sentence. To make a generalization, I try to make a statement about related ideas. The statement should give a rule or broad statement about how the ideas are alike.

PRACTICE AND ASSESS

STRATEGY I think I will read about how glassblowers blow glass.

SKILL Generalization: Though the process may be different, in general, glassblowing requires melted glass and blowing air.

WRITE Have students complete steps 1 and 2 of the Write to Read activity. You might consider using this as a whole class activity.

Monitor Progress

Generalize

If... students are unable to complete **Write to Read** on p. 380,	then... use Practice Book 3.2 p. 143 to provide additional practice.

Tech Files
ONLINE

For a Web site that explores the Spanish words used in the selection, have students use a student-friendly search engine to do an Internet search using the keywords *common Spanish words*.

Build Background Use ELL Poster 30 to build background and vocabulary for the lesson concept of being free to follow your dreams.

▲ **ELL Poster** 30

Build Background

ACTIVATE PRIOR KNOWLEDGE

BEGIN A PROBLEM AND SOLUTION CHART about overcoming problems in order to follow your dreams.

- Have students think of a time when they wanted to do something but were unable to. Invite them to record their problem, including what they wanted to achieve and why they could not accomplish it.

- Next ask students to consider how they solved the problem and achieved their goal. If they did not overcome the problem, have them think about steps they took or steps they should have taken to overcome the problem. Encourage students to add the information to the graphic organizer.

- Tell students that, as they read, they should consider the problem Elena encounters in following her dream. Ask them to note how Elena solves her problem.

> **Problem**—I wanted to be a soccer player.
>
> ⬇
>
> **Solution**—I went to soccer practice and joined a soccer team.

▲ **Graphic Organizer** 20

BACKGROUND BUILDING AUDIO This week's audio presents Mexican folk songs from the selection. After students listen, discuss what they thought about the songs.

Background Building Audio

Introduce Vocabulary

WORD RATING CHART

Create word rating charts using the categories *Know, Have Seen,* and *Don't Know.*

Word Rating Chart

Word	Know	Have Seen	Don't Know
burro	✔		
bursts		✔	
factory	✔		
glassblower			✔
puff			
reply			
tune			

▲ **Graphic Organizer** 4

Read each word to students and have them place a check mark in one of the three columns: *Know* (know and can use), *Have Seen* (have seen or heard the word; don't know meaning), *Don't Know* (don't know the word).

Activate Prior Knowledge

Have students share where they may have seen some of these words. Point out that some of this week's words have synonyms *(tune/melody; bursts/explodes).*

Context Clues • Synonyms

Check charts with students at the end of the week and have them make changes to their ratings.

Discuss the meanings of some of the vocabulary words with students. Ask the following questions to clarify word meanings.

- Why don't you *reply* when I ask you a question?
- What is the name of that *tune* I've heard you humming all day?
- Did you see the piñata *burst* and spill all the goodies?

Use the Multisyllabic Word Routine on p. DI·1 to help students read multisyllabic words.

Lesson Vocabulary

WORDS TO KNOW

T **burro** a donkey, used to carry loads

T **bursts** breaks open or opens suddenly

T **factory** a building or group of buildings where people and machines make things

T **glassblower** a person who shapes glass objects by blowing air from the mouth through a tube into a blob of hot, liquid glass at the other end of the tube

T **puff** to swell up

T **reply** to answer someone by words or actions

T **tune** a piece of music; melody

MORE WORDS TO KNOW

serenade music played to someone outside at night

shriek to make a loud, sharp, shrill sound

T= Tested Word

Vocabulary

Directions Match each word on the left with its meaning. Draw a line from the word to its definition.

1. tune — swells
2. burro — answer
3. bursts — melody
4. reply — explodes
5. puffs — donkey

Check the Words You Know
___glassblower ___puffs
___factory ___burro
___tune ___reply
___bursts

Directions Choose the word from the box that best completes each sentence. Write the word on the line.

glassblower   6. The _____ made cups out of melted glass.

burro   7. A _____ will get you safely down the steep and rocky hillside.

factory   8. My mother works in a _____ that makes computers.

reply   9. You should always _____ politely when someone asks you a question.

bursts   10. A balloon _____ if you blow too much air into it.

Write a Story
On a separate sheet of paper, write a story about an animal that can sing. Use as many vocabulary words as possible.
Students' answers should incorporate vocabulary words from this lesson in a story about an animal that can sing.

Home Activity Your child has identified and used vocabulary words from *Elena's Serenade*. Read a story or poem about an animal with your child. Encourage him or her to use this week's vocabulary words as you talk about what you read.

▲ **Practice Book 3.2** p. 144

Vocabulary Strategy

OBJECTIVE

 Use context clues to determine word meanings with synonyms.

INTRODUCE

Discuss the context clues strategy for synomyms using the steps on p. 382.

TEACH

- Have students read "At the Glassblower's," paying attention to how vocabulary is used.
- Model using context clues to determine the meaning of *puffs.*

Think Aloud **MODEL** The word *puffs* on p. 383 refers to something the glassblower does again. I look back to see that she blew into a pipe. *Puffs* must mean the same thing as "blows."

Words to Know

| glassblower |
| bursts |
| puffs |
| factory |
| burro |
| tune |
| reply |

Remember

Try the strategy. Then, if you need more help, use your glossary or a dictionary.

Vocabulary Strategy
for Synonyms

Context Clues Sometimes when you are reading, you will see a word you don't know. The words nearby may help you figure out its meaning. Perhaps you will see a synonym for the word. A synonym is a word that has the same or almost the same meaning as another word. Look for a word you know that might be a synonym. See if it will help you understand the meaning of the word you don't know.

1. Look at the words around the word you don't know. Can you use them to figure out the meaning?

2. Perhaps the author used a synonym. Look for a word you know that might be a synonym, and use it to figure out the meaning of the unfamiliar word.

3. Try the synonym in place of the word in the sentence. Does it make sense?

As you read "At the Glassblower's," look for synonyms to help you understand the meanings of the vocabulary words.

382

DAY 2 Grouping Options

Reading
Whole Group Discuss the Question of the Day. Then use pp. 382–384.

Group Time Differentiated Instruction
Read *Elena's Serenade.* See pp. 380f–380g for the small group lesson plan.

Whole Group Use pp. 407a and 407i.

Language Arts
Use pp. 407e–407h and 407k–407m.

Strategic Intervention

 Context Clues Have students work in pairs to follow the steps on p. 382. Encourage them to list clues and synonyms for an unknown word and then decide together the best meaning for it.

ELL

Access Content Use ELL Poster 30 to preteach vocabulary. Choose from the following to meet language proficiency levels.

Beginning Point out clues on p. 383 that show that a *tune* is the same thing as a song or a melody played in music.

Intermediate After reading, students can create a Venn diagram to show words that belong with music, with making things, and with both.

Advanced Teach the lesson on pp. 382–383. Have students report on those words that have cognates in their home languages.

Resources for home-language words may include parents, bilingual staff members, bilingual dictionaries, or online translation sources.

At the GLASSBLOWER'S

You and some friends are watching a glassblower make beautiful glass pieces. The glassblower explains what she does. First she mixes sand, soda ash, and limestone together and heats them until they become liquid. Then she takes a hollow iron pipe about 5 feet long and dips one end into the liquid glass. She blows gently into the other end of the pipe, and a hollow glass bulge suddenly bursts out. She puffs again if she wants to make the bulge bigger. She twirls, stretches, and cuts the glass while it is soft. Then she removes the glass from the pipe and sets it aside to cool.

In a glass factory, the blowing might be done using molds and machines, but in this shop it is all done by hand. Here, you see glass vases, glass ornaments, and glass animals. A tiny glass burro, or donkey, even has a tiny saddle. Sets of glass chimes dangling from the ceiling play a tune when the wind blows. Their song sounds like tinkling bells. Everything shines and sparkles in the sunlight.

Your friends ask what you like best, and you reply, "I like when a new shape appears at the end of the pipe. What an amazing craft!"

Your friends smile and answer, "We think so too."

Words to Write

Write about a special glass object that you own or have seen. Describe it. Use words from the Words to Know list.

383

PRACTICE AND ASSESS

- Have students determine the meanings of the remaining words and explain the context clues and synonyms they used.
- Point out that synonyms and context clues do not work with every word. Students may have to use the glossary or a dictionary to find the exact meaning of some words.
- If you began word rating charts (p. 382b), have students reassess their ratings.
- Have students complete Practice Book 3.2, p. 145.

WRITE Writing should include vocabulary words that identify and describe a glass object that is special to the student.

Monitor Progress

↻ Context Clues

If... students need more practice with the lesson vocabulary,	**then...** use Tested Vocabulary Cards.

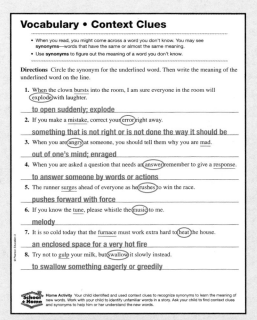

Vocabulary • Context Clues

- When you read, you might come across a word you don't know. You may see **synonyms**—words that have the same or almost the same meaning.
- Use **synonyms** to figure out the meaning of a word you don't know.

Directions Circle the synonym for the underlined word. Then write the meaning of the underlined word on the line.

1. When the clown bursts into the room, I am sure everyone in the room will explode with laughter.
   to open suddenly; explode
2. If you make a mistake, correct your error right away.
   something that is not right or is not done the way it should be
3. When you are angry at someone, you should tell them why you are mad.
   out of one's mind; enraged
4. When you are asked a question that needs an answer, remember to give a response.
   to answer someone by words or actions
5. The runner surges ahead of everyone as he rushes to win the race.
   pushes forward with force
6. If you know the tune, please whistle the music to me.
   melody
7. It is so cold today that the furnace must work extra hard to heat the house.
   an enclosed space for a very hot fire
8. Try not to gulp your milk, but swallow it slowly instead.
   to swallow something eagerly or greedily

Home Activity Your child identified and used context clues to recognize synonyms to learn the meaning of new words. Work with your child to identify unfamiliar words in a story. Ask your child to find context clues and synonyms to help him or her understand the new words.

▲ **Practice Book 3.2** p. 145

Prereading Strategies

GENRE STUDY

Fantasy

Elena's Serenade is a fantasy. A fantasy could not really happen. Some of the characters, the setting, or the events could not be real.

PREVIEW AND PREDICT

Have students preview the selection title and cover illustration. Discuss the meaning of the word *serenade*. Take a picture walk through the book. Ask students to predict what the story will be about. Encourage them to use lesson vocabulary as they talk about what they expect to read.

Strategy Response Log

Graphic Organizer Have students make a three-column chart (Graphic Organizer 26). In the first column, they should list characters from the story. As they read, they should fill in the second column with facts about the characters. Students will update their graphic organizers by making generalizations in the Strategy Response Log activity on p. 393.

Genre

Fantasy is a made-up story that could never happen. What makes this story a fantasy?

384

ELL

Activate Prior Knowledge Invite students to tell about a time when an adult did not believe in their ability to do something. Explain that Elena has a similar experience in the story.

Consider having students read the selection summary in English or in students' home languages. See the Multilingual Summaries in the ELL Teaching Guide, pp. 208–210.

Serenade

by Campbell Geeslin   illustrated by Ana Juan

What happens when
Elena plays her serenade?

385

SET PURPOSE

Read the first page of the selection aloud to students. Have them consider their preview discussion and tell what they hope to find out as they read.

Remind students to look for facts about things and people in the story. These facts can help them make generalizations as they read.

STRATEGY RECALL

Students have now used these before-reading strategies:

- preview the selection to be aware of its genre, features, and possible content;
- activate prior knowledge about that content and what to expect of that genre;
- make predictions;
- set a purpose for reading.

Remind students to be aware of and flexibly use the during-reading strategies they have learned:

- link prior knowledge to new information;
- summarize text they have read so far;
- ask clarifying questions;
- answer questions they or others pose;
- check their predictions and either refine them or make new predictions;
- recognize the text structure the author is using, and use that knowledge to make predictions and increase comprehension;
- visualize what the author is describing;
- monitor their comprehension and use fix-up strategies.

After reading, students will use these strategies:

- summarize or retell the text;
- answer questions they or others pose;
- reflect to make new information become part of their prior knowledge.

Audio CD   AudioText

Guiding Comprehension

 1 Setting • Inferential

In what country does Elena live?

Mexico

2  **Generalize • Critical**

What kinds of people get to be glassblowers? How do you know?

Possible response: Adult men are glass-blowers. Elena's father believes children are too young to blow glass and girls should not be glassblowers, only boys.

Monitor Progress
⟳ **Generalize**

If... students are unable to form a valid generalization,	**then...** use the skill and strategy instruction on p. 387.

Tech Files
ONLINE

Students can find out more about glassblowing by searching the Internet. Have them use a student-friendly search engine and the keyword *glassblowing*.

EXTEND SKILLS

Simile

Tell students that authors sometimes use similes to compare two unlike things that are alike in some way. A simile uses the words *like* or *as*. Have students review the last sentence on p. 386 and identify the simile and its meaning. (*I am mad as a wet hen*; Elena is very angry.)

1 In Mexico the sun is called *el sol*, and the moon is called *la luna*. I am called Elena.

My papa is a glassblower. He puffs out his cheeks, blows into a long pipe, and a bottle appears at the other end, just like magic.

One afternoon I find an old pipe of Papa's. I ask him if he will teach me to be a glassblower too, but he shakes his head. "You are too little, Elenita, and the hot **2** glass might burn you. Besides, who ever heard of a girl glassblower?"

Even though I am mad as a wet hen, I don't let Papa see my tears.

386

ELL

Extend Language Draw a T-chart (Graphic Organizer 25) on the board. Label the first column *Spanish* and the second column *English*. Write the Spanish words *el sol* from the text in the first column. Then write the English translation *the sun* in the second column. Repeat with the other two Spanish words on pp. 386–387. Encourage Spanish speakers to identify other Spanish words, using the images on the pages as a prompt. Complete the chart in a similar method.

When I get home, my brother Pedro asks, "Why the sad face, Elena?"

"I want to blow glass, but Papa says I'm too little and anyway, who ever heard of a girl glassblower?"

"Monterrey is where the great glassblowers are," Pedro says. "You should go there."

Should I? I'm scared to leave Papa, but maybe I *should.*

The next morning I borrow a pair of Pedro's trousers, hide my hair under his old *sombrero,* and set out. Since girls aren't supposed to be glassblowers, I'll pretend that I am a boy.

387

 SKILLS ⬌ STRATEGIES IN CONTEXT

Generalize

TEACH

- Tell students that authors may give ideas about things or people. Good readers can make a statement about all of the things or people together. The statement may be about how they are mostly alike or are alike in some way.

- Explain to students that they should be able to support their statements with examples from the texts and from their own experiences.

- Model how to generalize.

Think Aloud **MODEL** The question asks me to make a generalization, or a conclusion, about glassblowers. I know that Elena is a young girl. She went to Papa and asked him to teach her to blow glass. He told her she was too little and that girls are not glassblowers. I can conclude from his reply to Elena that he thinks children are not old enough to be glassblowers and that girls should not be glassblowers. Most glassblowers must be men.

PRACTICE AND ASSESS

Have students examine the text on pp. 386–387. Ask them to make a generalization about when the author uses words in italics. *(The author puts Spanish words and words that should be emphasized in italics.)*

Time for SOCIAL STUDIES

Location Skills

Using a map to find Monterrey, you would first look at North America. Next, you would look for the country, Mexico. Mexico is divided into states, like the states of the United States. Monterrey is located in the state of Nuevo León. You will find Monterrey in the northeastern corner of Mexico. It is approximately 150 miles away from the Texas border. Study a map of North and South America. What are some other places you could use to help explain where Monterrey is located?

Guiding Comprehension

3 Simile • Literal

Reread the first sentence on p. 388. What two things does the author compare?

el sol (the sun) and Papa's furnace

4 Imagery • Literal

What words does the author use to help the reader "hear" the music from the pipe?

pree-tat-tat, clip-clop

5  Vocabulary • Context Clues

Reread the third paragraph on p. 388. What context clues on pp. 388–389 help you learn the meaning of the word *burro*? What does the word mean?

Clues: *clip-clop*, the way a burro trots along, the burro offers to take Elena somewhere on his back; Meaning: a small donkey

Monitor Progress
Context Clues

If... students have difficulty using context to determine the meaning of *burro*,	**then...** use the vocabulary strategy instruction on p. 389.

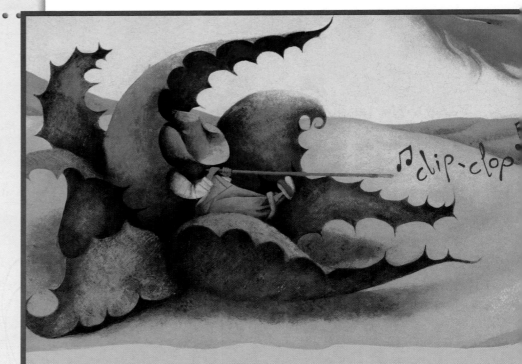

El sol blazes like Papa's furnace, and the road is long. I get hotter and hotter until, at last, I must rest. To pass the time, I puff out my cheeks and blow on my pipe. What is that? A pretty sound comes out!

Ever so gently I blow again. The notes get higher, *pree-tat-tat, pree-tat-tat*. I can hardly believe my ears— my pipe is making music!

I blow, easy and then harder, *pree-tat-tat*, until I find all the notes for a happy song called "Burro Serenade." I make the music go *clip-clop, clip-clop*, just the way a burro trots along.

Over and over I play the tune, my heart flying higher with every note. At last there are no mistakes.

388

ELL

Extend Language Guide students as they continue to add to the Spanish/English chart. In addition, help students understand the definition of difficult or unfamiliar vocabulary, such as *furnace* and the meaning of *higher,* as it is used on p. 388.

clip-clop ♪ clip-clop ♪

From behind a cactus Burro trots up and says, "Oh, *señor,* I was lost and lonely until I heard my song. Now I am smiling, see? May I take you someplace?"

"*Sí,*" I say. "I am on my way to Monterrey to learn to be a glassblower."

"If you can make music, I'm sure you can make glass," Burro says. I climb on his back, and off we go.

It is almost evening when we overtake Roadrunner, limping along. "Oh, *Señor* Roadrunner," I say, "you are supposed to fly like the wind. *Qué pasa?*"

389

Women in the Workforce

Time for SOCIAL STUDIES

"Traditional jobs for women" is a concept that has been losing meaning since WWII. During the war (1939–1945), women were called upon to fill jobs left vacant by men serving in the Armed Forces. Women worked factory, technical, and professional jobs by operating machinery, serving as managers, and performing research and development in industries such as manufacturing, medicine, and engineering. Today it is common to find female doctors, engineers, pilots, lawyers, and managers.

VOCABULARY STRATEGY
Context Clues

TEACH

- Remind students that when they read an unfamiliar word, they can use context clues and illustrations to determine the word's meaning. Point out that the clues may be in the same sentence as the word. The clues may also be in another sentence or paragraph.

- Model using context clues to determine the meaning of the word *burro*.

Think Aloud **MODEL** I read the word *burro* twice in the third paragraph on p. 388. I am not sure what it means. The first time it is used, it is in the name of a song. The next time it is used, the words *clip-clop* describe the way a burro moves. On p. 389 a burro comes to Elena and offers to take her on his back. I also see a small donkey in the illustration. The word *burro* must mean "small donkey."

PRACTICE AND ASSESS

Have students use context clues to determine the meaning of *tune* in the last paragraph on p. 388. (Clues include *play the tune, every note, heard my song, you can make music*; Meaning: song)

EXTEND SKILLS

Homograph

Point out the word *wind* on p. 389. Tell students that this word is a homograph. Homographs are words that are spelled the same but are pronounced differently and have different meanings. *Wind* pronounced (wind), as used in the story, is air that is in motion. *Wind* can also be pronounced (wīnd) which means to move or go in a crooked way.

Guiding Comprehension

6 Point of View • Inferential

Who does the author use to tell the story?

Elena.

7 Repetition • Critical

What idea does the author repeat?

Elena meets an animal in need. Her music helps the animal.

8 **REVIEW** Main Idea • Inferential

So far, what is the story all about?

Elena helps animals that she meets on her way to learn to be a glassblower.

Monitor Progress

REVIEW **Main Idea**

If... students have difficulty identifying the main idea,	then... use the skill and strategy instruction on p. 391.

6 Roadrunner sighs. "I might as well be a turtle. Every time I try to run, one of my legs forgets how. Even a rock can go faster."

"Let's try this," I say. "I will blow my pipe slowly, and you step along with the music." I wonder if the steady beat of *"La Marcha Grande de Mejico"* will help. I sound out the notes until I have it just right.

Roadrunner's limp changes to a march. "Oh, that music makes me proud to be a Mexican!" he exclaims.

TUM, tum, TUM, tum. I play faster like a drum. *TUMtumTUMtumTUMtum.*

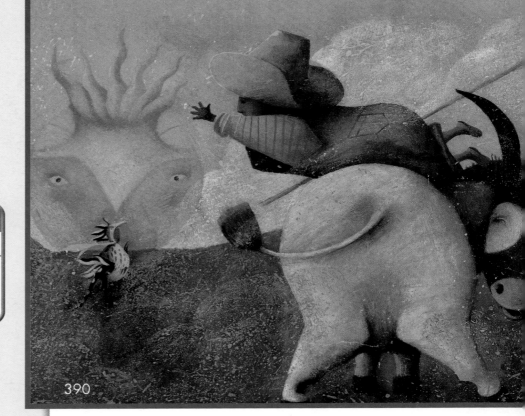

390

Access Content/Understanding Idioms Help students understand unfamiliar words and phrases. For example, read the sentence "Coyote throws back his head." Model the action and have students copy you.

Suddenly, Roadrunner surges ahead. "Where are you going?" he calls back to me.

"I am on my way to Monterrey to learn to be a glassblower!" I shout.

"You play such a fine march, certainly you'll make a fine glassblower." His voice fades away as he disappears in a cloud of dust.

That evening, after *la luna grande* has risen, Burro lies down and I use him as a pillow. We have traveled all day, and we are tired. As I drift off to sleep, I think of home.

Sometime during the night I am awakened by awful howling. *La luna grande* is high in the sky and the desert is golden. Coyote runs toward us, chased by an owl, two bats, and a lizard who are hurling rocks at him.

"*Qué pasa, Señor* Coyote?" I ask.

His tongue hangs out and he puffs and puffs. "When *la luna* is bright, I sing—I can't help myself. But everyone hates my song."

"Let me hear you," I say.

Coyote throws back his head. *"Ouchowahooooo!"* he howls.

"Ay yah!" I cry.

The owl hoots, the bats shriek, and the lizard covers his ears.

391

SKILLS ←→ STRATEGIES IN CONTEXT

Main Idea REVIEW

TEACH

- Remind students that all stories, passages, and articles have a main idea. For fiction, the main idea is what the story is all about.

- Model answering the question "What is the story all about?"

Think Aloud

MODEL There is not a sentence in the story that tells what the story is mostly about. I must put it in my own words. I ask myself, "What is the big idea?" Elena is on her way to learn to be a glassblower. She meets animals that need her help. The music she blows through her pipe helps the animals. That is what the story is mostly about.

PRACTICE AND ASSESS

- Have students return to pp. 386–387 and identify the main idea. Have them answer the question "What are these two pages all about?" *(Elena decides to go to Monterrey to learn to be a glassblower after her father refuses to teach her.)*

- To assess students, use Practice Book 3.2, p. 146.

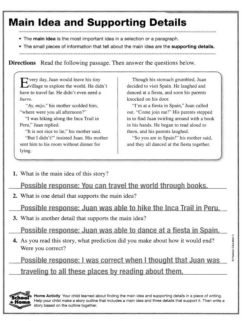

▲ **Practice Book 3.2** p. 146

Guiding Comprehension

9 **Personification • Inferential**
What human traits does the author give Burro, Roadrunner, and Coyote?
They have feelings and can talk.

10 **Draw Conclusions • Critical**
Text to World **Think about the animals Elena has met. Look at the illustrations. Describe the environment, or the natural world, in which Elena lives. Where does it remind you of?**
Responses will vary but should include a description of a desert.

11 **Predict • Critical**
What do you think will happen when Elena meets the people in the factory? What clues in the story helped you make your prediction?
Responses will vary but should be logical and well supported by text, text clues, and/or common knowledge.

9 "Listen to this," I say, "and sing along." I take my pipe and blow, very softly, a low note. It is the beginning of a song my papa used to sing to me, *"Cielito Lindo."*

"Hmmm, that sounds sweet as honey," Coyote says. "Let me try." He clears his throat and begins, "For when our hearts sing together, *ci-e-li-to lin-do,* love comes along . . ." His voice is soft and low.

"Bravo!" I shout.

"Bravo!" cry the owl, the bats, and the lizard.

The happy Coyote asks me where I am going. "I am on my way to Monterrey to become a glassblower."

"If you could teach me to sing, you can do anything!" he declares.

Then, as Coyote sings his sweet love song to *la luna,* Burro and I slip back into sleep.

10

392

ELL

Access Content/Understanding Idioms Help students understand unfamiliar phrases, such as "slip back into sleep" and "the furnace's giant mouth is full of bubbling glass."

Next morning, Burro and I start off with the sunrise, and at last we get to Monterrey. There are many houses and buildings, and everyone is in a hurry. Before me is a factory where the furnace's giant mouth is full of bubbling glass.

"*Adiós, mi amigo,*" I say to Burro and then step inside.

FÁBRICA DE VÍDRIO

393

STRATEGY SELF-CHECK

Predict

Remind students to make generalizations about people and things as they read. Explain that the generalizations can help students make valid predictions.

Students can use the earlier generalization about Papa to predict what Elena will encounter at the glassblowing factory. Have them check their predictions and refine them if necessary as they read pp. 394–395.

SELF-CHECK

Students can ask themselves these questions to assess their ability to use the skill and strategy.

- Did I use generalizations to help make a prediction?
- Did I use facts and events that happened earlier in the story to make the prediction?
- Did I think about text clues and what I already know to help me make a correct prediction?
- How can predicting help me be a more active reader?

Monitor Progress	
Generalize	
If... students have difficulty using generalizations to make predictions,	then... revisit the skill lesson on pp. 380–381. Reteach as necessary.

Strategy Response Log

Update Graphic Organizer Have students revisit the graphic organizer and add facts or make revisions as necessary. Ask them to complete the third column by writing a generalization about each character.

If you want to teach this story in two sessions, stop here.

Develop Vocabulary

PRACTICE LESSON VOCABULARY

Students orally respond yes or no to each question and provide a reason for each answer.

1. **Is *donkey* a synonym for *burro*?** (*Yes, a* burro *is a small donkey.*)
2. **Do people live in a *factory*?** (*No, people work in a* factory.)
3. **Do you *puff* your cheeks when you blow up a balloon?** (*Yes, you* puff *your cheeks because you fill them with air when you blow up a balloon.*)

BUILD CONCEPT VOCABULARY

Review previous concept words with students. Ask if students have come across any words today in their reading or elsewhere that they would like to add to the Concept Web.

Guiding Comprehension

If you are teaching the story in two days, discuss generalizations so far and review the vocabulary.

12 Character • Critical

Why does Elena speak in a low voice when she speaks to the men?

Possible response: She wants them to believe she is a boy because she believes that people think girls cannot be glass-blowers.

13 🔄 Generalize • Inferential

What clues in the story help you draw the conclusion that the men in the factory do not take Elena seriously when they first see her?

Clues: The men laugh. The boss winks at the other men as he tells Elena to blow glass. The men laugh at her when she begins to blow music.

Monitor Progress
🔄 **Generalize**
If... students are unable to make a generalization, **then...** use the skill and strategy instruction on p. 395.

DAY 3 Grouping Options

Reading
Whole Group Discuss the Question of the Day.

Group Time Differentiated Instruction
 *Elena's Serenade.* See pp. 380f–380g for the small group lesson plan.

Whole Group Discuss the Reader Response questions on p. 401. Then use p. 407a.

Language Arts
Use pp. 137e–137h and 137k–137m.

In front of me, four big men stand stiff as soldiers, puffing on long pipes. As their balloon cheeks shrink, glass bubbles appear and turn into tall bottles, medium bottles, and tiny bottles.

"What do you want?" their boss yells at me.

I cough and in a low voice I say, *"Por favor, Señor . . .*
12 I want to be a glassblower."

The men laugh. The boss winks and says, "Okay, *muchacho.* Let's see what you can do."

I twirl the end of my pipe in the hot glass just the way Papa does.

What is going to happen?

I close my eyes and gulp a deep breath. I puff out my cheeks and begin to play a song called *"Estrellita,"* about a little star.

When the men hear music, they laugh even harder.
13 I think they will never stop, but then . . .

I remember how my pipe helped Burro, how it helped Roadrunner and Coyote.
I blow, strong and steady, and when I open my eyes, I have made a star!

394

ELL

Fluency Lead a choral reading of p. 394, demonstrating how to read text that contains an ellipses. For example, "Por favor, Señor . . . I want to be a glassblower."

The men's mouths drop open in surprise.

I tap the star off into the sand to cool, and then I play *"Estrellita"* again. At the end of my pipe another glass star bursts out.

The men try to blow music too, but only burping noises and crooked bottles come from their pipes.

"Welcome, little glassblower!" the boss says, and shakes my hand. He puts my stars in the factory windows where they twinkle like real stars.

As soon as the children in Monterrey see them, they all want one. The stars sell faster than I can blow them.

395

Glassblowing

Time for SOCIAL STUDIES

Glassblowers heat a mass of glass to soften it. They then attach it to a tube. When the glassblowers blow air through the tube, the air expands the glass and forms a bubble. They then swing the glass, roll it on a smooth surface, or use tools to mold it while the glass is still soft. The technique is more than 1,000 years old.

SKILLS ↔ STRATEGIES IN CONTEXT

Generalize Predict

TEACH

- Remind students that they should make a broad statement about the things and people they read about. This is called a generalization. It is like drawing a conclusion.
- Clues in the story can help readers make a generalization.
- Have students evaluate their predictions about the factory workers' response to Elena.
- Model identifying the clues used to make the generalization.

Think Aloud **MODEL** When Elena speaks to the men, they laugh. The boss winks at the other men as he tells her to blow the glass. They all laugh when she begins to play music. I can conclude that the men do not take her seriously. This supports my prediction about how the factory workers would act toward Elena. They do not believe she is old enough to be a glassblower.

PRACTICE AND ASSESS

Have students work in pairs to make a generalization about the men after Elena blows a glass star. Also have them make a generalization about Elena. To assess, make sure their generalizations are logical and well supported by text.

Guiding Comprehension

14 **Realism and Fantasy • Inferential**

What details from the text on pp. 396–397 help you know that this story is a fantasy?

Elena blows a song about a swallow through the pipe, and the glass turns into a swallow. It grows and grows until it is larger than a burro. Then the huge glass bird flies Elena to her home.

15 **REVIEW Main Idea • Critical**

What is this part of the story all about?

Elena thinks of the past. She wants to see Papa, so she goes home.

Monitor Progress

REVIEW Main Idea

If... students are unable to identify the main idea,	then... use the skill and strategy instruction on p. 397.

One night, when I am working alone, I get tired of playing *"Estrellita."* I twirl a huge glass glob onto the end of my pipe and begin a song called *"La Golondrina."* It is about a swallow gliding over the sea.

A glass bird appears. As I play, its wings grow long. I play on, and it becomes the size of Roadrunner. I take a quick breath to play more, and the glass bird grows as big as Coyote. I blow and blow, and my swallow becomes bigger than Burro.

I tap the bird off and the glass cools. The swallow's great wings stretch from one wall to the other.

ELL

Context Clues Assist students as they use context clues to identify the meaning of *swallow* as it is used on p. 396.

Oh, I wish Papa could see what I can do!

After sliding open the factory's big back door, I push my bird out into the alley. I climb on and play *"La Golondrina"* again. Slowly the swallow rises into the air.

I'm flying! Down below, the lights shine from hundreds of windows with glass stars in them.

As I play my pipe the bird flies higher. I turn south, and when I see my town below, I play softer and softer and finally stop. The bird glides down onto a field of lilies. I run home, climb in the window, and curl up in my own little bed. **14** **15**

397

Main Idea REVIEW

TEACH

- Remind students that the main idea is what the story is mostly about.
- Model putting the main idea into your own words.

 Think Aloud **MODEL** The question asks me to tell what *this part* of the story is all about. I begin by rereading pp. 396–397. I restate the main events and what this part of the story is all about. It is about Elena going home.

PRACTICE AND ASSESS

Have students reread pp. 394–395 and identify what this part of the story is all about. *(Elena convinces the men she is a glassblower.)*

Guiding Comprehension

16 **Plot • Critical**

Text to World What was Elena's plan? When have you had a plan to convince someone you could do something?

Responses will vary but should include relevant information.

17 **Vocabulary • Synonyms**

Reread the last two paragraphs on p. 399. What is a synonym for the word *reply*?

answer

Monitor Progress
Synonyms
If... students are unable to identify a synonym, **then...** use the vocabulary skill and strategy instruction on p. 399.

18 **Author's Purpose • Inferential**

Question the Author Why do you think the author wrote the story?

Possible response: To entertain the reader and to teach a lesson about following your dreams and not judging someone by their age or gender.

Strategy Response Log

Summarize When students finish reading the selection, provide this prompt: Imagine that you want to tell a friend what *Elena's Serenade* is about. In four or five sentences, explain its important points.

The next morning, when Papa goes off to work, I get up. I have a plan all figured out. I put on Pedro's pants and *sombrero* again, and then I tear a *tortilla* in half and paste it onto my chin with flour and water.

I take my pipe and run straight to Papa's factory.

"*Buenos días, señor,*" I say, in an old man's shaky voice. "I am a glassblower, come all the way from Monterrey."

"Why, grandfather," Papa says politely, "you aren't as tall as your pipe. How can you blow glass?"

398

ELL

Extend Language Have students add to their Spanish/English charts. Encourage them to name words that are new to them, including vocabulary words from the story.

I twirl hot glass onto the end and begin to play a song called *"La Mariposa,"* about how pretty butterflies are. A glass butterfly floats from my pipe and flutters about, its wings chiming.

"Qué bonita!" Papa exclaims. "If only my daughter were here to see this."

"But she is!" I shout, and rip off my *tortilla* beard and toss the *sombrero* in the air.

"Is that you, Elena?" Papa asks, squinting.

"At your service, Papa," I reply and laugh. Then I tell him about all the funny and amazing things that happened on my trip to Monterrey.

18

399

VOCABULARY SKILL

Synonyms

TEACH

- Remind students that a synonym is a word that means the same, or about the same, as another word.

- Remind them to use context clues to learn the meaning of an unfamiliar word. Then they can identify a synonym for the word.

- Model identifying a synonym.

 Think Aloud **MODEL** Papa asks Elena a question. She answers him, and the sentence uses the word *reply*. *Reply* must mean "to answer." *Answer* and *respond* are synonyms for *reply*.

PRACTICE AND ASSESS

Have students identify the synonym for the word *exclaims* in the second paragraph on p. 399. *(cries out with strong feelings)*

Predict

Have students make a new generalization about Papa's view of his daughter and about Elena's view of herself. Ask them to evaluate their earlier predictions and to make predictions about Elena's future. Use Practice Book 3.2, p. 147.

SELF-CHECK

Students can ask themselves these questions to assess understanding of the story.

- Did I use generalizations to make predictions about the story's future events?
- Was my prediction correct? If not, did I make changes to my prediction?
- Do I understand how my generalizations can help me predict Elena's future?

Monitor Progress

⟳ Generalize

If... students are having difficulty using generalizations to make predictions,	then... use the Reteach lesson on p. 407b.

Generalize • Predict

- When you read, you find facts or ideas about things or people. Sometimes, you can make a **general statement** about them.
- A **general statement** tells how things or people are all alike in some way.

Directions Read the following passage. Then answer the questions below.

> Five kids were studying under the big oak tree near the town's square. They watched as other kids their age played on the swings. They didn't have time to play. They were all doing their best to keep their grades the highest in their class. Maria looked around when she heard a deep voice. She thought the voice said, "Go play."
>
> Then Carlo and Manuel began to explain something, but stopped in mid-sentence. The boys looked at each other with mouths open. "Go have some fun," a deep voice said. "You're a kid only once." Now everybody looked around. The tree shook as if it were hit by a great wind. "Go and play!" it thundered. All five kids were out of there in a flash.

1. What is a general statement you can make about what you read?

   <u>Possible response: You should work hard but also make time</u>
   <u>for fun.</u>

List three ideas that helped you make a general statement about this story.

2. <u>None of the five kids were playing.</u>

3. <u>The five kids didn't have time to play.</u>

4. <u>The five kids cared a lot about their grades.</u>

5. Who did you predict was speaking to the kids? Was your prediction correct?

   <u>Possible response: I predicted the tree was talking. I was right.</u>

 Home Activity Your child learned about making generalizations. Look through the newspaper for an article that makes a generalization. Help your child point out the ideas or facts in the article that contribute to the generalization that was made.

▲ **Practice Book 3.2** p. 147

Now every day Papa and I work side by side at our great furnace. Papa blows bottles and pitchers and drinking glasses. I blow birds, stars, butterflies, and songs.

On Saturdays tourists come from all over to dance to the music and to try to catch a glass butterfly. If you close your eyes and sit absolutely still, you may hear their wings chiming like little glass bells. Listen. . . .

400

Develop Vocabulary

PRACTICE LESSON VOCABULARY

As a class, use a Word to Know to complete each sentence.

1. **If you put too much air in a balloon, it** (bursts).

2. **When someone asks you a question, you should** (reply).

3. **Another word for** *song* **is** (tune).

BUILD CONCEPT VOCABULARY

Review previous concept words with students. Ask if students have come across any words today in their reading or elsewhere that they would like to add to the Concept Web.

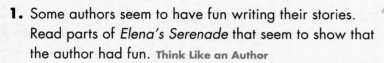

Reader Response

Open for Discussion Which parts of *Elena's Serenade* might be hard to believe? Suppose you asked Burro, Roadrunner, and Coyote about these parts. What would they say?

1. Some authors seem to have fun writing their stories. Read parts of *Elena's Serenade* that seem to show that the author had fun. **Think Like an Author**

2. What did you learn about Elena? How might she act in other situations? **Generalize**

3. What did you predict would happen when Elena met Roadrunner? Did you change your prediction as you read? If so, why? **Predict**

4. If prizes were given to unusual glassblowers, do you think Elena would get one? Make a list of reasons why she should—or should not. Use words from the Words to Know list. **Vocabulary**

Look Back and Write Elena pretends that she is an old man. Does Papa believe her? Look back at pages 398–399. Tell why you think as you do.

Meet author **Campbell Geeslin on page 421** and illustrator **Ana Juan on page 423.**

401

Reader Response

Open for Discussion **Personal Response**

MODEL It's hard to believe that the animals would talk to Elena. If I asked Burro, Roadrunner, and Coyote about these parts, they might let me know that animals have their own ways of talking.

Comprehension Check **Critical Response**

1. Responses will vary but should include entertaining text. ***Author's Purpose***

2. Elena believes in herself. She is brave and kind. Elena might show these qualities in other situations. ***Generalize***

3. Responses will vary but should include relevant predictions. ***Predict***

4. Responses will vary but should show an understanding of the words and Elena's glassblowing abilities. ***Vocabulary***

Look Back and Write For test practice, assign a 10–15 minute time limit. For assessment, see the Scoring Rubric at the left.

Retell

Have students retell *Elena's Serenade*.

Scoring Rubric **Look Back and Write**

Top-Score Response A top-score response will use details from pp. 398–399 of the selection to tell whether they think Elena's papa believes she is an old man and to explain why they think this way.

Example of a Top-Score Response Elena dresses up like an old glassblower. Her papa pretends to believe she is an old man. He calls her "grandfather." Elena proves she is a glassblower by making a butterfly. Papa pretends to be very surprised when Elena takes off her sombrero and beard.

For additional rubrics, see p. WA10.

Monitor Progress

Check Retelling Rubric 4 3 2 1

| If... students have difficulty retelling the selection, | then... use Retelling Cards and the Scoring Rubric on p. 402 to assist fluent retelling. |

SUCCESS PREDICTOR

Check Retelling Have students use illustrations and other text features to guide their retellings. Let students listen to other retellings before attempting their own.

SUCCESS PREDICTOR

Write Now

Look at the Prompt Explain that each sentence in the prompt has a purpose.

- Sentence 1 presents a topic.
- Sentence 2 suggests students think about the topic.
- Sentence 3 tells what to write—notes.

Strategies to Develop Focus

Have students

- mark important ideas in the text with self-stick notes.
- look at the first sentence of each paragraph to find important ideas.
- include only important ideas in notes.

NO: Visitors enjoy lovely view

YES: Statue on island in New York Harbor

For additional suggestions and rubric, see pp. 407g–407h.

Write Now

Paragraph

Prompt

Elena's Serenade describes a girl who makes special music.

Think about a character or person you know well.

Now write a paragraph about that person, using logical organization.

Writing Tr...

Organize your **paragraph** by ... ideas in an orde... makes sense.

Student Model

Writer uses quotation marks to indicate words from story.

Details support idea that Elena is determined.

Paragraph has **organization**: topic sentence, followed by details and a conclusion.

> Elena knows what she wants, and she work... reach her goals. She tells Papa she wants to be... glassblower. He tells her that girls cannot do t... job. Elena is "mad as a wet hen," but she does... give up. She dresses like a boy and walks across... desert to a factory. Some people might be sca... of desert animals, but Elena helps them all. W... the factory men laugh at her, Elena blows gla... and surprises them. Finally, Elena works with P... making her dream come true.

Use the model to help you write your own good paragrap...

402

Scoring Rubric Narrative Retelling

Rubric 4 3 2 1	4	3	2	1
Connections	Makes connections and generalizes beyond the text	Makes connections to other events, stories, or experiences	Makes a limited connection to another event, story, or experience	Makes no connection to another event, story, or experience
Author's Purpose	Elaborates on author's purpose	Tells author's purpose with some clarity	Makes some connection to author's purpose	Makes no connection to author's purpose
Characters	Describes the main character(s) and any character development	Identifies the main character(s) and gives some information about them	Inaccurately identifies some characters or gives little information about them	Inaccurately identifies the characters or gives no information about them
Setting	Describes the time and location	Identifies the time and location	Omits details of time or location	Is unable to identify time or location
Plot	Describes the problem, goal, events, and ending using rich detail	Tells the problem, goal, events, and ending with some errors that do not affect meaning	Tells parts of the problem, goal, events, and ending with gaps that affect meaning	Retelling has no sense of story

Retelling Plan

☑ **Week 1** Assess Strategic Intervention students.

☑ **Week 2** Assess Advanced students.

☑ **Week 3** Assess Strategic Intervention students.

☑ **Week 4** Assess On-Level students.

☑ **This week** assess any students you have not yet checked during this unit.

Use the Retelling Chart on p. TR16 to record retelling.

Selection Test To assess with *Elena's Serenade*, use Selection Tests, pp. 117–120.

Fresh Reads for Differentiated Test Practice For weekly leveled practice, use pp. 175–180.

Hints for Writing Good Paragraphs

- Write an opening sentence that "sets up" your topic or main idea and engages readers. Consider a topic sentence, a question, or an interesting fact.
- Use transition words and phrases such as *first, after, but, also, however, then, for example,* and *on the other hand* to connect ideas, sentences, and paragraphs.
- Make sure each sentence in the paragraph supports the topic or main idea.
- Write a conclusion that wraps things up but is more than a repeating of ideas or "The end."

403

Writer's Checklist

☑ **Focus** Do notes include only most important ideas?

☑ **Organization** Are notes in the same order as ideas in the text?

☑ **Support** Are important dates and names included in notes?

☑ **Conventions** Are capital letters used where needed? Do punctuation and abbreviations used make sense?

Social Studies in Reading

OBJECTIVES

- Examine features of expository nonfiction.
- Practice a test-taking strategy.
- Compare and contrast across texts.

PREVIEW/USE TEXT FEATURES

As students preview "Leading People to Freedom," have them look at the maps and art. After they preview, ask:

- **How does the map on p. 406 help you understand information?** (*It shows where things took place.*)

- **What does the illustration on p. 407 show? Why did the author likely include it?** (*It shows how slaves escaped. The author likely included it to show the danger and bravery of slaves on the Underground Railroad.*)

Link to Social Studies

Remind students to use keywords in their search for information. You may want to make a list of research topics to avoid duplication.

DAY 4 Grouping Options

Reading
Whole Group Discuss the Question of the Day.

Group Time Differentiated Instruction
Read "Leading People to Freedom." See pp. 380f–380g for the small group lesson plan.

Whole Group Use pp. 407a and 407j.

Language Arts
Use pp. 407e–407h and 407k–407m.

Social Studies in Reading

LEADING PEOPLE TO FREEDOM

BY JULIA NASSER PADGETT

Expository Nonfiction

Genre

- **Expository nonfiction explains specific details of a topic.**

- **Expository nonfiction gives facts in a clear, organized way.**

Text Features

- **Maps or other graphics are often used to show where events took place.**

Link to Social Studies

Use the library or the Internet to research other people who worked on or used the Underground Railroad to escape slavery. Share what you learn in a brief report.

404

Content-Area Vocabulary | Social Studies

escape	to free yourself and get away from captivity
outwit	outsmart
slavery	being owned by and having to work for someone else

Access Content Help students understand the concept of slavery. Also make sure they understand the time period discussed in the text.

It is one thing to follow your own dream of freedom. It is quite another to bravely risk that freedom to help others be free. Harriet Tubman did just that. Harriet Tubman was born into slavery in Maryland in 1820. Slavery is the owning of a person by another person. When she was a child, Harriet Tubman was sent away from her family to work in the fields. There she heard other slaves talk about wanting to be free. It was then that Harriet Tubman first heard of the Underground Railroad. It wasn't a real railroad with trains and stations, however. The Underground Railroad was a secret system that provided slaves with help and the opportunity to escape slavery and find freedom.

To keep things as secret as possible, the Underground Railroad even had its own code language. The "trains" were the people who were running to freedom. The "conductors" were the people who led slaves on their journey to parts of the northern United States and Canada. The "stations" were churches, homes, and stores of free African Americans and white people who believed that slavery was wrong.

Predict Can you make a prediction about Harriet Tubman?

405

Economic Opportunity

Time for SOCIAL STUDIES

Harriet Tubman began life as a slave. At the time, even free women had few opportunities, but that gradually changed. Until World War II, most women worked at home. Slowly they began to enter the workforce in greater numbers. During the Second World War, women went to work in factories while men served in the military. They received education and training that let them succeed in these jobs that had been only for men. Today women work in different jobs. While some women choose to work in the home, others can be found in jobs ranging from a bulldozer driver to a doctor, from a lawyer to a manager.

EXPOSITORY NONFICTION

Use the sidebar on p. 404 to guide discussion.

- Expository nonfiction gives facts about a topic in a clear, organized way.

- Ask students why the author included the map on p. 406. Why would a map be used in an expository nonfiction selection? *(The map presents information about where something happened in an easy-to-understand way.)*

- Discuss with students the information they can learn by studying the visuals and captions.

Audio CD AudioText

Predict

Students should make the prediction after reading p. 405. Ask students to identify details and make generalizations to help them make their predictions.

Strategies for Nonfiction

USE GRAPHIC SOURCES Explain that students will be asked to read expository non-fiction articles and answer questions about these articles on standardized tests. When an article has graphic sources, we can use them to locate information to answer test questions. Provide the following strategy.

Use the Strategy

1. Read the title of a map or graphic source. Make sure you understand what is shown in a map. Use the map key to help you understand its main idea. Also decide if the graphic source shows historical information or present-day information.

2. When you read a test question, see if a graphic source can help you identify the answer.

3. Use the graphic source and the text to answer the question correctly.

GUIDED PRACTICE Have students discuss how they would use the map on p. 406 to answer the following question.

What information is presented in the map?

INDEPENDENT PRACTICE After students answer the following test question, discuss the process they used to find information.

Describe one of the Underground Railroad routes.

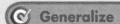
Ⓒ Generalize

Possible response: The slaves who escaped on the Underground Railroad were brave and determined to live in freedom.

When she was 29 years old, Harriet Tubman used the Underground Railroad to escape from slavery. She did this by walking through the cold woods at night and by getting help from people at the stations. She finally found freedom when she arrived in Philadelphia. When she discovered what it meant to be free, she wanted to lead other slaves to freedom. She soon began working on the Underground Railroad.

Harriet Tubman risked her life on 19 trips to help over 300 slaves find freedom, including her family. She showed courage by facing danger without fear. She used this courage and her intelligence to outwit the slave owners. Harriet Tubman spent her life helping African Americans build new lives in freedom.

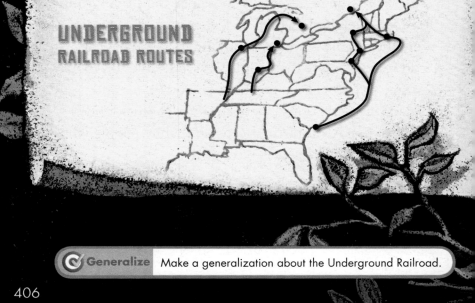

UNDERGROUND RAILROAD ROUTES

Ⓒ **Generalize** Make a generalization about the Underground Railroad.

406

🅔🅛🅛

Test Practice Review the map with students, helping them understand its content. Have them describe orally the content of the map before they answer the Guided and Independent Practice questions. You may also pair English Language Learners with proficient English speakers.

Reading Across Texts

Harriet Tubman and Elena each showed courage in seeking a certain freedom. What freedom did each want?

Writing Across Texts Write a brief paragraph explaining each freedom, and tell which means the most to you.

407

CONNECT TEXT TO TEXT

Reading Across Texts

Have students revisit selection 1 before answering the question. You may want to chart the information in a two-column chart with the headings "Elena" and "Harriet Tubman."

Writing Across Texts Remind students to include all information relevant to the topic. Students should identify the person, Elena or Harriet Tubman, and the freedom she sought. Students should follow up with an explanation of why freedom is important to them.

Fluency Assessment Plan

☑ **Week 1** Assess Advanced students.

☑ **Week 2** Assess Strategic Intervention students.

☑ **Week 3** Assess On-Level students.

☑ **Week 4** Assess Strategic Intervention students.

☑ **This week assess any students you have not yet checked during this unit.**

Set individual goals for students to enable them to reach the year-end goal.

• Current Goal: 110–120 wcPM

• Year-End Goal: 120 wcPM

To develop fluent readers, use Fluency Coach.

MORE READING FOR
Fluency

To practice fluency with text comprised of previously taught phonics elements and irregular words, use Decodable Reader 30.

DAY 5 Grouping Options

Reading
Whole Group
Revisit the Question of the Week.

Group Time
Differentiated Instruction
Reread this week's Leveled Readers. See pp. 380f–380g for the small group lesson plan.

Whole Group
Use pp. 407b–407c.

Language Arts
Use pp. 407d–407h and 407k–407n.

CHARACTERIZATION
Fluency

DAY 1

Model Reread "Manuelo, the Playing Mantis" on p. 380m. Model how to make changes in your voice to bring the characters to life.

DAY 2

Readers' Theater Read aloud p. 387. Have students notice characterization as you read. Have students practice doing reader's theater readings of p. 387 in groups of three: a narrator, Pedro, and Elena.

DAY 3

Model Read aloud p. 389. Have students notice how your voice changes as you read the dialogue. Have students practice reading the dialogue on this page with a partner, taking turns being Elena and Burro.

DAY 4

Readers' Theater Groups of three practice reading aloud p. 399, three times, readers' theater style. Students should read with characterization.

Monitor Progress | Check Fluency wcPM

As students reread, monitor their progress toward their individual fluency goals. Current Goal: 110–120 words correct per minute. End-of-Year Goal: 120 words correct per minute.

If... students cannot read fluently at a rate of 110–120 words correct per minute,
then... make sure students practice with text at their independent level.
Provide additional fluency practice, pairing nonfluent readers with fluent readers.

If... students already read at 120 words correct per minute,
then... they need not reread three to four times.

SUCCESS PREDICTOR

DAY 5

Assessment
Individual Reading Rate Use the Fluency Assessment Plan and do a one-minute timed reading of either selection from this week to assess students in Week 5. Pay special attention to this week's skill, characterization. Provide corrective feedback for each student.

RETEACH

 Generalize

TEACH

Explain that when you generalize, you make a general or broad statement that applies to several examples. Students can complete Practice Book 3.2, p. 148, on their own, or you can complete it as a class. Review how to read the graphic organizer before students begin the activity. Explain that the facts should come from the passage.

ASSESS

Have students review pp. 389–392. Ask them to list facts and details about Elena, then make a generalization about her personality *(Fact—Elena helps the animals, and the animals thank Elena; Generalization—Elena is a caring person).*

For additional instruction for generalize, see DI·56.

EXTEND SKILLS

Details and Facts

TEACH

Details are small pieces of information. Facts are pieces of information that can be proven to be true. Details can help you remember important information, visualize the story events, and justify your predictions, conclusions, generalizations, and feelings related to the story.

- Look for details that help you understand the plot, characters, and setting.
- As you read, try to decide which details are important.
- Use details to help you decide why the author wrote a selection.

Read aloud the first paragraph on p. 386. With students, list important facts and details on the board.

ASSESS

Have students work with a partner to reread p. 388. Invite them to identify important facts and details. Ask:

1. **Why is it important to remember the details you listed?**

2. **How do the details help you understand why the author wrote *Elena's Serenade?***

OBJECTIVES

- Make generalizations.
- Identify important facts and details.

Skills Trace	
Generalize	
Introduce/Teach	TE: 3.3 354–355, 3.4 60–61, 3.6 380–381
Practice	PB: 3.1 133, 137, 138; 3.2 23, 27, 28, 36, 46, 56, 143, 147, 148
Reteach/Review	**TE: 3.3 379b, DI•55; 3.4 85b, 101, 127, DI•54; 3.5 161; 3.6 407b, DI•56**
Test	Selection Test: Unit 6 Benchmark Test: Unit 4

ELL

Access Content Reteach the skill by reviewing the Picture It! lesson on generalizing in the ELL Teaching Guide, pp. 204–205.

Generalize

- When you read, you may find facts or ideas about things or people. Sometimes, you can make a **general statement** about them.
- A **general statement** tells how things or people are all alike in some way.

Directions Read the following story. Fill in the chart with four ideas or facts from the story. Then write a general statement about what you read.

Alma had a pet parrot. Its name was Pepé. Alma wrote children's stories. She really liked what she did. But lately, Alma couldn't think of a thing to write about. Pepé told her to write a story about a parrot who could talk. So Alma wrote the story.

Her boss did not like it. Alma was sad. She was afraid she'd never write a good story again. Pepé told her another idea. Once again, she used Pepé's idea. And again, her boss did not like it. Alma stopped listening to Pepé. Now she thinks of her own ideas.

Idea/Fact
1. Possible response: Alma had a talking parrot.

Idea/Fact
2. Possible response: The parrot gave Alma ideas about what to write.

Idea/Fact
3. Possible response: Alma's boss didn't like her new stories.

Idea/Fact
4. Possible response: Alma came up with her own ideas.

5. **General Statement**
Possible response: Some of your best ideas and work come from yourself.

Home Activity Your child learned about making generalizations. Read a book together that was written many years ago. Find the generalizations in the book and the ideas that contributed to making the generalizations. Then discuss with your child whether that generalization could still be made today.

▲ **Practice Book 3.2** p. 148

Vocabulary and Word Study

Context Clues

SYNONYMS Remind students that they can use context clues and synonyms to determine the meaning of unfamiliar words. Have students list any unknown words they encountered as they read *Elena's Serenade.* They can create a chart showing the unknown word, helpful context clues and synonyms, and their definition of the word. Students can confirm word meanings using a dictionary.

Word	Context Clue Synonym	Meaning
soft	low	quiet
mad		
furnace		

Following Your Dreams

LOOKING BACK Remind students of the unit theme: Freedom. Discuss the unit focus question: What does freedom mean? Ask students how the Concept Vocabulary from each week of this unit relates to the unit theme and unit focus question. Ask students if they have any words or categories to add. If time permits, create a Unit Concept Web.

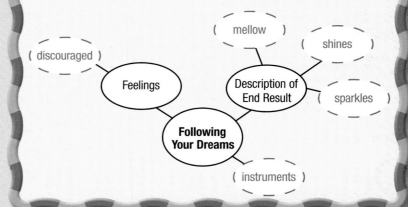

Glass Words

Some words, such as *glassblower*, have to do with glass. Have partners use reference sources to make lists of words of things that are made of glass and their definitions. Students can illustrate their favorite glass-related words.

Some Glass Words

bottles	mugs
eyeglasses	windows
plates	marbles
containers	table tops
bricks	ornaments

Monitor Progress

Check Vocabulary

If... students suggest words or categories that are not related to the concept,	**then...** review the words and categories on the Concept Web and discuss how they relate to the lesson concept.

SUCCESS PREDICTOR

Speaking and Listening

SPEAKING

Song, Rap, or Poem

SET-UP Students recite a poem from memory or perform a song or rap for the class.

PLANNING Have students think of a short song, rap, or poem they can memorize and present. Performances should be less than three minutes. Encourage students to select a piece that uses figurative language techniques, such as similes, metaphors, or sensory language. Remind students to consider using notes or props during their presentations.

DELIVERY Provide time for students to rehearse their song, rap, or poem aloud. Share these delivery suggestions:

- Stand tall.
- Use a clear voice with emotion.
- Smile and make eye contact.
- Move with the rhythm.
- Keep the rhythm lively to maintain audience interest.

LISTENING

Listen to Song or Poem

Have students listen to their classmates recite a poem, song, or rap. Then have them answer these questions orally.

1. **What forms of sound devices or poetic elements did the speaker use?** *(Responses will vary but may include rhyme, alliteration, repetition.)*

2. **How did the song or poem make you feel? Was it uplifting? Scary?** *(Responses will vary.)*

3. **Did the poem or song have a repetitive pattern or beat? Did the rhythm of the song or poem help you enjoy the listening experience? Why or why not?** *(Possible response: Yes, the poem rhymed. I like listening to rhyming poems because I can follow and remember them.)*

Listening Tips
- Listen for rhythm and repetitive patterns.
- Be polite and courteous.
- Do not stand up or leave during the performance.
- Sit quietly and attentively.

Support Vocabulary Use the following to review and extend vocabulary and to explore lesson concepts further:
- ELL Poster 30, Days 3–5 instruction
- Vocabulary Activities and Word Cards in ELL Teaching Guide, pp. 206–207

Assessment For information on assessing students' speaking, listening, and viewing, see the ELL and Transition Handbook.

SUCCESS PREDICTOR

Grammar Quotations

OBJECTIVES

- Define and identify quotations.
- Use quotations in writing.
- Become familiar with quotation assessment on high-stakes tests.

Monitor Progress

Grammar

If... students have difficulty with quotations,	then... see The Grammar and Writing Book pp. 224–227.

DAILY FIX-IT

This week use Daily Fix-It Transparency 30.

Spiral REVIEW

Support Grammar See the Grammar Transition lessons in the ELL and Transition Handbook.

▲ **The Grammar and Writing Book**
For more instruction and practice, use pp. 224–229.

DAILY FIX-IT

1. Tina and me enjoy the naturel world in the desert. *(I; natural)*

2. Tina said "I thouht I saw a snake." *(said,; thought)*

READING-GRAMMAR CONNECTION

Write this sentence from *Elena's Serenade* on the board:

> *"Let me hear you," I say.*

Explain that this is a **quotation;** the quotation marks indicate the speaker's exact words. A comma separates the speaker's words from the rest of the sentence.

Display Grammar Transparency 30. Read aloud the definitions and sample sentences. Work through the items.

Quotations

Quotation marks (" ") show the exact words of a speaker in a conversation.
- Use a comma to separate the speaker's exact words from the rest of the sentence.
- Use a capital letter to begin the first word inside the quotation marks.
- Put the punctuation mark that ends the quotation inside the quotation marks.
  "I want to be a glassblower," said Elena.
  "Is that a hard job?" I asked.
  She replied, "You need good lungs!"
Quotation marks also indicate many kinds of titles, such as song, poem, and story titles.
  Elena played "Burro Serenade."

Directions Write *C* if a sentence is correct. If it is not correct, make the corrections that are needed.
1. " There are different ways to make glass into objects," Ben said. _____
2. " You can blow the hot glass with a blowpipe, Kit said. _____
3. Taylor said, "You can press the glass into a mold." _____
4. Kevin added, "You can pour hot glass into a mold." **C**

Directions Write each sentence. Add a comma and quotation marks where they are needed.
5. You can make many useful and pretty things with glass, Sara exclaimed.
   "You can make many useful and pretty things with glass," Sara exclaimed.
6. Mr. Parker said You can make beautiful vases.
   Mr. Parker said, "You can make beautiful vases."
7. I asked Are some lamps made of glass?
   I asked, "Are some lamps made of glass?"

Unit 6 Elena's Serenade   Grammar **30**

▲ **Grammar Transparency** 30

DAILY FIX-IT

3. Doesnt the warm sun in the desert feel pleasent? *(Doesn't; pleasant)*

4. The desert animels rests during the day. *(animals; rest)*

GUIDED PRACTICE

Review the concept of quotations.

- A **quotation** shows the exact words of a speaker in a conversation.

- Use a comma to separate the speaker's exact words from the rest of the sentence.

- Use a capital letter to begin the first word inside the **quotation marks.**

- Put the punctuation mark that ends the sentence inside the quotation marks.

HOMEWORK Grammar and Writing Practice Book p. 117. Work through the first two items with the class.

Quotations

Quotation marks (" ") show the exact words of a speaker in a conversation.
- Use a comma to separate the speaker's exact words from the rest of the sentence.
- Use a capital letter to begin the first word inside the quotation marks.
- Put the punctuation mark that ends the quotation inside the quotation marks.
  "I can play music on my pipe," said Elena.
  She asked, "Shall I play for you?"
  We replied, "That's a great idea!"
Quotation marks also indicate many kinds of titles, such as song, poem, and story titles.
  We read "Elena's Serenade."

Directions Underline the part of each sentence that is a quotation.
1. "I want to play the flute," said Jeremy.
2. "I will teach you," replied Ms. Foster.
3. Ms. Foster said, "Everyone will enjoy your songs."

Directions Write the sentences. Add quotation marks and commas where they are needed.
4. Some of my songs are happy said Jeremy.
   "Some of my songs are happy," said Jeremy.
5. Ms. Foster exclaimed You play beautifully!
   Ms. Foster exclaimed, "You play beautifully!"
6. Jeremy can play a song named Paco's Dog.
   Jeremy can play a song named "Paco's Dog."

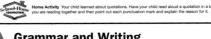

Home Activity Your child learned about quotations. Have your child read aloud a quotation in a book you are reading together and then point out each punctuation mark and explain the reason for it.

▲ **Grammar and Writing Practice Book** p. 117

DAY 3 — Apply to Writing

DAILY FIX-IT

5. Roadrunners are birds and they usual live in the desert. *(birds,; usually)*

6. Joe said, "Roadrunners are abel to run 15 miles per hour". *(able; hour.")*

USE QUOTATIONS IN WRITING

Explain that using quotations that show exactly what people said makes stories and articles more vivid and interesting.

Interesting: The little girl said she wanted to be a glassblower.

More Interesting: The little girl said, "I want to be a glassblower!"

• Have students review something they have written to see if they can use quotations to make it more interesting.

HOMEWORK Grammar and Writing Practice Book p. 118

Quotations

Directions Write a quotation in a sentence to answer each question. Use *I replied, I answered, I said,* and *I exclaimed.*
Possible answers:

1. "What is your favorite kind of music?" Jeremy asked.
"Pop music is my favorite," I said.

2. "What musical instruments do you know how to play?" Nicole asked.
"I can play the piano," I answered.

3. "What other musical instrument would you like to play?" Chris asked.
"I would like to play the guitar," I replied.

4. "What is your favorite kind of dancing?" Anna asked.
"I like ballet," I said.

5. "Why do you like music?" Steven asked.
"Music makes me happy," I exclaimed.

Directions Imagine a conversation you might have with a friend about learning to play a musical instrument. Write three sentences of the conversation. Use quotation marks and other punctuation correctly.
Possible answer: "I'm taking piano lessons," Jamal said. "What songs have you learned to play?" I asked. "I just had my first lesson yesterday!" exclaimed Jamal.

▲ **Grammar and Writing Practice Book** p. 118

DAY 4 — Test Preparation

DAILY FIX-IT

7. Tina said, "I wonder if there are wolfs in the desert. *(wolves; desert.")*

8. Coyotes live in the desert and they are members of the dog family to. *(desert,; too)*

STANDARDIZED TEST PREP

Test Tip

You may be asked to identify which words should go inside quotation marks. In addition to showing the exact words of people, quotation marks indicate many kinds of titles, such as song, poem, and story titles. Titles of longer works such as books are indicated with italics in print or underlined in handwriting.

Examples: Jane read a story called "A Big Lizard." I read a poem called "Desert Nights."

HOMEWORK Grammar and Writing Practice Book p. 119

Quotations

Directions Mark the letter of the words that should go inside quotation marks.

1. The desert is great, Tim said.
A Tim said
B The desert
C The desert is great,
D The desert is great, Tim

2. Look at the cactus, I responded.
A Look
B Look at the cactus,
C I
D I said

3. Tim said, There are bushes too.
A Tim said,
B Tim said, There
C There are
D There are bushes too.

4. I said, There is not much water.
A There is not much water.
B I said, There
C There is not
D not much water.

5. It is hot and dry, Tim exclaimed.
A Tim said.
B It is hot and dry,
C It is hot
D hot and dry, Tim

6. Do animals live here? I asked.
A Do animals live here?
B Do animals?
C live here? I asked
D I asked.

7. Some like hot weather, Tim said.
A hot weather, Tim said.
B Some like
C Some like hot weather,
D Tim said.

8. I said, I like it too.
A I said,
B I like
C I said, I like
D I like it too.

▲ **Grammar and Writing Practice Book** p. 119

DAY 5 — Cumulative Review

DAILY FIX-IT

9. Coyotes, wolves and foxs are all members of the dog family. *(wolves,; foxes)*

10. Chris and him hear coyotes howling in the desert in july. *(he; July)*

ADDITIONAL PRACTICE

Assign pp. 224–227 in The Grammar and Writing Book.

EXTRA PRACTICE Grammar and Writing Practice Book p. 151.

TEST PREPARATION Grammar and Writing Practice Book pp. 157–158.

ASSESSMENT

CUMULATIVE REVIEW Grammar and Writing Practice Book p. 120

Quotations

Directions Write C if a sentence is correct. If it is not correct, make the corrections that are needed.

1. Mr. Sanchez said, "You can make beautiful glass by blowing." ____

2. "It is an interesting art," exclaimed Julio. **C**

3. "You use a blowpipe to make a glass ball," Mr. Sanchez added. ____

4. "It looks really hard!" Carla said. ____

5. "Glassblowing takes a lot of practice," Mr. Sanchez said. ____

Directions Write each sentence. Add a comma and quotation marks where they are needed.

6. People have been blowing glass for thousands of years Ms. Rice said.
"People have been blowing glass for thousands of years," Ms. Rice said.

7. She added The blowpipe was invented long ago.
She added, "The blowpipe was invented long ago."

8. Colonists built a glass factory in Jamestown in 1608 Anita said.
"Colonists built a glass factory in Jamestown in 1608," Anita said.

9. Glassmakers used big furnaces in the 1700s added Ms. Rice.
"Glassmakers used big furnaces in the 1700s," added Ms. Rice.

▲ **Grammar and Writing Practice Book** p. 120

Writing Workshop Write Good Paragraphs

OBJECTIVES

- Identify the characteristics of a good paragraph.
- Write a good paragraph that includes a strong conclusion.
- Focus on organization/paragraphs.
- Use a rubric.

Genre Writing Good Paragraphs
Writer's Craft Strong Conclusions
Writing Trait Organization/Paragraphs

ELL

Organization/Paragraphs Make sure English learners can decode words in the prompt. Work with students to complete a cloze sentence that addresses the prompt and could be used to launch writing.

Writing Trait

IDEAS/FOCUS The paragraph focuses on a specific setting.

ORGANIZATION/PARAGRAPHS Details are arranged in a logical order according to the things that live in the desert. The paragraph ends with a strong conclusion.

VOICE The writer's voice is original and knowledgeable.

WORD CHOICE The writer uses vivid and precise words to describe a setting.

SENTENCES Sentences of different lengths and kinds are used.

CONVENTIONS Grammar and mechanics are excellent, including use of quotations.

DAY 1 Model the Trait

READING-WRITING CONNECTION

- *Elena's Serenade* is a fantasy about a girl who wants to become a glassblower, like her father.
- Ideas in *Elena's Serenade* are expressed in a series of well-developed paragraphs.
- Students will **write a good paragraph** with a strong ending.

MODEL ORGANIZATION/ PARAGRAPHS

Discuss Writing Transparency 30A. Then discuss the model and the writing trait of organization/paragraphs.

 Think Aloud I see that the writer has written a paragraph called "Life in the Desert." The paragraph has a topic sentence that gets the reader's attention and tells the main idea of the paragraph. The next ten sentences provide supporting details about the main idea. The conclusion vividly sums up the paragraph's main idea.

Writing Good Paragraphs

A **good paragraph** has a topic sentence that tells the paragraph's main idea. It has supporting details that tell more about the main idea and are organized in a logical way. A good paragraph ends with a strong conclusion.

Life in the Desert

Topic sentence gets readers' interest and states paragraph's main idea. The desert seems like a hot, empty place, but it is really full of life. In "Elena's Serenade," Elena goes to the desert. She says, "*El sol* blazes like Papa's furnace."

Next 10 sentences provide supporting details. They are arranged in two groups: plants and animals. Deserts are not only hot. They are also very dry. Still, plants that need little water grow there. These include cactuses, grasses, and even some trees. When it does rain, wildflowers and plants bloom. Many animals like the dry, hot desert climate. Snakes and lizards live under rocks during the day. Foxes and jackrabbits may also spend time in the desert.

Conclusion vividly sums up paragraph's main idea. When you think of a desert, you may think of a dead brown landscape. But you will find that nature has amazing variety there.

Unit 6 Elena's Serenade Writing Model **30A**

▲ **Writing Transparency** 30A

DAY 2 Improve Writing

WRITER'S CRAFT
Strong Conclusions

Display Writing Transparency 30B. Read the directions and work together to decide whether each conclusion is the strongest possible for the paragraph.

Think Aloud STRONG CONCLUSIONS Tomorrow we will write a paragraph about someone we know. How will I organize my sentences into a logical order? I will start with a strong topic sentence, followed by facts, descriptions, and examples that support the topic sentence. Finally, I will write a conclusion that sums up the main idea of the paragraph.

GUIDED WRITING Some students may need more help with strong conclusions. Review some paragraphs from other selections and discuss their conclusions with students.

Strong Conclusions

A **strong conclusion** sums up the main idea of a paragraph in a vivid way.

Directions Read the paragraph and each conclusion. Write why each conclusion is or is not the strongest conclusion for the paragraph.

A mountaintop looks beautiful from far away, but it is a harsh place for people who visit. The higher you go, the worse the weather gets. At the top of a high mountain, snow swirls in a stiff wind. Temperatures are below freezing.

1. Mountains are very beautiful.
   <u>No; it doesn't sum up the main idea of the paragraph.</u>

2. So everyone should climb mountains.
   <u>No; it doesn't sum up the main idea of the paragraph.</u>

3. Unless you are an experienced mountain climber, the best way to enjoy a tall mountain is from the ground.
   <u>Yes; it sums up the main idea and holds readers' interest.</u>

Directions Write a strong conclusion for the following paragraph.

The rain forest is a noisy and colorful part of the natural world. Monkeys screech, frogs croak, and insects chirp. The plants create a lush green world that contrasts with the brilliant reds and yellows of flowers and birds.
<u>Possible answer: A rain forest has more sights and sounds than the most exciting adventure movie.</u>

Unit 6 Elena's Serenade Writer's Craft **30B**

▲ **Writing Transparency** 30B

DAY 3 — Prewrite and Draft

READ THE WRITING PROMPT

on page 402 in the Student Edition.

Elena's Serenade *describes a girl who makes special music.*

Think about a character or person you know well.

Now write a paragraph about that person, using logical organization.

Writing Test Tips

- Begin with a strong topic sentence that makes a generalization about the story setting.
- Brainstorm facts, descriptions, and examples to support the topic sentence.
- Write a conclusion that sums up the paragraph's main idea and keeps readers' interest.

GETTING STARTED Students can do any of the following:

- With a partner, make a list of interesting people you know.
- With a group, make a concept web with *Lively Story Characters* in the center.
- Discuss with the class interesting people and stories in the selections you have read.

DAY 4 — Draft and Revise

EDITING/REVISING CHECKLIST

☑ Does the paragraph focus on a specific setting?

☑ Do vivid details elaborate on the setting?

☑ Are quotations used correctly to add interest?

☑ Are related words spelled correctly?

☑ Are abbreviations punctuated correctly?

See *The Grammar and Writing Book,* pp. 228–233.

Revising Tips

Organization/ Paragraphs

- Write a topic sentence that states the paragraph's main idea.
- Use well-organized details to support the main idea.
- Write a vivid conclusion that sums up the main idea.

PUBLISHING Students can read their paragraphs aloud in small groups. Some students may wish to revise their work later.

ASSESSMENT Use the scoring rubric to evaluate students' work.

DAY 5 — Connect to Unit Writing

Research Report

Week 1	Taking Notes 303g–303h
Week 2	Outlining 331g–331h
Week 3	Informational Paragraph 353g–353h
Week 4	Writing About a Picture 379g–379h
Week 5	Write Good Paragraphs 407g–407h

PREVIEW THE UNIT PROMPT

Write a research report about a monument or statue that symbolizes freedom in the United States. Discuss the monument itself, its history, and why it is important. Find information in sources such as books, magazines, CD-ROMs, and the Internet.

APPLY

- A research report is an informational article based on research.
- In a research report, each paragraph contains a topic sentence and details that support the topic sentence.

Writing Trait Rubric

	4	3	2	1
Organization/ Paragraphs	Ideas well developed from beginning to end; strong closure	Ideas that progress from beginning to end; good closure	Some sense of movement from beginning to end; weak closure	No sense of movement from beginning to end or closure
	Paragraph organized with exceptional logic	Paragraph organized adequately	Paragraph not clearly organized	Paragraph not organized

OBJECTIVES

- Use known words to decode and define related words.
- Review multisyllabic words with prefixes and suffixes.
- Blend and read related words and multisyllabic words with prefixes and suffixes.
- Apply decoding strategies: blend longer words.

ELL

Support Phonics English language learners will benefit from studying related words in English. Have students create word webs for related words and have them indicate whether the words are nouns, verbs, adjectives, or adverbs. Encourage students to create parallel word webs for related words in their home language.

See the Phonics Transition Lessons in the ELL and Transition Handbook.

Related Words

Directions Choose the word that best matches each clue. Write the word on the line.

1. coverings for the body	cloth clothes	clothes
2. a person who plays sports	athlete athletics	athlete
3. a person's handwritten name	sign signature	signature
4. a tub for washing	bath bathe	bath
5. the world of living things and the outdoors	natural nature	nature

Directions Read each pair of related words. Underline the parts that are spelled the same but pronounced differently. Write a sentence using one of the words in each pair.
Sentences will vary.

6. feel	felt	I felt tired so I went to bed.
7. keep	kept	I keep my coat in my locker.
8. decide	decision	I made a decision about what to do tonight.
9. mean	meant	I didn't mean to break the plate.
10. define	definition	What is the definition of this word?
11. volcano	volcanic	I read about a volcano that erupted.
12. please	pleasant	Please pass the salt.
13. relate	relative	Bill is my relative.
14. sign	signal	I didn't see the stop sign.
15. repeat	repetition	Please repeat the question.

Home Activity Your child read and wrote related words that have parts that are spelled the same but pronounced differently, as in *cloth* and *clothes*. Discuss the meanings of the related words on the page above. Then work together to write a story that uses some of the words.

▲ **Practice Book 3.2** p. 149

Related Words

TEACH

Remind students that they have learned many words that are similar. Write the words *able, ability, deal,* and *dealt.*

- How do you pronounce the first word? *(able)*
- What does *able* mean? (having the skill to accomplish a task)
- How is the second word similar to the first? (It looks and sounds something like *able.* It begins like *able.*)

MODEL When I come to an unfamiliar word, I think about similar words I already know. Often words that look and sound similar are related. That means they have similar meanings. The word *able* describes a person who can do something well. *Ability* is a noun that means "skill." I can use what I know about *able* to help me understand what *ability* means. By thinking about related words and using context clues if the word is in a sentence, I can usually figure out the new word without looking it up.

Model blending *deal* and *dealt.* Then have students blend the words with you and explain how their meanings are similar and how they are different.

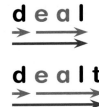

PRACTICE AND ASSESS

DECODE LONGER WORDS Write these words. Have students read them and explain how the meanings of the similar words are related.

single   singular   courtesy   courteous

describe   description   add   additional

READ WORDS IN CONTEXT Write these sentences. Have individuals read them and point out related words in each. The related words are underlined.

It's almost time for <u>dinner</u> so let's look for a good place to <u>dine</u>.

The piece of cake <u>crumbled</u> into tiny <u>crumbs</u> when I picked it up.

The job of a <u>goalie</u> is to keep the other team from scoring a <u>goal</u>.

A <u>historian</u> is a person who studies <u>history</u>.

To assess, observe whether students recognize related words.

Review Word Parts

REVIEW PREFIXES AND SUFFIXES

CONNECT Review the meanings of affixes. Write this sentence: *Her cheerfulness made us feel at home.*

- We learned to decode longer words by dividing them into word parts.
- Read the sentence to yourself. Raise your hand when you see a word that has a base word and two suffixes. *(cheerfulness)*
- How do we divide the word into parts? *(cheer/ful/ness)*
- How does dividing the word into parts help us figure it out? **(The parts are easier to read than the whole word. We know each part, so we can just put the parts together to read the word.)**

Continue in the same way with the sentence *I wonder what is in the unopened box.*

PRACTICE AND ASSESS

DECODE LONGER WORDS Have individuals read the following words. Model chunking and blending the words one syllable at a time from left to right as needed.

mismanagement	distrustfully	replacement	oversleeping
previewing	midyear	shamefully	unpleasantness
overjoyed	disinterested	disorderly	misconduct

READ WORDS IN CONTEXT Have students read these sentences. Then, to check meaning, have them give their own sentence for the underlined word.

Our fear of the <u>darkness</u> turned out to be <u>needless</u>.

<u>Rebuilding</u> the model for the science fair was a big job.

The <u>outfielder</u> ran to catch the ball.

The whole problem was the result of my <u>carelessness</u>.

To assess, note how well students read the multisyllabic words.

Vocabulary TiP

You may wish to explain the meanings of these words.

disorderly — not neat, unorganized

misconduct — bad behavior

mismanagement — leading in an unskilled or disorganized way

Spelling & Phonics Related Words

OBJECTIVE

● Spell related words.

Generalization

Connect to Phonics Related words often have parts that are spelled the same but pronounced differently: *cloth*, *clothes*.

Spelling Words

1. cloth	9. deal
2. clothes	10. dealt
3. nature	11. please
4. natural	12. pleasant
5. able	13. sign
6. ability	14. signal
7. mean	15. signature
8. meant	

Challenge Words

16. equal	19. major
17. equation	20. majority
18. equator	

ELL

Spelling/Phonics Support See the ELL and Transition Handbook for spelling support.

PRETEST

Use the Dictation Sentences from Day 5 to administer the pretest. Read the word, read the sentence, and then read the word again. Guide students in self-correcting their pretests and correcting any misspellings.

Monitor Progress

Spelling

If... students misspell more than 4 pretest words,	then... use words 1–8 for Strategic Intervention.
If... students misspell 1–4 pretest words,	then... use words 1–15 for On-Level practice.
If... students correctly spell all pretest words,	then... use words 1–20 for Advanced Learners.

HOMEWORK Spelling Practice Book, p. 117

Related Words

Generalization Related words often have parts that are spelled the same but pronounced differently: **cloth**, **clothes**.

Word Sort Sort the list words by words you know how to spell and words you are learning to spell. Write every word.

words I know how to spell	words I'm learning to spell
1. Answers will vary.	9. Answers will vary.
2.	10.
3.	11.
4.	12.
5.	13.
6.	14.
7.	15.
8.	

Spelling Words
1. cloth
2. clothes
3. nature
4. natural
5. able
6. ability
7. mean
8. meant
9. deal
10. dealt
11. please
12. pleasant
13. sign
14. signal
15. signature

Challenge Words
16. equal
17. equation
18. equator
19. major
20. majority

Challenge Words

words I know how to spell	words I'm learning to spell
16. Answers will vary.	18. Answers will vary.
17.	19.
	20.

School + Home **Home Activity** Your child is learning to spell related words. To practice at home, have your child study each word that he or she wrote in the second column on this page, spell the word with eyes shut, and then write it.

▲ **Spelling Practice Book** p. 117

TEACH

Related words often begin the same but are spelled differently. Demonstrate this by writing the spelling words on the board in pairs and having students sound out the syllables of each word. Guide students in identifying the different sounds produced by the same letter combinations.

mean meant

USE THE DICTIONARY Have students use a dictionary to find the different meanings of the related spelling words.

HOMEWORK Spelling Practice Book, p. 118

Related Words

Spelling Words

cloth	clothes	nature	natural	able
ability	mean	meant	deal	dealt
please	pleasant	sign	signal	signature

Replacing Words Write list words to take the place of the underlined words.

1. I jumped out of the tub and put on my shirt and shorts. — 1. clothes
2. It has been a nice day. — 2. pleasant
3. Did you write your name on the card? — 3. sign
4. Dogs have the skill to hear high-pitched sounds. — 4. ability
5. Mom made a kerchief from a scrap of blue fabric. — 5. cloth
6. Tom is never cruel to animals. — 6. mean
7. We went to the mountains to enjoy the environment. — 7. nature
8. Sara gave six cards to each player. — 8. dealt

Missing Words Write the missing word.

9. She has a natural talent for music.
10. His hand signal warned me to stop.
11. A bat is the only mammal that is able to fly.
12. That's not what I meant .
13. I can do what I please on Saturday morning.
14. Her signature is on the credit card.
15. My big sister knows how to deal with most emergencies.

School + Home **Home Activity** Your child spelled related words. Have your child pronounce each list word and use the word in a sentence.

▲ **Spelling Practice Book** p. 118

DAY 3 Connect to Writing

WRITE A STORY

Have students write a story or play using at least three spelling words. Have students read their work aloud, or collect them into a book to share with other students.

Frequently Misspelled Words

want   whole

These words are difficult for third-graders to spell. Alert students to these frequently misspelled words and encourage them to think carefully before spelling.

HOMEWORK Spelling Practice Book p. 119

Related Words

Proofread a Paragraph Circle four spelling errors and cross out the sentence that does not belong in the paragraph. Write the words correctly.

When I grow up, I want to design clothes. I think I would be good at this. I have the abilty to draw, and I like to deal with people. I like to sketch outfits that please my friends. My best friend is Rosa. I am learning about cotton, wool, and other kinds of cloth.

Spelling Words
cloth
clothes
nature
natural
able
ability
mean
meant
deal
dealt
please
pleasant
sign
signal
signature

1. __want__   2. __ability__
3. __please__   4. __cloth__

Proofread Words Circle the word that is spelled correctly. Write it.

Frequently Misspelled Words
want
whole

5. My bus driver is a (pleasant) plesant person.
   __pleasant__
6. Wave to signel (signal) if you need help.
   __signal__
7. Will you be abel (able) to come to the party?
   __able__
8. Simon was reading a book about the wonders of (nature) natur.
   __nature__

Home Activity Your child spelled related words. Have your child point out a pair of related list words and explain how the spellings differ.

▲ **Spelling Practice Book** p. 119

DAY 4 Review

REVIEW RELATED WORDS

Have students create a matching game using the related spelling words. Students can exchange their games with others to solve each puzzle.

Spelling Strategy
Related Words

Even though they have different sounds, related words include the same letter combinations, which makes spelling them easier.

HOMEWORK Spelling Practice Book p. 120

Related Words

Spelling Words

cloth	clothes	nature	natural	able
ability	mean	meant	deal	dealt
please	pleasant	sign	signal	signature

Riddle Write the missing words. Then use the numbered letters to solve the riddle.

What has eighteen legs and catches flies?

1. You have a __ smile.   p l e a s a n t
2. I like being out in __.   n a t u r e
3. What do you __?   m e a n
4. Are you __ to sit up?   a b l e
5. Will you __ help?   p l e a s e

a b a s e b a l l   t e a m

Hidden Words Each of the list words below contains a shorter list word related in spelling and meaning to the longer word. Circle the short word. Write both words.

6. c l o t h e s   6. __cloth, clothes__
7. d e a l t   7. __deal, dealt__
8. s i g n a t u r e   8. __sign, signature__
9. m e a n t   9. __mean, meant__
10. s i g n a l   10. __sign, signal__

Home Activity Your child has been learning to spell related words. Pronounce a list word. Ask your child to name a related word and spell it.

▲ **Spelling Practice Book** p. 120

DAY 5 Posttest

DICTATION SENTENCES

1. Put a cloth over the basket.
2. I need to buy new clothes for school.
3. Let's go on a nature walk.
4. It's natural for some animals to sleep during the day.
5. She is able to jump rope.
6. He has the ability to sail a boat.
7. The puppy did not mean to hurt you.
8. I meant to tell you the story.
9. Dad got a good deal on the car.
10. Mom dealt the cards for the game.
11. Please sit down for dinner.
12. The day was sunny and pleasant.
13. Where is the stop sign?
14. The signal is red when a train comes.
15. I can't read her signature.

CHALLENGE

16. Two cups equal one pint.
17. Write the equation on your paper.
18. Find the equator on the map.
19. The brain is a major organ.
20. The majority of my friends live near me.

OBJECTIVES

- Formulate an inquiry question that is connected to this week's lesson focus.
- Effectively and efficiently find, evaluate, and communicate information related to an inquiry question using electronic sources.

New Literacies

Day 1	Identify Questions
Day 2	Navigate/Search
Day 3	Analyze
Day 4	Synthesize
Day 5	Communicate

NEW LITERACIES

Internet Inquiry Activity

EXPLORE FOLLOWING YOUR DREAMS

Use the following 5-day plan to help students conduct this week's Internet inquiry activity on following your dreams. Remind students to follow classroom rules when using the Internet.

DAY 1

Identify Questions Discuss the lesson focus question: *When are you free to follow your dreams?* Brainstorm ideas for specific inquiry questions about following dreams. For example, students might want to find out how to start a pet-sitting business, or how to prepare for a career as an astronaut. Have students work individually, in pairs, or in small groups to write an inquiry question they want to answer.

DAY 2

Navigate/Search Review how to evaluate Web sites. Remind students to check for the timeliness of the information and the general appearance of the site. Tell students that organizations sometimes pay to have their sites listed among the first ten shown on certain search engines. Remind students to consider these factors as well as the content of the sites when selecting sites to analyze on Day 3.

DAY 3

Analyze Encourage students to explore the Web sites they identified on Day 2. Tell them to scan each site for information that may help to answer their inquiry questions. Have students analyze information for credibility, reliability, and usefulness. Take notes or print out valuable information.

DAY 4

Synthesize Have students synthesize information from Day 3. Remind them that when they synthesize, they combine relevant information and ideas from several sources to find an answer to their inquiry questions.

DAY 5

Communicate Have students share their inquiry results. They can use a word processing program to create a short journal entry about following your dreams.

RESEARCH/STUDY SKILLS
Chart/Table

OBJECTIVES
- Review terms and ideas related to charts and tables.
- Organize information in a table.

TEACH

Ask students what kind of information they have seen organized in a chart or table. If necessary, give examples such as schedules, calendars, price lists, and multiplication facts. Show an example of a table as you discuss these terms and ideas.

- Both terms *chart* and *table* can describe the same thing.
- Most tables have boxes.
- Charts and tables have horizontal rows and/or vertical columns.
- Tables usually have a title that summarizes the included information.
- The words in the rows and columns tell you what information is given.

Invite students to name their dream job. Record several dream jobs, and select four or five for a class vote. Ask students which of these jobs they would choose. Use tallies to record results of the vote on the chalkboard. Have students make a table to organize the data. Before students make their tables, discuss the answers to the following questions.

1. How will you label the columns in your table? *(with the job choices)*

2. What information do the columns provide? *(the number of votes for each job choice)*

ASSESS

As students organize the information in a table, check that they properly label the rows and columns and write a title. Make sure the numbers they use are accurate.

For more practice or to assess students, use Practice Book 3.2, p. 150.

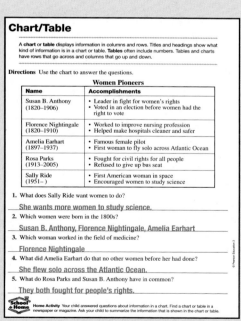

▲ **Practice Book 3.2** p. 150

Assessment Checkpoints *for the Week*

Selection Assessment

Use pp. 117–120 of Selection Tests to check:

 Selection Understanding

 Comprehension Skill *Generalize*

 Selection Vocabulary

burro	*puff*
bursts	*reply*
factory	*tune*
glassblower	

Leveled Assessment

- On-Level
- Strategic Intervention
- Advanced

Use pp. 175–180 of Fresh Reads for Differentiated Test Practice to check:

 Comprehension Skill *Generalize*

 REVIEW **Comprehension Skill** *Character*

 **Fluency** *Words Correct Per Minute*

Managing Assessment

Use Assessment Handbook for:

 Observation Checklists

 Record-Keeping Forms

 Portfolio Assessment

Unit 6
Concept Wrap-Up

Unit Poetry

Use the poetry on pp. 408–411 to help students appreciate poetry and further explore their understanding of the unit theme, Freedom. It is suggested that you

- **read the poems aloud**
- **discuss and interpret the poems with students**
- **have students read the poems for fluency practice**
- **have students write interpretive responses**

Unit Wrap-Up

Use the Unit Wrap-Up on pp. 412–413 to discuss the unit theme, Freedom, and to have students show their understanding of the theme through cross-curricular activities.

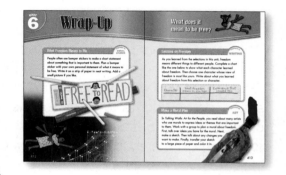

Unit Project

On p. 283, you assigned students a unit-long inquiry project, researching symbols of freedom. Students have investigated, analyzed, and synthesized information during the course of the unit as they researched. Schedule time for students to present what they have learned about the symbol they chose. The project rubric can be found to the right.

Unit Inquiry Project Rubric			
4	**3**	**2**	**1**
• Research is accurate and highly detailed. Sources are relevant to inquiry question. • List of resources about symbols of freedom is useful and organized.	• Research is accurate but not thorough. Most sources are relevant to inquiry question. • List of resources about symbols of freedom is useful but not organized as well as it could be.	• Research is not accurate and has little information that is relevant to inquiry question. • List of resources about symbols of freedom is not always helpful and not well-organized.	• Research is not accurate and does not include information that is relevant to inquiry question. • List of resources about symbols of freedom is not complete, helpful, or organized.

Unit 6
Reading Poetry

Model Fluent Reading

Point out that this poem is also the first verse of a famous song—our national anthem. Explain that you will read the song rather than sing it. Ask students to listen for the sense, or meaning, of these familiar words. Then read the text slowly, pausing as punctuation indicates.

Discuss the Poem

1 **Setting • Literal**

At what time of day is the song set?

It is set at daybreak ("at the dawn's early light").

2 **Paraphrase • Inferential**

In your own words, tell what happened the night before. What role did the flag play in that event?

Possible responses: There was a battle. During the battle, the flag continued to wave.

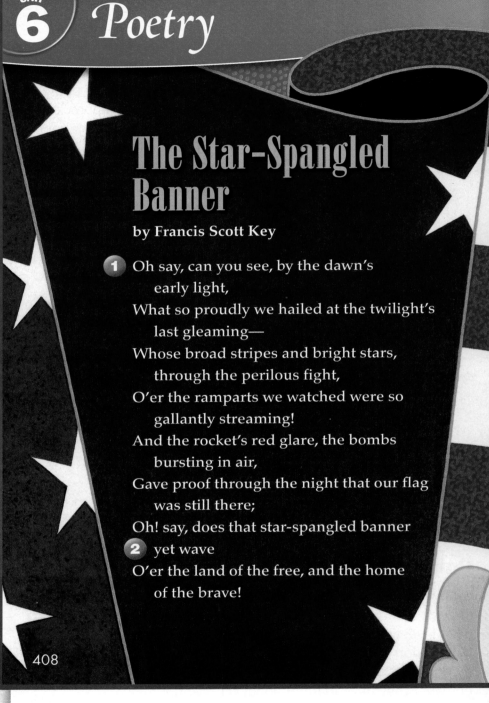

UNIT 6 Poetry

The Star-Spangled Banner

by Francis Scott Key

1 Oh say, can you see, by the dawn's
early light,
What so proudly we hailed at the twilight's
last gleaming—
Whose broad stripes and bright stars,
through the perilous fight,
O'er the ramparts we watched were so
gallantly streaming!
And the rocket's red glare, the bombs
bursting in air,
Gave proof through the night that our flag
was still there;
Oh! say, does that star-spangled banner
2 yet wave
O'er the land of the free, and the home
of the brave!

408

Practice Fluent Reading

Have students take turns reading "I Watched an Eagle Soar" in groups of three or four. As they read, have students imagine they are addressing an important adult in their lives. Encourage them to use a tone that is both respectful and excited. When students have finished, have them listen to the AudioText of the poem and compare and contrast their readings with the CD recording.

Audio CD   AudioText

I Watched an Eagle Soar

by Virginia Driving Hawk Sneve

Grandmother,
I watched an eagle soar
high in the sky
until a cloud covered him up.
Grandmother,
I still saw the eagle
behind my eyes.
1 2

409

✏️ WRITING POETRY

Explain to students than an *anthem* is a song of praise or tribute. Then have students work in groups to write their own poetic tribute to the American flag. Allow students to illustrate their poems and display them in the classroom.

Model Fluent Reading

Tell students that the speaker in this poem is describing something she respects—nature—to someone she respects—her grandmother. Read the poem aloud in a reverent voice. As you read, have students imagine they are the grandmother. What do they picture in their heads?

Discuss the Poem

1 Sequence • Interpretation
What two events does the speaker describe?
Watching an eagle fly in the sky, and then "seeing" the eagle when she closes her eyes.

2 Figurative Language • Interpretation
What else might it mean to "see" something "behind your eyes"?
Possible responses: It might also mean to imagine something, or to remember something.

EXTEND SKILLS

Symbolism

Explain that a symbol is a person, place, event, or object that has a meaning in itself but suggests other meanings as well. In "The Star-Spangled Banner," for example, the flag is a real object, but it also stands for American ideals such as courage and freedom. In "I Watched an Eagle Soar," the main event—seeing an eagle fly across the sky—really happens. But when the speaker closes her eyes and "sees" the eagle again, the event becomes symbolic. It now suggests the act of imagination—of "seeing" something in the mind's eye.

Unit 6
Reading Poetry

Model Fluent Reading

Explain that in "Words Free as Confetti," the poet celebrates words and shows a deep affection for them. As you read the poem aloud, have students listen for all the different ways the poet expresses "word love."

Discuss the Poem

1 Imagery • Literal

What do words taste like to the poet? smell like? feel like? sound like?

They taste like sweet plums and old lemons; smell like warm almonds or tart apples; feel like grass, dandelions, cactus, cement, and icicles; and sound like the ocean or a lullaby.

2 Simile • Inferential

In what ways are words like confetti?

They both "rise and dance and spin."

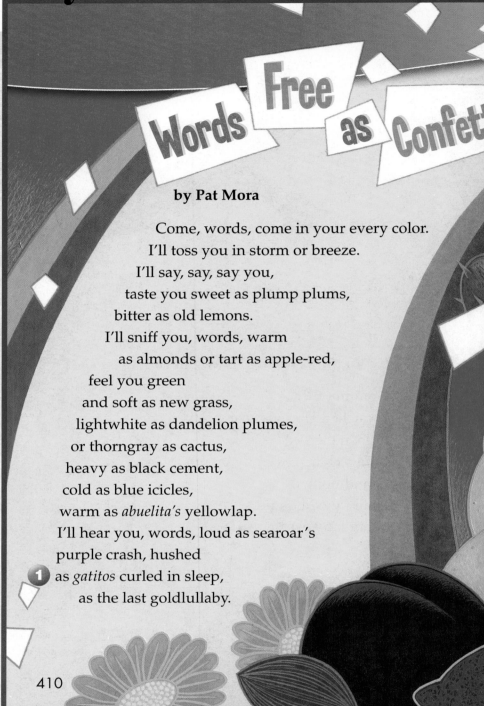

Words Free as Confetti

by Pat Mora

Come, words, come in your every color.
I'll toss you in storm or breeze.
I'll say, say, say you,
   taste you sweet as plump plums,
   bitter as old lemons.
I'll sniff you, words, warm
   as almonds or tart as apple-red,
   feel you green
   and soft as new grass,
   lightwhite as dandelion plumes,
   or thorngray as cactus,
   heavy as black cement,
   cold as blue icicles,
   warm as *abuelita's* yellowlap.
I'll hear you, words, loud as searoar's
purple crash, hushed
1 as *gatitos* curled in sleep,
   as the last goldlullaby.

410

EXTEND SKILLS

Invented Words

Explain that authors sometimes invent, or make up, words to express certain ideas or shades of meaning. Then point out the words *thorngray, yellowlap, searoar, goldlullaby,* and *chestnutwind* in this poem. Ask students how the poet invented these words. (She invented each one by putting two other words together.) Guide students to see that in this poem, the author wants to show how fun and free words can be. To do this, she experiments with words and uses them in new, surprising ways.

 Practice Fluent Reading

Have partners practice reading "Words Free as Confetti" aloud, each student taking one sentence. (Before they begin, have them locate each of the poem's twelve periods.) Remind students that the poem is a celebration and that their voices should reflect this. When they are finished, have them listen to the AudioText of the poem and then discuss how their own readings were similar or different.

Audio CD AudioText

I'll see you long and dark as tunnels,
   bright as rainbows,
   playful as chestnutwind.
I'll watch you, words,
   rise and dance and spin. **2**
I'll say, say, say you
in English,
in Spanish,
I'll find you.
Hold you.
Toss you.
   I'm free too.
   I say *yo soy libre,*
   I am free
      free, free,
         free as confetti.
            3 **4**

411

Discuss the Poem

3 **Generalize • Inferential**
Why does the poet think words are so wonderful?

Possible response: She thinks they are wonderful because you can use them to describe anything.

4 **Draw Conclusions • Inferential**
How are confetti, words, and the speaker all the same?

They are all free.

Connect Ideas and Themes

Remind students that this unit explores some different meanings of the word *freedom*. Have students tell what they think each poet in this group is trying to say about freedom. How might each poet define freedom? Why might each poet value that kind of freedom? Then have students offer their own definitions of freedom. Jump-start the discussion by writing these sentence stems on the board: *True freedom is freedom from....; True freedom is freedom to....*

WRITING POETRY

Have students choose one of the definitions for *freedom* generated in Connect Ideas and Themes, or come up with another one. Then have students think of an object that could symbolize or stand for that kind of freedom (much as the flag represents political freedom in "The Star-Spangled Banner," and confetti represents poetic freedom in "Words Free as Confetti"). Then have students use that symbol in a poem about freedom.

Unit 6
Wrap-Up

OBJECTIVES

- Critically analyze unit theme.
- Connect content across selections.
- Combine content and skills in meaningful activities that build literacy.
- Respond to unit selections through a variety of modalities.

FREEDOM

Discuss the Big Idea

What does freedom mean?

Write the unit theme and Big Idea question on the board. Ask students to think about the selections they have read in the unit. Discuss how each selection and lesson concept can help them answer the Big Idea question from this unit.

Model this for students by choosing a selection and explaining how the selection and lesson concept address the Big Idea.

UNIT 6 Wrap-Up

What Freedom Means to Me

connect to SOCIAL STUDIES

People often use bumper stickers to make a short statement about something that is important to them. Plan a bumper sticker with your own personal statement of what it means to be free. Write it on a strip of paper in neat writing. Add a small picture if you like.

412

What does it mean to be free?

Lessons on Freedom

connect to
WRITING

As you learned from the selections in this unit, freedom means different things to different people. Complete a chart like the one below to show what each character learned about freedom. Then choose one character whose view of freedom is most like yours. Write about what you learned about freedom from this selection or character.

Character	What freedom means to him/her	Experience that caused this

Make a Mural Plan

connect to
ART

In *Talking Walls: Art for the People,* you read about many artists who use murals to express ideas or themes that are important to them. Work with a group to plan a mural about freedom. First, talk over ideas you have for the mural. Next, make a sketch. Then talk about any changes you want to make. Finally, transfer your sketch to a large piece of paper and color it in.

413

ACTIVITIES

What Freedom Means to Me

Make a Bumper Sticker Introduce the activity using examples of actual bumper stickers to help students understand that their sayings should be creative and make the point in just a few words.

Lessons on Freedom

Write a Short Essay Model the activity by discussing one of the selections and filling in the chart, working with the class as a group. Have students write a summary statement telling what they learned about freedom from the character they chose and then write the essay.

Make a Mural Plan

Design a Mural Before students join their assigned groups, explain the steps they will follow to make their plan. You may want to have every member in a group submit a mural plan. The group can discuss each idea and then come to consensus about one idea. Visit each group to hear their ideas before they make a sketch of their mural.

Glossary

How to Use This Glossary

This glossary can help you understand and pronounce some of the words in this book. The entries in this glossary are in alphabetical order. There are guide words at the top of each page to show you the first and last words on the page. A pronunciation key is at the bottom of every other page. Remember, if you can't find the word you are looking for, ask for help or check a dictionary.

The entry word is in dark type. It shows how the word is spelled and how the word is divided into syllables.

The pronunciation is in parentheses. It also shows which syllables are stressed.

Part-of-speech labels show the function or functions of an entry word and any listed form of that word.

a·dore (ə dôr′), *VERB.* to love and admire someone very greatly: *She adores her mother.* ❑ *VERB.* **a·dores, a·dored, a·dor·ing.**

Sometimes, irregular and other special forms will be shown to help you use the word correctly.

The definition and example sentence show you what the word means and how it is used.

424

Aa

ad·mire (ad mir′), *VERB.* to look at with wonder, pleasure, and approval: *We all admired the beautiful painting.* ❑ *VERB* **ad·mires, ad·mired, ad·mir·ing.**

air·port (âr′pôrt′), *NOUN.* an area used regularly by aircraft to land and take off. An airport has buildings for passengers and for keeping and repairing aircraft.

at·tempt (ə tempt′), *VERB.* to try: *She attempted to climb the mountain.* ❑ *VERB* **at·tempts, at·tempt·ed, at·tempt·ing.**

at·ten·tion (ə ten′shən), *NOUN.* careful thinking, looking, or listening: *Give me your attention while I explain this math problem.*

at·tic (at′ik), *NOUN.* the space in a house just below the roof and above the other rooms.

av·er·age (av′ər ij), *NOUN.* the quantity found by dividing the sum of all the quantities by the number of quantities. The average of 3 and 5 and 10 is 6 (because 3 + 5 + 10 = 18, and 18 divided by 3 = 6).

Bb

bak·er·y (bā′kər ē), *NOUN.* a place where bread, pies, cakes, and pastries are made or sold.

batch (bach), *NOUN.* a quantity of something made at the same time: *a batch of cookies.*

board (bôrd), **1.** *NOUN.* a broad, thin piece of wood for use in building: *We used 10-inch boards for shelves.* **2.** *NOUN.* a group of people managing something; council: *a board of directors.*

boil (boil), *VERB.* to cause a liquid to bubble and give off steam by heating it: *He boils some water for tea.* ❑ *VERB* **boils, boiled, boil·ing.**

bow (bou), *VERB.* to bend the head or body in greeting, respect, worship, or obedience: *The people bowed before the queen.* ❑ *VERB* **bows, bowed, bow·ing.**

braid·ed (brād′ed), *ADJECTIVE.* woven or twined together: *The warm, braided bread was delicious.*

---

bur·ro (bėr′ō), *NOUN.* a donkey used to carry loads or packs in the southwestern United States and Mexico.

burros

burst (bėrst), *VERB.* to break open or be opened suddenly: *The trees had burst into bloom.* ❑ *VERB* **bursts, burst·ed, burst·ing.**

a in hat	ō in open	sh in she
ā in age	ò in all	th in thin
â in care	ô in order	ᴛʜ in then
ä in far	oi in oil	zh in measure
e in let	ou in out	ə = a in about
ē in equal	u in cup	ə = e in taken
ėr in term	ů in put	ə = i in pencil
i in it	ü in rule	ə = o in lemon
ī in ice	ch in child	ə = u in circus
o in hot	ng in long	

425

Cc

can·vas (kan′vəs), *NOUN.* a strong, heavy cloth made of cotton. It is used to make tents, sails, and certain articles of clothing, and for artists' paintings.

card·board (kärd′bôrd′), *NOUN.* a stiff material made of layers of paper pulp pressed together, used to make cards, posters, boxes, and so on.

cel·e·brate (sel′ə brāt), *VERB.* to do something special in honor of a special person or day: *We celebrated my birthday with a party.* ❑ *VERB* **cel·e·brates, cel·e·brat·ed, cel·e·brat·ing.**

celebrate

---

chill·y (chil′ē), *ADJECTIVE.* cold; unpleasantly cool: *It is a rainy, chilly day.*

chore (chôr), *NOUN.* a small task or easy job that you have to do regularly: *Feeding our pets is one of my daily chores.* ❑ *PLURAL* **chores.**

clam·ber (klam′bər), *VERB.* to climb something, using your hands and feet; scramble: *We clambered up the cliff.* ❑ *VERB* **clam·bers, clam·bered, clam·ber·ing.**

clog (klog), *NOUN.* a shoe with a thick, wooden sole.

clogs

clutch (kluch), *VERB.* to grasp something tightly: *I clutched the railing to keep from falling.* ❑ *VERB* **clutch·es, clutched, clutch·ing.**

426

---

col·lage (kə läzh′), *NOUN.* a picture made by pasting things such as parts of photographs, newspapers, fabric, and string onto a background.

collage

com·plain (kəm plān′), *VERB.* to say that you are unhappy, annoyed, or upset about something: *We complained that the room was too cold.* ❑ *VERB* **com·plains, com·plained, com·plain·ing.**

con·tin·ue (kən tin′yü), **1.** *VERB.* to keep up; keep on; go on: *The rain continued all day.* **2.** *VERB.* to go on with something after stopping for a while: *The story will be continued next week.* ❑ *VERB* **con·tin·ues, con·tin·ued, con·tin·u·ing.**

---

cot·ton (kot′n), *ADJECTIVE.* cloth made from soft, white fibers that grow in fluffy bunches on the cotton plant: *I like to wear cotton in hot weather.*

cou·ra·geous (kə rā′jəs), *ADJECTIVE.* full of courage; fearless; brave.

crev·ice (krev′is), *NOUN.* a narrow split or crack: *Tiny ferns grew in crevices in the stone wall.* ❑ *PLURAL* **crev·ic·es.**

crown (kroun), *NOUN.* a head covering of precious metal worn by a royal person, such as a queen or a king.

crys·tal (kris′tl), *NOUN.* a hard, solid piece of some substance that is naturally formed of flat surfaces and angles. Crystals can be small, like grains of salt, or large, like some kinds of stone.

a in hat	ō in open	sh in she
ā in age	ò in all	th in thin
â in care	ô in order	ᴛʜ in then
ä in far	oi in oil	zh in measure
e in let	ou in out	ə = a in about
ē in equal	u in cup	ə = e in taken
ėr in term	ů in put	ə = i in pencil
i in it	ü in rule	ə = o in lemon
ī in ice	ch in child	ə = u in circus
o in hot	ng in long	

427

---

curious • determined

cur·i·ous (kyùr′ē əs), *ADJECTIVE.* strange; odd; unusual: *I found a curious, old box in the attic.*

cur·rent (kèr′ənt), **1.** *NOUN.* a flow or stream of water, electricity, air, or any fluid: *The current swept the stick down the river.* **2.** *ADJECTIVE.* of or about the present time: *current events.*

cus·tom (kus′təm), *NOUN.* an old or popular way of doing things: *The social customs of many countries differ from ours.*

cus·tom·er (kus′tə mər), *NOUN.* someone who buys goods or services: *Just before the holidays, the store was full of customers.*

Dd

de·li·cious (di lish′əs), *ADJECTIVE.* very pleasing or satisfying; delightful, especially to the taste or smell: *a delicious cake.*

depth (depth), *NOUN.* the distance from the top to the bottom: *The depth of the well is about 25 feet.*

de·scribe (di skrīb′), *VERB.* to tell in words how someone looks, feels, or acts, or to record the most important things about a place, a thing, or an event: *The reporter described the awards ceremony in detail.* ❑ *VERB* **de·scribes, de·scribed, de·scrib·ing.**

des·ert (dez′ərt), *NOUN.* a dry, sandy region without water and trees: *In northern Africa there is a great desert called the Sahara.*

desert

de·ter·mined (di tèr′mənd), *ADJECTIVE.* with your mind made up: *Her determined look showed that she had decided what to do.*

disappear • encourage

dis·ap·pear (dis′ə pir′), *VERB.* to vanish completely; stop existing: *When spring came, the snow disappeared.* ❑ *VERB* **dis·ap·pears, dis·ap·peared, dis·ap·pear·ing.**

dis·cov·er·y (dis kuv′ər ē), *NOUN.* something found out: *One of Benjamin Franklin's discoveries was that lightning is electricity.*

dough (dō), *NOUN.* a soft, thick mixture of flour, liquid, and other things from which bread, biscuits, cake, and pie crusts are made.

drift (drift), *VERB.* to carry or be carried along by currents of air or water: *A raft drifts if it is not steered.* ❑ *VERB* **drifts, drift·ed, drift·ing.**

drown (droun), *VERB.* to die or cause to die under water or other liquid because of lack of air to breathe: *We almost drowned when our boat overturned.* ❑ *VERB* **drowns, drowned, drown·ing.**

Ee

ech·o (ek′ō), *VERB.* to be heard again: *Her shout echoed through the valley.* ❑ *VERB* **ech·oes, ech·oed, ech·o·ing.**

en·cour·age (en kèr′ij), *VERB.* to give someone courage or confidence; urge on: *We encouraged our team with loud cheers.* ❑ *VERB* **en·cour·ag·es, en·cour·aged, en·cour·ag·ing.**

encourage

a in hat	ò in open	sh in she
ā in age	ô in all	th in thin
â in care	ô in order	ŦH in then
ä in far	oi in oil	zh in measure
e in let	ou in out	ə = a in about
ē in equal	u in cup	ə = e in taken
ėr in term	ù in put	ə = i in pencil
i in it	ü in rule	ə = o in lemon
ī in ice	ch in child	ə = u in circus
o in hot	ng in long	

enthusiastic • flight

en·thu·si·as·tic (en thü′zē as′tik), *ADJECTIVE.* eagerly interested; full of enthusiasm: *My little brother is enthusiastic about going to kindergarten.*

ex·pres·sion (ek spresh′ən), *NOUN.* the act of putting into words or visual medium: *freedom of expression.*

Ff

fab·ric (fab′rik), *NOUN.* a woven or knitted material; cloth. Velvet, denim, and linen are fabrics. ❑ *PLURAL* **fab·rics.**

fac·tor·y (fak′tər ē), *NOUN.* a building or group of buildings where people and machines make things.

fa·mous (fā′məs), *ADJECTIVE.* very well known; noted: *The famous singer was greeted by a large crowd.*

fare·well (fâr′wel′), *ADJECTIVE.* parting; last: *a farewell kiss.*

feast (fēst), *NOUN.* a big meal for a special occasion shared by a number of people: *The breakfast that she cooked was a real feast.*

fes·ti·val (fes′tə vəl), *NOUN.* a program of entertainment, often held annually: *a summer music festival.*

festival

fierce (firs), *ADJECTIVE.* wild and frightening: *The fierce lion paced in his cage.*

fierce

flight¹ (flīt), *NOUN.* a set of stairs from one landing or one story of a building to the next. ❑ *PLURAL* **flights.**

flight • glum

flight² (flīt), *NOUN.* act of fleeing; running away; escape; *The flight of the prisoners was discovered.*

fool·ish (fü′lish), *ADJECTIVE.* without any sense; unwise: *It is foolish to cross the street without looking both ways.*

fo·reign (fôr′ən), *ADJECTIVE.* outside your own country: *She travels often in foreign countries.*

fra·grant (frā′grənt), *ADJECTIVE.* having a sweet smell or odor: *These cinnamon buns are very fragrant.*

Gg

gawk (gòk), *VERB.* to stare at someone or something in a rude way; gape: *People driving by gawked at the accident.* ❑ *VERB* **gawks, gawked, gawk·ing.**

gig·gle (gig′əl), *NOUN.* a silly or uncontrolled laugh.

gin·ger·ly (jin′jər lē), *ADVERB.* with extreme care or caution: *He walked gingerly across the ice.*

glar·ing (glâr′ing), *ADJECTIVE.* staring angrily.

glass·blow·er (glas blō′ər), *NOUN.* a person who shapes glass objects by blowing air from the mouth through a tube into a blob of hot, liquid glass at the other end of the tube.

glassblowers

glum (glum), *ADJECTIVE.* gloomy; dismal; sad: *I felt very glum when my friend moved away.*

a in hat	ò in open	sh in she
ā in age	ô in all	th in thin
â in care	ô in order	ŦH in then
ä in far	oi in oil	zh in measure
e in let	ou in out	ə = a in about
ē in equal	u in cup	ə = e in taken
ėr in term	ù in put	ə = i in pencil
i in it	ü in rule	ə = o in lemon
ī in ice	ch in child	ə = u in circus
o in hot	ng in long	

Glossary

goal (gōl), *NOUN.* something desired: *Her goal was to be a scientist.*

grace·ful (grās′fəl), *ADJECTIVE.* beautiful in form or movement: *He is a graceful dancer.*

gul·ly (gul′ē), *NOUN.* a ditch made by heavy rains or running water.

Hh

hand·ker·chief (hang′kər chif), *NOUN.* a soft, usually square piece of cloth used for wiping your nose, face, or hands.

her·it·age (her′ə tij), *NOUN.* traditions, skills, and so on, that are handed down from one generation to the next; inheritance: *Freedom is our most precious heritage.*

home·sick (hōm′sik′), *ADJECTIVE.* very sad because you are far away from home.

hov·er (huv′ər), *VERB.* to stay in or near one place in the air: *The two birds hovered over their nest.* ❏ *VERB* **hov·ers, hov·ered, hov·er·ing.**

Ii

ig·nore (ig nôr′), *VERB.* to pay no attention to something or someone: *The driver ignored the traffic light and almost hit another car.* ❏ *VERB* **ig·nores, ig·nored, ig·nor·ing.**

in·gre·di·ent (in grē′dē ənt), *NOUN.* one of the parts of a mixture: *The ingredients of a cake usually include eggs, sugar, flour, and flavoring.* ❏ *PLURAL* **in·gre·di·ents.**

ingredient

in·ter·na·tion·al (in′tər nash′ə nəl), *ADJECTIVE.* between or among two or more countries: *A treaty is an international agreement.*

Jj

jan·i·tor (jan′ə tər), *NOUN.* someone whose work is taking care of a building or offices. Janitors do cleaning and make some repairs.

jour·ney (jėr′nē), *NOUN.* a long trip from one place to another: *I'd like to take a journey around the world.*

joy·ful (joi′fəl), *ADJECTIVE.* causing or showing joy; glad; happy: *joyful news.*

Kk

knead (nēd), *VERB.* to press or mix together dough or clay into a soft mass: *The baker was kneading dough to make bread.* ❏ *VERB* **kneads, knead·ed, knead·ing.**

knead

Ll

la·bel (lā′bəl), *VERB.* to put or write a label on something: *She labeled her backpack with her name and address.* ❏ *VERB* **labels, labeled, label·ing.**

lib·er·ty (lib′ər tē), *NOUN.* freedom: *In 1865, the United States granted liberty to all people who were enslaved.*

lo·cal (lō′kəl), *ADJECTIVE.* about a certain place, especially nearby, not far away: *I go to a local doctor.*

loop (lüp), *VERB.* to form a line, path, or motion shaped so that it crosses itself: *The plane looped twice in the air above the ground.* ❏ *VERB* **loops, looped, loop·ing.**

a in hat	ò in open	sh in she
ā in age	ō in all	th in thin
â in care	ô in order	ᴛʜ in then
ä in far	oi in oil	zh in measure
e in let	ou in out	ə = a in about
ē in equal	u in cup	ə = e in taken
ėr in term	ü in put	ə = i in pencil
i in it	ü in rule	ə = o in lemon
ī in ice	ch in child	ə = u in circus
o in hot	ng in long	

432

433

Mm

med·al (med′l), *NOUN.* a piece of metal like a coin, given as a prize or award. A medal usually has a picture or words stamped on it: *She received two medals in gymnastics.* ❏ *PLURAL* **med·als.**

mem·o·ry (mem′ər ē), *NOUN.* a person, thing, or event that you can remember: *One of my favorite memories is my seventh birthday party.* ❏ *PLURAL* **mem·o·ries.**

men·tion (men′shən), *VERB.* to tell or speak about something: *I mentioned your idea to the group that is planning the picnic.* ❏ *VERB* **men·tions, men·tioned, men·tion·ing.**

min·er·al (min′ər əl), *NOUN.* a solid substance, usually dug from the Earth. Minerals often form crystals. Coal, gold, sand, and mica are minerals. Some minerals, such as iron, sodium, and zinc, are nutrients. ❏ *PLURAL* **min·er·als.**

mix·ture (miks′chər), *NOUN.* a mixed condition: *At the end of the move, I felt a mixture of relief and disappointment.*

mod·el (mod′l), *NOUN.* a small copy of something: *A globe is a model of the Earth.* ❏ *PLURAL* **mod·els.**

mur·al (myùr′əl), *NOUN.* a large picture painted on a wall. ❏ *PLURAL* **mur·als.**

mural

Nn

nar·row (nar′ō), *ADJECTIVE.* not wide; having little width; less wide than usual for its kind: *a narrow path.*

narrow

na·tive (nā′tiv), *ADJECTIVE.* belonging to someone because of that person's birth: *The United States is my native land.*

Oo

out·run (out run′), *VERB.* to run faster than someone or something: *She can outrun her older sister.* ❏ *VERB* **out·runs, out·ran, out·run·ning.**

o·ver·night (ō′vər nīt′), *ADVERB.* during the night: *She likes to stay overnight with friends.*

Pp

pace (pās), *NOUN.* a step: *He took three paces into the room.* ❏ *PLURAL* **pac·es.**

pale (pāl), *ADJECTIVE.* not bright; dim: *a pale blue.*

peak (pēk), *NOUN.* the pointed top of a mountain or hill: *We saw the snowy peaks in the distance.*

ped·es·tal (ped′i stəl), *NOUN.* a base on which a column or a statue stands.

pedestal

perch (pėrch), *VERB.* to come to rest on something; settle; sit: *A robin perches on the branch.* ❏ *VERB* **perch·es, perched, perch·ing.**

a in hat	ò in open	sh in she
ā in age	ō in all	th in thin
â in care	ô in order	ᴛʜ in then
ä in far	oi in oil	zh in measure
e in let	ou in out	ə = a in about
ē in equal	u in cup	ə = e in taken
ėr in term	ü in put	ə = i in pencil
i in it	ü in rule	ə = o in lemon
ī in ice	ch in child	ə = u in circus
o in hot	ng in long	

434

435

pitcher•quarry

pitch·er¹ (pich′ər), *NOUN*. a container made of china, glass, or silver, with a lip at one side and a handle at the other. Pitchers are used for holding and pouring out water, milk, and other liquids.

pitch·er² (pich′ər), *NOUN*. a player on a baseball team who pitches to the catcher. The batter tries to hit the ball before it gets to the catcher.

pitcher

pla·teau (pla tō′), *NOUN*. a large, flat area in the mountains or high above sea level.

pop·u·lar (pop′yə lər), *ADJECTIVE*. liked by most people: *a popular song.*

pos·ses·sion (pə zesh′ən), *NOUN*. something owned; property: *Please move your possessions from my room.* ❑ *PLURAL* **pos·ses·sions.**

pre·cip·i·ta·tion (pri sip′ə tā′shən), *NOUN*. the amount of water that falls from the air in a certain time.

pub·lic (pub′lik), *ADJECTIVE*. of or for everyone; belonging to the people: *public libraries.*

puff (puf), *VERB*. to swell up: *He puffs up his cheeks when he plays his trumpet.* ❑ *VERB* **puffs, puffed, puff·ing.**

pum·per·nick·el (pum′pər nik′əl), *NOUN*. a kind of rye bread. It is dark and firm.

Qq

quar·ry (kwôr′ē), *NOUN*. a place where stone is dug, cut, or blasted out for use in putting up buildings. ❑ *PLURAL* **quar·ries.**

436

raindrop•ruin

Rr

rain·drop (rān′drop′), *NOUN*. the water that falls in drops from the clouds. ❑ *PLURAL* **rain·drops.**

rec·i·pe (res′ə pē), *NOUN*. a set of written directions that show you how to fix something to eat: *Please give me your recipe for bread.*

reed (rēd), *NOUN*. a kind of tall grass that grows in wet places. Reeds have hollow, jointed stalks. ❑ *PLURAL* **reeds.**

reeds

re·luc·tant·ly (ri luk′tənt lē), *ADVERB*. unwillingly.

re·ply (ri plī′), *VERB*. to answer someone by words or action: *He replied with a shout.* ❑ *VERB* **re·plies, re·plied, re·ply·ing.**

res·i·dent (rez′ə dənt), *NOUN*. someone living in a place, not just a visitor: *The residents of the town are proud of its new library.* ❑ *PLURAL* **res·i·dents.**

rhythm (riŦH′əm), *NOUN*. the natural strong beat that some music or poetry has. Rhythm makes you want to clap your hands to keep time.

riv·et (riv′it), *VERB*. to fasten something with metal bolts. ❑ *VERB* **riv·ets, riv·et·ed, riv·et·ing.**

ru·in (rü′ən), *VERB*. to destroy or spoil something completely: *The rain ruined our picnic.* ❑ *VERB* **ru·ins, ru·ined, ru·in·ing.**

a in hat	ō in open	sh in she
ā in age	ò in all	th in thin
â in care	ô in order	ŦH in then
ä in far	oi in oil	zh in measure
e in let	ou in out	ə = a in about
ē in equal	u in cup	ə = e in taken
ėr in term	ů in put	ə = i in pencil
i in it	ü in rule	ə = o in lemon
ī in ice	ch in child	ə = u in circus
o in hot	ng in long	

437

scoop•souvenir

Ss

scoop (sküp), *NOUN*. a tool like a small shovel used to dip up things. A cuplike scoop is used to dish up ice cream.

scram·ble (skram′bəl), *VERB*. to make your way, especially by climbing or crawling quickly: *We scrambled up the steep, rocky hill, trying to follow the guide.* ❑ *VERB* **scram·bles, scram·bled, scram·bling.**

sculp·tor (skulp′tər), *NOUN*. an artist who makes things by cutting or shaping them. Sculptors make statues of marble, bronze, and so on.

sculptor

se·re·nade (ser′ə nād′), *NOUN*. music played or sung; tune.

set·tle (set′l), *VERB*. to set up the first towns and farms in an area: *The English settled New England.* ❑ *VERB* **set·tles, set·tled, set·tling.**

shriek (shrēk), *VERB*. to make a loud, sharp, shrill sound. People sometimes shriek because of terror, anger, pain, or joy. ❑ *VERB* **shrieks, shrieked, shriek·ing.**

sleek (slēk), *ADJECTIVE*. soft and shiny; smooth: *sleek hair.*

snick·er (snik′ər), *VERB*. to laugh in a sly, silly way: *The children snickered to each other.* ❑ *VERB* **snick·ers, snick·ered, snick·er·ing.**

snug (snug), *ADJECTIVE*. fitting your body closely: *That coat is a little too snug.*

so·cial (sō′shəl), *ADJECTIVE*. concerned with human beings as a group: *Schools and hospitals are social institutions.*

sou·ve·nir (sü′və nir′), *NOUN*. something given or kept as a reminder; keepsake: *She bought a pair of moccasins as a souvenir of her trip out West.*

438

spare•summit

spare (spâr), **1.** *ADJECTIVE*. extra: *a spare tire.* **2.** *VERB*. to show mercy to someone; decide not to harm or destroy: *He spared his enemy's life.* ❑ *VERB* **spares, spared, spar·ing.**

stamp (stamp), **1.** *NOUN*. a small piece of paper with glue on the back; postage stamp. You put stamps on letters or packages before mailing them. ❑ *PLURAL* **stamps.** **2.** *VERB*. to bring down your foot with force: *He stamped his foot in anger.* ❑ *VERB* **stamps, stamped, stamp·ing.**

stir (stėr), **1.** *VERB*. to mix something by moving it around with a spoon, stick, and so on: *Stir the sugar into the lemonade.* **2.** *VERB*. to move something: *The wind stirred the leaves.* ❑ *VERB* **stirs, stirred, stir·ring.**

stoop¹ (stüp), *NOUN*. a forward bend of the head and shoulders: *My uncle walks with a stoop.*

stoop² (stüp), *NOUN*. a porch or platform at the entrance of a house. ❑ *PLURAL* **stoops.**

stroke (strōk), **1.** *NOUN*. the act of hitting something; blow: *I drove in the nail with several strokes of the hammer.* **2.** *NOUN*. a single complete movement made over and over again: *He rowed with strong strokes of the oars.*

strug·gle (strug′əl), *VERB*. to try hard; work hard against difficulties: *The swimmer struggled successfully against the tide.* ❑ *VERB* **strug·gles, strug·gled, strug·gling.**

sum·mit (sum′it), *NOUN*. the highest point; top: *We climbed to the summit of the mountain.*

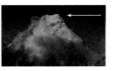

summit

a in hat	ō in open	sh in she
ā in age	ò in all	th in thin
â in care	ô in order	ŦH in then
ä in far	oi in oil	zh in measure
e in let	ou in out	ə = a in about
ē in equal	u in cup	ə = e in taken
ėr in term	ů in put	ə = i in pencil
i in it	ü in rule	ə = o in lemon
ī in ice	ch in child	ə = u in circus
o in hot	ng in long	

439

Glossary

sup·port (sə pôrt′), *VERB.* to help; aid: *Parents support and love their children.* ❑ *VERB* **sup·ports, sup·port·ed, sup·port·ing.**

swoop (swüp), *VERB.* to come down fast on something, as a hawk does when it attacks: *Bats are swooping down from the roof of the cave.* ❑ *VERB* **swoops, swooped, swoop·ing.**

sym·bol (sim′bəl), *NOUN.* an object, diagram, icon, and so on, that stands for or represents something else: *The olive branch is the symbol of peace.*

Tt

tab·let (tab′lit), *NOUN.* a small, flat surface with something written on it.

tempt (tempt), *VERB.* to appeal strongly to; attract: *That cake is tempting me.* ❑ *VERB* **tempts, tempt·ed, tempt·ing.**

tide (tīd), *NOUN.* the rise and fall of the ocean about every twelve hours. This rise and fall is caused by the gravitational pull of the moon and the sun. ❑ *PLURAL* **tides.**

torch (tôrch), *NOUN.* a long stick with material that burns at one end of it.

torch

tra·di·tion (trə dish′ən), *NOUN.* a custom or belief handed down from parents to children. ❑ *PLURAL* **tra·di·tions.**

treas·ure (trezh′ər), *NOUN.* any person or thing that is loved or valued a great deal: *The silver teapot is my parents' special treasure.*

tune (tün), *NOUN.* a piece of music; melody: *popular tunes.*

twi·light (twī′līt′), *NOUN.* the faint, soft light reflected from the sky after sunset.

twist (twist), *NOUN.* a braid formed by weaving together three or more strands of hair, ribbon, or yarn: *She wore her hair in a twist at the back of her head.*

440

Uu

un·a·ware (un′ə wâr′), *ADJECTIVE.* not aware; unconscious: *We were unaware of the approaching storm.*

un·for·get·ta·ble (un′fər get′ə bəl), *ADJECTIVE.* so good or so wonderful that you cannot forget it: *Winning the race was an unforgettable experience.*

un·veil (un vāl′), *VERB.* to remove a veil from; uncover; disclose; reveal: *She unveiled her face.* ❑ *VERB* **un·veils, un·veiled, un·veil·ing.**

Vv

val·ley (val′ē), *NOUN.* a region of low land that lies between hills or mountains. Most valleys have rivers running through them.

valley

vi·o·lent·ly (vī′ə lənt lē), *ADVERB.* acting or done with great force: *He violently signaled for the train to stop.*

Ww

wa·ter·fall (wȯ′tər fȯl′), *NOUN.* a stream of water that falls from a high place. ❑ *PLURAL* **wa·ter·falls.**

waterfall

a in hat	ȯ in open	sh in she
ā in age	ȯ in all	th in thin
â in care	ȯ in order	ŦH in then
ä in far	oi in oil	zh in measure
e in let	ou in out	ə = a in about
ē in equal	u in cup	ə = e in taken
ėr in term	ú in put	ə = i in pencil
i in it	ü in rule	ə = o in lemon
ī in ice	ch in child	ə = u in circus
o in hot	ng in long	

441

English/Spanish Selection Vocabulary List

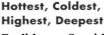

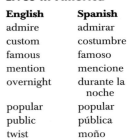

Unit 4

Wings

English	Spanish
attention	atención
complained	quejarse
drifting	flotando
giggle	risita
glaring	mirada feroz
looping	dando la vuelta
struggled	tuvo dificultad
swooping	volando en picado

Hottest, Coldest, Highest, Deepest

English	Spanish
average	promedio
depth	profundidad
deserts	desiertos
outrun	correr más rápido que
peak	cima
tides	mareas
waterfalls	cataratas

Rocks in His Head

English	Spanish
attic	ático
board	consejo
chores	quehaceres
customer	cliente
labeled	rotuló
spare	de repuesto
stamps	estampillas

Unit 5

America's Champion Swimmer: Gertrude Ederle

English	Spanish
celebrate	celebrarán
continued	siguió
current	corriente
drowned	se ahogó
medals	medallas
stirred	revolvió
strokes	brazadas

Fly, Eagle, Fly!

English	Spanish
clutched	agarraron
echoed	hicieron eco
gully	barranco
reeds	juncos
scrambled	luchó por salir
valley	valle

Suki's Kimono

English	Spanish
cotton	algodón
festival	festival
graceful	elegante
handkerchief	pañuelo
paces	pasos
pale	claro
rhythm	ritmo
snug	ceñido

How My Family Lives in America

English	Spanish
admire	admirar
custom	costumbre
famous	famoso
mention	mencione
overnight	durante la noche
popular	popular
public	pública
twist	moño

442

443

Good-Bye, 382 Shin Dang Dong

English	Spanish
airport	aeropuerto
curious	curiosa
delicious	deliciosa
described	descrito
farewell	despedida
homesick	nostálgico
memories	memorias
raindrops	gotas de lluvia

Jalapeño Bagels

English	Spanish
bakery	panadería
batch	hornada
boils	hierva
braided	trenzado
dough	masa
ingredients	ingredientes
knead	amasa
mixture	mezcla

Me and Uncle Romie

English	Spanish
cardboard	cartón
feast	festín
fierce	feroz
flights	tramos (de escalera)
pitcher	lanzador
ruined	arruinado
stoops	pórticos
treasure	tesoro

Unit 6

The Story of the Statue of Liberty

English	Spanish
crown	corona
liberty	libertad
models	maquetas
symbol	símbolo
tablet	lápida
torch	antorcha
unforgettable	inolvidable
unveiled	descubrió

Happy Birthday Mr. Kang

English	Spanish
bows	inclina
chilly	frío
foolish	tonto
foreign	extranjero
narrow	estrechas
perches	se posa
recipe	receta

Talking Walls: Art for the People

English	Spanish
encourages	anima
expression	expresión
local	locales
native	natales
settled	se asentaron
social	sociales
support	apoyar

444

445

English/Spanish Selection Vocabulary List

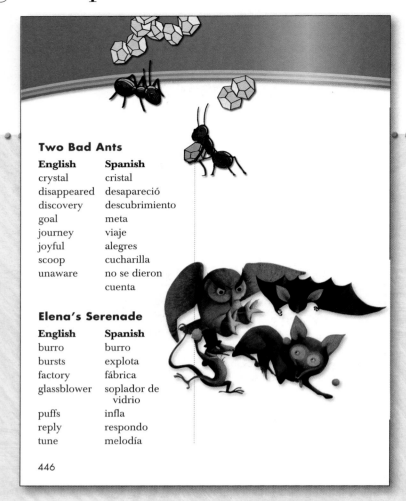

Two Bad Ants

English	Spanish
crystal	cristal
disappeared	desapareció
discovery	descubrimiento
goal	meta
journey	viaje
joyful	alegres
scoop	cucharilla
unaware	no se dieron cuenta

Elena's Serenade

English	Spanish
burro	burro
bursts	explota
factory	fábrica
glassblower	soplador de vidrio
puffs	infla
reply	respondo
tune	melodía

446

Acknowledgments

Text

16: updated From *Wings* by Christopher Myers. Published by Scholastic Press/Scholastic Inc. Copyright © 2000 by Christopher Myers. Reprinted by permission; **40:** From *Hottest, Coldest, Highest, Deepest* by Steve Jenkins. Copyright © 1998 by Steve Jenkins. Reprinted by permission of Houghton Mifflin Company. All rights reserved; **56:** Excerpt from *Factastic Book of Comparisons* by Russell Ash. Text copyright © 1997 Russell Ash. Compilation and illustrations © 1997 Dorling Kindersley Limited, London. Reprinted by permission; **64:** *Rocks in His Head* by Carol Otis Hurst. Text copyright © 2001 by Carol Otis Hurst. Used by permission of HarperCollins Publishers; **78:** From *Everybody Needs a Rock*. Text copyright © 1974 by Byrd Baylor. Reprinted with permission of Atheneum Books for Young Readers, Simon & Schuster Children's Publishing Division. All rights reserved; **90:** Text from *America's Champion Swimmer: Gertrude Ederle,* copyright © 2000 by David A. Adler, reprinted by permission of Harcourt, Inc. Illustrations from *America's Champion Swimmer: Gertrude Ederle* by David A. Adler, illustrations, copyright © 2000 by Terry Widener, reproduced by permission of Harcourt, Inc.; **108:** "Women Athletes" from Women in History: Wilma Rudolph website, www.lkwdpl.org. Courtesy of Women In History, www.lkwdpl.org/wihohio; **116:** From *Fly, Eagle, Fly!* Text copyright © 2000 by Christopher Gregorowski. Illustrations copyright © 2000 by Niki Daly. Reprinted with permission of Margaret K. McElderry Books, an Imprint of Simon & Schuster Children's Publishing Division. All rights reserved; **132:** (Updated) *Purple Coyote* by Cornette, Illustrated by Rochette. Copyright © 1997 by L'Ecole des Loisirs, Paris. First American edition 1999–Originally published in France by Pastel, 1997. English translation copyright © 1999 by Random House Inc. Published by arrangement with Random House Children's Books, a division of Random House, Inc. New York, New York. All rights reserved. Reprinted by permission; **138:** From *Because I Could Not Stop My Bike* by Karen Jo Shapiro. Text copyright © 2003 by Karen Jo Shapiro. Illustration copyright © 2003 by Matt Faulkner. Used with permission of Charlesbridge Publishing, Inc. All rights reserved; **139:** (Updated) "By Myself" from *Honey, I Love* by Eloise Greenfield. Text Copyright © 1978 by Eloise Greenfield. Used by permission of HarperCollins Publishers. Reprinted by permission of Nancy Gallt Literary Agency; **141:** "Written at the Po-Shan Monastery" by Hsin Ch'i-chi, translated by Irving Y. Lo from Sunflower Splender edited by Liu, Wu-chi and Irving Yucheng Lo, 1990. Reprinted by permission of Indiana University Press; **150:** *Suki's Kimono* written by Chieri Uegaki and Illustration by Stéphane Jorisch, is used with the permission of Kids Can Press, Ltd., Toronto. www.kidscanpress.com. Text © 2003 Chieri Uegaki. Illustrated © 2003 Stéphane Jorisch; **174:** From *How My Family Lives in America*. Copyright © 1992 by Susan Kuklin. Reprinted with permission of Simon & Schuster Books for Young Readers, Simon & Schuster Children's Publishing Division. All rights reserved; **192:** From *Scott Foresman Social Studies Communities 2003*. Copyright © 2003 Pearson Education, Inc. Reprinted by permission of Pearson Education, Inc.; **198:** (Updated) Reprinted with permission of the National Geographic Society from *Good-Bye, 382 Shin Dang Dong* by Frances Park and Ginger Park. Copyright © 2002 Frances Park and Ginger Park. Illustrations © 2002 Yangsook Choi; **218:** (Updated) Lyrics from *It's a Small World* by Richard M. Sherman & Robert B. Sherman. Words and Music by Richard M. Sherman and Robert B. Sherman. © 1963 Wonderland Music Company, Inc. Reproduced by permission; **224:** From *Jalapeño Bagels*. Copyright © 1996 by Natasha Wing. Reprinted with permission of Atheneum Books for Young Readers, Simon & Schuster Children's Publishing Division. All rights reserved; **240:** "A Happy Heart", "Native Foods", and "The Spanish Flavor" from *Viva Mexico! - The Foods* by George Ancona, 2002. Reprinted with permission of Marshall Cavendish; **248:** From *Me and Uncle Romie: A Story Inspired by the Life and Art of Romare Bearden* by Claire Hartfield, illustrated by Jerome Lagarrigue, copyright © 2002 by Claire Hartfield, text. Used by permission of Dial Books for Young Readers, A Division of Penguin Young Readers Group, A Member of Penguin Group (USA) Inc., 345 Hudson Street, New York, NY 10014. All rights reserved; **272:** (Updated) www.FactMonster.com. © Pearson Education, published as FactMonster.com; **276:** "My Friend in School" from *DeShawn Days*. Text copyright © 2001 by Tony Medina. Permission arranged with Lee & Low Books Inc., New York NY 10016; **278:** "Lunch Survey", from *Swimming Upstream: Middle Grade Poems* by Kristine O'Connell George. Text copyright © 2002 by Kristine O'Connell George. Reprinted by permission of Clarion Books, an imprint of Houghton Mifflin Company. All rights reserved; **279:** "Saying Yes" is copyright by Diana Chang. Reprinted by permission of the author; **288:** *The Story of the Statue of Liberty* by Betsy C. Maestro, illustrations by Maestro Giulio. Text copyright © 1986 by Betsy Maestro. Illustrations copyright © 1986 by Giulio Maestro. Used by permission of HarperCollins Publishers; **302:** From *Scott Foresman Social Studies Communities 2003*. Copyright © 2003 Pearson Education, Inc. Reprinted by permission of Pearson Education, Inc.; **308:** From *Happy Birthday Mr. Kang* by Susan L. Roth. Copyright © 2001 Susan L. Roth. Reprinted with permission of the National Geographic Society; **352:** (Updated) "Nathaniel's Rap" from *Nathaniel Talking* by Eloise Greenfield. Copyright © 1988 by Eloise Greenfield. Reprinted by permission of Gallt Literary Agency; **358:** (Updated) *Two Bad Ants* by Chris Van Allsburg. Copyright © 1988 by Chris Van Allsburg. Reprinted by permission of Houghton Mifflin Company. All rights reserved; **384:** From *Elena's Serenade*. Text copyright © 2004 by Campbell Geeslin. Illustrations copyright © 2004 by Ana Juan. Reprinted with permission of Atheneum Books for Young Readers, Simon & Schuster Children's Publishing Division. All rights reserved; **409:** "I Watched an Eagle Soar" from *Dancing Teepees: Poems of the North American Indian Youth* by Virginia Driving Hawk Sneve. Copyright © 1989 by Virginia Driving Hawk Sneve. Reprinted from *Dancing Teepees: Poems* by permissions of Holiday House, Inc.; **410:** "Words Free as Confetti" from *Confetti: Poems for Children*. Text copyright © 1996 by Pat Mora. Permission arranged with Lee and Low Books, Inc., New York, NY 10016.

447

Illustrations

Cover: ©Mark Buehner; **4, 10, 142-143** Bill Mayer; **13-15** Kris Wiltse; **30-35** Kyle Still; **78-85, 194-195** Franklin Hammond; **113, 355** Scott Gustafson; **145, 224-238, 439** Antonio Castro; **147-149** Shelly Hehenberger; **171** Chris Lensch; **218** Sachiko Yoshikawa; **276-278** Laurie Keller; **352-353** Jan Spivey Gilchrist; **404-406** Neil Shigley; **408-410** Stephen Daigle; **435** Teresa Flavin; **436** Wendell Minor.

Photography

Every effort has been made to secure permission and provide appropriate credit for photographic material. The publisher deeply regrets any omission and pledges to correct errors called to its attention in subsequent editions.

Unless otherwise acknowledged, all photographs are the property of Scott Foresman, a division of Pearson Education.

Photo locators denoted as follows: Top (T), Center (C), Bottom (B), Left (L), Right (R), Background (Bkgd).

6 (TR) ©Jeremy Horner/Getty Images, (TC) ©Royalty-Free/Corbis; **8** ©1991/Faith Ringgold; **16** Getty Images; **28** Getty Images; **37** (TR) ©Comstock, Inc., (BR) ©Royalty-Free/Corbis; **38** ©Dale Wilson/Masterfile Corporation; **39** (T) Getty Images, (TC) ©Ken Welsh/Age Fotostock, (BR) ©Royalty-Free/Corbis; **56** (TC, TR, CC) Getty Images, (BR) ©James Balog/Getty Images; **59** (BR, TR) Getty Images; **61** (TR) Brand X Pictures, (BR) ©Jonathan Blair/Corbis, (TR) ©Richard T. Nowitz/Corbis; **62** ©Maurice Nimmo/Frank Lane Picture Agency/Corbis; **63** (TL) ©Bill Ross/Corbis, (TR) ©Art Wolfe/Getty Images, (BR) ©Richard T. Nowitz/Corbis; **80** ©Art Wolfe/Getty Images; **87** ©Creasource/ Masterfile Corporation; **88** Brand X Pictures; **89** (T) ©Bill Bachmann/PhotoEdit, (BC) ©David Young-Wolff/PhotoEdit; **108** (TR) ©Underwood & Underwood/Corbis, (BC) ©George Silk/Time Life Pictures/Getty Images; **110** ©George Silk/Time Life Pictures/Getty Images; **111** (CL) ©George Silk/Time Life Pictures/Getty Images, (CR) ©Bettmann/Corbis; **114** Getty Images; **115** (TR, BR) ©Royalty-Free/Corbis; **144** ©Jeremy Horner/Getty Images; **166** (BR) Getty Images, (BC) ©Christie's Images/Peter Harholdt/Corbis, (BR) Art Resource, NY; **167** (TR) Art Resource, NY, (CR) ©Lynn Goldsmith/Corbis; **168** (TR) ©Historical Picture Archive/Corbis, (CR) ©Werner Forman/Corbis, (BR) Getty Images; **169** (CR) Getty Images, (TR) Corbis, (BR) ©Pavlovsky Jacques/Corbis; **172** Getty Images; **173** Getty Images; **174** Getty Images; **179** Jupiter Images; **182** Getty Images; **185** (BR) ©Creative Concept/Index Stock Imagery; **190** (TL, BR) Getty Images; **192** (BR) Morton Beebe/Corbis, (TR) Getty Images; **193** (BR) ©Steve Vidler/SuperStock, (TR) Getty Images; **196** ©Ed Bock/Corbis; **197** (TR) ©Tom Stewart/Corbis, (TC) Getty Images; **221** (T, BL) Getty Images, (CR) ©Royalty-Free/ Corbis; **222** Getty Images; **223** ©Royalty-Free/Corbis; **240-243** George Ancona; **245** (TL) ©Alan Schein Photography/ Corbis, (TR, CR) Getty Images; **246** Getty Images; **247** Getty Images; **272** (TR) ©Terry W. Eggers/Corbis, (BR) ©David Zimmerman/Corbis; **273** AP/Wide World Photos; **274** ©Duomo/Corbis; **275** (CR) ©David Thomas/PictureArts/Corbis, (BR) ©Royalty-Free/Corbis; **280** ©Jeremy Horner/Getty Images; **282** ©1991/Faith Ringgold; **283** (CR) "Reach High and You Will Go Far" © 2000 Art and Photography by Joshua Sarantitis. All Rights Reserved. Sponsored by the Philadelphia Mural Arts Program; **285** (TL) Corbis, (TR) ©Royalty-Free/Corbis, (BR) Getty Images; **286** ©Richard Berenholtz/Corbis; **287** ©Gail Mooney/Corbis; **302** (TR) ©Bettmann/Corbis, (CC) ©Jim Erickson/Corbis Stock Market; **303** ©Robert Holmes/Corbis; **306** ©Royalty-Free/Corbis; **307** Getty Images; **328** (TC) ©Steve Kaufman/Corbis, (R) ©Darrell Gulin/Corbis; **329** (TL) ©Erik Freeland/Corbis, (BR) ©Claus Meyer/Minden Pictures; **330** (TL) ©Jeff Vanuga/Corbis, (BL) ©Comstock Inc.; **331** (T) ©Jim Zipp/Photo Researchers, Inc., (BR) ©Jeff Vanuga/Corbis; **333** (T) ©Matthias Kulka/Corbis, (T) Getty Images; **337** ©Meg Saligman; **339** ©Ben Valenzuela; **340-341** ©Hector Ponce/Rich Puchalsky; **343** (C) "Reach High and You Will Go Far" ©2000 Art and Photography by Joshua Sarantitis. All Rights Reserved. Sponsored by the Philadelphia Mural Arts Program; **344** ©Paul Botello; **346** Getty Images; **347** ©David Botello; **348** Courtesy of the U.S. Capitol Historical Society; **349** (TL, B) ©Meg Saligman; **357** (T) ©M. Bahr/Peter Arnold, Inc., (CC) ©Michael & Patricia Fogden/Corbis; **378** ©Ron Watts/Corbis; **379** ©Royalty-Free/Corbis; **381** (T) ©K. M. Westermann/Corbis, (TC) ©James L. Amos/Corbis; **382** ©Kelly-Mooney Photography/Corbis; **383** ©George B. Diebold/Corbis; **412** ©1991/Faith Ringgold; **413** ©1991/Faith Ringgold; **419** Courtesy, Kids Can Press; **421** (C) ©Scholastic, Inc., (T) Philip Groshong/©Cincinatti Opera; **422** Photo of Niki Daly used with permission of Simon & Schuster, Inc.; **423** ©Ana Juan; **431** ©Walt Anderson/Visuals Unlimited; **432** (BL) ©Lawrence Migdale, (BR) Getty Images; **434** The National Park Service; **436** ©Robert Lindholm/Visuals Unlimited; **437** ©K. M. Westermann/Corbis; **438** ©Jeff Greenberg/Visuals Unlimited; **439** ©Vincent Besnault/Stone/Getty Images; **440** SuperStock; **441** Getty Images; **442** ©AFP/Getty Images; **443** ©Bob Stefko/Imagebank/Getty Images; **444** ©Manfred Rutz/Taxi/Getty Images; **445** ©Galen Rowell/Corbis; **446** ©David Madison/Imagebank/Getty Images; **447** SuperStock; **448** Getty Images.

Glossary

The contents of the glossary have been adapted from *Thorndike Barnhart School Dictionary,* copyright © 2001, Pearson Education, Inc.

448

Unit 6
Monitoring Fluency

Ongoing assessment of student reading fluency is one of the most valuable measures we have of students' reading skills. One of the most effective ways to assess fluency is taking timed samples of students' oral reading and measuring the number of words correct per minute (WCPM).

How to Measure Words Correct Per Minute—WCPM

Choose a Text
Start by choosing a text for the student to read. The text should be:
- narrative
- unfamiliar
- on grade level

Make a copy of the text for yourself and have one for the student.

Timed Reading of the Text
Tell the student: As you read this aloud, I want you to do your best reading and to read as quickly as you can. That doesn't mean it's a race. Just do your best, fast reading. When I say begin, start reading.

As the student reads, follow along in your copy. Mark words that are read incorrectly.

Incorrect	Correct
• omissions	• self-corrections within 3 seconds
• substitutions	• repeated words
• mispronunciations	
• reversals	

After One Minute
At the end of one minute, draw a line after the last word that was read. Have the student finish reading but don't count any words beyond one minute. Arrive at the words correct per minute—WCPM—by counting the total number of words that the student read correctly in one minute.

Fluency Goals
Grade 3 End-of-Year Goal = 120 WCPM

Target goals by unit

Unit 1 80 to 90 WCPM	**Unit 4** 95 to 105 WCPM
Unit 2 85 to 95 WCPM	**Unit 5** 102 to 112 WCPM
Unit 3 90 to 100 WCPM	**Unit 6** 110 to 120 WCPM

More Frequent Monitoring
You may want to monitor some children more frequently because they are falling far below grade-level benchmarks or they have a result that doesn't seem to align with their previous performance. Follow the same steps above, but choose 2 or 3 additional texts.

Fluency Progress Chart Copy the chart on the next page. Use it to record each student's progress across the year.

Writing

Assessment

Student Tips for Making Top Scores in Writing Tests

1 Use transitions such as those below to relate ideas, sentences, or paragraphs.

in addition	nevertheless	finally	however
then	instead	therefore	as a result
for example	in particular	first	such as

2 Write a good beginning. Make readers want to continue.
- I shouldn't have opened that green box.
- Imagine being locked in a crate at the bottom of the sea.
- When I was four, I saw a purple dog.
- Have you ever heard of a talking tree?

3 Focus on the topic.
If a word or detail is off-topic, get rid of it. If a sentence is unrelated or loosely related to the topic, drop it or connect it more closely.

4 Organize your ideas.
Have a plan in mind before you start writing. Your plan can be a list, bulleted items, or a graphic organizer. Five minutes spent planning your work will make the actual writing go much faster and smoother.

5 Support your ideas.
- Develop your ideas with fully elaborated examples and details.
- Make ideas clear to readers by choosing vivid words that create pictures. Avoid dull *(get, go, say)*, vague *(thing, stuff, lots of)*, or overused *(really, very)* words.
- Use a voice that is appropriate to your audience.

6 Make writing conventions as error-free as possible.
Proofread your work line by line, sentence by sentence. Read for correct punctuation, then again for correct capitalization, and finally for correct spelling.

7 Write a conclusion that wraps things up but is more than a repeating of ideas or "The end."
- After all, he was my brother, weird or not.
- The Internet has changed our lives for better and for worse.
- It's not the largest planet but the one I'd choose to live on.
- Now tell me you don't believe in a sixth sense.

Writing Traits

Rubric

Focus/Ideas

Organization/
Paragraphs

Voice

Word Choice

Sentences

Conventions

- **Focus/Ideas** refers to the main purpose for writing and the details that make the subject clear and interesting. It includes development of ideas through support and elaboration.

- **Organization/Paragraphs** refers to the overall structure of a piece of writing that guides readers. Within that structure, transitions show how ideas, sentences, and paragraphs are connected.

- **Voice** shows the writer's unique personality and establishes a connection between writer and reader. Voice, which contributes to style, should be suited to the audience and the purpose for writing.

- **Word Choice** is the use of precise, vivid words to communicate effectively and naturally. It helps create style through the use of specific nouns, lively verbs and adjectives, and accurate, well-placed modifiers.

- **Sentences** covers strong, well-built sentences that vary in length and type. Skillfully written sentences have pleasing rhythms and flow fluently.

- **Conventions** refers to mechanical correctness and includes grammar, usage, spelling, punctuation, capitalization, and paragraphing.

Writing Workshop

Research Report

OBJECTIVES

● Develop an understanding of a research report.

● Find information in printed and electronic resources.

● Write good paragraphs with topic sentences.

● Establish criteria for evaluating a research report.

Key Features

Research Report

In a research report, a writer gathers and organizes facts from several sources.

● Is an informational article based on research

● Has complete, accurate information

● Presents facts in an organized way

● Has clear topic sentences and supporting details

Connect to Weekly Writing

Week 1	Taking Notes 303g–303h
Week 2	Outlining 331g–331h
Week 3	Informational Paragraph 353g–353h
Week 4	Write About a Picture 379g–379h
Week 5	Write Good Paragraphs 407g–407h

Strategic Intervention

See Differentiated Instruction p. WA8.

Advanced

See Differentiated Instruction p. WA9.

ELL

See Differentiated Instruction p. WA9.

Additional Resource for Writing

Writing Rubrics and Anchor Papers, pp. 34–38.

WA2 *Freedom*

Writing Prompt: Freedom

Write a research report about a monument or statue that symbolizes freedom in the United States. Discuss the monument itself, its history, and why it is important. Find information in sources such as books, magazines, CD-ROMs, and the Internet.

Purpose: Give information about a monument

Audience: Classmates interested in history

READ LIKE A WRITER

Look back at *The Story of the Statue of Liberty.* Point out that to write the article, the author gathered and organized information about the Statue of Liberty, a symbol of freedom in America. Explain that a research report also contains information that the writer gathers and organizes.

EXAMINE THE MODEL AND RUBRIC

GUIDED WRITING Read the model aloud. Have students identify the topic sentence and detail sentences in each paragraph. Discuss how the model reflects traits of good writing.

The Lincoln Memorial

The Lincoln Memorial in Washington, D.C., is one of our country's great monuments. It stands for freedom because it honors Abraham Lincoln. Lincoln, the United States president during the Civil War, helped bring freedom to all Americans.

The Lincoln Memorial is built of white marble. It is rectangular and has 36 columns. It looks like an ancient Greek building. The 36 columns stand for the 36 states in the United States when Lincoln was president.

Inside the Lincoln Memorial are three rooms. A statue of Lincoln sitting in a chair is in the center room. It is 19 feet tall! The other rooms display paintings and two of Lincoln's most famous speeches. They are the Gettysburg Address and the Second Inaugural Address.

The Lincoln Memorial was dedicated in 1922. It has the Potomac River on one side. The Washington Monument can be seen on the other side. The Lincoln Memorial is beautiful. It overlooks Washington and honors a great president. For all these reasons, the Lincoln Memorial is one of Americans' favorite monuments.

▲ **Writing Transparency** WP36

Traits of a Good Research Report

Focus/Ideas	Report focuses on a monument to freedom in the United States.
Organization/ Paragraphs	The report consists of several good paragraphs with topic sentences and a strong conclusion.
Voice	Writer shows thoughtfulness, originality, and thoroughness of research.
Word Choice	Writer uses vivid and precise words. (*rectangular, ancient Greek*).
Sentences	Writer uses sentences of different kinds and includes both simple and compound sentences.
Conventions	Writer has good control of spelling, grammar, capitalization, and usage.

▲ **Writing Transparency** WP37

FINDING A TOPIC

- With students, brainstorm some monuments that stand for freedom, such as the Washington Monument, Lincoln Memorial, and the Liberty Bell. Write a list on the board, raising questions that need clarification and/or direct investigation.

- Have students sort through memories of statues and monuments they have visited by looking through journals and photo albums.

- Have students investigate Washington, D.C., finding pictures and facts about monuments located there.

Tech Files ONLINE **ONLINE INVESTIGATION** Students can easily access information online with the right search engines and keywords. They can narrow broad topics *(monuments)* by using several keywords *(Washington, D.C., monuments)*. They can sift through information quickly to select or refine a subject. Remind students to take accurate notes and write sources.

PREWRITING STRATEGY

GUIDED WRITING Display Writing Transparency WP38. Model how to complete a K-W-L Chart.

Think Aloud **MODEL** This student knows some general facts about the Washington Monument. The student asks questions about the monument that can be answered by finding information in the library and online. The controlling question will help focus the research.

PREWRITING ACTIVITIES

- Have students use Grammar and Writing Practice Book p. 180 to research and narrow their topic.

- Students can make an outline based on the notes they take during research.

Outline

I. Appearance
   A. Tall, thin pillar
   B. 55 feet square at bottom
   C. Pyramidion at top
   D. White marble

K-W-L Chart

Fill out this K-W-L chart to help you organize your ideas.

Topic Washington Monument

What I **Know**	What I **Want** to Know	What I **Learned**
The Washington Monument is in Washington, D.C.	How tall is the Washington Monument?	The Washington Monument is 555 feet tall.
It honors our first President.	When was it built?	It was begun in 1848 and completed in 1884.
It is tall and white.	What is inside it?	The inside is hollow, with an elevator and 898 steps.

Controlling Question

Why is the Washington Monument so special to Americans?

Unit 6 Research Report • PREWRITE   Writing Process **38**

▲ **Writing Transparency** WP38

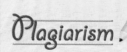

Plagiarism

Tell students to take notes on the sources they use. Any exact phrases or sentences they use must appear in quotation marks. They should also acknowledge others' ideas and wording that is close to the original.

K-W-L Chart

Directions Fill out this K-W-L chart to help you organize your ideas.

Topic _____

What I **Know**	What I **Want** to Know	What I **Learned**
Answers should include details about each element of the research report.		

Controlling Question _____

180 Unit 6   Grammar and Writing Practice Book

▲ **Grammar and Writing Practice Book** p. 180

Writing Workshop

1 PREWRITE — 2 DRAFT — 3 REVISE — 4 EDIT — 5 PUBLISH

Think Like a Writer

Write an Interesting Introduction Your first paragraph tells your readers the main topic of your report and its focus. The first paragraph should also be interesting so that readers will want to keep reading. You might use a question, a quotation, or an interesting anecdote to both state the report's topic and motivate readers to keep reading.

Support Writing If students include home-language words in their drafts, help them find English words to replace them. Resources can include
• conversations with you
• other home-language speakers
• bilingual dictionaries, if available
• online translation sources

Topic and Detail Sentences

A topic sentence tells the main idea of a paragraph. Detail sentences give supporting facts, descriptions, and examples about the main idea.

Directions Decide how you will organize your paragraphs. Then write a topic sentence and supporting details for each paragraph.

Paragraph 1
Topic Sentence **Answers should be topic**
Detail Sentences **sentences and supporting details on the research topic.**

Paragraph 2
Topic Sentence _____
Detail Sentences _____

Paragraph 3
Topic Sentence _____
Detail Sentences _____

Paragraph 4
Topic Sentence _____
Detail Sentences _____

Grammar and Writing Practice Book   Unit 6 **181**

▲ **Grammar and Writing Practice Book** p. 181

WRITING THE FIRST DRAFT

GUIDED WRITING Use Writing Transparency WP39 to practice using topic sentences.

• Remind students that the topic sentence states the main idea of a paragraph, and all the supporting sentences focus on that topic.

• Have students decide which topic sentence best states the main idea of each group of detail sentences in Exercise 1, and think of a topic sentence to go with the details in Exercise 2.

MODEL A topic sentence states a main idea. I can see how the main idea in each topic sentence here is reflected in a group of details. Details in item 1, such as the experiments with crops, the improved copying device, and the founding of the University of Virginia, name Jefferson's different interests. Item 2 mentions the white marble, round dome, and water reflecting on white columns—all aspects of the monument's beauty. Item 3 mentions the handshake and the round table, both changes Jefferson introduced.

Topic and Detail Sentences

A **topic sentence** tells the main idea of a paragraph. The topic sentence is often the first sentence of an informational paragraph.

Directions Read the three topic sentences below. Write the sentence that would be the best topic sentence for each numbered group of details. **Possible answers:**

The Jefferson Memorial is one of the most beautiful monuments in Washington. Jefferson started new customs that made the presidency seem less formal. After retiring from the presidency, Jefferson pursued many interests.

1. He experimented with new crops and farming techniques. He improved a copying device called the *polygraph* to preserve all the letters he wrote. In 1825, he founded the University of Virginia.
After retiring from the presidency, Jefferson pursued many interests.

2. The Jefferson Memorial is made of white marble. It has a round dome and is at the edge of a body of water that reflects its white columns.
The Jefferson Memorial is one of the most beautiful monuments in Washington.

3. He requested that people greet the President with a handshake rather than a bow. He seated dinner guests at round tables so that everyone would feel equally important.
Jefferson started new customs that made the presidency seem less formal.

Directions Write a topic sentence for the following details.
Some monuments honor great people. Other monuments honor people who fought in wars. Still others honor ideas, such as freedom.
Monuments are built for a variety of purposes.

Unit 6 Research Report • DRAFT   Writing Process **39**

▲ **Writing Transparency** WP39

WRITER'S CRAFT Strong Conclusions

Here are some ways writers can conclude a research report.
• Use a quotation.
• Give a final interesting example.
• Ask a question or make a suggestion in the form of a command.

DRAFTING STRATEGIES

• Have students review their K-W-L charts and notes before they write.

• Students can make a generalization from their notes to serve as a topic sentence for each paragraph.

• Remind them to keep their audience and purpose in mind.

• Students may use one of the ideas above for a conclusion.

• Have students use Grammar and Writing Practice Book, p. 181 to organize their paragraphs.

WRITER'S CRAFT Elaboration

COMBINE SENTENCES Explain that one way to elaborate is to combine sentences. Students can combine two short simple sentences to make a compound sentence. They can also combine two sentences with the same subject or the same predicate.

| Choppy | The Washington Monument is beautiful. Most Americans recognize the Washington Monument. |
| Improved | The Washington Monument is beautiful, and most Americans recognize it. |

Use Grammar and Writing Practice Book p. 182 to practice elaboration by combining sentences.

REVISING STRATEGIES

GUIDED WRITING Use Writing Transparency WP40 to model revising. Point out the Revising Marks, which students should use when they revise their work.

MODEL This is part of the research report about the Washington Monument.

First, the writer has revised the topic sentence. Second, the writer combines two short, choppy sentences to make one compound sentence. In the last sentence, the writer has added words to make the details more precise.

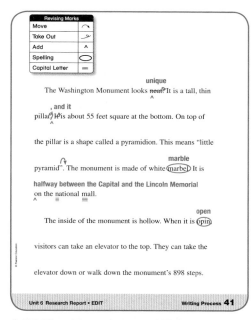

Revising Marks	
Move	⌒
Take Out	✄
Add	∧
Spelling	◯
Capital Letter	═

                  unique

The Washington Monument looks ~~neat~~. It is a tall, thin

    , and it

pillar. It is about 55 feet square at the bottom. On top of

the pillar is a shape called a pyramidion. This means "little

                      marble

pyramid". The monument is made of white ◯marble◯. It is

halfway between the Capital and the Lincoln Memorial

on the national mall.

                              open

   The inside of the monument is hollow. When it is ◯opin◯

visitors can take an elevator to the top. They can take the

elevator down or walk down the monument's 898 steps.

Unit 6 Research Report • EDIT   **Writing Process 41**

▲ **Writing Transparency** WP41

PEER REVISION Write the Revising Checklist on the board or make copies to distribute. Students can use this checklist to revise their research reports. Have partners read one another's first drafts. Remind them to be courteous and specific with suggestions.

Citing Sources You may want to have students list their sources at the end of the research report. Here are examples.

Internet Article "Statues and Memorials: The Washington Monument." November 3, 2003. www.thepagesofhistory.com

Magazine Markham, Lois. "Washington, D.C." *Kids Discover* (2002): 10–12.

Book Nelson, Kristin L. *The Washington Monument.* Lerner Publications, 2003. pp. 8–10.

Trait Checklist

REVISING

Focus/Ideas
✔ Is the research report focused on facts about a monument?
✔ Does the report have details that support the main ideas?

Organization/Paragraphs
✔ Does each paragraph have a topic sentence and supporting sentences?

Voice
✔ Does the report show that the writer is interested in the topic?

Word Choice
✔ Are vivid, precise words used?

Sentences
✔ Have short, choppy sentences or sentences with the same subjects or predicates been combined?

Elaboration
Combine Sentences

When you **combine sentences,** you join two sentences that are about the same topic. You make them into one sentence.
• You can join two simple sentences and make a compound sentence. Add a comma and a conjunction such as *and, but,* or *or.*
• You can combine two sentences that have the same subject or the same predicate.

Directions Use the word in ( ) to combine each pair of sentences. Remember to add a comma.

1. There are many monuments in Washington. Many people visit them. (and)
There are many monuments in Washington, and many people visit them.

2. Some monuments honor presidents. Others honor soldiers and other ordinary people. (but) **Some monuments honor presidents, but others honor soldiers and other ordinary people.**

Directions Combine the sentences. Use the underlined words only once in your new sentence.

3. Some monuments <u>are made of white marble</u>. Some statues <u>are made of white marble</u>.
Some monuments and statues are made of white marble.

182 Unit 6   **Grammar and Writing Practice Book**

▲ **Grammar and Writing Practice Book** p. 182

Writing Workshop

1 PREWRITE 2 DRAFT 3 REVISE **4 EDIT** 5 PUBLISH

Monitor Progress

Differentiated Instruction

If... students are using commas incorrectly,	then... review the grammar lesson on pp. 379e–379f.

Editing Checklist

✔ Did I capitalize proper nouns?

✔ Did I use quotation marks correctly?

✔ Do my subjects and verbs agree?

✔ Did I spell words with a schwa sound in an unaccented syllable correctly?

Support Writing Invite students to read their drafts aloud to you. Observe whether they seem to note any spelling or grammatical errors by stumbling or self-correcting. Return to those errors and explain how to correct them. Use the appropriate Grammar Transition Lessons in the ELL and Transition Handbook to explicitly teach the English conventions.

EDITING STRATEGY

LINE BY LINE Suggest that students use an editing strategy. They can check their work one line at a time. Have them focus on areas such as subject-verb agreement, capitalization, comma usage, and spelling.

GUIDED WRITING Use Writing Transparency WP41 to model the process of editing line by line. Indicate the Proofreading Marks, which students should use when they edit their work. Write the Editing Checklist on the board or make copies to distribute. Students can use this checklist to edit their work.

 MODEL I am going to edit the paper by looking at one line at a time. The first two lines look good. In the third sentence, I see that the end punctuation mark is outside the quotation marks. It should be inside the quotation marks. In the next line, I see a misspelled word, *marbel.* I correct the spelling to *marble.* I capitalize *National Mall* because it is the name of a special place. Another misspelled word, *opin,* must be changed to *open.*

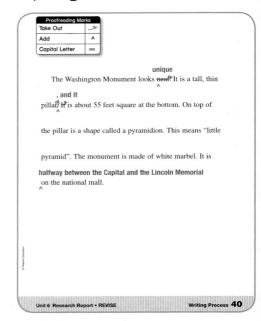

Proofreading Marks	
Take Out	↶
Add	∧
Capital Letter	=

unique
The Washington Monument looks neat. It is a tall, thin
, and it
pillar. It is about 55 feet square at the bottom. On top of
the pillar is a shape called a pyramidion. This means "little
pyramid". The monument is made of white marbel. It is
halfway between the Capital and the Lincoln Memorial
on the national mall.

Unit 6 Research Report • REVISE   Writing Process **40**

▲ **Writing Transparency** WP40

 **OFFLINE**

USING TECHNOLOGY Students who have written or revised their reports on computers should keep these points in mind as they edit:

- If your program has a grammar checker, use it to check the grammar. But do not rely on this feature exclusively. A good grammar book is the best resource.

- Do not rely on search engines for getting consistent accurate information. Note that you can access reliable information from encyclopedias, dictionaries, and other reference sources online.

- If your work is more than a single page, you may wish to use the header or footer feature in the menu to include a page number.

SELF-EVALUATION

Prepare students to fill out a Self-Evaluation Guide. Display Writing Transparency WP42 to model the self-evaluation process.

Think Aloud

MODEL I would give the report a *4*.

Focus/Ideas The report focuses on the Washington Monument.

Organization/Paragraphs Each paragraph has a topic sentence and details that support the main idea.

Voice The writer shows interest and enthusiasm in the topic.

Word Choice The writer uses vivid words (*giant, unique, hollow*).

Sentences Sentences are of different lengths and kinds.

Conventions Grammar, capitalization, and spelling are excellent.

EVALUATION Assign Grammar and Writing Practice Book p. 183. Tell students that when they evaluate their own reports, assigning a score of 3, 2, or even 1 does not necessarily indicate a bad paper. The ability to identify areas for improvement in future writing is a valuable skill.

The Washington Monument

What is the tallest building in Washington, D.C.? No, it is not a giant office building. It is the Washington Monument. This 555-foot-tall building was completed in 1884 to honor America's first President.

The Washington Monument looks unique. It is a tall, thin pillar, and it is about 55 feet square at the bottom. On top of the pillar is a shape called a pyramidion. This means "little pyramid." The monument is made of white marble. It is halfway between the Capitol and the Lincoln Memorial on the National Mall.

The inside of the monument is hollow. When it is open, visitors can take an elevator to the top. They can take the elevator down or walk down the monument's 898 steps.

The cornerstone of the Washington Monument was laid in 1848 on an important date: July 4. From that day on, the building has been a symbol of freedom and a great monument to George Washington, the "Father of Our Country."

Unit 6 Research Report • PUBLISH   Writing Process **42**

▲ **Writing Transparency** WP42

Self-Evaluation Guide
Research Report

Directions Think about the final draft of your report. Then rate yourself on a scale of from 4 to 1 (4 is the highest) on each writing trait. After you fill out the chart, answer the questions.

Writing Traits	4	3	2	1
Focus/Ideas				
Organization/Paragraphs				
Voice				
Word Choice				
Sentences				
Conventions				

1. What is the best part of your research report?
   Students' responses should show that they have given thought to the reports they have written.

2. Write one thing you would change about this research report if you had the chance to write it again.

Grammar and Writing Practice Book   Unit 6 **183**

▲ **Grammar and Writing Practice Book** p. 183

Scoring Rubric Research Report

Rubric 4 3 2 1	4	3	2	1
Focus/Ideas	Report well focused on topic	Report generally well focused	Report needing sharper focus	Report lacking focus
Organization/ Paragraphs	Strong topic sentences and many supporting details	Fairly strong topic sentences and good details	Inadequate topic sentences and details	No topic sentences; few details
Voice	Interested, informed voice	Voice somewhat interested, informed	Vaguely interested voice	Uninterested or uninformed voice
Word Choice	Many vivid, precise words	Some vivid, precise words	Few vivid, precise words	No use of vivid, precise words
Sentences	Clear, varied sentences	Mostly clear sentences with some variety	Some unclear sentences; little variety	Incoherent sentences; no variety
Conventions	Few, if any, errors	Few errors	Errors that detract from writing	Seriously flawed writing

For 6-, 5-, and 3-point Scoring Rubrics, see pp. WA11–WA14.

Writing Workshop

Research Report
Differentiated Instruction

Strategic Intervention

MODIFY THE PROMPT

Show students a book with facts about and illustrations of important American statues and monuments, such as the Liberty Bell, the Washington Monument, the Jefferson Memorial, and the Lincoln Memorial. Briefly explain what each monument honors and why it is unique.

WRITING PROMPT: Freedom

Write a research report about a monument or statue that symbolizes freedom in the United States. Discuss the monument itself, its history, and why it is important. Find information in sources such as books, magazines, CD-ROMs, and the Internet.

Purpose: Give information about a monument

Audience: Classmates interested in history

Pick One

MODIFY INSTRUCTION

ALTERNATIVE PROMPTS

ALTERNATIVE PROMPTS: Expository Writing

Strategic Intervention Find an article about a monument in an encyclopedia. Write three facts about the monument in your own words. Write a topic sentence that states the main idea of your facts. Add sentences with supporting details.

On-Level You are writing a travel brochure for people who want to visit monuments in Washington, D.C., Find facts about one monument in two sources. Write two or three paragraphs with facts that visitors would want to know.

Advanced Write a research report about a monument that honors a group of people, such as the Vietnam Veterans Memorial or the U.S. Marine Corps War Memorial. Explain why this memorial is especially important to a particular group of people.

PREWRITING SUPPORT

- Have students who are working on the same topic work together to find information on the Internet or in the library.

- Show a film or slide show on American monuments and other symbols of freedom such as the Liberty Bell and the Statue of Liberty.

- Interview students about the topic they have chosen for their research reports. Take notes on students' remarks. Circle ideas that could serve as topic sentences.

OPTIONS

- Give students the option of writing a group report under your supervision.

CHECK PROGRESS Segment the assignment into manageable pieces. Check work at intervals, such as notes, outlines, and first drafts, to make sure writing is on track.

Advanced

MODIFY THE PROMPT

Expect advanced writers to produce a report with some details that are not found in every source. Look for strong focus and organization. Expect students to use vivid, precise words. The research report should be 300–400 words. Require at least four sources and a bibliography.

APPLY SKILLS

- As students revise their work, have them consider ways to improve it.
- Combine sentences for variety.
- Include at least one quotation.
- Write a strong conclusion.

OPTIONS

- Students can follow these steps to create their own class rubrics.
  1. Read examples of class research reports and rank them 1–4, with 4 the highest.
  2. Discuss how they arrived at each rank.
  3. Isolate the six traits and make a rubric based on them.

CHECK PROGRESS Discuss the students' Self-Evaluation Guides. Work with students to monitor their growth and identify their strengths and weaknesses as writers.

ELL

MODIFY THE PROMPT

Allow beginning speakers to name key ideas they would like to include in their report. Help them restate the ideas in complete sentences. Record the sentences and have students copy them.

BUILD BACKGROUND

- Write the word *research* on the board. Underline the word part *search.* Explain that when people research, they search in books, magazines, and other sources for facts already gathered by someone else. Since the facts were previously found and written, research report writers must give credit to those writers and not copy their words. Discuss the list of Key Features of a research report that appears in the left column of p. WA2.

OPTIONS

- As students write their reports, guide them toward books, magazines, or Web sites that provide comprehension support through features such as the following:

  detailed photographs or illustrations

  labeled diagrams

  strong picture/text correspondence

  text in the home language

- For more suggestions on scaffolding the Writing Workshop, see the ELL and Transition Handbook.

CHECK PROGRESS You may need to explain certain traits and help students fill out their Self-Evaluation Guides. Downplay conventions and focus more on ideas. Recognize examples of vocabulary growth and efforts to use language in more complex ways.

Scoring Rubric | Look Back and Write

2 points The response indicates that the student has a complete understanding of the reading concept embodied in the task. The response is accurate, complete, and fulfills all the requirements of the task. Necessary support and/or examples are included, and the information given is clearly text-based.

1 point The response indicates that the student has a partial understanding of the reading concept embodied in the task. The response includes information that is essentially correct and text-based, but the information is too general or too simplistic. Some of the support and/or examples may be incomplete or omitted.

0 points The response indicates that the student does not demonstrate an understanding of the reading concept embodied in the task. The student has either failed to respond or has provided a response that is inaccurate or has insufficient information.

Scoring Rubric | Look Back and Write

4 points The response indicates that the student has a thorough understanding of the reading concept embodied in the task. The response is accurate, complete, and fulfills all the requirements of the task. Necessary support and/or examples are included, and the information is clearly text-based.

3 points The response indicates that the student has an understanding of the reading concept embodied in the task. The response is accurate and fulfills all the requirements of the task, but the required support and/or details are not complete or clearly text-based.

2 points The response indicates that the student has a partial understanding of the reading concept embodied in the task. The response that includes information is essentially correct and text-based, but the information is too general or too simplistic. Some of the support and/or examples and requirements of the task may be incomplete or omitted.

1 point The response indicates that the student has a very limited understanding of the reading concept embodied in the task. The response is incomplete, may exhibit many flaws, and may not address all requirements of the task.

0 points The response indicates that the student does not demonstrate an understanding of the reading concept embodied in the task. The student has either failed to respond or has provided a response that is inaccurate or has insufficient information.

Scoring Rubric — Narrative Writing

Rubric 4 3 2 1

	6	5	4	3	2	1
Focus/Ideas	Excellent, focused narrative; well elaborated with quality details	Good, focused narrative; elaborated with telling details	Narrative focused; adequate elaboration	Generally focused narrative; some supporting details	Sometimes unfocused narrative; needs more supporting details	Rambling narrative; lacks development and detail
Organization/Paragraphs	Strong beginning, middle, and end; appropriate order words	Coherent beginning, middle, and end; some order words	Beginning, middle, and end easily identifiable	Recognizable beginning, middle, and end; some order words	Little direction from beginning to end; few order words	Lacks beginning, middle, end; incorrect or no order words
Voice	Writer closely involved; engaging personality	Reveals personality	Pleasant but not compelling voice	Sincere voice but not fully engaged	Little writer involvement, personality	Careless writing with no feeling
Word Choice	Vivid, precise words that bring story to life	Clear words to bring story to life	Some specific word pictures	Language adequate but lacks color	Generally limited or redundant language	Vague, dull, or misused words
Sentences	Excellent variety of sentences; natural rhythm	Varied lengths, styles; generally smooth	Correct sentences with some variations in style	Correctly constructed sentences; some variety	May have simple, awkward, or wordy sentences; little variety	Choppy; many incomplete or run-on sentences
Conventions	Excellent control; few or no errors	No serious errors to affect understanding	General mastery of conventions but some errors	Reasonable control; few distracting errors	Weak control; enough errors to affect understanding	Many errors that prevent understanding

Scoring Rubric — Narrative Writing

Rubric 4 3 2 1

	5	4	3	2	1
Focus/Ideas	Excellent, focused narrative; well elaborated with quality details	Good, focused narrative; elaborated with telling details	Generally focused narrative; some supporting details	Sometimes unfocused narrative; needs more supporting details	Rambling narrative; lacks development and detail
Organization/Paragraphs	Strong beginning, middle, and end; appropriate order words	Coherent beginning, middle, and end; some order words	Recognizable beginning, middle, and end; some order words	Little direction from beginning to end; few order words	Lacks beginning, middle, end; incorrect or no order words
Voice	Writer closely involved; engaging personality	Reveals personality	Sincere voice but not fully engaged	Little writer involvement, personality	Careless writing with no feeling
Word Choice	Vivid, precise words that bring story to life	Clear words to bring story to life	Language adequate but lacks color	Generally limited or redundant language	Vague, dull, or misused words
Sentences	Excellent variety of sentences; natural rhythm	Varied lengths, styles; generally smooth	Correctly constructed sentences; some variety	May have simple, awkward, or wordy sentences; little variety	Choppy; many incomplete or run-on sentences
Conventions	Excellent control; few or no errors	No serious errors to affect understanding	Reasonable control; few distracting errors	Weak control; enough errors to affect understanding	Many errors that prevent understanding

Scoring Rubric — Narrative Writing

Rubric 4 3 2 1

	3	2	1
Focus/Ideas	Excellent, focused narrative; well elaborated with quality details	Generally focused narrative; some supporting details	Rambling narrative; lacks development and detail
Organization/Paragraphs	Strong beginning, middle, and end; appropriate order words	Recognizable beginning, middle, and end; some order words	Lacks beginning, middle, end; incorrect or no order words
Voice	Writer closely involved; engaging personality	Sincere voice but not fully engaged	Careless writing with no feeling
Word Choice	Vivid, precise words that bring story to life	Language adequate but lacks color	Vague, dull, or misused words
Sentences	Excellent variety of sentences; natural rhythm	Correctly constructed sentences; some variety	Choppy; many incomplete or run-on sentences
Conventions	Excellent control; few or no errors	Reasonable control; few distracting errors	Many errors that prevent understanding

Scoring Rubric — Descriptive Writing

Rubric 4 3 2 1

	6	5	4	3	2	1
Focus/Ideas	Excellent, focused description; well elaborated with quality details	Good, focused description; elaborated with telling details	Description focused; good elaboration	Generally focused description; some supporting details	Sometimes unfocused description; needs more supporting details	Rambling description; l development and detai
Organization/ Paragraphs	Compelling ideas enhanced by order, structure, and transitions	Appealing order, structure, and transitions	Structure identifiable and suitable; transitions used	Adequate order, structure, and some transitions to guide reader	Little direction from beginning to end; few transitions	Lacks direction and identifiable structure; no transitions
Voice	Writer closely involved; engaging personality	Reveals personality	Pleasant but not compelling voice	Sincere voice but not fully engaged	Little writer involvement, personality	Careless writing with no feeling
Word Choice	Vivid, precise words that create memorable pictures	Clear, interesting words to bring description to life	Some specific word pictures	Language adequate; appeals to senses	Generally limited or redundant language	Vague, dull, or misused words
Sentences	Excellent variety of sentences; natural rhythm	Varied lengths, styles; generally smooth	Correct sentences with variations in style	Correctly constructed sentences; some variety	May have simple, awkward, or wordy sentences; little variety	Choppy; many incomple run-on sentences
Conventions	Excellent control; few or no errors	No serious errors to affect understanding	General mastery of conventions but some errors	Reasonable control; few distracting errors	Weak control; enough errors to affect understanding	Many errors that preve understanding

Scoring Rubric — Descriptive Writing

Rubric 4 3 2 1

	5	4	3	2	1
Focus/Ideas	Excellent, focused description; well elaborated with quality details	Good, focused description; elaborated with telling details	Generally focused description; some supporting details	Sometimes unfocused description; needs more supporting details	Rambling description; lacks development and detail
Organization/ Paragraphs	Compelling ideas enhanced by order, structure, and transitions	Appealing order, structure, and transitions	Adequate order, structure, and some transitions to guide reader	Little direction from beginning to end; few transitions	Lacks direction and identifiable structure; no transitions
Voice	Writer closely involved; engaging personality	Reveals personality	Sincere voice but not fully engaged	Little writer involvement, personality	Careless writing with no feeling
Word Choice	Vivid, precise words that create memorable pictures	Clear, interesting words to bring description to life	Language adequate; appeals to senses	Generally limited or redundant language	Vague, dull, or misused words
Sentences	Excellent variety of sentences; natural rhythm	Varied lengths, styles; generally smooth	Correctly constructed sentences; some variety	May have simple, awkward, or wordy sentences; little variety	Choppy; many incomplete or run-on sentences
Conventions	Excellent control; few or no errors	No serious errors to affect understanding	Reasonable control; few distracting errors	Weak control; enough errors to affect understanding	Many errors that prevent understanding

Scoring Rubric — Descriptive Writing

Rubric 4 3 2 1

	3	2	1
Focus/Ideas	Excellent, focused description; well elaborated with quality details	Generally focused description; some supporting details	Rambling description; lacks development and detail
Organization/ Paragraphs	Compelling ideas enhanced by order, structure, and transitions	Adequate order, structure, and some transitions to guide reader	Lacks direction and identifiable structure; no transitions
Voice	Writer closely involved; engaging personality	Sincere voice but not fully engaged	Careless writing with no feeling
Word Choice	Vivid, precise words that create memorable pictures	Language adequate; appeals to senses	Vague, dull, or misused words
Sentences	Excellent variety of sentences; natural rhythm	Correctly constructed sentences; some variety	Choppy; many incomplete or run-on sentences
Conventions	Excellent control; few or no errors	Reasonable control; few distracting errors	Many errors that prevent understanding

Scoring Rubric — Persuasive Writing

Rubric 4 3 2 1

	6	5	4	3	2	1
Focus/Ideas	Persuasive argument carefully built with quality details	Persuasive argument well supported with details	Persuasive argument focused; good elaboration	Persuasive argument with one or two convincing details	Persuasive piece sometimes unfocused; needs more support	Rambling persuasive argument; lacks development and detail
Organization/ Paragraphs	Information chosen and arranged for maximum effect	Evident progression of persuasive ideas	Progression and structure evident	Information arranged in a logical way with some lapses	Little structure or direction	No identifiable structure
Voice	Writer closely involved; persuasive but not overbearing	Maintains persuasive tone	Persuasive but not compelling voice	Sometimes uses persuasive voice	Little writer involvement, personality	Shows little conviction
Word Choice	Persuasive words carefully chosen for impact	Argument supported by persuasive language	Uses some persuasive words	Occasional persuasive language	Generally limited or redundant language	Vague, dull, or misused words; no persuasive words
Sentences	Excellent variety of sentences; natural rhythm	Varied lengths, styles; generally smooth	Correct sentences with variations in style	Carefully constructed sentences; some variety	Simple, awkward, or wordy sentences; little variety	Choppy; many incomplete or run-on sentences
Conventions	Excellent control; few or no errors	No serious errors to affect understanding	General mastery of conventions but some errors	Reasonable control; few distracting errors	Weak control; enough errors to affect understanding	Many errors that prevent understanding

Scoring Rubric — Persuasive Writing

Rubric 4 3 2 1

	5	4	3	2	1
Focus/Ideas	Persuasive argument carefully built with quality details	Persuasive argument well supported with details	Persuasive argument with one or two convincing details	Persuasive piece sometimes unfocused; needs more support	Rambling persuasive argument; lacks development and detail
Organization/ Paragraphs	Information chosen and arranged for maximum effect	Evident progression of persuasive ideas	Information arranged in a logical way with some lapses	Little structure or direction	No identifiable structure
Voice	Writer closely involved; persuasive but not overbearing	Maintains persuasive tone	Sometimes uses persuasive voice	Little writer involvement, personality	Shows little conviction
Word Choice	Persuasive words carefully chosen for impact	Argument supported by persuasive language	Occasional persuasive language	Generally limited or redundant language	Vague, dull, or misused words; no persuasive words
Sentences	Excellent variety of sentences; natural rhythm	Varied lengths, styles; generally smooth	Carefully constructed sentences; some variety	Simple, awkward, or wordy sentences; little variety	Choppy; many incomplete or run-on sentences
Conventions	Excellent control; few or no errors	No serious errors to affect understanding	Reasonable control; few distracting errors	Weak control; enough errors to affect understanding	Many errors that prevent understanding

Scoring Rubric — Persuasive Writing

Rubric 4 3 2 1

	3	2	1
Focus/Ideas	Persuasive argument carefully built with quality details	Persuasive argument with one or two convincing details	Rambling persuasive argument; lacks development and detail
Organization/ Paragraphs	Information chosen and arranged for maximum effect	Information arranged in a logical way with some lapses	No identifiable structure
Voice	Writer closely involved; persuasive but not overbearing	Sometimes uses persuasive voice	Shows little conviction
Word Choice	Persuasive words carefully chosen for impact	Occasional persuasive language	Vague, dull, or misused words; no persuasive words
Sentences	Excellent variety of sentences; natural rhythm	Carefully constructed sentences; some variety	Choppy; many incomplete or run-on sentences
Conventions	Excellent control; few or no errors	Reasonable control; few distracting errors	Many errors that prevent understanding

Scoring Rubric — Expository Writing

Rubric 4 3 2 1	6	5	4	3	2	1
Focus/Ideas	Insightful, focused exposition; well elaborated with quality details	Informed, focused exposition; elaborated with telling details	Exposition focused, good elaboration	Generally focused exposition; some supporting details	Sometimes unfocused exposition needs more supporting details	Rambling exposition; lacks development and detail
Organization/ Paragraphs	Logical, consistent flow of ideas; good transitions	Logical sequencing of ideas; uses transitions	Ideas sequenced with some transitions	Sequenced ideas with some transitions	Little direction from beginning to end; few order words	Lacks structure and transitions
Voice	Writer closely involved; informative voice well suited to topic	Reveals personality; voice suited to topic	Pleasant but not compelling voice	Sincere voice suited to topic	Little writer involvement, personality	Careless writing with no feeling
Word Choice	Vivid, precise words to express ideas	Clear words to express ideas	Words correct and adequate	Language adequate but may lack precision	Generally limited or redundant language	Vague, dull, or misused words
Sentences	Strong topic sentence; fluent, varied structures	Good topic sentence; smooth sentence structure	Correct sentences that are sometimes fluent	Topic sentence correctly constructed; some sentence variety	Topic sentence unclear or missing; wordy, awkward sentences	No topic sentence; many incomplete or run-on sentences
Conventions	Excellent control; few or no errors	No serious errors to affect understanding	General mastery of conventions but some errors	Reasonable control; few distracting errors	Weak control; enough errors to affect understanding	Many errors that prevent understanding

Scoring Rubric — Expository Writing

Rubric 4 3 2 1	5	4	3	2	1
Focus/Ideas	Insightful, focused exposition; well elaborated with quality details	Informed, focused exposition; elaborated with telling details	Generally focused exposition; some supporting details	Sometimes unfocused exposition needs more supporting details	Rambling exposition; lacks development and detail
Organization/ Paragraphs	Logical, consistent flow of ideas; good transitions	Logical sequencing of ideas; uses transitions	Sequenced ideas with some transitions	Little direction from beginning to end; few order words	Lacks structure and transitions
Voice	Writer closely involved; informative voice well suited to topic	Reveals personality; voice suited to topic	Sincere voice suited to topic	Little writer involvement, personality	Careless writing with no feeling
Word Choice	Vivid, precise words to express ideas	Clear words to express ideas	Language adequate but may lack precision	Generally limited or redundant language	Vague, dull, or misused words
Sentences	Strong topic sentence; fluent, varied structures	Good topic sentence; smooth sentence structure	Topic sentence correctly constructed; some sentence variety	Topic sentence unclear or missing; wordy, awkward sentences	No topic sentence; many incomplete or run-on sentences
Conventions	Excellent control; few or no errors	No serious errors to affect understanding	Reasonable control; few distracting errors	Weak control; enough errors to affect understanding	Many errors that prevent understanding

Scoring Rubric — Expository Writing

Rubric 4 3 2 1	3	2	1
Focus/Ideas	Insightful, focused exposition; well elaborated with quality details	Generally focused exposition; some supporting details	Rambling exposition; lacks development and detail
Organization/ Paragraphs	Logical, consistent flow of ideas; good transitions	Sequenced ideas with some transitions	Lacks structure and transitions
Voice	Writer closely involved; informative voice well suited to topic	Sincere voice suited to topic	Careless writing with no feeling
Word Choice	Vivid, precise words to express ideas	Language adequate but may lack precision	Vague, dull, or misused words
Sentences	Strong topic sentence; fluent, varied structures	Topic sentence correctly constructed; some sentence variety	No topic sentence; many incomplete or run-on sentences
Conventions	Excellent control; few or no errors	Reasonable control; few distracting errors	Many errors that prevent understanding

Unit 6
Monitoring Fluency

Ongoing assessment of student reading fluency is one of the most valuable measures we have of students' reading skills. One of the most effective ways to assess fluency is taking timed samples of students' oral reading and measuring the number of words correct per minute (WCPM).

How to Measure Words Correct Per Minute—WCPM

Choose a Text

Start by choosing a text for the student to read. The text should be:

• narrative
• unfamiliar
• on grade level

Make a copy of the text for yourself and have one for the student.

Timed Reading of the Text

Tell the student: As you read this aloud, I want you to do your best reading and to read as quickly as you can. That doesn't mean it's a race. Just do your best, fast reading. When I say *begin*, start reading.

As the student reads, follow along in your copy. Mark words that are read incorrectly.

Incorrect	Correct
• omissions	• self-corrections within 3 seconds
• substitutions	• repeated words
• mispronunciations	
• reversals	

After One Minute

At the end of one minute, draw a line after the last word that was read. Have the student finish reading but don't count any words beyond one minute. Arrive at the words correct per minute—WCPM—by counting the total number of words that the student read correctly in one minute.

Fluency Goals

Grade 3 End-of-Year Goal = 120 WCPM

Target goals by unit

Unit 1 80 to 90 WCPM	**Unit 4** 95 to 105 WCPM
Unit 2 85 to 95 WCPM	**Unit 5** 102 to 112 WCPM
Unit 3 90 to 100 WCPM	**Unit 6** 110 to 120 WCPM

More Frequent Monitoring

You may want to monitor some students more frequently because they are falling far below grade-level benchmarks or they have a result that doesn't seem to align with their previous performance. Follow the same steps above, but choose 2 or 3 additional texts.

Fluency Progress Chart Copy the chart on the next page. Use it to record each student's progress across the year.

· See also Assessment Handbook p. 158

Fluency Progress Chart, Grade 3

Name

WCPM

	1	2	3	4	5	6	7	8	9	10	11	12	13	14	15	16	17	18	19	20	21	22	23	24	25	26	27	28	29	30
145																														
140																														
135																														
130																														
125																														
120																														
115																														
110																														
105																														
100																														
95																														
90																														
85																														
80																														
75																														
70																														
65																														
60																														
55																														
50																														

Timed Reading

· See also Assessment Handbook p. 164

Name   **Date**

Assessment Chart

Unit 6

Day 3 Retelling Assessment			Day 5 Fluency Assessment			Reteach	Teacher's Comments	Grouping
The assessed group is highlighted for each week.	Benchmark Score	Actual Score	*The assessed group is highlighted for each week.*	Benchmark WCPM	Actual Score	✓		
The Story of the Statue of Liberty Main Idea and Details								
Strategic	1–2		Strategic	Less than 110				
On-Level	3		On-Level	110–120				
Advanced	4		Advanced*	110–120				
Happy Birthday Mr. Kang Cause and Effect								
Strategic	1–2		Strategic	Less than 110				
On-Level	3		On-Level	110–120				
Advanced	4		Advanced*	110–120				
Talking Walls: Art for the People Fact and Opinion								
Strategic	1–2		Strategic	Less than 110				
On-Level	3		On-Level	110–120				
Advanced	4		Advanced*	110–120				
Two Bad Ants Plot and Theme								
Strategic	1–2		Strategic	Less than 110				
On-Level	3		On-Level	110–120				
Advanced	4		Advanced*	110–120				
Elena's Serenade Generalize								
Strategic	1–2		Strategic	Less than 110				
On-Level	3		On-Level	110–120				
Advanced	4		Advanced*	110–120				
Unit 6 Benchmark Test Score								

WEEK 1   WEEK 2   WEEK 3   WEEK 4   WEEK 5

* **RECORD SCORES** Use this chart to record scores for the Day 3 Retelling, Day 5 Fluency, and Unit Benchmark Test Assessments.

*Students in the advanced group should read above grade-level materials.

* **REGROUPING** Compare the student's actual score to the benchmark score for each group level and review the Questions to Consider. Students may move to a higher or lower group level, or they may remain in the same group.

* **RETEACH** If a student is unable to complete any part of the assessment process, use the weekly Reteach lessons for additional support. Record the lesson information in the space provided on the chart. After reteaching, you may want to reassess using the Unit Benchmark Test.

Assess and Regroup

FYI In Grade 3 there are opportunities for regrouping every five weeks—at the end of Units 2, 3, 4, and 5. These options offer sensitivity to each student's progress although some teachers may prefer to regroup less frequently.

End-of-Year Performance

There is no need to regroup at the end of Unit 6. To assess students' end-of-year performance, consider their scores for

- Unit 5 Retelling
- Fluency (WCPM)
- Unit 5 Benchmark Test and/or End-of-Year Benchmark Test

Group Time

On-Level

To continue On-Level or to move into the On-Level group, students should

- score 3 or better on their cumulative unit rubric scores for Retelling
- meet the current benchmark for fluency (110–120 WCPM), reading On-Level text such as Student Edition selections
- score 80% or better on the Unit 6 Benchmark Test
- be capable of working in the On-Level group based on teacher judgment

Strategic Intervention

Students would benefit from Strategic Intervention if they

- score 2 or lower on their cumulative unit rubric scores for Retelling
- do not meet the current benchmark for fluency (110–120 WCPM)
- score below 60% on the Unit 6 Benchmark Test
- are struggling to keep up with the On-Level group based on teacher judgment

Advanced

To move to the Advanced group, students should

- score 4 on their cumulative unit rubric scores for Retelling
- read fluently at the rate of 140 WCPM
- score 95 on the Unit 6 Benchmark Test
- read above grade-level material (110–120 WCPM) with speed, accuracy, and expression. You may try them out on one of the Advanced leveled readers.
- use expansive vocabulary and ease of language in retelling.
- are capable of handling the problem solving and investigative work of the Advanced group based on teacher judgment

QUESTIONS TO CONSIDER

- What types of test questions did the student miss? Are they specific to a particular skill or strategy?
- Does the student have adequate background knowledge to understand the test passages or selections for retelling?

- Has the student's performance met expectations for daily lessons and assessments with little or no reteaching?
- Is the student performing more like students in another group?
- Does the student read for enjoyment, different purposes, and with varied interests?

Benchmark Fluency Scores

Current Goal: **110–120 WCPM**

End-of-Year Goal: **120 WCPM**

Leveled Readers

Table of Contents

Unit 6 Week 1

🔍 **MAIN IDEA**

🔍 **TEXT STRUCTURE**

LESSON VOCABULARY crown, liberty, models, symbol, tablet, torch, unforgettable, unveiled

The Statue of Liberty

SUMMARY This book is about the origins of the Statue of Liberty, a symbol of freedom in America. It also gives information about Paris and New York City.

INTRODUCE THE BOOK

BUILD BACKGROUND Discuss with students the title and the author of *The Statue of Liberty: From Paris to New York City.* Ask students whether the title and the photograph on the cover give them any clues as to what this book is about.

ELL Invite students to talk about important statues or buildings in their home countries.

PREVIEW/USE TEXT FEATURES Ask students how the photographs, captions, and labels in this book give them a glimpse into 1880s life in Paris and New York.

TEACH/REVIEW VOCABULARY Review vocabulary words with students. Then, write a list of definitions in one column and the vocabulary words in the other and have students match the words to the correct definitions.

TARGET SKILL AND STRATEGY

🔍 **MAIN IDEA** Remind students that the *main idea* is the most important idea about a topic. Model a way of determining the main idea of this book by asking these questions: In a few words, what is this book about? *(the Statue of Liberty)* What are the most important ideas about this topic? *(The statue was offered as a symbol of friendship and took several years to complete.)*

🔍 **TEXT STRUCTURE** Remind students that a way to find the main idea is to recognize how the book is organized. Call attention to the heads, photographs, and captions. These elements will help students gain significant information, and students can learn more about the times during which the statue was created from the photographs and captions.

READ THE BOOK

Use the following questions to support comprehension.

PAGE 4 What does the map on page 4 tell you about the city of Paris? *(Possible responses: There are many roads; the river Seine runs through the center of Paris; there is a right and left bank.)*

PAGE 6 Why do you think Bartholdi made models of every part of the Statue of Liberty before he built it? *(Possible response: Building a small model can save time by giving an idea of what it will look like when large.)*

PAGE 9 What is the main idea of this passage? *(New York City in the 1880s was full of amazing sights, including the Brooklyn Bridge.)*

TALK ABOUT THE BOOK

READER RESPONSE
1. Paris in the 1880s was a very old and beautiful city.
2. Responses will vary, but students' diagrams should show the likenesses and differences of New York City and Paris.
3. *Unforgettable:* not able to forget; *Forgettable:* able to be forgotten; *Unpacked:* took out of packing; *Packed:* put into packing; *Unveiled:* took off a covering; *Veiled:* covered
4. Responses will vary.

RESPONSE OPTIONS

WRITING Ask students to imagine they are the Statue of Liberty in New York and have them write postcards to Paris about their new life here.

CONTENT CONNECTIONS

SOCIAL STUDIES Suggest students make up and draw their own symbols of freedom. Post the symbols in class.

Main Idea

- The **main idea** is the most important idea about the topic.
- Sometimes the main idea is stated in a sentence, but when it isn't, you have to figure it out and state it in your own words.

Directions Read the following passages from the story *The Statue of Liberty: From Paris to New York City*. Circle the correct main idea in each.

1. What was New York City like in 1886? At night the city was ablaze with light. New York City was the first city in the world lighted by electricity!
   a. New York City was a busy city.
   b. New York in 1886 was full of light.
   c. New York City was the first city to have electricity.

2. The Statue of Liberty was being unveiled. Thousands of New Yorkers watched the unforgettable sight from the shores of Manhattan.
   a. Thousands of New Yorkers came to the shores.
   b. The Statue of Liberty was unveiled.
   c. People like to see new statues.

3. The Paris of today still has much of the charm of the old city. But not everything in Paris is old. There are new parks and gardens. You can ride down wide, tree-lined avenues where you will see new railroad stations, government buildings, and theaters.
   a. Paris has many parks and gardens.
   b. Paris today is a mixture of old and new.
   c. You can have a lot of fun in Paris.

Directions Look at the main ideas written below. Can you think of a supporting detail for each idea? For example, if the main idea is "Bob loves to sing," a supporting detail might be "and he is always giving musical concerts." Try it yourself!

4. My dog Skip loves the park. _____

_____

5. Keeping your teeth clean is important. _____

_____

114

Name _____

Vocabulary

Directions Fill in the missing letters for each vocabulary word. Then use the word in a sentence.

Check the Words You Know			
___crown	___liberty	___models	___symbol
___tablet	___torch	___unforgettable	___unveiled

1. __r__wn _____

_____

2. __ __b__ __ty _____

_____

3. t__ __ch _____

_____

4. __ __for__et__able _____

_____

5. m__de__s _____

_____

6. __ __mbol _____

_____

7. t__ __let _____

_____

8. un__ei__ed _____

_____

115

Signs, Songs, and Symbols...

Signs, Songs, and Symbols of America
by Alma Ransford

MAIN IDEA

TEXT STRUCTURE

LESSON VOCABULARY crown, liberty, models, symbol, tablet, torch, unforgettable, unveiled

SUMMARY This book gives students information about the creation, meaning, and importance of cultural icons of the United States.

INTRODUCE THE BOOK

BUILD BACKGROUND Discuss with students what signs, symbols, or songs they already know.

PREVIEW/USE TEXT FEATURES Ask students how they think the captions and subheads in this book help them understand what the material is about.

TEACH/REVIEW VOCABULARY Review with students the dictionary meaning of each vocabulary word. Then invite students to create their own definitions and write a simple illustrative sentence for each vocabulary word.

ELL Suggest students make flashcards, writing a riddle for each vocabulary word on one side and the word on the other.

TARGET SKILL AND STRATEGY

MAIN IDEA Remind students that the *main idea* is the most important idea about a topic. The main idea is sometimes not stated directly, but the text can give details and clues. Ask students to read a paragraph. Use a graphic organizer for main ideas and details so that students can keep track of this information as they read the selection.

TEXT STRUCTURE Remind students that *text structure* is the way a selection is organized and that recognizing text structure can help them determine the main idea. Tell students that this selection connects important ideas using descriptions and definitions.

READ THE BOOK

Use the following questions to support comprehension.

PAGE 4 What is the main idea of this page and what are two supporting details? *(Possible response: Main idea: America has many symbols. Supporting details: the flag, the bald eagle)*

PAGE 11 Why would the cartoon encourage people to join the armed forces? *(It feels as if Uncle Sam is asking you directly.)*

PAGE 14 How does the heading give you an idea of what the topic will be about? *(The heading is about government buildings, which makes me think the topic is about buildings.)*

TALK ABOUT THE BOOK

READER RESPONSE

1. Main Idea: Our country has important songs about it. Details: Francis Scott Key wrote a poem that became a song. George M. Cohan met a Civil War veteran who inspired him to write a song about the flag.
2. The headings point out the topic of each section.
3. unforgettable, unveiled, *un*; Sentences will vary.
4. Possible response: He didn't think the flag would still be there. Yes, I would have been amazed to see the flag still there.

RESPONSE OPTIONS

WRITING Ask students to research the turkey and the bald eagle. Then have students write about why the turkey could have been our national bird.

CONTENT CONNECTIONS

SOCIAL STUDIES/MUSIC/ART Divide students into groups and invite them to form their own country and create lyrics for a short national song, a symbol, and a flag. Groups can share with the class.

Time for SOCIAL STUDIES

Main Idea

- The **main idea** is the author's most important point about a topic.
- Sometimes the main idea is not stated directly in a selection, but the details of a selection can give you clues.

Directions Read the following passages. Then write down the main idea and list two details from the passage that support your answer.

> Our flag has thirteen stripes to remind us of our first colonies. There is a star for each state. The colors all mean something. Red is for hardiness, white is for innocence, blue stands for justice. Betsy Ross sewed the first flag.

1. Main idea: _____

_____

2. Supporting detail: _____

_____

3. Supporting detail: _____

_____

> Francis Scott Key watched the British attack during the War of 1812. When he looked out after a terrible battle, he saw that our flag was still waving. This inspired him to write a poem about it, *The Star Spangled Banner*, which was set to music. This song later became our national anthem.

4. Main idea: _____

_____

5. Supporting detail: _____

_____

6. Supporting detail: _____

_____

114

Vocabulary

Directions Use five of these vocabulary words to write a story about the signs and symbols of America. Then write definitions for the words you don't use in your story.

Check the Words You Know

___crown ___liberty ___models ___symbol
___tablet ___torch ___unforgettable ___unveiled

1. _____

_____

_____

_____

_____

_____

_____

_____

_____

2. _____

3. _____

4. _____

© Pearson Education 3

115

French Roots in North America

French Roots
in North America
by Sharon Franklin

MAIN IDEA

TEXT STRUCTURE

LESSON VOCABULARY assembly line, bilingual, descendants, echo chamber, fortified, immigrants, influence, strait

---

SUMMARY This book shows students how French culture can still be found where the French once ruled.

INTRODUCE THE BOOK

BUILD BACKGROUND Discuss with students what they know about France and French culture.

ELL Invite students to discuss the parts of their cultures that they find in the United States.

PREVIEW/USE ILLUSTRATIONS Ask students how making the book look like a travel journal adds interest to the topic.

TEACH/PREVIEW VOCABULARY Review the vocabulary words with students. Give students sentences with words used correctly or incorrectly. Ask students to mark sentences "true" or "false" and to correct "false" sentences.

TARGET SKILL AND STRATEGY

MAIN IDEA Remind students that the *main idea* is the most important idea about a topic. Review a recent book with students and discuss what the main idea is and which details support their answer. Remind students to try to determine the main idea and supporting details as they read this book.

TEXT STRUCTURE Remind students that *text structure* is the way material is organized, including description and definition, which is how this text is organized. Remind students that understanding text structure can help them determine the main idea. Suggest they take notes as they read.

READ THE BOOK

Use the following questions to support comprehension.

PAGE 4 How did the author record her trip? What does each different recording method add to the story? *(journal writing: tells us the narrator's inner thoughts; video and postcards: gives visuals and descriptions; interviews: gives someone else's thoughts on the subject)*

PAGE 8 What is the main point of the paragraph about Detroit? *(Antoine de la Mothe Cadillac started a settlement called Fort Pontchartrain du Détroit.)*

PAGE 9 Why do you think the author used a series of photographs and captions in the text structure? *(The photos make it look realistic.)*

TALK ABOUT THE BOOK

READER RESPONSE

1. Main Idea: There is still much of the old French culture throughout North America. Details and sentences will vary.
2. Chapter titles point out the main idea and the places. They get me ready to read about them.
3. *Influence* can be used as a verb and it means "to convince." Sentences will vary.
4. Quebec City: people speak French; Detroit: streets have French names; New Orleans: has a French colonial center; St. Louis: a French name; St. Lucia: has French food, music, and language

RESPONSE OPTIONS

WRITING Invite students to write their own postcards from places in the text.

CONTENT CONNECTIONS

SOCIAL STUDIES/ART Suggest students write and illustrate a travel brochure about one of the cities.

Time for SOCIAL STUDIES

Main Idea

- The **main idea** is the most important idea about a reading selection.
- Sometimes it is stated at the beginning, middle, or end of the selection; but sometimes it isn't and you must figure it out yourself.

Directions Below are groups of three sentences. Write *M* next to the sentence that is the main idea and *D* next to the sentences that are the supporting details.

_____ **1.** No trip to Detroit is complete without a visit to the Henry Ford car museum.

_____ **2.** Because of the automobile industry, Detroit is called Motor City.

_____ **3.** Detroit is the home of the automobile industry.

_____ **4.** In the 1820s, the French fur-trading families began to lose their influence.

_____ **5.** The first major in the local army was an English-speaking doctor.

_____ **6.** The population grew to include Germans, Irish, and others.

_____ **7.** The strongest tradition in St. Lucia is African, but there is a large amount of French culture.

_____ **8.** French is still spoken in St. Lucia.

_____ **9.** There is a great deal of French music in St. Lucia.

10. What was the main idea of *French Roots in North America?*

_____

_____

© Pearson Education 3

114

Name_____

Vocabulary

Directions Unscramble the vocabulary words. Write the letter of the correct definition on the line.

Check the Words You Know

___assembly line   ___bilingual   ___descendants   ___echo chamber
___fortified   ___immigrants   ___influences   ___strait

_____   **1.**   gualbiiln   _____

_____   **2.**   mmgistnari   _____

_____   **3.**   stiart   _____

_____   **4.**   fluinensec   _____

_____   **5.**   blyssaem enli   _____

_____   **6.**   roftideif   _____

_____   **7.**   hoec hamcber   _____

_____   **8.**   cendesdants   _____

a.   what you are if you speak two languages

b.   things that have effects on someone or something

c.   a narrow strip of water that connects two larger bodies of water

d.   people who leave one country and settle in another

e.   room or space with walls that reflect sound so that an echo is made

f.   made stronger against attack

g.   in a factory, work passing from one person or machine to the next

h.   people who are related to someone who lived in the past

115

The Sights and Sounds of...

The Sights and Sounds of **New York City's Chinatown** *by Christine Wolf*

◎ **CAUSE AND EFFECT**

◎ **GRAPHIC ORGANIZERS**

LESSON VOCABULARY bows, chilly, foolish, foreign, narrow, perches, recipe

SUMMARY This book describes New York City's Chinatown, the people who live there, as well as the sights and sounds and traditions of this lively neighborhood.

INTRODUCE THE BOOK

BUILD BACKGROUND Discuss with students what they know about Chinatown. Ask them whether they have ever visited Chinatown in New York or another city. What do they remember about their visit? What surprised them the most?

PREVIEW/USE PHOTOS AND CAPTIONS Invite students to review the photographs, charts, and captions. Ask students what they think the text will be about.

ELL Have students tell what is unique about their neighborhood. Tell them that a city's Chinatown is also a unique area of the city.

TEACH/REVIEW VOCABULARY Encourage student pairs to find the vocabulary words in the text. Have them define the words and then work together to write a sentence for each word.

TARGET SKILL AND STRATEGY

◎ **CAUSE AND EFFECT** Remind students that an *effect* is what happened, and a *cause* is why something happened. Have students read page 8. Ask: What is one reason the older generation feels that their traditions are slipping away? (*Younger Chinese do not bow to their elders.*)

◎ **GRAPHIC ORGANIZERS** Remind students that *graphic organizers* are a visual way to arrange information. Have students look at the table on page 8. Help them explore the reasons (right-hand column) for four Chinese traditions (left-hand column).

READ THE BOOK

Use the following questions to support comprehension.

PAGE 7 What languages will you hear in Chinatown? (*Chinese and English*)

PAGE 8 Why do many Chinese people practice Tai Chi? (*to exercise their minds and bodies*)

PAGE 12 Does the Chinese New Year happen on the same day as our New Year? (*No, it happens sometime in January or February.*)

TALK ABOUT THE BOOK

READER RESPONSE
1. Streets are crowded and busy; important Chinese traditions are falling away; there are many choices of food and other products.
2. Sights: narrow winding streets; crowds of Chinese people and tourists; food markets; seasonal festivals; Sounds: spoken Chinese; traffic noises; music from seasonal festivals
3. Response will vary but may include: chilly, narrow, crowded, loud, colorful, traditional
4. Answers will vary but may include speaking politely, saying please and thank you, and listening to what you are told.

RESPONSE OPTIONS

WRITING Have students imagine that they are attending the New Year's parade in Chinatown. Have them describe the sights, sounds, and smells.

CONTENT CONNECTIONS

Time for **SOCIAL STUDIES**

SOCIAL STUDIES Have students research Chinese immigration on the Internet or in the library. What were the years when the highest numbers of Chinese people came to this country?

Name _____

Cause and Effect

- A **cause** is *why* something happened.
- An **effect** is *what* happened.

Directions For each cause, write an effect. Use *The Sights and Sounds of New York City's Chinatown* to help you. The same cause may have different effects.

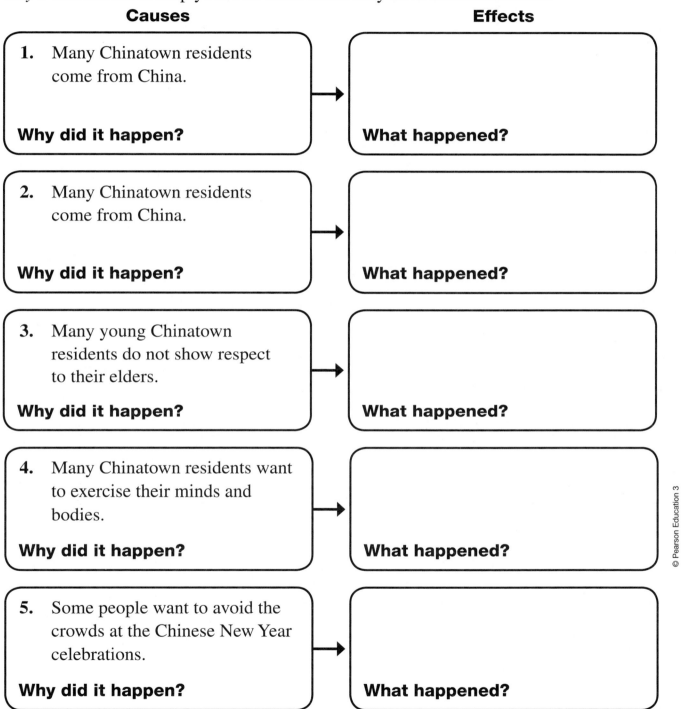

Causes

1. Many Chinatown residents come from China.

 Why did it happen?

2. Many Chinatown residents come from China.

 Why did it happen?

3. Many young Chinatown residents do not show respect to their elders.

 Why did it happen?

4. Many Chinatown residents want to exercise their minds and bodies.

 Why did it happen?

5. Some people want to avoid the crowds at the Chinese New Year celebrations.

 Why did it happen?

Effects

What happened?

What happened?

What happened?

What happened?

What happened?

118

Vocabulary

Directions Fill in the blank with the word from the box that matches the definition.

Check the Words You Know

___ bows   ___ chilly
___ foolish   ___ foreign
___ narrow   ___ perches
___ recipe

1. _____ from a country other than your own

2. _____ places to view things from high above

3. _____ leans forward to show respect

4. _____ silly; not wise

5. _____ instructions for cooking

6. _____ having a small width; not very wide

7. _____ slightly cold

Directions Write a paragraph about Chinatown as described in *The Sights and Sounds of New York City's Chinatown.* Use at least three vocabulary words.

_____

_____

_____

_____

_____

_____

_____

_____

© Pearson Education 3

119

Caring for Your Pet Bird

CAUSE AND EFFECT

GRAPHIC ORGANIZERS

LESSON VOCABULARY bows, chilly, foolish, foreign, narrow, perches, recipe

SUMMARY This book tells how to care for a pet bird. Birds make wonderful pets, especially if they receive the right kind of care and feeding. This book describes what to do to make your bird happy and healthy.

INTRODUCE THE BOOK

BUILD BACKGROUND Ask students if any of them have a pet bird. If so, ask them to tell the class what they do to care for their bird. Have them share their pets' names. Ask them if their pets are able to speak, and if so, what they can say.

PREVIEW/USE ILLUSTRATIONS Suggest students skim the text and look at the illustrations and captions. Ask them what clues these elements give as to what this book might be about.

ELL Ask students whether any of them have pet birds. If so, have each share the pets' names. Have each share with the class how to say *bird* in their native language.

TEACH/REVIEW VOCABULARY Ask students why they think the word *foreign* may be used in a book on birds. Ask them to look at the other vocabulary words and predict their use in a book about keeping birds as pets.

TARGET SKILL AND STRATEGY

CAUSE AND EFFECT Remind students that an *effect* is what happened, and a *cause* is why it happened. Have students read pages 12–13. What could cause a bird to get chilly? (*cold drafts near the cage*) What could happen to a bird that is left in the sun? (*could become overheated*)

GRAPHIC ORGANIZERS A *graphic organizer* is a visual way to organize information. Have students make two columns on a sheet of paper. Have them label the right-hand column *Likes* and the left-hand column *Does not like*. Then, as they read the text, have them fill in things pet birds like and dislike.

READ THE BOOK

Use the following questions to support comprehension.

PAGE 5 Which birds can be taught how to talk? (*birds of the parrot family—parrots, parakeets, lovebirds, cockatiels, macaws, and conures*)

PAGE 11 Why does a bird need to have grit in its diet? (*It doesn't have teeth.*)

PAGE 12 What could happen if a bird is kept in a draft? (*It could get chilly.*)

TALK ABOUT THE BOOK

READER RESPONSE
1. It can get lonely or anxious.
2. Things to Do Before You Bring Your Bird Home: get a cage, make sure the cage has several perches, get toys, get things for bird to chew on. Things to Do After You Bring Your Bird Home: change the water every day, change the newspaper every day, give it a bowl of water to bathe in, give bird grit, give bird a mineral block, keep bird warm and quiet, give bird 10–12 hours of darkness per day
3. chilly, warm; Sentences will vary.
4. zebra finch; Responses will vary.

RESPONSE OPTIONS

WRITING Have students imagine that they are going to the pet store to pick out a pet bird. Have them write about how they decided on a particular bird and what they will name it. Describe the bird in detail.

CONTENT CONNECTIONS

SCIENCE Have students pick out one of the birds mentioned in the article and research it on the Internet or in the library. What country is the bird native to? What is its native habitat? Have each student report back to the class.

TIME FOR Science

Cause and Effect

- A **cause** is why something happened.
- An **effect** is what happened.

Directions Use *Caring for Your Pet Bird* to fill in each missing cause or effect.

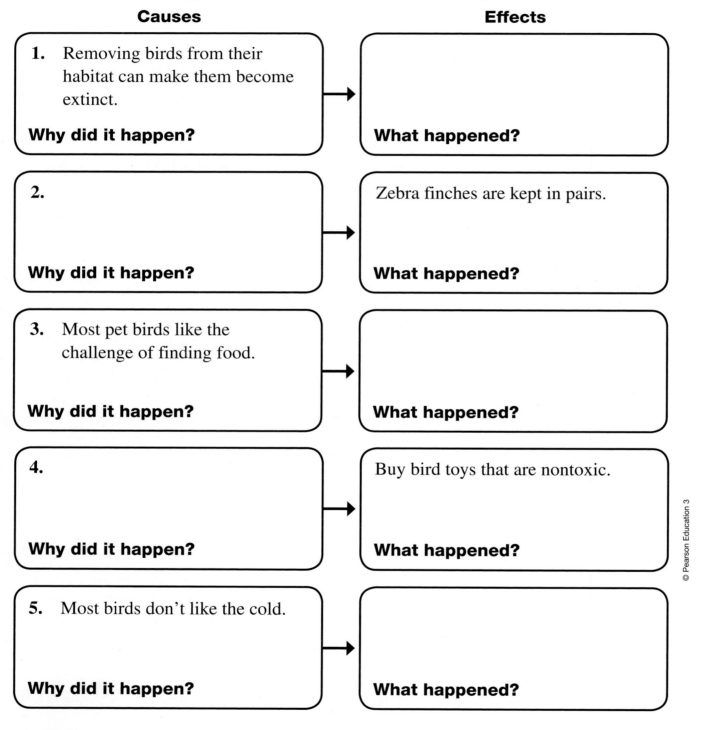

Causes

1. Removing birds from their habitat can make them become extinct.

Why did it happen?

2.

Why did it happen?

3. Most pet birds like the challenge of finding food.

Why did it happen?

4.

Why did it happen?

5. Most birds don't like the cold.

Why did it happen?

Effects

What happened?

Zebra finches are kept in pairs.

What happened?

What happened?

Buy bird toys that are nontoxic.

What happened?

What happened?

© Pearson Education 3

118

Vocabulary

Directions Fill in the blank with the word from the box that matches the definition.

Check the Words You Know

___ bows	___ chilly
___ foolish	___ foreign
___ narrow	___ perches
___ recipe	

1. _____ *adj.* from a country other than your own

2. _____ *n.* places to view things from high above

3. _____ *v.* leans forward to show respect

4. _____ *adj.* silly; not wise

5. _____ *n.* instructions for cooking

6. _____ *adj.* having a small width; not very wide

7. _____ *adj.* slightly cold

Directions Write a brief paragraph discussing how to care for a pet bird. Use at least three vocabulary words.

_____

_____

_____

_____

_____

_____

_____

_____

119

China's Gifts to the World

CAUSE AND EFFECT

GRAPHIC ORGANIZERS

LESSON VOCABULARY bristles, dialects, diverse, expedition, flourished, ingredien inspiration, literate, muffled, techniques, translation

SUMMARY This book describes the art and culture of China. It focuses on the ancient art of calligraphy, describing the process by which calligraphers make their own ink and study how to make the 50,000 characters in the Chinese written language.

INTRODUCE THE BOOK

BUILD BACKGROUND Discuss with students what they know about China. What do they know about the art of calligraphy? If possible bring in a photo or picture of a Chinese character.

PREVIEW/USE ILLUSTRATIONS AND CAPTIONS Suggest students skim the text and look at the illustrations and captions. Ask students what clues these text elements give for what this book might be about.

ELL Ask students to look at the historical map on page 4. Have them trace the trade routes and, if they can, identify the countries that the routes passed through.

TEACH/REVIEW VOCABULARY To reinforce the contextual meaning of the word *literate* on page 6, discuss with students how the phrase *can read* might help them guess the meaning of the world *literate.* Do this with other vocabulary words in the story.

TARGET SKILL AND STRATEGY

CAUSE AND EFFECT Remind students that an *effect* is what happened, and a *cause* is why something happened. Have the students read pages 9–10. Ask: Why was the poet Li Po sent to jail?

GRAPHIC ORGANIZERS Remind students that *graphic organizers* are visual ways to organize information during reading. Students can use graphic organizers to strengthen their understanding of the text. Have students create a cause-and-effect chart and fill it in as they read whenever they come to an event or happening that was caused by another event.

READ THE BOOK

Use the following questions to support comprehension.

PAGE 5 How was China kept isolated from the rest of the world for so many years? *(It is surrounded by tall mountains and a huge desert.)*

PAGE 11 Read the poem by Li Po. What feeling does this poem give you? *(Responses will vary but may include: peaceful, calm, happy, alone.)*

PAGE 15 Look at the table. Why is it important to make all the ink you will need at one time? *(It is difficult to make two batches of ink that are exactly the same color.)*

TALK ABOUT THE BOOK

1. The language is written in pictures instead of letters.
2. brushes; ink sticks; ink stones; paper
3. Antonyms: *diverse,* same; *flourished,* fared poorly; *literate,* illiterate, not able to read or write; *muffled,* clear, sharp
4. practicing to use a brush ("mo"); copying from a model ("lin"); writing your own thoughts and developing your own style ("xie"); Reasons will vary.

RESPONSE OPTIONS

WRITING Imagine that you are travelling to China with the young Marco Polo in the late 1200s. Describe the things that you see, smell, and taste along the way. Describe what it is like to see Chinese writing for the first time.

CONTENT CONNECTIONS

Time for **SOCIAL STUDIES**

SOCIAL STUDIES There were many things that the Chinese developed before the Europeans. Make a list of some of the things that the book says were first invented in China.

Name _____

Cause and Effect

- A **cause** is why something happened.
- An **effect** is what happened.

Directions Skim through *China's Gifts to the World* to find the text on the following topics. For each topic, list one cause and one effect.

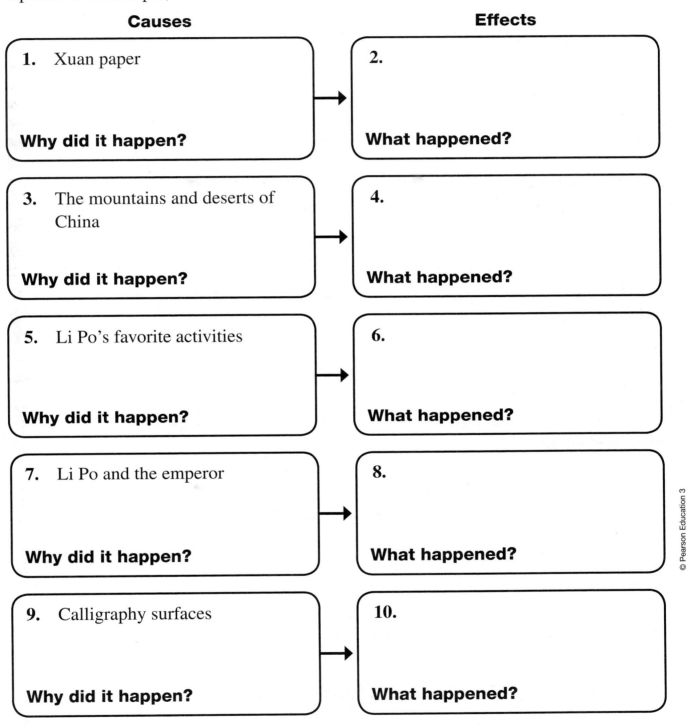

Causes

1. Xuan paper

Why did it happen?

Effects

2.

What happened?

3. The mountains and deserts of China

Why did it happen?

4.

What happened?

5. Li Po's favorite activities

Why did it happen?

6.

What happened?

7. Li Po and the emperor

Why did it happen?

8.

What happened?

9. Calligraphy surfaces

Why did it happen?

10.

What happened?

118

© Pearson Education 3

Vocabulary

Directions Fill in the blank with the word from the box that matches the definition.

Check the Words You Know

___ bristles	___ dialects	___ diverse
___ expedition	___ flourished	___ ingredient
___ inspiration	___ literate	___ muffled
___ techniques	___ translation	

1. _____ *v.* steadily grew, expanded

2. _____ *n.* something that stimulates a person to be creative

3. _____ *n.* the hairs on a brush

4. _____ *adj.* unable to be heard; wrapped with material to deaden the sound

5. _____ *n.* one of several substances mixed together to make a new substance

6. _____ *n.* a journey with a specific purpose

7. _____ *n.* methods of doing something

Directions Write a paragraph about China using the words *dialects, diverse, literate,* and *translation.*

_____

_____

_____

_____

_____

_____

_____

119

A Different Drawing

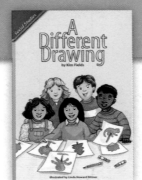

◎ **FACT AND OPINION**

◎ **MONITOR AND FIX UP**

LESSON VOCABULARY encourages, expression, local, native, settled, social, support

SUMMARY
In this story, a girl is encouraged to draw what she feels. It supports the lesson concept of freedom of expression in a free society.

INTRODUCE THE BOOK

BUILD BACKGROUND Ask students to name a favorite book. Say: Suppose a law said that everyone had to read the same kind of book. Would that be okay? Why or why not?

PREVIEW/USE ILLUSTRATIONS Have students look at the pictures in the book. Ask: Who is the story about? Where does it happen? Have students read the heading on page 16. Discuss with students whether this page is part of the story.

TEACH/REVIEW VOCABULARY Discuss the vocabulary words. Reinforce word meaning by asking students to complete sentences for each vocabulary word. For example: A person who helps is a person who_____.

ELL Students may have difficulty with *wavy* (page 3), *lollipops* (page 4), and *octopus* (page 11). Restate the terms, and draw pictures that they can label in both English and their home languages.

TARGET SKILL AND STRATEGY

◎ **FACT AND OPINION** Remind students that a *statement of fact* tells something that can be proved true or false by reading, observing, or asking an expert. A *statement of opinion* tells ideas or feelings. It cannot be proved true or false. Turn to page 5 and read the sentence: "They grow all around the state." Ask: Can you prove this statement true or false? How? Look at the statement on page 5: "Well, you got it *wrong*." Ask: Is this a statement of fact, or a statement of opinion? *(It is Nat's opinion.)*

◎ **MONITOR AND FIX UP** Remind students that as they read they should check to see if they understand what they are reading. One way to check is by asking questions. Suggest that each time students turn a page, they write a question about the story up to that point and try to answer it.

READ THE BOOK
Use the following questions to support comprehension.

PAGES 3–7 How do the children try to solve the big problem? *(First Sue offers to help. Then Nat shows everyone how to make lollipop trees.)*

PAGES 10–11 Why do you think Sue wants to draw a tree that looks like an octopus? *(Possible response: Sue enjoys drawing.)*

PAGE 12 Read what Amy said. Is it a statement of fact or a statement of opinion? Why? *(It is a statement of opinion. Possible response: It can't be proved true or false.)*

TALK ABOUT THE BOOK

READER RESPONSE
1. Responses will vary.
2. Responses will vary.
3. grows naturally in a certain place
4. He explained that sometimes kids want to do what is easiest, and sometimes they want to do the same things that other kids do.

RESPONSE OPTIONS

WRITING Encourage students to express themselves by writing a letter to the editor supporting or opposing Nat's opinion in the story.

CONTENT CONNECTIONS

SOCIAL STUDIES Have students look up the First Amendment. Have them list the freedoms it protects. Lead the class in a discussion of these basic rights.

Fact and Opinion

- A statement of **fact** is a statement that can be proved true or false.
- A statement of **opinion** is a statement of someone's judgment, belief, or way of thinking about something.

Directions Write *F* beside statements of fact and *O* beside statements of opinion.

1. _____ Trees have leaves and branches.

2. _____ There is only one way that you should draw a tree.

3. _____ Sue's trees were better than the other kids' trees.

4. _____ Mr. Martinez encouraged his students to do their best.

5. _____ You should do what other kids tell you to do.

6. _____ There are all sorts of trees.

7. _____ All trees should not look like lollipops.

8. _____ Freedom of expression means that we can express ourselves in many different ways.

Directions Read the statement: Sue's drawings are better than everyone else's drawings. Is this a fact or an opinion? Why?

9–10. _____

_____

_____

_____

_____

© Pearson Education 3

122

Vocabulary

Directions Write the word that best completes each sentence.

> ## Check the Words You Know
>
> ___encourages ___expression ___local ___native
> ___settled ___social ___support

1. A great painting can be an _____ of joy.

2. I was born and raised in this town. I am a _____.

3. They discussed the problem and _____ it by coming to an agreement.

4. Sue _____ the other kids to draw the trees any way they like.

5. Nat talked to many kids. He is very _____.

6. Sue went to the _____ art supply store to buy markers.

7. Mr. Martinez will _____ you, no matter how you draw a tree.

Directions Use the words *local*, *support*, and *expression* in a short paragraph.

_____

_____

_____

_____

_____

_____

_____

123

A Whole World in One City

A Whole World in One City
by Juliette Ruiz
illustrated by Bill Peterson

FACT AND OPINION

MONITOR AND FIX UP

LESSON VOCABULARY encourages, expression, local, native, settled, social, support

SUMMARY In this story, a young girl learns about the diversity of expression in Chicago's ethnic neighborhoods. The story supports the lesson concept of freedom of expression in a free society.

INTRODUCE THE BOOK

BUILD BACKGROUND List a few customs that come from other countries. Lead a discussion about how many Americans follow these customs that come from other countries.

PREVIEW/USE ILLUSTRATIONS Have students look at the pictures in the book. Ask: What is the most important character doing? Have students read the heading on page 20. Ask: What is the purpose of this part of the book?

TEACH/REVIEW VOCABULARY Distribute cards for each of the vocabulary words. Make additional word cards for *human, help, born here, peopled, face, cheers, nearby.* Ask students to show the vocabulary word that best matches each.

ELL Give students word cards for the lesson vocabulary. Have them sort the cards by the number of syllables in each word.

TARGET SKILL AND STRATEGY

FACT AND OPINION Remind students that a *statement of fact* tells something that can be proved true or false by reading, observing, or asking an expert. A *statement of opinion* tells ideas or feelings. It cannot be proved true or false. Turn to page 4 and find the sentence: *Chicago has many different neighborhoods.* Ask: Can you prove this statement true or false? If yes, it is a statement of fact. How can you prove it? Next, explain that some words are clues to statements of opinion. Turn to page 5 and find the sentence: *That's much more fun, isn't it?* Ask: Is this a statement of fact or a statement of opinion? Which words are clues? *(much more)* Note that a statement of opinion cannot be proved true or false.

MONITOR AND FIX UP Remind students that they should check their understanding as they read. One way is by asking questions, such as: *What happened in the middle?* If they can't answer their questions, they can do things to fix up, such as reread or use a dictionary.

READ THE BOOK

Use the following questions to support comprehension.

PAGES 5–6 Why do you think Lily's dad wanted to show her Chicago? *(Possible response: He wanted her to feel good about staying there.)*

PAGES 10–11 Why do you think so many Polish immigrants settled in the same area? *(Possible response: They felt comfortable with people who shared the same customs.)*

PAGE 15 Bobak's had one hundred different kinds of sausage. Is this a statement of fact or a statement of opinion? *(It is a statement of fact. It can be proved true or false.)*

TALK ABOUT THE BOOK

READER RESPONSE
1. Responses will vary.
2. Students could reread, read on, or ask for help.
3. Responses should include italicized words in the story.
4. Possible responses: No, Lily's family is not unique. Many people are interested in the cultures to be found in the United States.

RESPONSE OPTIONS

WRITING Have students write a letter to a pen pal from one of the neighborhoods in the story. They should explain their family and community traditions.

CONTENT CONNECTIONS

SOCIAL STUDIES Have students use a reference source to find facts about one of the countries of origin in the story.

Time for SOCIAL STUDIES

Fact and Opinion

- A statement of **fact** is a statement that can be proved true or false.
- A statement of **opinion** is a statement of someone's judgment, belief, or way of thinking about something. Although statements of opinion cannot be proved true or false, they can be supported or explained.

Directions Write *F* beside statements of fact and *O* beside statements of opinion.

1. _____ Chicago has many different neighborhoods.

2. _____ It's much more fun to take the bus or the train.

3. _____ Mexican ice cream tastes better than regular ice cream.

4. _____ Pilsen is the largest Mexican neighborhood in any city in the country.

5. _____ The Polish neighborhood has better food than the Mexican neighborhood.

6. _____ It is better to feel like you're not stuck in just one place.

7. _____ The streets were filled with pagodas, fish markets, and restaurants.

8. _____ The Chicago Food Market has the best fish.

Directions Write your own opinion of what it would be like to live in a city with many different cultures.

_____

_____

_____

_____

© Pearson Education 3

122

Vocabulary

Directions Fill in the blank with the word that best completes each sentence.

> ## Check the Words You Know
>
> ___encourages ___expression ___local ___native
> ___settled ___social ___support

1. She doesn't play much with other kids. She is not very _____.

2. Lily shopped at the _____ fish market in her neighborhood.

3. Lily's family moved to many places, then _____ in Chicago.

4. Lily's grandmother _____ her to keep a diary.

5. I was born in Chicago, so that makes me a _____ of Chicago.

6. At first, Lily did not _____ her family's move to Chicago.

7. When Lily saw the colorful neighborhood, she had an excited

_____ on her face.

Directions Use the words *encourages*, *social*, *local*, and *expression* in a short paragraph about your community.

_____

_____

_____

_____

_____

_____

_____

_____

123

The Huge Paintings of . . .

Social Studies

Biography

The **Huge Paintings** of Thomas Hart Benton

by Peggy Bresnick Kendler

FACT AND OPINION

MONITOR AND FIX UP

LESSON VOCABULARY ally, appreciated, encouraged, enlisted, expression, legacy, murals, native, social, support

SUMMARY This is a biography of the American muralist, Thomas Hart Benton. It supports the lesson concept of freedom of expression in a free society.

INTRODUCE THE BOOK

BUILD BACKGROUND Discuss what students know about murals. If they have seen a public mural or helped make one, have them share their experiences.

PREVIEW/USE TEXT FEATURES Ask students to look at the table of contents. Discuss how it helps them to easily locate information in the book. Also discuss why each photo and art reproduction has a caption. Ask: How do captions add to your understanding of the images and text?

TEACH/REVIEW VOCABULARY Form student pairs. Have each partner write a cloze sentence for one of the vocabulary words. Ask them to exchange sentences and fill in the correct word. Have children repeat the activity until all the words have been used at least once.

ELL Make a set of cards for the vocabulary words and another set for definitions. Have students play a memory game by pairing words and definitions.

TARGET SKILL AND STRATEGY

FACT AND OPINION Remind students that a *statement of fact* tells something that can be proved true or false by reading, observing, or asking an expert. A *statement of opinion* tells ideas or feelings. It cannot be proved true or false. Explain that some words are clues to statements of opinion. Words such as *I believe* or *I think* and *beautiful* or *best* often signal an opinion.

MONITOR AND FIX UP Remind students that they should check their understanding as they read. One way is by asking questions, such as: *What does this mean?* If they can't answer their questions, they can do things to fix up, such as reread or use a dictionary.

READ THE BOOK

Use the following questions to support comprehension.

PAGES 6–7 Do you think Benton's early childhood affected his later work as an artist? Why or why not? *(Possible response: Yes, he met many of the kinds of people he painted later in life.)*

PAGES 16–17 Why did the author include the story about Benton and President Truman? *(to inform and entertain)*

PAGE 19 Do you like Benton's paintings? Why or why not? *(Possible response: I like them because they are very colorful and lively.)*

TALK ABOUT THE BOOK

READER RESPONSE
1. Facts and opinions will be based on the work being done in the mural shown on page 13.
2. He painted murals because he needed large spaces to get his ideas across.
3. Other definitions: living or liking to live with others; liking company; connected with fashionable society; Sentences will vary.
4. Responses will vary based on students' choice of paintings.

RESPONSE OPTIONS

WRITING Have students write a paragraph that compares the work of Benton and Picasso.

CONTENT CONNECTIONS

SOCIAL STUDIES Explain to students that Benton was one of many artists employed under New Deal art programs during the Great Depression. Have students conduct research about how these programs helped artists and society in general. Have them share their findings.

Time for **SOCIAL STUDIES**

Fact and Opinion

- A statement of **fact** is a statement that can be proved true or false.
- A statement of **opinion** is a statement of someone's judgment, belief, or way of thinking about something.

Directions Write *F* beside statements of fact and *O* beside statements of opinion. Then explain what makes the statement a fact or an opinion.

_____ **1.** Thomas Hart Benton is a famous muralist.

_____

_____

_____ **2.** Thomas Hart Benton is the best of the American muralists.

_____

_____

_____ **3.** His father wanted his son to go into politics.

_____

_____

_____ **4.** Art institutes are better schools than military institutes.

_____

_____

_____ **5.** New York City is the best place for an artist to live.

_____

_____

122

Vocabulary

Directions Draw a line from the word to its meaning.

Check the Words You Know

___ally   ___appreciate   ___encouraged   ___enlisted
___expression ___legacy   ___mural   ___native
___social   ___support

1. ally   *n.* a local resident

2. appreciate   *n.* example, illustration, or demonstration

3. enlisted   *n.* backing, encouragement, help

4. encouraged   *n.* a friend or helper

5. expression   *v.* gave support to

6. legacy   *n.* a large wall painting

7. mural   *n.* a gift left by someone

8. native   *v.* to be grateful for

9. social   *v.* joined or signed on

10. support   *adj.* relating to human society

Directions Using at least two of the vocabulary words above, write one statement of fact and one statement of opinion.

_____

_____

_____

_____

_____

_____

123

Leo and the School of Fish

PLOT AND THEME

VISUALIZE

LESSON VOCABULARY crystal, disappeared, discovery, goal, journey, joyful, scoop, unaware

SUMMARY Leo is a young fish who is tired of always swimming in a school of fish. So one day he discovers a shipwreck and swims off alone to explore it. In the wreck, he encounters several dangerous situations, so he decides to return to the safety of his school.

INTRODUCE THE BOOK

BUILD BACKGROUND Ask students what they know about fish and the ocean. Have them describe trips they've taken to an aquarium or movies they've seen that have shown fish swimming in schools.

PREVIEW/USE ILLUSTRATIONS Invite students to look at all the illustrations in the book. Ask students how the illustrations give clues to the meaning of the story.

ELL Have students describe a trip to the ocean. Have they ever gone fishing in the ocean? Have they ever been to an aquarium? Have them talk about any of these experiences.

TEACH/REVIEW VOCABULARY Encourage student pairs to find the vocabulary words in the text. Have them define the words and then work together to write a sentence for each word.

TARGET SKILL AND STRATEGY

PLOT AND THEME Remind students that the *plot* is the sequence of events that take a story from the beginning to the middle to the end. Also, remind students that stories usually have one big idea or *theme*. Discuss with them what they think the big idea is in a familiar story like "The Tortoise and the Hare" *(slow and steady wins the race)*. Have them tell the plot of the story by recalling what happens at the beginning, in the middle, and at then end of the story.

VISUALIZE Remind students that when we *visualize,* we form pictures in our minds about what is happening in the story. Encourage students to try to visualize the scenes and characters in *Leo and the School of Fish* as they read it. Have them try to activate all their senses: sight, smell, taste, touch, and hearing.

READ THE BOOK

Use the following questions to support comprehension.

PAGE 4 What does Leo's friend Gil think about swimming in a school? *(that it's cool)*

PAGE 6 What does Gil say to Leo about the ship? *(that it could be dangerous, that he might get eaten)*

PAGE 9 What was the first danger Leo found on the ship? *(a lanternfish with its mouth open)*

TALK ABOUT THE BOOK

READER RESPONSE

1. Possible responses: Beginning: Leo is bored of always swimming in his school. Middle: Leo swims into an old ship and encounters dangers. End: Leo returns to the safety of his school.

2. Possible responses should include colorful verbs, adjectives, and adverbs.

3. Responses will vary.

4. Possible response: Advantages of doing things in a group include enjoying safety in numbers, getting help when you need it, and learning from others. Advantages of doing things alone are that you don't have to compromise, and you can do whatever you want.

RESPONSE OPTIONS

WRITING Have students imagine that they are a fish swimming in a large school. Ask students: What is it like to swim in a group? What did you see during the day? How does staying in a large group allow you to be safer from larger creatures who could eat you?

CONTENT CONNECTIONS

SCIENCE Have students research schools of fish. Assign each student a different type of fish. Have them draw pictures of their fish. Once they have gathered all their information, have them share it with the class.

TIME FOR Science

Plot and Theme

- The **plot** is an organized pattern of events.
- The **theme** is the "big idea" of a story.

Directions Fill in the graphic organizer about the story elements in *Leo and the School of Fish*.

Title _____

This story is about _____

_____
(name the characters)

This story takes place _____

_____
(where and when)

The action begins when _____

_____

Then, _____

_____

Next, _____

_____

After that, _____

_____

The story ends when _____

_____

Theme: _____

© Pearson Education 3

126

Vocabulary

Directions Fill in the blank with the word from the box that fits best.

Check the Words You Know

___crystal   ___disappeared   ___discovery   ___goal

___journey   ___joyful   ___scoop   ___unaware

1. Leo didn't listen to his friend Gil and set off on his _____.

2. The fisherman tried to _____ the fish out of the water with the net.

3. The flashing _____ caught Leo's eye.

4. Leo was hoping to make an exciting _____ on his adventure.

5. The fish in the school were _____ when Leo returned safely.

6. Leo swam so fast it looked as if he _____.

7. Leo's _____ was to explore the ship.

8. Leo was _____ of what would happen on his journey.

Directions Write a brief paragraph discussing Leo's journey, using as many vocabulary words as possible.

_____

_____

_____

_____

_____

_____

_____

_____

_____

127

Goldilocks and the Three Bears

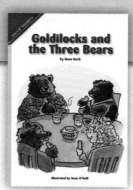

Goldilocks and the Three Bears
by Rosa Koch
Illustrated by Sean O'Neill

Unit 6 Week 4

🌀 **PLOT AND THEME**

🌀 **VISUALIZE**

LESSON VOCABULARY crystal, disappeared, discovery, goal, journey, joyful, scoop, unaware

SUMMARY This is a retelling of the traditional fairy tale.

INTRODUCE THE BOOK

BUILD BACKGROUND Ask students if they know the story of *Goldilocks and the Three Bears*. Have them tell the story in their own words.

PREVIEW/USE ILLUSTRATIONS Have the students look through the illustrations in the book. Do the illustrations seem to tell the story of Goldilocks in the same way that they remember it?

ELL Have each student tell the story of Goldilocks, if they know it, or another fairy tale, perhaps one from their native country.

TEACH/REVIEW VOCABULARY Encourage student pairs to find the vocabulary words in the text. Have them define the words and then work together to write a sentence for each word.

TARGET SKILL AND STRATEGY

🌀 **PLOT AND THEME** Remind students that the *plot* is the events in a story from the beginning to the middle to the end. Also, remind students that stories usually have one big idea. Discuss with students what they think is the *theme* of a familiar story such as "The Tortoise and the Hare" *(slow and steady wins the race)*. Have them tell the plot of the story by recalling what happens at the beginning, in the middle, and at the end of the story, including problems that arise and how they are resolved.

🌀 **VISUALIZE** Remind students that when we *visualize,* we form pictures in our minds about what is happening in the story. Encourage students to try to visualize the scenes and characters in *Goldilocks and the Three Bears* as they read it. Have them try to activate all their senses: sight, smell, taste, touch, and hearing.

READ THE BOOK

Use the following questions to support comprehension.

PAGE 4 Why was Billy Bear lonely? *(He lived in the forest far from his friends in town.)*

PAGE 5 What was special about Mom Bear's chair? *(It was covered in soft green velvet.)*

PAGE 9 What sort of crystal animal does Goldilocks break? *(a bunny)*

TALK ABOUT THE BOOK

READER RESPONSE

1. Wording may vary: Problem: Dad Bear is angry because of the damage done to the house. Beginning: The Bear Family goes out for a walk; Middle: Goldilocks enters their house, eats their oatmeal, breaks a chair, and goes to sleep in Billy's bed. End: The Bears return home. Solution: They forgive Goldilocks.

2. Responses may vary: hungry, excited, happy, smiling

3. Responses may vary: Goldilocks discovers that she is in Billy Bear's house; that she's too heavy for Billy Bear's chair; that Billy Bear's bed is just right for her. The Bears learn that someone has broken into their house; that a crystal animal and a chair have been broken; that Goldilocks is sleeping in Billy Bear's bed.

4. Responses may vary.

RESPONSE OPTIONS

WRITING Have the students write about a time when they were selfish and did something they regretted but were forgiven. How did it feel to be forgiven?

CONTENT CONNECTIONS

SCIENCE Have students research as much as they can find out about bears. Assign each group of students a different type of bear. Once they have gathered all their information, have them share it with the class.

TIME FOR Science

Name _____

Plot and Theme

- The **plot** is an organized pattern of events.
- The **theme** is the "big idea" of a story.

Directions Fill in the table below, which will guide you through a summary of the plot and end with your naming the theme of *Goldilocks and the Three Bears*.

Title _____

This story is about _____

_____
            (name the characters)

This story takes place _____

_____
            (where and when)

The action begins when _____

_____

Then, _____

_____

Next, _____

_____

After that, _____

_____

_____

The story ends when _____

_____

Theme: _____

126

Vocabulary

Directions Fill in the blank with the word from the box that fits best.

Check the Words You Know

___crystal	___disappeared	___discovery	___goal
___journey	___joyful	___scoop	___unaware

1. Mom Bear made breakfast with one large _____ of oatmeal.

2. Goldilocks _____ from the Bears' house in a rush.

3. Goldilocks did not knock the _____ vase off the shelf.

4. The thought of oatmeal for breakfast made Papa Bear feel _____.

5. The Bears were _____ that Goldilocks was upstairs sleeping.

6. The _____ of the Bears' walk was to let the oatmeal cool.

7. The Bears made a big _____ when they returned home.

8. Goldilocks will be more careful on her next _____.

Directions Write a brief paragraph discussing Goldilocks's visit to the Bears' house, using as many vocabulary words as possible.

_____

_____

_____

_____

_____

_____

_____

_____

_____

127

A Fantastic Field Trip

Life Science

A Fantastic Field Trip

by C. Truman Rogers
illustrated by Dan Bridy

Unit 6 Week 4

◉ PLOT AND THEME

◉ VISUALIZE

LESSON VOCABULARY announcement, budge, entomological, exhibition, expenses, nuisances

---

SUMMARY This is a science fiction story in which a group of nine year olds visits a special zoo for giant bugs. While they are at the zoo, they see butterflies the size of small cars, fleas that can jump more than 150 feet, and a wasps' nest as big as a garage.

INTRODUCE THE BOOK

BUILD BACKGROUND Discuss with students what they know about insects, especially butterflies. Have they ever watched a butterfly emerge from a cocoon? Have they ever collected butterflies or other insects?

PREVIEW/USE ILLUSTRATIONS Invite students to look at all of the illustrations in the book. Ask students to predict what will happen in the story from looking at the pictures. Discuss with students which illustrations seem realistic and which seem like fantasy.

ELL Have students describe their favorite insects. How do insects in their home countries differ from insects in this country?

TEACH/REVIEW VOCABULARY Encourage student pairs to find the vocabulary words in the text. Have them define the words and then work together to write a sentence for each word.

TARGET SKILL AND STRATEGY

◉ PLOT AND THEME Remind students that the *plot* is the events in a story from the beginning to the middle to the end. Also, remind students that stories usually have one big idea, or *theme.*

◉ VISUALIZE Remind students that when we *visualize,* we form pictures in our minds about what is happening in the story. Encourage students to try to visualize the scenes and characters in *A Fantastic Field Trip* as they read it. Have them try to activate all their senses: sight, smell, taste, touch, and hearing.

READ THE BOOK

Use the following questions to support comprehension.

PAGE 5 Who paid for the students' trip to the entomological zoo? *(The students raised their own money.)*

PAGE 7 Why was Mrs. Appleby late for the trip? *(She had been stuck in traffic.)*

PAGE 13 Where were the insects kept? *(in underground halls)*

TALK ABOUT THE BOOK

READER RESPONSE

1. Possible responses: giant butterflies, pupas as big as soccer balls, the loud sounds of the insects, fleas that could jump more than 150 feet, giant ladybugs
2. Possible response: thousands of lightning bugs
3. Possible response: relating to bugs
4. Possible response: I saw giant insects, fleas that could jump more than 150 feet, and thousands of lightning bugs.

RESPONSE OPTIONS

WRITING Have students imagine that they found a giant butterfly in their backyard. What would they do with it? Have students imagine they could fly on the back of the butterfly. Where would they go, and what would they see?

CONTENT CONNECTIONS

SCIENCE Have students research as much as they can find out about butterflies. Assign each student a different butterfly. They can use the Internet or the library. Have them draw a picture of their butterfly. Once they have gathered all their information, have them share it with the class.

Plot and Theme

- The **plot** is an organized pattern of events.
- The **theme** is the "big idea" of a story.

Directions Fill in the table below, which will guide you through a summary of the plot and end with your naming the theme of *A Fantastic Field Trip*.

1. Title _____

2. This story is about _____

_____

(name the characters)

_____

3. This story takes place _____

_____

(where and when)

4. The action begins when _____

_____

_____

5. Then _____

_____

_____

6. Next, _____

_____

7. After that, _____

_____

8. The story ends when _____

_____

9. Theme: _____

126

Vocabulary

Directions Fill in the blank with the word from the box that fits best.

Check the Words You Know

___announcement	___budge	___entomological
___exhibition	___expenses	___nuisances

1. We heard the _____ that blared "Put on your sunglasses!"

2. The _____ zoo was a place that was all about bugs.

3. The Bug Kids raised money to pay for their trip's _____.

4. They tried to open the door but it wouldn't _____.

5. The entomological _____ housed many gigantic insects.

6. Although insects can be fascinating, some of them can be _____.

Directions Write a brief paragraph discussing the Bug Kids' trip to the Entomological Zoo, using as many vocabulary words as possible.

_____

_____

_____

_____

_____

_____

_____

_____

_____

_____

© Pearson Education 3

127

Glass Blowing
by J. Matteson Claus

◎ **GENERALIZE**

◎ **PREDICT**

LESSON VOCABULARY burros, bursts, factory, glassblower, puff, reply, tune

Glass Blowing

SUMMARY Readers explore the history and methods of making things of glass. Detailed illustrations and photographs support the concepts in the text. Readers can make predictions, compare methods, and make generalizations about glass blowing.

INTRODUCE THE BOOK

BUILD BACKGROUND Discuss with students the unique characteristics of glass. It is able to withstand heat; it is easy to clean; it is smooth; it can be clear or colored; it comes in many shapes.

PREVIEW/USE TEXT FEATURES As students look through the headings, photographs, and illustrations, ask them to comment on things they find surprising.

TEACH/REVIEW VOCABULARY Play Memory with synonyms by writing each of the following vocabulary words and their synonyms on separate index cards: *burros—donkeys; puff—breathe; tune—adjust; factory—plant; bursts—blasts; reply—answer.* You may want to point out the meaning for each vocabulary word, especially *puff* and *tune.* Place the cards facedown. Students then take turns turning over two cards at a time.

ELL Have students play Synonym Memory with a word and matching picture on one side of each card. Adding a picture will help these students recognize synonyms.

TARGET SKILL AND STRATEGY

◎ **GENERALIZE** Review with students that when they read about several people, things, or ideas that are alike, they can often make a general statement about them. Read the first sentence on page 14. Point out that the word *much* is a clue word. Group students in pairs and assign each pair a page of text. Ask each pair of students to write a general statement from facts on that page. As a class, have students evaluate the *generalizations* by looking at facts in the text.

◎ **PREDICT** Students need to pay attention to details in the text when making generalizations and *making predictions.* Stop and practice this skill after students have read page 6. Guide students to look for details that will help them predict what will be next. Write students' predictions on the board. Then as predictions are confirmed as correct or incorrect, pause and encourage class discussion.

READ THE BOOK

Use the following questions to support comprehension.

PAGE 3 What does the author mean by comparing glass to gold? *(At one time glass was rare and highly valued, like gold.)*

PAGE 8 What is the first step of glass blowing? *(melting the ingredients)*

PAGE 12 What are some things that glass is used for? *(Possible responses: TV screens, drinking glasses)*

TALK ABOUT THE BOOK

READER RESPONSE
1. Responses will vary.
2. Possible response: Glass is recyclable, so glass containers may be used more than plastic.
3. Possible response: If glass blowers puff too hard, the bubbles will burst.
4. Possible response: make the glass, gather it, blow a bubble, shape it, and cool it in a special oven

RESPONSE OPTIONS

WRITING Ask students to create a time line showing the history of glass using what they have just read.

CONTENT CONNECTIONS

SOCIAL STUDIES Arrange with your librarian to have additional books or videos on glass and glass blowing for students to browse after reading.

Time for **SOCIAL STUDIES**

Generalize

- To **generalize** is to make a broad statement or rule that applies to many examples.
- When you make a generalization, you look for similarities or differences among facts and examples in the text.

Directions Complete the graphic organizer below. Find facts from the text that support the generalization.

Generalization
Blowing glass is usually difficult to do by hand.

Supporting Examples

| 1.

2. | 3.

4. | 5.

6. |

Directions Write a generalization about glass factories. Then write three facts that support the generalization.

7. Generalization:

_____

_____

8–10. Supporting examples:

_____

_____

_____

130

Name _____

Vocabulary

Directions First unscramble each word. Then use the word in a sentence.

Check the Words You Know

___ burros   ___ bursts
___ factory   ___ glassblower
___ puff   ___ reply
___ tune

1. etnu   _____

_____

2. tbsru   _____

_____

3. fufp   _____

_____

4. yrfaotc   _____

_____

5. orbusr   _____

_____

6. ypelr   _____

_____

7. bssalgrewol   _____

_____

© Pearson Education 3

131

Traditional Crafts of Mexico

◎ **GENERALIZE**

◎ **PREDICT/CONFIRM PREDICTIONS**

LESSON VOCABULARY burros, burst, factory, glassblower, puff, reply, tune

SUMMARY Readers learn about Mexican culture by exploring various traditional crafts. Readers can make generalizations from similarities among crafts and regions of Mexico. Topics are organized to support readers' predictions.

INTRODUCE THE BOOK

BUILD BACKGROUND Discuss with students any recent crafts they have made at school. Or ask students if they have made any crafts outside of school. Have students describe what they made, what materials they used, and whether it was difficult.

ELL Build background and develop vocabulary by encouraging students to discuss crafts of their native culture. Ask students to share native-language words related to crafts.

PREVIEW/USE TEXT FEATURES Direct students to look through the book and to pay attention to the headings, map, illustrations, and photographs. Ask students to share with the class anything that is familiar to them. Encourage students to comment on what they already know about crafts or Mexico.

TEACH/REVIEW VOCABULARY Write the vocabulary words on cards. Turn the cards over and mix them up. Have students choose two cards. They must then use the two words in one sentence. Students can work as a class or in small groups of three or four.

TARGET SKILL AND STRATEGY

◎ **GENERALIZE** Review with students that when they read about several people, things, or ideas that are alike, they can often make a *generalization* about them. Group students in pairs. Assign each a different craft discussed in the text. Have pairs write a general statement about their topic. Next have pairs trade statements and evaluate them by looking at facts in the text.

◎ **PREDICT/CONFIRM PREDICTIONS** Making predictions requires students to look at details in the text. Stop and practice this skill after students have read page 7. Guide students to look for details that will help them predict what will be next. Write students' predictions on the board. Discuss as predictions are confirmed as correct or incorrect.

READ THE BOOK

Use the following questions to support comprehension.

PAGE 5 What does the statement "The Mayan civilization was at its peak" mean? *(The Maya were at the height of their glory.)*

PAGES 12–13 What are some differences and similarities between making a rug and making a basket? *(Both are woven. A rug can take 300 hours to make; a medium-size basket takes less than an hour.)*

PAGE 17 Which craft is highly valued in Mexico? *(needlework)*

TALK ABOUT THE BOOK

READER RESPONSE
1. Possible responses: colorful, handmade, traditional techniques
2. Possible response: techniques might be lost forever
3. Possible response: glass + blower = glassblower; Responses will vary.
4. Responses will vary.

RESPONSE OPTIONS

WRITING Have students write instructions or steps in a process on how to make something simple such as a mask, collage, poster, or hat.

CONTENT CONNECTIONS

ART Have students make a mask to wear on their favorite holiday. Require that the mask's colors, decorations, and/or shape closely relate to the holiday.

Name _____

Generalize

- To **generalize** is to make a broad statement or rule that applies to many examples.
- When you make a generalization, you look for similarities or differences among facts and examples in the text.

Directions Complete the graphic organizer below. Find facts and examples from the text that support the generalization.

> **Generalization** Many Mexican crafts, first made by ancient Indian groups, are still made the same way.

Supporting Examples

1.

2.

3.

4.

5.

6.

Directions Write a generalization about Mexican crafts. Then write three facts that support the generalization.

Generalization:

7. _____

Supporting examples:

8. _____

9. _____

10. _____

130

Name _____

Vocabulary

Directions Choose a word from the box that best completes each sentence.

```
┌─────────────────────────────────────────┐
│       Check the Words You Know           │
│   ___ burros        ___ burst            │
│   ___ factory       ___ glassblower      │
│   ___ puff          ___ reply            │
│   ___ tune                               │
└─────────────────────────────────────────┘
```

1. I can play a beautiful _____ on my flute.

2. *Arboles de la vida,* "trees of life," are known for their _____ of leaves and clay figures.

3. When decorating masks, people use a _____ of yarn to represent hair.

4. Many poor people moved closer to a _____ in hopes of getting a job.

5. Some Mexicans travel using _____ .

6. If you asked me if I would like to go to Mexico, I would _____ "Yes!"

7. The _____ sells his colorful vases at the market.

Directions Using as many vocabulary words as possible, write two generalizations about traditional Mexican crafts.

_____

_____

_____

_____

_____

_____

_____

131

Jackie Robinson

Biography

Social Studies

Jackie Robinson
by Morgan Lloyd

⟲ **GENERALIZE**

⟲ **PREDICT/CONFIRM PREDICTIONS**

LESSON VOCABULARY adversity, descending, discrimination, guise, legacy, scholarships, segregated, sharecropper, strike

SUMMARY Learn about the struggles African Americans faced under the laws of segregation through the achievements of Jackie Robinson. The introduction prepares the reader to predict the difficulties Jackie encountered throughout his life, while photographs help the reader visualize the time period.

INTRODUCE THE BOOK

BUILD BACKGROUND To help students appreciate Jackie Robinson's achievements, discuss the discrimination African Americans faced before and during the Civil Rights Movement. Clarify the meaning of the phrase *civil rights*.

ⒺⓁⓁ Build background and vocabulary by discussing the game of baseball. Explain the difference between the minor and major league teams. Discuss the popularity of the Brooklyn Dodgers and the famous athletes on that team.

PREVIEW/USE TEXT FEATURES Prompt students to look at the table of contents. Ask students how they think the information about Jackie is organized.

TEACH/REVIEW VOCABULARY Practice finding the meaning of unfamiliar words by using context clues. Begin with the word *segregated* at the top of page 5. Ask students to tell its meaning in their own words and explain which context clues helped them understand the word. Repeat this process for each vocabulary word.

TARGET SKILL AND STRATEGY

⟲ **GENERALIZE** Review with students that when they read about several people, things, or ideas that are alike, they can often make a *general statement* about them.

⟲ **PREDICT/CONFIRM PREDICTIONS** Both making generalizations and *making predictions* requires students to look at details in the text. Stop and practice this skill after students have read page 18. Guide students to look for details that will help them predict how Jackie will be treated in major league baseball.

READ THE BOOK

Use the following questions to support comprehension.

PAGE 7 What general statement can you make about Jackie's childhood? *(It was difficult.)*

PAGE 10 Why did Jackie believe that a college degree would not help him get a good job? *(African Americans did not have many economic choices even when they had a college degree.)*

PAGE 17 What character trait did Jackie show by not reacting to attackers? *(self-discipline)*

TALK ABOUT THE BOOK

READER RESPONSE
1. Possible responses: They did not have contracts, were forced to work for lower wages, and were restricted in where they could eat and sleep while on the road.
2. Possible response: Baseball might not have become integrated for a long time.
3. Possible response: by adding the suffix *-tion* to make the words *discrimination* and *segregation;* Additional responses will vary.
4. Possible responses: Event and Date—Born, 1919; Left army, 1944; First major league game, 1947; Died, 1972

RESPONSE OPTIONS

WRITING Have students write a fictional journal entry from the point of view of a spectator at Opening Day for the Brooklyn Dodgers in 1947.

CONTENT CONNECTIONS

SOCIAL STUDIES Students can learn more about the Civil Rights Movement by researching on the Internet or at the library.

Time for
SOCIAL
STUDIES

Generalize

- To **generalize** is to make a broad statement or rule that applies to many examples. When you make a generalization, you look for similarities or differences among facts and examples in the text.

Directions Read the following passage. Then answer the questions below.

After he retired from baseball, Jackie and his wife Rachel participated in voter registration drives to register African American voters. They raised money to support Martin Luther King, Jr.'s organization, the Southern Christian Leadership Conference (SCLC). Jackie spoke out against segregation and tried to get other athletes involved in the Civil Rights Movement. He once said, "A life is not important except for the impact it has on other lives." Jackie's life was dedicated to service.

What generalization did the author make about Jackie's life?

1. _____

What four facts and examples from the passage support the generalization?

2. _____

3. _____

4. _____

5. _____

Directions Write your own generalization about Jackie Robinson. Then write four examples that support the generalization.

Generalization:

6. _____

Supporting examples:

7. _____

8. _____

9. _____

10. _____

130

© Pearson Education 3

Vocabulary

Directions Synonyms are words that have similar meanings. Draw a line to match the synonyms.

> ## Check the Words You Know
>
> ___ adversity   ___ descending   ___ discrimination
> ___ guise   ___ legacy   ___ scholarships
> ___ segregated ___ sharecropper ___ strike

1. discrimination

2. guise

3. strike

4. scholarships

5. legacy

a. protest—an act that shows disapproval

b. heritage—lasting customs of a group of people

c. awards—prizes given for achievement

d. bias—unfair dislike

e. charade—a false act

Directions Antonyms are words that have the opposite meaning. Draw a line to match the antonyms.

6. adversity

7. descending

8. discrimination

9. segregated

10. sharecropper

f. planter—a plantation owner

g. integrated—to become joined or combined

h. ascending—moving upward

i. privilege—a special advantage or right

j. easiness—without challenge

131

The Statue of Liberty: From Paris to New Yory City LR1

 Main Idea, LR2

1. b **2.** b **3.** b

Possible responses given. **4.** He loves to play frisbee on the lawn. He loves to roll on the grass. He naps under a tree. **5.** You can get cavities if you don't brush. Your teeth won't be healthy. Your teeth won't look good.

Vocabulary, LR3

1. crown **2.** liberty **3.** torch **4.** unforgettable **5.** models **6.** symbol **7.** tablet **8.** unveiled

Sentences will vary.

The Sights and Sounds of New York City's Chinatown LR10

 Cause and Effect, LR11

Possible responses given. **1.** Throughout Chinatown, you can hear people speaking Chinese. **2.** Many Chinese traditions are maintained in Chinatown. **3.** Some older residents of Chinatown are disappointed in the younger generation. **4.** Some Chinatown residents practice Tai Chi. **5.** Some people watch the celebrations from perches high above the city streets.

Vocabulary, LR12

1. foreign **2.** perches **3.** bows **4.** foolish **5.** recipe **6.** narrow **7.** chilly

Responses will vary.

A Different Drawing LR19

 Fact and Opinion, LR20

1. F **2.** O **3.** O **4.** F **5.** O **6.** F **7.** O **8.** F **9–10.** Opinion; It is a statement of someone's judgment.

Vocabulary, LR21

1. expression **2.** native **3.** settled **4.** encourages **5.** social **6.** local **7.** support

Paragraphs will vary.

Leo and the School of Fish LR28

 Plot and Theme, LR29

Leo and the School of Fish; a fish named Leo; under the sea; Leo swims away from the school to look at a ship. Leo confronts a lantern fish. He confronts a moray eel. He gets caught in a net but is able to swim through it. He rejoins the school. It's best to stick with the group.

Vocabulary, LR30

1. journey **2.** scoop **3.** crystal **4.** discovery **5.** joyful **6.** disappeared **7.** goal **8.** unaware

Responses will vary.

Glass Blowing LR37

 Generalize, LR38

1. need very hot furnace—2,500°F; **2.** need safety goggles and gloves; **3.** cannot blow too gently; **4.** cannot blow too hard; **5.** glass breaks easily; **6.** must be cooled slowly

Vocabulary, LR39

Possible responses given. **1.** *tune;* The musician played a beautiful tune on her guitar. **2.** *bursts;* When you blow too hard through the rod, the glass bubble bursts. **3.** *puff;* You need to puff through a rod to make a bubble. **4.** *factory;* Glass bottles are made in a factory. **5.** *burros;* Burros were used to pull wagons. **6.** *reply;* I will reply to your question when I finish this work. **7.** *glassblower;* A glassblower wears safety goggles and gloves.

Signs, Songs, and Symbols of America   LR4

 Main Idea, LR5

Possible responses given. **1.** Everything about our flag is symbolic. **2.** Each of the colors stands for something. **3.** The thirteen stripes remind us of our colonies. **4.** Francis Scott Key wrote our national anthem. **5.** He was inspired by watching a battle. **6.** He wrote a poem that was set to music.

Vocabulary, LR6

1–4. Responses will vary.

Caring for Your Pet Bird   LR13

Cause and Effect, LR14

Possible responses given. **1.** In the United States it is illegal to import birds from many countries. **2.** Zebra finches don't like to be lonely. **3.** Place interesting treats in different parts of your bird's cage. **4.** Birds like to chew on their toys. **5.** Make sure there are no cold drafts near the cage.

Vocabulary, LR15

1. foreign **2.** perches **3.** bows **4.** foolish **5.** recipe **6.** narrow **7.** chilly
Responses will vary.

A Whole World in One City   LR22

Fact and Opinion, LR23

1. F **2.** O **3.** O **4.** F **5.** O **6.** O **7.** F **8.** O
Responses will vary.

Vocabulary, LR24

1. social **2.** local **3.** settled **4.** encourages **5.** native **6.** support **7.** expression
Responses will vary.

Goldilocks and the Three Bears LR31

Plot and Theme, LR32

Possible responses given. **Title:** Goldilocks and the Three Bears **About:** Goldilocks, Dad Bear, Mom Bear, and Billy Bear. **Takes place:** in the house of the Bear family. **Begins:** Mom Bear makes oatmeal that is too hot to eat. The family goes for a walk while it cools. **Then:** Goldilocks wanders by their house. She goes inside to taste the oatmeal. **Next:** She tastes the oatmeal, breaks their chairs and a glass figure, and falls asleep in Billy Bear's bed. **After that:** The Bears return and find the things she's broken. They also find her asleep in Billy Bear's bed. She wakes up, says she's sorry, and runs off. **Ends:** Billy Bear stops her and says he forgives her. **Theme:** It is best to respect the property of others.

Vocabulary, LR33

1. scoop **2.** disappeared **3.** crystal **4.** joyful **5.** unaware **6.** goal **7.** discovery **8.** journey
Responses will vary.

Traditional Crafts of Mexico   LR40

Generalize, LR41

1. The Maya made pottery. **2.** The Aztecs made pottery, cloth, baskets, and metal work. **3.** Today, there are Mexican folk artists. **4.** Today, pottery is made without a wheel. **5.** Today, people carve wood by hand. **6.** People still embroider. Possible responses given. **7.** Most modern Mexican crafts are colorful. **8.** Some pottery is green, blue, yellow, and mauve. **9.** Weavers use natural dyes to make colorful baskets. **10.** Some masks are decorated with colorful feathers.

Vocabulary, LR42

1. tune **2.** burst(s) **3.** puff **4.** factory **5.** burros **6.** reply **7.** glassblower
Responses will vary.

Answer Key for Advanced-Level Reader Practice

French Roots in North America — LR7

Main Idea, LR8
1. D **2.** D **3.** M **4.** M **5.** D **6.** D **7.** M **8.** D **9.** D **10.** The French have influenced North America.

Vocabulary, LR9
1. a, bilingual **2.** d, immigrants **3.** c, straits **4.** b, influences **5.** g, assembly line **6.** f, fortified **7.** e, echo chamber **8.** h, descendants

China's Gifts to the World — LR16

Cause and Effect, LR17
Possible responses given. **1.** It doesn't tear easily and can't be damaged by insects. **2.** Artwork drawn on Xuan paper has lasted a long time. **3.** China has huge mountains and deserts. **4.** They kept China isolated from Europe for many years. **5.** Li Po loved nature, friends, and spending time alone. **6.** He often took time off for "wandering." **7.** The emperor thought Li Po wanted to create a new kingdom. **8.** He had Li Po sent to jail. **9.** Calligraphers can paint their characters on any surface. **10.** Some artists draw on silk.

Vocabulary, LR18
1. flourished **2.** inspiration **3.** bristles **4.** muffled **5.** ingredients **6.** expedition **7.** techniques
Responses will vary.

The Huge Paintings of Thomas Hart Benton — LR25

Fact and Opinion, LR26
1. F; Many people have written about him; many people know him. **2.** O; You cannot prove it, but you can compare him to other artists and like his art more. **3.** F; His father sent him to military school and expressed a desire for him to go into politics. **4.** O; You cannot prove that this is true. **5.** O; You cannot prove this is true.

Vocabulary, LR27
1. *n.* friend or helper **2.** *v.* to be grateful for **3.** *v.* joined or signed on **4.** *v.* gave support to **5.** *n.* example, illustration, or demonstration **6.** *n.* a gift left by someone **7.** *n.* a large wall painting **8.** *n.* a local resident **9.** *adj.* relating to human society **10.** *n.* backing, encouragement, help

A Fantastic Field Trip — LR34

Plot and Theme, LR35
Possible responses given. **Title:** A Fantastic Field Trip **The story is about** the Bug Kids (Emma, Jacob, Kayla, Luke, Carlos, Lily), Mr. Edwards, Mrs. Appleby, and Elvis. **This story takes place** at the school and at the Entomological Zoo. **The action begins when** the Bug Kids take off in the school van for the zoo. They arrive at their hotel, where they spend one night. **Then** at the Entomological Zoo, they visit the butterflies, and some are huge. **Next,** they visit wasps and cicadas, which are also huge. **After that,** they visit fleas that can jump 150 feet. **The story ends when** they return home. **Theme:** One should have respect for insects.

Vocabulary, LR36
1. announcement **2.** entomological **3.** expenses **4.** budge **5.** exhibition **6.** nuisances
Responses will vary.

Jackie Robinson — LR43

Generalize, LR44
1. Jackie's life was dedicated to service. **2.** participated in voter registration drives **3.** raised money to support the SCLC **4.** spoke out against segregation **5.** tried to get other athletes involved in the Civil Rights Movement.
Possible responses given. **6.** Jackie Robinson was a role model. **7.** Jackie was a talented athlete. **8.** Jackie did not react to insults. **9.** Jackie was involved in the Civil Rights Movement. **10.** He worked to help others.

Vocabulary, LR45
1. d **2.** e **3.** a **4.** c **5.** b **6.** j **7.** h **8.** i **9.** g **10.** f

Differentiated Instruction

Table of Contents

Routine Cards

Oral Rereading Routine

Use this Routine when students read orally.

1 Read Have students read the entire book orally.

2 Reread For optimal fluency, students should reread the text three or four times.

3 Provide Feedback Listen as students read and provide corrective feedback regarding their oral reading and their use of decoding strategies.

Choral Reading Routine

Use this Routine when students read chorally.

1 Select a Passage Choose an appropriate passage from the selection.

2 Divide into Groups Assign each group a part to read.

3 Model Have students track the print as you read.

4 Read Together Have students read along with you.

5 Independent Reading Have the groups read aloud without you. Monitor progress and provide feedback. For optimal fluency, students should reread three to four times.

Fluent Word Reading Routine

Teach students to read words fluently using this Routine.

1 Connect Write an example word. Isolate the sound-spelling or word structure element you will focus on and ask students to demonstrate their understanding.

2 Model When you come to a new word, look at all the letters in the word and think about its vowel sound. Say the sounds in the word to yourself and then read the word. Model reading the example words in this way. When you come to a new word, what are you going to do?

3 Group Practice Write other similar words. Let's read these words. Look at the letters, think about the vowel sounds, and say the sounds to yourself. When I point to the word, let's read it together. Allow 2-3 seconds previewing time for each word.

Paired Reading Routine

Use this Routine when students read in pairs.

1 Reader 1 Begins Students read the entire book, switching readers at the end of each page.

2 Reader 2 Begins Have partners reread; now the other partner begins.

3 Reread For optimal fluency, students should reread three or four times.

4 Provide Feedback Listen as students read. Provide corrective feedback regarding their oral reading and their use of decoding strategies.

© Pearson Education, Inc.

Advanced

ROUTINE

1 Extend Comprehension

SKILL CAUSE AND EFFECT Tell students that a cause-and-effect relationship is not always obvious and that sometimes there is more than one cause or reason for an effect, or more than one effect from a cause. Have students think of several causes or reasons why Sam might want his grandfather to set the bird free.

STRATEGY GRAPHIC ORGANIZERS Have students use a cause-and-effect graphic organizer with more than one box for the effects. In the "cause" box, have them write, "Mrs. Kang gives Mr. Kang a birthday party." Then ask students to list at least two effects.

2 Read *Happy Birthday Mr. Kang,* pp. 318–325

BEFORE READING Have students recall what has happened in the selection so far. Remind them to look for causes and their effects and to write them on a graphic organizer as they read the remainder of the story.

CRITICAL THINKING Have students read pp. 318–325 independently. Encourage them to think critically. For example, ask:

- Why do you think Mr. Kang set the bird free even though his wife and friends wanted him to keep his *hua mei* caged?
- Why do you think the bird came back to him?

AFTER READING Have students complete the Strategy Response Log activity (p. 324). Meet with them to have them share their summaries. Then have students imagine that Mr. Kang keeps a diary. Have them write the entry he might have recorded on the Sunday he gave his *hua mei* freedom. Tell students to include details about Mr. Kang's feelings and how they changed from early in the morning to later in the day.

DAY 3

AudioText

Group Time

ROUTINE

DAY 4

Audio CD AudioText

1 Practice Retelling

REVIEW STORY ELEMENTS Help students identify the main characters and the setting of *Happy Birthday Mr. Kang*. Then guide them in using the Retelling Cards to list story events in sequence. Prompt students to include important details.

RETELL Using the Retelling Cards, have students work in pairs to retell *Happy Birthday Mr. Kang*. Monitor retelling and prompt students as needed. For example, ask:

PEARSON Scott Foresman Grade 3 **Retelling Cards**

- What is the problem in this story?
- What is the author trying to tell us or teach us?

If students struggle, model a fluent retelling.

2 Read "Back to the Wild"

BEFORE READING Read the genre information on p. 328. Explain that an interviewer will ask an expert questions and take notes on the answers or even tape-record them, and then write down each question and its answer.

Read the rest of the panel on p. 328. Point out examples of different colored print. Show students that the interviewer's initials are in green and the expert's initials are in red after their first appearance. Call attention to the questions in dark print. Then have students scan the pages and examine the photographs for details.

DURING READING Have students read along with you while tracking the print or do a choral reading of the selection. Discuss the opening page to be certain that students understand why Molly Jean Carpenter is considered an expert. Stop to discuss difficult language, such as *recover* and *aggressive*.

AFTER READING Have students share their reactions to the selection. Then guide them through the Reading Across Texts and Writing Across Texts activities, prompting if necessary.

- Why was Mr. Kang's *hua mei* away from its natural home? Why was Copernicus?
- How did Mr. Kang's *hua mei* react to being set free? How did Copernicus react?
- Should all animals be set free? When might animals be better off in homes or clinics?

Monitor Progress

Word and Selection Reading

If... students have difficulty reading multisyllabic words in the selection,	**then...** have them look for and read meaningful parts in the words or have them chunk words with no recognizable parts.
If... students have difficulty reading along with the group,	**then...** have them follow along as they listen to the AudioText.

Advanced

ROUTINE

1 Read "Back to the Wild"

CRITICAL THINKING/CREATIVE THINKING Have students read pp. 328–331 independently. Encourage them to think critically and creatively. For example, ask:

- What steps are taken before an animal is released back into the wild? Why?
- Do you think it was hard for Molly Jean Carpenter to see Copernicus fly away? Explain.
- Why might it be hard for parents to see their older children "fly away," or leave home?

AFTER READING Have students meet with you to discuss Reading Across Texts. Have students do Writing Across Texts independently.

2 Extend Genre Study

RESEARCH Have students use online resources or print resources to find other examples of interviews. Have them make a list of the experts who were interviewed and note their areas of expertise.

WRITE Have students conduct an interview with an animal expert (a veterinarian, a zoo animal caretaker, a pet shelter worker) either in person, by phone, or by e-mail. Help them find out about the expert and politely request the interview. Tell students to prepare a list of interview questions beforehand. Encourage them to use initials and dark or otherwise special print when they write the final interview. Meet with students as they share their interviews.

DAY
4

AudioText

Group Time

ROUTINE

① Reread for Fluency

MODEL Read aloud pp. 3–5 of the Leveled Reader *The Sights and Sounds of New York City's Chinatown*, emphasizing appropriate phrasing. Have students note how you read entire groups of words together. Then read p. 6 word-by-word. Have students tell you which model was better. Tell students that reading in meaningful phrases helps readers better understand what they read.

PRACTICE Have students reread passages from *The Sights and Sounds of New York City's Chinatown* with a partner or individually. For optimal fluency, they should reread three or four times.
As students read, monitor fluency and provide corrective feedback. Assess the fluency of students in this group using p. 331a.

② Retell Leveled Reader *The Sights and Sounds of New York City's Chinatown*

Model how to use the question headings and photographs to retell the selection. Then ask students to retell the book, one question-and-answer section at a time. Prompt them as needed.

- What is this section mostly about?
- What did you learn from reading this section?

DAY 5

Leveled Reader
Database
ONLINE
PearsonSuccessNet.com

Monitor Progress

Fluency

If... students have difficulty reading fluently,	then... provide additional fluency practice by pairing nonfluent readers with fluent ones.

For alternate Leveled Reader lesson plans that teach **Cause and Effect, Graphic Organizers,** and **Lesson Vocabulary,** see pp. LR10–LR18.

On-Level

DAY 5

1 Reread for Fluency

ROUTINE

MODEL Read aloud p. 3 of the Leveled Reader *Caring for Your Pet Bird,* emphasizing appropriate phrasing. Have students note how you read entire groups of words instead of reading word-by-word. Discuss how reading in meaningful phrases helps readers better understand what they read.

PRACTICE Have students reread passages from *Caring for Your Pet Bird* with a partner or individually. For optimal fluency, they should reread three or four times. As students read, monitor fluency and provide corrective feedback. Students in this group are assessed in Week 3.

2 Retell Leveled Reader *Caring for Your Pet Bird*

Have students use headings and photographs as a guide to summarize the important facts they learned from each section of the book. Prompt as needed.

- What was this selection mostly about?
- Tell me about the steps I need to follow to care for a bird.

Advanced

1 Reread for Fluency

ROUTINE

PRACTICE Have students reread passages from the Leveled Reader *China's Gifts* to the World with a partner or individually. As students read, monitor fluency and provide corrective feedback. If students read fluently on the first reading, they do not need to reread three or four times. Students in this group were assessed in Week 1.

2 Revisit Leveled Reader *China's Gifts to the World*

RETELL Have students retell the Leveled Reader *China's Gifts to the World.*

NOW TRY THIS Have students complete their projects. You may wish to see whether they need any additional supplies. Ask them to present their calligraphy.

Group Time

Leveled Reader Database

ONLINE

PearsonSuccessNet.com

Strategic Intervention

ROUTINE

1 Preteach Phonics

SYLLABLES *-TION, -SION, -TURE.* Tell students that there are some common word parts that appear in many different words. Write *nation.* How many syllables do you hear in *nation? (two)* What is the first syllable? *(na)* What is the second syllable? *(tion)* Which syllable have you seen in many other words? *(tion)* Model blending *nation.* Then have students blend *nation* with you. Repeat this process for the syllables *-sion* and *-ture,* using the words *television* and *future.*

2 Preview Decodable Reader 28

BEFORE READING Review the words on Decodable Reader p. 97. Then have students blend these story words: *earn, inventor, surrounded, creaked, alarmed, invisible, reverse, spoonful, gasped.* Be sure students understand the meanings of words such as *alarmed* and *reverse.*

Use the Picture Walk Routine on p. DI·1 to guide students through the text.

3 Read Leveled Reader *A Different Drawing*

REINFORCE CONCEPTS This week's concept is *freedom of expression.* People can express themselves, or show what they think or feel, by saying, doing, or writing something. How do you express yourself?

BEFORE READING Using the Picture Walk Routine on p. DI·1, guide students through the text focusing on key concepts and vocabulary. Ask questions such as:

p. 7 The girl in the pink sweater is Sue. How is Sue's drawing the same as the other drawings? How is it different? *(Sue's drawing is a tree like the others, but it looks more real then the other trees.)*

p. 12 What kinds of trees did Sue draw? *(all kinds, even trees that look like an octopus and a monkey)*

Read pp. 3–4 aloud. Then do a choral reading of pp. 5–8. Have students read and discuss the remainder of the book with a partner. Ask: We are free to express ourselves in many different ways. How do the students' tree drawings show this? *(They are all different. Some look like real trees, and some don't.)*

Monitor Progress

Word and Selection Reading

If... students have difficulty reading story words from the Decodable Reader,	**then...** reteach them by modeling blending or reading multisyllabic words.
If... partners have difficulty reading the Leveled Reader on their own,	**then...** have them follow along as they listen to the Online Leveled Reader Audio.

For alternate Leveled Reader lesson plans that teach
🔾 **Fact and Opinion,** 🔾 **Answer Questions,**
and **Lesson Vocabulary,** see pp. LR19–LR27.

On-Level

❶ Build Background

DEVELOP VOCABULARY Write the word *downhearted* and ask students to define it in their own words. *(When you are downhearted, you feel sad.)* Show me how a downhearted person might look. Repeat this activity with the word *excited* and other words from the Leveled Reader *A Whole World in One City.* Use the Concept Vocabulary Routine on p. DI·1 as needed.

❷ Read Leveled Reader *A Whole World in a City*

BEFORE READING Have students create a three-column chart titled *Chicago Neighborhoods* with the headings *Mexican, Polish,* and *Chinese.* This book tells how people in various Chicago neighborhoods are free to express themselves and the cultures they came from. As you read, look for details about ways the people express themselves through art, food, music, and other activities. Record the information on your chart.

DURING READING Have students follow along as you read pp. 3–8. Then let them complete the book on their own. Remind students to add facts on their chart as they read.

AFTER READING Have students compare the facts on their charts. Point out that details they learn about the ways people express themselves in different neighborhoods will help them as they read tomorrow's selection, *Talking Walls: Art for the People.*

Advanced

❶ Read Leveled Reader *The Huge Paintings of Thomas Hart Benton*

BEFORE READING Recall the Read Aloud "Indescribably Arabella." Why do you think the two lonely people appreciated Arabella's talents when others didn't? *(The two people knew that Arabella was expressing herself as only she could, and they liked that she was different.)* Today you will read about a famous American painter whose art is an expression of how he felt about life in the United States.

CRITICAL THINKING Have students read the Leveled Reader independently. Encourage them to think critically. For example, ask:

- Why might Thomas Hart Benton's honest paintings upset some people?
- Select your favorite Thomas Hart Benton painting. What do you think he was trying to express through this piece of art?

AFTER READING Have students review the selection to find four or more unfamiliar words and determine their meanings through context or the dictionary. Then ask them to write each word in a sentence about themselves or draw a picture of themselves that conveys the meaning of the word. Have students meet with you to discuss the selection and their sentences or pictures.

❷ Independent Extension Activity

NOW TRY THIS Assign "Now Try This" on pp. 22–23 of *The Huge Paintings of Thomas Hart Benton* for students to work on throughout the week.

Talking Walls: Art for the People

Group Time

ROUTINE

Audio CD · AudioText

DAY 2

1 Reread for Fluency

Use Decodable Reader 28.

2 Word Study/Phonics

LESSON VOCABULARY Use p. 334b to review the meanings of *encourages, expression, local, native, settled, social,* and *support.* Have students blend decodable words: *encourages, expression, local, native, settled,* and *support.* Then say and spell the nondecodable word *social.* Have individuals practice with word cards.

DECODING MULTISYLLABIC WORDS Write *festivals* and model how to chunk the word. I see a chunk at the beginning of the word: *fes.* I see a part in the middle: *ti.* I see a chunk at the end of the word: *vals.* I say each chunk slowly: *fes ti vals.* I say the chunks fast to make a whole word: *festivals.* Is it a real word? Yes, I know *festivals.*

Use the Multisyllabic Word Routine on p. DI·1 to help students read these other words from *Talking Walls: Art for the People: artistic, muralists, depict, democracy, seamstress, interprets, fashioned, extending, graduated, accomplished* and *residents.* Be sure students understand the meanings of words such as *depict* and *fashioned.*

3 Read *Talking Walls: Art for the People,* pp. 336–343

BEFORE READING Yesterday we read about a girl who expressed herself through art. Today we will read about artists called muralists who are free to express themselves by creating huge paintings on walls.

Using the Picture Walk Routine on p. DI·1, guide students through the text, asking questions such as those listed below. Then read the question on p. 337. Together, set a purpose for reading.

pp. 340–341 On p. 340 is a mural. On p. 341, you can see two sections of that mural close up. What do you notice about the mural?

p. 343 This mural is painted on the side of a building. What do you notice about the top of it? *(It goes above the building.)*

DURING READING Follow the Guiding Comprehension routine on pp. 338–343. Have students read along with you while tracking the print or do a choral reading of the selection. Stop every two pages to ask what students have learned so far. Prompt as necessary.

- What did you learn about the mural "Immigrant" by Hector Ponce?
- What are pp. 342 and 343 about?

AFTER READING What have you learned so far? What do you think you will learn about tomorrow? Reread passages as needed.

Monitor Progress

Word and Selection Reading

If... students have difficulty reading multisyllabic words in the selection,	**then...** have them look for and read meaningful parts in the words or have them chunk words with no recognizable parts.
If... students have difficulty reading along with the group,	**then...** have them follow along as they listen to the AudioText.

Advanced

1 Extend Vocabulary

GLOSSARY Choose and read a sentence or passage containing a word from the glossary, such as this sentence from p. 9 of *The Huge Paintings of Thomas Hart Benton:* "When World War I began, Thomas enlisted in the navy." Look up the word *enlisted* in the glossary. What does it mean? *("joined" or "signed on")* How did you find the word's meaning? *(I found the glossary in the back of the book and used the first letters of the word to help me find it in alphabetical order. I read the meaning, and then I tried it in the sentence to see if it made sense.)* A glossary is helpful because it gives the meanings of important words in the book. Remind students to use the strategy as they read *Talking Walls: Art for the People.*

2 Read *Talking Walls: Art for the People,* pp. 336–343

BEFORE READING In *The Huge Paintings of Thomas Hart Benton* you read about the enormous murals that the artist created. Today you will read a selection about other famous muralists who express themselves by painting on walls. As you read, think about the different ways people can express themselves.

In their Strategy Response Logs (p. 336), have students write two questions that they would like to have answered as they read. As they read, they can record answers to their questions in their Strategy Response Logs (p. 343).

CRITICAL THINKING AND PROBLEM SOLVING Have students read pp. 336–343 independently. Encourage them to think critically and solve problems. For example, ask:

- Why do you think Hector Ponce decided to paint on the walls of a meat market in Los Angeles?
- Joshua Sarantitis encourages people to reach for the future through education. What does this mean? How might a person accomplish this goal?

AFTER READING Have partners discuss the selection. Tell them to share their Strategy Response Log questions and answers. Then have students draw pictures that show how they would express the meaning of reaching for the future through education. Meet with them to discuss their art. Display their paintings horizontally on a wall of the classroom. Encourage them to compose a title for the mural.

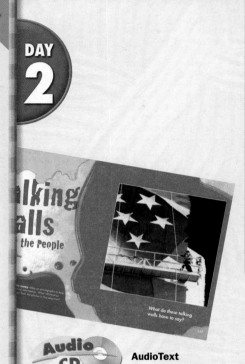

DAY 2

AudioText

Talking Walls: Art for the People
Group Time

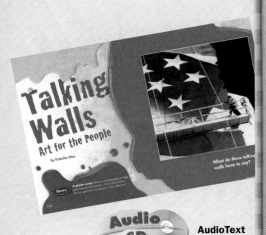

DAY
3

Audio CD AudioText

Monitor Progress

Word and Selection Reading

If... students have difficulty reading multisyllabic words in the selection,	**then...** have them look for and read meaningful parts in the words or have them chunk words with no recognizable parts.
If... students have difficulty reading along with the group,	**then...** have them follow along as they listen to the AudioText.

Strategic Intervention

ROUTINE

1 Reinforce Comprehension

SKILL FACT AND OPINION Have students tell what a statement of fact is *(something that can be proved true or false)* and what a statement of opinion is *(an idea or feeling about something)*. Have them list clue words that can signal statements of opinion. *(great, best, worst)* If necessary, review the meaning and provide a model. A statement of fact can be proved true or false. For example, *There are different kinds of murals* is a statement of fact. It can be proved by looking in a reference or art book. *Murals are the best kind of art* is an opinion. It cannot be proved; it is just someone's judgment. The word *best* helps me see that it is an opinion.

Read these statements and have students decide whether they are statements of fact or opinion.

- Murals that show festivals are more fun to see than those that show history. *(opinion)*
- Hector Ponce came from El Salvador to the United States. *(fact)*

2 Read *Talking Walls: Art for the People*, pp. 344–349

BEFORE READING Have students retell what they have learned from the selection so far. Ask: What does Joshua Sarantitis do before he creates a mural? Model how to answer the question. I skim the selection until I find the name Joshua Sarantitis on p. 342. Then I reread the first paragraph on p. 342 and summarize what it says. Then ask: What makes the mural on p. 343 so beautiful? Solicit some answers, and then model using the Answer Questions strategy. To answer this question, you need to combine what is in the text with your own ideas. I reread the second paragraph on p. 342 and study the mural. The text helps me notice details I might have missed. Then I think about what I like best about the mural. I must use my own judgment to decide what is most beautiful about it. Remind students to use the Answer Questions strategy as you read and discuss the rest of *Talking Walls*. **STRATEGY Answer Questions**

DURING READING Follow the Guiding Comprehension routine on pp. 344–349. Have students read along with you while tracking print or do a choral reading.

- What are pp. 344–345 about?
- What did you learn about muralists?

AFTER READING How do muralists express their feelings? Reread with students as needed. Tell them that tomorrow they will read "Nathaniel's Rap," a poem in which a boy expresses his feelings.

DAY 3

Advanced

ROUTINE

1 Extend Comprehension

🎯 **SKILL FACT AND OPINION** Have students write a short paragraph about the mural "Community of Music" on p. 339 that includes both facts and opinions. Ask students to use a yellow marker to highlight the statements of fact in their writing. Invite students to meet with you to discuss what they could do to prove the facts. Encourage them to explain their opinions and tell why they cannot be proved true or false.

🎯 **STRATEGY ANSWER QUESTIONS** Remind students that some questions can be answered by finding information right there in the text. Other questions require students to combine what is in the text with their own knowledge or judgment. Ask students to write one question that can be answered using information in the text on pp. 336–343 and one question that would require combining that text with their own ideas or judgment. Have students share their questions and discuss how they would go about answering them.

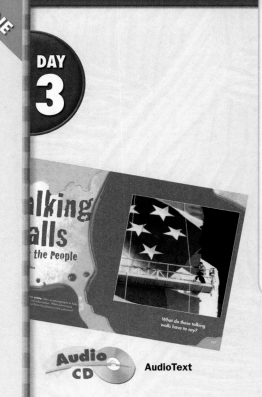

Audio CD   **AudioText**

2 Read *Talking Walls: Art for the People,* pp. 344–349

BEFORE READING Have students recall what they have learned so far. Remind them to look for facts and opinions as they read the remainder of the selection.

CRITICAL AND CREATIVE THINKING Have students read pp. 344–349 independently. Then ask questions to encourage critical and creative thinking. For example ask:

- What do the symbols in "A Shared Hope" represent?
- How are all the murals in this selection similar? What do they have in common?
- How do these murals show the importance of freedom of expression?
- What would life be like without freedom of expression?

Remind students to use the Answer Questions strategy as they answer these questions. As they answer a question, ask: How did you find an answer to this question?

AFTER READING Have students complete the Strategy Response Log activity (p. 348). Then have them compile a list of the things they read, the art they saw, and the movies they watched during the past week. Have them use the list to write a description of what their life would be like if there was no freedom of expression. Allow time for students to share their descriptions with you and the class.

Group Time

DAY 4

Poetry

Nathaniel's Rap
by Eloise Greenfield

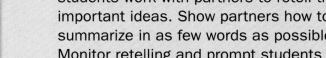

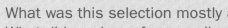

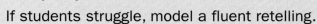

Audio CD **AudioText**

① Practice Retelling

REVIEW MAIN IDEAS Help students identify the main ideas in *Talking Walls: Art for the People.* List the ideas students mention. Then ask questions to help students differentiate between essential and nonessential information.

RETELL Using the Retelling Cards, have students work with partners to retell the important ideas. Show partners how to summarize in as few words as possible. Monitor retelling and prompt students as needed. For example, ask:

- What was this selection mostly about?
- What did you learn from reading this selection?
- Why do you think the author wrote this selection?

If students struggle, model a fluent retelling.

Retelling Cards
Grade 3
PEARSON Scott Foresman

② Read "Nathaniel's Rap"

BEFORE READING Read the genre information on p. 352. A rap is a type of poem that includes rhyme and has short lines with a very strong rhythm, or beat. Encourage students to share what they know about rap.

Read the rest of the panel on p. 352. Explain that Nathaniel will be the person talking in this poem. Where there is no punctuation, have students point out where they should pause. Before you begin, note the print size changes and discuss how the lines should be read.

DURING READING Have students read along with you while tracking the print or do a choral reading of the selection.

AFTER READING Have students share their reactions to the poem and discuss any difficult language or parts of the poem that were problematic. Then guide them through the Reading Across Texts and Writing Across Texts activities, prompting if necessary.

- What is the main thing the muralists would want you to know about their art?
- What is the main thing Nathaniel would want you to know about his rap?

Monitor Progress

Word and Poetry Reading

If... students have difficulty reading multisyllabic words in the poem,	**then...** have them look for and read meaningful parts in the words or have them chunk words with no recognizable parts.
If... students have difficulty reading along with the group,	**then...** have them follow along as they listen to the AudioText.

Advanced

① Read "Nathaniel's Rap"

CRITICAL THINKING Have students read pp. 352–353 independently. Encourage them to think critically. For example, ask:

- What kind of person is Nathaniel? Would you like to have him as a friend?
- Nathaniel says, "I'm talking about my philosophy." What does he mean by this?
- Why do you think rapping is so popular with many young people?

AFTER READING Have students meet with you to discuss Reading Across Texts. Have students do Writing Across Texts independently.

② Extend Genre Study

RESEARCH Have students use books, music collections, and online resources to find raps and other poems they like. Have them make a list of their favorites, noting how they feel when they read or hear each selection and why it makes them feel that way.

WRITE Have students work together to write a rap. Have them meet with you and recite the rap several times before presenting it to the class. Encourage the audience to snap and tap to the rhythm.

AudioText

Group Time

Leveled Reader
Database
ONLINE

PearsonSuccessNet.com

Strategic Intervention

ROUTINE

1 Reread for Fluency

MODEL Read aloud pp. 3–4 of the Leveled Reader *A Different Drawing* with fluency, self-correcting when you make one or two mistakes. Discuss how students should read silently in a similar way, with accuracy and self-correcting when they misread a word, in order to better understand. Then tell students that you are going to read the same pages silently. Model how to focus on the material you are reading. Then model inappropriate silent reading behavior, such as looking around the room. Have students tell you which model was better.

PRACTICE Have students find a quiet place in the classroom to reread passages from *A Different Drawing* silently. Remind students to block out noise and self-correct. Students in this group are assessed in Weeks 2 and 4.

2 Retell Leveled Reader *A Different Drawing*

Model how to skim the book, retelling as you skim. Then ask students to retell the story, one page at a time. Prompt them as needed.

- What is the problem in this story?
- How is the problem solved?

Monitor Progress

Fluency

If... students have difficulty reading fluently,	then... provide additional fluency practice by pairing nonfluent readers with fluent ones.

For alternate Leveled Reader lesson plans that teach **Fact and Opinion**, **Answer Questions**, and **Lesson Vocabulary**, see pp. LR19–LR27.

On-Level

1 Reread for Fluency   ROUTINE

MODEL Tell students that good silent readers block out other noises and concentrate on what they are reading. Point out that they also self-correct when they misread or skip a word. Then model, reading p. 3 of the Leveled Reader *A Whole World in One City.* First read it aloud, and then read it silently. Discuss how being a good silent reader helps you understand and remember what you read.

PRACTICE Have individuals find a comfortable place to reread passages from *A Whole World in One City* silently. Remind them to self-correct if they misread or skip a word. Then have partners reread passages aloud. For optimal fluency, students should reread three or four times. As students read, monitor fluency and provide corrective feedback. Assess the fluency of students in this group using p. 353a.

2 Retell Leveled Reader *A Whole World in One City*

Have students use the illustrations as a guide to retell *A Whole World in One City.* Prompt as needed.

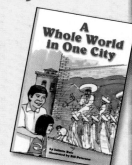

- Where does this story take place?
- Has anything like this happened to you?
- What is the author trying to tell us or teach us?

Advanced

1 Reread for Fluency   ROUTINE

PRACTICE Have students silently reread passages from the Leveled Reader *The Huge Paintings of Thomas Hart Benton.* Students in this group were assessed in Week 1.

2 Revisit Leveled Reader *The Huge Paintings of Thomas Hart Benton*

RETELL Have students retell the Leveled Reader *The Huge Paintings of Thomas Hart Benton.*

NOW TRY THIS Have students complete their charts and drawings. You may wish to review their charts and see whether they need any additional art supplies. Have them share their mini-murals with classmates.

Two Bad Ants

Group Time

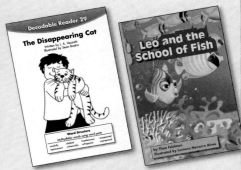

Leveled Reader Database ONLINE

PearsonSuccessNet.com

❶ Preteach Phonics

MULTISYLLABIC WORDS USING AFFIXES Tell students that prefixes and suffixes can be added to base words. Write *unselfish*. What is the base word in *unselfish*? *(self)* What word part do you see at the beginning of *unselfish*? *(the prefix* un-*)* What word part do you see at the end of *unselfish*? *(the suffix* -ish*)* When you come to a longer word, look closely for a prefix, a suffix, or both. You can divide the word and look at each word part; then the word becomes much easier to read. Model blending *unselfish*.

❷ Preview Decodable Reader 29

BEFORE READING Review the words on Decodable Reader p. 105. Then have students blend these story words: *discouraged, remarkable, unacceptable, recalled, impossibly, uncomfortable, ownership, misbehaved, squirmed, refreshments*. Be sure students understand words such as *discouraged* and *remarkable*.

Use the Picture Walk Routine on p. DI·1 to guide students through the text.

❸ Read Leveled Reader *Leo and the School of Fish*

REINFORCE CONCEPTS This week's concept is *too much freedom*. What might happen in a classroom where there were no rules? How might too much freedom be a problem?

BEFORE READING Using the Picture Walk Routine on p. DI·1, guide students through the text focusing on key concepts and vocabulary. Ask questions such as:

pp. 4–5 Why do you think these fish are swimming together in a group? *(They are safe; they like each other.)* A group of fish is called a school. When fish swim together they are safer.

pp. 8–9 This fish wants freedom from the school. Where does he go? What does he see?

Read pp. 3–4 aloud. Then do a choral reading of pp. 5–8. Have students read and discuss the remainder of the book with a partner. Ask: What might Leo say about having too much freedom?

Monitor Progress

Word and Selection Reading

If... students have difficulty reading story words from the Decodable Reader,	then... reteach them by modeling blending or reading multisyllabic words.
If... partners have difficulty reading the Leveled Reader on their own,	then... have them follow along as they listen to the Online Leveled Reader Audio.

For alternate Leveled Reader lesson plans that teach
🔁**Plot and Theme,** 🔁**Visualize,** and
Lesson Vocabulary, see pp. LR28–LR36.

On-Level

ROUTINE

❶ Build Background

DEVELOP VOCABULARY Write the word *fascinated* and ask students to define it in their own words. *(When you are fascinated by something, you are really interested in it.)* Give an example of something that you are fascinated by. Use the word *fascinated* when you tell about it. *(Possible responses: I'm fascinated by snakes, video games, soccer.)* Repeat this activity with the word *intruder* and other words from the Leveled Reader *Goldilocks and the Three Bears*. Use the Concept Vocabulary Routine on p. DI·1 as needed.

❷ **Read** Leveled Reader *Goldilocks and the Three Bears*

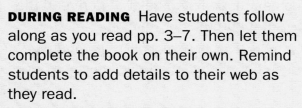

BEFORE READING Have students create webs with *selfish* in the center. This book tells how Goldilocks used her freedom in a selfish way. As you read, look for ways Goldilocks was selfish. Record the information on your web.

DURING READING Have students follow along as you read pp. 3–7. Then let them complete the book on their own. Remind students to add details to their web as they read.

AFTER READING Have students compare the details on their webs. Point out that details about Goldilocks using freedom in a selfish way will help them as they read tomorrow's selection, *Two Bad Ants*.

Advanced

ROUTINE

❶ **Read** Leveled Reader *A Fantastic Field Trip*

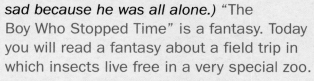

BEFORE READING Recall the Read Aloud "The Boy Who Stopped Time." For a while Julian was free to do as he pleased. How did his feelings about this freedom change? *(First he was happy and excited. Then he became sad because he was all alone.)* "The Boy Who Stopped Time" is a fantasy. Today you will read a fantasy about a field trip in which insects live free in a very special zoo.

CREATIVE THINKING Have students read the Leveled Reader independently. Encourage them to think critically and creatively. For example, ask:

- What is mysterious about the zoo?
- Why do you think the author wrote the story this way?
- How could you add to the story to explain the size of the insects?

AFTER READING Have students select five or more unfamiliar words and determine their meanings. Then have students use the words as they write a short story about one of the giant insects escaping from the zoo. Have students meet with you to discuss their stories and how they used the words. Invite students to share their stories.

❷ Independent Extension Activity

CREATE A MURAL Assign the article on p. 22 of *A Fantastic Field Trip*. Then have students find facts about other insects that might live in the Entomological Zoo. Throughout the week, have students work on a mural, drawing and labeling giant insects that are based on scientific facts.

Two Bad Ants

Group Time

ROUTINE

Audio CD AudioText

1 Reread for Fluency
Use Decodable Reader 29.

2 Word Study/Phonics

LESSON VOCABULARY Use p. 356b to review the meanings of *crystal, disappeared, discovery, goal, journey, joyful, scoop,* and *unaware.* Have students blend decodable words: *disappeared, discovery, goal, journey, joyful, scoop, unaware.* Then say and spell the nondecodable word *crystal.* Have students practice with word cards.

DECODING MULTISYLLABIC WORDS Write *whirlpool* and model how to use meaningful word parts to read it. First I ask myself if I see any parts I know. I see *whirl* at the beginning of the word and *pool* at the end. I know that *whirl* means "to spin" and that a *pool* is a place where there is water. So I think a whirlpool is spinning water.

Use the Multisyllabic Word Routine on p. DI·1 to help students read these other words from *Two Bad Ants: delicious, departed, surrounded, twilight, anxiously, echoing, delicate, unnatural, hovered,* and *violently.* Be sure students understand the meanings of words.

3 Read *Two Bad Ants,* pp. 358–367

BEFORE READING Yesterday we read how having too much freedom put Leo the fish in danger. Today we will read how two ants end up in an unsafe place because they don't use their freedom wisely.

Using the Picture Walk Routine on p. DI·1, guide students through the text, asking questions such as those listed below. Then read the question on p. 359. Together, set a purpose for reading.

pp. 362–363 Why do the plants look so big? *(because the ants are so small)* Yes, in this story the author and illustrator wants you to see the world the way ants see it.

p. 365 Where are the ants going? *(into a house)* The ants have left their underground home and are now crawling into a kitchen window.

DURING READING Follow the Guiding Comprehension routine on pp. 360–367. Have students read along with you while tracking the print or do a choral reading. Stop every two pages to ask what students have learned so far. Prompt as necessary.
• When the other ants return home, what do the two ants do? Why?
• How do the two ants end up in a boiling brown lake?

AFTER READING What has happened so far? What do you think will happen next? Reread passages as needed.

Monitor Progress

Word and Story Reading

If... students have difficulty reading multisyllabic words in the selection,	**then...** have them look for and read meaningful parts in the words or have them chunk words with no recognizable parts.
If... students have difficulty reading along with the group,	**then...** have them follow along as they listen to the AudioText.

Advanced

1 Extend Vocabulary

WORD STRUCTURE Choose and read a sentence or passage containing a difficult word with a prefix or suffix, such as this sentence from p. 18 of *A Fantastic Field Trip:* "Everyone stopped to watch an adult cicada crawl out of its skin, almost like unwrapping a present." *What does the word* unwrapping *mean? (the opposite of wrapping) How did you figure out the word's meaning? (I looked at the prefix and the base word. The prefix* un- *can mean "the opposite of," so* unwrapping *is the opposite of wrapping.)* Using word structure is helpful because it can help you figure out the meaning of an unknown word. Remind students to use the strategy as they read *Two Bad Ants.*

2 Read *Two Bad Ants,* pp. 358–367

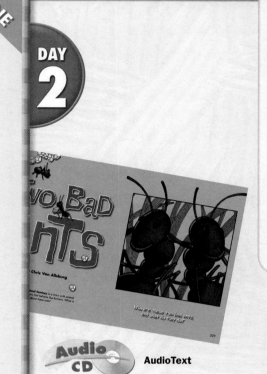

AudioText

BEFORE READING In "The Boy Who Stopped Time," you read about Julian, who found himself alone when he didn't obey family rules. Today you will read a story about two ants who find themselves alone when they don't follow the rules of their ant colony.

Have students predict why the ants in the story are bad. Have them enter their responses in their Strategy Response Logs (p. 358).

CREATIVE THINKING Have students read pp. 358–367 independently. Encourage them to think creatively. For example, say:

• The two ants want to eat the tasty treasure every day, forever. What does this remind you of from another story? What does it remind you of from your own life?

AFTER READING Have partners discuss the selection and share their Strategy Response Log entries. Have them revise their old predictions or make a new prediction about the rest of the story for their Strategy Response Logs (p. 367). Then have students answer the question: Can you ever have too much of a good thing? Have them support their opinion with examples. Encourage them to think of examples other than those that relate to food or drink. When students are finished, have them meet with you to discuss their opinions.

Two Bad Ants

Group Time

DAY 3

Audio CD — **AudioText**

ROUTINE

1 Reinforce Comprehension

◉ **SKILL PLOT AND THEME** Ask students what the story's plot tells. *(the beginning, middle, and end of the story)* Have them tell what the theme of a story is. *(the big idea)* If necessary, review the meaning and provide a model. The important events in a story make up the plot. The plot has a beginning, a middle, and an end. The "big idea" of a story is the theme. The theme can be stated in one sentence. Share the plot and theme of a familiar story, such as "The Wizard of Oz," with the class.

Guide students to identify the plot and theme of *Leo and the School of Fish*. What is the plot of *Leo and the School of Fish*? What happens at the beginning? *(Leo is bored so he leaves his school and swims alone to a sunken ship.)* What happens in the middle? *(Leo meets dangers, such as an anglerfish, a fork, a moray eel, and a net.)* What happens at the end? *(Leo is happy to swim in safety with his school of fish.)* What is the theme, or "big idea," of the story? *(Be happy with what you have.)*

2 Read *Two Bad Ants,* pp. 368–375

BEFORE READING Have students retell what happened in the story so far. Ask: What happens when the ants are scooped up from the crystals? Reread p. 367 and model how to visualize the scene. As I read this page, I try to picture in my mind how the ants see things. To them a spoon looks like a giant silver scoop. They can feel each crystal of sugar. When the sugar is dropped into coffee, look out for the ants! In my mind I can see them falling down, down, down into a boiling brown lake. Remind students to visualize as they read the rest of *Two Bad Ants*. ◉ **STRATEGY Visualize**

DURING READING Follow the Guiding Comprehension routine on pp. 368–375. Have students read along with you while tracking print or do a choral reading. Stop every two pages to ask students what has happened so far. Prompt as necessary.

• Where did the ants go after they left the "lake" in the cup?
• What happened after the ants went into the holes in the wall?

AFTER READING How did having too much freedom become a problem for the ants? Reread with students for comprehension as needed. Tell them that tomorrow they will read "Hiking Safety Tips," a list of rules that can help hikers safely enjoy the freedom of walking in natural places.

Monitor Progress

Word and Story Reading

If... students have difficulty reading multisyllabic words in the selection,	then... have them look for and read meaningful parts in the words or have them chunk words with no recognizable parts.
If... students have difficulty reading along with the group,	then... have them follow along as they listen to the AudioText.

Advanced

1 Extend Comprehension

◉ SKILL PLOT AND THEME Have students explain the problem that all the ants were trying to solve at the beginning. Then have them identify the event in the middle that changes the main problem in the story. Ask students how they will recognize the theme of this story.

◉ STRATEGY VISUALIZE Have a volunteer reread p. 367 while others close their eyes. Then ask questions such as:

- How did you use your senses to visualize this story event? What could you see, hear, smell, taste, and touch in your mind?
- Would you like to live in an ant's world? Why or why not?

2 Read *Two Bad Ants*, pp. 368–375

BEFORE READING Have students recall what has happened in the story so far. Remind them to think about the plot and theme and to visualize as they read the remainder of the story.

CRITICAL THINKING Have students read pp. 368–375 independently. Encourage them to think critically. For example, ask:

- Why do you think the author wrote this story?
- What story details did you use to figure out the "big idea"?

AFTER READING Have students complete the Strategy Response Log activity (p. 374). Then have them select a major story event that would make a good preview, or trailer, for a movie. Have students write a description of the scene that would catch people's attention and make them want to see the movie. Have them meet with you to discuss why they chose this scene.

DAY **3**

AudioText

Group Time

DAY 4

Hiking Safety Tips

Audio CD AudioText

Monitor Progress

Word and Selection Reading

If... students have difficulty reading multisyllabic words in the selection,	**then...** have them look for and read meaningful parts in the words or have them chunk words with no recognizable parts.
If... students have difficulty reading along with the group,	**then...** have them follow along as they listen to the AudioText.

ROUTINE

1 Practice Retelling

REVIEW STORY ELEMENTS Help students identify the main characters and the setting of *Two Bad Ants*. Then guide them in using the Retelling Cards to list story events in sequence. Prompt students to include important details.

RETELL Using the Retelling Cards, have students work in pairs to retell *Two Bad Ants*. Monitor retelling and prompt students as needed. For example, ask:

- Where and when does this story take place?
- What are the ants like?
- What is the author trying to tell us or teach us?

If students struggle, model a fluent retelling.

2 Read "Hiking Safety Tips"

BEFORE READING Read the genre information on p. 378. Discuss with students why not all online sources can be trusted to have good or useful information. Even if a source has information you can trust, it may not be exactly the information you're looking for. To read an online source, you can click on a link to its site. A link is often underlined or in blue.

Read the rest of the panel on p. 378. Point out the Web site address and the key word on p. 379. Have students scan the first computer screen to find three sites and the extra information after each link.

DURING READING Have students read along with you while tracking the print or do a choral reading of the selection. Stop to point out each computer screen and the information it shows.

AFTER READING Have students share their reactions to the selection. Then guide them through the Reading Across Texts and Writing Across Texts activities, prompting if necessary.

- What happened when the ants wanted a drink? How would having water with them have helped?
- How would you tell the ants that they should carry their own snacks?

Advanced

1 Read "Hiking Safety Tips"

PROBLEM SOLVING Have students read pp. 378–379 independently. Encourage them to problem solve. Ask "what if" questions. For example, ask:

- What if you type in a keyword but no Web sites appear?
- What if your topic has hundreds of links?
- What if you are not sure that the facts you find are true?

AFTER READING Discuss Reading Across Texts. Have students do Writing Across Texts independently. Have them share their letters with you.

2 Extend Genre Study

RESEARCH Have students use the Internet to find more information on hiking safety tips. Tell them to skim the Web site names, noting the links that might be useful by reading the descriptions.

WRITE Have students create a Web site showing a list of kitchen safety tips for kids and parents who cook together. Encourage them to use a feature that will make the tips easy to read on the screen, such as different colored print (as in the selection), bullets, or numbers. Remind them to include a Web site address.

AudioText

Two Bad Ants

Group Time

DAY 5

① Reread for Fluency

MODEL Read aloud pp. 3–4 of the Leveled Reader *Leo and the School of Fish* at the appropriate pace. Read the words accurately and with expression. Then read the pages too fast and again too slowly. Have students tell you which model was best. Discuss how reading all the words correctly, with expression, and at the proper pace helps a reader enjoy and understand a selection.

PRACTICE Have students reread passages from *Leo and the School of Fish* with a partner or individually. For optimal fluency, they should reread three or four times. As students read, monitor fluency and provide corrective feedback. Assess the fluency of students in this group using p. 379a.

② Retell Leveled Reader *Leo and the School of Fish*

Model how to use the illustrations to retell the story. Then ask students to retell the story, one page at a time. Prompt them as needed.

- What is happening on this page?
- What is Leo's problem on this page?
- How does this story remind you of other stories?

Monitor Progress

Fluency

If... students have difficulty reading fluently,	then... provide additional fluency practice by pairing nonfluent readers with fluent ones.

For alternate Leveled Reader lesson plans that teach
Plot and Theme, Visualize, and
Lesson Vocabulary, see pp. LR28–LR36.

DAY 5

On-Level

1 Reread for Fluency
ROUTINE

MODEL Read aloud p. 8 of the Leveled Reader *Goldilocks and the Three Bears,* emphasizing accuracy and the appropriate pace. Have students note the expression in your voice. Discuss how reading with accuracy and appropriate pace, rate, and expression helps a reader understand and enjoy selections.

PRACTICE Have students reread passages from *Goldilocks and the Three Bears* with a partner or individually. For optimal fluency, they should reread three or four times. As students read, monitor fluency and provide corrective feedback. Students in this group were assessed in Week 3.

2 Retell Leveled Reader *Goldilocks and the Three Bears*

Have students use the illustrations as a guide to retell *Goldilocks and the Three Bears.* Prompt as needed.

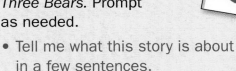

- Tell me what this story is about in a few sentences.
- What was the author trying to tell us?

Advanced

1 Reread for Fluency
ROUTINE

PRACTICE Have students reread passages from the Leveled Reader *A Fantastic Field Trip* with a partner or individually. As students read, monitor fluency and provide corrective feedback. If students read fluently on the first reading, they do not need to reread three or four times. Students in this group were assessed in Week 1.

2 Revisit Leveled Reader *A Fantastic Field Trip*

RETELL Have students retell the Leveled Reader *A Fantastic Field Trip.*

CREATE A MURAL Have students complete their projects. You may wish to review their sources and see whether they need any additional supplies or resources. Have them meet with you to discuss their mural and decide on the best place to display it.

Group Time

Leveled Reader
Database
ONLINE
PearsonSuccessNet.com

Strategic Intervention

ROUTINE

1 Preteach Phonics

RELATED WORDS Tell students that many words are similar. Write *imagine* and *image.* How do you pronounce the first word? *(imagine)* What does *imagine* mean? *(to picture something in your mind)* How is the second word similar to the first? *(It looks like the beginning of* imagine.*)* An image is a picture of something or someone. *Imagine* can help me understand what *image* means. Blend and read each word and have students blend the words with you.

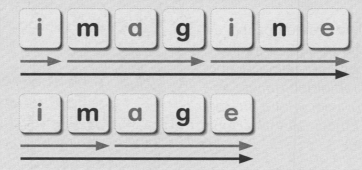

2 Read Decodable Reader 30

BEFORE READING Review the words on Decodable Reader p. 113. Then have students blend these story words: *injured, medicine, department, firehouse, alarm, sirens, wailing, sooty, protected, station, ability.* Be sure students understand the meanings of words such as *injured* and *wailing.*

Use the Picture Walk Routine on p. DI·1 to guide students through the text.

3 Read Leveled Reader *Glass Blowing*

REINFORCE CONCEPTS This week's concept is *freedom to create.* People want to be free to make and do things that are important to them. What do you like to make? What is your favorite activity? Are you free to do these things? Explain.

BEFORE READING Using the Picture Walk Routine on p. DI·1, guide students through the text focusing on key concepts and vocabulary. Ask questions such as:

pp. 8–9 This book is about the art of glassblowing. The first step is to melt the ingredients. What do glassblowers need for this? *(fire)*

Read pp. 3–4 aloud. Then do a choral reading of pp. 5–8. Have students read and discuss the remainder of the book with a partner. Ask: What are some things created with glass?

Monitor Progress

Word and Selection Reading

If... students have difficulty reading story words from the Decodable Reader,	**then...** reteach them by modeling blending or reading multisyllabic words.
If... partners have difficulty reading the Leveled Reader on their own,	**then...** have them follow along as they listen to the Online Leveled Reader Audio.

For alternate Leveled Reader lesson plans that teach ⟳Generalize, ⟳Predict, and **Lesson Vocabulary,** see pp. LR37–LR45.

On-Level

ROUTINE

① Build Background

DEVELOP VOCABULARY Write the word *instruments* and ask students to define it (*things you play to make music*) and to give examples. Then ask students to draw and label several musical instruments, each on a separate sheet of paper. Have students compile the labeled drawings in a Musical Instrument Picture Glossary. Repeat this activity with the word *crafts* and other words from the Leveled Reader *Traditional Crafts of Mexico.* Use the Concept Vocabulary Routine on p. DI·1 as needed.

② Read Leveled Reader *Traditional Crafts of Mexico*

BEFORE READING Have students create webs with *Mexican Crafts* in the center. This book is about crafts that are made right in the artist's home. As you read, look for facts about crafts that the people of Mexico create. Record the information on your web.

DURING READING Have students follow along as you read pp. 3–7. Then let them complete the book on their own. Remind students to add facts to their webs as they read.

AFTER READING Have students compare the facts on their webs. Point out that facts they learn about Mexican crafts will help them as they read tomorrow's selection, *Elena's Serenade.*

Advanced

ROUTINE

① Read Leveled Reader *Jackie Robinson*

BEFORE READING Recall the Read Aloud "Manuelo the Playing Mantis." How do you know that it was important to Manuelo to create music? (*He was very sad when he couldn't, but he kept trying.*) Today you will read about Jackie Robinson, an African American who created an important change in Major League Baseball.

CRITICAL THINKING/PROBLEM SOLVING Have students read the Leveled Reader independently. Encourage them to think critically and solve problems. For example, ask:

- Do you think the way Jackie Robinson and Branch Rickey solved the color barrier was the best approach? Explain.
- If you could say something to Jackie Robinson, what would it be?
- What might you and others do today to help all people be treated fairly?

AFTER READING Have students review the selection to find five unfamiliar words and determine their meanings by using context clues or a dictionary. Have them write each word on an index card and its meaning on a separate card. Then have partners turn their word and meaning cards facedown and play a memory game to match words with meanings. Meet with students afterward to discuss the selection.

② Independent Extension Activity

NOW TRY THIS Assign "Now Try This" on pp. 22–23 of *Jackie Robinson* for students to work on throughout the week.

Elena's Serenade
Group Time

AudioText

Strategic Intervention

ROUTINE

1 Reread for Fluency

Use Decodable Reader 30

2 Word Study/Phonics

LESSON VOCABULARY Use p. 382b to review the meanings of *burro, bursts, factory, glassblower, puff, reply,* and *tune*. Students can blend all of the words. Practice reading the words from word cards.

DECODING MULTISYLLABIC WORDS Write *squinting* and model how to use meaningful word parts to read it. First I look for parts I know. I see the ending *-ing*. I also notice the base word *squint*. I say the parts of the word: *squint ing*. Then I read the word: *squinting*.

Use the Multisyllabic Word Routine on p. DI·1 to help students read these other words from *Elena's Serenade: serenade, furnace, overtake, Roadrunner, steady, awakened, Coyote, medium, burping, swallow,* and *chiming*. Be sure students understand the meanings of words such as *serenade* and *chiming*.

3 Read *Elena's Serenade,* pp. 384–393

BEFORE READING Yesterday we read about the five steps glassblowers follow to create glass. Today we will read a about a girl named Elena who wants to be free to learn to be a glassblower.

Using the Picture Walk Routine on p. DI·1, guide students through the text, asking questions such as those listed below. Then read the question on p. 385. Together, set a purpose for reading.

pp. 386–387 This is Elena and her father. What does Elena's papa do? *(He is a glassblower.)* Yes, and Elena would like to be a glassblower too.

pp. 388–389 Elena is under the hat. What comes out of her glassblowing pipe? *(music and sounds)* What a surprise! Her pipe plays a serenade.

DURING READING Follow the Guiding Comprehension routine on pp. 386–393. Have students read along with you while tracking the print or do a choral reading. Stop every two pages to ask what has happened so far. Prompt as necessary.

• Where did this story take place?
• What was Elena's problem?
• What happened when Elena played a march for Roadrunner?

AFTER READING What has happened so far? What do you think will happen next? Reread passages with students as needed.

Monitor Progress

Word and Story Reading

If... students have difficulty reading multisyllabic words in the selection,	then... have them look for and read meaningful parts in the words or have them chunk words with no recognizable parts.
If... students have difficulty reading along with the group,	then... have them follow along as they listen to the AudioText.

Advanced

ROUTINE

1 Extend Vocabulary

CONTEXT CLUES Choose and read a sentence or passage containing a difficult word, such as this passage from p. 12 of *Jackie Robinson:* "Still, Rickey was cautious. He did not go public with his plans to sign an African American player but instead pretended he had plans to start a new African American team. . . ." What does the word *cautious* mean? *(careful, not taking chances)* How did you figure out the word's meaning? *(I used the details about Rickey not telling anyone what he was doing.)* Discuss why context clues are helpful, and remind students to use the strategy as they read *Elena's Serenade.*

2 Read *Elena's Serenade,* pp. 384–393

BEFORE READING In *Jackie Robinson,* you read how Jackie Robinson wanted to be free to follow his dream of becoming a major league baseball player. Today you will read a fantasy about a girl who follows her dream. As you read, think about people, either real or make-believe, who followed their dreams.

For their Strategy Response Logs (p. 384), have students make a three-column chart. In the first column, they should list the characters from the story. As they read, they can complete the second column with facts about the characters. During and after reading they can write generalizations about the characters in the third column (p. 393).

CREATIVE THINKING/PROBLEM SOLVING Have students read pp. 384–393 independently. Encourage them to think creatively and solve problems. For example, ask:

- What advice would you give Elena about following her dreams?
- What would you do to help each of the animals solve its problem?

AFTER READING Have partners discuss the selection and share their Strategy Response Log entries. Have them add facts and generalizations to their charts. Then have students put themselves in the role of an advice columnist. Have them write and answer a letter that Elena might write about her problem. Meet with students to discuss their columns.

Elena's Serenade
Group Time

Audio CD   **AudioText**

Monitor Progress

Word and Story Reading

If... students have difficulty reading multisyllabic words in the selection,	**then...** have them look for and read meaningful parts in the words or have them chunk words with no recognizable parts.
If... students have difficulty reading along with the group,	**then...** have them follow along as they listen to the AudioText.

Strategic Intervention

ROUTINE

1 Reinforce Comprehension

SKILL GENERALIZE Have students tell what it means to *generalize* (*to make a statement or rule that fits a lot of examples*) and list clue words that you might use when you generalize (*all, most, always*). If necessary, review the meaning and provide a model. When you read a story, you learn lots of details about things or people. Sometimes you can make a general statement, or a generalization, about the things or people based on what you learned. A generalization tells how the things or people are alike in some way. *Most glassblowers wear safety goggles and gloves* is a generalization. It tells how glassblowers are alike. The word *most* is a clue that the statement is a generalization.

Read aloud the following statements. Have students identify which of the ideas is a generalization (*Most roadrunners are fast*) and which word is a clue (*most*).

> **Most roadrunners are fast.**
> **Roadrunner limps along.**
> **Elena helps Roadrunner go faster.**

2 Read *Elena's Serenade*, pp. 394–400

BEFORE READING Have students retell what happened in the story so far. Ask: What did you predict would happen when Elena met Coyote? What clues in the story helped you make your prediction? Reread pp. 388–390 and model how to predict. I use story events that happened earlier to help me predict what might happen next. Elena plays music that helps Burro. Then her serenade helps Roadrunner. I used the events as clues to predict that Elena's music would help Coyote. Remind students to make predictions as they read the rest of *Elena's Serenade*. **STRATEGY Predict**

DURING READING Follow the Guiding Comprehension routine on pp. 394–400. Have students read along with you while tracking print or do a choral reading. Stop every two pages to ask what has happened so far. Prompt as necessary.

- What happened when Elena finally got to the glassblowing factory?
- How did Elena get back home?

AFTER READING How did Elena follow her dream of having the freedom to create? Reread with students for comprehension as needed. Tell them that tomorrow they will read "Leading People to Freedom," a selection about people who showed bravery in following their dream of freedom.

Advanced

ROUTINE

1 Extend Comprehension

SKILL GENERALIZE Have students imagine what it would be like if no one was allowed the freedom to create art. Have them suggest generalizations about what the world would be like.

STRATEGY PREDICT Ask students what they do to predict when they read *(use things that have happened and their own prior knowledge to predict what will happen).* Have a volunteer reread p. 387. Ask questions such as:

- What did you predict would happen when Elena left home dressed as a boy?
- Did knowing this story was a fantasy help you make your prediction? Explain.

2 Read *Elena's Serenade,* pp. 394–400

BEFORE READING Have students recall what has happened in the story so far. Remind them to make generalizations and predictions as they read the remainder of the story.

CRITICAL THINKING Have students read pp. 394–400 independently. Encourage them to think critically and creatively. For example, ask:

- What parts of this story are fantasy?
- What message is the author trying to tell you?
- In what other ways might the author tell you this message?

AFTER READING Have students complete the Strategy Response Log activity (p. 398). Then have them discuss how the story would be different if it were realistic fiction. What if the characters and events were like people and events in real life? Who might Elena help? How might she solve her problem? Have students write the story as realistic fiction. Have them meet with you to read aloud their new versions.

DAY
3

AudioText

Group Time

Strategic Intervention

DAY 4

1 Practice Retelling

REVIEW STORY ELEMENTS Help students identify the main characters and the setting of *Elena's Serenade.* Then guide them in using the Retelling Cards to list story events in sequence. Prompt students to include important details.

RETELL Using the Retelling Cards, have students work in pairs to retell *Elena's Serenade.* Monitor retelling and prompt students as needed. For example, ask:

- What is Elena like?
- Tell me what this story is about in a few sentences.
- How does this story remind you of other stories?

If students struggle, model a fluent retelling.

Grade 3 Retelling Cards

2 Read "Leading People to Freedom"

BEFORE READING Read the genre information on p. 404. Explain that one way authors organize facts in expository nonfiction is to put them in the order in which they happened in real life. That is how the expository nonfiction selection "The Story of the Statue of Liberty," which we read at the beginning of this unit, was organized.

Read the rest of the panel on p. 404. Have students scan the pages, stopping to discuss what the map on p. 406 shows. Ask: Why do you think the author included this map?

DURING READING Have students read along with you while tracking the print or do a choral reading of the selection. Stop to clarify Underground Railroad terms, such as *trains, conductors,* and *stations.*

AFTER READING Have students share their reactions to the selection. Then guide them through the Reading Across Texts and Writing Across Texts activities, prompting if necessary.

- What would Elena say if you asked her, "What did you want to do? Why?"
- What would Harriet Tubman say if you asked her, "What did you want to do? Why?"

Audio CD **AudioText**

404

Monitor Progress

Word and Selection Reading

If... students have difficulty reading multisyllabic words in the selection,	**then...** have them look for and read meaningful parts in the words or have them chunk words with no recognizable parts.
If... students have difficulty reading along with the group,	**then...** have them follow along as they listen to the AudioText.

Advanced

1 Read "Leading People to Freedom"

CRITICAL THINKING Have students read pp. 404–407 independently. Encourage them to think critically. For example, ask:

- In what way did Harriet Tubman work for the freedom to create?
- Do you think this is an important selection for students to read? Explain.

Have students write a review of the selection. Ask them to describe the impact it will have on other readers and why they feel this way. Have students meet with you to discuss the selection and share their review.

AFTER READING Discuss Reading Across Texts. Have students do Writing Across Texts independently.

2 Extend Genre Study

RESEARCH Have students use online resources or print sources to find other examples of expository nonfiction about Harriet Tubman. Have them make a list of titles, noting the types of maps or other graphics that were used in each selection.

WRITE Have students write a short nonfiction article that tells about Harriet Tubman's early life as an enslaved person, or about her later life as she helped hundreds to find their own freedom. Encourage students to include a map or other graphic organizer in their articles.

DAY 4

AudioText

Elena's Serenade

Group Time

ONLINE

PearsonSuccessNet.com

Strategic Intervention

ROUTINE

1 **Reread for Fluency**

MODEL Read aloud pp. 3–5 of the Leveled Reader *Glass Blowing*. Have students note how you read all the words with expression and pacing. Then read pp. 3–5 in a monotone. Have students tell you which model was better. Discuss how students should read with expression and pacing to better understand the selection.

PRACTICE Have students reread passages from *Glass Blowing* with a partner or individually. For optimal fluency, they should reread three or four times. As students read, monitor fluency and provide corrective feedback. Assess any students you have not yet checked during this unit.

2 **Retell Leveled Reader *Glass Blowing***

Model how to use the section headings to retell the book. Then ask students to retell the book, one section at a time. Prompt them as needed.

- What did you learn from reading this section?
- Tell me about the steps I need to follow in glass blowing.

Monitor Progress

Fluency

If... students have difficulty reading fluently,	then... provide additional fluency practice by pairing nonfluent readers with fluent ones.

For alternate Leveled Reader lesson plans that teach ◔ **Generalize,** ◔ **Predict,** and **Lesson Vocabulary,** see pp. LR37–LR45.

On-Level

1 Reread for Fluency ROUTINE

MODEL Read aloud p. 3 of the Leveled Reader *Traditional Crafts of Mexico,* emphasizing expression and proper rate. Have students note that you read with expression and at a rate that was not too fast or too slow. Discuss how reading at the appropriate rate with expression will help them understand and remember what they read.

PRACTICE Have students reread passages from *Traditional Crafts of Mexico* with a partner or individually. For optimal fluency, students should reread three or four times. As students read, monitor fluency and provide corrective feedback. Assess any students you have not yet checked during this unit.

2 Retell Leveled Reader *Traditional Crafts of Mexico*

Have students use section headings and photos as a guide to summarize the important facts they learned from each section of the book. Prompt as needed.

- What is this section mostly about?
- What did you learn from reading this book?

Advanced

1 Reread for Fluency ROUTINE

PRACTICE Have students reread passages from the Leveled Reader *Jackie Robinson* with a partner or individually. As students read, monitor fluency and provide corrective feedback. If students read fluently on the first reading, they do not need to reread three or four times. Assess any students you have not yet checked during this unit.

2 Revisit Leveled Reader *Jackie Robinson*

RETELL Have students retell the Leveled Reader *Jackie Robinson.*

NOW TRY THIS Have students complete their reports or biographies. You may wish to review their sources. Have students meet with you to read their work before sharing it with a parent or the class.

Main Idea/Details

Determining the main idea in a text helps readers distinguish between important and less important information. When students can correctly identify the main idea, they understand the gist of what they read. Use this routine to teach main idea.

1 EXPLAIN ITS USE

Explain that finding the main idea is an important tool in helping students understand and remember what they read.

2 DEFINE TOPIC SENTENCE

Explain that the topic is the subject, what the selection is all about. The main idea is the most important idea about the topic. The main idea can be stated in a sentence.

3 MODEL FINDING THE MAIN IDEA

Read a nonfiction paragraph with a stated main idea. Have students identify the topic by asking: *What is this paragraph about?* Then model how you determine the main idea.

4 FINDING SUPPORTING DETAILS

Explain that supporting details are small pieces of information that tell more about the main idea. Model how to identify supporting details.

5 USE A GRAPHIC ORGANIZER

Have students find the main idea and supporting details in a nonfiction selection. Use a main idea chart to help students organize their thoughts.

Choose passages carefully to practice this succession of skills:

- Paragraphs: stated main idea (Grades 2–6); implied main idea (Grades 3–6)

- Articles: stated main idea (Grades 4–6); implied main idea (Grades 4–6)

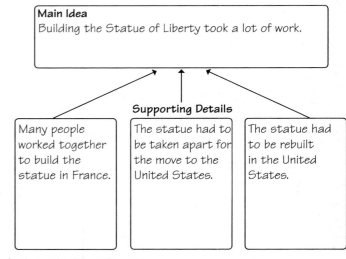

▲ **Graphic Organizer** 16

Research on Main Idea/Details

"When great readers are reading this stuff that has so many ideas in it, they have to listen to that mental voice tell them which words, which sentences or paragraphs, and which ideas are most important. Otherwise they won't get it."

Ellin Oliver Keene and Susan Zimmermann,
Mosaic of Thought

Keene, Ellin Oliver, and Susan Zimmermann. *Mosaic of Thought: Teaching Comprehension in a Reader's Workshop.* Heinemann, 1997, p. 86.

Cause and Effect

Students who are able to connect what happens in a selection to the reason why it happens can better understand what they read. In fiction, this skill will help them figure out why characters do what they do. In nonfiction, it will give them a better grasp of factual information. Use the following routine to teach cause and effect.

1 DEMONSTRATE CAUSE AND EFFECT

Remind students that an effect is what happens. A cause is why it happened. Demonstrate by turning out the lights. Ask:

What is the effect? (It is dark.)

What is the cause? (You turned off the lights.)

2 IDENTIFY CAUSE AND EFFECT

Write this sentence on the board: *Because it is raining, I took my umbrella to school.* Explain that sometimes a sentence has a clue word such as *because, so,* or *since* that signals a cause-and-effect relationship. Have volunteers circle the cause (*it is raining*) and the effect (*I took my umbrella*) and underline the clue word (*because*).

3 APPLY TO A SELECTION

Read with students a story that has causes and effects. Several causes can lead to one effect: Sunshine <u>and</u> water make flowers grow. One cause can lead to several effects: Leaving a bike in the hallway can cause someone to trip <u>and</u> break an arm.

4 RECORD CAUSES AND EFFECTS

Have students use a cause and effect chart to record the causes and effects in the selection.

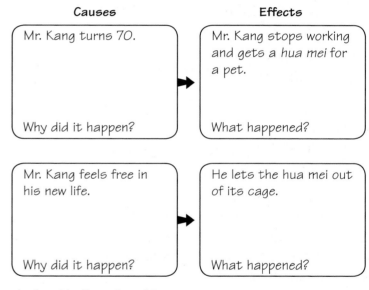

▲ **Graphic Organizer** 19

Research on Cause and Effect

"A great deal of our thought process has to do with cause and effect. To be fully fluent thinkers, children need to learn the logic of cause and effect."

Stanley Greenspan and Serena Weider,
Learning to Think Abstractly

Greenspan, Stanley, and Serena Weider. "Learning to Think Abstractly." *Scholastic Early Childhood Today* (May/June 1998).

Fact and Opinion

When students can identify statements of fact and opinion, they are able to make critical judgments concerning what they hear, read, and write. Use this routine to help students recognize statements of fact and statements of opinion and distinguish between them.

1 DEFINE FACT AND OPINION

Explain a statement of fact can be proved true or false. A statement of opinion is someone's judgment, belief, or way of thinking about something. It cannot be proved true or false, but it can be supported or explained.

2 GIVE EXAMPLES

Write three statements on the board:

Charlotte's Web was published in 1952. E. B. White wrote Charlotte's Web. You should read Charlotte's Web.

Ask: *Which sentences are statements of fact? (the first two) How can you tell?* Elicit ways the facts could be verified, such as looking at the book or asking the school librarian. Talk about other ways to check statements of fact (observing, weighing, measuring, asking an expert).

Ask: *Which sentence is a statement of opinion? (the third one)* Point out the judgment word *should.* Explain opinions often contain judgment words such as *should, I think, cute,* and *best.*

3 PROVIDE PRACTICE

- Partners can read nonfiction selections and use a T-chart to list statements of fact and opinion.

- Have small groups read newspaper editorials. Students can list opinions and their supporting arguments.

Facts	Opinions
1. Murals are usually painted on walls.	1. Murals make neighborhoods look better.
2. Joshua Sarantitis talks to people in the neighborhood before painting.	2. Sarantitis's mural is beautiful.
3. David Botello painted "Dreams of Flight" at a public housing project in Los Angeles.	3. "Dreams of Flight" is an inspirational work of art.

▲ **Graphic Organizer** 25

Research on Fact and Opinion

"Students will—and should—argue about the difference between fact and opinion . . .; they will often dispute one another about inferences . . . . The point of such discussions is to help students sensitize themselves to the kinds of statements they encounter and make them aware of the inferences of others."

Thomas G. Devine,
Teaching Reading Comprehension

Devine, Thomas G. *Teaching Reading Comprehension.* Allyn and Bacon, Inc., 1986.1992, p. 238.

Plot

When students have a clear understanding of the typical plot structure of stories, they can tell which events are most important and why they happen. Use this routine to support students' understanding of plot.

1 REVIEW PLOT

For third graders, review plot as the beginning, middle, and end of a story. Help them chart the beginning, middle, and end of familiar stories.

2 TEACH NEW TERMS

For more advanced readers, introduce the following terms: *problem, rising action, climax,* and *resolution.* Tell students these words describe a common plot structure.

3 IDENTIFY THE PROBLEM

Have students look for a problem or goal in a story you have read. Explain they might see a conflict:

- between two characters,

- between a character and nature, such as a character trying to survive in the desert, or

- within a character, as when a character needs to make a decision.

Show students how to record the problem on a plot structure map.

4 RECORD PLOT STRUCTURE

Have students identify and record the major events in the story, the climax (when the problem is directly confronted), and the resolution (when the problem is resolved).

Title
Two Bad Ants

This story is about
two ants who go on a journey.

This story takes place
in an ant hole and a person's home.

The action begins when
ants go to find crystals for their queen.
Then,
the ants find the crystals
in someone's home.

Next,
two ants stay behind to eat more crystals.
After that,
they end up in a cup of coffee
and in a toaster.
The story ends when
the ants arrive back at the ant hole.
Theme:
Sometimes home is the best place to be.

▲ **Graphic Organizer** 10

Research on Plot

"By studying plot, children can learn to identify patterns that appear over and over again in the books they read. With older students, plot maps can be drawn to focus on key events in particular chapters or to discover the shapes of whole books."

Linda DeGroff and Lee Galda,
"Responding to Literature: Activities for Exploring Books"

DeGroff, Linda, and Lee Galda. "Responding to Literature: Activities for Exploring Books." In *Invitation to Read: More Children's Literature in the Reading Program,* edited by Bernice E. Cullinan, International Reading Association, 1992.

Generalize

Recognizing generalizations helps students judge the validity of an argument. Making their own generalizations helps students understand and summarize texts. Use this routine to teach generalizing.

1 DEFINE GENERALIZATION

Explain that a *generalization* is a broad statement or rule that applies to many examples. A *valid generalization* is well supported by facts and logic. A *faulty* one is not well supported.

2 DISCUSS CLUE WORDS

Students should look for clue words that signal generalizations as they read. List words on the board:

all	none
most	few
always	never
generally	in general

3 MODEL GENERALIZING

Explain that when readers generalize, they think about a number of examples and decide what they have in common. After reading a passage containing several facts, model how to generalize.

4 SCAFFOLD GENERALIZING

Before students write their own generalizations, have them practice choosing the most valid generalization for several paragraphs. You may also ask them to complete stems, such as: *The climate in the Arctic is generally _____ .*

5 PRACTICE GENERALIZING

Have students record a generalization and examples in a web.

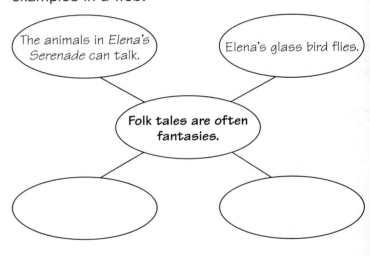

▲ **Graphic Organizer** 15

Research on Generalizing

"To be able to create a summary of what one has just read, one must discern the most central and important ideas in the text. One also must be able to generalize from examples or from things that are repeated. In addition, one has to ignore irrelevant details."

National Reading Panel,
Teaching Children to Read

National Reading Panel. *Teaching Children to Read: Reports of the Subgroups.* National Institute of Child Health & Human Development, National Institutes of Health, 2000, p. 4-92.

Providing students with reading materials they can and want to read is an important step toward developing fluent readers. A running record allows you to determine each student's instructional and independent reading level. Information on how to take a running record is provided on pp. DI•59–DI•60.

Instructional Reading Level

Only approximately 1 in 10 words will be difficult when reading a selection from the Student Edition for students who are at grade level. (A typical third-grader reads approximately 105–120 words correct per minute.)

- Students reading at grade level should read regularly from the Student Edition and On-Level Leveled Readers, with teacher support as suggested in the Teacher's Editions.
- Students reading below grade level can read the Strategic Intervention Leveled Readers. Instructional plans can be found in the Teacher's Edition and the Leveled Reader Teaching Guide.
- Students who are reading above grade level can read the Advanced Leveled Readers. Instructional plans can be found in the Teacher's Edition and the Leveled Reader Teaching Guide.

Independent Reading Level

Students should read regularly in independent-level texts in which no more than approximately 1 in 20 words is difficult for the reader. Other factors that make a book easy to read include the student's interest in the topic, the amount of text on a page, how well illustrations support meaning, and the complexity and familiarity of the concepts. Suggested books for self-selected reading are provided for each lesson on p. TR14 in this Teacher's Edition.

Guide students in learning how to self-select books at their independent reading level. As you talk about a book with students, discuss the challenging concepts in it, list new words students find in sampling the book, and ask students about their familiarity with the topic. A blackline master to help students evaluate books for independent reading is provided on p. DI•58.

Self-Selected/Independent Reading

While oral reading allows you to assess students' reading level and fluency, independent reading is of crucial importance to students' futures as readers and learners. Students need to develop their ability to read independently for increasing amounts of time.

- Schedule a regular time for sustained independent reading in your classroom. During the year, gradually increase the amount of time devoted to independent reading.
- Encourage students to track the amount of time they read independently and the number of pages they read in a given amount of time. Tracking will help motivate them to gradually increase their duration and speed. Blackline masters for tracking independent reading are provided on pp. DI•58 and TR15.

Choosing a Book for Independent Reading

When choosing a book, story, or article for independent reading, consider these questions:

_____ 1. Do I know something about this topic?

_____ 2. Am I interested in this topic?

_____ 3. Do I like reading this kind of book (fiction, fantasy, biography, or whatever)?

_____ 4. Have I read other things by this author? Do I like this author?

If you say "yes" to at least one of the questions above, continue:

_____ 5. In reading the first page, was only about 1 of every 20 words hard?

If you say "yes," continue:

_____ 6. Does the number of words on a page look about right to me?

If you say "yes," the book or article is probably at the right level for you.

Silent Reading

Record the date, the title of the book or article you read, the amount of time you spent reading, and the number of pages you read during that time. Remember to capitalize the first word, last word, and every important word in a book title.

Date	Title	Minutes	Pages

Taking a Running Record

A running record is an assessment of a student's oral reading accuracy and oral reading fluency. Reading accuracy is based on the number of words read correctly. Reading fluency is based on the reading rate (the number of words correct per minute) and the degree to which a student reads with a "natural flow."

How to Measure Reading Accuracy

1. Choose a grade-level text of about 80 to 120 words that is unfamiliar to the student.

2. Make a copy of the text for yourself. Make a copy for the student or have the student read aloud from a book.

3. Give the student the text and have the student read aloud. (You may wish to record the student's reading for later evaluation.)

4. On your copy of the text, mark any miscues or errors the student makes while reading. See the running record sample on page TR20, which shows how to identify and mark miscues.

5. Count the total number of words in the text and the total number of errors made by the student. Note: If a student makes the same error more than once, such as mispronouncing the same word multiple times, count it as one error. Self-corrections do not count as actual errors. Use the following formula to calculate the percentage score, or accuracy rate:

$$\frac{\text{Total Number of Words} - \text{Total Number of Errors}}{\text{Total Number of Words}} \times 100 = \text{percentage score}$$

Interpreting the Results

- A student who reads **95–100%** of the words correctly is reading at an **independent level** and may need more challenging text.

- A student who reads **90–94%** of the words correctly is reading at an **instructional level** and will likely benefit from guided instruction.

- A student who reads **89%** or fewer of the words correctly is reading at a **frustrational level** and may benefit most from targeted instruction with lower-level texts and intervention.

How to Measure Reading Rate (WCPM)

1. Follow Steps 1–3 above.

2. Note the exact times when the student begins and finishes reading.

3. Use the following formula to calculate the number of words correct per minute (WCPM):

$$\frac{\text{Total Number of Words Read Correctly}}{\text{Total Number of Seconds}} \times 60 = \text{words correct per minute}$$

Interpreting the Results

An appropriate reading rate for a third-grader is 105–120 (WCPM).

Running Record Sample

Running Record Sample

Dana had recently begun volunteering at the animal rescue shelter where her mom worked as a veterinarian. The shelter was just across the bay from their house.

Dana was learning many different jobs at the shelter. She fed the dogs and cleaned their cages. She played catch with the dogs in the shelter's backyard. Dana's favorite job, however, was introducing people to the dogs waiting for adoption. Whenever a dog found a new home, Dana was especially pleased!

The road to the shelter crossed over the bay. Dana looked for boats in the channel, but there were none. Dana's mom turned on the radio to listen to the news as they drove. The weather reporter announced that a blizzard might hit some parts of the state.

—From *A Day with the Dogs*
On-Level Reader 3.3.4

Symbols

Accurate Reading
The student reads a word correctly.

Omission
The student omits words or word parts.

Hesitation
The student hesitates over a word, and the teacher provides the word. Wait several seconds before telling the student what the word is.

Mispronunciation/Misreading
The student pronounces or reads a word incorrectly.

Self-Correction
The student reads a word incorrectly but then corrects the error. Do not count self-corrections as actual errors. However, noting self-corrections will help you identify words the student finds difficult.

Insertion
The student inserts words or parts of words that are not in the text.

Substitution
The student substitutes words or parts of words for the words in the text.

Running Record Results	▶	**Reading Accuracy**	▶	**Reading Rate—WCPM**
Total Number of Words: **126**		$\dfrac{126-5}{126} = \dfrac{121}{126} = .9603 = 96\%$		$\dfrac{121}{64}$ x 60 = 113.43 = 113 words correct per minute
Number of Errors: **5**				
Reading Time: **64 seconds**		Accuracy Percentage Score: **96%**		Reading Rate: **113 WCPM**

Teacher Resources

Table of Contents

Elsa   from p. 304m

At last the week of waiting ended. On our return we fired a shot and Elsa came rushing out of the bush, overjoyed to see us. She was thin but not hungry, for she showed no interest in the buck we had brought her.

After this we paid her short visits at frequent intervals, and although she was always delighted to see us it was quite obvious that she could manage without us. I went to England for a long time that summer, and after my return she was particularly pleased to see me.

We had always hoped that she would find a mate and that one day she would walk into our camp followed by a family.

You can imagine our great joy when a few months later she swam across the river followed by three fine cubs.

Indescribably Arabella   from p. 332m

"Now please dance, Arabella, for you make us very happy."

So Arabella kicked and turned…and jumped…and whirled…all in her own special way. And the two people were so very happy and loved Arabella's dancing so very much that they clapped and clapped their hands.

Now Arabella performs for the whole neighborhood, so you see she has become famous after all

And she is also, always, indescribably Arabella.

The Boy Who Stopped Time   from p. 354m

hard to read by himself. He wished Miss Bruning, the children's librarian, could help as she had many times before.

He went to the movie theater, but the picture wasn't moving, and the silence and stillness crept into him. He felt sleepy and dozed off. Julian didn't know how long he had slept because when he woke up everything was exactly the same. Then he remembered how he had stopped the clock so he wouldn't have to go to sleep.

Listening to the silence within himself, Julian pedaled to the town park. He looked at all the children frozen in their play. Now his feeling of silence started to become a feeling of sadness, and he knew that he wanted to go home.

He took the back road home. Cows and horses stood motionless in the fields, and high above, an airplane hung in the sky. He was very tired when he arrived and very happy to find everything waiting for him just as he had left it.

He put his bike away, went inside, peeked in at his mom, climbed up on the chair, and started the clock pendulum swinging. His mother's lullaby began again. He got down and silently returned the chair to its place. The lullaby ended, the clock went *ding-dong,* and his mother said, "It's time, Julian."

He took one last look out the window. His father was throwing another stone on the pile. Down by the creek, the deer had gone, and over the meadow honeybees gathered nectar in the evening sun. Julian smiled to himself and quietly went to bed.

Manuelo the Playing Mantis from p. 380m

No sooner had Debby whispered this than Manuelo attached the stick to the walnut shell. He watched as the nimble spider spun four strong silken threads from one end of the stick to the other.

"All we need now is a bow," said Debby. "Can you think of something that will do the trick?"

"Yes, yes! I know!" exclaimed Manuelo. "I saw a bluebird's feather that should make a splendid bow." And indeed it did.

At last, Manuelo was ready to play his cello. Taking the bow in his right hand, he began moving it softly across the silken strings. And as he bowed back and forth, the most beautiful melody filled the night air.

Gradually from the grassy glade, from behind the fig tree, and from out of the pond, crickets, grasshoppers, katydids, and frogs came creeping forward, making a wide circle around Manuelo.

As they listened, each creature could not resist joining in with the cello's mellow music. Soon everyone was taking part in the concert with clicking, fiddling, wing-singing, and deep-throated croaking. Never was there a more glorious insect symphony!

On and on far into the night, Manuelo played to everyone's delight.

And every summer night thereafter, Manuelo played his cello.

Unit 1

	Vocabulary Words	Spelling Words

Boom Town

Vocabulary Words

boom   mending
business   pick
coins   skillet
fetched   spell
laundry

Short Vowels VCCV

happen	supper	traffic
lettuce	subject	suggest
basket	lesson	puppet
winter	spelling	
sister	napkin	
monster	collar	

What About Me?

Vocabulary Words

carpenter   merchant
carpetmaker   plenty
knowledge   straying
marketplace   thread

Plurals -s, -es

pennies	wishes	crashes
inches	pockets	supplies
plants	lists	pencils
families	copies	
bodies	parties	
glasses	bunches	

Alexander, Who Used to Be Rich Last Sunday

Vocabulary Words

college   nickels
dimes   quarters
downtown   rich
fined

Adding -ed, -ing, -er, and -est

using	pleased	funniest
getting	emptied	angrier
easiest	leaving	shopped
swimming	worried	
heavier	strangest	
greatest	freezing	

If You Made a Million

Vocabulary Words

amount   million
check   thousand
earned   value
expensive   worth
interest

Long Vowel Digraphs

clean	display	Sunday
agree	window	float
teeth	shadow	thrown
dream	cheese	
grain	peach	
coach	braid	

My Rows and Piles of Coins

Vocabulary Words

arranged
bundles
dangerously
errands
excitedly
steady
unwrapped
wobbled

Vowel Sounds in *out* and *toy*

proud	avoid	annoy
shower	thousand	appoint
hour	prowl	broil
amount	employ	
voyage	bounce	
choice	poison	

Unit 2	Vocabulary Words	Spelling Words

Penguin Chick

Vocabulary Words
cuddles
flippers
frozen
hatch
pecks
preen
snuggles

Syllable Pattern V/CV, VC/V

finish	rapid	tulip
pilot	female	camel
even	lemon	salad
wagon	pupil	
music	focus	
silent	robot	

A Day's Work

Vocabulary Words
excitement
gardener
motioned
sadness
shivered
shocked
slammed

Words Ending in -le

handle	little	juggle
trouble	gentle	uncle
simple	poodle	riddle
people	pickle	
middle	noodle	
table	saddle	

Prudy's Problem and How She Solved It

Vocabulary Words
collection
enormous
realize
scattered
shiny
strain

Compound Words

sunglasses	snowstorm	campground
football	earring	sandbox
homework	scarecrow	toothbrush
haircut	blueberry	
popcorn	butterflies	
railroad	lawnmower	

Tops & Bottoms

Vocabulary Words
bottom
cheated
clever
crops
lazy
partners
wealth

Words with spl, thr, squ, str

splash	street	throne
throw	split	strawberry
three	splurge	squeeze
square	thrill	
throat	strength	
strike	squeak	

William's House

Vocabulary Words
barrels
cellar
clearing
pegs
spoil
steep

Digraphs sh, th, ph, ch, tch

father	weather	athlete
chapter	catch	trophy
other	fashion	nephew
alphabet	shrink	
watch	pitcher	
English	flash	

Unit 3 — Vocabulary Words — Spelling Words

The Gardener

Vocabulary Words

beauty	humor
blooming	recognizing
bulbs	showers
doze	sprouting

Contractions

let's	haven't	they'd
he'd	hasn't	wasn't
you'll	she'd	didn't
can't	they'll	
I'd	when's	
you'd	we'd	

Pushing Up the Sky

Vocabulary Words

antlers
imagined
languages
narrator
overhead
poked

Prefixes un-, re-, mis-, dis-

unhappy	dislike	unknown
recall	replace	dishonest
disappear	mislead	react
unload	disagree	
mistake	rewrite	
misspell	unroll	

Night Letters

Vocabulary Words

blade
budding
dew
fireflies
flutter
notepad
patch

Consonant Sounds /j/ and /k/

clock	crack	jacket
large	edge	badge
page	pocket	orange
mark	brake	
kitten	change	
judge	ridge	

A Symphony of Whales

Vocabulary Words

anxiously	melody
bay	supplies
blizzards	surrounded
channel	symphony
chipped	

Suffixes -ly, -ful, -ness, -less

beautiful	illness	fairness
safely	helpful	cheerful
kindness	daily	painful
finally	suddenly	
spotless	wireless	
worthless	quietly	

Volcanoes: Nature's Incredible Fireworks

Vocabulary Words

beneath
buried
chimney
earthquakes
fireworks
force
trembles
volcanoes

Words with wr, kn, mb, gn

thumb	wrist	lamb
gnaw	crumb	knob
written	assign	knit
know	wrench	
climb	knot	
design	wrinkle	

Unit 4

	Vocabulary Words		Spelling Words

Wings	attention complained drifting giggle	glaring looping struggled swooping	**Irregular Plurals** wolves · sheep · elves knives · heroes · banjos feet · scarves · halves men · mice children · geese women · cuffs
Hottest, Coldest, Highest, Deepest	average depth deserts outrun	peak tides waterfalls	**Vowels with *r*** third · earth · thirsty early · word · workout world · perfect · earn certain · verb dirty · nerve herself · worm
Rocks in His Head	attic board chores customer	labeled spare stamps	**Prefixes *pre-, mid-, over-, out-*** prepaid · prefix · overdue midnight · Midwest · outside overflow · pretest · outfield outdoors · midpoint outline · outgoing overgrown · overtime
America's Champion Swimmer: Gertrude Ederle	celebrate continued current drowned	medals stirred strokes	**Suffixes *-er, -or, -ess, -ist*** dentist · seller · chemist editor · tutor · investor artist · tourist · conductor hostess · organist actress · lioness swimmer · shipper
Fly, Eagle, Fly!	clutched echoed gully reeds scrambled valley		**Syllable Pattern VCCCV** monster · instant · address surprise · inspect · substance hundred · pilgrim · children complete · contrast control · explode sample · district

Unit 5

	Vocabulary Words		Spelling Words

Suki's Kimono

Vocabulary Words:
cotton	paces
festival	pale
graceful	rhythm
handkerchief	snug

Syllable Patterns CVVC, CVV

create	studio	trio
medium	violin	stadium
piano	duo	audio
idea	patio	
radio	rodeo	
video	pioneer	

How My Family Lives in America

Vocabulary Words:
admire	overnight
custom	popular
famous	public
mention	twist

Homophones

to	hour	right
too	stair	new
two	stare	knew
week	flour	
weak	flower	
our	write	

Good-Bye, 382 Shin Dang Dong

Vocabulary Words:
airport	farewell
curious	homesick
delicious	memories
described	raindrops

Vowel Sound in *ball*

small	also	applause
almost	author	walnut
always	false	lawn
because	already	
straw	flaw	
drawn	sausage	

Jalapeño Bagels

Vocabulary Words:
bakery	dough
batch	ingredients
boils	knead
braided	mixture

More Vowel Sound in *ball*

thought	cough	trough
fought	talk	chalk
bought	daughter	stalk
taught	ought	
caught	sought	
walk	brought	

Me and Uncle Romie

Vocabulary Words:
cardboard	pitcher
feast	ruined
fierce	stoops
flights	treasure

Suffixes -y, -ish, -hood, -ment

rocky	movement	bumpy
foolish	neighbor-hood	payment
rainy	childish	sleepy
childhood	parenthood	shipment
selfish	crunchy	
treatment		

Unit 6   Vocabulary Words   Spelling Words

The Story of the Statue of Liberty

Vocabulary Words

crown	tablet
liberty	torch
models	unforget-table
symbol	unveiled

Vowel Sounds in *tooth* and *cook*

few	cushion	glue
school	noodle	Tuesday
true	bookmark	bushel
goose	balloon	
fruit	suit	
cookie	chew	

Happy Birthday Mr. Kang

Vocabulary Words

bows	narrow
chilly	perches
foolish	recipe
foreign	

Schwa

above	family	item
another	travel	gallon
upon	afraid	melon
animal	nickel	
paper	sugar	
open	circus	

Talking Walls: Art for the People

Vocabulary Words

encourages	settled
expression	social
local	support
native	

Words with -tion, -sion, -ture

question	direction	sculpture
creature	culture	vision
furniture	vacation	celebration
division	mansion	
collision	fiction	
action	feature	

Two Bad Ants

Vocabulary Words

crystal	journey
disappeared	joyful
discovery	scoop
goal	unaware

Multisyllabic Words

leadership	carefully	reappeared
gracefully	unbearably	unprepared
refreshment	ownership	oncoming
uncomfortable	unaccept-able	misbehaving
overdoing	impossibly	
remarkable		

Elena's Serenade

Vocabulary Words

burro	puffs
bursts	reply
factory	tune
glassblower	

Related Words

cloth	mean	sign
clothes	meant	signal
nature	deal	signature
natural	dealt	
able	please	
ability	pleasant	

Grade 2 Vocabulary

Use this list of second grade tested vocabulary words for leveled activities.

A

above
adventure
afternoon
ago
alone
America
angry
animals
answer
aunt

B

bank
bases
basket
bear
beautiful
been
behind
believe
birthday
blame
blankets
block
borrow
bought
branches
break
brought
build
building
bumpy
burning
buy

C

campfire
cattle
caught
certainly
chased
cheers

chewing
chuckle
clattering
climbed
clothes
clubhouse
clung
collects
company
couldn't
country
cowboy
crawls

D

daughters
door
dripping
drum

E

early
either
enough
everybody
everywhere
exploring
eyes

F

fair
family
faraway
father
favorite
field
finally
fingers
flag
flashes
freedom
friend
front

fruit
full

G

galloped
giant
gone
grabbed
great
greatest
guess

H

half
harvest
heard
herd
hours

I

idea
important
insects

J

jingle

L

laugh
learn
lightning
listen
live
love

M

machines
many
masks
minute
money
mother
move

N

neighbor
nicknames

O

often
once
only

P

parents
people
picnic
picture
pieces
plate
pleasant
pond
pounds
pours
powerful
practice
present
pressing
pretended
pretty
probably
promise
pull

Q

question
quickly
quilt

R

railroad
roar
rolling
root

S

sailed
scared
school
science
second
shall
shed
shoe
sign
signmaker
silver
skin
smooth
soil
someone
somewhere
sorry
special
stars
station
storm
straight
stripes
strong
stuffing

T

taught
tears
their
though
threw
thunder
tightly
today
together
tomorrow
toward
townspeople
trails

treat
trouble
truest
trunks

U

unpacked

V

very
village
vine
voice

W

wagged
warm
wash
watch
water
whatever
whole
woman
won
wondered
wonderful
word
work
world
worst
wrapped

Y

you're
youngest

Grade 4 Vocabulary

Use this list of fourth grade tested vocabulary words for leveled activities.

A

aboard
affords
amazed
amphibians
ancestors
ancient
anticipation
appeared
aquarium
astronauts
atlas
aviator
avoided
awkward

B

bargain
bawling
bewildered
biologist
bluff
boarding school
bow
brilliant
brisk
bustling

C

canopy
capable
capsule
cargo
celestial
chant
chorus
cockpit
colonel
conducted
Constitution
continent
convergence
cord

coward
coyote
cradle
crime
crumbled
curiosity

D

dangle
dappled
daring
depart
destruction
dignified
dismay
docks
dolphins
dormitory
draft
drag
dudes
duke
dungeon

E

elegant
enchanted
endurance
escape
etched
exhibit
expected

F

fascinated
favor
flex
flexible
forbidding
forecasts
fouled
fragrant
frost
furiously

G

generations
genius
glacier
gleamed
glider
glimpses
glint
glorious
grand
granite
grizzly

H

hangars
hatch
heaves
homeland
hoop
horizon
howling
humble

I

icebergs
immense
impressive
inland

J

jersey

L

lagoon
lassoed
link
lizard
longed
loomed
lunar
lurking

M

magician
majesty
manual
marveled
massive
mechanical
memorial
migrating
minister
miracle
module
monument

N

naturalist
navigation
noble
numerous

O

offended
outspoken

P

palettes
parlor
payroll
peasant
peculiar
politics
pollen
pollinate
porridge
positive
prairie
preserve
prideful
pulpit
pulses

Q

quaint
quarantine
quivered

R

recalls
reference
reptiles
reseat
resemblance
reservation
responsibility
rille
rim
riverbed
roundup
rudder
ruins
rumbling
runt

S

salamanders
scan
scent
scholars
sculptures
seeker
selecting
shatter
shielding
shimmering
shrieked
slithered
slopes
society
solemnly
solo
species
speechless
spurs
staggered

stalled
stern
still
stumped
summoning
surface
surge
swatted

T

taunted
temple
terraced
terror
thickets
timid
torrent
towering
translate
trench
triumph
tropical
trudged

U

unbelievable
uncover

V

vain
vanished
vehicle

W

wharf
wilderness
wondrous

Y

yearned

Legibility

When handwriting is legible, letters, words and numbers can be read easily. Handwriting that is not legible can cause problems for the reader and make communication difficult. Legibility can be improved if students are able to identify what is causing legibility problems in their handwriting. Focus instruction on the following five elements of legible handwriting.

Size

Letters need to be a consistent size. Students should focus on three things related to size: letters that reach to the top line, letters that reach halfway between the top and bottom line, and letters that extend below the bottom line. Writing letters the correct size can improve legibility. Often the letters that sit halfway between the top and bottom line cause the most problems. When students are writing on notebook paper, there is no middle line to help them size letters such as *m, a, i*, and *r* correctly. If students are having trouble, have them draw middle lines on their notebook paper.

Shape

Some of the most common handwriting problems are caused by forming letters incorrectly. These are the most common types of handwriting problems:

• round letters such as *a, o,* and *g* are not closed
• looped letters such as *i, e,* and *b* have no loops
• letters such as *i, t,* and *d* have loops that shouldn't be there

Have students examine one another's writing to indicate which words are hard to read, and then discuss which letters aren't formed correctly. They can then practice those particular letters.

Spacing

Letters within words should be evenly spaced. Too much or too little space can make writing difficult to read. A consistent amount of space should also be used between words in a sentence and between sentences. Suggest that students use the tip of their pencil to check the spacing between words and the width of their pencil to check the spacing between sentences.

Slant

Correct writing slant can be to the right or to the left, or there may be no slant at all. Slant becomes a legibility problem when letters are slanted in different directions. Suggest that students use a ruler to draw lines to determine if their slant is consistent.

Smoothness

Written letters should be produced with a line weight that is not too dark and not too light. The line should be smooth without any shaky or jagged edges. If students' writing is too dark, they are pressing too hard. If the writing is too light, they are not pressing hard enough. Usually shaky or jagged lines occur if students are unsure of how to form letters or if they are trying to draw letters rather than using a flowing motion.

D'Nealian™ Cursive Alphabet

a b c d e f g
h i j k l m n
o p q r s t u
v w x y z

A B C D E F G
H I J K L M N
O P Q R S T U
V W X Y Z . , ' ?

1 2 3 4 5 6
7 8 9 10

D'Nealian™ Alphabet

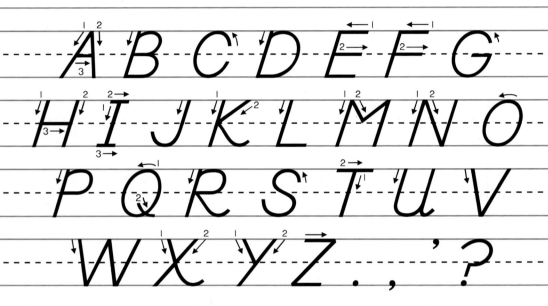

a b c d e f g h i
j k l m n o p q r s t
u v w x y z

A B C D E F G
H I J K L M N O
P Q R S T U V
W X Y Z . , ' ?

1 2 3 4 5 6
7 8 9 10

Manuscript Alphabet

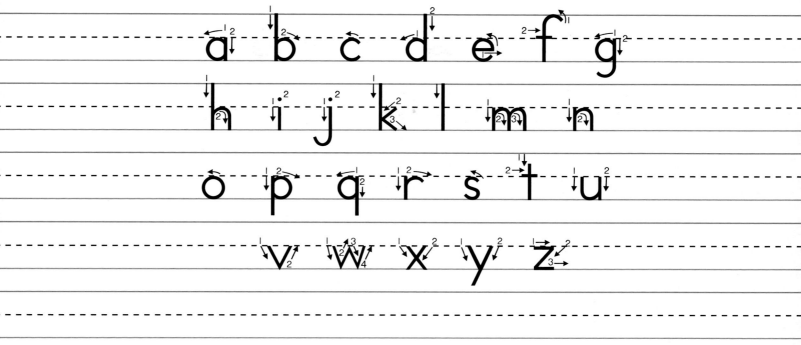

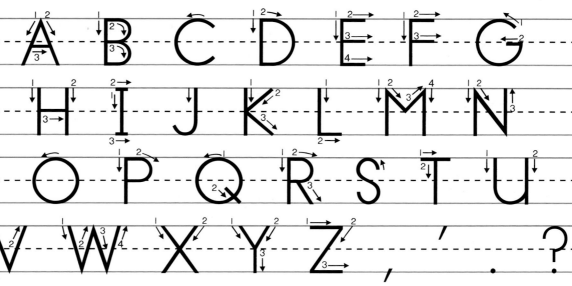

Unit 6 *Freedom*

	Below-Level	On-Level	Advanced

The Statue of Liberty

To Read Aloud!
Liberty!
by Allan Drummond (Farrar, Straus & Giroux, 2002) A small boy stands at the feet of the Statue of Liberty to signal when it is time to unveil her. As New York waits, the boy recounts the story of this country's symbol of freedom.

Uncle Sam and Old Glory: Symbols of America
by Delno C. West and Jean M. West (Simon & Schuster, 1999) This book presents the backgrounds of American symbols, such as Uncle Sam and the Liberty Bell.

O, Say Can You See? America's Symbols, Landmarks, and Important Words
by Sheila Keenan (Scholastic, 2004) This colorful book presents a lighthearted look at familiar symbols of the United States.

Brooklyn Bridge
by Lynn Curlee (Simon & Schuster, 2001) This book describes the planning, construction, and history of the Brooklyn Bridge, celebrated as one of the greatest landmarks and grandest sights in New York City.

Happy Birthday Mr. Kang

To Read Aloud!
The Colors of Freedom: Immigrant Stories
by Janet Bode (Franklin Watts, Inc. 1999) Newly arrived teenaged immigrants describe their experiences in America, recount traditions of their countries, and present short stories and poems.

Minty: A Story of Young Harriet Tubman
by Alan Schroeder (Puffin, 2000) As a young slave, Harriet Tubman was a spirited girl with a dream of freedom, whose rebellious spirit often got her into trouble.

Rechenka's Eggs
by Patricia Polacco (Philomel Books, 1988) Rechenka is an artist who paints beautiful eggs. But one day, a very special egg reveals a work of art inside.

Fly Away Home
by Eve Bunting (Clarion, 1991) A homeless boy who lives in an airport with his father, moving from terminal to terminal and trying not to be noticed, is given hope when he sees a trapped bird find its freedom.

Talking Walls

To Read Aloud!
The School Mural
by Sarah Vazquez (Steck-Vaughn, 1991) The students in Mrs. Sanchez's class create a mural to celebrate their school's 50th anniversary.

Diego
by Jeanette Winter, Jonah Winter (Bantam Doubleday Dell, 1994) Told in Spanish and English, this story of Diego Rivera, the great muralist, discusses his childhood and how it influenced his art.

The Paint Brush Kid
by Clyde Robert Bulla (Random House, 1998) Gregory paints pictures of Uncle Pancho's childhood in Mexico on the man's house. When the house is slated for demolition, a plan is hatched to save it.

Murals: Walls That Sing
by George Ancona (Marshall Cavendish, 2003) This colorful photo-essay provides a fascinating look at outdoor murals and the communities they represent.

Two Bad Ants

To Read Aloud!
Bad Day at Riverbend
by Chris Van Allsburg (Houghton Mifflin, 1995) The sheriff and his men can't figure out what the shiny, colorful material is that's beginning to cover their coloring-book town.

Ant
by Karen Hartley (Heinemann, 2001) Part of the Bug Book series, this easy-to-read work presents an overview of the life cycle, physical characteristics, and habitat of the ant.

Just a Dream
by Chris Van Allsburg (Houghton Mifflin, 1990) A young litterbug dreams of a future earth that is overcrowded and polluted. This nightmare scares him into becoming a more nature-conscious person.

Insectlopedia: Poems and Paintings
by Douglas Florian (Hartcourt, 1998) This beautifully illustrated book presents twenty-one short, simple, and fun poems about such insects as the inchworm, ant, cricket, and ladybug.

Elena's Serenade

To Read Aloud!
For the Love of the Game: Michael Jordan and Me
by Eloise Greenfield (HarperCollins, 1997) A poetic exhortation tells children to find their paths in life and to excel in them, accompanied by paintings by Jan Spivey Gilchrist.

Gabriella's Song
by Candace Fleming (Aladdin, 2001) A young girl finds music all around her as she walks about the city of Venice, Italy, and she shares her song with everyone she meets.

Frida
by Jonah Winter (Scholastic, 2002) This tribute to the Mexican painter, Frida Kahlo, tells about her life as an artist and how she turned challenges into art.

Angela Weaves a Dream: The Story of a Young Maya Artist
by Michele Sola (Hyperion, 1997) Angela's grandmother teaches her how to create the seven sacred weaving patterns passed down from one generation to the next in southern Mexico.

See also *Assessment Handbook*, p. 119

Unit 6 Reading Log

Name _____

Dates Read	Title and Author	What is it about?	How would you rate it?	Explain your rating.
From _____ to _____			Great 5 4 3 2 1 Awful	
From _____ to _____			Great 5 4 3 2 1 Awful	
From _____ to _____			Great 5 4 3 2 1 Awful	
From _____ to _____			Great 5 4 3 2 1 Awful	
From _____ to _____			Great 5 4 3 2 1 Awful	

Unit 6 Narrative Retelling Chart

Selection Title _____   Name _____   Date _____

Retelling Criteria/Teacher Prompt	Teacher-Aided Response	Student-Generated Response	Rubric Score (Circle one.)
Connections Has anything like this happened to you? How does this story remind you of other stories?			4 3 2 1
Author's Purpose Why do you think the author wrote this story? What was the author trying to tell us?			4 3 2 1
Characters Describe _____ (character's name) at the beginning and end of the story.			4 3 2 1
Setting Where and when did the story happen?			4 3 2 1
Plot Tell me what the story was about in a few sentences.			4 3 2 1

Summative Retelling Score   4   3   2   1

Comments _____
_____

Unit 6 Expository Retelling Chart

Name _____ Date _____

Selection Title _____

Retelling Criteria/Teacher Prompt	Teacher-Aided Response	Student-Generated Response	Rubric Score (Circle one.)		
Connections Did this selection make you think about something else you have read? What did you learn about as you read this selection?			4	3	2 1
Author's Purpose Why do you think the author wrote this selection?			4	3	2 1
Topic What was the selection mostly about?			4	3	2 1
Important Ideas What is important for me to know about _____ (topic)?			4	3	2 1
Conclusions What did you learn from reading this selection?			4	3	2 1

Summative Retelling Score 4 3 2 1

Comments _____
_____

Reading

Concepts of Print and Print Awareness	Pre-K	K	1	2	3	4	5
Develop awareness that print represents spoken language and conveys and preserves meaning	•	•	•				
Recognize familiar books by their covers; hold book right side up	•	•					
Identify parts of a book and their functions (front cover, title page/title, back cover, page numbers)	•	•	•				
Understand the concepts of letter, word, sentence, paragraph, and story	•	•	•				
Track print (front to back of book, top to bottom of page, left to right on line, sweep back left for next line)	•	•	•				
Match spoken to printed words	•	•	•				
Know capital and lowercase letter names and match them	•	• T	•				
Know the order of the alphabet	•	•	•				
Recognize first name in print	•	•	•				
Recognize the uses of capitalization and punctuation		•	•				
Value print as a means of gaining information	•	•	•				

Phonological and Phonemic Awareness	Pre-K	K	1	2	3	4	5
Phonological Awareness							
Recognize and produce rhyming words	•	•	•				
Track and count each word in a spoken sentence and each syllable in a spoken word	•	•	•				
Segment and blend syllables in spoken words			•				
Segment and blend onset and rime in one-syllable words		•	•				
Recognize and produce words beginning with the same sound	•	•	•				
Identify beginning, middle, and/or ending sounds that are the same or different	•	•	•				
Understand that spoken words are made of sequences of sounds	•	•	•				
Phonemic Awareness							
Identify the position of sounds in words		•	•				
Identify and isolate initial, final, and medial sounds in spoken words	•	•	•				
Blend sounds orally to make words or syllables		•	•				
Segment a word or syllable into sounds; count phonemes in spoken words or syllables		•	•				
Manipulate sounds in words (add, delete, and/or substitute phonemes)	•	•	•				

Phonics and Decoding	Pre-K	K	1	2	3	4	5
Phonics							
Understand and apply the **alphabetic principle** that spoken words are composed of sounds that are represented by letters	•	•	•				
Know letter-sound relationships	•	• T	• T	• T			
Blend sounds of letters to decode		•	• T	• T	• T		
Consonants, consonant blends, and consonant digraphs		•	• T	• T	• T		
Short, long, and r-controlled vowels; vowel digraphs; diphthongs; common vowel patterns			• T	• T	• T		
Phonograms/word families		•	•	•	•		
Word Structure							
Decode words with common word parts		•	• T	• T	• T	•	•
Base words and inflected endings			• T	• T	•	•	•
Contractions and compound words			• T	• T	• T	•	•
Suffixes and prefixes			• T	• T	• T	•	•
Greek and Latin roots						•	•
Blend syllables to decode words			• T	• T	• T	•	•
Decoding Strategies							
Blending strategy: Apply knowledge of letter-sound relationships to decode unfamiliar words		•	•	•	•		
Apply knowledge of word structure to decode unfamiliar words		•	•	•	•	•	•
Use context and syntax along with letter-sound relationships and word structure to decode		•	•	•	•	•	•
Self-correct			•	•	•	•	•

Fluency	Pre-K	K	1	2	3	4	5
Read aloud fluently with accuracy, comprehension, appropriate pace/rate; with expression/intonation (prosody); with attention to punctuation and appropriate phrasing			• T	• T	• T	• T	• T
Practice fluency in a variety of ways, including choral reading, partner/paired reading, Readers' Theater, repeated oral reading, and tape-assisted reading		•	•	•	•	•	•

• instructional opportunity   **T** tested in standardized test

	Pre-K	K	1	2	3	4	5	6
x toward appropriate fluency goals by the end of each grade			•T	•T	•T	•T	•T	•T
d regularly in independent-level material			•	•	•	•	•	•
d silently for increasing periods of time				•	•	•	•	•

cabulary (Oral and Written)

	Pre-K	K	1	2	3	4	5	6
rd Recognition								
ognize regular and irregular high-frequency words	•	•	•T	•T				
ognize and understand selection vocabulary		•	•	•T	•	•	•	•
erstand content-area vocabulary and specialized, technical, or topical words			•	•	•	•	•	•
rd Learning Strategies								
elop vocabulary through direct instruction, concrete experiences, reading, listening to text read-aloud	•	•	•	•	•	•	•	•
knowledge of word structure to figure out meanings of words			•	•T	•T	•T	•T	•T
context clues for meanings of unfamiliar words, multiple-meaning words, homonyms, homographs			•	•T	•T	•T	•T	•T
grade-appropriate reference sources to learn word meanings	•	•	•	•	•T	•T	•T	•T
picture clues to help determine word meanings	•	•	•	•	•			
new words in a variety of contexts	•	•	•	•	•	•	•	•
nine word usage and effectiveness		•	•	•	•	•	•	•
te and use graphic organizers to group, study, and retain vocabulary			•	•	•	•	•	•
end Concepts and Word Knowledge								
emic language	•	•	•	•	•	•	•	•
sify and categorize	•	•	•	•	•	•	•	•
nyms and synonyms			•	•T	•T	•T	•T	•T
ographs, homonyms, and homophones				•	•T	•T	•T	•T
iple-meaning words			•	•	•T	•T	•T	•T
ted words and derivations					•	•	•	•
ogies						•		•
notation/denotation						•	•	•
ative language and idioms			•	•	•	•	•	•
riptive words (location, size, color, shape, number, ideas, feelings)	•	•	•	•	•	•	•	•
utility words (shapes, colors, question words, position/directional words, and so on)	•	•	•	•	•			
and order words	•	•	•	•	•	•	•	•
sition words						•	•	•
origins: Etymologies/word histories; words from other languages, regions, or cultures					•	•	•	•
tened forms: abbreviations, acronyms, clipped words			•	•	•	•	•T	•

xt Comprehension

	Pre-K	K	1	2	3	4	5	6
mprehension Strategies								
ew the text and formulate questions	•	•	•	•	•	•	•	•
nd monitor purpose for reading and listening	•	•	•	•	•	•	•	•
ate and use prior knowledge	•	•	•	•	•	•	•	•
e predictions	•	•	•	•	•	•	•	•
tor comprehension and use fix-up strategies to resolve difficulties in meaning: adjust reading rate, d and read on, seek help from reference sources and/or other people, skim and scan, summarize, text features				•	•	•	•	•
te and use graphic and semantic organizers		•	•	•	•	•	•	•
ver questions (text explicit, text implicit, scriptal), including *who, what, when, where, why, what if, how*	•	•	•	•	•	•	•	•
ok back in text for answers			•	•	•	•	•	•
swer test-like questions			•	•	•	•	•	•
erate clarifying questions, including *who, what, where, when, how, why,* and *what if*	•	•	•	•	•	•	•	•
ognize text structure: story and informational (cause/effect, chronological, compare/contrast, ription, problem/solution, propostion/support)	•	•	•	•	•	•	•	•
marize text		•	•	•	•	•	•	•
call and retell stories	•	•	•	•	•	•	•	•
entify and retell important/main ideas (nonfiction)	•	•	•	•	•	•	•	•
entify and retell new information		•	•	•	•	•	•	•
alize; use mental imagery		•	•	•	•	•	•	•
strategies flexibly and in combination			•	•	•	•	•	•

Comprehension Skills

	Pre-K	K	1	2	3	4	5
Author's purpose			• T	• T	• T	• T	• T
Author's viewpoint/bias/perspective					•	•	•
Categorize and classify	•	•	•	•			
Cause and effect		•	• T	• T	• T	• T	• T
Compare and contrast		•	• T	• T	• T	• T	• T
Details and facts		•	•	•	•	•	•
Draw conclusions		•	• T	• T	• T	• T	• T
Fact and opinion				• T	• T	• T	• T
Follow directions/steps in a process	•	•	•	•	•	•	•
Generalize					• T	• T	• T
Graphic sources		•	•	•	•	• T	• T
Main idea and supporting details		• T	• T	• T	• T	• T	• T
Paraphrase			•	•	•	•	•
Persuasive devices and propaganda				•	•	•	•
Realism/fantasy		•	• T	• T	• T	•	•
Sequence of events		• T	• T	• T	• T	• T	• T

Higher Order Thinking Skills

	Pre-K	K	1	2	3	4	5
Analyze				•	•	•	•
Describe and connect the essential ideas, arguments, and perspectives of a text			•	•	•	•	•
Draw inferences, conclusions, or generalizations, support them with textual evidence and prior knowledge	•		•	•	•	•	•
Evaluate and critique ideas and text				•	•	•	•
Hypothesize						•	•
Make judgments about ideas and text			•	•	•	•	•
Organize and synthesize ideas and information			•			•	•

Literary Analysis, Response, & Appreciation

	Pre-K	K	1	2	3	4	5
Genre and Its Characteristics							
Recognize characteristics of a variety of genre	•	•	•	•	•	•	•
Distinguish fiction from nonfiction		•	•	•	•	•	•
Identify characteristics of literary texts, including drama, fantasy, traditional tales		•	•	•	•	•	•
Identify characteristics of nonfiction texts, including biography, interviews, newspaper articles		•	•	•	•	•	•
Identify characteristics of poetry and song, including nursery rhymes, limericks, blank verse	•	•	•	•	•	•	•
Literary Elements and Story Structure							
Character	•	• T	• T	• T	• T	• T	• T
Recognize and describe traits, actions, feelings, and motives of characters		•	•	•	•	•	•
Analyze characters' relationships, changes, and points of view		•	•	•	•	•	•
Analyze characters' conflicts				•		•	•
Plot and plot structure	•	• T	• T	• T	• T	• T	• T
Beginning, middle, end	•	•	•	•	•		
Goal and outcome or problem and solution/resolution		•	•	•	•	•	•
Rising action, climax, and falling action/denouement; setbacks						•	•
Setting	•	• T	• T	• T	• T	• T	
Relate setting to problem/solution						•	•
Explain ways setting contributes to mood						•	•
Theme		•	• T	• T	•	•	•
Use Literary Elements and Story Structure	•		•	•	•	•	•
Analyze and evaluate author's use of setting, plot, character				•	•	•	•
Identify similarities and differences of characters, events, and settings within or across selections/cultures	•	•	•	•	•	•	•
Literary Devices							
Allusion							
Dialect						•	•
Dialogue and narration	•	•	•	•	•	•	•
Exaggeration/hyperbole					•	•	•
Figurative language: idiom, jargon, metaphor, simile, slang			•	•	•	•	•

• instructional opportunity   **T** tested in standardized test